ISBN 978-1-330-78665-9
PIBN 10105278

English
Français
Deutsche
Italiano
Español
Português

www.forgottenbooks.com

Mythology Photography **Fiction**
Fishing Christianity **Art** Cooking
Essays Buddhism Freemasonry
Medicine **Biology** Music **Ancient
Egypt** Evolution Carpentry Physics
Dance Geology **Mathematics** Fitness
Shakespeare **Folklore** Yoga Marketing
Confidence Immortality Biographies
Poetry **Psychology** Witchcraft
Electronics Chemistry History **Law**
Accounting **Philosophy** Anthropology
Alchemy Drama Quantum Mechanics
Atheism Sexual Health **Ancient History**
Entrepreneurship Languages Sport
Paleontology Needlework Islam
Metaphysics Investment Archaeology
Parenting Statistics Criminology
Motivational

HE FACE OF THE DEEP.

THE FACE OF THE DEEP:

A DEVOTIONAL COMMENTARY

ON

THE APOCALYPSE.

BY THE LATE

CHRISTINA G. ROSSETTI,

AUTHOR OF "SEEK AND FIND," "TIME FLIES," ETC.

"Thy judgments are a great deep."—PSALM xxxvi. 6.

THIRD EDITION.

PUBLISHED UNDER THE DIRECTION OF THE TRACT COMMITTEE.

LONDON:
SOCIETY FOR PROMOTING CHRISTIAN KNOWLEDGE,
NORTHUMBERLAND AVENUE, W.C.; 43, QUEEN VICTORIA STREET, E.C.
NEW YORK: E. & J. B. YOUNG & CO.
1895.

Richard Clay & Sons, Limited
London & Bungay.

TO

My Mother,

FOR THE FIRST TIME

TO HER

BELOVED, REVERED, CHERISHED MEMORY.

PREFATORY NOTE.

IF thou canst dive, bring up pearls. If thou canst not dive, collect amber. Though I fail to identify Paradisiacal "bdellium," I still may hope to search out beauties of the "onyx stone."

A dear saint—I speak under correction of the Judgment of the Great Day, yet think not then to have my word corrected —this dear person once pointed out to me Patience as our lesson in the Book of Revelations.

Following the clue thus afforded me, I seek and hope to find Patience in this Book of awful import. Patience, at the least: and along with that grace whatever treasures beside God may vouchsafe me. Bearing meanwhile in mind how "to him that knoweth to do good, and doeth it not, to him it is sin."

Now if any deign to seek Patience in my company, I pray them to remember that One high above me in the Kingdom of Heaven heads our pilgrim caravan.

O, ye who love to-day,
Turn away
From Patience with her silver ray :
For Patience shows a twilight face,
Like a half-lighted moon
When daylight dies apace.

But ye who love to-morrow,
Beg or borrow
To-day some bitterness of sorrow :
For Patience shows a lustrous face
In depth of night her noon ;
Then to her sun gives place.

THE APOCALYPSE.

CHAPTER I.

1. **The Revelation of Jesus Christ, which God gave unto Him, to show unto His servants things which must shortly come to pass; and He sent and signified it by His angel unto His servant John:**
2. **Who bare record of the word of God, and of the testimony of Jesus Christ, and of all things that he saw.**

"Things which must shortly come to pass."—At the end of 1800 years we are still repeating this " shortly," because it is the word of God and the testimony of Jesus Christ : thus starting in fellowship of patience with that blessed John who owns all Christians as his brethren (*see* ver. 9).

More marvellous than many marvels subsequently revealed is that initiatory marvel, the dignity of Him Who ministers to His own servants. For God Almighty it is Who gives to Jesus Christ His Co-Equal Son a Revelation for man. It reaches us through Angel and Apostle, but these are the channel, not the fountain-head, as St. Paul writes to his Corinthian converts : " What hast thou that thou didst not receive ? now if thou didst receive it, why dost thou glory, as if thou hadst not received it ? "

Wherefore are we God's creatures ? To the end that He may do us good. Wherefore are we Christ's servants ? To the end that He may save us. And how helped He His fallen creatures ? By taking their damage upon Himself. And how took He in hand to save His servants ? By sacrificing Himself for them. Did He at all need us as servants ? Nay, but we needed Him.

Thee we needed, Thee we need, O Only Almighty, All-merciful Redeemer. As Thou for us who needed Thee, so grant that we may spend ourselves for any who need us ; nor desire to have servants or dependents or inferiors except so far as we may do them good, requiting to them what Thou hast done to us.

[Such cannot be our honest theory, unless it be likewise our honest practice.]

We may not connect so human a virtue as patience with the blessed Angels, because exemption from sin seems to entail incapacity for certain graces. But St. John, of like passions with ourselves, may indeed have needed patience to "prophesy again before many peoples, and nations, and tongues, and kings" of that "whole world" whereof he himself avers that it lieth in wickedness.

"The Revelation of Jesus Christ, which God gave unto Him, to show unto His servants things which must . . . come to pass."—Christ reveals to us these things, and by virtue of His Spirit dwelling in us, these and all things reveal to us Christ. For while this Book abounds in the terror of the Lord, through and above tumult of multitudes and their voice as of voluminous waters or of mighty thunderings sounds the dear word, "It is I ; be not afraid."

Teach us, O Lord, to fear Thee without terror, and to trust Thee without misgiving : to fear Thee in love, until it please Thee that we shall love Thee without fear.

"To show unto His servants."—The promise is to "His servants" only, in accordance with our Lord's own words : "If any man will do His Will, he shall know of the doctrine. . ." : he, not another. Obedience is the key of knowledge, not knowledge of obedience. Yet this showing is not the same as explaining : truths or events are certified to us, and in consequence we know them ; but it by no means follows that we can account for them or foresee the time or the manner of their coming to pass. Even St. Paul was content to class himself with his hearers when he wrote, "We know in part." And St. Peter attests how the prophets "inquired and searched diligently . . . searching what, or what manner of time the Spirit of Christ which was in them did signify . . . Unto whom it was revealed, that not unto themselves, but unto us they did minister . . ."

Seems it a small thing to minister rather than to be ministered unto ? Nay : for thus did the Lord Jesus, Who likewise said, " It is more blessed to give than to receive."

"The goodly fellowship of the Prophets praise Thee."

Things there are which "the angels desire to look into."

Somewhat of the manifold Wisdom of God was not known
unto the principalities and powers in heavenly places until the
Church brought it to light.

"Therefore, with Angels and Archangels, and with all the
company of heaven, we laud and magnify Thy Glorious Name,
evermore praising Thee."

O Gracious Saviour, Who declaredst unto St. Peter, "What
I do, thou knowest not now; but thou shalt know hereafter";
give us grace now to answer Thee with his final submission,
that hereafter we may adore Thee with his insight.

O Gracious Saviour, Who bestowedst upon St. John a great
glory of humility when he bare record how Thou saidst not of
him, "He shall not die," grant unto us in mortal life humility,
and in life immortal glory.

> Heaven is not far, though far the sky
> 　Overarching earth and main.
> It takes not long to live and die,
> 　Die, revive, and rise again.
> Not long: how long? Oh long re-echoing song!
> O Lord, how long?

"Who bare record of the word of God, and of the testimony
of Jesus Christ." Elsewhere St. John writes: "If we receive
the witness of men, the witness of God is greater." All truth
is venerable, let who will propound it; now an Apostle, at
another time Caiaphas. Our Lord Himself said: "Ye sent
unto John, and he bare witness unto the truth. But I receive
not testimony from man." Clearly then the Truth is to be
believed not for his word's sake who records it, but for His
Verity's sake Who reveals it.

O Lord Jesus Christ, who art Truth and Wisdom, reveal
Thyself unto us, we beseech Thee. Thou art not far from
every one of us. Grant us good-will to draw nigh unto Thee,
Who deignest to draw nigh unto us.

"Who bare record . . . of all things that he saw." Blessed
he who once and again saw and believed. None the less
Christ's promise stands sure to ourselves: "Blessed are they
that have not seen, and yet have believed."

O Saviour of men, Who sufferest not Thy beloved Disciple
to exclude us, even us, from any height or depth of beatitude,
give us grace to be of those blessed who not seeing believe.

**3. Blessed is he that readeth, and they that hear the
words of this prophecy, and keep those things which
are written therein, for the time is at hand.**

" Understandest thou what thou readest?" asked Philip the
Deacon of the Ethiopian Eunuch. And he said, " How can I,
except some man should guide me?" Whereupon flowed forth
to him the stream of light, knowledge, and love. Yet not then
did his illumination commence : it already was his in a measure to enjoy, respond to, improve, even before his father in
God preached Christ unto him. What could he do before
that moment? He could study and pray, he could cherish
hope, exercise love, feel after Him Whom as yet he could not
intelligently find.

So much at least we all can do who read, or who hear, this
Book of Revelations : thus claiming, and by God's bounty
inheriting, the covenanted blessing of such readers and hearers.
Any who pray and love enjoy already no stinted blessing.
Even the will to love is love.

A reader and hearers stand in graduated degrees of knowledge or of ignorance, as the case may be. The reader studying at first hand is in direct contact with God's Word : hearers
seek instruction of God through men. The reader requires
most gifts : hearers may exercise fully as much grace. Most
of us are hearers : having performed conscientiously the duty
of hearers, we shall be the less prone to make mistakes if ever
providentially promoted to be readers. Our dearest Lord,
Who deigned to become the pattern of every grade of aspirant,
as a Boy showed hearers how to hear (St. Luke ii. 46, 47) ; and
as a Man showed readers how to read (St. Luke iv. 16—27).

> Lord, I am feeble and of mean account ;
> Thou Who dost condescend as well as mount,
>   Stoop Thou Thyself to me
> And grant me grace to hear and grace to see.
>
> Lord, if Thou grant me grace to hear and see
> Thy very Self Who stoopest thus to me,
>   I make but slight account
> Of aught beside wherein to sink or mount.

It suffices not to read or to hear the words of this prophecy,
except we also " keep those things which are written therein."
How keep them? One part in one way, another part in
another : the commandments by obedience, the mysteries by
thoughtful reception ; as blessed Mary, herself a marvel, kept
mysterious intimations vouchsafed to her, and pondered them
in her heart. Yet never had she gone on in pursuit of all
mysteries and all knowledge if she had not first answered in

simple obedience : "Behold the handmaid of the Lord; be it unto me according to thy word."

O bountiful Lord, to Whom they who do the will of God are as brother and sister and mother, number us in that blessed company, that here we may obey and suffer as Thy patient exiles, and hereafter rule and rejoice as Thy nearest and dearest.

"Blessed are they . . . for the time is at hand." Even now, eighteen centuries later, we know not when that cry shall be made, "Behold, the Bridegroom cometh; go ye out to meet Him." Nevertheless the time was then at hand, for so the Bible certifies us, and still must it be at hand. What time? Doubtless the time of fulfilment after fulfilment until all be fulfilled. Likewise also that (so to say) secondary time when each one of us, having done with mortal life and probation, shall await judgment. For truly the end of all flesh is at hand, whether or not we possess faith to realize how a thousand years and one day are comparable in the Divine sight.

"A thousand years in Thy sight are but as yesterday when it is past, and as a watch in the night."

Blessed are the wise virgins whose lamps burn on unto the endless end. "Blessed are those servants, whom the Lord when He cometh shall find watching." "If ye know these things, happy are ye if ye do them."

"The time is at hand," ever at hand; yet it waits long for us: "Who knoweth if he will return and repent?" But if we will not return or repent, "iniquity shall be to you as a breach ready to fall . . . whose breaking cometh suddenly at an instant."

O Lord God of time and eternity, Who makest us creatures of time to the end that when time is over we may attain to Thy blessed eternity; with time, Thy gift, give us also wisdom to redeem the time, lest our day of grace be lost. For our Lord Jesus' sake. Amen.

> Astonished Heaven looked on when man was made,
>   When fallen man reproved seemed half forgiven ;
> Surely that oracle of hope first said
>   Astonished Heaven.
>
> Even so while one by one lost souls are shriven,
>   A mighty multitude of quickened dead ;
> Christ's love outnumbering ten times sevenfold seven.
>
> Even so while man still tosses high his head,
>   While still the All-holy Spirit's strife is striven ;—
> Till one last trump shake earth, and undismayed
>   Astonished Heaven.

4. John to the seven churches which are in Asia : Grace be
unto you, and peace, from Him which is, and which
was, and which is to come ; and from the seven Spirits
which are before His throne ;

5. And from Jesus Christ, Who is the faithful Witness, and
the first begotten of the dead, and the Prince of the
kings of the earth. Unto Him that loved us, and washed
us from our sins in His own blood,

6. And hath made us kings and priests unto God and His
Father; to Him be glory and dominion for ever and
ever. Amen.

"John to the seven Churches."—Gracious the speaker,
because his mouth was filled with a grace not his own. Whoso
speaketh for God must take heed to speak like God. If St.
Paul made himself all things to all men, that he might by all
means save some, how much more Christ ! St. John saluteth,
but not with his own salutation : "What hast thou that thou
hast not received ? "

Nothing perhaps ever brought more vividly home to me the
condescension, not of the servant, but of the Master, than once
when at a Communion which was to me almost a sick Communion, the Celebrant in administering moved a chair slightly
for my greater convenience. "He knoweth whereof we are
made ; He remembereth that we are but dust."

"Grace be unto you, and peace."—Before we tremble, God
reassures us. "Yea, like as a father pitieth his own children,
even so is the Lord merciful unto them that fear Him."

O God Almighty, by Whom and before Whom we all are
brethren, grant us so truly to love one another, that evidently
and beyond all doubt we may love Thee. Through Jesus
Christ Thy Son, our Lord and Brother. Amen.

"Grace . . . and peace."—"Thou shalt keep him in
perfect peace whose mind is stayed on Thee : because he
trusteth in Thee."

"From Him which is, and which was, and which is to
come."—Not "was—is—is to come." "Is" abides perpetual,
unalterable, dominant. Antecedent to creatures, antecedent
to time, is revealed to our finite conception by "was": out-
lasting time, by "is to come" : whilst parallel with creatures,
with time, with all beginnings and all ends, abides the eternal
"is." We creatures of time, who might instinctively have
written "was—is—is to come," are thus helped, not indeed
to understand, but to adore the inconceivable, eternal,

absolute Unchangeableness of God. We run a course; not so He.

"And from the Seven Spirits which are before His throne."— These words appear to correspond with those of Isaiah : "The Spirit of the Lord . . . the Spirit of wisdom and understanding, the Spirit of counsel and might, the Spirit of knowledge and of the fear of the Lord." Also with the description of the golden candlestick in the Mosaic Tabernacle : "And thou shalt make a candlestick of pure gold . . . And thou shalt make the seven lamps thereof : and they shall light the lamps thereof, that they may give light . . ."

A mystery confronts us. We read of Seven, yet we dare not think except as of One.

"O God the Holy Ghost, proceeding from the Father and the Son : have mercy upon us, miserable sinners." "Lighten our darkness, we beseech Thee, O Lord."

Multitude no less than Unity characterizes various types of God the Holy Spirit. Water indefinitely divisible, and every portion equivalent in completeness to the whole. Fire kindling unlimited flames, each in like manner complete in itself. Dew made up of innumerable drops : so also rain, and if we may make the distinction, showers. A cloud as a cloud is one, while as raindrops it is a multitude. And as in division each portion is a complete whole devoid of parts, so equally in reunion all portions together form one complete whole similarly devoid of parts : let drops or let flames run together, and there exists no distinction of parts in their uniform volume.

"Before His throne."—As the golden candlestick stood before the Holy of Holies.

"And from Jesus Christ, Who is the Faithful Witness."— Not John, but Jesus : or rather Jesus through John, and John only because of Jesus. St. John, the Apostle of love, becomes here the mouthpiece of very Love. So that in this Apocalypse not glories only, joys unutterable, perfection, are witnessed to us by Love, but terrors likewise, doom, the Judgment, the opened Books, the lake of fire. Love reveals to us these things, threatens now that it may spare then, shows us destruction lest we destroy ourselves.

—Let us not in all our tremblings forget or doubt that it is Faithful Love which speaketh.

> My God, Thyself being Love Thy heart is love,
> And love Thy Will and love Thy Word to us,
> Whether Thou show us depths calamitous
> Or heights and flights of rapturous peace above.

O Christ the Lamb, O Holy Ghost the Dove,
  Reveal the Almighty Father unto us ;
  That we may tread Thy courts felicitous,
Loving Who loves us, for our God is Love.
Lo, if our God be Love through heaven's long day,
  Love is He through our mortal pilgrimage,
  Love was He through all aeons that are told.
We change, but Thou remainest ; for Thine age
  Is, Was, and Is to come, nor new nor old ;
We change, but Thou remainest : yea, and yea!

"The Faithful Witness" demands faith : "the First Begotten of the dead" invites hope : "the Prince of the kings of the earth" challenges obedience. Now faith may be dead, hope presumptuous, obedience slavish. But "He that loved us" thereby wins our love : and forthwith by virtue of love faith lives, hope is justified, obedience is enfranchised.

Loveless faith is dead, being alone. Loveless hope leads to shame. Loveless obedience makes fair the outside, but within is rottenness. Balaam seems to exemplify all three.

"Without shedding of blood is no remission," wherefore Christ washed us from our sins in His own blood.

But God Almighty declared of old : "Surely your blood of your lives will I require." Whence it follows that if after such cleansing we give ourselves over to pollution, we become guilty of the Blood of the Lord, and bring upon ourselves destruction. Our sins crucified Him once, and He forgave and cleansed us : if by obstinate sin we crucify the Son of God afresh, who shall again cleanse or forgive us? for there remaineth no more offering for sins.

Lord, by Thy Love of us, that great Love wherewith Thou hast loved us, let not our latter end be worse than our beginning.

"Kings and Priests."—At the least and lowest, each of us king with subject self to rule ; priest with leprous self to examine and judge. At one step higher "the King's face gives grace," and we edify our brethren. "Let your light so shine before men, that they may see your good works, and glorify your Father which is in Heaven." Another step upward, and we execute our priestly function of intercession, offering up prayers and thanks for all men : and highest of all, we offer up ourselves to God in will and in deed as His reasonable and lively sacrifice, beseeching Him to sanctify and accept our self-oblation.

O Good Lord God, Who uniting us with Thine everlasting King and Priest Jesus Christ, makest us unworthy in Him to be Thy kings and priests, constitute us what Thou requirest, endow us with what Thou desirest. Give us royal hearts to give back ourselves to Thee Who bestowest all, and priestly hearts to sacrifice ourselves to Thee, and keep back nothing, through the grace of Thine indwelling Holy Spirit, by Whom Christ dwells in His members. We ask this for His sake, for Whose sake we cannot ask too much. Amen.

> Long and dark the nights, dim and short the days,
> Mounting weary heights on our weary ways,
>   Thee our God we praise.
> Scaling heavenly heights by unearthly ways,
> Thee our God we praise all our nights and days,
>   Thee our God we praise.

"The First begotten of the dead." — "The Firstborn of every creature."—" He is not a God of the dead, but of the living : for all live unto Him."—"To this end Christ both died, and rose, and revived, that He might be Lord both of the dead and living." Thus tenderly does God provide for all estates of men, whether dead or alive. Though His elect be dead, He accounts and keeps them alive in Christ, and blots not their names out of the book of His remembrance, and suffers not earth so to cover their blood that they should be overlooked, and knows whence to recover their dust, and holds their souls in His hand. "The souls of the righteous are in the hand of God, and there shall no torment touch them . . . They are in peace."

St. Paul has left us words of mutual comfort : " I would not have you to be ignorant, brethren, concerning them which are asleep, that ye sorrow not, even as others which have no hope. For if we believe that Jesus died and rose again, even so them also which sleep in Jesus will God bring with Him. For this we say unto you by the word of the Lord, that we which are alive and remain unto the coming of the Lord, shall not prevent them which are asleep. For the Lord Himself shall descend from heaven with a shout, with the voice of the archangel, and with the trump of God : and the dead in Christ shall rise first : then we which are alive and remain shall be caught up together with them in the clouds, to meet the Lord in the air : and so shall we ever be with the Lord."

And years before, as one whom his mother comforteth, saintly Martha had been comforted by Christ Himself : " I am the resurrection and the life : he that believeth in Me, though he were dead, yet shall he live : and whosoever liveth and believeth in Me shall never die." Amen, Good Lord.

B

[Our Church Palms are budding willow twigs.]

> While Christ lay dead the widowed world
>   Wore willow green for hope undone ;
> Till, when bright Easter dews impearled
>   The chilly burial earth,
> All north and south, all east and west,
>   Flushed rosy in the arising sun ;
> Hope laughed, and faith resumed her rest,
>   And love remembered mirth.

"The seven Churches in Asia" on whom first alighted so great a benediction ceased centuries ago to flourish locally : nevertheless the Divine salutation has not returned unto God empty. All Christendom being the abode of the Son of peace, peace rests upon it and will rest to the end, although without respect of particular place or particular person. Those Seven Churches are representative of the entire Church Militant, the number seven standing for completeness : as seven tints paint the rainbow, and Wisdom hews out her seven pillars, and after seven weeks of years dawned the new year of the Jewish Jubilee, and a mystical seventh day closes the great week of time.

Yet as to forgiveness, seven sums not up our debt :— "Peter . . . said, Lord, how oft shall my brother sin against me, and I forgive him? till seven times? Jesus saith unto him, I say not unto thee, Until seven times : but, Until seventy times seven."

O Christ our God, Who of us requirest so much, suffer us to plead with Thyself for more than that measure which from us Thou requirest. For Thine own love's sake.

"Shall mortal man be more just than God? shall a man be more pure than his Maker?"

> If thou be dead, forgive and thou shalt live ;
>   If thou hast sinned, forgive and be forgiven ;
> God waiteth to be gracious and forgive,
>   And open heaven.
>
> Set not thy will to die and not to live ;
>   Set not thy face as flint refusing heaven ;
> Thou fool, set not thy heart on hell : forgive
>   And be forgiven.

How can man effectually ascribe to Christ "glory and dominion for ever and ever"? Not merely by uttering Amen, but by *living* Amen. To use the grace of God's most bountiful salutation, thereby attaining His peace, constitutes us His faithful servants and patient saints : servants who shall see His face and serve Him in perfection ; saints in whom He shall be glorified when He cometh to be admired in all them that believe.

"Lord, I believe; help Thou mine unbelief."

Lord Jesus, what joy was that, what covetable good, for whose sake Thou didst endure the Cross, despising the shame? Not for glory and dominion for ever and ever simply and for their own sake. Already Thou hadst glory with the Father before the world was, and dominion and fear were with Thee before man transgressed Thy commandment. Nay, rather, it was that as the bridegroom rejoiceth over the bride, so mightest Thou rejoice over us. If Thou hadst given no more than all the substance of Thy house for love, it might have been contemned: but Thou hast given Thyself. What shall we give Thee in return? What shall we not give Thee?

7. Behold, He cometh with clouds; and every eye shall see Him, and they also which pierced Him: and all kindreds of the earth shall wail because of Him. Even so, Amen.

Once to Nicodemus our Lord said: "Verily, verily, I say unto thee, We speak that we do know, and testify that we have seen: and ye receive not our witness." So now St. John, on the threshold of his revelation, cries to us: "Behold"—being about to make us see with his eyes and hear with his ears, if only we will understand with hearts akin to his own.

Dare we then aspire to become like St. John? Wherefore not, when we are bidden and invited to become like Christ?

Our likeness to St. John (if by God's grace we assume any vestige of such glory) must include faith and love, but need not involve more than an elementary degree of knowledge.

Humility and prayer will guard us against culpable misunderstanding, but may not for the present confer understanding. I once heard a teacher instruct his class that Joshua when he bade the sun stand still, himself rightly conceived the astronomical position, whilst he spoke according to the opinion of his hearers. Wherefore suppose this? Faith alone, not knowledge, seems essential to the miracle.

Similarly in our present study faith is required of us, and faith may consist with either ignorance or knowledge. We are bound to believe and obey: we may live, and haply we may die, before being called upon to recognize hidden meanings.

St. John himself, illuminated as he was beyond mortal wont, becomes our pattern of a gracious partial ignorance when he records how the Lord said not of him, "He shall not die; but,

If I will that he tarry till I come, what is that to thee?"
Certain disciples thinking to understand, misinterpreted: he
himself abiding by the simple letter of God's word, awaited
what the day should bring forth.

"Behold, He cometh with clouds."—"Behold, the Bridegroom cometh; go ye out to meet Him." Who shall go out?
Nay, who shall tarry within? "The virgins love Thee"; and
the wise virgins at length after patient watching and waiting go
out. The foolish virgins too go out; but alas! they are not of
those who shall go in to the marriage. They that are in the
graves go out, some to everlasting life, some to shame and
everlasting contempt. The sea casts up her dead. North and
south, east and west, the winds, the ends of heaven, all give
back, all bring back, the dead. A very great army.

"And every eye shall see Him."—All impelled in one
direction, all looking in one direction. Even a very small
crowd doing the same thing at the same instant has a thrilling,
awful power; as once when I saw the chorus of a numerous
orchestra turn over their music sheets at the same moment, it
brought before me the Day of Judgment.

"He cometh with clouds."—"Clouds and darkness are
round about Him; righteousness and judgment are the habitation of His throne." But we know not whether at that
supreme moment any one will even notice clouds, or angels,
or subordinate terrors. Now is our time to notice and avail
ourselves of them, if we aim at living by every word that proceedeth out of the mouth of God.

Each common cloud in this our cloudy climate may serve
to remind us of the cloud of the Ascension, and of the clouds
of the second Advent. Also of that great cloud of witnesses
who already compass us about, who one day will hear our
doom pronounced; who perhaps will then for the moment
become as nothing to us when we stand face to face with
Christ our Judge: "At the brightness of His presence His
clouds removed."

"Truly the light is sweet, and a pleasant thing it is for the
eyes to behold the sun." Good also are clouds when they
recall our thoughts to Christ; yea, good is a horror of great
darkness, if thereby He vouchsafe us a revelation.　　•

O all-sufficing Lord Jesus, our fear and our hope, nourish
in us the fear Thou requirest, and the hope Thou acceptest;
that by fear we may become bold in obedience, and by hope
indomitable in perseverance, lest we fall and perish at Thy
presence.

Ah, Lord, we all have pierced Thee : wilt Thou be
　Wroth with us all to slay us all?
Nay, Lord, be this thing far from Thee and me :
　By whom should we arise, for we are small,
　By whom if not by Thee ?

Lord, if of us who pierced Thee Thou spare one,
　Spare yet one more to love Thy face,
And yet another of poor souls undone,
　Another, and another—God of grace,
　Let mercy overrun.

We all have pierced Him, and wicked Christians far more
cruelly than did those who of old knew not what they did.
Yet to those men who handled the nails and the spear (to any
of them who repented not) seems to appertain one special pang
of recognition, their pang and not another's—a pang not
awaiting any who even from the left hand can answer, Lord,
when saw we Thee?

No retributive agony for offences against our neighbour may
equal the sight of Christ Himself recognized too late.　Yet
may it be but the extreme instance of what we incur daily,
hourly, by such offences, whether of commission, omission,
malign influence.　What will it be to meet again those whom
we would have the mountains fall upon, and the hills cover?
souls whose blood cries out against us? some twofold more
child of hell of our own making?　What will it be to depart
with our victims into everlasting fire prepared for the devil and
his angels?　O my God, what would it be by some miracle of
Thy mercy ourselves to stand safe while we behold one whom
we have corrupted depart into everlasting punishment?

David when he beheld his own misdeed visited upon his
people "spake unto the Lord . . . and said, Lo, I have sinned,
and I have done wickedly; but these sheep, what have they
done? let Thine hand, I pray Thee, be against me . . ."—
David, a man after God's own heart, saintly in his penitence.
Long before him Moses, by the grace of God, had freely identified himself for love's sake with his self-destroyed people :
"Moses returned unto the Lord, and said, Oh, this people have
sinned a great sin, and have made them gods of gold.　Yet
now, if Thou wilt, forgive their sin; and if not, blot me, I pray
Thee, out of Thy book which Thou hast written."　And once
again, centuries afterwards, St. Paul, rapt out of himself by love,
deliberately put on record : "I could wish that myself were
accursed from Christ for my brethren."　For the spiritual world
also has had its giants, mighty men that were of old, men of
renown.

Now we have been created small, and not great, and further, we may have stunted and dwarfed ourselves by sin; and if so (at least for the present) it may both seem and be simply hopeless for us to aim at heights or at depths.   Still, however ignominious our level, the person we have wronged has a present, urgent, instant claim upon us, and if we can do nothing else by way of reparation, we can pray for him.   "Yes, verily, and by God's help so I will."

O Lord God, Almighty and All-merciful, cleanse those whom I have defiled, heal those whom I have wounded, strengthen those whom I have enfeebled, set right those whom I have misled, recall to Thyself those whom I have alienated from Thee.   I pray Thee, save these sinners, save all sinners, and amongst all sinners save me the sinner.   For Jesus' sake, the Friend of sinners.   Amen.

"All kindreds of the earth shall wail because of Him"—or, as in the Revised Version : "All the tribes of the earth shall mourn over Him."   The two translations suggest different trains of thought.

The first seems to set before us those whose resurrection bodies being still of the earth earthy, their resurrection cannot but be the resurrection of damnation.   "Kindreds of the earth," and by their own free will wedded to earth, the union abides indissoluble even while earth and all that is therein are being burnt up because the Day of the Lord is come. "There shall be wailing and gnashing of teeth."   They whose whole lives have clamoured to God to depart from them must abide by the awful sentence, "Depart from Me."

But the second reading has a different sound, rather as if all souls alike should go forth and weep bitterly,—alike, yet how unlike.   Saints mourning because they have never mourned enough over the sins which slew their Beloved, because they have never loved enough the Beloved of their souls.   "They shall look upon Me Whom they have pierced, and they shall mourn for Him as one mourneth for his only son, and shall be in bitterness for Him, as one that is in bitterness for his firstborn."

Yet not to picture saints as mourning when the days of mourning are ended, I set aside my own thought, and dwell upon it only so far as to realize vividly the unworthiness of even the most worthy, and (if such grace be granted me) to nurse tenderness and contrition in my own hard heart.

Lord, now give us tears, yea, always tears so long as they shall be to Thy glory ; tears acceptable to Thee, stored in Thy bottle; tears which Thou Thyself wilt wipe away.

Thy lovely saints do bring Thee love,
  Incense and joy and gold ;
Fair star with star, fair dove with dove,
  Beloved by Thee of old.
I, Master, neither star nor dove,
  Have brought Thee sins and tears ;
Yet I too bring a little love
  Amid my flaws and fears.
A trembling love that faints and fails
  Yet still is love of Thee,
A wondering love that hopes and hails
  Thy boundless love of me ;
Love kindling faith and pure desire,
  Love following on to bliss,
A spark, O Jesus, from Thy fire,
  A drop from Thine abyss.

"Even so, Amen."—"Amen" alone closed the doxology
(ver. 6), but here where judgment is the theme, St. John doubles
his assent.   A lesson of adhesion to the revealed Will of God,
be that Will what it may: a foreshowing of the perfected will
and mind of all saints at the separating right and left of the
final division : an example of the conformity we must now pray
and strive after : even so, Amen..

**8. I am Alpha and Omega, the beginning and the ending,
saith the Lord, which is, and which was, and which is
to come, the Almighty.**

" I am Alpha and Omega."—Thus well-nigh at the opening
of these mysterious Revelations, we find in this title an instance
of symbolical language accommodated to human apprehension ;
for any literal acceptation of the phrase seems obviously and
utterly inadmissible.   God condescends to teach us somewhat
we can learn, and in a way by which we are capable of learning
it.   So, doubtless, either literally or figuratively, throughout
the entire Book.

Such a consideration encourages us, I think, to pursue our
study of the Apocalypse, ignorant as we may be.   Bring we
patience and prayer to our quest, and assuredly we shall not
be sent empty away.   The Father of lights may still withhold
from us knowledge, but He will not deny us wisdom.

" Open Thou mine eyes, that I may behold wondrous things
out of Thy law."

If a letter of the alphabet may be defined as a unit of
language, then under this title "Alpha and Omega" we may
adore God as the sole original Existence, the Unit of Existence

whence are derived all nations, and kindreds, and people, and tongues; yea, all other existences whatsoever.

This title derived from human language seems to call especially upon "men confabulant" for grateful homage. As said of old the wise son of Sirach: "The Lord hath given me a tongue for my reward, and I will praise Him therewith." Or as the sweet Psalmist of Israel declared: "I will sing and give praise with the best member that I have."

Alas! that men often pervert their choicest gifts to their soul's dire destruction. For St. James bears witness against the tongue: "The tongue is a little member, and boasteth great things. Behold, how great a matter a little fire kindleth! And the tongue is a fire, a world of iniquity: so is the tongue among our members, that it defileth the whole body, and setteth on fire the course of nature; and it is set on fire of hell . . . The tongue can no man tame; it is an unruly evil, full of deadly poison."

O Lord Jesus Christ, Wisdom and Word of God, dwell in our hearts, I beseech Thee, by Thy most Holy Spirit, that out of the abundance of our hearts our mouths may speak Thy praise. Amen.

"The beginning and the ending."—"The beginning" absolutely and in every sense, antecedent to all, cause of all, origin of all.

Not so "the ending"; for by God's merciful Will whilst all creatures have a commencement, many abide exempt from any end, being constituted to share His own eternity. Yet in a different sense God is "the Ending" of all creation, inasmuch as all permanent good creatures converge to His Beatific Presence, find their true unalterable level at His right hand, rejoice in His joy, and rest in His rest for ever and ever. In Him all, out of Him none, attain to fulness of life immortal. "He that dwelleth in the secret place of the Most High, shall abide under the shadow of the Almighty."

Contrariwise, obstinate sinners who finally and of set purpose approach not unto Him by attraction of love, dash themselves against Him in endless rebellion of hatred; as miry waves upheaved over and over again from the troubled deep might shatter themselves over and over again against the Rock of Ages.

"Fear ye not me? saith the Lord: will ye not tremble at My presence, which have placed the sand for the bound of the sea by a perpetual decree, that it cannot pass it: and though the waves thereof toss themselves, yet can they not prevail; though they roar, yet can they not pass over it?"

" If I ascend up into heaven, Thou art there : if I make my
bed in hell, behold, Thou art there."

" The Almighty."—

> O Lord Almighty, Who hast formed us weak,
>> With us whom Thou hast formed deal fatherly ;
> Be found of us whom Thou hast deigned to seek,
>> Be found that we the more may seek for Thee ;
> Lord, speak and grant us ears to hear Thee speak ;
>> Lord, come to us and grant us eyes to see ;
> Lord, make us meek, for Thou Thyself art meek ;
>> Lord, Thou art Love, fill us with charity.
> O Thou the Life of living and of dead,
>> Who givest more the more Thyself hast given,
> Suffice us as Thy saints Thou hast sufficed ;
>> That beautified, replenished, comforted,
> Still gazing off from earth and up at heaven,
> We may pursue Thy steps, Lord Jesus Christ.

Christ said : " I will forewarn you whom ye shall fear.   Fear
Him, which after He hath killed hath power to cast into hell ;
yea, I say unto you, Fear Him "—words to awaken fear : may
it be a godly fear.

Meanwhile in these words of dread lies a great encouragement.   The power to destroy us is limited to the Almighty,
and He is the All-merciful.

" O God, Who declarest Thy almighty power most chiefly in
showing mercy and pity ; mercifully grant unto us such a
measure of Thy grace, that we, running the way of Thy
commandments, may obtain Thy gracious promises, and be
made partakers of Thy heavenly treasure ; through Jesus Christ
our Lord.   Amen."

" The Lord appeared to Abram, and said unto him, I am
the Almighty God ; walk before Me, and be thou perfect."—
"When the Almighty scattered kings for their sake : then were
they as white as snow in Salmon."

Because our God is Almighty, therefore can He demand of
us purity and perfection, for by aid of His preventing grace we
can respond to His demand.   Thanks be to Him, through
Jesus Christ our Righteousness.

How light a heart befits one whose burden the Almighty deigns
to carry with him.   " Why art thou so heavy, O my soul : and
why art thou so disquieted within me? Oh, put thy trust in God."

**9. I John, who also am your brother, and companion in
tribulation, and in the kingdom and patience of Jesus
Christ, was in the island that is called Patmos, for the
word of God, and for the testimony of Jesus Christ.**

" Your brother, and companion . . . in the kingdom . . .
of Jesus Christ."—Thus far St. John addresses all baptized
Christians; but not necessarily all, as concerns "tribulation"
and "patience." The first and obvious privileges are ours by
Royal gift; the second and less obvious are likewise ours
potentially and in the germ, yet neither effectually nor in
maturity unless our own free will co-operate with God's pre-
disposing grace.

Patience is a great grace; but is it at all a privilege? Yes,
surely. The patient soul, lord of itself, sits imperturbable amid
the jars of life and serene under its frets. " Let patience have
her perfect work, that ye may be perfect and entire, wanting
nothing." - Hence we infer that where patience is perfect,
nought else will remain imperfect.

Tribulation cannot but be a privilege, inasmuch as it makes
us so far like Christ.

O Tender Lord Jesus, Who layest not upon us more than
we can bear, give us patience in tribulation; a courageous, sweet
patience; a patient, indomitable hope.

"I John . . . was in the isle that is called Patmos, for
the word of God, and for the testimony of Jesus Christ."—All
for edification, nothing for self-glorification: so much and no
more does St. John tell us of his confession and exile.

Christians should resemble fire-flies, not glow-worms; their
brightness drawing eyes upward, not downward.

**10. I was in the Spirit on the Lord's day, and heard behind
me a great voice, as of a trumpet,**

**11. Saying, I am Alpha and Omega, the First and the Last:
and, What thou seest, write in a book, and send it unto
the seven churches which are in Asia; unto Ephesus,
and unto Smyrna, and unto Pergamos, and unto
Thyatira, and unto Sardis, and unto Philadelphia, and
unto Laodicea.**

"I was in the Spirit on the Lord's day."—Rome and St.
John had come to an issue. Rome had power of life and
death, chains and sentence of banishment on its side: St. John
on his side had the defence of the Most High and the shadow
of the Almighty. "Where the Spirit of the Lord is, there is
liberty," neither was the Word of God bound. Immovable as
Patmos the rock amid buffeting winds and waves, St. John
stood fast in the liberty wherewith Christ had made him
free.

Earth cannot bar flame from ascending,
Hell cannot bind light from descending,
Death cannot finish life never ending.

Eagle and sun gaze at each other,
Eagle at sun, brother at Brother,
Loving in peace and joy one another.

O St. John, with chains for thy wages,
Strong thy rock where the storm-blast rages,
Rock of refuge, the Rock of Ages.

Rome hath passed with her awful voice,
Earth is passing with all her joys,
Heaven shall pass away with a noise.

So from us all follies that please us,
So from us all falsehoods that ease us,—
Only all saints abide with their Jesus.

Jesus, in love looking down hither,
Jesus, by love draw us up thither,
That we in Thee may abide together.

"A great voice, as of a trumpet, saying . . ."—Now if the trumpet give an uncertain sound, who shall prepare himself to the battle? But this trumpet voice uttereth no uncertain sound, but a great alarum, sounding an alarm in God's holy mountain, and bidding every soul make ready against the sounding of that other trumpet-blast which will compel a response from living and dead, one and all.

If we entertain any uncertainty as to this voice, the uncertainty lurks in ourselves, not elsewhere. So when long ago sundry men appeared " as trees, walking," any peculiarity observed resided in the vision of him who gazed, not in the appearance of them who walked.

Speak, Lord, for Thy servant heareth. Grant us ears to hear, eyes to see, wills to obey, hearts to love : then declare what Thou wilt, reveal what Thou wilt, command what Thou wilt, demand what Thou wilt. Amen.

The clause, " I am Alpha and Omega, the First and the Last," is here omitted by the Revised Version. Very nearly the same words have already occurred (ver. 8) and will recur (xxi. 6 ; xxii. 13).

"What thou seest, write in a book, and send it . . ."— " Write," and forthwith St. John wrote. "Send it," and when the moment came, means of transmission would be forthcoming. Could St. John forecast those means? Very probably not ; but like another blessed saint before him, he did what he could.

Not so we. We make sure that the first step which depends on ourselves can be taken, but we indulge misgivings as to the second step which depends upon God alone. Whereupon we omit that first step divinely put within our own power. God condescends to trust us, and we will not trust Him.

> Lord, I am here.—But, child, I look for thee
>   Elsewhere and nearer Me.—
> Lord, that way moans a wide insatiate sea :
>   How can I come to Thee ?—
> Set foot upon the water, test and see
>   If thou canst come to Me.—
> Couldst Thou not send a boat to carry me,
>   Or dolphin swimming free ?—
> Nay, boat nor fish if thy will faileth thee :
>   For My Will too is free.—
> O Lord, I am afraid.—Take hold on Me :
>   I am stronger than the sea.—
> Save, Lord, I perish.—I have hold of thee,
>   I made and rule the sea,
> I bring thee to the haven where thou wouldst be.

"To the seven Churches which are in Asia."—What St. John saw and wrote concerns Christendom of to-day, no less directly and urgently than it concerned the seven Churches of the Apostolic day. The great voice as of a trumpet adjures every soul within hearing.

As a matter of history, those seven Churches were in the main swept away long ago, misbelief ravaging and occupying their territory. Their charge has been transferred to us, their burden laid upon us : it is we who are called upon to overcome. Amen !

12. And I turned to see the voice that spake with me. And being turned, I saw seven golden candlesticks;
13. And in the midst of the seven candlesticks one like unto
-   the Son of man, clothed with a garment down to the foot, and girt about the paps with a golden girdle.
14. His head and his hairs were white like wool, as white as snow; and His eyes were as a flame of fire;
15. And His feet like unto fine brass, as if they burned in a furnace; and His voice as the sound of many waters.
16. And He had in His right hand seven stars : and out of His mouth went a sharp two-edged sword : and His countenance was as the sun shineth in his strength.

"When Thou saidst, Seek ye My face ; my heart said unto Thee, Thy face, Lord, will I seek."

At the call of Jesus the saints turn as doves to their windows. Are then their faces ever set from and not towards their Lord ? Yes, by a figure, and so far as to confirm what St. John himself elsewhere avers: "If we say that we have no sin, we deceive ourselves." Mortal saints at the best are such as St. Paul describes himself as being: "Not as though I had already attained, either were already perfect: but I follow after, if that I may apprehend that for which also I am apprehended of Christ Jesus."

Christ is our fountain-head and our abyss ; we begin from Him, we end in Him. What He maketh us we are ; what He bestoweth upon us we possess. We, as it were, pour and empty ourselves and our treasures into Him, yet we enrich Him not: what have we that we have not received? The gifts He giveth us are and remain His: we only ourselves, unless we abide in Him, retain neither life nor portion.

"All the rivers run into the sea; yet the sea is not full; unto the place from whence the rivers come, thither they return again "—this is true of earth's sea and of all which it typifies: full it is, yet not filled, and it moans as with a craving unappeasable.

Let us not refuse fulness to choose emptiness. " Behold your God ! . . . Behold, the nations are as a drop of a bucket . . . And Lebanon is not sufficient to burn, nor the beasts thereof sufficient for a burnt offering."

" I sleep, but my heart waketh: it is the voice of my Beloved." As sleep with a wakeful heart soon to be fully awakened, as the needle's trembling to and fro to find its rest, so is the saint's turning from and turning back to Christ. The sanctified heart was neither slumbering nor estranged, but the face had as it were perforce been turned away while the feet sped on some Divine errand. " Turn again then unto thy rest, O my soul." " I turned myself to behold Wisdom."

"And being turned, I saw seven golden candlesticks ; and in the midst of the seven candlesticks One like unto the Son of man."—St. John first saw, or at least he first mentions having seen, not the One like unto the Son of man, but the seven surrounding candlesticks. Even in that overwhelming Presence, and at that moment of visible reunion, those likewise he beheld : thus vividly bringing home to us the precept: " That he who loveth God love his brother also."

O Gracious Lord Omniscient, Who hast forewarned us that if we love not the brother we see neither can we love Thyself unseen ; replenish us with such grace that we may love our brethren much for Thy sake, and Thee much more for Thine own sake. And if any love us, grant us our heart's desire that from love of us they may ascend to the supreme love of Thee. Amen, merciful Lord Jesus, Amen.

Moreover, who were they that St. John saw?

Not (so far as we read) St. James his brother and fellow-heir, not St. Peter with whom he had walked in the House of God as a friend, not one by one any of those elect persons whom he loved in the truth, and to one of whom he wrote: "And now I beseech thee . . . that we love one another." He beheld, and merely in a figure, congregations of Christians, the majority of whom he may never have seen face to face in the flesh.

Now St. John wrote by inspiration of the Holy Ghost. "Saith He it altogether for our sakes? For our sakes, no doubt, this is written."

If St. John, a man so greatly beloved and so greatly corresponding to the Divine Love, recovered not in that moment of ecstasy the visible presence of saints personally dear to him, much more may we believe that from our frail selves the prospect of such reunions is kept veiled purposely and in mercy. As it is and thus relegated to the background of celestial prevision, the hope of reunion eclipses all earthly hopes: placed in the foreground, it might block out even our hope of the Beatific Vision.

O Gracious Lord God, Who deignest to make of man Thy mirror, that we in one another may behold Thine Image and love Thyself; unto every one of us grant, I beseech Thee, thus to love and thus to be beloved. For our Lord Jesus Christ's sake, Son of God and Son of man. Amen.

"Seven golden candlesticks."—"The King's Daughter is all glorious within: her clothing is of wrought gold." "Is not . . . the body [more] than raiment?" So likewise the light of the candlestick is more than the gold thereof.

Exterior gifts and privileges adorn and dignify Christ's Bride, interior grace makes and keeps her His. True alike of church, of congregation, of two or three gathered together, of each solitary soul.

The golden candlestick is the vessel appointed to honour: the light freely received must freely be given forth. The *gold* is personal, yet by sympathy becomes common to all: if "one member be honoured, all the members rejoice with it." The *light* too is personal, but by emission is shared by all: set on its candlestick it gives light to all that are in the house.

"Remember the words of the Lord Jesus, how He said, It is more blessed to give than to receive."

> O Lord, on Whom we gaze and dare not gaze,
> Increase our faith that gazing we may see,
> And seeing love, and loving worship Thee
> Through all our days, our long and lengthening days.
> O Lord, accessible to prayer and praise,
> Kind Lord, companion of the two or three,
> Good Lord, be gracious to all men and me,
> Lighten our darkness and amend our ways.
> Call up our hearts to Thee, that where Thou art
> Our treasure and our heart may dwell at one ;
> Then let the pallid moon pursue her sun,
> So long as it shall please Thee, far apart,—
> Yet art Thou with us, Thou to Whom we run,
> We hand in hand with Thee and heart in heart.

"Moses hid his face ; for he was afraid to look upon God."

The unutterable, unapproachable Majesty of "One like unto the Son of man" bids us fall prostrate. "Be not rash with thy mouth, and let not thine heart be hasty to utter anything before God: for God is in heaven, and thou upon earth: therefore let thy words be few."

I believe in Jesus Christ, God's only Son, our Lord, co-eternal and co-equal with the Father.

Daniel the prophet "beheld . . . and the Ancient of Days did sit, Whose garment was white as snow, and the hair of His head like the pure wool. . . . A fiery stream issued, and came forth from before Him. . . . And, behold, One like the Son of man came with the clouds of heaven, and came to the Ancient of Days." So now St. John beheld "One like unto the Son of man, clothed with a garment down to the foot, and girt about the paps with a golden girdle. His head and His hairs were white like wool, as white as snow ; and His eyes were as a flame of fire ; and His feet like unto fine brass, as if they burned in a furnace."

Daniel beheld a garment white as snow, but saith not that it was girded. St. John beheld a girded garment, but nameth not its colour. God, as God, is not girded: "The Father Incomprehensible, the Son Incomprehensible, and the Holy Ghost Incomprehensible. And yet they are not three Incomprehensibles, but One Incomprehensible." God, as Christ, is girded: "He took on Him the seed of Abraham." Once even He deigned to say: "How am I straitened . . . !" God inhabiteth eternity: Christ was sent forth in the fulness of time, and before His Passion spake saying: "My time is at hand."

The white garment recalls that light which no man can approach unto, wherein God dwelleth. But Isaiah in vision beheld Christ red in His apparel when, wearing the girded garment, He proclaimed Himself Mighty to save.

Our Lord's own gracious words express to us the mystery of His eternal glory with the Father, and of His somewhile self-restriction to the limitations and poverty of time : " I have glorified Thee on the earth : I have finished the work which Thou gavest Me to do. And now, O Father, glorify Thou Me with Thine own Self with the glory which I had with Thee before the world was."

" Clothed with a garment down to the foot."—Behold our great High Priest !

Now under the Mosaic dispensation, how was Aaron the first high priest clothed, and wherewith were his sacred vestments overclothed ? King David partially informs us :— " Behold, how good and how pleasant it is for brethren to dwell together in unity ! It is like the precious ointment upon the head, that ran down upon the beard, even Aaron's beard : that went down to the skirts of his garments ; as the dew of Hermon, and as the dew that descended upon the mountains of Zion : for there the Lord commanded the blessing, even life for evermore."

That unction symbolic of God the Holy Spirit overflowed not Aaron's person only, but his robe also : in like manner Christ's Divine graces overflowing from Himself the Head, pour down upon His members, until the least little one whose life is hid with Christ may sing merrily : " I will greatly rejoice in the Lord, my soul shall be joyful in my God ; for He hath clothed me with the garments of salvation, He hath covered me with the robe of righteousness, as a bridegroom decketh himself with ornaments, and as a bride adorneth herself with her jewels." For if brotherly unity be like that precious ointment, then is that precious ointment under some one of its many aspects like brotherly unity : which unity with one another, yea, with Christ Himself, it lies within our own option to clench and perpetuate according to His benign announcement : " Whosoever shall do the will of God, the same is My brother, and My sister, and mother."

God's commandment is exceeding broad, not by us limitable. Amongst its incalculable treasures we here find our own commanded blessing, even life for evermore,—Christ, Who is our life. " The King . . . asked life of Thee, and Thou gavest it Him, even length of days for ever and ever."

"And girt about the paps with a golden girdle."—This girdle lying next the Sacred Heart, as it were binds and constrains it. Now gold Christ hath in common with the saints who all together make up the Church's golden candlestick. The precious sons of Zion, comparable to fine gold, flesh of His flesh and bone of His bone, may seem memorialized in this golden girdle which, not for malediction but for benediction, Christ weareth for a girdle wherewith He is girded continually.

O Lord, Who so hast loved us, Who so lovest us, grant us grace so to love Thee that we may never fall away from Thy love.

"His eyes were as a flame of fire."—"Who among us shall dwell with the devouring fire? who among us shall dwell with everlasting burnings? He that walketh righteously, and speaketh uprightly . . . Thine eyes shall see the King in His beauty."

God is Light: Christ is Light of Light, Very God of Very God. His eyes are light, all-seeing: "Yea, the darkness is no darkness with Thee, but the night is as clear as the day: the darkness and light to Thee are both alike."

O Lord, Who beholding Adam and Eve in their misery didst find comfort for them, Who beholding David in his pollution spakest the word that he should not die; Thou, Lord, Who hast beheld all sinners from the first sinner, and wilt behold us all even unto the last; turn Thy face from our sins, but turn it not from us.

These are the very Eyes which I myself at the last day may look upon, and which will look upon me.

"In the Day of Judgment, good Lord, deliver us."

> O Jesu, gone so far apart
> Only my heart can follow Thee,
> That look which pierced St. Peter's heart
> Turn now on me.
>
> Thou Who dost search me thro' and thro'
> And mark the crooked ways I went,
> Look on me, Lord, and make me too
> Thy penitent.

"His feet like unto fine brass, as if they burned in a furnace."—"I will make the place of My feet glorious."

These dazzling Feet before which the sun running his course as a giant and the moon walking in brightness are ashamed, whence came they? Out of great tribulation. These are they which went about doing good, and grew weary along the paths of Palestine, and climbed Calvary, and were nailed to a cross. These are they which a penitent sinner and an accepted saint washed with tears, kissed, anointed with precious ointment, dried with tresses of hair. These are they which in infancy a Virgin Mother swaddled, and which after the Resurrection holy women were permitted to touch.

No cross, no crown : no humiliation, no glory. Such is the rule for fallen man. And Christ, Who took upon Himself our nature and calls us brethren, exempted not Himself from the common lot.

He willed thus to become like us. We by following Him shall in our turn put on a measure of His likeness. To-day He denies not to His beloved crosses and humiliations : to-morrow what will He deny to them whom He invests with crowns and glory? "What shall be done unto the man whom the king delighteth to honour?"

I have read of a holy person who said : "O my feet, ye shall tread upon the stars." Feet that would climb up into heaven must wend their way thither by treading in Christ's footsteps. "Feet was I to the lame," said righteous Job, whose end was better than his beginning.

Now to walk in Christ's incomparable footsteps is both easy and difficult. The easiness lies in our surroundings, the difficulty in ourselves. Flesh is weak, and spirit too often unwilling ; otherwise London or any other neighbourhood might become to us holy as Palestine. There waits in every direction abundant good to be done, if only we have the will patiently to do it, first counting the cost. For though no literal mountain obstruct our path, mountainous opposition may confront us ; and if it please not God to remove it, then in His strength, weary and heartsore as we may be, we must surmount it, "looking unto Jesus." "But as for me, my feet were almost gone ; my steps had well-nigh slipped."

"No man can come to Me, except the Father which hath sent Me draw him."

"Draw me, we will run after Thee."

"Feet have they, but they walk not," writes the Psalmist, in his description of idols : and he appends thereto, "They that make them are like unto them." Thus we behold the idolater furnished with useless feet; and so far like him appears the sluggard, standing here all the day idle on feet useless because unused.

"O thou that art named the house of Jacob, is the Spirit of

the Lord straitened? are these His doings? do not My words
do good to him that walketh uprightly? . . . Arise ye, and
depart; for this is not your rest."

"I thought on my ways, and turned my feet unto Thy
testimonies."

How beautiful upon the celestial mountains will be those
feet which, ever following in the steps of Jesus, at length
ascend into the hill of the Lord, and stand in His holy place!
Surely it is no mean privilege here to wash feet which shall be
dazzling there. It is good to wash them, it is better to follow
them. Worthily to wash the saints' feet we need ourselves to
be saints. It is a blessed communion of mutual service which
our tender Lord enjoins upon us when He says: "Ye also
ought to wash one another's feet"—having first by His
loveliest example commended to us His lovely precept.

"What shall I say? He hath both spoken unto me, and
Himself hath done it."

> What will it be, O my soul, what will it be
> To touch the long-raced-for goal, to handle and see,
> To rest in the joy of joys, in the joy of the blest,
> To rest and revive and rejoice, to rejoice and to rest!

"His voice as the sound of many waters."—Blessed be God
Who hath vouchsafed us the revelation: "Many waters cannot
quench love, neither can the floods drown it." Our loving
Lord hath declared: "My sheep hear My voice, and I know
them, and they follow Me"—"Every one that is of the truth
heareth My voice."

> We are of those who tremble at Thy word;
> Who faltering walk in darkness toward our close
> Of mortal life, by terrors curbed and spurred:
> We are of those.
>
> We journey to that land which no man knows,
> Who any more can make his voice be heard
> Above the clamour of our wants and woes.
>
> Not ours the hearts Thy loftiest love hath stirred,
> Not such as we Thy lily and Thy rose:—
> Yet, Hope of those who hope with hope deferred,
> We are of those.

Centuries before St. John, the Prophet Ezekiel beheld and
heard the Divine Glory and Voice: "Behold, the Glory of
the God of Israel came from the way of the east: and His
Voice was like a noise of many waters: and the earth shined
with His Glory."

It is the same Voice and the same Glory. "I am the Lord, I change not; therefore ye sons of Jacob are not consumed."

Still waters are silent; flowing waters find a voice. This "voice as the sound of many waters" seems to address man not from the eternal calm of Christ's Godhead; but rather from that veritable and accessible Humanity which He assumed, which can be touched with a feeling of our infirmities, which was symbolized by the smitten rock whence water gushed out, and which on the cross yielded water as well as blood from a pierced side.

Therefore, though it be a Voice to shake not earth only, but also heaven, to us who are bone of His bone and flesh of His flesh, it conveys not awe alone, but therewith courage and comfort. It hath "a sound of abundance of rain" when it certifies the outpouring of God the Holy Ghost in the waters of Baptism; and a tone of tender reassurance in the protest that the waters of Noah shall no more go over the earth; and a promise to saints that the one cup of cold water shall by no means remain unrequited; and a hope for penitents that God keepeth a bottle for our tears. It crieth: "Ho, every one that thirsteth, come ye to the waters": and lo! these are waters of comfort beside which the Lord Himself will lead us.

The Prayer-book version of that lovely twenty-third Psalm gives "waters of comfort," whilst its Bible equivalent is "still waters." If we may figuratively connect one phrase with our Lord's Godhead, the other with His Manhood, then indeed are we reminded of God's promise to make His elect "partakers of the Divine Nature."

God the Son clothed Himself with our nature to the intent that He might clothe us with His own.

"There was no more spirit in her. And she said to the King . . . The half was not told me . . . Because the Lord loved Israel for ever, therefore made He thee King, to do judgment and justice."

> Lord, Thou art fulness, I am emptiness:
> Yet hear my heart speak in its speechlessness
> Extolling Thine unuttered loveliness.

"And He had in His right hand seven stars."—In His mortal day our Lord had said: "My sheep hear My voice, and I know them, and they follow Me: and I give unto them eternal life; and they shall never perish, neither shall any man pluck them out of My hand. My Father, which gave them Me, is greater

than all ; and no man is able to pluck them out of My Father's
hand. I and My Father are one."

· "His right hand doth embrace me," saith peacefully the
Bride of the Canticles.

All weareth, all wasteth,
A'l flitteth, all hasteth,
All of flesh and time :—
Sound, sweet heavenly chime,
Ring in the unutterable, eternal prime.

Man hopeth, man feareth,
Man droopeth :—Christ cheereth,
Compassing release,
Comforting with peace,
Promising rest where strife and anguish cease.

Saints waking, saints sleeping,
Rest well in safe keeping ;
Well they rest to-day
While they watch and pray,—
But their to-morrow's rest what tongue shall say ?

"Out of His mouth went a sharp two-edged sword."—Thus
in the Epistle to the Hebrews : "The word of God is quick,
and powerful, and sharper than any two-edged sword, piercing
even to the dividing asunder of soul and spirit, and of the
joints and marrow, and is a discerner of the thoughts and
intents of the heart."

Four points I note : life, keenness, in the weapon ; depth,
subtilty, in the wound. That which probes and sunders me
will never of its own proper nature slay me ; for life it is, not
death, that thus cleaves its way into my heart of hearts. It will
do its work exquisitely, for it is sharp ; and thoroughly by
reason of the might and skill of Him Who wields it. It may
not spare for my crying ; nevertheless not a hair of my
head need perish, and dear is my blood in His sight Who
smites me.

No mere surface work can possibly be this saving work of
which the text speaks : a religion without depth is not Christ's
religion. The necessity of depth is set forth in the Parable of
the Sower: the seed enters not at all into the first refuse soil,
and barely penetrates into the second ; in the third it perishes
from a different cause ; in the fourth and good ground alone
does it take root downward and bear fruit upward.

Are we afraid of a dividing asunder of our very selves? Nay,
and if we be, let fear nerve us to endure it ; for more dreadful
will be the cutting asunder of the reprobate servant.

This whole passage (vers. 13—16) sets our adorable Lord before us under an aspect which recalls St. Paul's prophecy concerning Him as the destroyer of antichrist : " Then shall that wicked be revealed, whom the Lord shall consume with the Spirit of His mouth, and shall destroy with the brightness of His . coming,"—and more remotely that Divine announcement concerning Leviathan : " He that made him can make His sword to approach unto him." Further on (xiii. 10) we shall read : " He that killeth with the sword must be killed with the sword," or according to the Revised Version : " If any man shall kill with the sword, with the sword must he be killed " : whence by analogy it appears that he who must be slain by the sword of Christ's mouth, cannot but be one whose own tongue has been a deadly sharp sword. So Daniel saith of the " little horn," that it had " a mouth speaking great things," and again : " a mouth that spake very great things."

Now without aiming at matters too wonderful for me which I know not, and amongst them must obviously be included those times and seasons which the Father hath put in His own power; and therefore without hazarding conjectures touching the coming of the last antichrist, I turn to St. John's first Epistle and read : " Little children, it is the last time : and as ye have heard that antichrist shall come, even now are there many antichrists; whereby we know that it is the last time . . . Who is a liar but he that denieth that Jesus is the Christ? He is antichrist, that denieth the Father and the Son . . . Every spirit that confesseth not that Jesus Christ is come in the flesh is not of God : and this is that spirit of antichrist, whereof ye have heard that it should come ; and even now already is it in the world."

Alas then for much which at this day is said and written amongst us upon whom the ends of the world are come. " And if one look unto the land, behold darkness and sorrow, and the light is darkened in the heavens thereof."

It is wiser to remain ignorant than to learn evil.

Evil knowledge acquired in one wilful moment of curiosity may harass and haunt us to the end of our time. And how after the end of our time ?

It is better to avoid doubts than to reject them.

To study a difficulty is too often to incur one.

" Who is blind as he that is perfect, and blind as the Lord's servant ? " They especially are bound to such reserve who have been in familiar contact with any living example of holy intellectual self-restraint : and amongst these am I, who for years enjoyed intercourse with one thus truly wise, and before me in many gifts and graces.

"And His countenance was as the sun shineth in his strength."—"The sun, which is as a bridegroom coming out of his chamber, and rejoiceth as a strong man to run a race. His going forth is from the end of the heaven, and his circuit unto the ends of it: and there is nothing hid from the heat thereof." "That was the true Light, which lighteth every man that cometh into the world": or as in the Revised Text: "There was the true light, even the light which lighteth every man, coming into the world."

What, *every* man? Yea, for the truth certifies it. Nevertheless, "that the righteous should be as the wicked, that be far from Thee: shall not the Judge of all the earth do right?" This Same is He Who having long made His sun to rise on the evil and on the good, will at length judge every man according to his works.

Job bears witness against sinners: "They are of those that rebel against the light; they know not the ways thereof, nor abide in the paths thereof." Here it is not the light that withdraws from them, but they that withdraw from the light. Whilst in the Answer from the Whirlwind we read: "Hast thou commanded the morning since thy days; and caused the dayspring to know his place; that it might take hold of the ends of the earth, that the wicked might be shaken out of it? . . . And from the wicked their light is withholden." Here the light seems to reveal and overwhelm, yet penally to be kept back.

And our Lord instructing Nicodemus declared: "This is the condemnation, that light is come into the world, and men loved darkness rather than light, because their deeds were evil. For every one that doeth evil hateth the light, neither cometh to the light, lest his deeds should be reproved. But he that doeth truth cometh to the light, that his deeds may be made manifest, that they are wrought in God,"—setting forth in harmony Divine free grace and human free will. And elsewhere He proclaims: "I am the Light of the world; he that followeth Me shall not walk in darkness, but shall have the light of life."

Does light reveal the colours of coloured objects, or does it impart colour to objects in themselves all alike colourless? Colour appears to be simply an analysis of light; if so, the withdrawal of light involves no mere disappearance of colour, but its absolute absence. Thus objects shut up in darkness would needs become part and parcel of that darkness, not because of any infliction from without, but because of what they themselves intrinsically are.

By an awful parallel this suggests how " he that hath the Son hath life ; and he that hath not the Son of God hath not life." How " he that hath not" must be deprived even of that which he seemeth to have. How amongst the lost there may not be found any mixed characters, any redeeming points such as used to endear many a wilful sinner even to penitents and saints. For "every good gift and every perfect gift is from above, and cometh down from the Father of lights." Cut off from the dayspring of colour, there can be no colour ; from the Source of goodness, no goodness ; from the Fountain of grace, no grace ; from the root of life, no life. " O Israel, thou hast destroyed thyself: but in Me is thine help." " To-day if ye will hear His voice, harden not your hearts."

Lord Jesus, Who lightest every man that cometh into the world, suffer us not for any snares of life or pains of death to fall from Thee.

But not only are we warned that he "that hath not" forfeits what seems his, elsewhere we see the one talent transferred from the slothful to the diligent servant. What does this indicate ? Can it be that so we are taught how heaven can be made heaven even to those who may enter it bereft of some they loved on earth?

If we analyze love, what is it we love in our beloved? Something that is lovable, not any hateful residuum ; something that kindles admiration, attracts fondness, wins confidence, nourishes hope, engrosses affection. If love arises from a mere misreading of appearances, then deeper insight may suffice to annul it. But if it arises from a genuine, though alas! transitory cause, then a transference of the endearing grace to another might seem the remedy. On earth the hollow semblance or the temporary endowment is believed in and preferred ; in heaven the perpetual reality. Crown and love together are transferred from Vashti to Esther ; the satisfied heart accepts Jacob as " very " Esau.

Not that flesh and blood may be able to endure the foresight. But as man's day so shall his strength be, and flesh and blood are not called to inherit the kingdom of God.

Lord Jesus, save us from any such experience, Thou Who loving Thine own lovest them unto the end. Amen.

> Light colourless doth colour all things else :
> Where light dwells pleasure dwells
> And peace excels.

Then rise and shine,
Thou shadowed soul of mine,
And let a cheerful rainbow make thee fine.

Light fountain of all beauty and delight
Leads day forth from the night,
Turns blackness white.
　Light waits for thee
　Where all have eyes to see :
　Oh well is thee and happy shalt thou be !

**17. And when I saw Him, I fell at His feet as dead. And
He laid His right hand upon me, saying unto me, Fear
not ; I am the First and the Last :**

**18. I am He that liveth, and was dead ; and, behold, I am
alive for evermore, Amen ; and have the keys of hell
and of death.**

" And when I saw Him, I fell at His feet as dead.' —" The
righteous, and the wise, and their works, are in the hand of
God : no man knoweth either love or hatred by all that is
before them. All things come alike to all : there is one event
to the righteous, and to the wicked ; to the good and to the
clean, and to the unclean. . . . There is one event unto
all." In this world and on the surface so it is : God's elect
seem to die, and their departure is taken for misery and their
end to be utter destruction ; yet are they in peace. Even St.
John the beloved Apostle when he beheld the glory of his
ascended Lord fell at His feet as dead : " cast down, but not
destroyed."

Another there is, "that wicked," whom the Lord shall
destroy with the brightness of His coming. God putteth a
boundless difference between clean and unclean even here,
where yet there is one event unto all.

The very holy are of all saints those most ready to fall at
Christ's feet as dead. Who else can realize so vividly His
Purity and their own defilement, His Glory and their own
shame ? With David they weep for love till they exceed ; with
Esther they faint in approaching their King : their eye seeth
Him, and they abhor themselves and repent in dust and
ashes ; they are jealous for His sake with a godly jealousy,
and jealousy is cruel as the grave. But He bringeth down to
the grave and bringeth up. And though the spirit fail from
before Him and the souls which He hath made, yet truly these
are they who hearing His Voice have turned to see Him that
speaketh with them, who know His Voice, and being raised
more and more continually to newness of life follow Him.

They come to Christ and He giveth them eternal life, as His own words of rebuke promise by implication : " Ye will not come to Me, that ye might have life."

He to whom Christ cometh for destruction hath not come to Christ.

Let us encourage ourselves though He slay us yet to trust in Him, by help of some of those parables of nature familiar to us all which speak of life reborn from lifelessness, or from death or from decay.   A leafless tree, a chrysalis, a buried seed, an egg.

> The twig sprouteth,
> The moth outeth,
> The plant springeth,
> The bird singeth :
> Tho' little we sing to-day,
> Yet are we better than they ;
> Tho' growing with scarce a showing,
> Yet, please God, we are growing.
>
> The twig teacheth,
> The moth preacheth,
> The plant vaunteth,
> The bird chanteth,·
> God's mercy overflowing
> Merciful past man's knowing.
> Please God to keep us growing
> Till the awful day of mowing.

St. John " heard " and endured to hear : not till he " saw " fell he as dead.   Hearing prepares for sight.   To-day is our day for hearing, faith, preparation.   Lord Almighty, so make it full of grace to each of us, for Jesu's sake.

Lord Jesus, how dare we at all times offer our petitions in Thy Name and for Thy sake? What, lovest Thou us so inexhaustibly that not one praying sinner of us all risks lighting upon the moment when it would not pleasure Thee for the Father to show us mercy, for the Holy Spirit to succour us? This, Lord, I believe. I believe that when I ask salvation in Thy Name, Thou Thyself askest it for me : yea, I believe that many times Thou intercedest for us when we ask not at all or ask amiss. " For Thy sake " investeth us with Thine own claims : what is done for us Thou accountest as done for Thee. " Thy sake " moveth God to pity us ; let Thy blessed sake move us likewise to pity each other. Give us grace to comfort ourselves and one another by memorials of Thy love ; much more comfort Thou us by assurance of Thy love.

" As dying, and behold we live ! "
    So live the Saints while time is flying;
Make all they make, give all they give,
    As dying ;

Bear all they bear without replying ;
    They grieve as tho' they did not grieve,
Uplifting praise with prayer and sighing.

Patient thro' life's long-drawn reprieve,
    Aloof from strife, at peace from crying,
The morrow to its day they leave,
    As dying.

" And He laid His right hand upon me, saying, Fear not."—
That same Right Hand which holdeth the seven stars and hath
the care of all the Churches is laid on one saint to comfort and
reassure him.

Think upon us all for good, think upon us each for good, O
good Lord Jesus !

Christ spake from the troubled sea : " Be of good cheer ;
it is I ; be not afraid." He saith in Heaven : " Fear not."
" Jesus Christ the Same yesterday, and to-day, and for ever."
" I am the First and the Last "—Christ's Godhead : " I
am He that liveth, and was dead : and behold, I am alive for
evermore, Amen "—Christ's Manhood.

There is no grief of ours which Christ cannot and will not
console. St. John falls as dead ; and his tender Master and
Friend forthwith brings to remembrance how He Himself had
verily been dead Who now was alive for evermore. In all our
afflictions He was afflicted. We have not an High Priest
which cannot be touched with the feeling of our infirmities.

In the Revised Version we read : " I am the First and the
Last, and the Living One ; and I was dead . . ." This
punctuation by removing "the Living One" from the second
to the first clause, seems to remove it from the Manhood to
the Godhead, setting forth with exceeding vividness Christ's
Unity of Person.

" Behold," He saith. Who shall behold? Shall St. John
and shall not I ? I also ; because for me no less than for St.
John He lived and was dead and is alive for evermore.
" Therefore with Angels and Archangels, and with all the
company of heaven, we laud and magnify Thy glorious Name ;
evermore praising Thee."

" And have the keys of hell and of death."—Here *hell* is
" Hades," the land of the shadow of death, the abode of
disembodied souls ; it is not *Gehenna,* the place of punishment.

Our Lord Jesus hath the keys of death and of Hades. He it is Who unlocked the gate for those we love and whose memory is blessed. He it is Who will once again unlock that gate for them in the day of the restitution of all things : He, not another. Surely they were not so greatly afraid or in any wise damaged what time He fixed the bounds of their habitation and brought them to their quiet lodging and settled them therein. "The lines are fallen unto me in pleasant places ; yea, I have a goodly heritage."

But I, Lord, am sore afraid. I am afraid of Thee, of death, of myself : yea, rather, I am afraid of Thee and of that because I fear mine own self. The sting of death is sin. God be merciful to me a sinner.

In that veiled land saints abide. Some saints who loved us on earth are there, saints whom we loved and love. If we call they do not answer. Surely one reason why they neither appear nor audibly respond to our desolate cry, may be that if it is hard for us now to love supremely God Whom we see not, it would be yet harder then were those who even in His eyes are lovely and desirable to woo us heavenward with unforgotten familiar human tenderness. Any of us who have lost our nearest and dearest may realize how keen would be the temptation to love—alas ! it may be to *go on* loving the creature more than the Creator.

This separation to them is not grievous, and for us it is safe.

Disembodied saints are there. And no sinners? On the contrary, who beside sinners? For these are the fruits of Christ's Passion, and He came not to call the righteous but sinners to repentance. "Lord, remember me when Thou comest into Thy Kingdom."

To join the congregation of cleansed sinners we too may aspire : let us aspire.

> Little Lamb, who lost thee ?—
> I myself, none other.—
> Little Lamb, who found thee ?—
> Jesus, Shepherd, Brother.
> Ah, Lord, what I cost Thee !
> Canst Thou still desire ?—
> Still Mine arms surround thee,
> Still I lift thee higher,
> Draw thee nigher.

"The keys of hell and of death."—No key need be preserved to the end were the door not at last to be re-opened. Many times opened to admit, once for all it will be re-opened to release. "There is hope in thine end."

19. Write the things which thou hast seen, and the things which are, and the things which shall be hereafter ;

20. The mystery of the seven stars which thou sawest in My right hand, and the seven golden candlesticks. The seven stars are the angels of the seven churches ; and the seven candlesticks which thou sawest are the seven churches.

"Write"—not any ecstasy of thy love even in this moment of reunion. "Write"—little for the indulgence of thine own heart, unless it be meat and drink to thee to do the Will of Him that sendeth thee, and to finish His work. "Write" that which shall glorify God, edify the Church, bear witness against the world. John the beloved and the true lover could endure this word : if it seems cold and disappointing to us, it seems so because we have not yet the mind of St. John ; much less the mind of Christ.

These who met after separation were not only God and man, Creator and creature, Lord and servant : they were likewise Friend and friend ; each to the other (if reverently we may say it) as his own soul. Yet still the standard is : If thou love Me keep My commandments ; and still the silence of the responsive soul makes answer : " Let my Lord speak ; for Thou hast strengthened me."

Love, to be love, must walk Thy way
　　And work Thy Will ;
　　Or if Thou say, "Lie still,"
Lie still and pray.

Love, Thine own Bride, with all her might
　　Will follow Thee,
　　And till the shadows flee
Keep Thee in sight.

Love will not mar her peaceful face
　　With cares undue,
　　Faithless and hopeless too
And out of place.

Love, knowing Thou much more art Love,
　　Will sun her grief,
　　And pluck her myrtle leaf,
And be Thy dove.

Love here hath vast beatitude :
　　What shall be hers
　　Where there is no more curse,
But all is good ?

The revelation and record are to be of things seen, and which are and which shall be ; not of opinions or of fancies. A world of mere opinions and mere fancies, of day-dreams and castles in the air, is antagonistic to the true and substantial world of revelation, and is more hollow and unavailing than was Jonah's gourd. "Now it is high time to awake out of sleep."

The mystery of the seven stars and the seven candlesticks is both revealed and explained. Thenceforward mystery after mystery will be revealed, but not necessarily explained. It is nobler to believe than to understand.

O only Lord God, Father of lights and Maker of darkness, send forth Thy light and Thy truth that they may lead us through dimness of things seen to clarity of things unseen. For our Lord Jesus Christ's sake, the Light of the world. Amen.

"Behold the height of the stars, how high they are !"

The star floats in heaven, and has no contact with earth except by sending thither its own radiance. It bestows light, and grasps at nothing in return. Earthborn clouds stop short at an immeasurable distance below its altitude : it is a celestial creature, a recluse by day, a watcher by night ; its bands regulate it within its assigned orbit, its sweet influences stream forth unbound to all within its radius. God Almighty, without Whom was not anything made that was made, made the stars also.

The candlestick is of gold, weighty, firm, and it cannot stand without a foundation. Its luminosity is derived, being no feature of its original self ; effectually kindled, yet ever liable to extinction. Without fuel the flame expires, without air it cannot exist : it cannot kindle or rekindle itself, or feed itself, or maintain itself. "What hast thou that thou didst not receive ? "

A Bishop and a Church should be congruous each with its symbol.

O God, our God, Who makest both high and low, grant unto the lofty to look down in Christ-like self-abasement, and unto the lowly to look up in Christ-like self-oblation. Accept Thy great and small, I beseech Thee, in Jesus Christ, Who loveth first and last. Amen.

CHAPTER II.

1. Unto the angel of the Church of Ephesus write ; These things saith He that holdeth the seven stars in His right hand, Who walketh in the midst of the seven .golden candlesticks.

" He telleth the number of the stars ; He calleth them all by their names."

Concerning Himself God Almighty proclaimed of old : " I AM THAT I AM," and man's inherent feeling of personality seems in some sort to attest and correspond to this revelation : I who am myself cannot but be myself. I am what God has constituted me : so that however I may have modified myself, yet do I remain that same I ; it is I who live, it is I who must die, it is I who must rise again at the last day. I rising again out of my grave must carry on that very life which was mine before I died, and of which death itself could not altogether snap the thread. Who I was I am, who I am I am, who I am I must be for ever and ever.

I the sinner of to-day am the sinner of all the yesterdays of my life. I may loathe myself or be amazed at. myself, but I cannot unself myself for ever and ever.

" O Lord, I am oppressed ; undertake for me."

There is no refuge, no hiding-place in multitude. The associated stars and candlesticks conceal not nor shelter that one star and one candlestick which God bringeth into judgment. Yet whilst no man may deliver his brother, there is dignity, joy, comfort, a present blessing and a future beatitude in the Communion of Saints.

> Lord, make me one with Thine own faithful ones,
>   Thy Saints who love Thee and are loved by Thee ;
>   Till the day break and till the shadows flee
> At one with them in alms and orisons :
> At one with him who toils and him who runs

And him who yearns for union yet to be ;
At one with all who throng the crystal sea
And wait the setting of our moons and suns.
Ah, my beloved ones gone on before,
    Who looked not back with hand upon the plough !
        If beautiful to me while still in sight,
        How beautiful must be your aspects now ;
    Your unknown, well-known aspects in that light
Which clouds shall never cloud for evermore.

2. I know thy works, and thy labour, and thy patience, and how thou canst not bear them which are evil: and thou hast tried them which say they are apostles, and are not, and hast found them liars :

3. And hast borne, and hast patience, and for My Name's sake hast laboured, and hast not fainted.

Our Lord saith, "I know," and proceedeth to enumerate the graces of His Church, as the bridegroom sets forth the loveliness of the bride. "Behold, thou art fair, My love; behold, thou art fair." He will not blame until first He hath praised : He lays the firm foundation of His approval before He upbraids for a spreading leprosy in her superstructure. He doth not change His affection though He must needs change His voice : "O, My dove, thou art in the clefts of the rock, in the secret places of the stairs, let Me see thy countenance, let Me hear thy voice : for sweet is thy voice, and thy countenance is comely. Take us the foxes, the little foxes, that spoil the vines : for our vines have tender grapes." He Who is Himself the True Vine, He best knoweth what shame it is, what loss, what ruin to any branch which is spoiled. Better the smart of to-day's pruning than of to-morrow's lopping.

The Church of Ephesus seems prepared to say : " All these things have I kept from my youth up : what lack I yet ? " and we to answer : " Surely the Lord's anointed is before Him." For how many of ourselves perform half the deeds which yet availed not to clear Ephesus?

Here are genuine works, not mere eye-service ; labour through the burden and heat of the day ; patience tried and not found wanting ; abhorrence of what is abominable ; sifting and upholding of truth to the unmasking of Satan, though he simulate an angel of light ; endurance outliving impulse ; and in this catalogue of virtues, two which appear at the beginning reappear at the end ; patience whose silver cord has not broken despite the long, strong strain put upon it, and labour now certified as done for Christ's Name's sake. Moreover, the doer of these great things fainteth not, but at the weakest moment is at least as Gideon with his three hundred of old, faint yet pursuing.

May not Ephesus aver : "Lo, these many years do I serve Thee, neither transgressed I at any time Thy commandment"? Nay, of a truth : Ephesus may not so much as plead trembling : "We are unprofitable servants : we have done that which was our duty to do."

4. Nevertheless I have somewhat against thee, because thou hast left thy first love.

Behold the worm in the gourd! All that gracious verdure and flourishing luxuriance is death-stricken. "The voice said, Cry. And he said, What shall I cry? All flesh is grass, and all the goodliness thereof is as the flower of the field : the grass withereth, the flower fadeth : because the Spirit of the Lord bloweth upon it : surely the people is grass. The grass withereth, the flower fadeth : but the word of our God shall stand for ever."

Love shaken, all totters. Love expiring, all perishes. For the first and great commandment is in effect : Thou shalt love the Lord thy God with all thy being, and with all thy powers. Whoso transgresses this commandment is verily guilty of the whole law.

Alas for each spiritual Ephesian who did run well, and afterwards loses ground.

It is not that such an one offers nothing, but he has voluntarily come down to offering less. He is as an ebbing, who was as a mounting wave. Many a leaf still green hangs long in autumn, but only the green leaves of spring attain to summer perfection. Ananias and Sapphira offered somewhat, for aught we know they offered much; but they possessed more than they offered, and what they withheld and the spirit in which they withheld it invalidated what they presented.

The Searcher of hearts saith not that Ephesus had renounced love, but that Ephesus had left its first love.
- Whereby one or both of two lapses may be understood : a decline from a standard once attained, or a turning aside from a former centre of attraction. Either lapse must perhaps entail the other ; the second inevitably the first.

O, my God, Fountain of Love, we know not but Thou knowest which of us hath fallen from first love. Have patience with us and we will pay Thee all, Thou Thyself furnishing

D

the love we owe.   If Thou furnish it not, whence shall we
fetch it?   Have pity, have mercy upon us and we will pay
Thee all, hiding ourselves in the merits of Jesus Christ.
Amen.

"Somewhat against thee," saith the patience and meekness
of Christ, Very God and Very Man.   He rejects not a scanty
remnant; rather He stoops to gather up the fragments that
remain, that nothing be lost.   In the former days having feasted
others on whole barley loaves He deigned Himself, as I suppose,
to eat of the broken victuals.   Now by a more amazing condescension He stoops to crave a revival of love.   He seeketh
His one strayed sheep, although not alone the ninety and
nine which went not astray are His, but so also are all the
beasts of the forest and the cattle upon a thousand hills.

Long ago God Almighty had said: "If I were hungry, I
would not tell thee"; now, on the contrary, He tells us, as
though to sinners might be applied that sacred sentence:
"Who knoweth if he will return and repent, and leave a
blessing behind him; even a meat offering and a drink offering
unto the Lord your God?"

"Thou hast left."—My fault, my own fault, my own most
grievous fault.

> O Shepherd with the bleeding Feet,
>   Good Shepherd with the pleading Voice,
>   What seekest Thou from hill to hill?
> Sweet were the valley pastures, sweet
>   The sound of flocks that bleat their joys,
>   And eat and drink at will.
> Is one worth seeking, when Thou hast of Thine
>   Ninety and nine?—
>
> How should I stay My bleeding Feet,
>   How should I hush My pleading Voice?
>   I Who chose death and clomb a hill,
> Accounting gall and wormwood sweet,
>   That hundredfold might bud My joys
>   For love's sake and good will.
> I seek My one, for all there bide of Mine
>   Ninety and nine.

O Lord, dost Thou seek us, and will not we seek Thee?
God forbid.

**5. Remember therefore from whence thou art fallen, and
repent, and do the first works; or else I will come
unto thee quickly, and will remove thy candlestick out
of his place, except thou repent.**

Ah, Lord, Who biddest us remember our shameful falls, re-member Thou Thy long-suffering and bounties. As righteous Zacharias attested Thy remembrance of Thy holy covenant, as St. Mary, blessed to all generations, bore witness that Thou hast holpen Israel in remembrance of Thy mercy, so for good remember us.

As the thief on his cross besought Thee, saying, " Lord, re-member me when Thou comest into Thy kingdom," so now and ·ever remember us.

By all that Thou alone rememberest, O Thou, Whose is the awful Book of Remembrance, for good and not for evil re-member us.

" Rejoice not against me, O mine enemy : when I fall, I shall arise ; when I sit in darkness, the Lord shall be a light unto me. I will bear the indignation of the Lord, because I have sinned against Him, until He plead my cause, and execute judgment for me : He will bring me forth to the light, and I shall behold His righteousness."

" Repent, and do the first works."

What wearied me once, must I do yet again?

" Yes."

Is there no alternative?

" None, except destruction, a certain fearful looking for of judgment and fiery indignation."

Is there no help?

" Not until thou begin to help thyself."

Is there any hope?

" Yea, assured and boundless hope. For if what man has done, man may do, much more what a man has once done, he, by God's help, may do again; and that very word, 'do the first works,' certifies that when formerly done they were acceptable. Do them once more, cease not to do them, do them with thy first love, do them with more love than ever because now thou more needest forgiveness, and at the eleventh hour well is thee and happy shalt thou be."

It often happens at church that wandering thoughts are recalled at a moment when no prayer specially interesting to ourselves is being offered ; we are tempted to catch up one we have missed, or to look forward to one still to come. Yet here at this very point lies our vantage-ground ; now is our oppor-tunity for self-discipline. By resolutely checking any indulgence of favourite petitions ; by instantly, simply, honestly concen-trating attention on the matter in hand, there seems good hope that gradually a habit of attention may be formed.

Shrink as we may from facing the consequences of our faults,
yet lost opportunities are and must remain lost. If I pray not
at the hour of prayer, the hour passes, and I have not prayed;
if I pray not the appointed prayer at the appointed moment,
the moment passes and I have not obeyed. In God's strength
let us face the consequences of our sins. Sins are worse than
their consequences.

To improve all our prayers is to improve our favourite
prayers amongst the rest.—Is not this appealing to a secondary
motive?—Yes; and I hope innocent secondary motives may
be called in to reinforce the prime motive; our whole strength
thus becomes concentrated in one effort made in one direction.
The spring-tide is strong, the neap-tide comparatively weak,
because the first obeys sun and moon attracting in unison, the
second is subject to their forces acting at cross purposes.

"Or else I will come unto thee quickly,"—the desire and
salvation of saints, the horror and overthrow of impenitent
sinners. He Who comes is the same; in them to whom He
comes lies all the difference. To such a word St. John will
afterwards reply: "Even so, come, Lord Jesus." Lord, teach
us to pray.

"Quickly."—Guilty fear mutters, "Art Thou come hither
to torment us before the time?" Innocence and sanctity cry
out, "Why tarry the wheels of His chariots?" Penitence re-
joins meekly: "The Lord is good unto them that wait for
Him, to the soul that seeketh Him. It is good that a man
should both hope and quietly wait for the salvation of the Lord."

"Remove thy candlestick out of his place."—He saith not
abolish or *extinguish*, but "remove"; surely there lingers a
gleam of hope for them whose candlestick is as yet only
removed. Judah carried afar into captivity, repented, and was
brought back to his own borders.

Repentance averts judgment, repentance reverses judgment,
repentance recovers "two legs, or a piece of an ear" out of
the very mouth of the lion.

To repentance all is promised. But alas! to us repentance
itself is not promised.

Lord Jesus, the Fountain opened for sin and for uncleanness,
Who promisest forgiveness to penitence, but reservest penitence
to Thyself to give or to deny; deny us not that penitence
which Thou acceptest, and which Thou alone canst give.

**6 But this thou hast, that thou hatest the deeds of the
Nicolaitanes, which I also hate.**

"Ye that love the Lord, hate evil; He preserveth the souls of His saints."

Good it is to hate what Christ hateth; better still to love what He loveth, and what He is. If hatred be our strongest feature of Christ-likeness, well may we betake ourselves to dust and ashes, to repentance and first works; for without love, to hate even the same object is to hate it out of a far different heart. Pride may hate much that is contemptible, fastidiousness much that is foul, softness much that is cruel; but what has pride or fastidiousness or sensual softness in common with Christ? If all human virtues are to be mistrusted, sifted, tested, not least that virtue of hatred which has for counterfeit a deadly sin.

Nevertheless Christ clearly commends hatred, and what He commends we are bound to aim at. For great saints there may be a direct royal road thither, for ordinary sinners a circuitous path may possibly prove safer if not shorter.

Extremes meet; therefore let us work our way round to hatred by way of love. A long round perhaps, but an absolutely safe one. Were we even to die in mid-pilgrimage we might hope to be accepted according to that we had, if not according to that we had not.

Moreover, however slowly, yet surely, love does infallibly breed a hatred akin to the Divine hatred. Such hatred absolute, unqualified, irreconcilable, is restricted to the one odious object. To love involves of necessity the capacity for hatred; how shall we not hate that which may sever ourselves from the supreme desire of our hearts, or may destroy others whom we love as ourselves?

And when we have learned so much of the science of love and hatred, we shall be ready to add: How much more shall we not hate that which doeth despite to the God of all goodness? Which solitary odious thing is sin.

The difficulty of hating aright is intensified by our predisposition towards hating amiss.

Lord of all power and might, bestow upon us, I beseech Thee, both love and hatred: but only that hatred which is a form and fruit of love. For Jesus Christ's sake. Amen.

"The deeds of the Nicolaitanes."—Commentators explain that the Nicolaitanes (*see also* ver. 15) were misbelievers of impure life. A suggestion which brands as their founder Nicolas of Antioch, seventh on the catalogue of the first-ordained seven deacons (Acts vi. 5, 6), is not to my knowledge supported by historical proof.

Whoever was their founder, their deeds and doctrines were hateful to Christ, Who is both righteousness and truth. St. John instructs us how "he that doeth righteousness is righteous"; thus doing, we shall keep free from the guilt of the Nicolaitanes; moreover thus doing we shall escape the contamination of their doctrines, in right of our Lord's own comforting declaration: "If any man will do His will, he shall know of the doctrine, whether it be of God."

To avoid the contagion of their example is the essential point. If still we feel curious to ascertain what the Nicolaitanes actually professed and did, although clearly such knowledge is not necessary to our salvation, let us rather ponder the words of St. Paul on a congruous subject: "It is a shame even to speak of those things which are done of them in secret,"—lest we should degrade ourselves like any against whom elsewhere he bears witness: "Unto them that are defiled and unbelieving is nothing pure; but even their mind and conscience is defiled."

Ignorance is often a safeguard and a privilege.

> Lord, make me pure :
> Only the pure shall see Thee as Thou art,
> And shall endure.
> Lord, bring me low ;
> For Thou wert lowly in Thy blessed heart:
> Lord, keep me so.

7. He that hath an ear, let him hear what the Spirit saith unto the churches; To him that overcometh will I give to eat of the tree of life, which is in the midst of the paradise of God.

Not the promise only, the preamble also is full of grace.

By it we are instantly reminded of that reiterated saying of our Lord's, recorded in their Gospels by SS. Matthew, Mark, Luke, but not (I believe) by St. John: "He that hath ears to hear, let him hear."

If I may venture to study both the similarity and the difference between the two forms, it seems to me that our Master's invitation has a wider and (if I may call it so) a more elementary sound. He appeals to all within reach of His blessed Voice: "To you is the word of this salvation sent." It was at the outset of a new dispensation, a first call of sinners to come out of the world and become saints. It was, as by the prophet of old, "Ho, every one." The words of winning mercy issued from the lips full of grace ; the Aspect of unutterable attraction,

as He spake, was visible to all who would behold. In that
day He called not the righteous, but sinners to repentance.

The message of the Spirit being addressed "unto the
Churches," suggests that the hearer who is called upon to hear
it is in heart no alien, but one already concerned in the import
of the message; one who, having actually started on his course,
now needs the advanced graces of perseverance and patience;
or at the very least one who, being predisposed with open face
to behold as in a glass the glory of the Lord, is apt to be
changed into the same image from glory to glory, even as by
the Spirit of the Lord. The mere word "an ear" instead of
"ears," reminding us of that single eye which is the light of
the body, suggests that this is the parallel ear, the purged ear
which hearing the Word of God is blessed, inasmuch as he that
heareth is a doer and not a hearer only.

But there is a quite different train of thought unconnected
perhaps with any argument to be founded on the words of our
text, yet to which these may lead us as to a blameless, pious
contemplation and exercise of devout gratitude. "An ear":
how does God accept the poorest offering if it be all a man
has to proffer. Thus elsewhere we are certified of the one-
eyed, one-footed, one-handed penitents who shall enter into
the kingdom of heaven. The lame and the blind might be
hated of David's soul; to the Son of David they are dear as
the apple of the eye.

Of old Abraham drew near, and said, Wilt Thou also
destroy the righteous with the wicked? and urging his intercession onward and downward, at length obtained a promise
of safety for all the cities of the plain, could ten righteous
be found in Sodom. He fixed ten as the extreme boundary
of what he dared implore; at ten he became dumb, and
opened not his mouth, for it was God's doing; could ten
not be found, Abraham acquiesced in the threatened destruction. But long ages afterwards, what saith God Almighty Himself of that Jerusalem which by the mouth of
Isaiah He once upbraided under the name of Sodom and
Gomorrah? Speaking yet again by the Prophet Jeremiah, He
saith: "Run ye to and fro through the streets of Jerusalem,
and see now, and know, and seek in the broad places thereof,
if ye can find a man, if there be any that executeth judgment,
that seeketh the truth; and I will pardon it."

Human charity laid hand on mouth at ten. Divine charity
sought and sifted, and would have pardoned for the sake
of one.

O God, all-Good, Father all-Merciful, Who didst provide Thine own Lamb for Thy Burnt Offering, even the One Man for Whom Thou soughtest; for His sake Who died in our stead that we should not also die, pardon and save us, the very sinners for whom He died.

"What the Spirit saith."—Is it then no longer Christ that speaketh? Surely it is the All-Holy Christ Who speaketh by His Spirit; and the All-Holy Spirit Who speaketh being One with the Father and the Son. Whatso each Divine Person doeth, the Godhead doeth.

This which I cannot understand, God helping me I will believe and hold fast.

With the ability to hear stands indissolubly connected the obligation to hear. He that hath an ear cannot make himself like him that hath none. He who has heard cannot make himself like him who has never heard. By shrinking from hearing more the sluggard or the coward bears witness against himself to having already heard somewhat.

"Unto the Churches."—Not only to that one Church primarily addressed, but to all Churches throughout all generations. To the Church of England now, as to the Church of Ephesus then.

A message to my neighbour! True; but equally a message to myself. If I long to improve my neighbour, the first step towards so doing is to improve myself: "And why beholdest thou the mote that is in thy brother's eye, but considerest not the beam that is in thine own eye? Or how wilt thou say to thy brother, Let me pull out the mote out of thine eye; and, behold, a beam is in thine own eye? Thou hypocrite, first cast out the beam out of thine own eye; and then shalt thou see clearly to cast out the mote out of thy brother's eye."

"To him that overcometh."—We are not here told what he overcometh in particular, but looking back it becomes clear that in this instance the foe to be overcome is the defaulter's own self; his accusation concerning neither word nor deed, but motive, the deep-seated spring of conduct, the inner man of the heart. "Ye did run well; who did hinder you?"

Ephesus appears like Ephraim of old: "Strangers have devoured his strength, and he knoweth it not; yea, gray hairs are here and there upon him, yet he knoweth it not." St. Paul writes: "As dying, and, behold, we live"; concerning Ephesus the sentence might be reversed: As living, and, behold, they die. If in full vitality they begin to die, how being half dead shall they retrieve their life? "With men it is impossible, but not with God; for with God all things are possible." "He giveth

more grace.   Wherefore He saith, God resisteth the proud, but
giveth grace unto the humble."

> O Christ the Life, look on me where I lie
> > Ready to die :
> O Good Samaritan, nay, pass not by.
>
> O Christ my life, pour in Thine oil and wine
> > To keep me Thine ;
> Me ever Thine, and Thee for ever mine.
>
> Watch by Thy saints and sinners, watch by all
> > Thy great and small :
> Once Thou didst call us all,—O Lord, recall.
>
> Think how Thy saints love sinners, how they pray
> > And hope alway,
> And thereby grow more like Thee day by day.
>
> O Saint of saints, if those with prayer and vow
> > Succour us now . . .
> It was not they died for us, it was Thou.

Even he "that overcometh" does not earn : it still is God
that "will give."

And what will He give ? "To eat of the tree of life which is
in the midst of the Paradise of God," thereby reversing Adam's
doom : "The Lord God said . . . Now, lest he put forth his
hand, and take also of the tree of life, and eat, and live for
ever : therefore the Lord God sent him forth from the garden
of Eden . . . And He placed at the east of the garden of
Eden cherubims, and a flaming sword which turned every way,
to keep the way of the tree of life."

Thus the eastern gate, the gate of light, shut out man into
darkness ; immortal cherubim barred him from the precincts
of life ; flame repelled him into the cold of death ; until the
times of refreshing should come from the Lord, and to Christ's
brethren every loss should be made up, yea, and much more
also.

Christ is our Tree of Life, whereof even now we eat and drink
in the Sacrament of His most Blessed Body and Blood ; even
now whilst, please God, we are overcoming, though we have
not yet overcome. "Blessed are ye that hunger now : for ye
shall be filled." He "the Branch," foretold by prophets, He
"the True Vine," revealed by His own lips, He now is mankind's centre to which turn eyes and hearts. Long ago the
Tree of Life so stood in the midst of Eden, and so in vision St.
John beheld it stand in the midst of the street of Holy New
Jerusalem (*see* ch. xxii. 2).

If we could forget the Vine's sweetness, can we forget how it left its sweetness to become our King? If we could forget the Tree of Life, can we forget that tree of death whereon Christ hung that so He might be indeed our life?

O our Saviour, grant us grace to love Thee in and above all Thy gifts, and to love Thy gifts because of Thee.

"The Paradise of God":—were it not "of God" it would not be Paradise. "In My Father's house are many mansions: if it were not so, I would have told you. I go to prepare a place for you. And if I go and prepare a place for you, I will come again, and receive you unto Myself; that where I am, there ye may be also."

Paradise is God's by right, man's by grace. In its midst Christ, Very God and Very Man, stands symbolized by the Tree of Life; later on we read of the Lamb "in the midst" of the Throne. In an awe-striking mystery we seem thus to behold Christ not centre of humankind alone, or of all creation alone; but even Christ in the Bosom of the Father, the Beloved Son in Whom the Father Himself is well pleased.

That Eden of earth's sunrise cannot vie
With Paradise beyond her sunset sky
   Hidden on high.

Four rivers watered Eden in her bliss,
But Paradise hath One which perfect is
   In sweetnesses.

Eden had gold, but Paradise hath gold
Like unto glass of splendours manifold
   Tongue hath not told.

Eden had sun and moon to make her bright;
But Paradise hath God and Lamb for light,
   And hath no night.

Unspotted innocence was Eden's best;
Great Paradise shows God's fulfilled behest,
   Triumph and rest.

Hail, Eve and Adam, source of death and shame!
New life has sprung from death, and Jesu's Name
   Clothes you with fame.

Hail Adam and hail Eve! your children rise
And call you blessed, in their glad surmise
   Of Paradise.

8. And unto the angel of the church in Smyrna write; These things saith the First and the Last, which was dead, and is alive.

He Who was made like unto us knoweth whereof we are made; and that we are but dust well may He remember Who died and was buried, although it was not possible that He should see corruption or be holden of death.. He feels with us as well as for us : He died, as we all must die; He lives again, as by His grace we all may rise to life everlasting. Thus He maketh Himself all things to all men, willing by all means to save us. His death and His life as it were salute.us: O ye dead, believe on Me and ye shall live ; O ye living, believe, and ye shall never die.

9. I know thy works, and tribulation, and poverty, (but thou art rich) and I know the blasphemy of them which say they are Jews, and are not, but are the synagogue of Satan.

The Searcher of hearts has no word of blame for Smyrna, only encouragement, approval, benediction. Her oblation is threefold : works, tribulation, poverty. Yet Ephesus exhibited a longer list of offerings, Ephesus whose heart was not right with God. "From all blindness and hardness of heart, good Lord, deliver us."

Of those three acceptable offerings, one alone properly appertained to Smyrna ; her works, that is; and even these were wrought only by aid of Divine grace. Tribulation, whether we regard it as simply equivalent to affliction, or tracing it to its root call it rather sifting, was her appointed discipline : poverty (unless voluntary) was her assigned condition.

O Gracious and Bounteous Lord God, Who furnishing our offering acceptest it, blessed be Thou for ever and ever, through Jesus Christ our Lord. Amen.

Nothing on earth is a substitute for performance of duty, be that duty what it may. Affliction cannot exempt us, nor great searchings of heart, nor poverty : these are conditions under which to work, not workers in our stead. "Is any among you afflicted? let him pray," prayer being practical and promotive of practice.

Yet deeds wrought in God become eminently glorious when wrought under stress of sorrow with patience and fear, with faith, hope, and charity. Such affliction will turn to gladness, such sifting and testing will certify, such poverty will enrich.

My God, openest Thou to us such possibilities, profferest Thou such vast grace and glory, and shall baptized Christians, being harnessed, turn themselves back in the day of battle? Not so, Lord Jesus, for Thine own sake.

"If thou faint in the day of adversity, thy strength is small."

"But thou art rich."—Neither is all wealth poor, nor all poverty rich. That widow who cast two mites into the sacred treasury, by so doing became rich, but had she kept them she had remained simply "a poor widow." God then sat in the congregation of princes visibly as Judge : still He sits invisibly : yet a little while and again He will sit visibly. Now He sits as a refiner and purifier of silver : then He will acknowledge every gift He has purified and accepted. God will be no man's debtor.

Then will come to light transfigured every offering in righteousness. The gold, frankincense, myrrh of wise men ; the boats and nets of fishermen ; the money of the exchanger ; the loaves and small fishes of disciples ; the ointment and alabaster box of loving women ; houses, lands ; a cup of cold water. All riches which have spread wings and flown away as eagles toward heaven, shall then reappear as treasures in heaven, where neither moth nor rust doth corrupt, and where thieves do not break through nor steal.

Is it difficult to realize the transcendent riches of poverty ? To me it should not be impossible. For once I knew a holy woman, who having given up one possession which was very dear to her, foresaw with delight the regaining it imperishable. To have known her long and intimately was a course of spiritual training : may it not turn to my condemnation.

> My God, wilt Thou accept, and will not we
>   Give aught to Thee?
> The kept we lose, the offered we retain
>   Or find again.
>
> Yet if our gift were lost, we well might lose
>   All for Thy use:
> Well lost for Thee, Whose Love is all for us
>   Gratuitous.

"The synagogue of Satan."—Evil neighbourhood ranks amongst the trials of the Church of Smyrna, all whose trials however were privileges and potential blessings. Still, whenever evil is the appointed channel of grace, there is obviously peril involved : as St. Paul warned his Corinthian flock, "evil communications corrupt good manners." Whilst doubly lovely by contrast appears that "lily among thorns," which surmounting them blossoms in their despite, elsewhere we read of good grain choked and ruined by thorns which sprung up in its company.

·" Lead us not into temptation " is one enjoined prayer. Yet when we fall into divers temptations we are to count it all joy, because the trying of faith worketh patience. " Blessed is the man that endureth temptation: for when he is tried, he shall receive the crown of life, which the Lord hath promised to them that love Him."

"I know the blasphemy of them," saith the Judge; yet knowing it, He permitted His outraged Church to sojourn within hearing of that blasphemy. A comfort to all Christians who involuntarily remain exposed to so keen a trial. "Hallowed by Thy name. Deliver us from evil."

" The synagogue of Satan."—As then certain non-Jews called themselves Jews, and composed in fact Satan's Synagogue, so now presumably there may be non-Christians, who calling themselves Christians, are the Church of Satan. Touching which ghastly possibility it is well to pray for others as for ourselves, but to mistrust ourselves rather than others. Myself in some degree I am bound to know and am bound to judge.

My permitted wanderings in prayer dishonour God's Holy Name. My indulged rebellious feelings deny His love.

O Merciful Lord Jesus, cast me not out, forget not me as I have forgotten Thee. For us all, Amen.

10. Fear none of those things which thou shalt suffer: behold, the devil shall cast some of you into prison, that ye may be tried; and ye shall have tribulation ten days: be thou faithful unto death, and I will give thee a crown of life.

" Fear none of those things which thou shalt suffer."—

O God our Father, Who callest us to be Thy children, give us filial fear and self-mistrustful fear ; and toward all beside courage indomitable, for our great Champion's sake, Jesus Christ. Amen.

> Cast down but not destroyed, chastened not slain :—
>   Thy Saints have lived that life, but how can I ?
>   I who thro' dread of death do daily die
> By daily foretaste of an unfelt pain.
> Lo, I depart who shall not come again ;
>   Lo, as a shadow I am flitting by ;
>   As a leaf trembling, as a wheel I fly,
> While death flies faster and my flight is vain.
> Chastened not slain, cast down but not destroyed :—
>   If thus Thy Saints have struggled home to peace,

> Why should not I take heart to be as they ?
> They too pent passions in a house of clay,
> Fear and desire and pangs and ecstasies ;
> Yea, then they joyed who now are overjoyed.

" Behold, the devil shall cast some of you into prison, that ye may be tried."—Though it be the devil's doing, yet are not those saints to fear.   They might be bound, but the Word of God could not be bound.   Moreover their bodies might be bound, but not their souls ; these would still sit in heavenly places with Christ Jesus.   Even their bodies, because temples of the Holy Ghost, would remain " Christ's freemen " while in bonds ; for where the Spirit of the Lord is, there is liberty. ·

What then could Satan bind?   Flesh and blood which shall not inherit the kingdom of God : the outer man of spiritual persons who used to spend themselves in going about to do good, and who would find and recover their strength in sitting still.

Thus Satan wrought evil in will but good in effect. Alleluia !

" The trying of your faith worketh patience.   But let patience have her perfect work, that ye may be perfect and entire, wanting nothing."

"And ye shall have tribulation ten days."—It may be that even the excellent souls addressed understood not what period that cipher indicated.   At any rate I assuredly understand it not.   But wisdom transcends understanding; and doubtless this word is capable of instructing us, God helping an honest endeavour.

There is comfort in the certainty that though the limit of any trial be hidden from me, by God that limit is prefixed and is all along well known ; the end is planned and adjusted from the beginning.   As the hairs of our head, so the throbs of our agony are all numbered.   Nor do "ten" seem so very many : one over, but nine remain, and so on and on ; till one by one all arrive, pass by, are finished.

Let us recall some Bible Tens, and fortify hope by cheerful meditation.

Ten commandments compose a complete scheme of righteousness.   Ten days even of tribulation will not be an excessive period wherein to practise their observance.

David had his instrument of ten strings whereon to worship God.   Our ten days of weeping may emit as sweet a harmony of prayer and praise, and as triumphant a note of victory.

Ten days are as ten talents for each good and faithful servant to employ profitably.

Ten days of darkness may shine to the glory of God, like ten lighted lamps of wise virgins, who with oil in their vessels go forth to meet the bridegroom.

Ten days of trial should be treasured more than ten pieces of silver : holy souls take jealous heed·lest one be wasted or lost.

Our ten days (alas !) at their best will by taint of sinfulness show more or less like ten lepers. At least let us secure that on each of them God be thanked and worshipped.

Ten days are as ten servants entrusted with ten pounds capable of multiplication.

Ten days of discipline may become as Hezekiah's ten degrees on the sundial certifying recovery : only, blessed be God ! they go forward and not backward.

O God, through Whose good Providence Daniel and his fellows flourished by reason of ten days' cheerful austerity; grant to us, I beseech Thee, like good will and ·a happy issue out of all our afflictions. For our Saviour Jesus Christ's sake. Amen.

Our Lord in His own Person was " faithful unto death," thereby winning the " Crown of Life " He weareth. Shall we bemoan ourselves because He bids us do as He once did, and be made like Him as He now is?

Faithful unto death. We often think of it as if it must demand a long as well as an unflinching effort; and so indeed it may demand, but we know not whether it will. One moment may suffice, for aught we truly know to the contrary. One moment's effort : the weakest might undertake so much.

Or if ever so long a strain be required, God's strength is always stronger than strong enough.

Let us not despise others or ourselves for a mere instinctive dread of death; while we observe that Christ Who by experience knew the bitterness of death, here sets death as the test of man's faithfulness and limit of his endurance. [If such a meaning may be understood as included in the charge to be faithful unto death.]

If we fear not, let us thank God and do valiantly. If we fear, let us thank God and take courage, offering up our fear to Him Who Himself was heard in that He feared.

Great is their grace who instead of choosing their offering simply offer whatever they have; as Jacob of old in extremity of danger took of that which came to his hand a present.

The faithful alone appear thoroughly furnished to treat of faithfulness. Yet since many truths admit of being vividly set forth by help of negatives, even unfaithfulness viewed as a sort of negation need not altogether strike us dumb, so long as we are hoping and aiming at obedience to Christ's injunction. If we cannot acquire faithfulness at once, let us patiently, humbly, anxiously, unlearn unfaithfulness. Till we can affirm truth, at least let us deny error.

The resolute unlearning of unfaithfulness is in fact the practice of faithfulness. "Cease to do evil; learn to do well," hang together. The Ten Commandments are mainly conveyed by negatives.

Be faithful unto death.   Christ proffers thee
  Crown of a life that draws immortal breath :
To thee He saith, yea, and He saith to me,
  "Be faithful unto death."

  To every living soul that same He saith,
" Be faithful : "—whatsoever else we be,
  Let us be faithful challenging His faith.

Tho' trouble storm around us like the sea,
  Tho' hell surge up to scare us and to scathe,
Tho' heaven and earth betake themselves to flee,
  " Be faithful unto death."

"I will give thee."—"Thou wilt not have earned, but I will give thee."

O Lord, Thy gift is better than any earnings, and Thou Thyself art better than Thy gift. "Thy love is better than wine."

"A crown of life."—Life had appeared no small boon, and must always have been beyond fallen man's utmost deserts. But Christ's promise goes far beyond bare life, and mounts up to dignity, beauty, a garment of praise. "For the Lord God is a sun and shield: the Lord will give grace and glory: no good thing will He withhold from them that walk uprightly."

We live after a sort, but all the while we are dying. We who dying live can form no conception of what the true, full, unstricken, undying life will be. Life, though along with many pleasures and alleviations, is now a matter of pains and aches, hunger and thirst, faintness and weariness: this is the life we experience. That other life will not be such; we realize not yet what it will be.

Once in his life "Israel said, It is enough; Joseph my son is yet alive: I will go and see him before I die." For the moment love and joy because of another's life cast out the sting though not the foresight of death.

O Lord Jesus, Who being yet alive art alive for evermore, and Who to every faithful soul art " better than ten sons," fill us with such love of Thee, and such joy in Thy joy, that for us also death in foresight may lose its sting. Amen for us all, Amen.

"A crown of life."—Of what fashion shall such a crown be ?

St. Paul speaks of an amaranthine crown, contrasting it with earth's fading crowns of victory. And later in this Book of Revelations we read of crowns of gold.

We may hope to discern in celestial crowns every adornment of all possible crowns. Gracefulness of leaves, loveliness of flowers, endearment (if I may call it so) of tendrils, permanence of gold, lustre and tints of jewels. Such crowns I hope to see on heads I have venerated and loved here.

Meanwhile, because our dear Lord, flower of humankind and comparable with fine gold (though fine gold sufficeth not to compare with Him), was contented on earth to be crowned with a crown of thorns ; let us be patient, contented, thankful, to wait on in hopes of a crown of life and glory.

" Go forth, O ye daughters of Zion, and behold King Solomon with the crown wherewith his mother crowned him in the day of his espousals, and in the day of the gladness of his heart."

If we be daughters of the spiritual Zion, let us obey this injunction though it send us along the way of sorrows.

Our King Whom we behold is not only the wisest of Men but is Very Wisdom Incarnate. He summons us to behold Him ; He waits if so be we will turn and behold Him. His Crown is a Crown of Thorns transcending any which Solomon in all his glory put on. His mother crowned Him therewith, Eve the mother of us all, Eve whose wilfulness brought in death, Eve to whom the victorious Seed was promised. And it was in the day of His espousals, when He betrothed to Himself His bride the Church, that in Will and purpose He assumed this crown, making ready to "leave His Father" and cleave unto His wife. Moreover it was in gladness of His heart that He put it on, in the eternal unbroken calm of Divine goodwill and good pleasure. Afterwards, for the joy that was set before Him, He endured the Cross, despising the shame ; and doubtless when beforehand He counted the cost, He anticipated also the ensuing joy. His Love (as it were) forgets the anguish, for joy of our new birth ; only never may our love forget it ; forget that glorious shame for our sakes against which He set His Face as a flint, that sorrow for our sakes like which there is no second sorrow.

E

11. He that hath an ear, let him hear what the Spirit saith unto the churches; He that overcometh shall not be hurt of the second death.

"Then shall be brought to pass the saying that is written, Death is swallowed up in victory."

Parallels cannot converge. If Christ the Life occupy and pervade us, death cannot annex us. Death may run alongside of us all our days, and hold out hands of invitation to seduce us, or clench fists and raise an outcry as though it could do us a mischief; but death and Christ's members tend towards different points; and there is nothing it can really effect to harm us so long as we cleave to Christ by faith, lean on Him by hope, hold Him fast and let Him not go by love. The first death (which is but the shadow of death) is indeed ours by birthright under a curse which God has long ago turned for the elect into a blessing; the second death, which alone is absolute, unmitigated death, has no fellowship with him that overcometh.

What then is he, are we, summoned to overcome? Without, fightings; within, fears.

Amen, by the grace of our Lord Jesus Christ, and the love of God, and the fellowship of the Holy Ghost. Amen.

12. And to the angel of the church in Pergamos write; These things saith He which hath the sharp sword with two edges;

"The word of God is quick, and powerful, and sharper than any two-edged sword, piercing even to the dividing asunder of soul and spirit, and of the joints and marrow, and is a discerner of the thoughts and intents of the heart."

If the powers which are His ordinance bear not the sword in vain, much less He from Whom all power is derived. On the other hand, if they are a terror not to good works but to evil, so and much more He also. "Wilt thou then not be afraid of the power? Do that which is good, and thou shalt have praise of the same."

"Sharp."—The sharpness guarantees nicety of operation, exactness to a hair's-breadth, no atom too much or too little affected by the stroke. "Two-edged."—None can evade that sword which cuts both ways.

But who is He that hath this deadly sword? He Who was Himself wounded for our transgressions, Who died in our stead that we should not also die. "I have no pleasure in the death of him that dieth, saith the Lord God: wherefore turn yourselves, and live ye."

O Lord Jesus, we fear Thee; but much more, Thou enabling us, we will trust and love Thee.

David, the man after God's own heart, was afraid because of the sword of the Angel of the Lord. Supreme dominion and supreme fear are with Him with Whom we have to do.

We may perhaps lawfully think thus of the two edges as under one of their aspects. One cuts asunder the evil servant penally, irremediably, by decree of the Supreme and Just Judge. The other, by tenderness of the Good Physician, wounds us for our own benefit and that afterwards He may heal us. "He that sinneth before his Maker, let him fall into the hand of the physician."

"Into Thy hands I commend my spirit: for Thou hast redeemed me, O Lord, Thou God of truth."

13. I know thy works, and where thou dwellest, even where Satan's seat is: and thou holdest fast My Name, and hast not denied My faith, even in those days wherein Antipas was My faithful martyr, who was slain among you, where Satan dwelleth.

In the Authorized Version all the Seven Churches alike are addressed in these same words: "I know thy works": whilst in the Revised Version this Church of Pergamos alone is not so addressed. Because the clause is here in one text omitted, whilst in both texts repeated throughout the corresponding passages, I here venture to pass it over. The Revised Version commences: "I know where thou dwellest; even where Satan's throne is"—thus supplying a second variation, *throne* for *seat*.

"Satan's seat," more especially when designated as his throne, recalls that phase of our Master's temptation when "the devil, taking Him up into an high mountain, showed unto Him all the kingdoms of the world in a moment of time. And the devil said unto Him, All this power will I give Thee, and the glory of them: for that is delivered unto me; and to whomsoever I will I give it." Elsewhere we read of "principalities, powers, rulers of the darkness of this world, spiritual wickedness in high places"; of "the prince of the power of the air"; of "the god of this world."

A common deadly inalienable peril thus appears to encompass the whole human race. Our enemy, further described as "a strong man armed," is no less than in some sort a prince.

Of his resources we know not the extent, of his armies we know not the number; but his being prince of the power of the air suggests that we are as closely beset by temptation as though this formed our atmosphere, as though at each breath we drew we inhaled it. "O wretched man that I am! who shall deliver me from the body of this death?"

Nevertheless our fathers in the flesh have resisted unto blood, striving against sin: why should not we? He that is on our side is greater than he that is against us: there is "a Stronger than he." "The breath of our nostrils" is "the Anointed of the Lord."

"I will hope continually, and will yet praise Thee more and more. My mouth shall show forth Thy righteousness and Thy salvation all the day; for I know not the numbers thereof."

"Thou holdest fast My Name, and hast not denied My faith"—the hidden allegiance of the heart, the open profession of loyalty. "With the heart man believeth unto righteousness; and with the mouth confession is made unto salvation."

When men (and women and children too) are called to martyrdom, not to deny amounts to plenary confession. But so long as the world says, Peace, peace, then oftentimes not to confess becomes virtually a denial.

O Jesus Christ, Who for love's sake desirest to confess and not to deny us before Thy Father; grant us such love of Thee that we too for love's sake may confess and never deny Thee before men.

"In those days."—No momentary trial: saintly impulse not enough, saintly endurance equally essential. Here then once more patience is in requisition : patience a tedious, indomitable grace.

"Whatsoever things were written aforetime were written for our learning, that we through patience and comfort of the Scriptures might have hope. Now the God of patience and consolation grant you to be like-minded one toward another according to Christ Jesus: that ye may with one mind and one mouth glorify God, even the Father of our Lord Jesus Christ."

"Antipas was My faithful martyr."—Men know him not now, how he lived or how he died. God alone knows him. Enough for blessed Antipas.

Hidden from the darkness of our mortal sight,
Hidden in the Paradise of lovely light,

Hidden in God's Presence worshipped face to face,
Hidden in the sanctuary of Christ's embrace.
Up, O Wills ! to track him home among the bless'd ;
Up, O Hearts l to know him in the joy of rest ;
Where no darkness more shall hide him from our sight,
Where we shall be love with love and light with light,
Worshipping our God together face to face,
Wishless in the sanctuary of Christ's embrace.

"Slain among you."—The blood of Martyrs is the seed of Saints : and " if it bear fruit, well." If it bear not fruit, the dust of martyrs cannot but testify against those among whom they were slain. Whoso has seen cannot revert to be as if he had not seen : whoso has heard cannot revert to be as if he had not heard. This latter point our Lord Himself attests in His charge to the Seventy : " Into whatsoever city ye enter, and they receive you not, go your ways out into the streets of the same, and say, Even the very dust of your city, which cleaveth on us, we do wipe off against you : notwithstanding be ye sure of this, that the kingdom of God is come nigh unto you."

So "where Satan dwelleth" turns out to have been in a city of saints from whose midst flashed forth a faithful martyr.

And to-day assuredly in our own midst he dwelleth ; making his neighbourhood known by hideous temptations to foulness, cruelty, self-ruin.

Here is the city and here is a cityful. But where are the saints ? and where, in will if not in deed, is the martyr ?

I trust such seemly inmates abide in my neighbour's habitation. Shall not one such abide likewise in my own ? Amen, God helping me.

14. But I have a few things against thee, because thou hast there them that hold the doctrine of Balaam, who taught Balac to cast a stumblingblock before the children of Israel, to eat things sacrificed unto idols, and to commit fornication.

"A few things."—Thus tenderly does our Lord speak, not breaking the bruised reed or quenching the smoking flax. Submit yourselves therefore to God. " Resist the devil, and he will flee from you. Draw nigh to God, and He will draw nigh to you."

15. So hast thou also them that hold the doctrine of the Nicolaitanes, which thing I hate.

Our Lord rebukes not Pergamos because Satan dwelt there, but because Balaamites and Nicolaitanes flourished there. The one intruder they had no power to eject; the others they could and therefore they were bound to discountenance.

At which announcement should we be more scared: that Satan kept his court amongst us, or that misbelievers and misdoers infested our neighbourhood? Very probably at the former; but the Mind of Christ seems otherwise.

"The doctrine of Balaam."—Yet studying Balaam's history (*see* Num. xxii. 23, 24; xxxi. 1—8, 16; and in addition Micah vi. 5—8, according to one view of the passage), his doctrine might to some of us have seemed his one strong point. He overflowed with knowledge, nor flinched from its eloquent exposition. Nevertheless and alas! he showed forth his faith by his works, which works were devilish. "The devils also believe." "Out of the abundance of the heart the mouth speaketh"; and out of the abundance of *his* heart proceeded that counsel which put a stumblingblock before Israel.

Knowledge then is not necessarily faith, neither is eloquence unction, neither is resource wisdom.

O my God, Who callest us to search Thy Scriptures of truth, furnish us, I beseech Thee, with faith, unction, wisdom; with willingness to shine to Thy glory, or not to shine at all so it be always to Thy glory. Grant us the life of the righteous, and a last end like his. For His sake Who alone is righteous and is our righteousness, Jesus Christ our Saviour. Amen.

Balaam put an outrageous stumblingblock in men's way, barefaced idolatry with-gross impurity being the result.

Are there no Balaams nowadays? We become Balaams when our influence lowers the tone of any who are about us.

What children are near me? What servants? What less educated persons? What individuals whose inclination it is rather to follow than to lead? I myself become a Balaam if I misuse my influence. Good Lord, deliver me.

Balaam has still to face at the Day of Judgment the wretched tools who adopted his policy, the wretched victims of his accursed counsel.

I myself must face on that Day and at that Bar all whom I have ever affected on earth, all who directly or remotely have responded to my influence for good or for evil. Good Lord, deliver us.

Lord, make us all love all : that when we meet
Even myriads of earth's myriads at Thy Bar,

We may be glad as all true lovers are
Who having parted count reunion sweet.
Safe gathered home around Thy blessed Feet,
  Come home by different roads from near or far,
  Whether by whirlwind or by flaming car,
From pangs or sleep, safe folded round Thy seat.
Oh, if our brother's blood cry out at us,
  How shall we meet Thee Who hast loved us all,
  Thee Whom we never loved, not loving him?
The unloving cannot chant with Seraphim,
  Bear harp of gold or palm victorious,
  Or face the vision Beatifical.

16. Repent; or else I will come unto thee quickly, and will fight against them with the sword of My mouth.

Lord, shall we repent, lest Thou come quickly unto us? Thy saints are praying: Even so, come, Lord Jesus.

Lord, if better may not as yet be, grant us the repentance which stayeth Thy coming; and lead us up to that loving penitence which longeth after Thee and inviteth Thee, and to which Thou wilt not say nay.

"With the sword of My mouth."—This Mouth which threatens to fight against obstinate sinners is the very Mouth which heretofore loved to say, Come unto Me,—Follow Me. To Christians thus it still speaketh. Under the elder Dispensation it spake not thus: not thus to Balaam with the living Voice of a Man our Brother, although by a miracle a rebuke was vouchsafed him. Wherefore if we Christians make ourselves like him, we make ourselves twofold more the child of hell. Our grace is fuller than was his grace, our knowledge clearer than his knowledge: he did despite to a Love that had still to be revealed; we do despite to a Love that now and for eighteen centuries past can call heaven and earth to witness, saying, What could I have done more that I have not done?

Lord, let not Thy life, Thy death, Thy resurrection for our sakes, Thy proffered grace, Thy longsuffering to usward, rise up in the Judgment with us to condemn us.

17. He that hath an ear, let him hear what the Spirit saith unto the churches; To him that overcometh will I give to eat of the hidden manna, and will give him a white stone, and in the stone a new name written, which no man knoweth saving he that receiveth it.

Already we eat of "the true bread from heaven" in the Blessed Sacrament of Christ's Body and Blood. Eating

thereof we receive strength to overcome; and truly it is
" hidden Manna " of virtue indiscernible by fleshly eyes and
carnal hearts.   Blessed are they who thus eat Bread in the
Militant Kingdom of God.   Afterwards, having overcome,
God's faithful soldier and servant will once more eat of the
hidden Manna in the peace of God's Triumphant Kingdom ;
no longer to sustain a life that may die, but to satisfy a life
that will live for ever.

The subtlest and profoundest of men cannot explain
mysteries ; the simplest person can appropriate and exult in
them.   On the very surface of this great promise it transpires
that as Christ is life to the faithful soul now, so He will be life
to the indefectible soul then.   This for the present suffices ;
if I am fain to know more, by overcoming I shall one day
attain to full knowledge.

Lord; Thou Thyself art here our Heavenly Food and
sustenance, and it passeth all understanding what there Thou
wilt be.   Already Thou art to us Strength and Sweetness, Life and
Joy, Safety and Sanctification.   What wilt Thou be to us then ?
Yea, Thou Thyself wilt not be changed : we shall be changed.
We shall see and flow together and wonder.   Amen l Amen !

" Hidden manna."—We often hide what is deepest and
dearest in us, yet one friend has cognizance of it.   Is it thus,
Lord, that Thou too hidest Thyself, and while thus hiding
revealest Thyself to Thy chosen ones ?

" A white stone, and in the stone a new name written."—
Here (if it be lawful) I read a promise of the everlasting
renewed innocence of the redeemed.   For their name shall
be inscribed on stone, which amongst earthly substances
excels in durability ; and that stone shall be white, as lambs,
doves, light, are white.   And as whiteness is not a colour, but
rather an absence of tints ; so innocence is not a virtue, but
rather an absence of guilt.

Each soul that overcometh will have its new name written
on whiteness ; and new indeed will it be when our name (God
grant it !) endorses innocence and not guilt.   For *now* " if we
say that we have no sin, we deceive ourselves, and the truth
is not in us."

The names of the twelve Apostles appear on foundation
stones ; the names of all faithful soldiers and servants on
white stones ; all alike imperishable in the Presence of God
Almighty.

Nevertheless as whiteness may again be defined not as
absence but rather as *invisibility* of colour, so these white stones

may be contemplated as white because of their proper stain-lessness, yet equally as coloured in response to that Divine Light which bathes them : even as the hueless diamond blazes with rainbow tints in answer to the sun's glory.

"In the stone a new name written, which no man knoweth saving he that receiveth it."—The reverse of our present ex-perience ; for now the saints are they who know not their own names, however unhesitatingly they name each other. Thus *Patience* will not discern herself, but will identify a neighbour as *Charity*, who in turn will recognize not herself, but mild Patience ; and they both shall know some fellow-Christian, as *Hope* or *Prudence* or *Faith ;* and every one of these shall be sure of the others, only not of herself.

But in the beatified life it shall be otherwise. When Christ shall call each happy, heavenly soul by name, as once He called " Mary " in an earthly garden, then each will perceive herself to be that which He calls her ; and will no more question her own designation than did those primitive creatures whom the first Adam named in the inferior Paradise.

"Which no man knoweth saving he that receiveth it."—"Thou shalt be called by a new name, which the mouth of the Lord shall name." Close, intimate, flawless as will be the com-munion of beatified saints with each other ; still closer, more intimate, perfect will be the communion between Christ and each saved soul. This is the supreme Fellowship which includes and entails the other, this is the supreme Union which the other is like unto. And so far as it is lawful to flesh and blood to meditate on matters not revealed (taking with us words, and turning to the Lord, and saying unto Him, Take away all iniquity, and receive us graciously), may we not even reverently ponder whether, after some transcendent, supersensual fashion, Christ and His own beloved one by one may not reciprocally have a love-name known to both and endeared to each, as it were a name (I mean) expressive of what He was and is to that one soul, and what that one soul to Him, and which as regards all others will pass man's or angel's understanding? " He that hath the bride is the Bridegroom," however the friend of the Bridegroom may stand and hear Him and rejoice greatly because of the Bridegroom's voice.

"That it may please Thee to give us true repentance ; to forgive us all our ignorances ; and to endue us with the grace of Thy Holy Spirit to amend our lives according to Thy holy Word ; We beseech Thee to hear us, good Lord."

Lord, shall there ever be a secret between Thee and me?—

Soul, is there not now already a secret between Me and thee? I know thy name now, whether thou be Impenitent Sinner or Sinful Penitent. I know it now; but none other knoweth it fully, neither dost thou thyself fully know it. Now in part thou knowest it: hereafter if thou be of those who overcome, thou shalt know even as thou art known.—

Lord, I pray Thee make me now what it will please Thee to call me then.—

Soul, canst thou drink of the cup that I drank of?—

Yea, Lord, Thou enabling me. Amen.

18. And unto the angel of the church in Thyatira write; These things saith the Son of God, Who hath His eyes like unto a flame of fire, and His feet are like fine brass.

"The Father judgeth no man, but hath committed all judgment unto the Son." "My defence is of God, which saveth the upright in heart. God judgeth the righteous, and God is angry with the wicked every day." "Remember not, Lord, our offences, nor the offences of our forefathers; neither take Thou vengeance of our sins: spare us, good Lord, spare Thy people, whom Thou hast redeemed with Thy most precious Blood, and be not angry with us for ever. Spare us, good Lord."

"Eyes like unto a flame of fire."—Omniscience from which nothing is concealed; unto which nothing is veiled, disguised, obscure. "Feet like fine brass."—Almighty Strength and Stability, before which all other strength and steadfastness become impotence.

This Who cannot err will be our Judge: This Whom none can gainsay will decree our sentence: as of old by Amos the Prophet He declared to revolted Israel: "Therefore thus will I do unto thee, O Israel: and because I will do this unto thee, prepare to meet thy God, O Israel. For, lo, He that formeth the mountains, and createth the wind, and declareth unto man what is his thought, that maketh the morning darkness, and treadeth upon the high places of the earth, The Lord, The God of hosts, is His Name."

19. I know thy works, and charity, and service, and faith, and thy patience, and thy works; and the last to be more than the first.

Good works to begin with, and abundant good works as

time progresses; and meanwhile charity which covers the
multitude of sins, and service which cannot go unrewarded,
and faith whereby it becomes possible to please God (*see* Heb.
ii. 6), and patience by which saints put on the likeness of
holy Job and of Job's most holy Redeemer;—charity which
never faileth, service which beginning on earth ends not in
heaven, faith which can remove mountains, patience which is
of hope in our Lord Jesus Christ and which fainteth not utterly
waiting for the Goodness of the Lord in the land of the living.

Thus even on earth are the elect arrayed in loveliness and
adorned with graces.   Not here are they crowned : perseverance entitles to a crown, final perseverance attains to one.   It
needs profound patience, patience born of love and sustained
by love, to achieve final perseverance.

> What is the beginning? Love.   What the course?   Love still.
> What the goal?   The goal is Love on the happy hill.
> Is there nothing then but Love, search we sky or earth?
> There is nothing out of Love hath perpetual worth :
> All things flag but only Love, all things fail or flee ;
> There is nothing left but Love worthy you and me.

" Thy works."—As we read that the last were more than the
first, they were surely works of charity towards men and service
towards God, wrought in faith and completed in patience.
Such is that path of the just which shineth more and more unto
the perfect day.

O God of all Goodness, Who on others hast bestowed such
grace that their last works excelled their first and their end was
exalted above their beginning ; grant us like grace, that by as
fair a path we may attain to as goodly a goal.   For the sake of
our Redeemer Jesus Christ.   Amen.

20. **Notwithstanding I have a few things against thee,**
    because thou sufferest that woman Jezebel, which
    calleth herself a prophetess, to teach and to seduce My
    servants to commit fornication, and to eat things
    sacrificed unto idols.

Pergamos and Thyatira have this in common ; both have
praise of God, whilst against both He bringeth forward " a few
things."

Man's estimate might incline in both cases to reverse the
proportion of virtues and vices ; but God is greater than our
heart, and knoweth all things.

" I am in a great strait : let me fall now into the hand of

the Lord; for very great are His mercies: but let me not fall into the hand of man."

"Because thou sufferest."—To put up willingly with abominable sin in our midst, even while holding aloof from any such malpractice, is so far to cast in our lot with sinners. To endure it unwillingly is what Christ Himself chose as a mortal Man to do, and is what He is pleased to exact from all successive generations of His disciples. Evil knowledge need not harm us whilst involuntary; but to court it without justifying cause is to court death, as Eve courted death by bye-path of knowledge. "Unto the pure all things are pure: but unto them that are defiled and unbelieving is nothing pure; but even their mind and conscience is defiled."

It becomes a matter of conscience what poems and novels to read, and how much of the current news of the day.

A second point also Pergamos and Thyatira have in common: false teachers. Yet I observe some difference between the quality of these; Balaam representing the pest of Pergamos, Jezebel that of Thyatira.

Jezebel (*see* her history in the First and Second Book of Kings), if we may take Jehu's word for her character, was an abandoned woman and a witch, besides being, as the Inspired Record shows, a nursing mother of idolatry. But whatever witch she may have been, there appears about her no trace of the genuine prophetess; any more than we infer that there was about that Thyatiran Jezebel, of whom it is expressly mentioned that she "calleth herself" a prophetess. Queen Jezebel therefore may have rivalled or surpassed Balaam in guilt, but seems not to have been his equal in gifts.

Whence a double consideration arises, if from these particular instances I am justified in generalizing. As Balaam in comparison with Jezebel, so men in comparison with women may usually be expected to exhibit keener, tougher, more workworthy gifts. Therefore if Jezebel the woman, going about to establish her equality with Balaam the man, poses as *prophetess* to his *prophet*, nothing is more likely than that she will have to eke out and puff up her pretensions by a whiff of imposture, conscious or unconscious imposture. [History repeats itself.]

21. And I gave her space to repent of her fornication; and she repented not.

Empty space, neutral space, is impossible; it must be occupied by accumulating guilt or by repentance unto progressive amendment.

Space is mine to-day by God's gift. Grant unto us all, I beseech Thee, O Lord, space to repent, and repentance while it is called to-day, repentance not to be repented of, repentance unto salvation. For Jesu's sake. Amen.

22. Behold, I will cast her into a bed, and them that commit adultery with her into great tribulation, except they repent of their deeds.

Any to whom space for repentance is still accorded, are still they whom God desireth to bring less *into* than *out of* great tribulation.

"Turn Thou us, O good Lord, and so shall we be turned. Thou sparest when we deserve punishment, and in Thy wrath thinkest upon mercy."

> O Lord, seek us, O Lord, find us
> In Thy patient care ;
> Be Thy Love before, behind us,
> Round us, everywhere :
> Lest the god of this world blind us,
> Lest he speak us fair,
> Lest he forge a chain to bind us,
> Lest he bait a snare.
> Turn not from us, call to mind us,
> Find, embrace us, bear ;
> Be Thy Love before, behind us,
> Round us, everywhere.

23. And I will kill her children with death ; and all the churches shall know that I am He which searcheth the reins and hearts : and I will give unto every one of you according to your works.

"And I will kill her children with death."—Doubtless "children that are corrupters," for by his prophet Ezekiel Almighty God protested aforetime : "The soul that sinneth, it shall die. The son shall not bear the iniquity of the father, neither shall the father bear the iniquity of the son : the righteousness of the righteous shall be upon him, and the wickedness of the wicked shall be upon him."

Yet as we read in Wisdom of "parents that killed with their own hands, souls destitute of help," so did this Jezebel make herself a murderess whether the children here denounced were hers according to the flesh, or hers only by an execrable discipleship.

"Let us also fear." All influence, my own influence, tends and cannot but tend either to preserve or to destroy.

"I the Lord thy God am a jealous God, visiting the iniquity of the fathers upon the children unto the third and fourth generation of them that hate Me."—"The wages of sin is death."

O my God, if for our own souls' sake we forbear not, yet grant us grace for the sake of those we love to cease from sin, lest we bring upon them a curse and not a blessing. At the least and lowest for their sakes, until by the same grace we attain to do all for the sake of Jesus Christ, Whose all-availing sake I now plead with Thee.

" And all the Churches shall know that I am He which searcheth the reins and hearts."—" When Thy judgments are in the earth, the inhabitants of the world will learn righteousness." Even the whole Church Militant herself is an inhabitant of the world, as our Blessed Lord in His unfathomable love for souls provided: " I pray not that Thou shouldest take them out of the world, but that Thou shouldest keep them from the evil."

" I am He which searcheth the reins and hearts."—An awful promise even to the righteous ; an awful threat to the impenitent wicked.

First Christ searcheth all the earth to find and reclaim souls. Next He searcheth each individual soul to prove and see what manner of soul it is. He sifts, as it were, our dust to detect the least germ of latent life. He examines the will, which is our strength (reins) ; the affections, which engross our heart. The will to love Him He accepts and quickens into love : the faintest emotion of love towards Him He acknowledges and is ready to confirm and develop.

He craves for our sake that we should love Him, but also He craves it for His own. He is not too lofty to ask our love, to seek for it, to desire it. He searches while there is hope : like the husbandman " who hath long patience " He waits.

But what if He whose hands most of all are mighty find nothing?

O Lord, what canst Thou find, except Thou first furnish it ? All is of Thy bounty, and but for Thine own gifts we can have no gift for Thee. I beseech Thee give us each some good gift, and receive it back as our gift to Thee.

"And I will give unto every one of you according to your works."—

I tremble at this word : but what word then would reassure me ? This is the Voice of the Just Judge ; would I desire rather to hear the voice of an unjust judge ? If justice be my destruction, could injustice be my salvation ? Nay.

How should injustice deliver me, if I be such as justice cannot deliver? From what do I need deliverance : from punishment ? Yes, and from very much besides punishment.

If I were saved from the punishment outside me, how save me from the punishment within ; from the fire, but how from the worm ?   Rescued from all else, how rescue me from myself ?

O Jesus, All Holy, All Just, All Merciful, deliver us from our perverse selves, and no other enemy can ruin us.   For Thine own sake.   Amen.

Again.   What other standard would I crave than this of work ? for work is voluntary, within my own option to do or leave undone.

Otherwise St. Paul could not thus write to his beloved Roman converts concerning the powers that be : " Rulers are not a terror to good works, but to the evil.   Wilt thou then not be afraid of the power ? do that which is good, and thou shalt have praise of the same : for he is the minister of God to thee for good."

What I do, I will to do : what I leave undone, I will to leave undone.   Who then is it that betrayeth me : Lord, is it I ?—It is I.

> Lord, carry me.—Nay, but I grant thee strength
> To walk and work thy way to Heaven at length.—
>
> Lord, why then am I weak ?—Because I give
> Power to the weak, and bid the dying live.—
>
> Lord, I am tired.—He hath not much desired
> The goal, who at the starting-point is tired.—
>
> Lord, dost Thou know ?—I know what is in man ;
> What the flesh can, and what the spirit can.—
>
> Lord, dost Thou care ?—Yea, for thy gain or loss
> So much I cared, it brought Me to the Cross.—
>
> Lord, I believe ; help Thou mine unbelief.—
> Good is the word ; but rise, for life is brief.
> The follower is not greater than the Chief :
> Follow thou Me along My way of grief.

24. But unto you I say, and unto the rest in Thyatira, as many as have not this doctrine, and which have not known the depths of Satan, as they speak ; I will put upon you none other burden.

A variation appears in the Revised Version :—" But to you I say, to the rest that are in Thyatira."—The. retrenchment of the word " and " (if correct) seems to convey the sense more clearly, by making the second clause of the sentence define the first instead of adding to it.

Blessed simplicity, not to hold false doctrine.   Blessed inexperience, which knows not depths of Satan.

From corrupt doctrine, foul knowledge, abcminable experience, good Lord, keep us; good Lord, deliver us. Keep rather than deliver, for deliverance brings not back innocence. Yet at the worst deliver us, that we may be Thy penitents, miracles of Thy pity. Amen.

"Depths of Satan."—Why dive into such depths, when deeper depths open before us?

"O the depth of the riches both of the wisdom and knowledge of God! how unsearchable are His judgments, and His ways past finding out! . . . For of Him, and through Him, and to Him are all things: to Whom be glory for ever. Amen."

We, no less than St. Paul's Ephesian converts, if "rooted and grounded in love, may be able to comprehend with all saints what is the breadth, and length, and depth, and height; and to know the love of Christ, which passeth knowledge."

"As they speak."—"Let the wicked be ashamed, and let them be silent in the grave. Let the lying lips be put to silence."

"I will put upon you none other burden."—None other than the burden Christ Himself has laid upon us, and which He elsewhere assures us is light.

A great writer has told us that Love carries a burden which is no burden.

"Why art thou so full of heaviness, O my soul? . . . Why go I thus heavily, while the enemy oppresseth me? . . . Why art thou so heavy, O my soul: and why art thou so disquieted within me? O put thy trust in God."

Christ's burden weighs heavily, not because of the burden's weight, but of the bearer's weakness. Blessed is he who embracing bears it. Not upon such a one laden with blessing, but upon another, his opposite, is woe pronounced: "Woe to him that increaseth that which is not his! how long? and to him that ladeth himself with thick clay!" "For what shall it profit a man, if he shall gain the whole world, and lose his own soul?"

Lord Jesus, I pray Thee bestow upon us that grace of strength whereby Thou didst uplift and comfort Daniel Thy saint :—

"O my Lord . . . my sorrows are turned upon me, and I have retained no strength. . . O man greatly beloved, fear not : peace be unto thee : be strong, yea, be strong."

25. But that which ye have already hold fast till I come.

Truly here are the patience, obedience, faith, of the

saints! Latter works must go on being more than former works, thus making last works most of all. Charity must never fail, but must abide. Service must to the end fulfil whatever it is our duty to do. Faith, though feeling companionless in a faithless generation because unwitting of God's seven thousand like-minded ones, must endure.

The Cross we have shouldered we must not lay down. The burnt sacrifice we have become we must continue to be though offered on a slow fire. Nor dare we say, It is finished, until Christ Himself say concerning us, It is finished; for He has pronounced : "No man, having put his hand to the plough, and looking back, is fit for the kingdom of God."

Such is our lot. Without our own will we were born to inherit it, without our own will we (most of us) were baptized into it : no will of ours can undo what is done.

All this, first and last, has befallen us by the Will of God.

And because by His Will, therefore it becomes possible for us to endure it, to profit by it, even by wonder-working grace to rejoice and be glad in it. Once let our will be conformed unto the Divine Will, and powers and pleasures shall be added unto us.

Even so, Lord God, conform our will to Thy Will, for our blessed self-sacrificing Saviour's sake. Amen.

Moreover we must not so dwell on our sore need of patience as to overlook faith, or worse still to overlook love. "Till I come," saith the Word, the Truth, in whom all Divine promises are Yea and Amen.

"Till I come." How long is that *till?* We cannot compute its days, weeks, months, years. But this we know : the remainder of time is the extent of that *till:* all eternity is the fullness of the ensuing thereafter.

Is time long? It may seem so, until it ends. Is eternity long? It is so, for it ends not.

Beloved, yield thy time to God, for He
  Will make eternity thy recompense ;
Give all thy substance for His Love, and be
  Beatified past earth's experience.
Serve Him in bonds, until He set thee free ;
  Serve Him in dust, until He lift thee thence ;
Till death be swallowed up in victory,
  When the great trumpet sounds to bid thee hence.
Shall setting day win day that will not set ?
  Poor price wert thou to spend thyself for Christ,
  Had not His wealth thy poverty sufficed :
    Yet since He makes His garden of thy clod,
Water thy lily, rose, or violet,
    And offer up thy sweetness unto God.

Must we then call our burden no burden? Not so, for Christ Himself by implication admits that a burden it is.

He, the Truth, requires of us the truth, the whole truth, and nothing but the truth. We are no more allowed to put sweet for bitter than bitter for sweet.

" Hold fast."—As one Greek whose grasping hands were hewn off, held fast the Persian vessel with his teeth; as the pilot of one burning ship held fast the helm while the flames consumed him; so, if we be called to any such supreme act, even so must each one of us hold fast our burden and birth-right till Christ come.

And if we be of those who oftentimes in the Blessed Sacrament of His Body and Blood show forth His Death till He come, we amongst all Christians are bound and are fortified thus to lose life and save it.

O Lord, Who assuredly wilt come ; in that tremendous Day suffer not our own privileges and our own words to rise up with us in the Judgment and condemn us.

We dwell upon terrors of Judgment : let us also dwell on its hopes. It will have a great sound of a trumpet, and the trumpet-blast is music. It will be with clouds, and God Almighty of old set His bow in the cloud. It will bring to sight angels. It will bring back saints ; the particular saints we having loved and lost, long for.

Yet, after all, these are but its minor hopes.

It will bring back Christ ; our supreme Hope, or else our supreme Fear. But the hope is in Him, the fear is in ourselves.

From ourselves and from our fear, good Lord, deliver us.

26. And he that overcometh, and keepeth My works unto the end, to him will I give power over the nations :

27. And he shall rule them with a rod of iron ; as the vessels of a potter shall they be broken to shivers ; even as I received of My Father.

The words *to keep Christ's works unto the end* suggest two branches of duty.

We are constantly to imitate, and by His strength made perfect in our weakness are as it were over and over again to reproduce, His blessed works. Because He prayed, we must pray. Because He went about doing good, we must do good. Because His meat was to do the will of Him that sent Him, so must ours be. Such are His works by us and through us.

And thus must we persevere to the end, lest we be not numbered amongst those who overcome.

We must also hold fast His works in us. The purifying grace of Baptism, the maturing grace of Confirmation, the sustaining grace of Holy Communion, we must hold fast. We holding fast what He bestows, He will continually bestow more and more. There is no limit to His bounties, nor can we assign a limit to our own capacity.

King Joash smote thrice and stayed, whilst he might have stricken five or six valid strokes. The miraculous flow of oil stayed only when the widow's receptacles were exhausted.

> O foolish Soul! to make thy count
>   For languid falls and much forgiven,
> When like a flame thou mightest mount
>   To storm and carry heaven.
>
> A life so faint,—is this to live?
>   A goal so mean,—is this a goal?
> Christ love thee, remedy, forgive,
>   Save thee, O foolish Soul.

He who in overcoming himself and all things has first exercised power, he it is on whom will be conferred power over the nations.

Unlike most of the rewards held out to our hope, this power appears to be punitive, destructive. Thank God, it is not ours at present; nor at present could aught like it by any possibility befit us common sort of Christians. He whom God may call to such an office, God by His Almighty Spirit will adapt to the call, and will keep safe in responding to it. Into His hands Fatherly, merciful, perfect, let us meanwhile commend and commit all men.

Nevertheless it cannot be without practical purpose that this prospect, "terrible as an army with banners," is opened to us. It brings home to our conviction that a day approaches, when, cost what it may, all the elect will be of one mind with God. Whatever He decrees they will uphold; whatever He inflicts they will approve. Even to the tenderest mother, the Divine good pleasure will then be altogether better than seven sons or than ten sons. Whom God pities not, neither will His saints pity: whom He saves not, neither will His saints yearn to save. They who are exalted to see Him as He is, will be like Him.

The punishment is greater than we can bear. God keep us from ever looking upon our beloved ones with changed eyes, or from being looked upon with changed eyes by them.

O my God, Who hast no pleasure in the death of him that dieth, preserve Thou them that are appointed to die; and when this dying life is fulfilled, bring us of Thy mercy to the life everlasting.   Through Jesus Christ our Life.   Amen.

"Even as I received of My Father."—The extreme instance vouching for all subordinate instances.   Christ, Who so long hath invited all men, saying, "Come unto Me," will at last say to those on His left hand, "Depart from Me."

O Lamb of God, from the Wrath of the Lamb, deliver us.

28. And I will give him the morning star.
29. He that hath an ear, let him hear what the Spirit saith unto the churches.

Elsewhere our Lord declares: "I am . . . the Bright and Morning Star." Thus (if the inference be allowable) here at the outset He promises to give Himself to him that overcometh.

To whom does a man give himself? To one whom he loves as himself.   Such is the standard of human self-gift; and Christ, Very Man no less than Very God, will not fall short of it.   To "the friend that is as His own soul" will He give Himself; giving Himself, He will withhold nothing.

We know not a millionth part of what Christ is to us, but perhaps we even less know what we are to Him.

O Lord, I cannot plead my love of Thee :
I plead Thy love of me ; —
The shallow conduit hails the unfathomed sea.

CHAPTER III.

I. **And unto the angel of the church in Sardis write; These things saith He that hath the seven Spirits of God, and the seven stars; I know thy works, that thou hast a name that thou livest, and art dead.**

If it be lawful to regard these "Seven Spirits of God" as that "One and the self-same Spirit," Who divideth to every man severally as He will, our Lord's preamble to the Church in Sardis corresponds with Isaiah's prophetic description of the Messiah: "The Spirit of the Lord shall rest upon Him, the Spirit of Wisdom and Understanding, the Spirit of Counsel and Might, the Spirit of Knowledge and of the Fear of the Lord; and shall make Him of quick understanding in the fear of the Lord: and He shall not judge after the sight of His eyes, neither reprove after the hearing of His ears."

Thus He Who telleth the number of the stars and calleth them all by their names, before He pronounces judgment on even one star, deigns to proclaim and certify His own infallible insight.

"I know thy works"—the works of Sardis, of all Christendom, of the whole world. Yea, and my works indeed, O Lord, Thou knowest: it is I myself who know them not fully. "Search me, O God, and know my heart: try me, and know my thoughts: and see if there be any wicked way in me, and lead me in the way everlasting."

"Thou hast a name that thou livest, and art dead."—Sardis with her name to live worked after a fashion, although dead. Centuries before the Psalmist had placed on record: "Men will praise thee, when thou doest well to thyself." And in our Lord's Sermon in the Plain we read: "Woe unto you, when all men shall speak well of you!"

Sardis doubtless in some sense did well unto herself, however cruel in truth were her tender self-mercies; and thus

earned the condemnation of God with the praise of men, inasmuch as that which is highly esteemed among men is abomination in the sight of God.   The particular works of Sardis are
not enumerated, but of this we may rest assured : so far as she
was a dead Church her works were infallibly dead works.
Yet works they were, and of such a semblance that men said
she lived : God and God only knew and testified that she was
dead.

And what avails man's word against God's word?

Her fair name and fame, her self-complacency, her lustre,
have passed away; yea, like as a dream when one awaketh, so
hath He made her image to vanish out of the city. A temporal
doom has long ago overtaken her : may it not be that an
eternal doom overhangs her!

Our Lord rebuked Sardis in the day of grace, lest at last He
should condemn her in the day of justice.

As once to her, so now if need is He speaks to us, to me.
In love He forewarns us all : " Many will say to Me in that
day, Lord, Lord, have we not prophesied in Thy Name? and
in Thy Name have cast out devils? and in Thy Name done
many wonderful works?   And then will I profess unto them,
I never knew you : depart from Me, ye that work iniquity."

Shall the dead rise up again and praise God?   Yea, the
dead also, if they will respond to the call of His grace.   As
avers the Father in the parable : " This my son was dead, and
is alive again ; he was lost, and is found."

" Comfort ye, comfort ye My people, saith your God."

**2. Be watchful, and strengthen the things which remain,
that are ready to die: for I have not found thy works
perfect before God.**

"What I say unto you I say unto all, Watch."   The watchful must watch on, the unwatchful must learn and practise
watchfulness. Every one of us is either watchful or unwatchful.
"Teach me, O Lord, the way of Thy statutes; and I shall
keep it unto the end."

Watchfulness is no easy duty.   When Elijah answered,
"Thou hast asked a hard thing," he made its coming to pass
depend on Elisha's own watchfulness : whence we may infer
that the boon being difficult of access, that on which it depended was not lightly to be achieved.   St. Peter, St. John,
St. James, for all their love, failed in watchfulness, while their
Saviour watched alone and agonized alone.

My God, if watchfulness taxes the strength of Thy saints

who live unto Thee, how shall the dead in trespasses and sins renew their vigil to praise Thee with songs in the night?—Nay, hath He spoken, and shall He not make it good? "O put thy trust in God : for I will yet thank Him, which is the help of my countenance, and my God."

"Strengthen the things which remain, that are ready to die." —God, Whose good pleasure hath chosen "things which are not," equally of His grace calls upon the dead to strengthen what remains and is ready to die. What He commands He renders possible. "He giveth power to the faint; and to them that have no might He increaseth strength." When Isaac asked, "Where is the lamb?" while as yet there appeared no lamb ; not Abraham himself can have understood the fullness of his own answer : "God will provide Himself a lamb."

Praise be to Thee, O God, Who both didst provide a lamb for Thyself, and Thyself becamest that Lamb which Thou providedst. Praise be to Thee, forasmuch as the ram offered in Isaac's stead was caught in a thicket by his horns; not weakness, but the sign of his strength holding him fast. Even so, not through weakness, but by Thine own Will, Strength, Glory, didst Thou stoop to become fast bound in the thicket of our troubles : nor wouldst Thou by any means pass out thence except as a Lamb for a burnt offering ; even the Lamb of God, which taketh away the sin of the world. Alleluia !

"Though He slay me, yet will I trust in Him."—This is one sort of dead man who shall live ; together with Christ's once-dead Body shall he arise. Perhaps for us the main point of that text roots itself in the word *will*. None predicates of him *he can* nor yet *he ought:* he alone says, and· says only, *I will*. He says not, I do ; for far from him be lying lips and a deceitful tongue. He says, I will : and the man who has the will to say, I will, has latent within him the power to bring to pass by God's assisting grace the purpose of that good will. His dew is as the dew of herbs, his earth shall cast out her dead.

When God demanded : "Son of man, can these bones live?" even Ezekiel could answer no more than, "O Lord God, Thou knowest." God alone, then as ever, knew what He would do.

We, every one of us, must at this moment be either dead or alive. Let us put it at the worst, and postulate that we are dead : what shall we do that we may come again to our border, and return into the land of the living? Sardis was bidden "strengthen those things which remain, that are ready to die": whence it follows: This do, and thou shalt live. And what if gazing within we discern nothing remaining; nothing even so far alive as to be ready to die? We still can lift up our eyes and look without, in obedience to St. Paul's precept: "Look not every man on his own things, but every man also on the things of others." Our neighbour languishes, is weak, wavers, is ready to perish: whoso strives by prayer, or by any other conceivable agency to uphold him, shall himself be upheld; even as Job, praying for his friends, received in his own person a blessing. "He that watereth shall be watered also himself."

If the light that is in us be as darkness that may be felt, let us work and walk by the light that is without us; until the day dawn, and the day-star arise in our hearts.

O Christ, the Resurrection and the Life; O Christ, Light of the world and of every man that cometh into the world, call Thy dead out of darkness of death into light of life. Say once again, yea, say again and again, Let there be light: and there shall be light.

> As froth on the face of the deep,
> As foam on the crest of the sea,
> As dreams at the waking of sleep,
> As gourd of a day and a night,
> As harvest that no man shall reap,
> As vintage that never shall be,
> Is hope if it cling not aright,
> O my God, unto Thee.

"I have not found thy works perfect before God"—or according to the Revised Version: "I have found no works of thine fulfilled before My God."—The former reading recalls our Lord's words in His Sermon on the Mount: "Be ye therefore perfect, even as your Father which is in heaven is perfect;" a precept so lofty that mortal man can appropriate it only in aim and intention, except so far as his being Christ's member clothes him with Christ's righteousness. The latter reading suggests works left incomplete even according to the standard of human completeness; beginnings broken off short, starts without careers, wishes instead of resolves, repentances still to be repented of. We are reminded of Lot's wife, the fig-tree leafy but fruitless, the son in the Parable who answered, I go, sir, and went not.

We look out of ourselves at these and such as these. God help us to look into ourselves, lest all the while we be such as they and know it not.

The way to hell is paved with good intentions.

3. Remember therefore how thou hast received and heard, and hold fast, and repent. If therefore thou shalt not watch, I will come on thee as a thief, and thou shalt not know what hour I will come upon thee.

Well may He Who beyond all others loves us, for that very love's sake bid us "Remember," lest all too late we should remember. For it has been said of old that there is no bitterer pang than in misery to remember past happiness. There shall be weeping and gnashing of teeth when the children of the kingdom being thrust out behold their birthright blessedness given to others that are better than they. "Son, remember," spake Abraham to Dives.

To-day it may be that if we choose we can forget; another day we shall not be able to choose, but must perforce remember what we have received and heard. Not through time and never through eternity can we make ourselves as though we had not received and heard.

We have heard the Word of God, the witness of saints, the voice of conscience whereby God the Holy Spirit speaks within us; these we must sooner or later remember.

We have received the Life of Baptism, the Strength of Confirmation, the Sustenance of Christ's most precious Body and Blood; these we must sooner or later remember.

Our startings aside have been from all these, our falls from all these. These we have held fast; or have let go.

And if we have let them go, can we ever again hope to hold them fast? Yea, saith our Judge: "Hold fast, repent."

Let us go forth in the strength of the Lord God, and make mention of His righteousness only.

O God Whose hand is not shortened that it cannot save, Who to him that hath no might increaseth strength, Who didst uphold St. Peter on the waters, convert him in the high priest's palace, restore him by the Sea of Tiberias, O our God, Who hast done all for us, now do all in us. Hold us fast, that we may hold Thee fast. Remember now our sins, that Thou mayest move us to repentance; and washing them away in Thy blood mayest remember them no more. Amen for Thine own sake, Lord Jesus, Amen.

Contempt and pangs and haunting fears—
  Too late for hope, too late for ease,
    Too late for rising from the dead ;
  Too late, too late to bend my knees,
    Or bow my head,
Or weep, or ask for tears.

Hark ! . . . One I hear Who calls to me :
  "Give Me thy thorn and grief and scorn,
    Give Me thy ruin and regret.
  Press on thro' darkness toward the morn :
    One loves thee yet :
Have I forgotten thee ? "

Lord, Who art Thou ? Lord, is it Thou
  My Lord and God, Lord Jesus Christ ?
    How said I that I sat alone
  And desolate and unsufficed ?
    Surely a stone
Would raise Thy praises now !

Once more the word is, Watch. In whatever mood, in de-
pression if need be, let us watch. As sings the Psalmist:
" I have watched, and am even as it were a sparrow, that sitteth
alone upon the house-top. Mine enemies revile me all the
day long ; and they that are mad upon me are sworn together
against me. For I have eaten ashes as it were bread ; and
mingled my drink with weeping ; and that because of Thine
indignation and wrath : for Thou hast taken me up, and cast
me down. My days are gone like a shadow ; and I am withered
like grass." For this woeful complaint is still a song : even
while he lies under the Divine indignation and wrath the
penitent sings and makes melody in his heart to the Lord.
By Whose gracious help we all may do likewise. Repentance
pleases God ; and that whereby we please God cannot be to
ourselves mere unmitigated grief.

Nor is it any trivial matter which depends upon our watchfulness. According as we watch, or watch not, Christ will
come to save or to punish.

"Watch therefore : for ye know not what hour your Lord
doth come. But know this, that if the good man of the house
had known in what watch the thief would come, he would have
watched, and would not have suffered his house to be broken
up. Therefore be ye also ready : for in such an hour as ye
think not the Son of Man cometh."

Shall He come to us " as a thief," Who would fain come to
us as a Bridegroom ?

" Yea, in the way of Thy judgments, O Lord, have we waited

for Thee; the desire of our soul is to Thy name, and to the remembrance of Thee. With my soul have I desired Thee in the night; yea, with my spirit within me will I seek Thee early." "I am my Beloved's, and His desire is toward me."

4. **Thou hast a few names even in Sardis which have not defiled their garments; and they shall walk with Me in white: for they are worthy.**

Primitive man arrayed in innocence needed no other robe. Fallen man God Himself deigned to clothe; and the garment of fallen man may (I think) be regarded as representing such sort and degree of holiness as being possible to a sinner is therefore required of him. For God Almighty is never that ruler who demands brick in a territory of no straw.

Absolute innocence on this side of the grave no soul can win back, yet holiness transcends innocence. A law, " Thou shalt not," hedged in innocence in the Garden of Eden; but St. Paul declares that " the fruit of the Spirit is love, joy, peace, longsuffering, gentleness, goodness, faith, meekness, temperance: against such there is no law."

" A few names even in Sardis."—Ten righteous would have preserved Sodom; one would have sufficed to save Jerusalem. Thus we discern that Abraham's persistence of intercession yet stopped short of the bounty of God's unsolicited Goodwill. Human tenderness pleaded *ten*, Divine yearning craved for *one*. Both however bore immediate reference to temporal punishment, not apparently to eternal judgment.

The " few " in Sardis safe themselves could not deliver their fellows. Their case corresponded with that set forth in Ezekiel's prophecy: " When the land sinneth against Me by trespassing grievously, then will I stretch out Mine hand upon it . . . Though these three men, Noah, Daniel, and Job, were in it, they should deliver but their own souls by their righteousness, saith the Lord God." Psalm xlix. (Prayer-Book version) throws light on the subject: " No man may deliver his brother, nor make agreement unto God for him; for it cost more to redeem their souls: so that he must let that alone for ever; yea, though he live long, and see not the grave." Truly did it cost more to redeem our souls, for it cost the life of that Man Who is the Lord's Fellow; had He lived long and not seen the grave, even He (so far as the Divine counsels have been revealed to us) must have let that alone for ever. Thus by a sort of harmony of contraries the Psalmist provides a

clue to the coming mystery of Redemption.   We recognize a
revelation of Divine Might where at first seemed but a statement of human impotence.   A veiled mystery flashes through
this verse; which verse of the Holy Bible may not veil a
mystery?

> Lord, grant us eyes to see and ears to hear
>   And souls to love and minds to understand,
>   And steadfast faces toward the Holy Land,
> And confidence of hope, and filial fear,
> And citizenship where Thy saints appear
>   Before Thee heart in heart and hand in hand,
>   And Alleluias where their chanting band
> As waters and as thunders fill the sphere.
> Lord, grant us what Thou wilt, and what Thou wilt
>   Deny, and fold us in Thy peaceful fold :
>   Not as the world gives, give to us Thine own :
> Inbuild us where Jerusalem is built
> With walls of jasper and with streets of gold,
>   And Thou Thyself, Lord Christ, for Corner Stone.

" A few names even in Sardis."—*A few* in a whole city, *a
few* out of an entire population.   Shall London cast the first
stone at Sardis?

O God, merciful and pitiful, Who hast created us all, and
knowest us all, if we be children teach us to honour Thee, and
if servants to fear Thee : yea, if we be stones teach us to
celebrate Thy praise.   For Jesus Christ's sake.   Amen.

"A few . . . which have not defiled their garments."
Who are these?   Baptized infants, and sweet souls of any age
unexperienced in mortal sin.

None beside these?   Thank God, the text says not so.   By
His grace it may (surely) include along with all who have never
defiled their garments those likewise who have not permanently
defiled them.

He Who has been pleased to promise that the elect human
family shall be made equal to the elect angels, can if He pleases
make the choir of penitents equal to that kindred choir which
by comparison need no repentance.   Once He vouchsafed to
say touching one sinful woman : " Her sins, which are many,
are forgiven ; for she loved much : but to whom little is forgiven,
the same loveth little."

"Judge nothing before the time, until the Lord come, Who
both will bring to light the hidden things of darkness, and will
make manifest the counsels of the hearts."   Only whilst we
have time let us love much.

"And they shall walk with Me in white."—The precarious

purity of mortal life shall become the indefectible purity of life immortal. As the bud becomes the lily, as the dawn the day, so white robes of earth shall reappear, transfigured as robes of heaven, white as no fuller on earth can white them. Such whiteness as we now are used to can scarcely abide unsullied unless it also abide intact ; thus trodden snow turns to mud ; whilst snow on mountain summits endures alone, inaccessible, stainless. Even so chaste virgins choose solitude for a bower; and recluses dwell apart and unknown, like unfound pearls; and great saints betaking themselves to heavenly places in Christ Jesus, move aloft like white sunny clouds of the sky.

Nevertheless, however good for the present distress, yet from the beginning God Himself declared that it is not good for man to be alone. No trace of solitude reappears in the next life, the life that lives for ever. Whatever we know, or know not, about Heaven, this beyond possibility of doubt is certified to us ; it will contain a great multitude that no man can number, and these congregated into one body, one community of saints. Nothing will ever any more separate them ; not night, for there is no night there ; not the sea, for they stand together upon that unearthly sea.

Yet all this accumulation of beatitude taken by itself could not satisfy us ; it would still be no more than a turning aside by the flocks of the companions. Christ's promise exceeds this. "They shall walk with Me." Herein is beatific love.

It is stated in our text (ver. 4) that those whose earthly garments have been undefiled, are the same who will be invested with a heavenly white garment. A second point, though unstated, may (I think) be inferred : those who like Enoch have "walked with God" on earth, are the same who shall walk with Him in Heaven.

Little as we know of blessed Enoch's personal history, yet the phrase "walked with God" tells us much. "Can two walk together, except they be agreed?" asks the Lord by the mouth of His Prophet Amos. Enoch's will must then have been conformed to the Divine Will. Moreover, exalted as it is to "sit together in heavenly places in Christ Jesus," blessed as it is to "sleep in Jesus"; yet of Enoch we are told not that he sat, still less if possible that he slept, but that he walked. He exerted himself, he made progress, he persevered, until "God took him.'

Amen, for us all.

"For they are worthy." —How "worthy"? when the same

Truth and Wisdom hath said : " None is good, save One, that is, God."

As Isaac received Rebekah into the tent, and himself was comforted ; as Boaz extended his protection to Ruth, and while loving and ennobling her rejoiced in her affection ; so our dear Lord enriches our poverty with His own wealth, covers our unworthiness with His own worthiness, sees in us of the travail of His Soul, and is satisfied.　He, Bridegroom of souls, saith to His beloved : " With all My goods I thee endow" : His Blessedness is as of the sun which gives, and ours is as of the moon which receives.　" It is more blessed to give than to receive."

" I am not worthy of the least of all the mercies, and of all the truth, which Thou hast showed unto Thy servant."

5. **He that overcometh, the same shall be clothed in white raiment, and I will not blot out his name out of the Book of Life, but I will confess his name before My Father, and before His angels.**
6. **He that hath an ear, let him hear what the Spirit saith unto the churches.**

Once again " he that overcometh " is the only person to win a prize.　Not even Christ's work for us can be substituted for the Holy Spirit's work in us.　By aid of Whose indwelling Might may every one of us watch, strengthen what languishes, remember, hold fast, repent, flee defilement.

Not that these are ever easy duties, but by help of grace they become possible : were they easy, we need not be incited to overcome.　And if possible to any, then are they possible to all, even to the most backward : for it is the same Almighty Spirit Who dwells and works in great and small, and Who many times has vouchsafed the race to the not-swift, and the battle to the not-strong.　One by one let us consider these particular points of duty.

Watch.　As failure may betide swift and strong, so may it betide watchers also : " Except the Lord keep the city, the watchman waketh but in vain."　Still, if watchfulness may, unwatchfulness must be rife with peril.　" The earth is weak, and all the inhabiters thereof : I bear up the pillars of it," came evidently to pass on that searching night of the Passion when our Lord watched alone, because the three whom He had bidden watch with Him slept.　On the other hand, under the elder and less helpful dispensation, Nehemiah with his

faithful adherents having prayed, set a watch day and night
against their foes and prospered ; and Habakkuk in the midst
of his prophecy protests: "I will stand upon my watch, and
set me upon the tower, and will watch to see what He will
say unto me, and what I shall answer when I am reproved."
Psalm cxxiii. furnishes us with the very words we need :
"Unto Thee lift I up mine eyes, O Thou that dwellest in
the heavens. Behold, as the eyes of servants look unto the
hand of their masters, and as the eyes of a maiden unto the
hand of her mistress ; so our eyes wait upon the Lord our
God, until that He have mercy upon us."

Strengthen what languishes. What desperate ruin it is by
letting slip the last opportunity and extinguishing the last
glimmer of light to do despite to Him Who breaks not the
bruised reed nor quenches the smoking flax, Christ's own
words and tears have revealed: "He beheld the city, and
wept over it, saying, If thou hadst known, even thou, at least
in this thy day, the things which belong unto thy peace ! but
now they are hid from thine eyes." For examples of self-
retrieval we turn to Joseph of Arimathæa, who being a disciple
of Jesus, but secretly for fear of the Jews, at length went in
boldly unto Pilate, and craved the Body of Jesus,—to Nicodemus, who first resorted to Jesus by night, later on spoke
however feebly in His defence, and at last shared with several
saints (women as well as men) the devotion and anguish of
His sepulture,—to St. Mark, who once hung back, but afterwards repented and went. "Hear my prayer, O Lord, and
with Thine ears consider my calling : hold not Thy peace at
my tears. For I am a stranger with Thee : and a sojourner,
as all my fathers were. O spare me a little, that I may recover
my strength : before I go hence, and be no more seen."

Remember. God Who bids us remember, Himself remembers : woe were it to mankind if He remembered not.
"Yea, many a time turned He His anger away, and did not
stir up all His wrath. For He remembered that they were
but flesh ; a wind that passeth away, and cometh not again."
Since He spake against His rebellious children, He doth
earnestly remember them still. To renegade Israel He even
saith: "I remember thee, the kindness of thy youth, the love
of thine espousals . . . I will yet plead with you." God
hath indeed not forgotten to be gracious, and graciously He
enjoins upon us the duty of ourselves remembering. Let us
call to mind a few points which we have received and heard :
—"Remember the Sabbath-day, to keep it holy." "Behold,

God exalteth by His power. . . . Remember that thou magnify
His work, which men behold. Every man may see it; man
may behold it afar off." "If a man live many years, and
rejoice in them all; yet let him remember the days of darkness; for they shall be many." "Remember now thy Creator
in the days of thy youth." St. Paul charges us "to remember
the words of the Lord Jesus, how He said, It is more blessed
to give than to receive." St. Jude exhorts us: "Remember
ye the words which were spoken before of the Apostles of our
Lord Jesus Christ; how that they told you there should be
mockers in the last time, who should walk after their own
ungodly lusts." And infinitely above even the Apostles, our
Master bade them and through them bids us: "Remember
the word that I said unto you, The servant is not greater than
his lord."—O Lord, the Better David, remember all Thine
own trouble; and for good remember us, remember me, when
Thou comest into Thy Kingdom.

Hold fast. Shall we fill our hands with possessions which
are not worth holding fast? "There is a sore evil which I
have seen under the sun, namely, riches kept for the owners
thereof to their hurt. But those riches perish by evil travail:
and he begetteth a son, and there is nothing in his hand." We
can carry nothing away when we die, neither the hurtful riches
denounced by the Preacher, nor the thick clay denounced by
the Prophet (*see* Hab. ii. 6). Hands preoccupied by such as
these cannot grasp veritable wealth: "How hardly shall they
that have riches enter into the kingdom of God!" Hands
emptied by showing mercy to the poor, are set free to hold fast
what God will require of us; hearts emptied of self are prepared
to receive and retain all He will demand; such blessed store as
righteousness, with Job who would not let it go; that which is
good, with the Thessalonian converts; the apostolic form of
sound words, with Timothy; our profession, and confidence,
and rejoicing of hope firm unto the end, with all faithful
Christians. Thus Jacob said: "I will not let Thee go, except
Thou bless me. . . . And He blessed him there." Yet because
God Himself is to us more than all His blessings, let us rather
protest with the Bride: "I found Him Whom my soul loveth:
I held Him, and would not let Him go."

Repent. There is no Divine promise which penitence may
not claim; no height, no depth of Divine Love secluded from
penitence. All is promised to the penitent, but repentance
itself is not promised to the sinner. Yet, O my God, how
otherwise should sinners be half so hopeful of repentance, as

now that it depends solely on Thy Goodwill? Thou Who biddest us repent, fulfil in us Thine own bidding. Thou Who hast declared concerning Israel : " I will heal their backsliding, I will love them freely," make us such as Thou canst heal and love. Thou Who art long-suffering to usward, not willing that any should perish, but that all should come to repentance ; bring us to repentance, for none else in heaven or in earth can bring us. Thou Who holdest out to us hope, let us not be disappointed of our hope. If we be lost, Christ thereby loseth the price of His most precious Blood : suffer us to plead Christ with Thee, and to say : Who shall countervail the King's damage ? Repentance is not promised to the impenitent, but to those who serve God all that they ask aright is promised ; Christians know this, say this, build and rest on this: thus prevailingly they implore for themselves fuller, deeper, ever renewed repentance ; thus availingly they might implore it for those who for themselves implore it not. O God of all Mercy and all Comfort, God the Father Who lovest us, God the Son Who lovest us, God the Holy Spirit Who lovest us, give us for whom Christ died grace to love our neighbour as ourself, and to pray for him as for ourself. Am I my brother's keeper? Yes.

Flee defilement. St. Mark records how when our Lord " had called all the people unto Him, He said unto them, Hearken unto Me every one of you, and understand : there is nothing from without a man, that entering into him can defile him : but the things which come out of him, those are they that defile the man. If any man have ears to hear, let him hear." So emphatically are all the people, every one of them, instructed that the spiritual garment contracts defilement not from without but from within. Purity follows a contrary rule to many other virtues. Many are promoted by dwelling on the antagonistic vices ; by coming, so to say, to close quarters with these, by waging war with them face to face, war to the death. Look hard at ill-temper, for instance ; and when you attain to appreciate its contemptible aspect, you may advance to discern and fall in love with the majesty of meekness. Not so with impurity : cover and turn away the eye lest it should behold it, stop the ear lest it should admit it ; for the blessed pure in heart who shall see God, copy their Lord the Holy One Who is of purer eyes than to behold evil, and Who cannot look on iniquity. Nor does this imperative duty of shunning contamination from without, at all clash with our Master's warning that defilement has its sole root within : the knowledge of foulness

G

welcomed, entertained, gloated over, breeds in us foulness like itself; it acts like blood poison which infused from without turns the man himself, or the woman herself, to a death-struck mass of corruption. Holy courage often befits us : in this single instance holy cowardice becomes man's only available courage; as Joseph fled, abandoning and risking all rather than do a great wickedness, and sin against God. Akin to our duty towards ourselves in this matter, is our duty towards others, especially towards the young : in their regard we may pray to be made perfect as our Father in heaven is perfect; Who vouchsafed to shield the innocent ignorance of young Samuel, even while denouncing by his mouth abominable and crying sin. " Finally, brethren, whatsover things are true, whatsoever things are honest, whatsoever things are just, whatsoever things are pure, whatsoever things are lovely, whatsoever things are of good report ; if there be any virtue, and if there be any praise, think on these things."

" The same shall be clothed in white raiment."—" Not unto us, O Lord, not unto us, but unto Thy Name give the praise." God will clothe us who cannot clothe ourselves. Wherefore we need not inquire either for earth or for heaven, " wherewithal shall we be clothed ? " for our Heavenly Father knoweth that we have need of many such things, and will without fail add them unto us if meanwhile we seek first His kingdom and righteousness. Whereof we enjoy already encouraging signs. As when He covered Adam and Eve after their shameful fall. Or as when under a similitude His love for Jerusalem is set forth : " I clothed thee also with broidered work, and shod thee with badgers' skin, and I girded thee about with fine linen, and I covered thee with silk. I decked thee also with ornaments, and I put bracelets upon thy hands, and a chain on thy neck. And I put a jewel on thy forehead, and earrings in thine ears, and a beautiful crown upon thine head. Thus wast thou decked with gold and silver ; and thy raiment was of fine linen, and silk, and broidered work . . . and thou wast exceeding beautiful. . . . And thy renown went forth among the heathen for thy beauty: for it was perfect through My comeliness, which I had put upon thee, saith the Lord God." Or as when the Father in the Parable arrays his prodigal son: " Bring forth the best robe, and put it on him ; and put a ring on his hand, and shoes on his feet." And how beautiful is whiteness for a garment we see illustrated on all sides : the dove "is covered with silver wings"; lambs wear a white fleece ; lilies and snowdrops are white, and there is a white

rose ; the swan floats in whiteness on blue waters, and over-
head white clouds float across the blue sky. Snow is white,
and so is a pearl ; and diamonds and light are colourless.

Nevertheless whiteness is not an absence but rather a compendium of colour. All tints when united in a perfectly
balanced harmony resolve themselves into whiteness, and
consequently all tints are capable of being re-developed from
whiteness. Thus colourless light paints the rainbow. And
thus celestial whiteness will not restrict but may rather gratify
the taste of all who wear it.

At the first moment *whiteness* does not suggest *colour :* yet
all colour being latent in it, we finally discern in its train every
lovely hue and gradation of hues. If thus it is with one word
characteristic of Heaven, how know we that it is not so with
every word?

To-day we hear by the hearing of the ear. So it was in her
day with the Queen of Sheba, who allured by what she heard
betook herself to the Holy Land ; and when she saw King
Solomon in his royalty, and saw those who served him,
"Behold," said she, "the half was not told me."

O Christ, our King and our Wisdom, bring us, I beseech
Thee, to Thy Holy Land which is very far off, that there our
eyes may see Thee in Thy Beauty.

"King Solomon gave unto the Queen of Sheba all her
desire, whatsoever she asked, beside that which Solomon gave
her of his royal bounty."

> All that we see rejoices in the sunshine,
>   All that we hear makes merry in the Spring :
> God grant us such a mind to be glad after our kind,
>   And to sing
>   His praises evermore for everything.

> Much that we see must vanish with the sunshine,
>   Sweet Spring must fail and fail the choir of Spring :
> But Wisdom shall burn on when the lesser lights are gone,
>   And shall sing
>   God's praises evermore for everything.

"I will not blot out his name out of the Book of Life."—
Human life is in two sections, life terminable and life interminable : and if I may so express it, the Book of Life appears
to be correspondingly in two volumes ; the Register of Baptism
for this world, and the Register of Final Perseverance for the
next. I say *of Baptism* because to us Christians the word of
this salvation is sent, and according to it we must judge ourselves, and abide the final Judgment : whereas as St. Paul

instructs us, "What have I to do to judge them also that are without? do not ye judge them that are within? But them that are without God judgeth." To Whose mercy in that day let us commend ourselves and every living soul.

That first volume is constituted our Book of Life to the extent of promise, privilege, possibility: it depends on ourselves to realize the possibility, perpetuate the privilege, claim fulfilment of the promise. It is also our patent of nobility: the Name that is above every name heads the "glorious, goodly, noble" list of those who please God; for He is not ashamed to call us brethren, He of Whom it is recorded, "Then said I, Lo, I come (in the volume of the book it is written of Me), to do Thy Will, O God."

> Thy Name, O Christ, as ointment is poured forth
>   Sweetening our names before God's Holy Face;
> Luring us from the south and from the north
>   Unto the sacred place.
>
> In Thee God's promise is Amen and Yea,
>   What art Thou to us? Prize of every lot,
> Shepherd and Door, our Life and Truth and Way:—
>   Nay, Lord, what art Thou not?

It is out of that first volume that names may be blotted: once entered in the second they become (thank God!) indelible. Change and vicissitude are confined to this life and this world: once safe in the next world the saved are safe for ever and ever. So our Lord deigned in effect to teach us all, when answering certain Sadducees, He said: "The children of this world marry, and are given in marriage: but they which shall be accounted worthy to obtain that world, and the resurrection from the dead, neither marry, nor are given in marriage: neither can they die any more: for they are equal unto the angels; and are the children of God, being the children of the resurrection." And further we gather hence by implication that not all shall "obtain . . . the resurrection from the dead": all must rise; but some will rise alive unto life, and some will rise dead unto damnation; in accordance with Christ's explicit statement elsewhere: "The hour is coming, in the which all that are in the graves shall hear His voice, and shall come forth; they that have done good, unto the resurrection of life; and they that have done evil, unto the resurrection of damnation."

Let us lay to heart each allusion to God's most awful Book. David mentions it where he prophesies against our Saviour's adversaries on Calvary; whose children, crucifying the Son of God afresh, and putting Him to an open shame, are the apostate Christians of successive generations: " Let them be blotted out of the Book of the living, and not be written with the righteous."

We meet with such a Book in the prophetic record of Daniel: "There shall be a time of trouble, such as never was since there was a nation even to that same time: and at that time thy people shall be delivered, every one that shall be found written in the Book. And many of them that sleep in the dust of the earth shall awake, some to everlasting life, and some to shame and everlasting contempt."

Malachi speaking of such a Book encourages the faithful: "Then they that feared the Lord spake often one to another: and the Lord hearkened, and heard it, and a Book of remembrance was written before Him for them that feared the Lord, and that thought upon His Name. And they shall be Mine, saith the Lord of hosts, in that day when I make up My jewels; and I will spare them, as a man spareth his own son that serveth him."

St. Paul too alludes confidently to the Book in question when he writes concerning certain saints: "Clement also, and . . . other my fellow-labourers, whose names are in the Book of Life." After which words no wonder that he goes on to say: "Rejoice in the Lord alway: and again I say, Rejoice."

Nor are we left in any shadow of doubt as to the standard according to which names will or will not abide in that Book. Long before any of the texts hitherto cited, we read concerning idolatrous Israel: "The Lord said unto Moses, Whosoever hath sinned against Me, him will I blot out of My Book."

"I will confess his name."—What is it that men confess? Something that they are, that they have done, that they admit; something personal, intimate: not things indifferent or alien.

Even so Christ in promising to confess the name of him that overcometh, promises to confess the name of one who is His member, bone of His bone, and flesh of His flesh, one Body and one Blood with Him; in whom He Himself has wrought the work of salvation, and by His Spirit has overcome.

Of which condescending Divine goodwill, St. Paul's declaration is the aspiring human correlative: "I am crucified with Christ: nevertheless I live; yet not I, but Christ liveth in me: and the life which I now live in the flesh, I live by the faith of the Son of God, Who loved me, and gave Himself for me"; from which exalted grace no Christian is excluded:

" Whatsoever ye do in word or deed, do all in the Name of the Lord Jesus."

We baptized Christians who bear the Name of Christ, and whom His Spirit indwells, are already one with Him. This union awaits not the future : it took place so many days, months, years ago; it now is, except we be reprobate ; it will ever abide, except we fall away. Immeasurable heights of hope, unmeasured depths of fear, open to us at the word : beyond either, the height and depth of Christ's Love. " He that hath ears to hear " hears His Voice pleading with the most lost, the most rebellious : " How shall I give thee up . . . ? how shall I deliver thee . . . ? how shall I make thee as Admah ? how shall I set thee as Zeboim ? Mine heart is turned within Me, My repentings are kindled together."

O Lord, wilt Thou be less to us than Adam was to his Eve ? for he prophesied : " Therefore shall a man . . . cleave unto his wife."

O Lord, cleave Thou to us, or we cannot cleave to Thee.

O Lord, wilt Thou require of us guilty more than Adam required of his innocent Eve ? when he bade not her weakness cleave to his strength, but promised that his strength should cleave to her weakness.

O Lord, cleave Thou to us, or we cannot cleave to Thee.

If our Lord had willed to keep secret the mutual love of each elect soul and Himself; and so had ascended alone with it into Heaven, or gone down alone with it into Hades, or dwelt alone with it in the uttermost parts of the sea, great and marvellous had been the condescension. How far greater, how transcendently marvellous, when He promises to confess the names of His faithful followers before His Father and before His angels. Before His Father, Whose equal He is as touching His Godhead, and Whose inferior He willed to become as touching His Manhood : before His own most noble creatures the angels, than whom He willed once to be made a little lower for us men and for our salvation.

In Him we hope, in ourselves we fear. Christ's words are clear as to our personal power to decide our own doom : " Whosoever therefore shall confess Me before men, him will I confess also before My Father which is in heaven. But whosoever shall deny Me before men, him will I also deny before My Father which is in heaven." " Whosoever shall confess Me before men, him shall the Son of Man also confess before the angels of God : but he that denieth Me before men, shall be denied before the angels of God."

Is it worse shame and ruin to be denied before God, or
before angels? Surely and beyond comparison, before God.
Yet Christ forewarns us of both contingent horrors : from both
then there is some help to be derived against that deadliest of
all our enemies, self.

Perhaps the utter inherent disproportion between the Infinite
Creator and the finite creature might seem to some perverse
minds to blunt the sting of rejection before God. But that our
elect fellow-creatures should behold us weighed and found
wanting, exhibits no colour of propriety : they stood, we might
have stood ; they overcame, we might have overcame. Their
steadfastness confronts our falling away, and condemns us.

**7. And to the angel of the church in Philadelphia write ;
These things saith He that is holy, He that is true,
He that hath the key of David, He that openeth, and
no man shutteth ; and shutteth, and no man openeth.**

The name of Philadelphia sets before us brotherly love and
the bliss of those who love as brethren. It invites us to pause
and refresh ourselves with an appropriate Psalm of David :—

" Behold, how good and how pleasant it is for brethren to
dwell together in unity ! It is like the precious ointment upon
the head, that ran down upon the beard, even Aaron's beard :
that went down to the skirts of his garments ; as the dew of
Hermon, and as the dew that descended upon the mountains
of Zion : for there the Lord commanded the blessing, even life
for evermore."

" 'The key of David " has doubtless mysteries and hidden
meanings to unlock. Here, meanwhile, it seems to fit the
words (or wards, to carry on the figure) both of this Apocalyptic
text and of this Psalm of Degrees ; opening to our contemplation
the grace and the corresponding blessing of unanimity, faithfulness, stability.

Graces, before they can become human graces, are primarily
and transcendently Divine Virtues or Attributes. Man's graces
are fruits of the Spirit : and in the human heart the Holy Spirit
bears His own proper fruits, not alien or arbitrary fruits. The
stability, faithfulness, unanimity, required of us, are first of all
exemplified in Christ ; Who being God became also Man, and
as Man received not the Spirit by measure.

" He that is Holy." To His Holiness Hannah bore exultant
witness : " There is none holy as the Lord : for there is none
beside Thee : neither is there any Rock like our God,"—thus

extolling also His Immutability. Which likewise are combined
by the Psalmist: "He hath commanded His covenant for
ever: holy and reverend is His Name,"—and by Isaiah : " To
whom then will ye liken Me, or shall I be equal? saith the
Holy One . . . Hast thou not known? hast thou not heard,
that the Everlasting God, the Lord, the Creator of the ends of
the earth, fainteth not, neither is weary?" Habakkuk celebrates with His Holiness His Eternity : "Art Thou not from
everlasting, O Lord my God, mine Holy One?" And centuries
later, after that the kindness and love of God our Saviour toward man appeared, the apostolic company (*see* Acts iv. 23, &c.)
praised God on this wise : " Of a truth against Thy Holy Child
Jesus, Whom Thou hast anointed, both Herod, and Pontius
Pilate with the Gentiles, and the people of Israel, were gathered
together, for to do whatsoever Thy hand and Thy counsel determined before to be done "—because heaven and earth may
pass away, but not God's Word.

And Chiefest among ten thousand, our Great High Priest
interceding for His own, whom having loved, He loved unto
the end, vouchsafed to pray for their perpetual safeguard and
indissoluble union even after the likeness of God's own Perfection : " Holy Father, keep through Thine own Name those
whom Thou hast given Me, that they may be one, as We are."

Heaven and the elements, earth and her main features, may
seem to us enduring in perpetuity ; but they are not so. God's
Will alone is established for ever, and His promise it is which
can never fail. Whence St. Peter deduces a lesson of personal
holiness : " The Lord is not slack concerning His promise . . .
The day of the Lord will come as a thief in the night ; in the
which the heavens shall pass away with a great noise, and the
elements shall melt with fervent heat, the earth also and the
works that are therein shall be burned up. Seeing then that
all these things shall be dissolved, what manner of persons
ought ye to be in all holy conversation and god'iness, looking
for and hasting unto the coming of the day of God, wherein
the heavens being on fire shall be dissolved, and the elements
shall melt with fervent heat? Nevertheless we, according to
His promise, look for new heavens and a new earth, wherein
dwelleth righteousness. Wherefore, beloved, seeing that ye
look for such things, be diligent that ye may be found of Him
in peace, without spot, and blameless."

"Who is like unto Thee, O Lord, among the gods? who
is like Thee, glorious in holiness, fearful in praises, doing
wonders?"

" He that is True."—On earth, and during His mortal life, the Only Begotten of the Father had been full of grace and truth toward all men. Once, speaking to certain Jews, He designated Himself as "a Man that hath told you the truth": while to Pontius Pilate He proclaimed : " To this end was I born, and for this cause came I into the world, that I should bear witness unto the truth. Every one that is of the truth, heareth My voice." All those were open sinners. To His saints He said : " I am the Way, the Truth, and the Life . . . I tell you the truth ; it is expedient for you that I go away: for if I go not away, the Comforter will not come unto you ; but if I depart, I will send Him unto you . . . When He, the Spirit of Truth, is come, He will guide you into all truth." And praying for the same beloved disciples, and for all who should believe on Him through their word, He said : " Sanctify them through Thy truth: Thy word is truth . . . And for their sakes I sanctify Myself, that they also might be sanctified through the truth."

Thus " grace and truth came by Jesus Christ." Glory be to Thee, O God, in His most Holy Name. Amen.

Beholding our Master, we behold Man in incomparably transcendent perfection : yet we ourselves, according to the Will and purpose of God, are designed in some sort and in miniature to become like Him. Beholding how in this life and in the next He is equally and unchangeably "the Truth" and " True," we become certified that this present life is the first stage of that future, ever-during life : strength, beauty, dignity, loveliness, delight, may be added ; but added only to what we are, never to what we are not. What we essentially are in this world, that we shall be in the other : what here we absolutely are not, we shall not be there.

If there is no truth in us now, either through wilful lack of faith or of sincerity, neither will there be any then.

" Purify your hearts, ye double-minded. Be afflicted, and mourn, and weep: let your laughter be turned to mourning, and your joy to heaviness. Humble yourselves in the sight of the Lord, and He shall lift you up."

O Lord Jesus Christ, have mercy, have mercy upon us. Amen.

Ah me, that I should be
Exposed and open evermore to Thee !—
" Nay, shrink not from My light,
And I will make thee glorious in My sight
With the overcoming Shulamite."—
Yea, Lord, Thou moulding me.

—Without a hiding-place
To hide me from the terrors of Thy Face.—
" Thy hiding-place is here
In Mine own heart, wherefore the Roman spear
For thy sake I accounted dear."—
My Jesus ! King of Grace.

—Without a veil, to give
Whiteness before Thy Face that I might live.—
" Am I too poor to dress
Thee in My royal robe of righteousness ?
Challenge and prove My love's excess."—
Give, Lord, I will receive.

—Without a pool wherein
To wash my piteous self and make me clean.—
"My Blood hath washed away
Thy guilt, and still I wash thee day by day :
Only take heed to trust and pray."—
Lord, help me to begin.

It was once pointed out to me by one whose was indeed a loving heart, that David had "a passion" for God. Such a dominant, absorbing passion, cries out in the familiar words : " Like as the hart desireth the water-brooks : so longeth my soul after Thee, O God. My soul is athirst for God, yea, even for the Living God : when shall I come to appear before the presence of God ? " Little as we " can understand his errors," still less perhaps can most of us hope to understand his sanctity : his errors we cannot but understand, so far as kindred errors of our own may serve to enlighten us ; but where in too many is the kindred sanctity to furnish a clue to his sanctity ?

Adam and Eve illustrate how impossible it is for man to know that which is utterly alien : they knew not and could not know evil until they had involved themselves in it. If we would fathom how it was that despite his sins David was yet a man after God's own heart, let us pray to love in some measure as he loved ; for without love we shall never understand either God or His saints.

And because David thus devotedly loved God, knowing none upon earth to desire in comparison of Him ; therefore (be other reasons what they may), doubtless does our Lord honour his name and memory by repeated and permanent association with His own Person ; permitting Himself to be designated and saluted as Son of David, in this world ; and in the other world laying claim to "the key of David," and afterwards announcing Himself as the Root and Offspring of David.

"The key of David" may haply give access to the treasure of David. Prophecy, vision, noble natural endowments, a very lovely song of one that hath a pleasant voice and can play well on an instrument, these were his and may never be ours; but pervading and excelling all these was that love without which even David would have been but as sounding brass or a tinkling cymbal. Which best gift is attainable by us all.

Safer than in David's hand, the master-key is in our own Saviour's hand. With it He can unlock what He pleases to whomsoever He will.

What is there, is there anything, from which Christ would exclude us? He so identifies His own with Himself that we must stand or fall according to this word: "Inasmuch as ye have done it unto one of the least of these My brethren, ye have done it unto Me. . . . Inasmuch as ye did it not to one of the least of these, ye did it not to Me." He shares with us His Name, He makes us partakers of the Divine Nature.

Even the key of David and its powers are promised by prophecy to "Eliakim the son of Hilkiah," and in words analogous to those of the Apocalyptic text: "The key of the house of David will I lay upon his shoulder; so he shall open, and none shall shut; and he shall shut, and none shall open."

But is not Eliakim a typical personage? I suppose so: still, to become typical, one must first be real.

O Gracious Lord, Who hast said: The disciple is not above his master, but every one that is perfect shall be as his master; Thee we adore, making answer: It is enough for the disciple that he be as his Master.

"And it was so, when the king saw Esther the queen standing in the court, that she obtained favour in his sight: and the king held out to Esther the golden sceptre that was in his hand. So Esther drew near, and touched the top of the sceptre. Then said the king unto her: What wilt thou, queen Esther? and what is thy request? it shall be even given thee to the half of the kingdom."

O Tender Lord, Who unto two disciples, one unnamed and both sad, didst once unlock in all the Scriptures things concerning Thyself, unlock to us, I beseech Thee, treasures of Thy word and wisdom. Thou, Who lovest and forgavest David, love us, forgive us, who in Thee are made akin to him. O Thou the more excellent David, Champion, Prophet, Shepherd, King, whether or not we be of a fair countenance amongst men, make us comely unto Thee. Whether or not we be sweet singers in Thy houses made with hands, grant us grace to

make melody in our hearts to Thee ; and say Thou to each of
us, Sweet is thy voice.   Show to us great mercy, bestow on us
sure mercies ; incorruption for this corruptible, immortality for
this mortal.   Be each of us Thy Jonathan, beloved and loving.
O Lord the Righteous Branch, make us also to bud, taking root
downward and bearing fruit upward.   O Lord the Rod of Jesse,
reject not our names from before Thy Mercy Seat, but make
the feeblest amongst us to be as David.   Thou Son of David,
have mercy on us.   Hosanna to the Son of David.   Amen.

Nevertheless, community of flesh and blood, confidence of
prayer, union of will, fervour of love, while they make us near
and dear to Christ with an unutterable nearness and dearness,
cannot in relative proportion add one cubit to the stature of
the creature worshipping the Creator, of man adoring God.
The Son of Mary, Son of God, is God the Son, Very God of
Very God.   "To everything there is a season, and a time to
every purpose under the heaven . . . a time to keep silence,
and a time to speak. . . .   Be not rash with Thy mouth, and
let not thine heart be hasty to utter any thing before God : for
God is in heaven, and thou upon earth : therefore let thy words
be few."   Before we study the *opening* and *shutting* with which
we now have to do, let us reverently contemplate that Eastern
Gate which Ezekiel beheld in vision, and from which mankind
is excluded : "He brought me to the gate, even the gate that
looketh toward the east : and, behold, the Glory of the God of
Israel came from the way of the east: His voice was like a noise
of many waters : and the earth shined with His glory. . . .
Then he brought me back the way of the gate of the outward
sanctuary which looketh toward the east ; and it was shut.
Then said the Lord unto me ; This gate shall be shut, it shall
not be opened, and no man shall enter in by it ; because the
Lord, the God of Israel, hath entered in by it, therefore it shall
be shut.   It is for the Prince."

Without adverting to the mystical interpretation of this
venerable Eastern Gate, it bids us bring awe, homage, adoration,
self-abasement, self-oblation, when we lift up hands and eyes
toward Him Whom our souls desire to love.

> Trembling before Thee we fall down to adore Thee,
>   Shamefaced and trembling we lift our eyes to Thee :
> O First and with the last ! annul our ruined past,
>   Rebuild us to Thy glory, set us free
>   From sin and from sorrow to fall down and worship Thee.
> Full of pity view us, stretch Thy sceptre to us,
>   Bid us live that we may give ourselves to Thee :

> O Faithful Lord and true! stand up for us and do,
>   Make us lovely, make us new, set us free,
> Heart and soul and spirit to bring all and worship Thee.

" He that openeth, and no man shutteth ; and shutteth, and no man openeth."—" When Thou hadst overcome the sharpness of death : Thou didst open the kingdom of heaven to all believers."

So mighty an opening has time already witnessed. A second correspondingly mighty it has still to behold, according to that prophecy of Ezekiel, where the great type sets before our eyes the yet greater anti-type : " Thus saith the Lord God ; Behold, O My people, I will open your graves, and cause you to come out of your graves, and bring you into the land of Israel. And ye shall know that I am the Lord, when I have opened your graves, O My people, and brought you up out of your graves."

Truly "no man shutteth." They who kill the body, and after that have no more that they can do, cannot debar from rising again those blessed bodies which once they slew, sawed asunder, burned to ashes, scattered to the four winds of heaven. Man proposeth, God disposeth. Man's extremity is God's opportunity.

> Bone to his bone, grain to his grain of dust :
>   A numberless reunion shall make whole
>   Each blessed body for its blessed soul,
> Refashioning the aspects of the just.
> Each saint who died must live afresh, and must
>   Ascend resplendent in the aureole
>   Of his own proper glory to his goal ;
> As seeds their proper bodies all upthrust.
> Each with his own not with another's grace,
>   Each with his own not with another's heart,
> Each with his own not with another's face,
> Each dovelike soul mounts to his proper place :—
>   O faces unforgotten ! if to part
> Wrung sore, what will it be to re-embrace?

O God, the only Creator of all things, uplift our spirits, I pray Thee, on the wings of Thy divine Dove ; that like birds of Thy first Paradise, they may fly above the earth in the open firmament of heaven. Cover us with silver wings of renewed innocence, with feathers like gold in the sunshine of Thy grace : that the waters of this troublesome world may bring forth abundantly to Thee the moving creature that hath life, and hath a tongue to sing Thy praises. For our Lord Jesu's sake. Amen.

" Doth the ploughman plough all day to sow? doth he open

and break the clods of his ground?" O our God, Who so
teachest him, forget not thine own Acre, and the holy seed
sown therein. For Christ's sake, the Firstfruits. Amen.

Let us take courage, contemplating some of the doors set
open, or ready to be set wide open, before every one of us.
And if all we observe be not doors, let us be thankful that they
all are openings for our benefit:—

"If thou shalt hearken diligently unto the voice of the Lord
thy God, to observe and to do all His commandments . . .
The Lord shall open unto thee His good treasure."—"The eyes
of the Lord are upon the righteous, and His ears are open
unto their cry."—"Open to me the gates of righteousness: I
will go into them, and I will praise the Lord: this gate of the
Lord, into which the righteous shall enter."—"Thou openest
Thine hand, and satisfiest the desire of every living thing."—
"We have a strong city; salvation will God appoint for walls
and bulwarks. Open ye the gates, that the righteous nation
which keepeth the truth, may enter in."—"In that day there
shall be a fountain opened to the house of David and to the
inhabitants of Jerusalem for sin and for uncleanness."—"Bring
ye all the tithes into the storehouse, that there may be meat
in Mine house, and prove Me now herewith, saith the Lord
of Hosts, if I will not open you the windows of heaven, and
pour you out a blessing, that there shall not be room enough
to receive it."—"Knock, and it shall be opened unto you."—
"Hereafter ye shall see heaven open. and the angels of God
ascending and descending upon the Son of Man."

Opening is suggestive of mercy; of Christ's arms spread wide
to draw all men unto Him, of His Heart pierced to shelter us.
Shutting suggests (though not always does it imply) durance
or exclusion, in accordance with which Job bears witness,
"He shutteth up a man, and there can be no opening,"—David
implores, "Let not the pit shut her mouth upon me,"—Jeremiah·
laments, "When I cry and shout, He shutteth out my prayer."
It is a fearful thing to fall into the hands of Him Who
shutteth and no man openeth. "When once the Master of
the house is risen up, and hath shut to the door, and ye begin
to stand without, and to knock at the door, saying, Lord, Lord,
open unto us; . . . He shall answer and say unto you, I
know you not whence ye are."—"The Bridegroom came, and
they that were ready went in with Him to the marriage; and
the door was shut. Afterward came also the other virgins,
saying, Lord, Lord, open to us. But He answered and said,
Verily I say unto you, I know you not."

Yet so long as the period of probation extends, even durance and exclusion may be blessed to man's safety; as befell Noah in the ark, when the Lord shut him in; Miriam also, when she was shut out of the camp as a step towards her restoration. These become to us spiritual symbols.

Our inexhaustible hope:—Jesus said, "I am the door of the sheep . . . I am the door; by Me if any man enter in, he shall be saved."

8. I know thy works: behold, I have set before thee an open door, and no man can shut it: for thou hast a little strength, and hast kept My word, and hast not denied My name. .

The Revised Version reads: "I know thy works (behold, I have set before thee a door opened, which none can shut), that thou hast a little power, and didst keep My word, and didst not deny My Name."

According to the first rendering, the "open door" seems to be a reward of the works summed up afterwards. The second rendering, by making the "door opened" parenthetical and so connecting the works directly with their ensuing summary, appears to announce that opened door as a bounty and safeguard rather than as a reward. While as to the good works themselves, the first version leads our thoughts to a habit of faith and courage; the second, to a distinct crisis of temptation overcome by those virtues.

The two translations combined kindle hope, gratitude, confidence, excite emulation. (A remark glib and impersonal, valuable only when personal and practical. The slothful servant has to be condemned out of his own mouth.)

The Church Triumphant dwells at large in the land that is very far off, "that goodly mountain." The Church Militant sojourns in "this world," whereof Christ declared: "The prince of this world cometh, and hath nothing in Me." Thus abides she within the enemy's camp, finding there no rest for the sole of her foot. Howbeit, in accordance with that great prophetic promise which our Lord vouchsafed to St. Peter, she is set upon a rock where the gates of hell shall not prevail against her. She stands as a city that is set on an hill, as a besieged city, compassed together on every side, hostile hosts swarming about her like bees. Their camp is "walled up to heaven," but its gates stand open, and the concentrated strength of hell cannot prevail to shut them upon her. For the true

Samson has passed through them once for all, and wrecked those gates; and Greater is He that is with her, than he that is against her.

"Let My people go, that they may serve Me." Each faithful soul is as the Church, for the Church is the congregation of all generations of faithful souls. "Ye are the children of the prophets."

"Thou hast a little strength."—Why not much strength? God knoweth.—Were it not better to have more? No, while God assigns no more.—With much, much could be done. With little, all can be done.—Give much, and I will glorify the Giver. Given much while disdaining little, and thou wouldst glorify thyself or Satan.—O wretched man that I am! Pray God to mend thee, and He will mend all else for thee.— If it be so, why am I thus? For the glory of God.—Yet fain would I like an angel excel in strength. Safer for thee like St. Paul, in weakness to be strong.

Can I know it?—Nay.—
Shall I know it?—Yea,
When all mists have cleared away
For ever and aye.—

Why not then to-day?—
Who hath said thee nay?
Lift a hopeful heart and pray
In a humble way.—

Other hearts are gay.—
Ask not joy to-day:
Toil to-day along thy way
Keeping grudge at bay.—

On a past May day
Flowers pranked all the way;
Nightingales sang out their say
On a night of May.—

Dost thou covet May
On an Autumn day?
Foolish memory saith its say
Of sweets past away.—

Gone the bloom of May,
Autumn beareth bay:
Flowerless wreath for head grown grey
Seemly were to-day.—

Dost thou covet bay?
Ask it not to-day:
Rather for a palm-branch pray;
None will say thee nay.—

"Hast kept My word, and hast not denied My name."—
They who keep Christ's Word, and deny not His Name, keep
their own life from going down to the pit. And this God
reckons to them for righteousness, and recompenses with an
inconceivable reward.

O Lord, Whose Word is a lantern unto our feet, and a light
unto our paths, I pray Thee make the law of Thy mouth
dearer unto us than thousands of gold and silver. O Lord,
Whose Name is a strong tower to the righteous, I pray Thee
give us wisdom to run into it and be safe.

To keep every word that proceedeth out of the mouth of
God, strains strength; or the young ruler, who had kept many
Divine precepts, had not at the last word gone away grieved.
Not to deny His Name, strains strength; or St. Peter had not
denied it. (Can I by possibility be called to wax stronger than
that young ruler whom Christ beholding loved; stronger than
St. Peter, whose love dared challenge his Lord's own witness?
"The things which are impossible with men, are possible with
God." Thank God, through Jesus Christ our Saviour.)

**9. Behold, I will make them of the synagogue of Satan,
which say they are Jews, and are not, but do lie; behold, I will make them to come and worship before
thy feet, and to know that I have loved thee.**

Thus translated, the promise reads as if the whole " synagogue
of Satan " should " come and worship." The Revised Version
seems rather to speak of some individuals so doing, not of all:
" Behold, I give of the synagogue of Satan, of them which say
they are Jews, and they are not, but do lie; behold, I will
make them to come and worship . . . ." I can but quote
both texts.

" Known unto God are all His works, from the beginning
of the world." He knoweth them, and He alone exhaustively.
To bear this in mind everywhere and always would go far to
curb rash judgment, and to still strife of tongues. I deem not
that you know, and you feel certain that I know not; He only
Who knoweth us both, knoweth all.

At the first flush we discern in this promise (ver. 9), glory to
Philadelphia, humiliation to that unseemly synagogue. And
humiliation indeed there may be, and in humiliations generally
we feel with instantaneous keenness the shame and sting.

Yet is there a gratuitous grace and unearned honour to that
offender, who being converted from the error of his ways,

H

retraces his steps even through the valley of humiliation. "There is a shame which is glory and grace."

For Satan's synagogue to bow down before Christ's saints, for those who lied even in calling themselves Jews, to know anything of the love wherewith Christ loves His own, may, in comparison with their former position, be at the least an approach "not far from the kingdom of God."

There dwells in this wide world no man or woman or child but either is, or is not, of the number of God's saints. We in Christendom, if we belong not to that illustrious company, yet abide within sight of it. God grant that the shining lights may shine, glow, radiate, more and more, and that the lookers-on glorifying the Father of all, may catch fire.

The self-assertion of Jews who were not genuine Jews, illustrates how "the fashion of this world passeth away." I know not whether at this day any one feels the pressure of that particular temptation.

There is one advantage in ignorance writing for ignorance ; the writer sets before the reader resources common to both. Only we must all beware of becoming as blind who lead the blind.

Yet, after all, neither knowledge nor ignorance is of first importance to Bible students : grace is our paramount need ; Divine grace, rather than any human gift. Acquirements and deficiencies sink to one dead level when lacking grace :—"Stay yourselves, and wonder ; cry ye out, and cry : they are drunken, but not with wine ; they stagger, but not with strong drink. For the Lord hath poured out upon you the spirit of deep sleep, and hath closed your eyes : the prophets and your rulers, the seers hath He covered. And the vision of all is become unto you as the words of a book that is sealed, which men deliver to one that is learned, saying, Read this, I pray thee : and he saith, I cannot ; for it is sealed : and the book is de-livered to him that is not learned, saying, Read this, I pray thee : and he saith, I am not learned."

Such considerations befit my own ignorance concerning the particular misbelievers branded as "the synagogue of Satan, which say they are Jews, and are not, but do lie." Still, something I gather from those words : an evil and not a good spirit swayed them ; they asserted what was in their own in-tention a claim to superiority ; in so doing they lied. Thus with threefold voice they warn all men to try the spirits whether they be of God ; to sit down in the lowest room ; to speak the truth without respect of persons.

O God, only Good, think upon Thy congregation whom Thou hast purchased and redeemed of old. Rule all hearts by Thy Most Holy Spirit; that humbly we may worship Thee, and truthfully confess Thee, owning ourselves unprofitable servants, and in honour preferring one another. To the praise of our Lord Jesus Christ. Amen.

"I will make them . . . . to know that I have loved thee." —Yea, gracious Lord, even while Thou waitest to call her also beloved who was not beloved. Thy waiting to love, is love. Thy forsaking for a small moment becomes, if we will, a step towards gathering with great mercies. Thy hiding Thy face in a little wrath for a moment, hinders not Thine everlasting kindness and overflow of mercy if we repent. Thy beloved ones, whom beholding we admire, are persons of like passions as we are: Thou lovest them, Thou waitest to love us; yea, already Thou lovest us, except we be reprobate.

Even so, God loved the world before it was reconciled to Him by the gift and sacrifice of His Only Begotten Son (*see* St. John iii. 16, 17). Even so, the father in the Parable loved his prodigal before ever he came in sight.

. Now Thou lovest us; when, O Lord, didst Thou not love us?

I pray Thee, Lord Jesus Christ, make those whom Thou lovest, and who return Thy love, mirrors of Thee unto their unloving brethren; that these too becoming enamoured of Thine image may reproduce it, light reflecting light, and ardour kindling ardour, until God be all and in all. Amen.

"I have loved thee."—"Thy love is better than wine." We know not all the features of lovableness which adorned these Philadelphian saints; but we are sure that lovable they were, inasmuch as Christ loved them. (A safe standard by which to estimate my neighbour. If I cannot love him, which is alien to love? he or I?)

10. Because thou hast kept the word of My patience, I also will keep thee from the hour of temptation, which shall come upon all the world, to try them that dwell upon the earth.

So far as I am aware the word *patience* is exclusively a New Testament word, although *patient* and *patiently* occur in both Testaments. Not that the virtue so named waited for these last days for illustration: on the contrary, St. James cites the Prophets and Job as examples of patience. Yet because patience in perfection was not found on earth until Christ trod our weary ways, it wakes a harmonious chord in our hearts to observe that till His blessed human lips spake the word, that word was not (unless I mistake) recorded in the Scriptures of Truth.

Once in the days of His mortality He had said to His disciples, "In your patience possess ye your souls;" but now in His glorious immortality He so far unites His suffering Church with Himself as to say, "Because thou hast kept the word of My patience."

O kind Lord, Who so identifiest Thy Church with Thyself that what Thou art she is accounted, and what she is Thou takest upon Thyself, grant that as Thy Desire is unto her, so her whole desire and longing may be unto Thee purely and without distraction, for ever and ever.

Patience goes with sorrow, not with joy. And by a natural instinct sorrow ranges itself with darkness, joy with light. But eyes that have been supernaturalized recognize, not literally only, but likewise in a figure, how darkness reveals more luminaries than does the day: to the day appertains a single sun; to the night innumerable, incalculable, by man's perception inexhaustible stars.

This is one of nature's revelations, attested by experience. God grant us to receive the parallel revelation of grace: then whatever tribulation befalls us will by His blessing work in us patience, and our patience will work experience, and our experience hope; "and hope maketh not ashamed; because the love of God is shed abroad in our hearts by the Holy Ghost which is given unto us."

What those saints kept was not patience merely, but "the word" of Christ's patience. At His word they kept patience; they kept it because of His will toward themselves, and subject to each jot and tittle of His revered law. He was their pattern and text-book of patience; because He bore contradiction of sinners, so did they; because He, when He was reviled, reviled not again, neither did they; because He prayed for His enemies, they likewise prayed for theirs.

Of these unknown, unrecorded Philadelphians do we then really and truly know such great things? Yea, such things as these, inasmuch as we are certified that they kept the Word of Christ's patience.

"As unknown, and yet well known."

> Patience must dwell with Love, for Love and Sorrow
> Have pitched their tent together here:
> Love all alone will build a house to-morrow,
> And sorrow not be near.

To-day for Love's sake hope, still hope, in sorrow,
    Rest in her shade and hold her dear :
To-day she nurses thee ; and lo ! to-morrow
    Love only will be near.

Patience is its own reward. It preoccupies the soul with a
sort of satisfaction which suppresses insatiable craving, vain
endeavour, rebellious desire. It keeps the will steadfast, the
mind disengaged, the heart quiet. Patience having little or
having nothing yet possesses all things; for through faith and
patience the elect inherit the promises. Here, in our text,
follows a momentous promise :—

"Because thou hast kept the word of My patience, I also will
keep thee from the hour of temptation, which shall come . . ."

Even so David's voice vibrates to us from a far-off century:
"Oh how plentiful is Thy goodness, which Thou hast laid up
for them that fear Thee: and that Thou hast prepared for
them that put their trust in Thee, even before the sons of
men ! Thou shalt hide them privily by Thine own Presence
from the provoking of all men : Thou shalt keep them secretly
in Thy tabernacle from the strife of tongues." And so of
old Isaiah bore witness : "A Man shall be as an hiding-place
from the wind, and a covert from the tempest; as rivers of
water in a dry place, as the shadow of a great rock in a weary
land."

The Philadelphian saints by patience obtained the special
promise we are considering. We ourselves a thousand and a
thousand times by impatience have forfeited our claim to it.
They thus were guaranteed exemption from an awful impending
trial; while we . . . ! Yet "hast Thou not reserved a blessing for me? Hast Thou but one blessing, my Father? bless
me, even me also, O my Father."

St. James, who by inspiration sets forth the praise of patience,
equally by inspiration blesses those who instead of being
sheltered from temptation are sustained under it: "Blessed
is the man that endureth temptation: for when he is tried, he
shall receive the crown of life, which the Lord hath promised
to them that love Him."

"Watch ye and pray, lest ye enter into temptation."

"Lead us not into temptation, but deliver us from evil."

"There hath no temptation taken you but such as is
common to man."

Draw freely, generously, hopefully upon patience; for the
more we draw upon it, so much is the strain upon it lessened.
On one memorable occasion had King Saul's patience held

out for perhaps a single hour longer, the Lord would have established his kingdom upon Israel "for ever."

God reserves many ways within His limitless resources whereby either from or under temptation to rescue as He pleases any soul He pleases. Death is one of His blessed ways: "The righteous perisheth, and no man layeth it to heart: and merciful men are taken away, none considering that the righteous is taken away from the evil to come. He shall enter into peace: they shall rest in their beds, each one walking in his uprightness." (Let us not then mourn inconsolably for our own "not lost, but gone before.") Or He can with a stroke fortify that weak point which would facilitate a given temptation, as blindness or deafness seals up eye or ear against pollution. Or He can deaden our faculty of enjoyment, and therewith our inclination to parley. Or He can replace an expelled vice by its antagonistic virtue, so that seven or seven times seven wicked spirits moaning and gibbering around our swept and garnished house should find no entrance there.

Nor can we while wheat and tares grow together foresee which ears quickly ripened and spared the brunt of wind and rain, will be garnered betimes as firstfruits of a multitudinous harvest. Not even their mother presenting her petition for the sons of Zebedee can have calculated that St. James would head the noble army of martyred Apostles, whilst St. John, the last survivor of their glorious company, would come to his grave in a full age, like as a shock of corn cometh in, in his season.

"The hour of temptation, which shall come upon all the world, to try them that dwell upon the earth."—The surface of the universe, or to bring my remark within a less unmanageable area, the surface of familiar nature and of society, presents incalculable if not infinite variety. Light stands out against darkness, growth against decay; the contrast of wedding and funeral stares us in the face. Divergences are the order of our day; insomuch that it even has been alleged that no two leaves can be found alike; and I for one am ready to believe it.

Yet the more we think over these diversities and such as these, the more (I suppose) we may discern something common underlying all that is individual. To take an instance: at one moment a wedding appears all life, a funeral all death; at another, both are perceived to be equally and at once an end and a beginning.

A step further, and I recognize that during this probational period not some influences only, but all influences as they touch us become our trials, tests, temptations; assayed by which we stand or fall, we are found wanting or not wanting, as genuinely as will be the case with us in the last tremendous Day of account.

Therefore while fear is quickened because of constant peril, any sort of unreasoning horror is abated, inasmuch as even the great last Judgment though supreme and final will not stand unprecedented and alone: over and over again we have been judged and condemned, or else acquitted; over and over again have fallen or stood to our own Master.

O my God, grant us the uprightness of saints, or at the least only such falls as they arise from. For Jesus Christ's merits' sake. Amen.

This "hour of temptation" was ordained to overtake all the world. Is it already past, is it passing, or is it still to come? To ourselves it may be present, or it may be future: it were rash to reckon any temptation assuredly past, whilst the liability to all temptation remains. The "old man" dies slowly, tediously, painfully: death-stricken by our Mighty Avenger of Blood, his life is indeed but death and corruption, yet "while there is life there is *fear.*"

"To try them that dwell upon the earth."—All alike must be. tried: not all alike will meet and pass through the trial. The qualification for trial is dwelling upon the earth: they who are least of the earth earthy will presumably fare best; inasmuch as this trial is not in order to confirm man upon the earth that now is, but to fit him for translation to that new heaven and new earth wherein shall dwell righteousness.

Foothold we must needs have, at least until we be made equal unto the angels; but let us pray against roothold. A foot may spurn the ground it cannot choose but tread; a root grasps and holds fast the soil whence it sucks subsistence, and whence it oftentimes cannot be wrenched except to die.

Sparrows and swallows are alike safe when once they have become denizens of the amiable tabernacles. But on earth, which is at best heaven's ante-chamber, it is wiser to construct a one-season's nest than a house for prolonged residence: the swallow of this generation is wiser than the sparrow.

Wisest of sparrows that sparrow which sitteth alone
  Perched on the housetop, its own upper chamber, for nest;
Wisest of swallows that swallow which timely has flown
  Over the turbulent sea to the land of its rest:
    Wisest of sparrows and swallows, if I were as wise!

Wisest of spirits that spirit which dwelleth apart
Hid in the Presence of God for a chapel and nest,
Sending a wish and a will and a passionate heart
Over the eddy of life to that Presence in rest :
Seated alone and in peace till God bids it arise.

Will the trial last for ever?—No, for some period which *an hour* represents. "Couldest not thou watch one hour?"

Will it overwhelm us?—No, for the promise is unto us and to our children: "God is faithful, Who will not suffer you to be tempted above that ye are able ; but will with the temptation also make a way to escape, that ye may be able to bear it."

When will it befall us?—"Of that day and hour knoweth no man . . . Watch therefore."

We fear. "He that feareth God shall come forth of them all."

We hope. "It is good that a man should both hope and quietly wait for the salvation of the Lord."

"And who is he that will harm you, if ye be followers of that which is good? But and if ye suffer for righteousness' sake, happy are ye : and be not afraid of their terror, neither be troubled; but sanctify the Lord God in your hearts : and be ready always to give an answer to every man that asketh you a reason of the hope that is in you with meekness and fear : having a good conscience."

11. Behold, I come quickly: hold that fast which thou hast, that no man take thy crown.

" Behold, I come quickly."—But some man would answer : Lord, sayest Thou that Thou comest quickly Who all these eighteen hundred years hast not come? Well may we pray that we may interpret.

Christ's blessed words are truth, sending forth wisdom by unnumbered channels. For He uses many seasons and modes of coming, besides and before that final coming when every eye shall see Him. To some exalted souls He has come ere now in vision and special revelation. To all His brethren down to the poorest and hungriest He comes, or is ready to come, in the Blessed Sacrament of His Body and Blood. To every man who loves Him and keeps His words He comes beyond the world's comprehension and makes His abode with him (*see* St. John xiv. 22, 23). To His beloved He comes in their death whereby they go to Him. In any or in all of these ways we believe and are sure that He kept faith with His faithful Philadelphians.

On the other hand, not the creature of time but only the Lord of time and eternity can pronounce on what is or is not *quickly* brought to pass. At eighteen we think a year long, at eighty we think it short: what terminable duration would seem long to us, what such duration would not seem short, if we had already passed out of time into eternity? Wherefore He alone Who saith "quickly" can define quickly.

O Gracious Lord Christ, Who lovest Thine elect with an everlasting love, keep us, I pray Thee, peaceful and trustful in our due ignorance until the day break and the shadows flee away.

> Oh knell of a passing time,
> Will it never cease to chime?
> Oh stir of the tedious sea,
> Will it never cease to be?
> Yea, when night and when day,
> Moon and sun pass away.
>
> Surely the sun burns low,
> The moon makes ready to go,
> Broad ocean ripples to waste,
> Time is running in haste,
> Night is numbered, and day
> Numbered to pass away.

"Hold that fast which thou hast."—Hold fast for one thing the word of Christ's patience. To let go patience would entail forfeit of both praise and promise.

With our little strength let us hold fast patience and whatever else has been entrusted to our keeping. Be we of no reputation and ever so small, God's blessing on our little strength will make it adequate, and will brace it to keep His commandments.

> I, Lord, Thy foolish sinner low and small,
> Lack all.
> His heart too high was set
> Who asked, What lack I yet?
> Woe's me at my most woeful pass!
> I, Lord, who scarcely dare adore,
> Weep sore:
> Steeped in this rotten world I fear to rot.
> Alas! what lack I not?
> Alas! alas for me! alas!
> More and yet more.—
>
> Nay, stand up on thy feet, betaking thee
> To Me.
> Bring fear; but much more bring
> Hope to thy patient King:
> What, is My pleasure in thy death?

I loved that youth who little knew
The true
Width of his want, yet worshipped with goodwill :
So love I thee, and still
Prolong thy day of grace and breath.
Rise up and do.—

Lord, let me know mine end, and certify
When I
Shall die and have to stand
Helpless on Either Hand,
Cut off, cut off, my day of grace.—
Not so : for what is that to thee?
I see
The measure and the number of thy day :
Keep patience, tho' I slay ;
Keep patience till thou see My Face.
Follow thou Me.

That which as yet "thou hast" is not thy crown, but on it depends thy crown. As safety depended on the steadfastness of the Alexandrian mariners (*see* Acts xxvii. 6, 30—32), so on our steadfastness here depends our coronation hereafter. And as then a delusive appearance of safety, or even perhaps a partial safety, had to be sacrificed to the general security, so our Lord has forewarned us, "He that findeth his life shall lose it : and he that loseth his life for My sake shall find it."

O Lord Whose symbol is the unchanging sun, enlighten us to be Thy faithful sequent moons ; waxing to Thee, waning to ourselves, walking in brightness, reflecting and spreading abroad Thy glory. Lighten our darkness, I beseech Thee, O Lord. Amen.

Can I hold fast my crown on purpose "that no man take" it ; and yet love my neighbour as myself? Yes, verily, and by God's help so I will.

For the Divine Treasury is never so scantily furnished that one man's enrichment depends on the impoverishment of another. Indeed the very contrary may be looked for, as is illustrated by a parallel case : "Whether one member suffer, all the members suffer with it ; or one member be honoured, all the members rejoice with it."

All is as God wills, and what He pleaseth to do He doeth. On the one hand the fall of Judas left an apostolic throne vacant for St. Matthias : on the other hand St. Paul out of due time became an Apostle in excess of the original Twelve. The Bounty of God never ceases, as it were, to appeal to man : "Prove Me now . . . if I will not—." "And yet there is room."

If I ruin myself the loss is mine, but my squandered blessing is not lost to the Church. The forfeited bishopric another takes. The forfeited mansion another will inhabit. God's House must needs be filled, though the door be shut in the face of ten thousand invited guests. The cast-out childrens' places will be occupied by elect children from east and west, and north and south.

Worst of all is it when self-ruin involves the ruin of others. There is a giving and taking which is mere absolute loss to both giver and receiver: "My son, if sinners entice thee, consent thou not. If they say, Come with us, . . . cast in thy lot among us; let us all have one purse: my son, walk not thou in the way with them; refrain thy foot from their path: for their feet run to evil . . . And they lay wait for their own blood; they lurk privily for their own lives." "The strange woman, . . . the stranger which flattereth with her words; which forsaketh the guide of her youth, and forgetteth the covenant of her God. For her house inclineth unto death, and her paths unto the dead. None that go unto her return again, neither take they hold of the paths of life."

"Thy crown."—What am I, to foresee a crown for myself? For my neighbour I will think out a crown.

Earthly maidens and brides wear garlands of blossoms which must wither: the heavenly Virgins and Brides shall wear amaranthine wreaths. So (please God) some whom I have known will be crowned. Far from crowned have I heretofore beheld them, meek, lowly, patient, obscure, perhaps unsightly, perhaps uncouth; but if I see them again "in all their glory," I shall see such persons as in his mortal day Solomon the magnificent could not vie with.

Crowns of righteousness await all the righteous; but not, it may be, crowns all alike, any more than stars beam all alike in their glory. If by way of figure and illustration earthly treasures correspond at all with heavenly treasures, pearls seem fit for purity, and most fine gold for sanctity, changeable opals with one abiding fire-spark for penitence, the perennial greenness of emeralds for hope that maketh not ashamed, diamonds sun-reproducing for faith, and for love carbuncles like coals of fire that hath a most vehement flame. Or rather, one and all for love: love being guard of purity, root of sanctity, spring of penitence, sustenance of hope, life of faith.

Is love then the only crowned virtue? Yes, only love: inasmuch as the others, divorced from love, would not be virtues.

Lord, I desire my crown.—Child, I also desired mine.—

Lord, what like will my crown be?—Call it not thine before
thou hast striven for it.—Lord, will it not be of glory?—Mine
once was of thorns.—Can a crown of thorns be in truth my
desire?—With desire I desired Mine.—Thorns, if so it must
be, to-day: but what to-morrow?—This day is called to-day:
to-morrow will take thought for the things of itself.

"My Beloved is mine, and I am His," saith the Bride of the
Canticles, and makes no mention of her own inferiority in the
gracious communion and so-far equality of love. Indeed, if
there be a difference, I think the Bridegroom may rejoice over
the Bride with a more absolute complacency of affection than
that wherewith she on her side worships Him: for He calls
her "My love," she Him "my Beloved"; "My love," as if she
were very love itself, "my Beloved," as if her love graced
Him.

Than this we need seek no sweeter marvel. To be classed
with it are two prophecies of Isaiah when set side by side:
"In that day shall the Lord of hosts be for a crown of glory,
and for a diadem of beauty, unto the residue of His people":
—"Thou shalt also be a crown of glory in the hand of the
Lord, and a royal diadem in the hand of thy God."

12. **Him that overcometh will I make a pillar in the temple
    of My God, and he shall go no more out: and I will
    write upon him the Name of My God, and the name
    of the city of My God, which is new Jerusalem, which
    cometh down out of Heaven from My God: and I
    will write upon him My new Name.**
13. **He that hath an ear, let him hear what the Spirit saith
    unto the churches.**

"A pillar"—great strength, the fruit and guerdon of a little
strength; absolute immovable stability, the outcome of the
effort to hold fast. Behold the choice work wrought out of
the costly material; wrought out by dint of blows, of cutting,
of shattering in a measure; but (thank God!) wrought out at
last. White and ruddy as alabaster; not all white lest it seem
cold, nor all ruddy lest it seem blood-stained; lilies, knops,
pomegranates;—nay, we know not what colours and devices
shall make it comely; but this we know, that it will be the
finished work of Him all Whose works were good in the
beginning; how much more, in the end and consummation of
all things!

Nor merely a pillar, but "a pillar in the Temple of My
God." A pillar adorns, dignifies, upholds the structure to

which it belongs. Even thus may it be with celestial pillars, yet never otherwise than where a Psalm speaks with the Voice of Christ: " I bear up the pillars of it." He Who was Strength to the weak on earth, will be Strength to the strong in Heaven : that which was founded on Rock here, will not be founded on sand there.

Can man uphold the glory of God? Yea, God so gracing him. Similarly we read of mortal men helping,—or rather, alas! of their not helping the victorious Lord of all : "They came not to the help of the Lord, to the help of the Lord against the mighty." Not that He needs our help : but whoso helps Him shares His Triumph ; whoso upholds His glory becomes invested with His Glory.

Good Lord, make me, me also of Thy votaries. Neither pray I for myself alone, but for all.

" And he shall go no more out."—

> Once within, within for evermore :
> There the long beatitudes begin :
> Overflows the still unwasting store,
> Once within.
>
> Left without are death and doubt and sin ;
> All man wrestled with and all he bore,
> Man who saved his life skin after skin.
>
> Blow the trumpet-blast unheard before,
> Shout the unheard-of shout for these who win,
> These, who cast their crowns on Heaven's high floor
> Once within.

" I will write upon him the Name of My God, and the name of the city of My God, which is new Jerusalem, . . . and I will write upon him My new Name."

Children bear their father's name, a wife her husband's. Thus the Divine Father bestows His own Name on His adopted children, and thus the Divine Bridegroom on His purchased bride ; and this to all eternity, as we see in the text.

But Christian Baptism is Baptism in the Name of the Most Holy Trinity, of Father, of Son, and of Holy Ghost. All through mortal life regenerate man bears that Sacred Name in Its fulness : God forbid that he who finally perseveres unto salvation, should then cease to bear It in unabated fulness of Perfection. [I write under correction : I repudiate my own thoughts if erroneous.]

Wherefore I humbly ponder whether " the name of the City of God, which is new Jerusalem," may hide at once and reveal the Supreme Name of that Divine Most Holy Spirit Who deigns to inhabit her. " In His temple doth every one speak of His glory "; and she is that Temple built of living stones; which stones are men, of whom each one severally is constituted a Temple of the Holy Ghost consecrated to worship God in spirit and in truth.

If such a train of thought be lawful, it seems to illustrate the Inscrutability of the Third Person of the Ever Blessed Trinity : a sacied Inscrutability of Mystery in the revelation to man of God the Holy Spirit, beyond what invests the corresponding revelation of God the Father or of God the Son. Even natural instinct attests as true the revelation of One Divine, universal Father: the heart's desire of all nations heretofore thirsted for, and now in some measure acknowledges, the revelation of God the Son. But Christ Himself said in reference to an operation of God the Holy Spirit, " The wind bloweth where it listeth, and thou hearest the sound thereof, but canst not tell whence it cometh, and whither it goeth "; and we are ready to answer : " Lo, He goeth by me, and I see Him not : He passeth on also, but I perceive Him not."

I think that a devout contemplation of our most approachable Master may help us to perceive and adore our " Other Comforter." During His earthly life Jesus engaged few followers ; and these in varying degrees of knowledge or of ignorance apprehended or apprehended not His Divinity ; but after His Resurrection, and again in greater splendour after His Ascension, light sprang up. Thus so long as eyes could see and ears hear and hands handle the Word of Life, Christ abode for the most part unseen, unheard, untouched ; but when a cloud had received Him out of sight, then it became possible for mankind at all times and in all places to behold Him with the eye of faith, listen to Him with the ear of hope, hold Him fast and not let Him go with the clasped hands of adoring love. So long as His Tabernacle was mortal it obscured the indwelling Deity : when His mortal put on immortality it revealed what till then it had veiled.

For more than these eighteen hundred years past it has pleased the Holy Spirit by choosing mortal men as His temples to dwell in houses made of dust and which must return to dust. The evidence He vouchsafes of His Presence consists in the supernatural endowments of His saints. Holy men, holy women, holy children, act like prisms to exhibit His Light : they are not that Light, but bear witness of that Light. Their love, joy, peace, longsuffering, gentleness, goodness, faith, meekness, temperance, bear witness to Him : these are His fruits, and the fruits declare the tree.

Now if Christ's mighty works, perfection of grace, un-measured plenitude of the Spirit, did not to the universal apprehension announce His Godhead so long as this was enshrined in a mortal though ever-immaculate Body,—no wonder is it that the Presence of God the Holy Ghost, in shrines so narrow, frail, flawed, polluted as are ordinary human hearts which have still to die, is often overlooked or denied : no wonder that His very Being should be denied by some who look for judgment, but behold oppression; for righteousness, but behold a cry.

An awful responsibility devolves on each Christian soul. You, I, are summoned and constituted to bear witness to the Person and Work of Almighty God the Holy Spirit; to be in some degree His evidence, His illustration, His proof. " O God, Thou knowest my foolishness ; and my sins are not hid from Thee . . . Let not those that seek Thee be con-founded for my sake, O God of Israel."

The saints are God's epistle known and read of all men : "tables of testimony . . . written with the finger of God."

"New Jerusalem, which cometh down out of heaven from My God."—Wherefore cometh she down ? and whither cometh she down ?

It seems to be the reverse of what our Redeemer spake concerning Himself : " No man hath ascended up to heaven, but He that came down from heaven, even the Son of Man which is in heaven."

He first descended, then ascended. His followers one by one slowly, painfully, precariously toil up from earth to the better country. And then after all we read that the New Jerusalem will come down !

Now if for the present this scarcely sounds to us like any phase of beatitude, it may prove to us none the less profitable : by setting us on our guard against fancying we know and comprehend what we neither know nor comprehend ; by inviting us to trust God implicitly, and not to lean to our own understanding ; by bringing home to us that God's perfect Will and not our own desire or imagination is the standard of beatitude.

O our God, teach us so to trust Thee that knowledge and ignorance may be alike welcome to us when of Thine ap-pointing. What we know we know only in part ; what we know not Thou knowest altogether. The darkness and light to Thee are both alike : therefore under the shadow of Thy wings will we rejoice. Through Jesus Christ our Lord. Amen.

" My New Name."—O Lord Whom we have loved as God, as Man, as Son of God, Son of Man, Son of David, Son of Mary, as Christ, as Jesus, what is that New Name, under which Thine own shall one day love Thee? I ask not to know it while It is secret. I ask that with all my brethren and all my sisters in Thee I may know, adore, love Thee under that New Name and under every Name through all eternity : for ever following on to know Thee ; ever learning, and coming to the knowledge of the truth, and learning still for ever.

> O Lord, I am ashamed to seek Thy Face
> As tho' I loved Thee as Thy saints love Thee :
> Yet turn from those Thy lovers, look on me,
> Disgrace me not with uttermost disgrace ;
> But pour on me ungracious, pour Thy grace
> To purge my heart and bid my will go free,
> Till I too taste Thy hidden Sweetness, see
> Thy hidden Beauty in the holy place.
> O Thou Who callest sinners to repent,
> Call me Thy sinner unto penitence,
> For many sins grant me the greater love :
> Set me above the waterfloods, above
> Devil and shifting world and fleshly sense,
> Thy Mercy's all-amazing monument.

14. And unto the angel of the church of the Laodiceans write ; These things saith the Amen, the faithful and true Witness, the beginning of the creation of God.

An " Angel " still though arraigned at the supreme bar. A " Church " still, though being weighed and found wanting. " Behold therefore the goodness and severity of God : on them which fell, severity ; but toward thee, goodness, if thou continue in His goodness : otherwise thou also shalt be cut off."

" The Amen."—Elsewhere the Voice of Inspiration affirms : " The Son of God, Jesus Christ . . was not yea and nay, but in Him was yea. For all the promises of God in Him are yea, and in Him Amen, unto the glory of God . . ." [Or according to the Revised Version : ". . . but in Him is yea. For how many soever be the promises of God, in Him is the yea : wherefore also through Him is the Amen, unto the glory of God . . ."]

To Balaam of old was revealed the immutability of God and of His Word : "God is not a man that He should lie ;

neither the son of man, that He should repent : hath He said
and shall He not do it? or hath He spoken, and shall He not
make it good?" In which utterance, as in a glass darkly, we
haply trace an allusion to the Mystery of our Lord's Incarnation : Who verily became a Man and the Son of Man neither
that He should lie nor repent, but to make good His plighted
word by bruising the serpent's head. He Who is the Truth
from all eternity, remains the Truth to all eternity. His faithfulness and truth are our shield and buckler.

In Him the promises are yea, wherefore the threatenings
likewise cannot but be yea. Indeed the several accomplish-
ments of promises and of threatenings, even if not interdependent, seem to be closely allied. As where we read:
"The righteous shall rejoice when he seeth the vengeance : he
shall wash his feet in the blood of the wicked. So that a man
shall say, Verily there is a reward for the righteous "—" The
day of vengeance is in Mine heart, and the year of My
redeemed is come "—" Behold, My servants shall eat, but ye
shall be hungry : behold, My servants shall drink, but ye shall
be thirsty : behold, My servants shall rejoice, but ye shall be
ashamed : behold, My servants shall sing for joy of heart, but
ye shall cry for sorrow of-heart, and shall howl for vexation of
spirit. And ye shall leave your name for a curse unto My
chosen "—" Judas . . . went immediately out : and it was night.
Therefore, when he was gone out, Jesus said, Now is the Son
of Man glorified, and God is glorified in Him "—" Then shall
the King say unto them on His Right Hand, Come, ye blessed
of My Father, inherit the kingdom prepared for you from the
foundation of the world. . . . Then shall He say also unto
them on the Left Hand, Depart from Me, ye cursed, into
everlasting fire, prepared for the devil and his angels. . . .
And these shall go away into everlasting punishment : but the
righteous into life eternal."

"The Faithful and True Witness."—Our Lord instructed
Nicodemus, saying : " We speak that we do know, and testify
that we have seen."

Lord, what is it which Thou hast seen in me? What now
seest Thou? What wilt Thou see at the awful day of my
death? What in the most awful Day of Thy Judgment?
Thou Who beholdest sin, kindle and behold in me repentance ;
that so at last even I may see the felicity of Thy chosen, may
see Thee in Thy beauty, may see Thee as Thou art. Amen.

There are some touching whom Christ forewarns us : " Then
will I profess unto them, I never knew you : depart from Me,

ye that work iniquity." "Search me, O God, and know my heart: try me, and know my thoughts: and see if there be any wicked way in me, and lead me in the way everlasting."

"The beginning of the creation of God."—"Without Him was not any thing made that was made." Thus is He the Source, Spring, Origin of creation.

Elsewhere we read: "A Body hast Thou prepared Me." This obviously and primarily refers to Christ's sacred Human Body. But as the Church is His Mystical Body no less truly than the other is His literal Body, we may (I think) attach a second signification to the same text, and adore Him as the Beginning especially of our own creation, inasmuch as we are made expressly and paramountly to bear so glorious a relation to Him: even before redeeming and quickening His members, He became Head of the race in order to redeem and quicken them. That human kind existed centuries before the Incarnation, alters not the order of beginning and sequence: creation dates not from commencement but rather from consummation. Thus we call not Adam as yet *created* whilst he remained no more than a lifeless body of clay; but only after God had breathed into his nostrils the breath of life. Christ the Source whence creation proceeds, stands as the Centre whence it radiates.

"Is anything too hard for the Lord?" He who can communicate life to the lifeless can even renew life in the dead.

O Jesus Christ All-Holy, Who beheldest in Thy beloved Mary Magdalene first seven devils, then Thine own image; in Thy beloved James and John first the fiery natural man, next the enkindled spiritual man; in Thy beloved Peter first three lapses, then three aspirations of love; in Thy beloved Thomas first doubt, then faith; in Thy beloved Paul first Thy persecutor, next Thy chosen vessel; in Thy beloved Mark, first one who answered, I will not, afterwards one who repented and went: us too behold, us too transform, us too accept; for which of us hast Thou not loved, O our All-Loving Lord?

Not that we should restrict meditation to mankind exclusively, when we worship Christ as the Beginning and Head of creation; God "having made known unto us the mystery of His Will, according to His good pleasure which He hath purposed in Himself: that in the dispensation of the fullness of times He might gather together in one all things in Christ, both which are in heaven, and which are on earth; even in Him: in Whom also we have obtained an inheritance." To widen thanksgiving is or ought to be to widen enjoyment.

"O all ye works of the Lord, bless ye the Lord: praise Him,
and magnify Him for ever."

**15. I know thy works, that thou art neither cold nor hot: I
would thou wert cold or hot.**
**16. So then because thou art lukewarm, and neither cold
nor hot, I will spue thee out of My mouth.**

I suppose the particular form of this tremendous anathema
may take its rise from the nauseating tendency of tepid water.
The cold or the hot may cause pleasure or exquisite pain : the
lukewarm simply invites expulsion.

Degradation it were and ruin to become an abhorring unto
all flesh : unspeakable degradation, ruin unutterable, to become
Christ's abhorrence. We must recollect what did not suffice to
make men so, before we can in the least estimate what consummate loathsomeness it is which will suffice. To be dead
sufficed not, for all whom He hath quickened were dead in
trespasses and sins. To lie in wickedness sufficed not, for the
whole world lieth in wickedness, and He came not to condemn
the world but to save the world. To be His enemies sufficed
not, for we were enemies when He reconciled us to God by His
death. To crucify Him sufficed not, for He interceded for
His crucifiers. To persecute Him sufficed not, for He brake
not in pieces like a potter's vessel Saul of Tarsus. To look
back from the plough sufficed not, for He reclaimed Mark
sister's son to Barnabas.

Christ in His mercy preserve us from ever sounding that
surpassing depth of Satan. Amen.

"I know thy works."—Every variety of perversity is possible
to free will. Some sinners work, and their work is their sin :
others work not, and their sin consists in their not working.
Yet not to work is in some sort to work amiss. "He that
gathereth not with Me scattereth."

"I know thy works, that thou art neither cold nor hot: I
would thou wert cold or hot."—Instinct and reason agree in
classing cold with death, heat with life : lukewarmness stands
midway between the twain, akin to both while stopping short
of either.

Like Israel under Ahab and Jezebel, the lukewarm Christian
halts between two opinions, and appears after a fashion to act
out the startling letter of two inspired sentences : "Be not
righteous over much. . . . Be not over much wicked." If he
be a guest, he wears a very decent cloak over his sins ; but

alas! he has not on a wedding garment. He is as a fountain which gives out water neither quite sweet nor quite bitter; as a sheep that is neither black nor white.

As lukewarmness stands between cold and heat, so indifference stands between love and hatred. If under the surface as well as upon the surface the two series correspond, at once light breaks in upon our subject. For indifference, so far as Holy Scripture instructs us, has no part whatsoever in the Divine Being. God Almighty we know is Love; and it is revealed that He can hate: but love and hatred alike preclude indifference. Thus indifference appears to involve absolute alienation from His Image and Likeness.

Yet, Lord Jesus, Thou breakest not the bruised reed, nor quenchest the smoking flax, and Thou praisest the little strength of Philadelphia. Wilt Thou not compassionate the little heat which is lukewarmness, and the languishing life which still is not death?

O Saviour, show compassion!
Because if Thou reject us, who shall receive us?
O Saviour, show compassion.
Because we are half dead, yet not wholly dead,
O Saviour, show compassion.
Because Thou art the Good Samaritan, the Good Physician; bind up our wounds pouring in Thine oil and Thy wine, take care of us, provide for us, set us forward on our way, bring us home. And because Thou lovest us, even for Thine own sake,
O Saviour, show compassion.

Without fully understanding wherefore so heinous, we yet cannot but understand from our text the precipitant-deathward tendency of lukewarmness. To face and investigate may help us to flee the danger.

And especially so because to face, investigate, and so far to grapple with the demon of lukewarmness, does then and there tend to rout him. Those are energetic acts; and energy infallibly clashes with a fault which is fostered by sloth, and in its turn fosters a low-born comfort.

A comfortable but insidious spiritual drowsiness seems one ailment symptomatic of lukewarmness. We know how physical heat and cold, however opposite to each other, so far agree that an excess of either disturbs rest: medium warmth, *lukewarmness*, woos and wins sound sleep.

Is this the time, is this the world, are we the persons safely to woo and win sound sleep? "Awake, thou that sleepest, and arise from the dead, and Christ shall give thee light."

"' I would thou wert cold or hot."—We seem to hear again the awful charge to Judas : " That thou doest, do quickly."

I ponder, Lord, the mystery of Thy words. For it never can be that Thou desirest my reprobation ; Thou Who didst undergo the chill of death, lest I should undergo the second death. Though I cannot fully comprehend it, I pray Thee prosper this word which Thou sendest me to the end where-unto Thou sendest it.

I hear another word of rebuke, yet of hope : " Now put off thy ornaments from thee, that I may know what to do unto thee."—Lord, grant me grace to strip myself of any subterfuges which hide me from myself but never from Thee ; of any whitening which overlays my foulness ; of any self-righteousness whereby I say Peace, peace, while there is no peace. For Thou hast declared that publicans and harlots go into the Kingdom of Heaven before Pharisees.

One broad difference I remark between lukewarmness and coldness : the difference between dying and death.

` The cold soul is a soul dead in trespasses and sins. A dead soul cannot requicken itself ; if it is to be quickened, it can be so only by an act external to itself infusing new life. The lukewarm soul is a dying soul : wherefore because a vestige of life remains to it, and so a vestige of power, it must co-operate with external aid in the task of arresting decay and reinforcing vitality.

Is it for such a reason as this, most gracious Master, that Thou wouldst some were cold rather than lukewarm ? For being cold we fall into Thy hand (and very great are Thy mercies), and not into the hand of man. But being lukewarm we partly fall into our own hands ; whilst because we are lukewarm we seem of all men least likely to stir up the gift that is in us, redeem the time, rend hearts and not garments, or take the Kingdom of Heaven by force.

Still I attain not to grasp Thy saying. Yet thus much I know : out of the abundance of the heart the mouth speaketh, and Thou art Love.

17. **Because thou sayest, I am rich, and increased with goods, and have need of nothing ; and knowest not that thou art wretched, and miserable, and poor, and blind, and naked :**

18. **I counsel thee to buy of Me gold tried in the fire, that thou mayest be rich ; and white raiment, that thou mayest be clothed, and that the shame of thy naked-**

ness do not appear; and anoint thine eyes with eye-salve that thou mayest see.

The Revised Version of this passage brings out with startling emphasis the self-complacency, arrogance, and destitution at once absolute and culpable of the offender: "Because thou sayest, I am rich, and have gotten riches, and have need of nothing ; and knowest not that thou art the wretched one, and miserable, and poor, and blind, and naked : I counsel thee to buy of Me gold refined by fire, that thou mayest become rich ; and white garments, that thou mayest clothe thyself, and that the shame of thy nakedness be not made manifest ; and eye-salve to anoint thine eyes, that thou mayest see."

"Because thou sayest . . ."—Presumedly not aloud in so many words, but rather like that fellow "fool" who saith in his heart, There is no God. Akin to both speakers is the rich fool of the Parable : "The ground of a certain rich man brought forth plentifully : and he thought within himself, saying, What shall I do, because I have no room where to bestow my fruits? And he said, This will I do : I will pull down my barns, and build greater ; and there will I bestow all my fruits and my goods. And I will say to my soul, Soul, thou hast much goods laid up for many years ; take thine ease, eat, drink, and be merry. But God said unto him, Thou fool, this night thy soul shall be required of thee : then whose shall those things be, which thou hast provided ? So is he that layeth up treasure for himself, and is not rich toward God."

Thus the covetous man and the lukewarm man have this in common : in their own eyes they do good unto themselves. Take we heed that we speak not well of them.

O All-seeing Lord, that which I know not and which Thou wouldest have me to know, teach Thou me. Expel my covetousness, even if by Thy good gift of poverty : enkindle my lukewarmness, even if in the furnace of affliction.

"I am rich, and increased with goods, and have need of nothing."—Of nothing? Alas ! as it would seem, not even of beatification. For the poor in spirit, and the hungry and athirst after righteousness, say not, "I am rich" ; neither the mourners, "I have need of nothing." Nor are the meek or the merciful engrossed by their own prosperity. Nor do the pure in heart set great store by aught short of God. Nor the peacemakers hug themselves because of that which may breed envy : though if persecution arise for the word or for righteousness' sake, such as they are not offended.

If a merry heart is a continual feast, a lukewarm heart is a continual lack. Worse still, it is a centre of spiritual creeping paralysis : a l airbreadth less of live man to-day, a hairbreadth less to-morrow; until unless the strong hand of Divine Grace should arrest decay, the dying man of so many days becomes the corpse of the ultimate morrow.

O Lord, Who extendedst mercy to him who believing craved help in his unbelief, extend mercy to all who half alive crave help in their half deadness. And for any who pray not for themselves vouchsafe to hear this prayer. Amen.

As dying,—and behold, we live !
　If Thou but give the word.
Give, Lord, the word : that we may give
　Thanks for a word unheard
　Till now, of pity not denied albeit deferred.

We lift to Thee our failing eyes,
　Our failing wills to Thee :
O Great Lord God of Battles, rise,
　Till foes and shadows flee,
And death being swallowed up of life shall cease to be.

" And knowest not that thou art wretched, and miserable, and poor, and blind, and naked."—For the lukewarm person is as one drunken but not with wine. " Yea, thou sha't be as he that lieth down in the midst of the sea, or as he that lieth upon the top of a mast."

What damps hope in such a case is not the wretchedness, misery, poverty, blindness, nakedness; but the self-ignorance. This ties our own feet from resorting to Christ, although it ties not His bounteous Hands; as He saith : " How often would I . . . and ye would not ! "—or as we read elsewhere : " He did not many mighty works there because of their unbelief ":—" He could there do no mighty work. . . And He marvelled because of their unbelief."

Glory be to God Who concedes not one only channel of grace, but many channels ; not one only point of access, but many points. Intercessory prayer is truly our Gate Beautiful: outside it sits the halting multitude of our brethren and sisters: we, by God's blessing on our weak walk and endeavour, can enter the Temple through that gate ; and not we ourselves alone, but so bringing others with us. Blessed are they who frequenting that Gate enter by it into the Presence of God; they are making ready for a future day whereon to enter into His Presence through a Gate of Pearl.

If we loved all mankind we should pray for them. If we prayed for all mankind we should love them. "Stir up, O Lord, the wills of Thy faithful people."

"I counsel thee."—"His Name shall be called . . . Counsellor." Most gracious Counsellor, He Who after guiding with counsel afterward receives to glory. Lord, suffer us not to be of those who forget Thy works and wait not for Thy counsel.   ◆

"With Him is wisdom and strength, He hath counsel and understanding. . . He discovereth deep things out of darkness, and bringeth out to light the shadow of death." "When we are judged, we are chastened of the Lord, that we should not be condemned with the world." O Lord, Who searchest us out and knowest us and understandest our thoughts long before; grant us grace in Thy sight.

"Doth not wisdom cry? . . . Counsel is mine, and sound wisdom : I am understanding ; I have strength." O Thou Who art a strength to the needy in his distress, strengthen us.

"Ointment and perfume rejoice the heart: so doth the sweetness of a man's friend by hearty counsel." Lord Jesus, Thine is the Name which is as ointment poured forth, and Thou hast called us friends. Give us grace to be sure that salutary is any bitterness of Thy sending, faithful are any wounds of Thine inflicting ; and that while Thou art our loving Father to correct us, Thou art still as our mother to comfort us.

"There is no wisdom nor understanding nor counsel against the Lord."

"I counsel thee to buy of Me gold tried in the fire, that thou mayest be rich."—But wherewith shall I come before the Lord, and bow myself before the High God ? Lo, there is nothing in my hand. Except Thou give me treasure in my sack's mouth I cannot traffick in Thy land.

"Ho, every one . . and. he that hath no money; come ye, buy . . . without money and without price."

Lord, I have nothing, and this Thou knowest. Turn not Thy Face away. I would fain borrow of Thee; so in the Great Day Thou shalt receive Thine own with usury. For I perceive that whilst first and last all is Thy gratuity, there must still be between us a sort of barter. As spake King David in the joy of his heart: "All things come of Thee, and of Thine own have we given Thee."

Wherefore, Thou helping me, I will break off my sins by showing mercy to the poor. Give Thou wings to my riches, and bid them fly as eagles towards heaven. By Thy grace I will lay up not corruptible treasures upon earth, but incorruptible in heaven. For he that hath pity upon the poor lendeth unto Thee, and I look that what I lay out it shall be paid me again. For earthly gold, which though it be tried seven times in the fire, perisheth, give me such imperishable gold as Thou usest for New Jerusalem and crowns of Thy saints triumphant. The gold of that land is good. The gold which I offer Thee must be purified in the fire; fire of self-denial, of self-sacrifice, of love; and if thus I that was lukewarm labour in the very fire, yet shall I not weary myself for very vanity.

Fire must one day try every man's work, of what sort it is.

" If therefore ye have not been faithful in the unrighteous mammon, who will commit to your trust the true riches?"

> I long for joy, O Lord, I long for gold,
> I long for all Thou profferest to me,
> I long for the unimagined manifold
> Abundance laid up in Thy treasury.
> I long for pearls, but not from mundane sea;
> I long for palms, but not from earthly mould;
> Yet in all else I long for, long for Thee,
> Thyself to hear and worship and behold.
> For Thee, beyond the splendour of that day
> Where all is day and is not any night;
> For Thee, beyond refreshment of that rest
> To which tired saints press on for its delight :—
> Or if not thus for Thee, yet Thee I pray
> To make me long so till Thou make me blest.

" And white raiment, that thou mayest be clothed, and that the shame of thy nakedness do not appear."—All our righteousnesses are as filthy rags: clothe Thou us with Thine own perfect righteousness, O Lamb of God without blemish and without spot. In which single prayer I petition for two things: that Thy righteousness be imputed to us unworthy, and that by operation of the Holy Spirit the Sanctifier, an image of Thy righteousness be wrought in us. We will not ask little when Thou offerest much, or keep lips half closed when Thou wilt fill a wide open mouth. Clothe us with the garments of salvation, cover us with the robe of righteousness, as a bridegroom decketh himself with ornaments, and as a bride adorneth herself with her jewels.

I ponder, gracious Saviour, this word : Clothe *us*,—cover *us:* as a bridegroom decketh *himself*, and as a bride adorneth *herself* (*see* Isa. lxi. 10). As because Thou lovest us Thou accountest that what we do to each other we do to Thee; can it even be that because of that same love, what Thou Thyself

doest unto us Thou accountest as doing it unto Thine own
Self, in some transcendent height and depth of love by human
tongue unutterable?

I know not: Thou knowest. Yet this I know: if the love
I imagine be not in that text, then is a better love latent there;
for the misconception of my heart attaineth not to the Truth
of Thine.

Whoso clothes the poor, weaves for himself (still more
obviously weaves for *herself*) a white garment. Whoso visits
the fatherless and widows in their affliction, and shuns the
world, keeps that garment unspotted. Of such was Dorcas;
of such also was St. Peter comforting the weeping widows who
displayed her handiwork.

" White raiment."—The spirit if not the letter of these words
seems by a secondary suggestion to go counter many a fashion
in dress. *White*, the symbol of innocence and purity; *the aim*,
simple, decorous, dignified decency. And this comely sober
array, the same for all; no single wearer ambitious of an exceptional effect, but all alike virgins that be fellows. For whosoever love God become as chaste virgins espoused to Christ,
be they married or single.

Of course in such a train of thought *white* need no more
be all literal white than *fellow virgins* need all be unmarried.
One may be a saint in a coat of many colours, whilst another
may be a sinner in silver tissue (for so the " royal apparel " of
King Herod, *see* Acts xii. 21, has been described).

From shame that is neither glory nor grace,
      Lord, defend us.
From shame which it were a shame to face even in thought,
      Lord, defend us.
From shame that worketh not repentance,
      Lord, defend us.
From shame that accompanieth perdition,
      Lord, defend us.
From shame irremediable, intolerable, everlasting,
      Lord, defend us.
From shame before pitiless devils and sinners,
Before unpitying Saints and Angels,
Before Thy Face not pitiful,   Lord, defend us.
Thou Who borest shame for our sake and in our stead,
      Defend us.
Thou Who didst set Thy Face as a flint and unashamed bear our shame,
      Defend us.
Thou Who enduredst the Cross despising the shame,
      Defend us.
From shame of Thee before men, and from that shame of us whereby Thou
 wilt requite it before Thy Father and before the holy Angels in the
 Dreadful Day,   Lord, defend us.

"And anoint thine eyes with eye-salve, that thou mayest see."—"Unto Thee lift I up mine eyes, O Thou that dwellest in the heavens. Behold, as the eyes of servants look unto the hand of their masters, and as the eyes of a maiden unto the hand of her mistress; so our eyes wait upon the Lord our God, until that He have mercy upon us. Have mercy upon us, O Lord, have mercy upon us."

What is this eye-salve? It imports us vitally to know, yet is it not here defined. "That which I see not, teach Thou me."

O Lord God Almighty, the most Holy Spirit, Who camest down in the likeness of Fire; bestow upon us, I beseech Thee, light and goodwill. Amen.

St. John in his First Epistle writes to his "little children . . . Ye have an Unction from the Holy One, and ye know all things." I think if we study that same Epistle, full as it is of illumination, we shall find that in it life, light, love, are indissolubly interconnected. If so, we shall surely not go far astray by concluding that, for our own enlightenment, love unflinchingly brought into practice will prove a safe, efficient, and most healing eye-salve. "He that saith he is in the light, and hateth his brother, is in darkness even until now. He that loveth his brother abideth in the light, and there is none occasion of stumbling in him. But he that hateth his brother is in darkness, and walketh in darkness, and knoweth not whither he goeth, because that darkness hath blinded his eyes:"—here love lets in light. Further on, it takes the place of sight in a case where sight is impossible: "No man hath seen God at any time. If we love one another, God dwelleth in us, and His love is perfected in us." Whilst yet again sight without love seems to be a sort of blindness: "If a man say, I love God, and hateth his brother, he is a liar: for he that loveth not his brother whom he hath seen, how can he love God Whom he hath not seen?" Nor would the following promise prove attractive to one who scanned his brother with a loveless eye: "If any man see his brother sin a sin which is not unto death, he shall ask, and He shall give him life for them that sin not unto death."

But here we must sift our love, lest under pretext of lynx-eyed goodwill towards our brother we exhibit rather the blindness of arrogant self-ignorance. For He Who alone is Life, Light, Wisdom, Love, has left us this solemn warning: "Why beholdest thou the mote that is in thy brother's eye, but considerest not the beam that is in thine own eye? Or how wilt thou say to thy brother, Let me pull out the mote out of thine eye; and, behold, a beam is in thine own eye? Thou hypocrite, first cast out the beam out-of thine own eye ; and then shalt thou see clearly to cast out the mote out of thy brother's eye."

Generalities we may at the same moment assent to and elude, as a duck's back receives, while remaining impervious to, drops of water.　Our defects, even if they swell to the enormous scale of generalities, are yet all made up of particulars; and if we are to repent and reform it must be by particulars, since it cannot be done by generalities.　Whoso breaks the law in one point is guilty of all ; but none the less, whoso breaks the whole law still breaks it point by point in separate breaches.

Defective love is defective all over, yet very probably it is particularly defective at some one point : if so, that is an obvious point to take in hand first.　For practical purposes (if we mean to be practical) efforts should be concentrated rather than diffused : and commence reformation somewhere we must, on pain of otherwise achieving it nowhere.　Every inch of a waste ground may equally need weeding, yet not the fabled Briareus himself could weed the whole simultaneously at one swoop.

Whilst we pray for love, let us act as if already possessed of love.　" He that hath a bountiful eye shall be blessed ; for he giveth of his bread to the poor."　Let us give of our bread to the poor ; and see whether God will not first bless us with the lacking bountiful eye, and afterwards bless us for its s ke.

Lord, I believe Thy word that the eye is not satisfied with seeing.　Give us, I beseech Thee, grace to love Thee Whom now we see not, and for Thy sake to love all whom we see ; and grant us one day to inherit the blessing of those who not having seen yet have believed and loved.

Life that was born to-day
Must make no stay,
　But tend to end
As blossom-bloom of May.
O Lord, confirm my root,
Train up my shoot,
　To live and give
Harvest of wholesome fruit.

Life that was born to die
Sets heart on high,
　And counts and mounts
Steep stages of the sky.
Two things, Lord, I desire
And I require ;
　Love's name, and flame
To wrap my soul in fire.

Life that was born to love
Sends heart above
Both cloud and shroud,
And broods a peaceful dove.
Two things I ask of Thee ;
Deny not me ;
Eyesight and light
Thy Blessed Face to see.

19. As many as I love, I rebuke and chasten : be zealous therefore, and repent.

O Christ, Who lovest all, we are not straitened in Thee, but we are straitened in our own hearts.

We know that Thou lovest us all, we all being liable to chastening.

Give us grace not to flee at Thy rebuke, although at the voice of Thy thunder we be afraid.

Thou Who knowest all the fowls of the mountains, and without Whom not one sparrow falls to the ground, have regard unto all of us, unto each of us.

Rebuke us in mercy and pity, not unto cursing and vexation, not that we should perish thereby.

Grant us wisdom to hear the rod and Who hath appointed it, lest we sit in the seat of the scornful who hear not rebuke.

"Open rebuke is better than secret love." Amen.

"As many as I love."—Ah, Lord, Who lovest all,
If thus it is with Thee why sit remote above,
Beholding from afar stumbling and marred and small
So many Thou dost love ?

Whom sin and sorrow make their worn reluctant thrall ;
Who fain would flee away but lack the wings of dove ;
Who long for love and rest ; who look to Thee, and call
To Thee for rest and love.

"Be zealous therefore, and repent."—I suppose it may be easier for many of us to repent, or at least to hope and trust that we repent, than to be zealous, or even to suppose that we are zealous. The Church of Corinth exhibits to all time a pattern of zealous repentance : "For behold this self-same thing, that ye sorrowed after a godly sort, what carefulness it wrought in you, yea, what clearing of yourselves, yea, what indignation, yea, what fear, yea, what vehement desire, yea, what zeal, yea, what revenge ! In all things ye have approved yourselves to be clear in this matter."

If nothing short of this be the imperative standard of repentance, God indeed be merciful to us sinners.

God Almighty declares that for us men and for our salvation
He Himself "was clad with zeal as a cloak"; whilst too
many of us His nominal servants are devoted body and soul
to soft clothing and delicate living, even if we be not clothed
in actual purple and fine linen and fare not sumptuously every
day.

Yet gazing, if merely as an outsider, at zeal, I recognize that
it is as fire which descending from heaven kindles earth to
consume it. Zeal knows little, and goes on to know less and
less, of self-indulgence and personal luxuries. Zeal so covets
earnestly the best gifts as to sell all to purchase the field of
hidden treasure, as to barter all the pearls once esteemed
goodly for the one pearl of great price. Zeal in the aforetime
sluggard cries out, "Here am I; send me"; and advances the
backslider beyond his former attainment. Zeal shouts for the
battle, and turns it to the gate, and wins it be the warrior weak
or strong; and wins the race be the runner swift or slow.
Zeal, loving righteousness and hating iniquity, sets the penitent
high in the congregation of saints; and makes his light so to
shine that men glorify their Father in Heaven. "Be zealous
therefore, and repent."

**20. Behold, I stand at the door, and knock: if any man
hear My voice, and open the door, I will come in to
him, and will sup with him, and he with Me.**

Lord, give us grace to behold.

This then is the reward of that wise obedience which
justifies God. "Behold," He saith: and with eyes healed and
enlightened the once lukewarm look and behold the King in
His beauty. They have silenced their own foolish boastings,
and so have ears to hear Him knock. They have "put on
their coats" and can rise instantly to open to Him. Neither
do they appear before their God empty: in clean hands they
bring gold tried in the fire as a tribute to Him Who gave it.

If beautiful upon the mountains were the feet of them who
brought good tidings, how infinitely beautiful are His Feet Who
enters the door of His beloved, and is Himself that very Good
published of old, our Salvation and our God! If we love
Him, and because He loves us, He makes Himself our Door of
entrance into the Paradise of God: and because He loves us,
and if we love Him, He makes us His door into a little
Paradise of His own, "a garden inclosed."

"I . . . will sup with him, and he with Me."—Blessed it
were to break our fast with Christ, and strengthened by that

meat to pursue our journey of however many days and nights
to the Mount of God. Blessed it were to dine with Him, and
start refreshed to follow Him across the storm-beaten sands of
this troublesome world. But to sup with Him is to end our
day with Him in (please God) the beatitude of final perseverance.

Again and again our kind Master comes in and sups with
each faithful soul in the Sacrament of His most Blessed Body
and Blood, the Sacrament of the Lord's Supper.

"Lord, evermore give us this Bread." "Is it nothing to
you, all ye that pass by?"

St. Peter once : "Lord, dost Thou wash my feet?"—
Much more I say : Lord, dost Thou stand and knock
At my closed heart more rugged than a rock,
Bolted and barred, for Thy soft touch unmeet,
Nor garnished nor in any wise made sweet?
Owls roost within and dancing satyrs mock.
Lord, I have heard the crowing of the cock,
And have not wept : ah, Lord, Thou knowest it.
Yet still I hear Thee knocking. Still I hear :
"Open to Me, look on Me eye to eye
That I may wring thy heart and make it whole ;
And teach thee love because I hold thee dear,
And sup with thee in gladness soul with soul,
And sup with thee in glory by and by."

**21. To him that overcometh will I grant to sit with Me in
My throne, even as I also overcame, and am set down
with My Father in His throne.**

**22. He that hath an ear, let him hear what the Spirit saith
unto the churches.**

· First and last there is no promise whatever except "to him
that overcometh." Each of the Seven Churches is confronted
by a particular foe, and encouraged to contend for a particular
prize ; but the only course for all alike is to overcome. No
Tree of Life, except for him who regains lost ground : no
immunity from the second death, except for him who endures
to the end : no hidden Manna, white stone, new name, except
for him who repents and amends : no dominion, no Morning
Star, except for him who by godly intolerance keeps himself
pure from the blood of all men : no white raiment or final
registration in the Book of Life, except for him who either
holds fast his integrity or rises from death of sin to life of
righteousness : no permanent incorporation into God's Temple,

no Divine Name, except for him who holding fast what he
has keeps patience till all be accomplished.

As with the Six, so with the Seventh and last Church: Overcome, and no good thing will God withhold. "Who among
us shall dwell with the devouring fire? who among us shall
dwell with everlasting burnings?" Well may heaven and
earth regard and wonder marvellously when the enkindled
lukewarm man sits down with Christ in His throne: for the
Lord our God is a consuming fire, even a Jealous God.

The sevenfold prize is not of man's earning but of God's
largesse: yet I think congruity is traceable between each phase
of righteousness and its allotted reward :—

1. He who regains lost ground, regains lost Paradise.

2. He who lives and believes till his mortal end, shall never
die.

3. Lo-ammi repenting, is renamed Ammi.

4. The witness on earth is the plenipotentiary in Heaven.

5. Life maintained or life regained, or else erasure from the
Book of Life.

6. Immutable amid mutability, permanent amid permanence.

7. "There are threescore queens."

"Even as I also overcame."—It is Thou, Lord, sayest,
"Even as I": for which of us had dared say it?

Thou overcamest in our stead, and happy are we if we overcome in Thy strength. Thou overcamest for us without our
help, and Thou wilt overcome in us and by us except we
hinder. Thanks be to Thee, O God.

> Lord, we are rivers running to Thy sea,
> Our waves and ripples all derived from Thee :
> A nothing we should have, a nothing be,
>   Except for Thee.

> Sweet are the waters of Thy shoreless sea,
> Make sweet our waters that make haste to Thee ;
> Pour in Thy sweetness, that ourselves may be
>   Sweetness to Thee.

"With Me in My throne, even as I . . . with My Father
in His throne."—This promise (if one may dare say so) ex-
hausts beatitude. This is indeed to call her beloved, which
was not beloved. Elsewhere our Lord says concerning His
own : "The glory which Thou gavest Me I have given them . . .
Father, I will that they also, whom Thou hast given Me, be
with Me where I am; that they may behold My glory, which
Thou hast given Me."

"My Father."—"My Father, and your Father . . . My God, and your God."

Our Father, which art in heaven, hallowed be Thy Name. Give us, I beseech Thee, daily grace to hallow It, for Thy Son our Lord Jesus Christ's sake. Amen.

"David said, Seemeth it to you a light thing to be a king's son in law, seeing that I am a poor man, and lightly esteemed?"

Who sits with the King in His Throne? Not a slave but a Bride,
  With this King of all Greatness and Grace Who reigns not alone ;
His Glory her glory, where glorious she glows at His side
  Who sits with the King in His Throne.

She came from dim uttermost depths which no Angel hath known,
Leviathan's whirlpool and Dragon's dominion worldwide,
  From the frost or the fire to Paradisiacal zone.

Lo, she is fair as a dove, silvery, golden, dove-eyed :
  Lo, Dragon laments and Death laments, for their prey is flown :
She dwells in the Vision of Peace and her peace shall abide
  Who sits with the King in His Throne.

CHAPTER IV.

1. After this I looked, and, behold, a door was opened in heaven: and the first voice which I heard was as it were of a trumpet talking with me; which said, Come up hither, and I will shew thee things which must be hereafter.

"After this I looked, and, behold . . ."—Let us too look, even if we should not behold. "Mine eyes fail with looking upward: O Lord, I am oppressed; undertake for me." "Then I saw that wisdom excelleth folly, as far as light excelleth darkness."

Far be it from me to think to unfold mysteries or interpret prophecies. But I trust that to gaze in whatever ignorance on what God reveals, is so far to do His will. If ignorance breed humility, it will not debar from wisdom. If ignorance betake itself to prayer, it will lay hold on grace.

As children may feel the awe of a storm, the beauty of sunrise or sunset, so at least I too may deepen awe, and stir up desire by a contemplation of things inevitable, momentous, transcendent. "Consider the work of God: for who can make that straight, which He hath made crooked? In the day of prosperity be joyful, but in the day of adversity consider."

The eagle strengthened with might gazes full at the sun. Glory be to God for all His gifts to all His creatures.

But God has not bidden us be mighty as eagles, but be harmless as doves. I suppose a dove may be no more fit than myself to look steadily at the sun: we both might be blinded by what would enlighten that stronger bird. The dove brings not much of her own to the sun, yet the sun caresses and beautifies her silver wings and her feathers like gold: it would be a sore mistake on the dove's part were she to say, Because I am not the eagle I am not a sun bird, and so were to cut herself off from the sun's gracious aspect.

And since five sparrows are sold for two farthings, and not one of them is forgotten before God, even the least and last of *birds* may take courage to court the light-giving, life-giving, munificent sun.

"After this,"—after, that is, a revelation, an alarum, a Great Voice of praise and rebuke, hope and fear. Rebuke and fear should not paralyse us : they should rather rouse us to instant exertion, instant obedience, instant prayer.

O Lord our God, deliver us, I beseech Thee, from idle tremblings and abject fear. It is Thou : give us grace not to be afraid, except with the fear of those who always fearing are happy. For Jesus Christ's sake. Amen.

"I looked."—If we will not look, we should not behold even though a door were opened in heaven for our enlightenment.

This Apocalypse is a celestial door opened to us : let us not, until we have looked, despair of seeing somewhat. Having looked, we shall not despair.

What shall we see? As it were the company of two armies ; life and good, death and evil. Wherefore choose life.

"Look how high the heaven is in comparison of the earth."

O my God, Who acceptedst Daniel when taking his life in his hand he set his face in prayer toward desolate Jerusalem, grant us such grace that night and day our eyes may be directed toward Thy heavenly Temple, and our faces set steadfastly toward New Jerusalem the mother of us all. For our Lord Jesu's sake. Amen.

"Those Seven ; they are the Eyes of the Lord, which run to and fro through the whole earth."

Lord Jesus, by indwelling of Thy Most Holy Spirit, purge our eyes to discern and contemplate Thee ; until we attain to see as Thou seest, judge as Thou judgest, choose as Thou choosest ; and having sought and found Thee, to behold Thee for ever and ever.

"I will stand upon my watch, and set me upon the tower, and will watch to see."

"A door was opened in heaven."—Jesus, Who hast deigned to call Thyself the Door of the sheep, lead us, I pray Thee, in and out, and provide for us pasture.

"And the first Voice which I heard was as it were of a trumpet talking with me."—The Revised Version reads : "And the first Voice which I heard, a Voice as of a trumpet speaking with me, One saying . . . ." This rendering more decidedly than the other, suggests that this may be the same Voice as that former Voice which spake (ch. i. 10). St. John was then "in the Spirit": but now (a verse later) he says: "And immediately I was in the Spirit." Thus we see how to him that hath shall be given; how the elect go from strength to strength until unto the God of gods appeareth every one of them in Sion. And when with eyes and heart fixed on God they at length appear before Him, then shall they one by one know how His Eyes and His Heart have been and are and will be upon them continually. [This remark is made under correction, lest "Spirit" and "spirit," occasionally so printed in the two verses alluded to, should negative the thought. The Revised Version prints "Spirit" in both verses alike.]

> Lord, dost Thou look on me, and will not I
>   Launch out my heart to Heaven to look on Thee?—
>   Here if one loved me I should turn to see,
> And often think on him and often sigh,
> And by a tender friendship make reply
>   To love gratuitous poured forth on me,
>   And nurse a hope of happy days to be,
> And mean "until we meet" in each good-bye.
> Lord, Thou dost look and love is in Thine Eyes,
>   Thy Heart is set upon me day and night,
>   Thou stoopest low to set me far above:
> O Lord, that I may love Thee make me wise;
>   That I may see and love Thee grant me sight;
>   And give me love that I may give Thee love.

"Come up hither."—Thus was St. John brought into the haven where he would be: but not to abide there. It was as when he leaned on His Master's Bosom, and after a while had to arise; as when he set off to follow, and after a while had to pause and tarry. Love laid him on his Master's Breast, love sped him along that blessed Foot-track; and equally it was love which constrained him to arise and depart from that Rest which was not at once to be his final rest, and to turn back from that "Way" which vouchsafed not yet to lead him home.

We reckon that love mighty which avails to enter heaven. How mighty must that love be which at God's behest turns back contentedly from heaven to earth!

"Come up hither."—*Hither* is a joyful word, but *come* a more joyful. *Hither* summons us to Mount Sion, and unto the City of the Living God, the heavenly Jerusalem, and to an innumerable company of Angels, to the general assembly and Church of the firstborn, which are written in heaven, and to the spirits of just men made perfect:—*Come* calls us to God the Judge of all, and to Jesus, the Mediator of the new covenant.

O Jesu, better than Thy gifts
  Art Thou Thine only Self to us !
Palm-branch its triumph, harp uplifts
  Its triumph-note melodious :
    But what are such to such as we ?
O Jesu, better than Thy saints
  Art Thou Thine only Self to us !
The heart faints and the spirit faints
  For only Thee all-Glorious,
    For Thee, O only Lord, for Thee.

"And I will shew thee things which must be hereafter."—
If it be the same Voice (*see* ante on "And the first Voice," &c.),
then is it "the Voice of my Beloved." It saith not now as in
the Song of songs, "Open to Me," but rather: I have opened
to thee. That first word appertains to earth and its duties,
this second word to Paradise and its privileges.

O Lord, Gracious without measure, beyond all measure, Who
hast said : "Whatsoever ye would that men should do to you,
do ye even so to them," if by love we now open to Thee, and
welcome Thee in time's sorrowful night; in eternity's rapturous
day open Thou to us, welcome Thou us, that we may enter
in and go out no more. Amen.

"I will shew thee things which must be hereafter."—The
personal honour thus promised is for St. John ; the grace is for
us all : the vision is his ; the revelation not his exclusively but
ours also, if we are penitent and obedient. As we read elsewhere : "Turn you at My reproof: behold, I will pour out My
Spirit unto you, I will make known My words unto you."

O Lord, Thou hast reproved the Churches, and we have
heard Thy reproof. Turn us, we beseech Thee, and teach us
by Thy most Holy Spirit the meaning of Thy sacred words.

"By terrible things in righteousness wilt Thou answer us, O
God of our salvation."

2. And immediately I was in the Spirit : and, behold, a throne was set in heaven, and One sat on the throne.

St. John records not "I was in the Spirit" for our discourage-
ment. On the contrary, in his First Epistle addressing all
obedient Christians he writes : "He that keepeth His commandments dwelleth in Him, and He in him. And hereby we
know that He abideth in us, by the Spirit which He hath
given us."

  "Come, Holy Ghost, our souls inspire,
  And lighten with celestial fire."

"Behold, a Throne was set in heaven."—We have beheld earthly thrones. Righteous they may be or unrighteous, gracious or tyrannical, from of old or of yesterday ; unlike each other in many ways, all alike in one way : they are crumbling with this crumbling world, are finishing with this finishing time ; to-day they judge, to-morrow they will be judged. For earthly thrones are probationary.

Not so the Heavenly Throne. In this He is set that judgeth right; the King of kings, Lord of lords, Judge of judges.

Yet we read : "A throne *was set*,"—suggesting (perhaps?) that whilst He Who sat on it was from eternity to eternity, yet that Throne itself was not from eternity although to eternity. For as we read on through this chapter of the Apocalypse, and markedly when we reach its final ascription of glory (*see* ver. 11), it appears as if creation were here gathered in solemn adoration around its Creator ; exceeding lofty creatures being constituted the mouthpiece of all, when everything that hath or that hath not breath praiseth the Lord. And if so, that word "was set" sends thought back into that eternity uninhabited of creatures, which (so far as human conception avails) preceded creation : not the creation of our actual world merely, but the formation of that chaos out of which it was evoked, and the beginning of that pre-creation which appears to have lapsed into chaos. For send our mind back as we may through the vast antecedent unknown of remote and yet more remote possible successive creations, yet beyond the utmost bound of the everlasting hills lies the infinite eternity of God Almighty, before it pleased Him to make all things out of nothing, and to be worshipped by ten thousand times ten thousand, and thousands of thousands.

When we consider even Thy heavens the work of Thy fingers, the moon and stars which Thou hast ordained, what is man that Thou art mindful of him ?

Much more when we consider Thee, what then is man ?

"The publican, standing afar off, would not lift up so much as his eyes unto heaven, but smote upon his breast, saying : God be merciful to me a sinner."

"And One sat on the throne."

O God Eternal, Who causest the vapours to ascend from the ends of the earth, let our prayer be set forth in Thy sight as the incense,
And be gracious unto us.
Thou Who art our Creator Blessed for ever,
Be gracious unto us.

Thou Who art the God and Father of our Lord Jesus Chist, for His sake
Who is God over all Blessed for ever,
                        Be gracious unto us.
Thou Who hast vouchsafed to us the glorious Gospel,
                        Be gracious unto us.
Thou Who art the Blessed and only Potentate, the King of kings and Lord
of lords,
                        Be gracious unto us.
Thou Who hatest nothing that Thou hast made,
                        Be gracious unto us.
Thou Who art Three Persons in One God,
                        Be gracious unto us.
We plead Christ Jesus made unto us Wisdom and Righteousness and
Sanctification and Redemption. Amen.

"Dominion and fear are with Him, He maketh peace in
His high places."

**3. And He that sat was to look upon like a jasper and a
sardine stone : and there was a rainbow round about
the throne, in sight like unto an emerald.**

If it be so, that in this transcendent vision we are permitted to
contemplate the Almighty Creator enthroned amid creation, then
I think that in particular some manifestation of the All Holy
Trinity in Unity may be revealed to the adoring eye of faith.
What is the Christian's manifestation of the Unapproachable
Trinity? Surely it is eminently Christ Himself, Who once
declared : "He that hath seen Me hath seen the Father" ;
Christ Himself Very God of Very God ; Christ Himself, Who
received not the Spirit by measure.
By "a jasper" need not (as I have read) be understood exclusively that opaque stone which now bears the name ; for of
yore translucent gems were included under the same designation. While thus we may picture it of dazzling brilliancy, per-
meated by pure light, and as it were swallowed up in radiations
of that light ; yet, as Moses of old at the Burning Bush, let us
also whilst we draw near to behold, be afraid even in a symbol
"to look upon God."   The "sardine stone" (or sardius, as I
have seen it explained) is a species of cornelian, which some write
carnelian, deriving the word not from *horn* but from *flesh ;* and
is a blood-red translucent gem, whence we may perhaps assume
an intimation of our Redeemer's Humanity.   The "rainbow"
has been thought to indicate that same Sacred Humanity, because surrounding the Throne it appears no less to surround
Him Who sat thereon, like as the Blessed Body enshrined the
"Incomprehensible" Divinity.   If so, the sardine stone may

remind us how the Godhead was not converted into flesh, but
the Manhood was taken into God : whilst the rainbow may
more especially bring home to us that in our Lord Himself
Very Man dwells the Fulness of the Godhead bodily.   Further
we are reminded that Christ as Man, over and beyond the
Indivisible Unity of the Divine Trinity, became a Temple of the
Holy Ghost.

For a rainbow being indissolubly connected with a cloud,
seems at once to suggest an emblematic allusion to the Most
Holy Spirit of God.   Its form shows that it proceeds ·from a
centre.   It exhibits to us what light is, by evolving the lovely
tints hidden in its whiteness.   It enables us to look on light
which viewed directly would blind us.   It conveyed hope to
Noah and his family all alone in a ruined world.   It gladdens
whoso beholds it : the eye that seeth it beareth witness to it.
What we look on is water, but transfigured by fire : fire and
water, two chief symbols of God the Holy Ghost.·

"Round about the Throne."—Not (please God) simply overarching the throne; but encircling it (as I have heard suggested) by its own *completely revealed* circle.   In this world
we observe no more than a larger or a smaller section of rainbow.   Thus even at its widest it overarches no wider area than
the eye can compass, and where it seems to touch earth or sea
we know that it touches them not.   We discern enough to feel
convinced that we see a portion only, not the whole; yet is
that portion so far complete in itself that it certifies to us that
whole which we see not : the part declares the unbroken,
continuous, unvaried whole.

And thus for the present the faithful "know in part" God
Almighty, so far as it pleases Him by His Spirit to reveal
Himself to them one by one in divers measures.   The least
recognize Him as on high protecting them ; the greatest realize
that He is in truth all around them embracing them.

Even a very little reading teaches that a number of different
tints belong to jewels of which we habitually think as exhibiting
some one fixed hue : thus though the ruby is red, the sapphire
blue, the emerald green, it does not follow that any one of
them· is restricted to that characteristic colour.   Perhaps such
variety of colour may be allowed for when this celestial rainbow is set before us as "in sight like unto an emerald."

Yet after all green remains as our standard colour for an
emerald.   Green seems the colour both of hope and of rest :
of hope because of sweet ever-renewed spring verdure; of rest
because of the refreshing repose green affords to strained

sight. Completed hope, completed rest, are celestial, not terrestrial.

> ". . . Look up and sing
> In hope of promised spring."

4. And round about the Throne were four and twenty seats: and upon the seats I saw four and twenty elders sitting, clothed in white raiment; and they had on their heads crowns of gold.

According to one theory, these twenty-four august Elders make up in some sort a figure of time or of a portion of time surrounding that Centre which rules it. Thus a fixed law dominates the Signs of the Zodiac, and thus the sun regulates days, weeks, months, years.

But if Time appears to meet us in the domain of Eternity, we may surely look for it not, so to say, in its own person, but as embodied in its permanent fruits. . Wherefore (in my avowed ignorance) I will for my own part connect these blessed Elders with the twofold Israel; the Twelve Tribes of the Old Dispensation, and the corresponding perfect number of the New.

A nation of kings and priests; they are clothed in priestly white raiment, and wear kingly crowns. Their " seats," according to the Revised Version, are "thrones." They are the family of the King of kings, the Divine royal family once of earth, now of heaven. Out of prison hath the sometime poor and wise child come to reign.

5. And out of the Throne proceeded lightnings and thunderings and voices: and there were Seven Lamps of Fire burning before the Throne, which are the Seven Spirits of God.

"Lightnings and thunderings and voices"—a message to every soul of man from "the Throne": a message not necessarily in articulate words, but greatly challenging our littleness. As when "God thundereth marvellously with His voice; great things doeth He, which we cannot comprehend." As when the lightnings say " Here we are." " There is neither speech nor language: but their voices are heard among them."

Lightnings, thunderings, voices: when our hearts misgive us and our spirits fail because of those things that are coming upon the earth, let us remember that they all proceed "out of the Throne."

Tumult and turmoil, trouble and toil,
   Yet peace withal in a painful heart;
Never a grudge and never a broil,
   And ever the better part.

O my King and my heart's own choice,
   Stretch Thy Hand to Thy fluttering dove;
Teach me, call to me with Thy Voice,
   Wrap me up in Thy Love.

"Seven Lamps of Fire burning before the Throne, which are the Seven Spirits of God."—Long ago I was impressed by a preacher's words. He explained this passage as revealing the Presence not of any creatures but of God the Holy Spirit in Person : for, he argued, had They been the highest of creatures they would have joined with their fellows in the hymn of praise to God Almighty; whence he inferred that That which praised not God, Was and Is and Is to come God.

That preacher's authority sanctions (I hope) what I endeavoured to think out on a former text (ch. i. ver. 4).

Once more we behold and adore that unspeakable Diffused Unity (if I may dare so express myself) which the All Holy Spirit Who is pleased to dwell in the innumerable hearts of faithful humankind reveals to our contemplation.

Sacrifices prefigured Christ. And since Christ "through the Eternal Spirit offered Himself," the fire of the sacrifice prefigured the Holy Ghost. We read concerning Abram's first great recorded sacrifice : " It came to pass, that, when the sun went down, and it was dark, behold a smoking furnace, and a burning lamp that passed between those pieces." And again we read how Abraham having laid the wood of the burnt offering upon Isaac his son " took the fire in his hand."

"Before the Throne "—as the Rainbow was "round about" the Throne : once more reminding us of that authoritative definition, "Proceeding from." Thus in a figure we discern how God the Holy Spirit is that Person of the All Holy Trinity Who vouchsafes to come into special nearness and contact with creation at large: creation itself being ranged round about the Throne in the person of the Elders; and before the Throne, when worshipping Him that sat thereon they fall down and cast down their crowns; in the midst of the Throne moreover, and round about the Throne, by reason of the four Living Creatures (*see* ver. 6).

In the beginning the Spirit of God Himself moved (or brooded) upon the face of the waters, recreating a world out of chaos by His own almighty act. He it was spake in time past unto the fathers by the Prophets. He it was came and went among the sons of men as He pleased. Century after century the human family lived and died before Christ was manifest in the Flesh : meanwhile generation after generation the Spirit strove with man, who oftentimes rebelled and vexed Him. And since the Ascension He has made regenerate man's heart His settled place wherein to abide for ever; according to our Lord's gracious promise to His Apostles : "I will pray the Father, and He shall give you another Comforter, that He may abide with you for ever; even the Spirit of Truth ; Whom the world cannot receive, because it seeth Him not, neither knoweth Him : but ye know Him; for He dwelleth with you, and shall be in you."

> O God the Holy Ghost Who art Light unto Thine elect,
>> Evermore enlighten us.
> Thou Who art Fire of Love
>> Evermore enkindle us.
> Thou Who art Lord and Giver of Life,
>> Evermore live in us.
> Thou Who art Holiness,
>> Evermore sanctify us.
> Thou Who bestowest Sevenfold Grace,
>> Evermore replenish us.
> As the Wind is Thy symbol,
>> So forward our goings.
> As the Dove,
>> So launch us heavenwards.
> As Water,
>> So purify our spirits.
> As a Cloud,
>> So abate our temptations.
> As Dew,
>> So revive our languor.
> As Fire,
>> So purge out our dross.

Be Thou, O Lord, before to guide us, behind to guard us, around to shelter us, within to perfect us.

As the Father loveth us for Jesu's sake, as Jesus for His own sake, so love Thou us, O Lord the Loving Spirit : until Thou Thyself bring home all Thy holy congregation to bless for evermore the Lord God, bowing down and worshipping the Lord and the King. Amen.

6. And before the Throne there was a sea of glass like unto crystal : and in the midst of the Throne, and round about the Throne, were four beasts full of eyes before and behind.

An untroubled sea, or it could not be "of glass": a pure sea, or it could not be "like unto crystal." But wherefore "before the Throne"?

However fathomless its depths, its surface (the thought is not my own) appears as a vast permanent mirror; reflecting all which surrounds it. It thus recalls Habakkuk's prophetic promise: "The earth shall be filled with the knowledge of the Glory of the Lord, as the waters cover the sea." So here in the better land we perceive a figure of that which (God willing) will convey to the redeemed a perfect knowledge of God Himself, and of each fellow saint who abode the day of His coming and stood when He appeared. Everything which is very good, all things lovely, the height of the heaven in comparison of the earth, the wide distance of the east from the west, all will be seen and known. For in that day and in fulness the delights of the Uncreated Wisdom shall be with the sons of men.

Knowledge seems, if I may so say, to be the key-note of this verse. The Living Creatures which abide "in the midst of the Throne, and round about the Throne" being likewise "full of eyes" must, in their degree, look on all things from the view-point of Almighty God Himself. Their eyes being "before and behind" suggest an exercise of foresight no less than of memory: and in them appears to be inherent an exemption from variableness or shadow of turning, according to the vision of Ezekiel: "They went every one straight forward: whither the spirit was to go, they went; and they turned not when they went."

Thus knowledge appears to be in them an original endowment, while to us it is held out as a prize at the goal. "So run, that ye may obtain."

7. And the first beast was like a lion, and the second beast like a calf, and the third beast had a face as a man, and the fourth beast was like a flying eagle.

Tradition assigns these four Living Creatures to the four Evangelists. St. John that Son of Thunder illuminated and unconsumed by "the Fire of God" inherits the sun-facing Eagle. St. Luke with his revelation of reconciling Love, the sacrificial Calf. The Lion and the Man remain for St. Matthew and St. Mark; of whom each sometimes takes one, sometimes the other: reasons have been alleged for either arrangement. If the Man is attributed to St. Matthew, we may connect it with his table of our Lord's Human genealogy: while St. Mark's

Lion may remind us how he alone notices that it was "with the wild beasts" that our Lord sojourned during Forty Days in the wilderness. Reversing the position (and not to enumerate other points), the Lion of the royal tribe of Judah befits St. Matthew in virtue of his unique narrative of the Adoration of the Magi when they worshipped Christ as King: the Man harmonizes with that special prominence of the Very Manhood which it has been thought characterizes St. Mark's Gospel.

Yet this venerable scheme need not (I hope) exclude the view that in these august Living Creatures; the Cherubim apparently of Ezekiel's visions; the Chariot of the Almighty Himself, whence the Psalmist sings, "He rode upon a Cherub, and did fly,"—that in them is perpetuated a sort of summary and memorial of those good gifts which God has lavished on man indeed pre-eminently, but likewise in varying degrees and after various fashions on beast, bird, and every inferior creature that hath life; all which creatures at the first were beheld to be very good. St. Paul writes: "The earnest expectation of the creature waiteth for the manifestation of the sons of God. For the creature was made subject to vanity, not willingly, but by reason of Him Who hath subjected the same in hope, because the creature itself also shall be delivered from the bondage of corruption into the glorious liberty of the children of God. For we know that the whole creation groaneth and travaileth in pain together until now. And not only they, but ourselves also, which have the firstfruits of the Spirit, even we ourselves groan within ourselves, waiting for the adoption, to wit, the redemption of our body":—thus opening our eyes to a mysterious element in those lower existences so familiar and often so friendly to us. We think of them in relation to man: yet surely the unnumbered multitudes of them which live, propagate, die "on the earth, where no man is; on the wilderness, wherein there is no man," may have some purpose independent of direct human profit, discipline, convenience. "O Lord, how manifold are Thy works! in wisdom hast Thou made them all."

Sacred association makes reverend to us lamb, lion, sheep (*see* Isa. liii. 7), dove, eagle (*see* Deut. xxxii. 11, 12), even leopard and bear (*see* Hos. xiii. 7, 8): and endears to us on inferior grounds hart, stork and sparrow, owl and pelican. All sentient creatures have a claim on us: and well may we admit and honour their claim, when we recollect Who vouchsafed to have respect to the much cattle of Nineveh.

O Good God, Who permitting to every man his temptation

preparest for him a way of escape, and hast constituted the present age a period of knowledge and of thirst after knowledge; give us grace never to pursue knowledge by avenues of cruelty or impurity, but keeping innocency to take heed to the thing that is right; lest headstrong lust of good and evil mislead us to choose the evil and refuse the good. Which God forbid, for His All Holy Son's sake. Amen.

If Cherubim transcendent in knowledge and accounted second in the ninefold celestial hierarchy exhibit any likeness to man's inferiors, well may I be contented to learn of these humble brethren. The serpent can teach me wisdom, the dove harmlessness, the ant prudent industry, the coney adaptability to circumstances, the locust self-government, the spider resource; lions and young ravens set me, in some sort, an example of prayer; dog and sow scare me from relapses into sin.

A Psalm asserts: "O Lord, Thou preservest man and beast"; or according to the Prayer-book version: "Thou, Lord, shalt save both man and beast." It were unwise to reflect on no statement besides "the beasts that perish"; or so to exalt man's spirit which goeth upward, over the beast's which goeth downward, as practically to ignore that the beast is endowed with any spirit at all. Land may cry out against an unrighteous owner, and furrows complain: how much more the moving creature that hath life.

8. And the four beasts had each of them six wings about him; and they were full of eyes within: and they rest not day and night, saying, Holy, Holy, Holy, Lord God Almighty, which was, and is, and is to come.

If these be the same living creatures as those Ezekiel beheld by the river Chebar, their aspect seems to have been revealed with a difference to St. John. To Ezekiel each appeared four-faced as Man, Lion, Ox, Eagle: St. John describes each individual as exhibiting one or other such face. Ezekiel assigns four wings to each; St. John six. Balancing together the two descriptions it may perhaps be thought that Ezekiel saw more of the physical aspect, exhibited in multiplied faces and in those hands and feet which he alone registers; St. John more of the spiritual significance, expressed by wings in greater number: these two revelations of the Cherubim thus corresponding respectively with the two dispensations; of which the elder dealt in carnal ordinances, the latter (thank God, our own) deals in spiritual realities.

"Full of eyes within" has, I believe, been understood as applying either to the person of the living creature, or else to his wings. One reading invites us to admire the depth of his intuition ; the other by a figure the aspiring loftiness of his contemplation.

Lord, if not for us are the eyes of a Cherub, yet grant us the receptiveness and goodwill of a Cherub ; that we may discern what Thou revealest, and may follow after to apprehend that for which also we are apprehended of Christ Jesus. For His sake. Amen.

> All things are fair, if we had eyes to see
> How first God made them goodly everywhere :
> And goodly still in Paradise they be,—
> All things are fair.
>
> O Lord, the solemn heavens Thy praise declare :
> The multi-fashioned saints bring praise to Thee,
> As doves fly home and cast away their care.
>
> As doves on divers branches of their tree
> Perched high or low, sit all contented there
> Not mourning any more ; in each degree
> All things are fair.

"They rest not."—I suppose by *rest not* we may understand *cease not, pause not, flag not ;* their endless worship being an endless contentment, their labour a labour of love, their exploration of unfathomable mysteries as it were a skylark's ever-ascending flight ; yet even at the same moment, as his sustained exaltation at his zenith on poised wings.

Rapture and rest, desire and satisfaction, perfection and progress, may seem to clash to-day : to-morrow the paradoxes of earth may reappear as the demonstrations of heaven.

These Living Creatures compounded of multiplied gifts and multiform beauties concentrate themselves in worship. Their worship is due exercise of their gifts ; the exercise of their gifts is worship.

God, who needeth not to be worshipped with men's hands, deigns to accept man's worship. Shall He dispose Himself to be worshipped, and shall not we worship ?

"Day and night."—Yet we look for no night there. Meanwhile though the ebb and flow of time sway not the natives of heaven, their perpetual adoration runs parallel with our night and day ; they worship while we wake, and worship on while we sleep. Alas for us, if while they rest not from worship, we worship not either while we labour or while we rest.

"Saying."—Isaiah of old beheld the six-winged Seraphim,

and heard one cry to another, saying, " Holy, Holy, Holy, is the Lord of hosts : the whole earth is full of His glory."

The Seraphim, spirits of love absorbed in God, in their hymn of Divine praise remember also the *hosts* their fellow-servants and the *earth* their fellow-creature.

The Cherubim, spirits of knowledge concentrated upon God, name and celebrate Him alone.

Yet Seraph ranks above Cherub, as love above knowledge.

" Saying, Holy, Holy, Holy, Lord God Almighty, which Was, and Is, and Is to come."—Worthy to be praised before praise waited on Him, before any creature existed to worship Him. Before the earth and the world, before the morning stars and the sons of God, before any extreme *before* mind can conceive, God was : three Persons, one God, always and evermore.

Three Persons : distinct, not separate ; alike, not the same. As our first Article of Religion declares : " There is but One Living and True God, Everlasting, without body, parts, or passions ; of infinite Power, Wisdom, and Goodness ; the Maker and Preserver of all things both visible and invisible. And in Unity of this Godhead there be Three Persons, of one Substance, Power, and Eternity ; the Father, the Son, and the Holy Ghost." As we ourselves year after year aver : " O Lord, Almighty, Everlasting God. Who art One God, One Lord ; not one only Person, but three Persons in One Substance. For that which we believe of the Glory of the Father, the same we believe of the Son, and of the Holy Ghost, without any difference or inequality."

Awful it is for feeble man to contemplate the Omnipotence of God, awful for finite man to contemplate His Eternity ; most of all awful is it for sinful man to contemplate His Sanctity. Yet may our awestruck weakness betake itself without shame to His Strength, our awestruck littleness to His Infinity : it is when we approach the presence of His Holiness that the shame of our face covers us, our comeliness is turned into corruption, and we retain no strength.

O God Almighty our Fear and our only Hope, Thou art in heaven and we upon earth, Thou art Holy and we unholy. . . But we plead Jesus Christ our Redeemer.

9. And when those beasts give glory and honour and thanks to Him that sat on the throne, who liveth for ever and ever,

Their service is clearly worship in spirit and in truth. Their recorded hymn by ascribing Holiness and Eternity, ascribes as bound up with them "glory and honour," but conveys not in set terms "thanks." Yet we are told that they give "thanks to Him that sat on the Throne." To overflow with thankfulness is virtually to render thanks. Thankless thanks, on the contrary, are no thanks at all.

These celestial impersonations of knowledge appear to have one only object of contemplation, God Almighty. Thus have they attained to know all they do know.

That same School of Cherubim is open to men,—is open to me.

True knowledge adores, gives thanks, loves, and ever follows on to know the love of Christ, which passeth knowledge.

"Let everything that hath breath praise the Lord." The Living Creatures ascribe glory to Him " Who liveth for ever and ever." Derived life praises its Fountain, imparted life its Bestower; life which began, the Unbeginning Life whence it began ; life which began yet which ends not, the Endless Life which sustains it endless.

> Love loveth Thee, and wisdom loveth Thee.
> The love that loveth Thee sits satisfied.
> Wisdom that loveth Thee grows million-eyed,
> Learning what was and is and is to be.
> Wisdom and love are glad of all they see ;
> Their heart is deep, their hope is not denied ;
> They rock at rest on time's unresting tide,
> And wait to rest thro' long eternity.
> Wisdom and love and rest, each holy soul
> Hath these to-day while day is only night :
> What shall souls have when morning brings to light
> Love, wisdom, rest, God's treasure stored above ?
> Palm shall they have and harp and aureole,
> Wisdom, rest, love—and lo ! the whole is love.

10. The four and twenty elders fall down before Him that sat on the Throne, and worship Him that liveth for ever and ever, and cast their crowns before the Throne, saying,

To sit on thrones is an exaltation, to wear crowns a dignity : to fall prostrate in worship is a loftier exaltation, to cast down tributary crowns an enhanced dignity. Blessed it is to receive, still more blessed to give.

What we have experienced, felt, done, bears witness to what we have not yet experienced, felt, done. The self-surrenders of earth rehearse in their rapturous triumph the all-surrendering self-surrender of heaven.

.The best gifts are those which can be given back to the Giver. Them it is generous to covet earnestly.

To press forward toward all the great things which may yet be ours annuls the pang caused by lesser matters we have missed. It is so even as concerns glories terrestrial when compared amongst themselves: home mountains and lakes may lightly be ignored by one who sets foot in Switzerland. How beyond all comparison does any comparison appear when terrestrial glories are set against celestial !

11. Thou art worthy, O Lord, to receive glory and honour and power; for Thou hast created all things, and for Thy pleasure they are and were created.

If in the present context we are allowed to view this majestic circle of crowned and enthroned Elders, with these multiform Living Creatures in their midst, as a representative compendium of creation, then we see and hear the universe justifying the ways of God. For they proclaim not solely "Holy, Holy, Holy," but also: "Thou art worthy, O Lord, to receive glory and honour and power: for Thou hast created all things, and for Thy pleasure they are and were created."

It is not at all times and in all places that *we* could as yet thus praise our Maker, except on trust and by an effort of love-illuminated faith. But courage ! our difficulty will end with this present distress, if we nerve ourselves to quit us like men and be strong.

Meanwhile it does indeed require a loving faith, trust, courage, to praise God for every creature. For every criminal, every ignorant soul, every child being trained to evil ; for some whose life seems well-nigh into'erable, for some whose death seems desperate. "Save me, O God : for the waters are come in, even unto my soul. I stick fast in the deep mire, where no ground is : I am come into deep waters, so that the floods run over me. I am weary of crying ; my throat is dry : my sight faileth me for waiting so long upon my God."

[Parenthetical, and to be skipped by all who please.—Just now I have been told an incident which is readily transformed into a parable.

Three newts and three frogs were sent up from Scotland. On being unpacked in London, two of the newts vanished forthwith from sight and were lost. Of the three frogs, one on being taken in hand croaked, moving to sympathy the heart of its captor. Humanity dictated that the remnant newt and all the frogs should be carried forth and manumitted at a neighbouring ornamental water; which was done. The fate of that newt and of one frog I do not know. Of the other two, one ensconced itself in a pipe; the second was then and there devoured by a duck. Who would have guessed that a frog born in Argyleshire would die in London?

Even if I fail to express my point to others, to myself there is something suggestive in the anecdote, reported (as I believe) with tolerable accuracy. The two vanishing newts presumably aimed at getting out of harm's way, while in reality by eluding powerful hands they cut themselves off from rescue. Their peers which (however perforce) faced apparent peril, may have attained safety,—except, indeed, for the final catastrophe of the one frog: but even this was a natural, not a monstrous, end for such as it. Nor shall the risk of being laughed at prevent my remarking that the croak of the helpless frog, yet not helpless because of that very faculty of helpless appeal lodged in it, sets before me much higher images.

We know on the highest Authority that not one sparrow is overlooked. " Are ye not much better than they ? "]

Ah Lord, Lord, if my heart were right with Thine
  As Thine with mine, then should I rest resigned
  Awaiting knowledge with a quiet mind
Because of heavenly wisdom's anodyne.
Then would Thy Love be more to me than wine,
  Then should I seek being sure at length to find,
  Then should I trust to Thee all humankind
Because Thy Love of them is more than mine.
Then should I stir up hope and comfort me
  Remembering Thy Cradle and Thy Cross ;
  How Heaven to Thee without us had been loss,
    How Heaven with us is Thy one only Heaven,
  Heaven shared with us through all eternity,
    With us long sought, long loved, and much forgiven.

" Thou hast created all things, and for Thy pleasure they are and were created."—If I would explain to my own comprehension how this can be : "all things, and for Thy pleasure they are,"—I should not succeed. Everything may have a bright side, everything may be a vehicle or a channel of good, or an imperfect form of good, or defective good, or good-excessive ; everything, except sin. Thus pain, suffering, privation, death may be good-producers. Wickedness alone, even should it be overruled to promote good, wickedness remains and must remain evil. The existence of evil silences me. I cannot understand; I can only trust : God, for Christ's sake, help me to trust.

Nevertheless for practical purposes all is clear as day. All things are and were created for the Divine good pleasure. Therefore I for one am capable of pleasing God, and it becomes me strenuously and gladly so to do. Because He hath no pleasure in the death of him that dieth, it becomes me to turn myself and live ; nor in wickedness, therefore must I cease to do evil and learn to do well ; nor in mere natural endowments (*see* Ps. cxlvii. 10), therefore I must sue out graces ; nor in "fools," therefore I must endeavour to get wisdom, and with all my getting to get understanding ; nor in sordid service (*see* Mal. i. 10), therefore I ought in spirit, and if it were possible even in the letter, to "fear God for nought."

I am bound myself to please God in the manner He appoints. I am not bound to account for His Will and pleasure at large.

"O Lord, let it be Thy pleasure to deliver me : make haste, O Lord, to help me. . . . Let all those that seek Thee be joyful and glad in Thee : and let such as love Thy salvation say alway, The Lord be praised."

CHAPTER V.

1. And I saw in the right hand of Him that sat on the Throne a book written within and on the backside, sealed with seven seals.

"In the Right Hand,"—the Hand of blessing. Whatever the import of the revelation, its being revealed is so far our blessing. He who warns desires to spare: as said Manoah's wife: "If the Lord were pleased to kill us, . . . neither would He have showed us all these things, nor would as at this time have told us such things as these";—or much more as the Lord Himself answered His prophet Habakkuk: "Write the vision, and make it plain upon tables, that he may run that readeth it."

O God most Merciful, Who warnedst even a generation of vipers to flee from the wrath to come, quicken us to bring forth fruits meet for repentance. We plead Jesus, only Jesus.

"Length of days is in her right hand; and in her left hand riches and honour." Thus Wisdom fills both her hands with blessings: yet I think a difference may be discernible between the twain.

By length of days may surely be understood life everlasting in accordance with David's words: "The King shall joy in Thy strength, O Lord; and in Thy salvation how greatly shall He rejoice! Thou hast given Him His heart's desire, and hast not withholden the request of His lips. . . . He asked life of Thee, and Thou gavest it Him, even length of days for ever and ever."

Solomon, whose gracious outset prefigured our Lord's fulness of grace, asked for himself "an understanding heart," and was answered: "Because thou hast asked this thing, and hast not asked for thyself long life; neither hast asked riches for thyself, nor hast asked the life of thine enemies; but hast asked for thyself understanding to discern judgment; behold I have done according to thy words: lo, I have given thee a wise and an understanding heart. . . . And I have also given thee that which thou hast not asked, both riches, and honour. . . . And if thou wilt walk in My ways, to keep My statutes and My commandments, as thy father David did walk, then I will lengthen thy days."

Thus Solomon's dutiful choice of a regal understanding heart won for him not simply the boon craved, but with it riches and honour, gifts of the left hand; which gifts correspond so far with that sunlight and rain which we see lavished on just and unjust, that they all alike come down from the Father of lights, and are all alike capable of promoting God's glory and man's salvation; while yet no one of them is guaranteed against such dire misuse as may pervert it into a means of destruction. Length of days, the gift statedly of the right hand, is promised to Solomon for nothing short of persevering obedience : wherefore we may understand thereby much more than even the most prolonged walk in this vain shadow.

Are we beset by shadows? Let us resolutely *walk* in them : for by sitting down we should fail ever to emerge from them.

Shadows to-day, while shadows show God's Will.
　　Light were not good except He sent us light.
　　Shadows to-day, because this day is night
Whose marvels and whose mysteries fulfil
Their course and deep in darkness serve Him still.
　　Thou dim aurora, on the extremest height
　　Of airy summits wax not over bright ;
Refrain thy rose, refrain thy daffodil.
Until God's Word go forth to kindle thee
　　And garland thee and bid thee stoop to us,
　　　Blush in the heavenly choirs and glance not down :
　　　To-day we race in darkness for a crown,
　　In darkness for beatitude to be,
　　In darkness for the city luminous.

" A book written within and on the backside, sealed with seven seals."—A book sealed, inscrutable : evidently containing a message, but that message withheld. Yet does it deliver a message by reason of that very withholding. St. John understood readily a call to humility, and wept (ver. 4) for his own and for the general unworthiness. Humility and penitence befitted St. John, and befit all the saints his fellows : it is the reckless sinners who act contrariwise, as at a former crisis was made clear to the prophet Isaiah : " In that day did the Lord God of Hosts call to weeping, and to mourning, and to baldness, and to girding with sackcloth : and behold joy and gladness, slaying oxen, and killing sheep, eating flesh, and drinking wine : let us eat and drink ; for to-morrow we shall die. And it was revealed in mine ears by the Lord of hosts, Surely this iniquity shall not be purged from you till ye die, saith the Lord God of hosts."

To humble ourselves, to repent, to stand alert at the rumour of a Divine message, such acts as these lie within our own power; acts whereby we all can please God. And if nothing further become possible to us, then surely even at such a point we shall not miss a blessing. "For My thoughts are not your thoughts, neither are your ways My ways, saith the Lord. For as the heavens are higher than the earth, so are My ways higher than your ways, and My thoughts than your thoughts. For as the rain cometh down, and the snow from heaven, and returneth not thither, but watereth the earth, and maketh it bring forth and bud, that it may give seed to the sower, and bread to the eater : so shall My word be that goeth forth out of My mouth : it shall not return unto Me void, but it shall accomplish that which I please, and it shall prosper in the thing whereto I sent it."

One whose memory I revere once suggested to me that if a person, not through any voluntary fault, knew no more than the Name of Jesus : that Name alone, beloved and cherished, might by God's grace suffice to salvation.

O God Only Wise, bless to us, I beseech Thee, all we know and all we know not. Grant us a ready mind; and accept us according to what we have and not according to what we have not, in our Lord Jesus Christ our All in all.

"Sealed with seven seals."—"There is nothing covered, that shall not be revealed ; and hid, that shall not be known." Lord, grant us sevenfold grace.

2. **And I saw a strong angel proclaiming with a loud voice, Who is worthy to open the book, and to loose the seals thereof?**

3. **And no man in heaven, nor in earth, neither under the earth, was able to open the book, neither to look thereon.**

4. **And I wept much, because no man was found worthy to open and to read the book, neither to look thereon.**

A question in form, in result a proclamation. He who proclaims is strong, but what he proclaims is a general weakness whence he himself is not exempt.

Since we read in the Prophecy of Daniel of "the man Gabriel," and in the Gospels and Book of Acts of *men* where it seems we must recognize *angels ;* so I suppose that here we may perhaps understand all creatures from human beings upwards to be intimated by "men" of heaven, earth, under the earth; and notably mankind at large whether living or dead.

Whereupon St. John wept. Wherefore? because the Book remained sealed and closed? He says not so, but because "no man was found worthy" to open, read, look. For saints bewail unworthiness rather than the penalty of unworthiness.

O Lord Jesus, Who on earth didst shed unselfish vicarious tears, and Who hast bestowed on us a treasure of tears; grant that we may never squander these goodly pearls on vanities, but may weep such blessed tears as Thou hast promised Thyself to wipe away.

"Who is worthy . . .?"—The solution was forthcoming, only not at once.

This world nowadays resounds with questions not yet answerable. I suppose an idiot might happen to propound a query, which not Solomon himself could then and there in his wisdom have answered. Among the first things which meet us when, following St. John afar off, we look through the "door opened in heaven," is a question left for the moment without an answer.

Heaven endured such discipline, and well may earth : St. John endured it, and well may I. "Trust in the Lord with all thine heart; and lean not unto thine own understanding."

Good Lord, Who requirest faith of us; if our faith be too weak to encounter doubtful disputations, I beseech Thee so far strengthen it that by Thy grace we may humbly avoid them.

O Lord Jesus, my Lord Jesus, Thou art Light to our darkness, Knowledge for our ignorance, Wisdom for our folly, Certainty for our doubts. Thou art our Way and our End; the Illumination of our way, the Glory of our end. Never shall we see, know, have, enjoy, aught permanent out of Thee; but in Thee (please God!) all : for whoso is one with Thee cannot but see with Thine Eyes, acquiesce in Thy Will, apprehend by Thine Understanding, possess by Thy Lordship, enjoy in Thy Good-pleasure. Yea, even while swaddled as babes in fleshly bands, Thy faithful servants being already joined to Thee, do already latently and potentially behold, know, choose, inherit, keep festival. The vigil of Thy Feast excels the high days of time; the threshold of Thy House, the presence-chamber of earth's palaces : "I had rather be a door-keeper in the house of my God, than to dwell in the tents of ungodliness." Or if as yet it be not thus with any, with me, Lord, make it thus to be with us all before we go hence and be no more seen. Amen.

5. And one of the elders saith unto me, Weep not: behold, the Lion of the tribe of Juda, the Root of David, hath prevailed to open the book, and to loose the seven seals thereof.

" One of the Elders."—Conjectured (I believe) by some to be St. James, own brother to St. John. What however we know with certainty of this beatified Elder is not his name, but his Christ-likeness. As once his Master on earth, so now he in heaven saith, " Weep not."

Jesus spake the word to a sonless mother in whom (reverent be the thought!) He may have contemplated a fore-image of His own blessed Mother in her bereavement.

The sympathetic Elder spake the same word to the appointed " son " of that blessed Mother, to a saint the days of whose mourning were not yet ended.

Jesus the Consolation of Israel spake, and it was done.

Pointing to Him, the Elder became a son of consolation.

Christ-likeness is the salient characteristic revealed to us of this celestial Elder. His name continues hidden, his previous history hidden : we know not, however we may attempt to guess, wherefore he rather than another was inspired to testify.

Would his name avail us aught, or his previous history, or even light cast on the secret of his predestination to that particular ministry ? We may safely conclude not, since they are unrevealed. Hidden they serve to check curiosity ; whilst in a manner they illustrate that the one and only aspect high or low need desire to be known by is Christ-likeness. Thus the saints are stamped, thereby they become recognizable ; and this is that accessible glory which we can if we will in common with them put on.

I saw a Saint.—How canst thou tell that he
Thou sawest was a Saint ?—
I saw one like to Christ so luminously
By patient deeds of love, his mortal taint
Seemed made his groundwork for humility.

And when he marked me downcast utterly
Where foul I sat and faint,
Then more than ever Christ-like kindled he ;
And welcomed me as I had been a saint,
Tenderly stooping low to comfort me.

Christ bade him, "Do thou likewise." Wherefore he
  Waxed zealous to acquaint
His soul with sin and sorrow, if so be
  He might retrieve some latent saint :—
"Lo, I, with the child God hath given to me!"

"Behold."—Commanded to behold, let us behold. The command is simple, the act of obedience simple.

Obedience will bring its own reward, for by obeying we shall presently contemplate Christ. We shall discern Him at work for us men and for our salvation, opening the book and loosing the seven seals thereof.

But if after all we cannot decipher the unsealed revelation?

We still shall have gazed on Him Who is the Author of the revelation : and Greater is He Who reveals than aught else which is revealed.

Lord Jésus, Who art Wisdom and the Word and Whose Name is called Wonderful ; whatever word be too hard for us, yet vouchsafe to us the wisdom hidden in that word. For Thine own sake, O God, Thou that doest wonders and declarest Thy strength.

"The Lion of the tribe of Juda."—Some if not all of the Jewish tribes derived, it would seem, their standard or coat-of-arms from the form of their father Jacob's blessing differently bestowed upon each. Jacob said : " Judah is a lion's whelp : from the prey, my son, thou art gone up : he stooped down, he couched as a lion, and as an old lion ; who shall rouse him up ? "

Therefore as the standard led the tribe, so this title "Lion of the tribe of Juda" denotes our Lord as Leader and Commander to the people. In the Song of Songs we read : " My Beloved is . . . the Chiefest among ten thousand," literally " Standard-bearer among ten thousand " : our omen of victory ; for never will it befall us " as when a standard-bearer fainteth."

" For thus hath the Lord spoken unto me, Like as the lion and the young lion roaring on his prey, when a multitude of shepherds is called forth against him, he will not be afraid of their voice, nor abase himself for the noise of them : so shall the Lord of hosts come down to fight for Mount Zion, and for the hill thereof."

And whereas in a prophecy of Redemption and Salvation we read : " When the enemy shall come in like a flood, the Spirit of the Lord shall lift up a standard against him,"—this same title Lion of the tribe of Juda seems to connect itself pointedly with the sacred Humanity of Jesus, according to those words of the Angel Gabriel instructing blessed Mary: "The Holy Ghost shall come upon thee, and the power of the Highest shall overshadow thee: therefore also that Holy Thing which shall be born of thee shall be called the Son of God."

"And on the east side toward the rising of the sun shall they of the standard of the camp of Judah pitch throughout their armies." Thus Judah of old by encamping toward the east prefigured the camp of Christ's faithful soldiers; in harmony with His declaration Who being the Light of the world said: "He that doeth truth cometh to the light, that his deeds may be made manifest, that they are wrought in God."

The disciple is called to be as his Master, the servant as his Lord. Because Christ is strong His Church likewise must wax strong. "Behold, the people shall rise up as a great lion, and lift up himself as a young lion: he shall not lie down until he eat of the prey, and drink the blood of the slain . . . He couched, he lay down as a lion, and as a great lion: who shall stir him up?" "The righteous are bold as a lion."

Yet let us not forget the terror also of this great Name of God. Even holy Job complains: "Thou huntest me as a fierce lion." Hosea in the Divine Name prophesies against Israel: "I will be unto Ephraim as a lion, and as a young lion to the house of Judah: I, even I, will tear and go away; I will take away, and none shall rescue him";—"I will be unto them as a lion: . . . there will I devour them like a lion."

"The lion hath roared, who will not fear?"

Lord, give me blessed fear
　And much more blessed love,
　That fearing I may love Thee here
　And be Thy harmless dove:

Until Thou cast out fear,
　Until Thou perfect love,
　Until Thou end mine exile here
　And fetch Thee home Thy dove.

"The Root of David."—It pleased our Lord on one occasion to propound a question touching the mystery of His relationship to David, without at the same time vouchsafing the answer:—

"While the Pharisees were gathered together, Jesus asked them, saying, What think ye of Christ? Whose Son is He? They say unto Him, The Son of David. He saith unto them, How then doth David in spirit call Him Lord, saying, The Lord said unto my Lord, Sit Thou on My right hand, till I make Thine enemies Thy footstool? If David then call Him Lord, how is He his Son?"

Lord, grant us receptive minds: and teach us by Thy Most Holy Spirit knowledge if Thou pleasest, and wisdom whereby to please Thee.

"In the beginning was the Word, and the Word was with God, and the Word was God. . . . All things were made by Him; and without Him was not anything made that was made."—If all things, then David.

The root is that which affords origin, stability, maintenance, to the plant. Root may exist without shoot, not shoot without root. The root supplies, the shoot receives, life and nourishment. The unseen root is the source and basis of all the luxuriant upgrowth. "What hast thou that thou didst not receive?"

"Hath prevailed."—The Revised Version substitutes "overcome" for "prevailed"; by that word reminding us how our own Lord has made Himself our Fellow. He Himself overcame before He bade His Seven Churches overcome. "Follow Me" is His word; not, Precede Me. "When He putteth forth His own sheep, He goeth before them."

Christ goes before us, leading us gently and encouraging us along the same path He long ago trod. When He saith, Do this, bear this, He has already done and borne much more for our sakes and in our stead. We peer into the valley of humiliation, and He goeth before us into Galilee. We gaze up the arduous ascent of perfection, and how beautiful upon the mountains are His feet!

By analogy:—to urge any one to suffer patiently, entails on the speaker, unless suffering be already in some measure his portion, the duty of assuming such fellowship of suffering as may justify urgency and avert scandal. Thus in penitentiary work, in reformatory work, self-denial must teach self-denial, and self-restraint, self-restraint. Otherwise, how flatter myself that my righteousness exceeds that of the Pharisees? "For they bind heavy burdens and grievous to be borne, and lay them on men's shoulders; but they themselves will not move them with one of their fingers."

An exemplary Sister speaking once of her Sister Superior in their common Order of Mercy, described that Superior's authority as exercised in postponing herself to her subordinates. To engross disadvantages was that Wise Virgin's form of coveting earnestly the best gifts.

"To open the Book, and to loose the seven seals thereof."—

Christ openeth, and no man shutteth. Our own eyes we can indeed shut, and can stop our ears; but we within radius of the Gospel cannot so cut ourselves off from revelation as to take up the position of heathens. Israel of old could not do so: "That which cometh into your mind shall not be at all, that ye say, We will be as the heathen, as the families of the countries, to serve wood and stone. As I live, saith the Lord God, surely with a mighty hand, and with a stretched out arm, and with fury poured out, will I rule over you." Neither afterwards could Israel by denying and rejecting their Messiah face to face revert to the position of their stiff-necked forefathers; for our Lord Himself declared: "If I had not come and spoken unto them, they had not had sin: but now they have no cloke for their sin."

Whether in great matters or small, whether for good or evil, done is done and cannot become not-done. A word may be retracted, but not recalled. A living soul once born must live or die, for it can never be dis-born. Eve could not unknow her foul knowledge, or Adam unchoose his ruinous choice.

And how many of their children in the anguish of inextinguishable existence have been ready to cry out: "Woe is me, my mother, that thou hast borne me!"

"Except the Lord keep the city, the watchman waketh but in vain."

O Lord Christ, Who hast said, Take heed what ye hear, how ye hear: give us grace to cast all our care on Thee Who carest for us.

Because Thou hast called us, give us grace to obey Thy call.

Because Thou showest us wonderful things in Thy Righteousness, give us grace to worship Thee trembling.

Because they that fear Thee lack nothing, give us grace to fear Thee.

Because they who seek Thee shall want no manner of thing that is good, give us grace to seek Thee until we find Thee.

Because Thou lovest them that love Thee, give us grace to love Thee.

Because Thou hast loved them that loved Thee not, give us grace to love Thee. Amen.

Hope is the counterpoise of fear
While night enthralls us here.

Fear hath a startled eye that holds a tear:
Hope hath an upward glance, for dawn draws near
With sunshine and with cheer.
Fear gazing earthwards spies a bier;

And sets herself to rear
A lamentable tomb, where leaves drop sere
Bleaching to congruous skeletons austere :
Hope chants a funeral hymn so sweet and clear
He seems true chanticleer
Of resurrection and of all things dear
In the oncoming endless year.

Fear ballasts hope, hope buoys up fear,
And both befit us here.

" And to loose the seven seals thereof."—" He shall deliver
thee in six troubles : yea, in seven there shall no evil touch
thee. In famine He shall redeem thee from death : and in
war from the power of the sword. . . . Neither shalt thou be
afraid of destruction when it cometh."

6. **And I beheld, and lo, in the midst of the Throne and of
the four beasts, and in the midst of the elders, stood a
Lamb as it had been slain, having seven horns and
seven eyes, which are the seven Spirits of God sent
forth into all the earth.**

If the preceding chapter (IV.) unfolds a vision of the Creator
surrounded and worshipped by His creation, this present
chapter appears more particularly to set before us in vision the
Redeemer, always well pleasing to God His Father, and to
Whom is given all power in Heaven and in earth.

Doubtless a thread of perfect sequence runs throughout
Divine Revelation, binding it into one sacred and flawless
whole. But not so do feeble eyes discern it. I can but study
piece by piece, word by word, unworthy even to behold the
little I seem to observe.

Much of this awful Apocalypse opens to my apprehension
rather a series of aspects than any one defined and certified
object. It summons me to watch and pray and give thanks;
it urges me to climb heavenward. Its thread doubtless consists
unbroken : but my clue is at the best woven of broken lights
and shadows, here a little and there a little. As when years
ago I abode some while within sight of a massive sea rock, I
used to see it put on different appearances : it seemed to float
baseless in air, its summit vanished in cloud, it displayed upon
its surface varied markings, it passed from view altogether in a
mist, it fronted me distinct and solid far into the luminous
northern summer night, still appearing many and various while
all the time I knew it to be one and the same,—so now this
Apocalypse I know to be one congruous, harmonious whole,
yet can I read it only as it were in disjointed portions, some to

myself inexplicable, some not unmistakably defined ; all nevertheless, please God, profitable to me for doctrine, for reproof,
for correction, for instruction in righteousness.

" Lo, in the midst of the Throne and of the four beasts, and
in the midst of the elders."—As the centre whence all proceeds, whither all converges. So St. Paul writes to the
Ephesians: " The Father of Glory . . . according to the
working of His mighty power, which He wrought in Christ,
when He raised Him from the dead, and set Him at His own
Right Hand in the heavenly places, far above all principality,
and power, and might, and dominion, and every name that
is named, not only in this world, but also in that which is to
come : and hath put all things under His feet, and gave Him
to be the Head over all things to the Church, which is His
body, the fulness of Him that filleth all in all."

Lord Jesus, lovely and pleasant art Thou in Thy high places,
Thou Centre of bliss, whence all bliss flows. Lovely also and
pleasant wast Thou in Thy lowly tabernacles, Thou sometime
Centre wherein humiliations and sorrows met.

Thou Who wast Centre of a stable, with two saints and harmless cattle and
some shepherds for Thy court,
Grant us lowliness.
Thou Who wast Centre of Bethlehem when Wise Men worshipped Thee,
Grant us wisdom.
Thou Who wast Centre of the Temple, with doves or young pigeons and
four saints about Thee,
Grant us purity.
Thou Who wast Centre of Egypt which harboured Thee and Thine in exile,
Be Thou our refuge.
Thou Who wast Centre of Nazareth where Thou wast brought up,
Sanctify our homes.
Thou Who wast Centre of all waters at Thy Baptism in the River Jordan,
Still sanctify water to the mystical washing away of sin.
Thou Who wast Centre of all desolate places during forty days and forty
nights,
Comfort the desolate.
Thou Who wast Centre of a marriage feast at Cana,
Bless our rejoicing.
Thou Who wast Centre of a funeral procession at Nain,
Bless our mourning.
Thou Who wast Centre of Samaria as Thou sattest on the well,
Bring back strayed souls.
Thou Who wast Centre of all heights on the Mount of Beatitudes,
Grant us to sit with Thee in heavenly places.
Thou Who wast Centre of sufferers by the Pool of Bethesda,
Heal us.
Thou Who was Centre of all harvest ground when Thou wentest through
the cornfields with Thy disciples,
Make us bring forth to Thee thirty, sixty, a hundredfold.

Thou Who wast Centre of mankind when Thou calledst unto Thee whom
  Thou wouldest,
> Grant us grace to obey Thy call.

Thou Who wast Centre of love in the Upper Chamber,
> Evermore give us that Bread.

Thou Who wast Centre of sorrows in Gethsemane,
> Console the sorrowful.

Thou Who wast Centre of the whole earth on Calvary,
> Reign over north and south, east and west.

Thou Who wast Centre of Life in Thy Sepulchre,
> Forget not our dust.

Remember us and ours, remember all, O our All in all.

Lord, remember us when Thou comest into Thy Kingdom. Amen.

"Stood a Lamb as it had been slain."—"Behold the Lamb
of God, which taketh away the sin of the world. . . . Behold
the Lamb of God!"

Not otherwise even in heaven than "as It had been slain."
Death will be abolished, pain over, tears wiped away, weakness
reinforced, loss made good, failure retrieved : these are remedi-
able, and will be remedied. No spot or blemish, wrinkle or
any such thing, will appear there. There all glories will con-
gregate : and glorious among glories will be the wounds made
by love. Now it is blessed to believe without seeing : then
blessed will it be to see what unseen we have believed. Then
wilt Thou show to Thine own with loving praise, what once
Thou showedst to St. Thomas with loving rebuke. Then shall
Thine own love Thee because, being all fair, Thou art also
"white and ruddy." And if they Thee, wilt Thou not likewise love them for their wounds made by love? Yea, all from
Thy most glorious martyrs downwards, who have been partakers
of Thy sufferings "more ruddy in body than rubies," Thou
wilt love.

> None other Lamb, none other Name,
>   None other Hope in heaven or earth or sea,
> None other Hiding-place from guilt and shame,
>   None beside Thee.
>
> My faith burns low, my hope burns low,
>   Only my heart's desire cries out in me
> By the deep thunder of its want and woe,
>   Cries out to Thee.
>
> Lord, Thou art Life tho' I be dead,
>   Love's Fire Thou art however cold I be :
> Nor heaven have I, nor place to lay my head,
>   Nor home, but Thee.

A lamb is a sort of personified innocence by reason of its

whiteness, its meek expression, its pathetic voice. Its curly softness suggests that by rights innocence is allied to comfort and cheerfulness. How beautiful is a lamb in green pastures beside still waters! In the natural course of events a lamb would grow old, and not till then would it die : a lamb would not naturally die as a lamb. Yet from ancient days lambs of sacrifice, by God's behest, have so far as in them lay taken the place of men, women, children, and been brought to the slaughter. Truly a lamb is to us a picture and memento of Divine Love.

"O Lamb of God : that takest away the sins of the world ;

"Grant us Thy peace.

"O Lamb of God : that takest away the sins of the world ;

"Have mercy upon us.

"O Christ, hear us."

It was once pointed out to me, that in the Bible the first mention of a lamb occurs in connection with Abraham's virtual sacrifice of Isaac : "Isaac spake unto Abraham his father, and said, My father : and he said, Here am I, my son. And he said, Behold the fire and the wood : but where is the lamb for a burnt offering? And Abraham said, My son, God will provide Himself a lamb for a burnt offering." And I think the observation is essentially correct, despite the "seven ewe lambs" of the preceding chapter ; inasmuch as these do not belong (so to say) to the same spiritual context. Yet, had I been aware of both texts, I should not (in *Seek and Find*) without a modifying clause have referred to Isaac's words as absolutely *first*.

[Which oversight invites me to two wholesome proceedings : to beg my reader's pardon for my errors ; and ever to write modestly under correction.]

"Having seven horns and seven eyes, which are the Seven Spirits of God sent forth into all the earth."—*Seven*, a number of completeness : *the horn*, a symbol of strength. Even during His Ministry, Christ deigned to announce the might of His inherent power : "I lay down My life, that I might take it again. No man taketh it from Me, but I lay it down of Myself. I have power to lay it down, and I have power to take it again."

If the "seven horns" may seem to indicate an attribute, the "Seven Eyes, which are the Seven Spirits of God," appear to show forth that Unutterable Sevenfold Spirit, Who being Very God proceedeth from the Father and the Son ; and Who having once vouchsafed amid audible and visible signs to be

M

"sent forth into all the earth" on the supreme Day of Pentecost, abides in and with the Church for ever.   That in sevenfold plenitude He should rest upon Christ "the Branch",
Isaiah prophesied, adding: ". . . and. shall make Him of
quick understanding in the fear of the Lord : and He shall not
judge after the sight of His eyes, neither reprove after the·
hearing of His ears"; the human faculties being, according to
the Hebrew Prophet, subordinated to that Divine Spirit Who
in St. John's present vision appears (if I dare so think) under
the figure of Seven Eyes.   Our Lord became "One Christ
. . . by taking of the Manhood into God": those two
Natures are His; and only those two, so far as Revelation
teaches.   Moreover we are expressly certified that "He took
not on Him the nature of angels": whence (if lawfully I may)
I infer that, on the evidence of the Apocalyptic text in question,
the "Seven Spirits of God" here named cannot be created
spirits, cannot but be the Creator Spirit.

Two prophecies of Zechariah without anticipating St. John's
vision seem to harmonize with it : "Hear now, O Joshua the
high priest, thou, and thy fellows, that sit before thee : . . .
behold, I will bring forth My Servant the BRANCH.   For
behold the stone that I have laid before Joshua; upon one
stone shall be seven eyes : behold, I will engrave the graving
thereof, saith the Lord of hosts, and I will remove the iniquity
of that land in one day" :—"Not by might, nor by power,
but by My Spirit, saith the Lord of hosts.   Who art thou, O
great mountain? before Zerubbabel thou shalt become a plain :
and he shall bring forth the headstone thereof with shoutings,
crying, Grace, grace unto it. . . .   The hands of Zerubbabel
have laid the foundation of this house; his hands shall also
finish it; and thou shalt know· that the Lord of hosts hath
sent me unto you.   For who hath despised the day of small
things? for they shall rejoice, and shall see the plummet in
the hand of Zerubbabel with those seven; they are the eyes
of the Lord, which run to and fro through the whole earth."

"Canst thou by searching find out God? canst thou find
out the Almighty unto perfection?"—Nay, my Master, I think
not to do so.   Yet hath it ere now pleased Thee to choose
and work by foolish things, weak things, base things, things
which are despised, yea, and things which are not.   That
which I know not, and which Thou requirest me to know,·
teach Thou me.   And teaching me, make me so far like
Jacob when he awaked out of sleep, that I too may say,
"Surely the Lord is in this place; and I knew it not": and

may fear, saying, " How dreadful is this place ! this is none
other but the House of God, and this is the Gate of Heaven " :
and may confess the munificence of Thy bounty, humbling
myself and saying, " I am not worthy of the least of all the
mercies, and of all the truth, which Thou hast showed unto
Thy servant."

**7. And He came and took the Book out of the Right Hand
of Him that sat upon the Throne.**

" For there is One God, and one Mediator between God
and men, the Man Christ Jesus ; Who gave Himself a ransom
for all." " For the Father judgeth no man, but hath committed all judgment unto the Son." " Jesus . . . spake . . .
saying, All power is given unto Me in heaven and in earth."

**8. And when He had taken the Book, the four beasts and
four and twenty elders fell down before the Lamb,
having every one of them harps, and golden vials full
of odours, which are the prayers of saints.**

As in the previous chapter, God the Creator, so now God
the Redeemer is Centre of worship to them that are round
about Him. God is very greatly to be feared and had in
reverence of all saints always ; yet now we seem to behold
these citizens and peers of Heaven carried away by a sudden
rapture of adoring love, a celestial ecstasy of satisfaction. If
the four Living Creatures be the Cherubim, the Song (vers. 9,
10) which speaks of Redemption becomes mysterious in their
mouths, unless we adopt the words of the Revised Version.
Or might we conceive the elders alone to have sung it ?

By considering them all, under whatever aspect, let us in
any case learn to aspire. Would we have it said of ourselves
to-day, or would we not far rather it were said of us to-morrow,
" It is not the voice of them that shout for mastery, neither is
it the voice of them that cry for being overcome : but the
noise of them that sing do I hear " ? We cannot in this life sit
at ease and make merry, eat, drink, and to-morrow die ; and
then on the morrow after sing a triumph song. Wherefore
blessed are those who now shout for mastery. Blessed are
even those who now cry for being overcome, if only they cry
to day while it is called to-day to Him that heareth prayer.

My God, give us grace to weep and lament while the world
rejoiceth, and in the end turn Thou our sorrow into joy. Give
us such present comfort in conforming our will to Thine that
we may have our songs in the night, songs of desire, songs of

hope. Give us, when day breaks and shadows flee away, songs of joy and love. Give us, and deny us what Thou wilt. For our Lord Jesu's sake. Amen.

Heavenly worship is fulness of joy and pleasures for evermore.

Earthly worship is too often a constraint and weariness.

Amongst the causes of this depressing difference certain appear to be removable, others not so. Some of the heavenly conditions of worship abide beyond our attainment, some are imitable. Presumably to assimilate the two systems of worship so far as feasible, might be a step secured towards informing the ritual of earth with the significance and sentiment of Heaven.

1. The Living Creatures from the midst of the Throne, and from round about the Throne, the Elders from their proper thrones, fall down. We, not in the midst, but afar off; we not on thrones, but more duly in dust and ashes, we are many times hampered by sloth or by false shame. Yet he alone "that overcometh" tempter, besetment, self, is he who can claim the promise to be set down in Christ's Throne at last.

Sloth and false shame, good Lord, overcome in us.

2. They have harps, worshipping the Lord in the beauty of holiness, the perfection of beauty. We, remote from such glories too often, neither do our best, nor bring our best. Yet of old such as we have been forewarned: "Cursed be the deceiver, which hath in his flock a male, and voweth, and sacrificeth unto the Lord a corrupt thing."

Hypocrisy, irreverence, a sacrilegious spirit, good Lord, cast out of us.

3. They have golden vials full of odours which are the prayers of saints. We in vessels of clay bring prayers of sinners, prayers mixed with sin, prayers (please God) mixed with tears.

Our tears in Thy bottle, our prayers in Thine own censer, good Lord, accept and make acceptable. Amen.

Whoso hath anguish is not dead in sin,
  Whoso hath pangs of utterless desire.
  Like as in smouldering flax which harbours fire,—
Red heat of conflagration may begin,
Melt that hard heart, burn out the dross within,
  Permeate with glory the new man entire,
  Crown him with fire, mould for his hands a lyre
Of fiery strings to sound with those who win.
Anguish is anguish, yet potential bliss,
  Pangs of desire are birth-throes of delight :
  Those citizens felt such who walk in white,

And meet but no more sunder with a kiss ;
Who fathom still unfathomed mysteries,
And love, adore, rejoice, with all their might.

Lord, make alms to be the golden vials of our prayer, and
the blessing of him that was ready to perish its upbearing
odours ; and let melody to Thee in our hearts be our harp,
with bands of love for its strings ; and exalt our present lowliness to become the step of our future throne ; and now grant
us grace to do what we can, that then Thou mayest empower
us to do what Thou wilt. Lord, for Thine own sake. Lord
Jesus, for the glory of Thy name. Amen.

The joy of Saints, like incense turned to fire
In golden censers, soars acceptable ;
And high their heavenly hallelujahs swell
Desirous still with still-fulfilled desire.
Sweet thrill the harpstrings of the heavenly choir,
Most sweet their voice while love is all they tell,
Where love is all in all, and all is well ;
Because their work is love and love their hire.
All clad in white and all with palm in hand,
Crowns too they have of gold and thrones of gold ;
The street is golden which their feet have trod,
Or on a sea of glass and fire they stand :
And none of them is young, and none is old,
Except as perfect by the will of God.

9 And they sung a new song, saying, Thou art worthy to
take the Book, and to open the seals thereof : for Thou
wast slain, and hast redeemed us to God by Thy blood
out of every kindred, and tongue, and people, and
nation ;

10. And hast made us unto our God kings and priests : and
we shall reign on the earth.

The Revised Version renders this Song of Praise somewhat
differently : " Worthy art Thou to take the Book, and to open
the seals thereof : for Thou wast slain, and didst purchase
unto God with Thy blood men of every tribe, and tongue,
and people, and nation, and madest them to be unto our God
a kingdom and priests ; and they reign upon the earth."

According to the first reading the blessed choir praise God
for their own lot : according to the second, apparently for the
lot of others. Wide the difference !

Nay, rather let us learn hence that it is only earthly narrow-
ness which insists on such difference as wide. Heavenly
large-heartedness seems scarcely to know *me* from *thee*, but
in its measure reflects the Mind of Christ when He said : " All

Mine are Thine, and Thine are Mine; and I am glorified in them." By Whose Divine grace St. Paul antedates final perfection for his Corinthian flock, when he writes: "That there should be no schism in the body; but that the members should have the same care one for another. And whether one member suffer, all the members suffer with it; or one member be honoured, all the members rejoice with it."

So that if, being "the body of Christ, and members in particular," we still rejoice not in the common joy, assuredly we are straitened not in Him but in ourselves.

"And they sung a new song."—The Church Militant is ever looking for new heavens and a new earth, wherein dwelleth righteousness. Under the sun there is nothing new: of mortal man himself it is written, "That which hath been is named already, and it is known that it is man"; and even concerning fierce searching individual temptation, St. Paul seems to imply a general rule when he writes to his Corinthian converts, "There hath no temptation taken you but such as is common to man."

Yet human instinct craves after something new; if not for a new pleasure, at least for a new sensation. And sanctified human instinct sets its hope above the sun: and while contentedly walking in the old paths of daily duty and reiterated discipline, knowing that for to-day the old is better; yet waits and hastens forward to be renewed, and strengthened to sustain a new perfection, where the Church Triumphant sings "a new song."

"It shall be one day which shall be known to the Lord, not day, nor night."

Lord Jesus, by Thy grace and gracious Will I will have my pearls not here, but new there for entrance gates; and my gold not here, but new there for a footway; and my jewels not here, but new there for garnishing; and my song not here, but new there for Thy praise; and my joy not here, but new there for Thy visible Presence. Amen.

> My heart is yearning :
> Behold my yearning heart ;
> And stoop low to satisfy
> Its lonely beseeching cry,
> For Thou its fulness art.
>
> Turn, as once turning
> Thou didst behold Thy Saint
> In deadly extremity ;
> Didst look, and win back to Thee
> His will frighted and faint.

Kindle my burning
From Thine unkindled Fire ;
Fill me with gifts and with grace
That I may behold Thy Face,
For Thee I desire.

My heart is yearning,
Yearning and thrilling thro'
For Thy Love mine own of old,
For Thy Love unknown untold,
Ever old, ever new.

"Thou art worthy to take the book, and to open the seals thereof: for Thou wast slain, and hast redeemed us to God by Thy Blood."—Our dear Lord is indeed everything to us. Here He stands before us altogether lovely both as our Redeemer and as our Example.

(Because Thy Love hath sought me,
All mine is Thine and Thine is mine :
Because Thy Blood hath bought me,
I will not be mine own but Thine.

I lift my heart to Thy Heart,
Thy Heart sole resting-place for mine :
Shall Thy Heart crave for my heart,
And shall not mine crave back for Thine ?)

But wherein our *Example?* Herein, I think.

He Who opens to mortal ken that Book of overwhelming judgments, mighty marvels, joys inconceivable, is the Same Who first tested by experience our wants and capacities, our strength and weakness. Well may He know whereof we are made Who assumed our flesh ; and remember that we are but dust Who, though it was not possible for Him to see corruption, lay down in a grave. He Who speaks to us is one of ourselves, infinitely above us indeed, yet none the less on our level ; incomparably unlike, yet essentially like us. He is in sympathy with us, He loves us, He has sacrificed Himself for us.

Any of us then who being older or better taught or placed by Providence on any other vantage ground, are called upon to educate or guide a neighbour ; as Aquila and Priscilla were promoted to instruct the highly-gifted zealous Apollos,—any of us so empowered may here learn from our Master opening the Sealed Book what graces ought to adorn us while exercising our privilege : sympathy, love, on occasion self-sacrifice.

We learn this, inasmuch as Christ Himself is here acclaimed "worthy" to unfold God's dealings, because ("for") He was slain and redeemed us to God by His Blood.

Lord Jesus Merciful and Patient, grant us grace, I beseech Thee, ever to teach in a teachable spirit; learning along with those we teach, and learning from them whenever Thou so pleasest. Word of God, speak to us, speak by us, what Thou wilt. Wisdom of God, instruct us, instruct by us if and whom Thou wilt. Eternal Truth, reveal Thyself to us, reveal Thyself by us in whatsoever measure Thou wilt.

"It is written in the prophets, And they shall be all taught of God."

Lord Jesus, the price of my Redemption was Thy Blood, Thy Life. Help me to love Thee.

> O Lord God, hear the silence of each soul,
>   Its cry unutterable of ruth and shame,
>   Its voicelessness of self-contempt and blame :
> Nor suffer harp and palm and aureole
> Of multitudes who praise Thee at the goal,
>   To set aside Thy poor and blind and lame ;
>   Nor blazing Seraphs utterly to outflame
> The spark that flies up from each earthly coal.
> My price Thy priceless Blood ; and therefore I
>   Price of Thy priceless Blood am precious so
>   That good things love me in their love of Thee :
>   I comprehend not why Thou lovedst me
> With Thy so mighty Love ; but this I know,
> No man hath greater love than thus to die.

"Hast redeemed us to God."—"What? know ye not that your body is the temple of the Holy Ghost which is in you, which ye have of God, and ye are not your own? For ye are bought with a price: therefore glorify God in your body, and in your spirit, which are God's."

Let not the thing formed say to Him that formed it, Why hast Thou made me thus?—It pleased Christ to redeem us whole, whence we know that our whole being is capable of serving God acceptably. Our body, our soul, our spirit, all are His and endowed for His service.

The body is a burden. "The corruptible body presseth down the soul, and the earthly tabernacle weigheth down the mind that museth upon many things." But for it we should escape aches, pains, death: this is its least and lowest burdensomeness. But for it we should abide impervious to sundry temptations, and not merely impervious but absolutely irrespective of them : this is an incalculable augment of its burden. Moreover we are certified that flesh and blood cannot inherit the Kingdom of God : so that after lifelong toil and trouble in cherishing and disciplining this burdensome body, it must be "changed" before man can arrive at perfection.

But Thou, Lord Christ, didst bear a heavier burden for our sake, even our guilt: a burden incapable of salutary discipline; intolerable to us who incurred it, and were it possible (as it would seem) all but intolerable to Thee. Thus didst Thou for us, for me. Love bore Thy burden which was mine: love, Thou sustaining me, shall bear my burden which is my own.

And since it is "to God" that we are redeemed, our very dust may well be dear in our own sight as it is in His.

"Out of every kindred, and tongue, and people, and nation." —Kindred, tongue, people, nation, will not (it appears) be obliterated from the Communion of Saints. Since in that blessed company similarities and varieties will alike become bonds of affection, motives of sympathy, we see as in a glass what they should even now already be to us who are militant here on earth. For earth holds heaven in the bud; our perfection there has to be developed out of our imperfection here; neither in heaven nor on earth, neither to-day nor to-morrow, neither by God nor by man, will grapes be gathered of thorns, or figs of thistles.

By grace love of kindred learns to embrace the whole human family. Language discriminates into groups; whilst speech, man's universal heritage, by grace brings home to our hearts the world-width of brotherhood. By grace the concentrated, I dwell among mine own people, expands until we also say with delighted welcome, Thy people shall be my people. By grace nations become bound and welded together in the unifying Presence of God (*see* Zech. viii. 20—23).

By grace; but not by nature. Now even kindred often lack warmth, tongues make discord, peoples encroach on one another, nations learn and practise war.—Lord, forgive and help us.

A lesson against antipathies. Every kindred, every tongue, every people, every nation, promises to be represented there and associate there: French with Germans, Italians with Austrians, English with Irish, whites with blacks, all ranks with all ranks, all men with all men,—an alarum against antipathies!

Saints are ready to receive all sinners: all sinners are not ready to receive saints. Abraham doubtless would have received into his bosom Dives his "son" as well as Lazarus: it was Dives who having held aloof from Lazarus in one world, was set down still more aloof from him in the other.

Much of earth will find no entrance into heaven. Not

sin alone: things which here have been allowable, inevitable, even expedient, will yet have to perish in the using.

To cling tenaciously to such as these is disproportionate, to cling passionately is idolatrous. God, Who alone can, help us to refrain our soul and keep it low like as a child that is weaned from his mother.

. Meanwhile,—if what I dwell upon, picture to myself, turn to, crave after, am overjoyed at possessing or acquiring, cannot be comforted in lacking or losing, be after all no more than something which must perish in the using; my own words condemn me.

From worshipping and serving the creature more than the Creator; from
striving to serve two masters;
Deliver us, Lord Jesus.
From laying up treasure for ourselves without being rich toward God;
from laying up treasures on earth and not in heaven;
Deliver us, Lord Jesus.
From building on the sand and not on the rock; from gaining though it
were the whole world and losing our own soul;
Deliver us, Lord Jesus.
From cleaving to anything apart from Thee; from loving anything in-
compatible with Thee;
Deliver us, Lord Jesus.
Until the day break and the shadows flee away; until we awake up after
Thy likeness and are satisfied therewith;
Deliver us, Lord Jesus. Amen and Amen.

They throng from the east and the west,
The north and the south with a song;
To golden abodes of their rest
They throng.

Eternity stretches out long:
Time, brief at its worst or its best,
Will quit them of ruin and wrong.

A rainbow aloft for their crest,
A palm for their weakness made strong!
As doves breast all winds to their nest,
They throng.

"And hast made us unto our God kings and priests."—Christ the King of kings hath kings for subjects; Christ the High Priest for ever hath priests for ministers; kings and priests unto His Father and our Father, unto His God and our God. Peaceable kings, infallible priests.

Lord, give us grace to seek peace and ensue it, holding fast Thy truth in a pure conscience; to serve Thee meekly on earth, gloriously in heaven, well pleasingly now and for ever-more. For our Redeemer's sake. Amen.

"And we shall reign on the earth."—Now, a trial ; then, a
reward. Now all earthly thrones are so far like King Herod's
that from them, as from the basest seat, one single step leads
to worms and corruption. Now earthly crowns are indeed of
gold and precious stones but, like one of yore, load as it were
a talent's weight on the head of the wearer. Not so the far
more exceeding and eternal weight of glory awaiting the better
life in Christ's triumphant kingdom. Thrones not precarious,
crowns not burdensome, in an universal peace : Ephraim no
more envying Judah, nor Judah vexing Ephraim.

**11. And I beheld, and I heard the voice of many angels
round about the Throne and the beasts and the elders :
and the number of them was ten thousand times ten
thousand, and thousands of thousands ;**

Thought fails before "the number of them" : no simile, no
symbol, conveys it to me. I suppose if every single thing I
have ever looked upon had been an Angel, yet all together
they might not sum up "the number of the fourth part" of
that celestial holy nation. Around the Throne and the Living
Creatures and the Elders they form a ring more glorious than
of fiery opals, they form a garland more lovely than of roses.

How know I that they are lovely and glorious?—I a sinner
know it, because certified that they have never sinned. Created
loveliness and lustre can be defaced by sin only. Every faithfully good creature abides in its degree as a mirror of God.

I dwell hopefully and aspiringly on the assurance that man
having been made a little lower than the Angels will one day
be made equal to them. But who are mounting to such
promotion? Not I, if I grudge them their present exceeding
highness,—if I would lower superiority to my baseness, instead
of by help of grace ascending to its level,—if wincing under
inferiority I rankle against excellence. David exhorts us not
to fret ourselves because of evil-doers : alas ! he writes not
down to the standard of those who fret themselves because of
the upright.

Lord Jesus, Who for love of us wast once made a little lower
than Thine own Angels ; make us, I pray Thee, for love of Thee
sacrificers of self, delighters in goodness, companions of all
who fear Thee : lest we should never see Thee as Thou art,
nor have part and lot with Thee.

"Round about."—In heavenly assemblies to encircle is as it
were to embrace, to embrace is to love. Created love finite
although unnumbered embraces its Creator, while abiding

within the Everlasting Arms which above, around, underneath, hold it in the embrace of Infinite Uncreated Love.

Lord God Almighty, suffer us not to withdraw from the embrace of Thy Love. Thy Love our consolation, Thy strong Love our safeguard, we sorely need. For oftentimes our contrarieties chill human love, leaving us lonely as sparrow on housetop, owl in desert, pelican in wilderness. Lord of Patience and Consolation, deign to fetch us back out of the loneliness of our perversity into meek charity with all. Then will our desolation not be wholly desolate, though we bear the reproach of our youth alone with Thee and keeping silence. For Jesus Christ's sake, ever Patient. Amen.

12. Saying with a loud voice, **Worthy is the Lamb that was slain to receive power, and riches, and wisdom, and strength, and honour, and glory, and blessing.**

"Saying."—The Elders *sang*, the Angels *say*. Throughout this Book of Revelation it is invariably (if I mistake not) the redeemed who sing. Nor elsewhere in Holy Scripture do I recall any mention of angelic songs; unless we except "The morning stars sang together," or "Sing, O ye heavens . . . Sing, O heavens." Yet who can think of Angels and not associate them with heavenly harmonies? Perhaps their speech is song.

The Angels render glory to the Lamb inasmuch as He was slain. Unlike the elders they say not wherefore, but are content simply to ascribe to Him all worthiness. They form the outer ring, others the inner. Thus standing without, they worship Him for gifts which He receives haply for others rather than for them. It is enough for them to fulfil His commandments, hearken unto the voice of His words, do His pleasure. As friends of the Bridegroom they stand without, rejoicing greatly because of the Bridegroom's voice : this their joy therefore is fulfilled.

In unselfed ecstasy they exult in that which is another man's, thereby glorifying God with that which is their own. Exalted on so eminent a pinnacle of the Temple they stand firm and cast not themselves down.

What grace sustains them? Greater grace than is lavished on us?

Grace does its natural work in upholding the upright: its supernatural work (if I may so say) in upraising the fallen. *This* it does for us, *that* for them.

O Lord their God and ours, while Thou wilt and to whatso-

ever point Thou wilt make Thy holy Angels excel and shame
us by gifts and glories: only let not Thy grace multiplied
towards ourselves bear in us less fruit of love. For Jesus
Christ's sake, slain for us. Amen.

Lord Jesus, Who wert pleased to live for us; make us
righteous: to die for us; make us holy: to rise again for us;
make us glorious.

God the Son once of free will assumed the form of a servant,
therefore and for evermore is He worthy of power,—once for
our sakes He became poor, therefore of riches,—once He
thought as a child, therefore of wisdom,—once He was slain
through weakness, therefore of strength,—once He endured the
Cross, therefore of glory,—once, yea many times He was
contradicted, reviled, blasphemed, therefore of blessing.

As Son of God these were always His in plenitude of perfection. As Son of Man He earned and receives them: for
Himself, but not for Himself alone; for Himself as Head of
mankind, for mankind as His members.

We must be congruous members of our Divine Head if we
desire to share His beatitude; we must tread the same steps if
we aspire to the same goal. Wherefore to serve becomes a
privilege; to lack, an endowment; to think simply, a profitable
exercise; to be sensible of weakness, a safeguard; to undergo
shame, a medicine; to endure provocations, a stimulus to
prayer.

This reverses the world's judgment; but the world and its
lust are to pass away.

> The world,—what a world, ah me!
> Mouldy, wormeaten, grey:
> Vain as a leaf from a tree,
> As a fading day,
> As veriest vanity,
> As the froth and the spray
> Of the hollow-billowed sea,
> As what was and shall not be,
> As what is and passes away.

**13. And every creature which is in heaven, and on the earth,
and under the earth, and such as are in the sea, and
all that are in them, heard I saying, Blessing, and
honour, and glory, and power, be unto Him that
sitteth upon the Throne, and unto the Lamb for ever
and ever.**

Absolute unanimity amongst all creatures. Though one
have more, another less, all swell the hymn of unalloyed,

unabated triumph. If stones also are crying out, it is not because any in heaven or on earth hold their peace : if those who still draw mortal breath speak, they supersede not voices from under the earth and from the sea. The present heaven and present earth must pass away, but meanwhile they praise God : the sea must be no more to morrow, yet to-day it magnifies its Maker.

Since all Holy Scriptures are written for our learning, this thirteenth verse cannot but be meet for us to ponder over. And it strikes me that whoever conscientiously and unflinchingly puts and keeps himself in harmony with this text, must find that for practical purposes even predestination itself is shorn of difficulties and terrors. For here we behold things transitory in company with things permanent uplifting praises : the former utilizing for praise the only time they have ; the latter for identical praise anticipating the eternity which awaits them. This is to take our Master at His word when He said : "Take therefore no thought for the morrow : for the morrow shall take thought for the things of itself." This is with Job to hold fast integrity come what may. This is with Shadrach, Meshach, and Abed-nego to silence the adversary : "O Nebuchadnezzar, we are not careful to answer thee in this matter. If it be so, our God Whom we serve is able to deliver us from the burning fiery furnace, and He will deliver us out of thine hand, O king. But if not, be it known unto thee, O king, that we will not serve thy gods, nor worship the golden image which thou hast set up."

"Go thou thy way till the end be."

For "power" the Revised Version substitutes "dominion," thereby recalling very pointedly our risen Lord's words to the eleven ; in which passage the Authorized Version again uses "power," which the Revised Version replaces by "authority" : —"All power is given unto Me in heaven and in earth. Go ye therefore, and teach all nations . . . and, lo, I am with you alway, even unto the end of the world."

"Unto Him that sitteth upon the throne, and unto the Lamb."—Lord Jesus, as Thou with the Eternal Father and the Eternal Spirit art One in Thy Godhead, deign, I pray Thee, to be One with Them in our humble apprehension and love ; that we may believe and feel that there is One Lord, One God, One Love, wherein to repose our hearts, souls, spirits. Amen.

"For ever and ever."—The Greek words (*see* margin of Revised Version) mean literally "unto the ages of the ages." This seems to condescend to our rooted habit of computation, measurement, estimate. An age we can realize : an age of ages (where each year is represented by an age?) we can in some sort imagine : and the vague undefined plural number conveys to us endlessness. Yet (if it be not irreverent to think so) I fancy that to some "for ever and ever," or, as I suppose one might equally express it, "for always and always," might appear if not more like *endlessness* yet to be more like *eternity*, if such a distinction may be assumed : because eternity having neither beginning nor middle nor end, seems to exhibit duration without sequence.

But in this passage where "unto the ages of the ages" is the phrase actually employed, I observe its adaptation to the matter in hand. All creatures, having had a beginning, speak in character if speaking with a birthright sense of time. And the Eternal Son of God, to Whom as Lamb of God the praise is addressed, had under that aspect even He Himself likewise a beginning: "When the fulness of the time was come, God sent forth His Son, made of a woman, made under the law, to redeem them that were under the law, that we might receive the adoption of sons."

> Voices from above and from beneath,
>   Voices of creation near and far,
> Voices out of life and out of death,
>   Out of measureless space,
>   Sun, moon, star,
>   In oneness of contentment offering praise.
>
> Heaven and earth and sea jubilant,
>   Jubilant all things that dwell therein ;
> Filled to fullest overflow they chant,
>   Still roll onward, swell,
>   Still begin,
>   Never flagging praise interminable.
>
> Thou who must fall silent in a while,
>   Chant thy sweetest, gladdest best at once ;
> Sun thyself to-day, keep peace and smile ;
>   By love upward send
>   Orisons,
>   Accounting love thy lot and love thine end.

14. And the four beasts said, Amen. And the four and twenty elders fell down and worshipped Him that liveth for ever and ever.

These Living Creatures which appear as if in some sort a compendium of animated nature, answer "Amen"—itself a summing up of praise. The Throne whereon He sitteth Who judgeth right, answers by their voice "Amen" to all His decrees and to all which He permits. Strength in the "Lion," acceptableness in the "Calf," intelligence in the "Man," loftiness in the "Eagle," every good gift and every perfect gift answers "Amen," to the praise and glory of the Father of Lights whence they came down.

Amen, O Lord : "dust to dust" also ascribeth to Thee glory. From the ends of the earth, from a heart in heaviness, from a "mouth in the dust" by foretaste of death, glory be to God on high, through Jesus Christ our Lord.   Amen.

We who have no door set open before us into visible Heaven, may yet look in with St. John's eyes.   And if with his heart as well as with his eyes, then shall we too be rapt into celestial regions and among harmonies superhuman.   With Elders our spirits may already fall prostrate in worship, with Living Creatures our wills may at once and for ever answer Amen.

Amen, which signifies both *So it is* and *So be it.*   God for Jesus' sake grant us grace now and for evermore to answer Amen to His perfect Will and Ways.

CHAPTER VI.

1. And I saw when the Lamb opened one of the seals, and I heard as it were the noise of thunder, one of the four beasts saying, Come and see.

He who had been redeemed by the Blood of the Lamb, he in whose stead Christ had died, he whom Jesus loved, "saw when the Lamb opened one of the seals." What that Wise Master and Gracious Lord did St. John could endure to behold, however awful, terrible, overwhelming in the result. He could endure because he was beloved and because he loved.

Lord, me also Thou hast redeemed by Thy Blood, in my stead also Thou hast died, me also Thou lovest (for which sinner hast Thou not loved?) ; yet I exceedingly fear and quake lest I should fall away. Thou hast not ceased to be my Wise Master and my Gracious Lord ; Thou lovest as Thou hast ever loved ; alas, it is I who love not as St. John loved.

Son of God, have mercy upon us. O Lord, let Thy mercy be showered upon us. O Lord, have mercy upon us ; have mercy upon us.

> Love still is Love, and doeth all things well,
> Whether he show me heaven or hell,
> > Or earth in her decay
> > Passing away
> > On a day.
>
> Love still is Love, tho' He should say, " Depart,"
> And break my incorrigible heart,
> > And set me out of sight
> > Widowed of light
> > In the night.
>
> Love still is Love, is Love, if He should say,
> " Come " on that uttermost dread day ,
> > " Come " unto very me,
> > " Come where I be,
> > Come and see."

Love still is Love, whatever comes to pass :
O Only Love, make me Thy glass,
    Thy pleasure to fulfil
      By loving still
      Come what will.

"Opened one of the seals."—Not the whole seven at once ; not forthwith to recompense all, or to make an end of all consuming as in a moment. Rather as it were remonstrating with mankind again and again : " The day of the Lord is great and very terrible ; and who can abide it ? Therefore also now, saith the Lord, turn ye even to Me with all your heart,"—and saying especially concerning the elect, as of old concerning Israel : " In measure when it shooteth forth, Thou wilt debate with it : He stayeth His rough wind in the day of the east wind."

So the waters of the Deluge mounted stage by stage, affording time not for the bitterness of death only, but also (please God !) for the salutary bitterness of repentance in sight of death.

O Merciful Redeemer, grant us repentance early in the morning, repentance at the third hour, at the sixth hour, at the ninth hour. O Most Merciful Saviour, grant us repentance at the eleventh hour ; grant us the eleventh hour for repentance. According to Thy Mercy saving us, Thou Who hast died our death and paid our penalty.

" As it were the noise of thunder."—That is, as appears, the voice of one of the Living Creatures. If we may assume that these speak in the order in which they are first named, then this thunderous voice appertains to him of the leonine aspect, with whom such a sound seems congruous. I have read how the natural lion setting his face toward the ground utters a tre- mendous reverberant roar far reaching and appalling : this celestial " Lion " now sets his face earthwards and summons all within hearing to " Come and see." For surely his word is not to St. John exclusively, but through him to us upon whom the ends of the world are come.

But if those four " Living Creatures " rest not day and night, saying, " Holy, Holy, Holy, Lord God Almighty, Which Was, and Is, and Is to come " : how is it that one after another they now say " Come and see " ? Perhaps partly to show us that charitable work interrupts not the flow of adoration. [Yet in such a case I must not be rash to utter anything with my mouth : for these are problems of heaven, while I am upon earth ; therefore should my words be few.]

O Lord, Who hast proclaimed by Thy servant, " Come and

see," blessed is the man whom Thou choosest and receivest unto Thee. Show us, I beseech Thee, wonderful things in Thy righteousness, O God of our salvation : Thou that art the hope of all the ends of the earth. For Jesus Christ's sake. Amen.

St. Paul has written: "Let the woman learn in silence with all subjection. But I suffer not a woman to teach." Yet elsewhere he wrote : "I call to remembrance the unfeigned faith . . . which dwelt first in thy grandmother Lois, and thy mother Eunice."

To expound prophecy lies of course beyond my power, and not within my wish. But the symbolic forms of prophecy being set before all eyes, must be so set for some purpose : to investigate them may not make us wise as serpents ; yet ought by promoting faith, fear, hope, love, to aid in making us harmless as doves. "Write the vision, and make it plain upon tables, that he may run that readeth it" :—God helping us, we all great and small can and will run.

A commentator I have turned to explains the remainder of this chapter as referring to the establishment on earth of Christ's Kingdom, and to successive events in the history of imperial ‛Rome. But since in Holy Scripture personage after personage, crisis after crisis, judgment after judgment, becomes at various points typical of some greater personage, crisis, judgment, thereafter to be looked for : I venture to trust that throughout this Book of Revelations underlying or parallel with the primary meaning, is often discernible a further signification which may be unfolded to us even while the other continues occult.

Nor surely need an ignorant man be accounted any great loser (so long as ignorance be his misfortune, not his fault) if Bible history becomes less his chronicle of individuals and nations than his parable of Christ and mankind. Abel will speak better things than ever when he is lost sight of in Christ. Isaac will be glorified when by his submission to death Christ is manifested and remembered. Moses will be sufficed when the Prophet like unto him supersedes him. Melchizedek and Aaron will vanish gloriously when by them Christ stands revealed : so David before his Son and Lord : so Solomon before the Sole Builder and Maker. The Paschal Lamb, the Scapegoat, will have fulfilled their end when they lead a worshipper to Christ : the Day of Atonement will avail him to whom it shadows forth Good Friday. The Deluge engulfing the old world, the eternal fire of the Cities of the plain, the fall of Jericho, of Assyria, of Babylon, the rejection of ancient Israel, will make wise unto salvation him to whom they bring home the final Day of account; and who with condemned Achan gives God the glory, and with ruined Manasseh betakes himself to penitence and prayer.

Glory be to Thee O God, with Whom are the treasures of wisdom and knowledge, and Who impartest to every man severally as Thou wilt. Glory be to Thee in the Church by Christ Jesus for ever and ever.

2. And I saw, and behold a white horse: and He that sat on him had a bow; and a crown was given unto Him: and He went forth conquering, and to conquer.

This verse, having been interpreted of our Blessed Lord and of the outset of His Gospel, harmonizes with the Psalmist's apostrophe: "Gird Thy sword upon Thy thigh, O Most Mighty, with Thy glory and Thy majesty. And in Thy majesty ride prosperously because of truth and meekness and righteousness; and Thy right hand shall teach Thee terrible things. Thine arrows are sharp in the heart of the King's enemies; whereby the people fall under Thee." Elisha also prophesied victory to Israel, in the words: "The arrow of the Lord's deliverance"; thus suggesting a type of this vision.

The horse (agent or vehicle of the rider) is white, the sign of innocence; showing how above His fellows our Lord is He Who, never doing evil that good may come, works by pure unmixed good to a good end. Horses were allowed only under restriction to ancient Israel; but now we see one advanced to signal honour; and are thus reminded that all things whereby they can serve God are lawful to Christians, who must not call any such creature common or unclean. The bow recalls to us the paternal blessing of Joseph, himself a hero of purity and eminent type of Christ: "Joseph is a fruitful bough, even a fruitful bough by a well: whose branches run over the wall: the archers have sorely grieved him, and shot at him, and hated him: but his bow abode in strength, and the arms of his hands were made strong by the hands of the Mighty God of Jacob; (from thence is the Shepherd, the stone of Israel:) even by the God of thy father, Who shall help thee; and by the Almighty, Who shall bless thee with blessings of heaven above, blessings of the deep that lieth under, blessings of the breasts, and of the womb: the blessings of thy father have prevailed above the blessings of my progenitors unto the utmost bound of the everlasting hills: they shall be on the head of Joseph, and on the crown of the head of him that was separate from his brethren." And again Job's protest of integrity which exhibits him also as a type of Christ, by its mention of diadem (though here the word is crown) and bow accords with the present vision: " When the ear heard me, then it blessed me; and when the eye saw me, it gave witness to me : because I delivered the poor that cried, and the fatherless, and him that had none to help him. The blessing of him that was ready to perish came upon me : and I caused the widow's heart to sing for joy. I put on righteousness, and it clothed me : my judgment was as a robe and a diadem. I was eyes to the blind, and feet was I to the lame. I was a father to the poor : and the cause which I knew not I searched out. And I brake the jaws of the wicked, and plucked the spoil out of his teeth . . . My glory was fresh in me, and my bow was renewed in my hand."

" And a crown was given unto Him."—Christ is the Priest Whose Self-oblation has found acceptance, the Captain Whose arm has brought salvation to His followers : " put the holy crown upon the mitre." This Crown *given* appears to be not the inalienable Crown of Supreme Divine Majesty, but rather the Crown of reinstated Human Royalty awarded by God to Man. It is the Crown of the only One born of woman Who in absolute perfection has striven lawfully and run well. It is the Mediatorial Crown honoured in heaven and on earth.

But receiveth He no Crown except from God ? Yes, verily. " Go forth, O ye daughters of Zion, and behold King Solomon with the crown wherewith his mother crowned him in the day of his espousals, and in the day of the gladness of his heart." Redeemed humanity crowns her beloved Son and Champion as her King for ever. Christ being God and Man is constituted between God and men the indissoluble link on whom descend blessings of heaven above, to Whom ascend blessings of the deep that lieth under, blessings unto the utmost bound of the everlasting hills.

Moreover inspired wisdom teaches us that " a virtuous woman is a crown to her husband." Which suggests that in the Mystical Marriage between Christ and the Church (whereof each earthly marriage is emblematic) the Bride is " crown " to the Bridegroom, accounted by His love not disgrace or drawback, but dignity and complement. " How great is His Goodness, and how great is His Beauty ! "

" But she that maketh ashamed is as rottenness in his bones." For not only do all the members in the One Body influence each other, but even the Divine head is honoured or dishonoured by them.   Christ keep us, keep me, from being " as rottenness."

Lord, of Whom a certain young man worshipping Thee once asked, What lack I yet?—we now worshipping Thee are bold rather to ask, What lackest Thou? Inasmuch as Thou hast said, Give Me thy heart: Lord, only grant us grace to give our hearts to Thee; and hold Thou them fast.   Then in Thy good pleasure shall we lack nothing.

"And He went forth conquering and to conquer."—Experience attests *conquering:* faith protests *and to conquer.*   Experience bears noble witness; but faith yet more noble, meets God as it were half-way and becomes His herald.

Experience follows and gives thanks; faith precedes and offers praise.   Experience keeps pace with time; faith outstripping time forestalls eternity.

Faith is the Elias of virtues, girt up and running before her advancing King.   Faith is the St. John Baptist of graces, her joy fulfilled without sight.

> Faith and Hope are wings to Love,
> Silver wings to golden dove.

Wings bear the bird heavenward: the bird animates, impels, directs the wings.

Bird without wings might do something: wings without bird could do nothing.

"And now abideth faith, hope, charity, these three; but the greatest of these is charity."

> Experience bows a sweet contented face,
>   Still setting to her seal that God is true:
>   Beneath the sun, she knows, is nothing new;
> All things that go return with measured pace,
> Winds, rivers, man's still recommencing race:—
>   While Hope beyond earth's circle strains her view,
>   Past sun and moon and rain and rainbow too,
> Enamoured of unseen eternal grace.
> Experience saith, "My God doth all things well";
>   And for the morrow taketh little care,
>   Such peace and patience garrison her soul:—
>   While Hope who never yet hath eyed the goal,
>   With arms flung forth and backward floating hair
> Touches, embraces, hugs the invisible.

This Who goeth forth conquering and to conquer is He, " Whose goings forth have been from of old, from everlasting." Before there was any to resist His Will He went forth to bless in the lovely work of creation.   He went forth for His own sake and for His creature's sake,

But evil having marred all, He again went forth for His own sake and for ours conquering and to conquer. He went forth from heaven to Bethlehem, from Jerusalem to Calvary without the gate, from the Sepulchre by way of Olivet back to Heaven. As He went He conquered sin and death for us, and then sat down on the Right Hand of the Majesty on High.

Now once more He goes forth, for us indeed but also with us one by one, to conquer sin and death in each separate human soul. He conquers with us; He offers not to conquer without us. "He hath showed thee, O man, what is good."

Neither has it pleased Him to conquer the heathen for His inheritance without the co-operation of their elder brethren in Christ. Some Christians are called to become literal Evangelists, and every Christian is at the least a minor missionary: example preaches more powerfully than words, intercession converts as mightily as sermons, alms supply the sinews of that war whose weapons are not carnal.

If all our forefathers had preached adequately by word and by example, wrestled in intercession, invested liberally in alms, spent themselves in missionary enterprise or at least in missionary zeal, doubtless Christ would have gone forth mightily with them to annex nations and races. It might have come to pass as Isaiah records : " The isles saw it, and feared ; the ends of the earth were afraid, drew near, and came. They helped every one his neighbour; and every one said to his brother, Be of good courage."

If our forefathers had then lived worthy of their vocation, thus it might have been. If we their children will now live worthy of ours, thus it yet may be.

A cowardly Christian shrinking from martyrdom risks suicide.

A scandalous Christian is Satan's right hand to strengthen evil.

An inconsistent Christian is his left hand to weaken good.

My God, Thou Who seest, knowest, siftest souls: how dare I look elsewhere and not within for cowardice, scandal, inconsistency, while Thou takest account of me and understandest me altogether?

Thou Who knowest me, be merciful unto me and correct me.

Thou Who knowest all, be merciful unto all and perfect us.

Amen, Gracious Lord Jesus, Amen.

3. And when He had opened the second seal, I heard the second beast say, Come and see.

The second living Creature resembled a Calf, one of the animals devoted to sacrifice, and thus an emblem of mercy. He summons St. John to contemplate an awful vision, as it would seem a mighty scourge sent in judgment. Yet is it mercy that gives the call, even while the sight is appalling to flesh and blood.

God in wrath remembers mercy.

Lord Jesus, while we tremble at Thy wrath, uphold us to confide in Thy mercy : for they that hope in Thee shall not be ashamed.

4. And there went out another horse that was red : and power was given to him that sat thereon to take peace from the earth, and that they should kill one another : and there was given unto him a great sword.

Red, the tint of blood ; the horse and his rider seem an impersonation of bloodshed. Our comfort is that the power was *given* and the great sword *given ;* recalling our Lord's own word to Pilate : "Thou couldest have no power at all against Me, except it were given thee from above."

Moreover, all follows : nothing now can precede, any more than it ever could outrun, our Saviour. Whatever Red Sea we are passing through or have still to pass, He has passed through it before us : even He Who in vision was beheld as red in His apparel when He made the depths of the sea a way for the ransomed to pass over.

Is there any peace under that domination ordained " to take peace from the earth "?　There remains that peace which the world neither gives nor takes away. Nothing happens irrespective of God's Will ; no sword can be unsheathed, unless He first have said : " Sword, go through the land."

Once too our Lord declared : " I came not to send peace, but a sword." Yet a sword of Christ's sending brings peace when welcomed for His sake and faced in His strength. Or even though the sword be Satan's sword, yet to ourselves it will become the sword of the Lord if whilst being slain we trust in Him.

But alas ! for those who "kill one another" filling up the measure of their fathers. Haman brought enlargement and great joy to captive Israel, nevertheless he with his sons miserably perished.

It is no part of duty to call that small which the Voice of Inspiration calls great. " Great " is the sword predicted : great must be the Church's searchings of heart if she would

be prepared with weapons not carnal to cope with and overcome that sword. Of yore " for the divisions of Reuben there
were great searchings of heart " : we too have shameful
divisions to our incalculable loss and hindrance, and woe is us
if we undergo not proportionate self-searchings. "Let us
search and try our ways, and turn again to the Lord. Let us
lift up our heart with our hands unto God in the heavens."

"If a kingdom be divided against itself, that kingdom
cannot stand. And if a house be divided against itself, that
house cannot stand."

> Such is Love, it comforts in extremity ;
> Tho' a tempest rage around and rage above,
> Tempest beyond tempest far as eye can see :
> Such is Love,
>
> That it simply heeds its mourning inward Dove,
> Dove which craves contented for a home to be
> Set amid the myrtles or an olive grove.
>
> Dove-eyed Love contemplates the Twelve-fruited Tree,
> Marks the bowing palms which worship as they move ;
> Simply sayeth, simply prayeth, "All for me !"
> Such is Love.

**5. And when He had opened the third seal, I heard the
third beast say, Come and see. And I beheld, and
lo a black horse ; and he that sat on him had a pair of
balances in his hand.**

The third Living Creature exhibiting "a face as a man"
summons his human brother (and with him humankind at
large) to view the black horse and his rider. If the Calf may
be interpreted as symbolizing Divine Compassion, the Man
suggests (in this context) an embodiment if not of human yet
still of fellow-creaturely sympathy.

If it becomes celestial creatures not of our blood to concern
themselves for us ; surely we ourselves of one common stock,
one common family, should plan and pray and yearn over each
other. The coming scourge has been interpreted as chastising
man not directly in his spiritual nature, but through the flesh.
For the black horse and his rider are viewed as a figure of
famine.

Behold a funeral traversing earth ! "And they shall pass
through it, hardly bestead and hungry : and it shall come to pass
that when they shall be hungry, they shall fret themselves, . . .
and look upward. And they shall look unto the earth ; and

behold trouble and darkness, dimness of anguish; and they shall be driven to darkness."

Famine: yet not absolute foodlessness; else, why the pair of balances?

But first let us note these Balances, the established insignia of Justice. Injustice never has a voice in the counsels of Providence: Justice always, except when silenced by Mercy. Which Mercy, whilst to us sinners gratuitous, is yet Justice and not Mercy to Him Who has taken our place, paid our penalty, made good our deficiency; even to Christ. To Whom be all gratitude, praise, love, for ever and ever.

To resume. The balances suggest scarcity short of literal nullity: hunger, but not necessarily starvation. Scarcity imposes frugality, exactness; a gathering up of fragments, with thanksgiving because there remain fragments to gather. No waste, latitude, margin; no self-pampering can be tolerated, but only a sustained self-denial: self must be stinted, selfishness starved, to give to him that needeth.

And as the poor never cease out of the land and are in various degrees standing representatives of famine, this self-stinting seems after all to be the rule and standard of right living; not a desperate exceptional resource, but a regular, continual, plain duty.

When the pinch of famine comes they will be prepared to bear it who already for charity's sake have learned and practised to suffer hunger. They who have kept the Fast of God's choosing by dealing their bread to the hungry will even in extremity know Whom they have trusted: "Although the fig tree shall not blossom, neither shall fruit be in the vines; the labour of the olive shall fail, and the fields shall yield no meat; the flock shall be cut off from the fold, and there shall be no herd in the stalls: yet I will rejoice in the Lord, I will joy in the God of my salvation."

"BECAUSE HE FIRST LOVED US."

I was hungry, and Thou feddest me;
  Yea, Thou gavest drink to slake my thirst:
O Lord, what love gift can I offer Thee
  Who hast loved me first?—

Feed My hungry brethren for My sake;
  Give them drink, for love of them and Me:
Love them as I loved thee, when Bread I brake
  In pure love of thee.—

Yea, Lord, I will serve them by Thy grace ;
  Love Thee, seek Thee, in them ; wait and pray :
Yet would I love Thyself, Lord, face to face,
  Heart to heart, one day.—

Let to-day fulfil its daily task,
  Fill thy heart and hand to them and Me :
To-morrow thou shalt ask, and shalt not ask
  Half I keep for thee.

God accepts dues as gifts.   Man receives gifts as dues.

An eminent physician once told me that there are people who would benefit in health by fasting : a secondary motive, yet surely not an unlawful one.   To perform a duty from a motive which is not wrong, may prove a step towards performing it from the motive which is right.   To leave it unperformed seems the last contrivance adapted to result in its performance.

6. And I heard a voice in the midst of the four beasts say, A measure of wheat for a penny, and three measures of barley for a penny ; and see thou hurt not the oil and the wine.

Whatever historical circumstances may here be indicated, the "Voice" which from the midst of the four Living Creatures speaks authoritatively, tempering judgment with mercy, may safely be listened to by us as the Divine Voice : for the Living Creatures are described as in the midst of the Throne and round about the Throne, and He is set in the Throne that judgeth right.

Discipline therefore, not inevitable destruction, may be confidently looked for, except we be reprobate : at the utmost "the destruction of the flesh, that the spirit may be saved in the day of the Lord Jesus."

A parable and prophecy of such severe tenderness was ages before vouchsafed through the Prophet Hosea : "Then said the Lord unto me, Go yet, love a woman beloved of her friend, yet an adulteress, according to the love of the Lord toward the children of Israel, who look to other gods, and love flagons of wine.   So I bought her to me for fifteen pieces of silver, and for an homer of barley, and an half homer of barley : and I said unto her, Thou shalt abide for me many days . . .   For the children of Israel shall abide many days without a king, and without a prince, and without a sacrifice, and without an image, and without an ephod, and without teraphim : afterward shall the children of Israel return, and seek the Lord their God, and David their king ; and shall fear the Lord and His goodness in the latter days." And earlier still Moses had declared to Israel assembled on the threshold of Canaan: "He humbled thee, and suffered thee to hunger, and fed thee with manna, which thou knewest not, neither did thy fathers know; that He might make thee know that man doth not live by bread only, but by every word that proceedeth out of the mouth of the Lord doth man live"—with a portion of which text our Blessed Saviour deigned to confute Satan in the wilderness.

"A measure of wheat for a penny, and three measures of barley for a penny."—A literal scarcity of material food: spiritual food cannot so be purchased: "Ho, every one that thirsteth, come ye to the waters, and he that hath no money; come ye, buy, and eat; yea, come, buy wine and milk without money and without price."

The next following clause in the verse under consideration we may hopefully appropriate as guarding our spiritual interests: "See thou hurt not the oil and the wine." *Oil* is a symbol of that "Unction from the Holy One" bestowed upon us when by Baptism we begin to live: *Wine* suggests that blessed life-sustaining Sacrament which verily and indeed feeds the faithful with the Body and Blood of Christ.

Happy we, if come what will that Table is still prepared before us against them that trouble us: if the Anointing Oil is not withheld from our children, nor from us our Cup of Blessing. "The Lord is my Shepherd; I shall not want."

If pursuing further such thoughts it be lawful to consider this "Oil" and "Wine" as symbolic not only of the gifts but also of the Divine Givers, Who indeed give Themselves: then may we reinforce hope by tenderness of grateful love, if so be the word "hurt" intimates how God the Son and God the Holy Spirit vouchsafe to account Themselves as of one Heart and one Mind with the Communion of Saints; so that what hurts the elect in some inscrutable sense hurts Them, after the manner of Christ's own express words: "Saul, Saul, why persecutest thou Me?"—and in harmony with the Apostolick injunction: "Grieve not the Holy Spirit of God."

Nevertheless the Prophet Amos predicted one period of surpassing famine: "Behold, the days come, saith the Lord God, that I will send a famine in the land, not a famine of bread, nor a thirst for water, but of hearing the words of the Lord: and they shall wander from sea to sea, and from the north even to the east, they shall run to and fro to seek the word of the Lord, and shall not find it. In that day shall the fair virgins and young men faint for thirst."

From such extremity God preserve us, or out of such extremity God recover us, for the all-availing sake of His Son Jesus. Amen.

7. And when He had opened the fourth seal, I heard the voice of the fourth beast say, Come and see.

This fourth amongst the Living Creatures appears to be the one " like a flying Eagle" assigned of old to St. John as his evangelical symbol.

Not merely like an eagle, but like a flying eagle ; one soaring or prompt to soar sunwards relinquishing earth for heaven, mounting with ever-renewed strength, " forgetting those things which are behind, and reaching forth unto those things which are before." Well may this lofty and gracious creature be the one to summon the Eagle of the Apostolick College to behold : for dread is the vision about to pass by, intolerable to flesh and blood, endurable only by men whose citizenship is already in heaven.

Yet by them gazed upon, dwelt upon, desired, embraced ; because they know that man cannot fully live except first he die. Therefore with a good courage they say "to corruption, Thou art my father : to the worm, Thou art my mother, and my sister." Therefore not bound with fetters and chains, but as free among the dead they oftentimes keep holy-day among the tombs, cleaving unto Christ the Resurrection and the Life, if by any means they may attain unto the resurrection of the dead.

O Lord God Omniscient, I thank Thee on behalf of all those who have not felt or who no longer are called to endure the pang of bereavement. I thank Thee for ourselves, who humbly trust that some we love rest safely in Paradise. Whom grant us grace to follow. In the Name of Jesus Christ. Amen.

Safe where I cannot lie yet,
  Safe where I hope to lie too,
Safe from the fume and the fret ;
  You, and you,
Whom I never forget.

Safe from the frost and the snow,
  Safe from the storm and the sun ;
Safe where the seeds wait to grow
  One by one
And to come back in blow.

8. And I looked, and behold a pale horse : and his name that sat on him was Death, and Hell followed with him. And power was given unto them over the fourth part of the earth, to kill with sword, and with hunger, and with death, and with the beasts of the earth.

Pallor of a visible death, as whiteness of leprosy is whiteness of death : leprosy is a type of sin, and the wages of sin is death. "Before their face the people shall be much pained : all faces shall gather blackness."

But not necessarily blackness of darkness for ever. Death appears mounted on a horse, not on a throne : he arrives, he passes by. And albeit there is one event to the righteous and to the wicked ; yet the righteous even while rendering to Death the things that are Death's enter their protest : " Rejoice not against me, O mine enemy : when I fall, I shall arise : when I sit in darkness, the Lord shall be a light unto me. I will bear the indignation of the Lord, because I have sinned against Him, until He plead my cause, and execute judgment for me : He will bring me forth to the light, and I shall behold His righteousness."

"And Hell followed with him."—Hell, otherwise Hades : Hades the coffin of mortality, the cradle of immortality. "An end is come, the end is come : it watcheth for thee ; behold, it is come."

Hades follows Death. Death reaps, Hades garners : Death reaps, to sow ; Hades garners, to reproduce.

Our tender Lord encourages the faithful : "I say unto you My friends, Be not afraid of them that kill the body, and after that have no more that they can do." Death then is one of those whom saints need not fear. And Hades includes Paradise.

Hades the intermediate abode appears (at least by a fanciful conjecture) to be fitly illuminated by intermediate light, twilight (otherwise, 'tween light). Twilight is one of two things : evening twilight is the dying of light into darkness : morning twilight, the vanishing of darkness into light.

God grant that to us it may prove the vanishing of darkness into light, for the True Light's sake, Jesus Christ.

"There is hope in thine end "—and my own fault it will be if there is not hope in mine.

> How know I that it looms lovely that land I have never seen,
> With morning-glories and heartease and unexampled green,
> With neither heat nor cold in the balm-redolent air?
> Some of this, not all, I know : but this is so :
> Christ is there.

How know I that blessedness befalls who dwell in Paradise,
The outwearied hearts refreshing, rekindling the worn-out eyes ;
All souls singing, seeing, rejoicing everywhere ?
  Nay, much more than this I know : for this is so :
    Christ is there.

O Lord Christ Whom having not seen I love and desire to love,
O Lord Christ Who lookest on me uncomely yet still Thy dove,
Take me to Thee in Paradise, Thine own made fair :
  For whatever else I know, this thing is so :
    Thou art there.

"And power was given unto them over the fourth part of the earth."—Once again our comfort is that the power is *given ;* the Giver regulates the gift. "What? shall we receive good at the hand of God, and shall we not receive evil?" said holy Job : and in this we are expressly certified that he sinned not with his lips. But for such an assurance and for other passages of Holy Scripture one might have hesitated to call anything of God's sending *evil.*

The "power" extended "over the fourth part of the earth," but no further. Not over the whole earth, nor at all into the other world ; nor indeed under the earth, where is God's Acre. It is a surface scourge : kiss the rod, and thou shalt abide as the profound sea whose surface is lashed and ploughed by winds, but whose depths repose in unbroken calm.

Alas for shallow persons who are all surface !

"Behold, a sower went forth to sow ; and when he sowed, some seeds . . . fell upon stony places, where they had not much earth : and forthwith they sprung up, because they had no deepness of earth : and when the sun was up, they were scorched ; and because they had no root, they withered away . . . He that received the seed into stony places, the same is he that heareth the word, and anon with joy receiveth it ; yet hath he not root in himself, but dureth for a while : for when tribulation or persecution ariseth because of the word, by and by he is offended."

Sorrow of saints is sorrow of a day,
  Gladness of saints is gladness evermore :
  Send on thy hope, send on thy will before
To chant God's praise along the narrow way.
Stir up His praises if the flesh would sway,
  Exalt His praises if the world press sore,
  Peal out His praises if black Satan roar
A hundred thousand lies to say them nay.
Devil and Death and Hades, threefold cord
  Not quickly broken, front thee to thy face ;

Front thou them with a face of tenfold flint :
Shout for the battle, David ! never stint
Body or breath or blood, but proof in grace
Die for thy Lord, as once for thee thy Lord.

"To kill with sword, . . . hunger, . . . death (or as in the margin *pestilence*), . . . beasts of the earth."—Ezekiel delivers a corresponding prophecy :—"The word of the Lord came again to me, saying, Son of man, when the land sinneth against Me by trespassing grievously, then will I stretch out Mine hand upon it, and will break the staff of the bread thereof, and will send famine upon it, and will cut off man and beast from it . . . If I cause noisome beasts to pass through the land, and they spoil it, so that it be desolate, that no man may pass through because of the beasts : . . . Or if I bring a sword upon that land, and say, Sword, go through the land ; so that I cut off man and beast from it : . . . Or if I send a pestilence into that land, and pour out My fury upon it in blood, to cut off from it man and beast : though Noah, Daniel, and Job, were in it, as I live, saith the Lord God, they shall deliver neither son nor daughter ; they shall but deliver their own souls by their righteousness. For thus saith the Lord God. How much more when I send My four sore judgments upon Jerusalem, the sword, and the famine, and the noisome beast, and the pestilence, to cut off from it man and beast ? "

If we may argue from the fuller prophecy to the briefer, we admit in both (because in one) what the Psalmist recognized and declared of old : " No man may deliver his brother : nor make agreement unto God for him ; for it cost more to redeem their souls : so that he must let that alone for ever ; yea, though he live long : and see not the grave." This familiar Prayer Book translation differs from the Bible Version ; but if I may here safely follow it, it darkly and in part by a negative affirms a Divine Mystery. For what " no man " can do, Christ did ; and therefore cannot but be God as well as man. And He did it not by living long and not seeing the grave, to which no covenanted redemptive virtue was attached ; but by being cut off out of the land of the living and making his grave with the wicked.

True, the scourge threatened by Ezekiel, revealed to St. John, is temporal, not eternal ; but since Noah, Daniel, Job, availed not for the lesser salvation, much more could they not avail for the greater.

What, Lord, have we then nothing but Thee?—Nothing out of Me, all in Me.—Amen, Lord.

"Evil shall hunt the wicked person to overthrow him" :—
but all in vain would it hunt the righteous man ; who being
even as the Mount Sion which may not be removed but
standeth fast for ever, echoes St. Paul's witness : "Who shall
separate us from the love of Christ? shall tribulation, or
distress, or persecution, or famine, or nakedness, or peril, or
sword? . . . Nay, in all these things we are more than
conquerors through Him that loved us. For I am persuaded,
that neither death, nor life, nor angels, nor principalities, nor
powers, nor things present, nor things to come, nor height, nor
depth, nor any other creature, shall be able to separate us from
the love of God, which is in Christ Jesus our Lord."

The sword has had its will of many a martyr, and yet has
despatched him to glory. Fasting devotees practise themselves
aforetime in famine. Pestilence damages not him who is
content to fall into the hand of the Lord. Prayer makes itself
heard out of the lion's mouth or from among the horns of the
unicorns. No antagonist can disconcert him to whom to live is
Christ and to die gain.

From any sword that would devour for ever,
> Lord, guard us.
From any hunger which Thou wilt not fill with good things,
> Lord, guard us.
From any sickness unto death and not for Thy glory,
> Lord, guard us.
From evil beasts,
> Lord, guard us.
From the venomous crooked serpent, from the roaring lion, from the
dragon and his angels,
> Lord, guard us.

9. And when He had opened the fifth seal, I saw under the altar the souls of them that were slain for the word of God, and for the testimony which they held :

"Do ye not know that . . . they which wait at the altar are
partakers with the altar?"

These blessed martyrs verily waited at the Altar when once
they were offered up as a whole burnt offering to God ; and
now St. John beholds them "partakers with the Altar"; so
identified with the Altar, that all which thenceforward is offered
thereon may be said to be offered likewise upon the sacrifice
and service of their faith.

All who are united to Christ are thereby united to one
another. The Communion of Saints flows in one continuous
stream from the One Fountain Head ; descends as one

o

unbroken chain link by link from that irremovable anchor of our only hope, the Cross of Christ.

The holy fear which to-day despises earthly terrors, mirrors and memorializes the holy fear of our fathers and mothers in the faith; holy courage, their courage; heavenly love, their love. A martyr of this generation is spiritual descendant of the martyrs of yore: even as (may I not say, *evidently ?*) St. Paul under the Roman sword was true son to St. Stephen who had interceded for him amid the Judæan stones.

"I saw . . . the souls of them that were slain for the word of God, and for the testimony which they held."—This most noble qualification applies to St. James, own brother of St. John, and to others amongst his familiar friends. But as before so now again we find not on either side any trace of human recognition, of human tenderness.

Perhaps this is for our sakes, lest we should presume so to people heaven with our own cherished dead as to turn them into idols in the very shrine and Presence of Christ.

Since he that keepeth his life shall lose it, it may be that oftentimes to keep our beloved would be to lose them. "Perhaps he therefore departed for a season, that thou shouldest receive him for ever." "Lord, all my desire is before Thee."

> It is not death, O Christ, to die for Thee:
> Nor is that silence of a silent land
> Which speaks Thy praise so all may understand:
> Darkness of death makes Thy dear lovers see
> Thyself Who Wast and Art and Art to Be;
> Thyself, more lovely than the lovely band
> Of saints who worship Thee on either hand
> Loving and loved thro' all eternity.
> Death is not death, and therefore do I hope:
> Nor silence silence; and I therefore sing
> A very humble hopeful quiet psalm,
> Searching my heart-field for an offering;
> A handful of sun-courting heliotrope,
> Of myrrh a bundle, and a little balm.

Every tree after its kind: the One Cross has ramified into unnumbered crosses. Every seed after its kind: the Corn of Wheat which died is replenishing the world-wide harvest-field.

Christ is Head of the Church: should a martyred Head have a pampered body? Lord Jesus, grant us grace to keep Easter Eve to-day and Easter Day to-morrow.

"The testimony which they held."—It is the same thing

over and over again : they only who have held, held fast, held
out, are they who shall come up with acceptance on God's
Altar. *Courage, patience,*—woe is me ! Yet, Lord, Thou canst
make us, make me, courageous and patient. Amen.

If I have wisdom, and then even because I am a coward, I
shall choose the less risk rather than the greater, the less
torment rather than the greater.

If I have wisdom, and then even because I am impatient,
I shall put up with the whip lest I incur the scorpion.

If I have wisdom . . . nay, but even if I have common sense !

10. And they cried with a loud voice, saying, How long, O Lord, holy and true, dost Thou not judge and avenge our blood on them that dwell on the earth?

" Vengeance is Mine ; I will repay, saith the Lord." Those
who are indefectibly of one mind and one will with God
Almighty thirst and cry out for His just judgment and
righteous vengeance.

Can these be they who in mortal life were ready to lay down
that life for their brethren? Yea, these same are they once
the "all things to all men" if by any means they might save
some; the echoes of Christ in intercession, the mirrors of
Christ in self-sacrifice.

Like Christ they became by grace, like Christ they cannot
but remain on the threshold of glory and throughout the
unending triumph of His Glory. What Christ is, that in their
several proportions they too must be : according to His
promise : "If any man serve Me, let him follow Me ; and
where I am, there shall also My servant be ":—*there* not
merely in celestial locality, but doubtless in spiritualized will
and illumination of wisdom.likewise.

O Lord, now is my soul troubled, and what shall I say?
Father, save us from that hour ; but for this cause hast Thou
revealed that hour. Father, glorify Thy Name. While there
is yet time, while there is yet hope, Lord, remember Jesus and
all His trouble for our sakes, for love of us. I plead Jesus
I plead only Jesus. Amen.

" Holy and True."—" Yea, let God be true, but every man
a liar ; as it is written, That Thou mightest be justified in
Thy sayings, and mightest overcome when Thou art judged. . . .
Is God unrighteous Who taketh vengeance? . . . God forbid :
for then how shall God judge the world?"

I know not what besetment hinders my neighbour, but in
some degree I know what hinders myself.

I quail before God's Holiness because I am not holy, before His Truth because I am not true. "God is love": and I am of a different mind from God, not because of my excess of love but because of my defect of love.

O God All-Holy our Father, pity us and renew us unto holiness.

O God All-True our Redeemer, compassionate us and conform us unto Thy Truth in righteousness.

O God All-Loving our Sanctifier, convert and perfect us.

O God All-Holy, All-True, All-Loving, Three Persons in One Godhead, we are they for whom Jesus was born and died and rose again and ascended into heaven, for whom He intercedes, whom He will judge. Behold us, consider us, succour us. I take refuge in the supreme Name of Jesus. Amen.

"On them that dwell on the earth."—They say not, On them that slew us; but, On them that dwell on the earth. Whoever then would clean escape from under their ban, can so do by ceasing to be a dweller and becoming a stranger and pilgrim upon earth. This road of safety lies open to all, to murderers of martyrs as freely as to succourers of saints. For either by innocence or by penitence any and every soul can quit earth and betake itself to Heaven.

And with how warm a heart the Martyrs do forgive and welcome their slayers is exemplified by St. James the Great: who (at least according to a legend) having by his superhuman sanctity of demeanour converted his accuser, received him with a kiss of peace; after which they suffered death together.

11. And white robes were given unto every one of them; and it was said unto them, that they should rest yet for a little season, until their fellow-servants also and their brethren, that should be killed as they were, should be fulfilled.

"He shall grow as the lily." Whiteness of purity, greenness of hope, fragrance of aspiration, a comely aspect, a head uplifted: once in their passion the martyrs became as lilies among thorns, and now in their rest they are beautiful as lilies in the garden of their Beloved. Is it not "to gather lilies" when He takes home His own unto Himself? Is it not to feed "among the lilies" when He sups with them and they with Him?

"Consider the lilies of the field, how they grow; they toil

not, neither do they spin : and yet I say unto you, That even Solomon in all his glory was not arrayed like one of these."

"White robes were given unto every one of them."—Israel in the wilderness gathering Manna "gathered, some more, some less. And when they did mete it with an omer, he that gathered much had nothing over, and he that gathered little had no lack." Similarly these elect souls have presumably not laboured all alike : some have borne the burden and heat of a long day, some have wrought but one hour ; yet in the sphere of their acceptance these have no lack and those nothing over. All are absolutely accepted, absolutely sanctified, absolutely perfected.

Does it follow that all the robes are on a par ? This point is not revealed. All are white : yet for aught we know one and another may differ in glory like stars, in beauty like flowers. However this may be, let not our eye be evil because God is good : those robes are *given*, and it is lawful for Him to do what He will with His own. Blessed be He Who freely gave every grace which He invests with glory, and freely bestows every glory wherewith He adorns grace.

"So then it is not of him that willeth, nor of him that runneth, but of God that sheweth mercy."

"And it was said unto them that they should rest yet for a little season."—In this world vehement desire is restless, in that better world it can rest. "Their strength is to sit still."

"A little season."—Already about eighteen centuries. But eternity dwarfs all time : that which will end may be prolonged, but cannot be long.

"Fellow-servants . . . brethren ', — designations of affection. And what their disembodied lovers look forward to with approval is that they be "killed." For martyrs know by experience that to die for Christ brings an accession of life ; and saints of every degree in honour prefer one another. "There is no fear in love ; but perfect love casteth out fear," not for self alone but for others also. "In the sight of the unwise they seemed to die : and their departure is taken for misery, and their going from us to be utter destruction ; but they are in peace." To be killed in Christ's cause is to be "fulfilled."

"All the rivers run into the sea ; yet the sea is not full." Man is a still wider sea, a still deeper ocean, a more insatiable abyss : this life and the resources of this life can never fill him. As one has proposed, expressing a thought too daring for me of myself to have entertained or uttered : The vast bed of ocean corresponds with the ocean whereof it is the bed: so man's vast emptiness corresponds with the Immensity of God Who fills him ; they correspond, God having fulness where man hath emptiness.

"Fellow-servants," one in duty : "brethren," one in love. Soul by soul each individual fulfilled, until the entire pre-destined number be fulfilled.

The generations of mankind shall not pass away, nor heaven and earth pass away, till all be fulfilled. Time must endure, eternity must stand back, till all be fulfilled.

Fulfil God's Will, and thou shalt be of the number of the fulfilled. I also, He prospering me. Amen.

> Once slain for Him Who first was slain for them,
>   Now made alive in Him for evermore,
>   All luminous and lovely in their gore
> With no more buffeting winds or tides to stem,
> The Martyrs look for New Jerusalem ;
>   And cry "How long?" remembering all they bore,
>   "How long?" with heart and eyes sent on before
> Toward consummated throne and diadem.
> "How long?"   White robes are given to their desire ;
>   "How long?" deep rest that is and is to be ;
>   With a great promise of the oncoming host,
> Loves to their love and fires to flank their fire :
>   So rest they, worshipping incessantly
>   One God, the Father, Son, and Holy Ghost.

12. And I beheld when He had opened the sixth seal, and, lo, there was a great earthquake ; and the sun be-came black as sackcloth of hair, and the moon became as blood ;

Darkness and earthquake waited on our Lord's Passion and Death : "the sun was darkened" and "the earth did quake." If on a saving Passion and life-restoring Death, how much more on a vain passion and destruction-preluding death ! "Great" now is the earthquake ; the sun now becomes "black as sackcloth of hair." The done done, and the undone left undone, earth is preparing to pass away, and she quakes. We know not whether the sun is passing away, or whether he will be relit.

That we know, *this* we know not : *that* concerns ourselves, *this* concerns us not. Practical utility, not idle amusement, appears to be one widely applicable rule according to which we are instructed or left ignorant. No good thing (but not, nothing whatever) will God withhold from them that walk uprightly.

O God All-Wise, let us not be as our mother Eve who thought to hanker after good knowledge denied, when in truth she hankered after evil knowledge kept back.

O God All-Good, let us not be as our father Adam who was not deceived, but rejected good and chose evil.

O God All-Merciful, we plead our only hope of mercy, Jesus, the Second Adam, made of a woman. Amen.

The sun being a figure of Christ (a figure authorized by the Bible) concerning whom Pilate said justly, "Behold the Man!" may presumably be in some sort a figure also of mankind. As a figure of Christ, its face was darkened at the Crucifixion, and is once more darkened towards the reprobate : as a figure of man, when all the tribes of the earth go mourning to their death it too puts on mourning. The luminous sun then is an emblem of the Living Christ and of all who live in Him : the lightless sun is an emblem of the Dying Christ, of Christ hiding His face from the incorrigible, and of all who die cut off from Him.

Now the moon is not mentioned in the Gospel narratives of the Crucifixion. Because the sun sets forth Christ, the moon which is that sun's mirror and follower cannot but set forth the Church. And the Church was not (so to say) born so early as the day of Calvary ; but by the end of the world she is even mature. Then therefore, though not till then, she appears unextinguished in heaven while the world is departing into darkness ; and exhibits her proper glory "as blood," for all her glory accrues to her through the Blood of the Lamb. [I trust such a train of thought is permissible.]

13. And the stars of Heaven fell unto the earth, even as a fig tree casteth her untimely figs, when she is shaken of a mighty wind.

The Son of Sirach observes : "All things are double one against another." This suggests that everything cognizable by the senses may be utilized as symbol or parable.

To such an exercise certain minds seem strongly drawn. Their horizon thereby recedes, depth is deepened, height heightened, width widened. Underlying any measurable depth, overtopping such height, encompassing such width, they apprehend That which nothing underlies, nothing overtops, nothing encompasses. To them matter suggests the immaterial ; time eternity. "One day telleth another : and one night certifieth another." Their world expands, and with their world their responsibilities, and with their responsibilities their peril.

The Tender Master Who adjusts our load, help us, whatever it amount to, to bear it : the Wise Master Who appoints our lot, help us, whatever it involve, to conform to it. And this with a cheerful hope : because it is "not that we are sufficient of ourselves to think anything as of ourselves; but our sufficiency is of God."

"The stars of heaven fell unto the earth."—He Who knoweth the number of the stars and calleth them all by their names, He alone can "loose the bands of Orion." Neither sparrow nor star shall fall to the ground without our Father, and we are of more value than many sparrows.

Meteors and shooting-stars rehearse to successive generations that great and terrible day. Nor can so much as one single unripe fig drop without sounding an alarm in our holy mountain. The fig tree bears last year's fruit and this year's fruit together, the ripe with the unripe : the unripe readily fall away, the ripe abide.

"A mighty wind."—But even the winds hear and obey God's word. He maketh the weight for them, and out of His treasuries He bringeth them : as after the Deluge to assuage the waters ; as at the Red Sea to open a passage to Israel ; as travelling from the wilderness to sift Job ; as across heaven to bring rain when earth languished under Ahab ; as rending the mountains to instruct Elijah ; as resuscitating the dead before the eyes of Ezekiel ; as arresting Jonah to the intent that he might return into the way of righteousness. "Therefore will we not fear." Or if still we fear, let us lay hold on that promise : "A Man shall be as an hiding-place from the wind." Yea, Lord Jesus, hide us as Thou hast promised.

"THOU SHALT HEAR A VOICE BEHIND THEE."

It was not warning that our fathers lacked,
　It is not warning that we lack to-day.
The Voice that cried, still cries : "Rise up and act :
　Watch alway,—watch and pray,—watch alway,—
　　　　　　　　　　All men."
Alas, if ought was lacked goodwill was lacked ;
　Alas, goodwill is what we lack to-day.
O gracious Voice, grant grace that all may act,
　Watch and act,—watch and pray,—watch alway.
　　　　　　　　　　Amen.

14. And the heaven departed as a scroll when it is rolled together ; and every mountain and island were moved out of their places.

Once, years ago in Normandy after a day of flooding rain, I beheld the clouds roll up and depart and the auspicious sky reappear. Once in crossing the Splugen I beheld that moving of the mists which gives back to sight a vanished world. Those veils of heaven and earth removed, beauty came to light. What will it be to see this same visible heaven itself removed and unimaginable beauty brought to light in glory and terror l auspicious to the elect, by aliens unendurable.

As a scroll rolled up the heavens shall depart. Meanwhile they are spread out above all humankind as an open scroll declaring the Glory of God.

David perused the open scroll to good purpose : "O Lord our Lord, how excellent is Thy Name in all the earth ! Who hast set Thy glory above the heavens. . . . When I consider Thy heavens, the work of Thy fingers, the moon and the stars, which Thou hast ordained ; what is man, that Thou art mindful of him ? and the son of man, that Thou visitest him ? . . . O Lord our Lord, how excellent is Thy Name in all the earth !"

Alas, O Lord God, we are not thus with Thee. Yet hast Thou made with us an everlasting covenant ordered in all things and sure in Jesus Christ. He is all our salvation, and even if we apprehend it not He is all our desire : for His sake make Thou us to grow in grace and in the saving knowledge of Thee. Amen.

"Every mountain and island were moved out of their places."—Faith, whose is the promise to remove mountains, will not fear "though the earth be removed, and though the mountains be carried into the midst of the sea ; though the waters thereof roar and be troubled, though the mountains shake with the swelling thereof."

Faith will not fear. Hope will look up and lift up the head. If now they abide, then also may they abide : yet neither now nor then except in company with love. Faith surmounts fear. Hope overbalances fear. Love casts out fear.

"Behold, He taketh up the isles as a very little thing." "According to their deeds, accordingly He will repay, fury to His adversaries, recompence to His enemies ; to the islands He will repay recompence." Nevertheless "He shall deliver the island of the innocent : and it is delivered by the pureness of thine hands."

England, our beloved England, seems naturally included in one or other of the foregoing texts. Innocence would avail for her protection ; but who among her millions dare challenge that safeguard? "Who can say, I have made my heart clean, I am pure from my sin?"

Penitence the restorer of purity is the substitute for irretrievably forfeited innocence. What innocence might have secured in some sense as a right, penitence secures as a grace. Innocence is strong without weakness. Penitence waxes strong in weakness.

> 15. And the kings of the earth, and the great men, and the rich men, and the chief captains, and the mighty men, and every bondman, and every free man, hid themselves in the dens and in the rocks of the mountains;
> 16. And said to the mountains and rocks, Fall on us, and hide us from the face of Him that sitteth on the Throne, and from the wrath of the Lamb:
> 17. For the great day of His wrath is come; and who shall be able to stand?

This general levelling is accounted for by the final clause: "Who shall be able to stand?" All, each, must either stand or fall: such as cannot stand, fall.

Herein consists a genuine distinction, here the man himself is in question: whereas those other points of difference enumerated in the text are accidental, temporary. To be a king or a captain; to be great, rich, mighty; even to be bond or free; is no more than the individual's appointed form of discipline in his proper vocation. Corruptible crowns perish in the using; sooner or later war will cease to be learned; greatness, riches, might of this world, cannot be expected to outlast the world to which they appertain; nor bonds or freedom of this mortal life, the mortality to which they are appended. These last two form the extreme instance: whoso grasps that even these are respectively a passing vanity or a passing vexation of spirit, abides in impregnable freedom though Pharaoh were his taskmaster.

Not that a slur attaches to any lawful condition or pursuit: what God hath made He is graciously willing to bear. A terrestrial crown may become the nucleus of a crown celestial. And so with the rest, or at most with one exception. *Bonds* surely will be stripped off at once and for ever from Christ's immortal freeman; unless haply they may reappear as an ornament of grace unto the head, and chains about the neck of one whose feet were hurt in the stocks whilst the iron entered into his soul, until the time came that his cause was known, the word of the Lord trying him.

Perhaps there is no convulsion of nature more rife with terror than an earthquake. What must that extremity of terror be which will call on earthquake for refuge and shelter !—and will be denied.

Sinners will then clamour to be hidden from the Face of God, not realizing how God's Face is about to be hidden from them.

" The wrath of the Lamb."—Words cannot utter it. " Is it not a grief unto death, when a companion and friend is turned to an enemy ? "

Lord, before the great day of Thy wrath overtake mankind, teach us, I beseech Thee, to discern between its good and its evil.

Thy wrath is the wrath of Holiness. It is the wrath of Love, for Thou art Love. Love while it hates still is Love. The day of Thy wrath, because it is Thy day, is also the day of Love, of Holiness.

Incorrigible sinners become the mark of Thy wrath ; them it tracks out, them it destroys. They appear to be (as it were) so fused into one mass with evil that these are no longer twain but one, inextricable, indistinguishable. They heaped up wrath against the day of wrath and revelation of Thy righteous judgment : their delight was in cursing, and it happens unto them ; they loved not blessing, and therefore is it far from them.

Thy righteous wrath lays hold of them, overwhelms them : these who shunned and abhorred righteousness are now forced into contact with it in one tremendous form. Sin mastered and prompted them hitherto, now righteousness dominates and overbears them : better, it may be, to be ruled in prison and darkness by "the rod of God," than at large to obey by choice the serpent of the diabolical enchanter.

Thy righteous wrath coerces, crushes, shivers them into some sort of conformity with Thy Will. It could not be better for them while they were in no sense conformed to it.

Sin was their evil of old ; and in the day of wrath not punishment, but sin remains their extreme evil. Sin rampant cannot be better than sin delivered to the tormentors.

Worse was it for Babel to be built than to be destroyed.

Grace withdrawn precludes grace resisted. Opportunity denied precludes opportunity set at nought. Time finished precludes time lost.

Such withdrawal, denial, finis, are amongst the last revealed dealings of God towards self-ruined man : and who shall dare pronounce them in no sense dealings of mercy? [These thoughts are less my own than derived from widely different sources.]

O Lamb of God, the spirit fails from before Thee and the souls which Thou hast made. I cannot understand, can only bow down before, the mystery of Thy wrath : preserve me from darkening counsel by words without knowledge. Behold, I am vile ; what shall I answer Thee ? I will lay my hand upon my mouth. Once have I spoken ; but I will not answer : yea, twice ; but I will proceed no further. O Lamb of God, Who camest not to destroy men's lives, but to save them, take away the sins of the world.

CHAPTER VII

1. And after these things I saw four angels standing on the four corners of the earth, holding the four winds of the earth, that the wind should not blow on the earth, nor on the sea, nor on any tree.

"After these things I saw."—Happen what may, the saints survive. The great saints? Yea, and the little saints along with them. Saints are all, every one of them "great fishes" drawn ashore at last in the unbroken net of salvation.

"Four angels . . . holding."—A period of suspense, preparation. Suspense is preparation, and should be utilized for preparation. That it should be, attests that it can be. That any one can so use it, certifies that all can. Suspense tempts one to do nothing: it ought contrariwise to stir one up to do everything.

For suspense though it may be prolonged indefinitely must sooner or later terminate; and must be succeeded by we know not what. Had we known what would follow, suspense could not have been suspense.

During suspense we can prepare ourselves for anything, only by preparing ourselves for everything. The prepared man secures "a happy issue" out of suspense whenever and whatever that issue may be. But the unprepared man . . .?

And since "the preparations of the heart in man" are "from the Lord," let us pray with David whose heart indited of good matters: "Create in me a clean heart, O God; and renew a right spirit within me." For Jesu's sake. Amen.

St. John saw four Angels standing on the four corners of the earth. They would equally have been standing there had he not seen them; and it may be so even now at this present moment.

Angels see us though we see them not, they hear us though

we hear them not: let it not be that they love us though we love them not.

Whether we love them or not, and even whether we love God or not, they love us so long as God loves us: because they are lovely, that is, love-like; and we know Who it is Whose Name is Love.

Glory be to Thee, O Lord God, Glory be to Thee for all created glories, for all ministries of mercy and judgment, for what eye hath seen, and what eye hath not seen, for Angels unfallen, for saints raised up to newness of life, for sinners with the possibilities of saints, for equality with angels accessible to man, for glory differing from glory, for glory that shall be revealed. Glory be to Thee for the Excellent Glory, for our knowledge of Thy Glory in the Face of Jesus Christ; Whom we plead, desiring to live and die unto Thy glory. Amen.

> Dear Angels and dear disembodied Saints
> Unseen around us, worshipping in rest,
> May wonder that man's heart so often faints
> And his steps lag along the heavenly quest,
> What while his foolish fancy moulds and paints
> A fonder hope than all they prove for best;
> A lying hope which undermines and taints
> His soul, as sin and sloth make manifest.
> Sloth, and a lie, and sin: shall these suffice
> The unfathomable heart of craving man,
> The heart that being a deep calls to the deep?
> Behold how many like us rose and ran
> When Christ life-Giver roused them from their sleep
> To rise and run and rest in Paradise !

This period of suspense is under one aspect a period of calm: the winds being withheld from blowing, earth, sea, and every tree stand still. Wherefore?

While we wait to know, let us practise ourselves in faith. "Be still, and know that I am God."

> Lord, grant us calm, if calm can set forth Thee;
> Or tempest, if a tempest set Thee forth;
> Wind from the east or west or south or north;
> Or congelation of a silent sea
> With stillness of each tremulous aspen tree.
>
> Still let fruit fall, or hang upon the tree;
> Still let the east and west, the south and north,
> Curb in their winds, or plough a thundering sea;
> Still let the earth abide to set Thee forth,
> Or vanish like a smoke to set forth Thee.

Earth with four corners, amenable to four winds and four angels, might seem but a small place.

And earth *is* small compared with space. And space is small compared with infinity.

Let us not lose our soul to gain the world, that smallest of three areas.

How escape four avenging winds, and four avenging angels? By entrenching ourselves betimes amid the four cardinal virtues: Prudence which seeks God while He may be found; Justice whereby (among other functions) man judges self, and so is not judged; Fortitude which even counts it happy to endure; Temperance which strives lawfully, and runs so as to obtain.

2. And I saw another angel ascending from the east, having the seal of the living God: and he cried with a loud voice to the four angels, to whom it was given to hurt the earth and the sea,

All alike angels, each with his particular office to fulfil, talent to use. Four to chastise, one to protect. The angel of protection exercises authority over those his brethren; salvation must be secured before destruction does its work; mercy delays judgment.

O Christ my God, if I know it not concerning any soul beside mine own, yet concerning mine own soul well know I that mercy delayeth judgment. Well I know it, yet not fully: Thou alone fully knowest the length, breadth, depth, height, of Thy mercy towards me; free mercy, renewed mercy, pursuing mercy, beseeching mercy. O my God, let it be prevailing, conquering, triumphant mercy over me, over all, lest we heap up wrath against the day of wrath by means of the longsuffering of Thy mercy: Thou Who camest not to condemn the world, but to save the world. Amen.

"Another angel ascending from the east."—As a star risen in the east manifested Christ, so now an angel rises in the east to manifest them that are Christ's. Instinctively I should picture an angel as descending, and not ascending on earthly embassies; but this angel visibly ascended: the east thereupon emitting a double light; an angel in his brightness; and an illuminating inference, that every Divine errand or calling whithersoever and whatsoever it may be exalts a faithful messenger, a dutiful servant.

To descend penitently into the valley of humiliation, to descend obediently and with a good courage into the valley of the shadow of death, is to ascend the hill of the Lord. To excavate the foundation forwards the erection of the Temple.

"Who is there among you of all His people? The Lord his God be with him, and let him go up."

"The seal of the Living God."—In Holy Baptism we certainly receive such a seal. But Baptism initiates: this seal seems to stamp the end rather than the beginning. Final perseverance, if it be not itself the seal, appears congruous with it.

To be sealed makes the members so far like their Head for Christ declared concerning Himself, "Him hath God the Father sealed." Which ineffable sealing I have seen explained as referring to a Jewish custom observed towards the Passover Lambs, according to which they were before sacrifice authoritatively inspected and certified as without blemish.

Whence it would seem that our Lord's "sealing" both attested His perfection and assigned Him to sacrifice. I know not whether a parallel on a lower level may be permitted to apply the same thought to His elect.

There is yet another sealing whereby the Bride prays to be indissolubly united to her Heavenly Bridegroom : "Set me as a seal upon Thine heart, as a seal upon Thine arm : for love is strong as death." And to this prayer each devoted soul may unblamed frame a parallel : Set Thyself as Seal upon my heart, as Seal upon mine arm ; that my love may wax strong as death. Amen.

A SORROWFUL SIGH OF A PRISONER.

Lord, comest Thou to me ?
My heart is cold and dead :
Alas that such a heart should be
The place to lay Thy head !

"The Living God."—"As the Father raiseth up the dead, and quickeneth them; even so the Son quickeneth whom He will. . . . As the Father hath life in Himself; so hath He given to the Son to have life in Himself." "The law of the Spirit of Life in Christ Jesus hath made me free from the law of sin and death. . . . And if Christ be in you, the body is dead because of sin ; but the Spirit is life because of righteousness."

"To whom it was given to hurt the earth and the sea."— Each duty, office, vocation, is God's gift whether to man or to angel. Man indulges ardours and reluctances, choices, recoils and preferences ; some gifts he styles trials, some burdens. Angels seem to see and feel no difference between calling and calling, opportunity and opportunity. Angels doubtless estimate the gift by the Giver : men too often the Giver by the gift; not, that is, by the intrinsic value of the gift, but rather by their own taste or distaste for it.

And indeed to flesh and blood it is in truth an appalling thing to be constituted a rod of God's anger. We shrink from reading of David : " He smote Moab, and measured them with a line, casting them down to the ground; even with two lines measured he to put to death, and with one full line to keep alive."

Well may we thank God for our exemptions.

We should naturally expect sooner or later to behold the four Angels execute their charge, perhaps by releasing the four winds. But we read not of the event in any such form. Earth and sea are smitten after a time, but not stately by those. " Be not wise in your own conceits."

3. Saying, Hurt not the earth, neither the sea, nor the trees, till we have sealed the servants of our God in their foreheads.

In like manner Sodom and Gomorrah could not be dealt with until " righteous Lot " had been rescued : " Haste thee, escape thither; for I cannot do anything till thou be come thither. . . . The sun was risen upon the earth when Lot entered into Zoar. Then the Lord rained upon Sodom and upon Gomorrah brimstone and fire from the Lord out of heaven ; and He overthrew those cities, and all the plain, and all the inhabitants of the cities, and that which grew upon the ground."

Thus are saints the salt of the earth ; preserving it from dissolution. Thus do the blessed meek inherit the earth.

Thus are they, thus do they. Gracious Lord Jesus, let it not be Thy rare saints only who are and do thus, but all souls with them.

" The servants of our God."—It might have sufficed for practical purposes to say simply, The servants of God : but the other is a loving form, and consequently a tongue of Angels.

" In their foreheads."—" Known unto God are all His works from the beginning of the world," is St. James's declaration. And St. Paul writes more particularly : " The foundation of God standeth sure, having this seal, The Lord knoweth them that are His."

God knoweth His own before they are sealed. The holy Angels who minister to such heirs of salvation must also previously know them, or how should they affix the seal? A seal made prominent on the forehead announces to all others whom it may concern the wearer's identity. And so on occasion of the great first Passover, the destroying Angel was admonished by a conspicuous sign, the blood of sacrifice, to pass over the doors of the exempt. And long afterwards in vision Ezekiel beheld a general slaughter, against which the safeguard was a mark set on the forehead: "And He called to the man clothed with linen, which had the writer's inkhorn by his side; and the Lord said unto him, Go through the midst of the city, through the midst of Jerusalem, and set a mark upon the foreheads of the men that sigh and that cry for all the abominations that be done in the midst thereof. And to the others he said in mine hearing, Go ye after him through the city, and smite: let not your eyes spare, neither have ye pity: slay utterly old and young, both maids, and little children, and women: but come not near any man upon whom is the mark; and begin at My sanctuary."

Perhaps by the seal we may further understand some distinct spiritual feature or gracious appearance whereby the Communion of Saints are enabled to recognize each other in love; whereby also the aliens recognizing the household of God will wax the more bitter to hate them without a cause, in accordance with our Lord's word to His disciples: "Ye shall be hated of all nations for My Name's sake."

We talk of the unrighteous hating the righteous: do they hate because they are unrighteous, or are they unrighteous because they hate? If at all the latter, I fear there are so-called and self-called righteous people who will scarcely if at all be saved.

"My God, I mean myself," said holy George Herbert. God grant us a like self-knowledge and humility.

Purlieus and Approaches which tend towards or border upon Hatred of the Righteous.

1. Antipathies tolerated.
2. Incompatibilities taken for granted.
3. Fastidiousness nursed on indifferent points.
4. Favoritism indulged.
5. Affront taken where none is meant.
6. Reciprocal angles, yours always in the wrong.
7. Reciprocal soreness, I always in the right.
8. Offence at distasteful doer, let him do or leave undone what he will.

Taking one a day, you will require a week and a day for your self-reform. I, alas! foresee requiring much more than a week and a day for mine.

Jesus Who didst touch the leper,
        Deliver us from antipathies.
Who didst dwell among the Nazarenes,
        Deliver us from incompatibility.
Who didst eat with some that washed not before meat,
        Deliver us from fastidiousness.
Who didst not promise the right hand or the left,
        Deliver us from favoritism.
Who didst condone Samaritan inhospitality,
        Deliver us from affront taking.
Who didst provide the sacred Didrachma,
        Deliver us from offence giving.
Who having called didst recall St. Peter,
        Deliver us from soreness.
Who didst love active Martha and contemplative Mary,
        Deliver us from respect of persons.
Deliver us to-day while it is called to-day, Thou Who givest us to-day and
    promisest us not to-morrow.

Whatever the "seal" may signify, its being impressed on the *forehead* suggests that it may be some sign definite, obvious, prominent, emphatic, calculated to be "known and read of all men," friends, unfriends, and foes; to catch their eye, even to force itself upon their notice.

Christians of some generation are (please God) to be sealed. But all Christians have once already by His mercy been sealed in Holy Baptism; and we cannot suppose that a crowning grace will contradict instead of harmonizing with an initiatory grace from the self-same Source.

Whence it ensues that if none but fearless, self-evident Christians can worthily undergo the final sealing, every Baptized man, woman, child, each in due proportion, is already pledged by the Baptismal seal to be a fearless, self-evident Christian.

Field-day harness, and parade carrying of bows, will profit a soldier nothing if he turn back in the day of battle.

4. And I heard the number of them which were sealed: and there were sealed an hundred and forty and four thousand of all the tribes of the children of Israel.

Then exulted Abraham, who having gone out not knowing whither he went, beheld as father of the faithful whither he and his seed after him had journeyed. Then Sarah had pleasure. Then Rebekah understood what good her life had done her. Then Rachel was comforted. Then Israel said tenfold more, "It is enough."

Dost thou thyself ask, What good shall my life do me? Resolve that God speeding thee it shall do thee this good, to be numbered among the nations of the saved; and thou too one day shalt say, It is enough.

"Of all the tribes."—Yet is not Dan named in the ensuing catalogue. Still, if we dwell on the literal twelve Patriarchs, Dan may doubtless have been represented through inter-marriages among kindred families. Moreover, Samson the Judge sprang from that tribe, and reappears in the goodly fellowship of heroes of faith (*see* Heb. xi. 32—34).

Whatever historical or prophetical meaning may be con-veyed by this omission of Dan, it at least serves to remind us how no perversity of man can ultimately thwart God's will or mar His work. Twelve tribes there were at the outset, and twelve tribes there are at the ingathering. In like manner the College of Apostles numbered twelve first and last, despite the apostasy of Judas. Sooner than the covenant with Abraham should fail, children would be raised up to him of stones.

We must not forget, however, that in Ezekiel's vision of the City whose name shall be "The Lord is there," Dan has his portion and his gate.

Dan no less than his peers inherited a prophetic benediction first from Jacob, afterwards from Moses:—"Dan shall judge his people, as one of the tribes of Israel. Dan shall be a serpent by the way, an adder in the path, that biteth the horse's heels, so that his rider shall fall backward. I have waited for Thy salvation, O Lord": "Dan is a lion's whelp: he shall leap from Bashan." Yet the second clause of the elder prophecy reads at the least equivocally: whatever the temporal character and tactics thus metaphorically conveyed, any obvious spiritual analogy seems to proclaim a curse rather than a blessing: a curse upon work such as the serpent com-passed in Eden when he likewise made the lord of this visible world to "fall backward." Read under so ominous a light, even the other clauses seem, if not to ring hollow, at least to give an uncertain sound; and we think fearfully of Dan as haply that wolf in sheep's clothing the Unjust Judge, sitting indeed to judge Christ's people, but "contrary to the law"; sitting "as" one of the tribes of Israel, but in truth no longer one of them, having gone out from them because not of them. Even the kingly prediction: "Dan is a lion's whelp: he shall leap from Bashan," reminds us that while God deigns to define His own Hill "as the hill of Bashan, an high hill as the hill of Bashan," yet for Bashan to vie with Zion would be as when

Eve set herself to become like God : and the lion which leaps from Bashan comes from the country of those "fat bulls" which closed the Messiah in on every side.

What immediately follows of the Sacred Text I once heard read like the roll-call, when victorious hosts muster to their colours. "And His banner over me was love."

5. **Of the tribe of Juda were sealed twelve thousand. Of the tribe of Reuben were sealed twelve thousand. Of the tribe of Gad were sealed twelve thousand.**
6. **Of the tribe of Aser were sealed twelve thousand. Of the tribe of Nepthalim were sealed twelve thousand. Of the tribe of Manasses were sealed twelve thousand.**
7. **Of the tribe of Simeon were sealed twelve thousand. Of the tribe of Levi were sealed twelve thousand. Of the tribe of Issachar were sealed twelve thousand.**
8. **Of the tribe of Zabulon were sealed twelve thousand. Of the tribe of Joseph were sealed twelve thousand. Of the tribe of Benjamin were sealed twelve thousand.**

Now is being made good every promise to the election. Now is being brought to pass the saying that is written, "Death is swallowed up in victory." Now is the beginning of the end.

Faith and hope look beyond the "little moment, until the indignation be overpast," and contemplate the final consummation.

Behold Juda praised of his brethren, supreme over his enemies, honoured by his nearest and dearest; replenished and lacking nothing, imperturbable in rest, royally sceptred; a rallying point to gracious men; his journey accomplished, his travail over, his cravings satisfied; gathered to his fathers and his people; coming short of nothing; delivered from all his adversaries. Behold Reuben renewed in strength, retrieved from lapses, excellent in dignity and in power; if once dead, now alive again; if once lost, now found; heretofore a little one, now twelve times a thousand; and from a small one become a strong nation. Behold Gad, having overcome all by whom ever he was overcome; enlarged, enriched, dominant; noble among the noble, because he executed the justice of the Lord and His judgments. Behold Aser, once hungry and athirst after 'righteousness, now satisfied; fed as it were with marrow and fatness, and all royal dainties; blessed with children, beloved of his brethren, anointed with oil, freely giving as freely he has received; as were his days, so was his strength, and as the eternal day, so shall his strength be. Behold Nepthalim loosed from all bonds; having a tongue, and therewith uttering praise; satisfied with favour, and full with the blessing of the Lord; possessing "the west and the south," even the kingdom of heaven glowing and luminous. Behold Manasses, as the branch of a fruitful bough abundantly watered; mighty and glorious; gone up from blessings of the deep that lieth under, to blessings of the heaven above. Behold Simeon purged from blood-guiltiness; his tongue singing of God's Righteousness; once scattered, now gathered for evermore. Behold Levi, having altogether left off from wrath and let go displeasure; holy, steadfast, approved, unworldly, unearthly; faithful to the word and the covenant, and now proving Him faithful Who promised; teacher of many, turner of many to righteousness, now shining as the stars for ever and ever; blessed in what he had, for the Lord was his inheritance; blessed in his work, for he waited on Him continually; exalted now to be Son of Consolation, peace around, and peace within. Behold Issachar, because sometime in faith he humbled and limited himself to serve, to bear, to render to all their dues, now at large and aloft in the rest that is good, and the land that is pleasant; because of old he dwelt in tents by faith, now ascended into the Hill of the Lord, and bringing many with him into that Temple which is the Presence of God; now where the sea is as of glass and fire, possessing for incorruptible treasure that Wisdom which the earthly sea saith is not with her. Behold Zabulon, brought safe unto the haven where he would be; having gone out from the world that is polluted, and having entered into that pure world whence none go out any more; offering the ever-acceptable sacrifice of righteousness. Behold Joseph, once strong in the earthly Israel, now tenfold strong in the heavenly; abiding in strength; the arms of his hands made strong by the hands of the Mighty God of Jacob; exalted and mighty for ever and ever; for temporal treasures having inherited eternal. Behold Benjamin, a vessel chosen unto honour, a chosen vessel unto God; having of yore coveted earnestly the best gifts, now dividing the spoil; beloved of the Lord, dwelling in safety by Him, covered of Him all the day long, placed at His Right Hand, gathered into His bosom.

"Happy is that people, that is in such a case: yea, happy is that people, whose God is the Lord."

9. After this I beheld, and lo, a great multitude, which no man could number, of all nations, and kindreds, and

people, and tongues, stood before the Throne, and
before the Lamb, clothed with white robes, and palms
in their hands;

As their praise was erst not of men but of God, so now their
number is known not to men but to God. "So many as the
stars of the sky in multitude, and as the sand which is by the
seashore innumerable."

"I beheld," says St. John: and you with your eyes, I with
mine (please God!) shall yet behold.

Looking forward to this, what terrestrial sight is worth
hankering after because of beauty or majesty? It will pass by
and be no more seen; no, nor peered after. What terrestrial
sight is worth avoiding because of horror or loathliness? It
will pass by and be no more shrunk from. I once grieved
and grudged because I could not betake myself to a vantage
ground whence to watch an eclipse: the grief might have
been simply blameless, but the grudge proved that I was in a
double sense loving darkness rather than light.

O Lord, grant us in Thy Light to see light; and aught
besides, reveal or hide from us according to Thy Will in Jesus
Christ, Light of Light. Amen.

One asked, "Lord, are there few that be saved? And He
said unto them, Strive to enter in at the strait gate: for many,
I say unto you, will seek to enter in, and shall not be able."
Yet now St. John beholds "a great multitude" of the saved.
Thank God.

"All nations, and kindreds, and people, and tongues."—
Never, since Babel, a unison: no longer, since the first
Christian Pentecost, an inevitable discord: for ever and ever,
a harmony. Babel dissolved the primitive unison into discord:
Pentecost reduced the prevalent discord to contingent harmony,
but reclaimed it not into unison.

Unison is faultless: harmony is perfect. On earth the
possibility of harmony entails the corresponding possibility of
discord. Even on earth, however, whoever chooses can himself or herself keep time and tune: which will be an apt
prelude for keeping eternity and tune in heaven.

"White robes."—"White as the light": for stainless and
spotless they sustain the Presence of the Very Light. Blessed
those sons and daughters for whom the best robe has been
brought forth without money and without price.

Neither was it of their own power or holiness that they
plucked palms and bore them before the Throne and before

the Lamb. Christ of Whom it is mystically written: "I said, I will go up to the palm tree, I will take hold of the boughs thereof,"—won all palms for all saints when on Calvary with His own right hand and with His holy arm He got Himself the victory. Christ it is Who triumphs in His triumphant redeemed: from Him they derive their victories, from Him their rewards. His Cross branched out into their crosses: His Cross, the one palm tree of victory, branches out into their palms.

> Thy Cross cruciferous doth flower in all
> And every cross, dear Lord, assigned to us:
> Ours lowly-statured crosses; Thine, how tall,
> Thy Cross cruciferous.
>
> Thy Cross alone life-giving, glorious:
> For Love of Thine, souls love their own when small
> Easy and light, or great and ponderous.
>
> Since deep calls deep, Lord, hearken when we call;
> When cross calls Cross racking and emulous:—
> Remember us, with him who shared Thy gall,
> Thy Cross cruciferous.

10. And cried with a loud voice, saying, Salvation to our God which sitteth upon the Throne, and unto the Lamb.

"I will sing a new song unto Thee, O God: and sing praises unto Thee upon a ten-stringed lute. Thou hast given victory unto kings."

Here we encounter a new word, "Salvation," in the chorus of perfected praise uplifted by new-comers into a new glory. Since time began no unfallen creature from the lowest to the highest could thus bless God. The dead alive again, the lost found, ascribing their salvation to God and to the Lamb, add to celestial language one more word, to celestial joys one more joy.

11. And all the angels stood round about the Throne, and about the elders and the four beasts, and fell before the Throne on their faces, and worshipped God,

Heretofore (ch. v. vers. 11, 12) when the Angels praised "the Lamb that was slain," we read not that they fell on their faces; but now beholding Him glorified in His saints and to be admired in all them that believe, they fall down in worship.

And in one sense this for which they fall down is a greater marvel than the other. For great and marvellous as are God's

works and ways, the marvel resides in the creature's apprehension of a truth newly revealed, and till then inscrutable and
unimaginable; not in the fact of any outcome whatsoever of
Goodness from Him Who is All Good of Love from Him
Who is Love. "He Himself knew what He would do" sets
forth not only the good pleasure of Christ, but the eternal,
uninterrupted, calm Will and Purpose of God.

But that man, of heart deceitful above all things and
desperately wicked, deathstruck and sin-relishing, endued with
free will, and so able to resist his Maker, should at length by
Divine patience, longsuffering and love unfeigned live once
more, and move, and have his being in God, his own free
will co-operating with Divine grace so that finally he is raised
up in heavenly places as a miracle and glorious, everlasting
monument of mercy; that man should do thus, and be thus,
transcends experience, baffles foresight, and is indeed a new
thing.

**12. Saying, Amen: Blessing, and glory, and wisdom, and
thanksgiving, and honour, and power, and might, be
unto our God for ever and ever. Amen.**

The rapturous Angels answer Amen to the triumph shout of
the enraptured redeemed. Amen they say first and last,
beginning and finishing in sympathy with a joy which primarily
befalls others. They exult when those who were beneath being
exalted to an equality, enter and stand within where they
themselves form the outer circle.

Alike in their former (ch. v. 12) and in their present chorus
of praise the Angels ascribe "Wisdom" to the Object of their
adoration. The first time it is to "the Lamb that was slain"
when He has prevailed to loose the Seven Seals; thereby
recalling St. Peter's statement: "Which things the Angels
desire to look into." The second time it is to God, when
before the Throne stand the saved arrayed in the garments
of salvation; thus reminding us of St. Paul's declaration aforetime: "To the intent that now unto the principalities and
powers in heavenly places might be known by the Church the
manifold wisdom of God."

**13. And one of the elders answered, saying unto me, What
are these which are arrayed in white robes? and
whence came they?**

A celestial model of catechetical instruction; the question
being propounded for the sake of the learner, not apparently
of the asker.

If this be the same elder who before spoke comfortably to
St. John, I note his personal gift of love : if it be another, I
note the general infusion and effusion of Divine charity.   As
I am now, I like to think him the same ; but as I hope to be
hereafter, I doubt not I shall then be well pleased whichever
way it turns out to have been.   For in the perfected Communion
of Saints surely the general glory of all will satisfy, no less than
the special glory proper to each will recreate.   I could more
imagine a perfected saint so immersed in universal love as to
be rapt out of the particular, than so absorbed in particular
love as to be estranged from the universal.

Thank God, I am not reduced to suppose either alternative.

In heaven all the redeemed are to be made like unto their
Redeemer; and I know, and am sure that Christ Who loves
us all, loves us each.

O Lord Jesus Who lovest each and all ; give us hearts wide
and deep to love all, exquisite and responsive to love each :
in proportion, or if it please Thee, out of proportion ; even
as Thou beyond all proportion lovest us.

"What are these which are arrayed in white robes ? "—The
white robes constitute one claim of these blessed ones on
celestial sympathy : not what they were originally, but what
has been wrought in them and for them establishes their
fellowship with the heavenly host.

How absolute and transcendent must be the spotless perfection of saints in glory, if not even St. John's experience in
mortal flesh availed to furnish him with an answer !

"What are these . . . and whence came they?"—In this
world and from the children of this world such questions might
mean : Are they common folk or gentry? learned or illiterate?
vulgar or refined? in or out of society? worth or not worth
knowing ?

The grave will set us at a different view-point.   There our
shallow earthly question will receive its answer out of all
mysteries and all knowledge.

If this be seemly and inevitable to-morrow, why not rectify
and elevate our standard (my standard) to-day ?

**14. And I said unto him, Sir, thou knowest. And he said
to me, These are they which came out of great tribulation, and have washed their robes, and made them
white in the blood of the Lamb.**

St. John, to our apprehension the most illuminated of the
Evangelists, makes himself, in accordance with St. Paul's

practice, a pattern of not stretching beyond the assigned measure. Here he humbly answers, "Sir, thou knowest"; and in his Gospel (*see* xxi. 23) he sets aside an inference which seemed to exalt him above his fellows.

Lord Jesus, shall he who lay on Thy Breast be humble, and will not we be humble? For very shame's sake clothe us with humility, that so we may become more like him and less unlike Thee. Amen.

"These are they which came out of great tribulation, and have washed their robes, and made them white in the blood of the Lamb."—Thus two points concur to produce the beatitude under contemplation: great tribulation, and the cleansing Blood of the Lamb. God hath joined them together; it is not for man to put them asunder. Yet this difference I observe: great tribulation could of its own virtue avail nothing without the Blood of the Lamb; whereas that most Precious Blood Divinely vouchsafed and applied could not but avail, though the redeemed were called out of great joy, and from green pastures, and from beside waters of comfort.

Indeed one striking instance occurs in the Old Testament, suggesting that whoso hath faith and hope enough may haply even in this world secure an approved felicity:—"And Jabez was more honourable than his brethren . . . . And Jabez called on the God of Israel, saying, Oh that Thou wouldest bless me indeed, and enlarge my coast, and that Thine hand might be with me, and that Thou wouldest keep me from evil, that it may not grieve me! And God granted him that which he requested." Whilst in the New Testament the history of the Holy Innocents seems almost a case in point: for small must have been their capacity for suffering who were spared foresight, and whom one blow or one grip sufficed in a moment to speed through the gate of death.

But presumably for most of us tribulation rather than ease constructs the safe road and the firm stepping-stone. Better to be taught with thorns of the wilderness and briars, than on no wise to be taught. Better great tribulation now than un-exampled tribulation hereafter.

> Good Lord, to-day
> I scarce find breath to say:
>   Scourge, but receive me.
> For stripes are hard to bear, but worse
> Thy intolerable curse;
>   So do not leave me.

Good Lord, lean down
In pity tho' Thou frown ;
    Smite, but retrieve me :
For so Thou hold me up to stand
And kiss Thy smiting hand,
    It less will grieve me.

" Tribulation," that is, sifting : sifting reclaims and releases good from bad, while aught of good remains. " Now no chastening for the present seemeth to be joyous, but grievous nevertheless afterward it yieldeth the peaceable fruit of righteousness unto them which are exercised thereby."

15. Therefore are they before the Throne of God, and serve Him day and night in His temple : and He that sitteth on the Throne shall dwell among them.

" Art Thou not from everlasting, O Lord my God, mine Holy One ? we shall not die. . . . Thou art of purer eyes than to behold evil, and canst not look on iniquity."

From everlasting to everlasting God is God, the Same yesterday and to-day and for ever. " Thou art the same, and Thy years shall have no end." " The righteous also shall give thanks unto Thy Name : and the just shall continue in Thy sight " :—the just shall, the unjust shall not. It is on pain of being cast out of the Divine Presence that we cling to sin.

The All-Holy desires to sanctify us, the All-Pure to purge us, that in the end He may set us up on high, and satisfy us with long life, and show us His salvation. Love desires the beloved ; Christ desires us : shall Love desire us, Christ desire us, in vain ? God forbid.

Lord Jesus, All-Pure, purify us that we may behold Thee. All-Holy, sanctify us that we may stand before Thee. All-Gracious, mould us that we may please Thee. Very Love, suffer us not to set at nought Thy Love. Suffer not devil, world, flesh, to destroy us. Suffer not ourselves to destroy ourselves ; us with whom Thou strivest, whom Thou desirest, whom Thou lovest.

" And serve Him day and night in His Temple."—Alas, Lord, that here on earth I have such tepid love for the habitation of Thy House, and the place where Thine Honour dwelleth ! Alas for any who are like me ! Grant us, I beseech Thee, if not yet delight at least perseverance in resorting to Thy most amiable tabernacles. Give us grace to do what we can, and of Thy free Grace do Thou for us and in us what we cannot. Give us grace to serve Thee in spite of ourselves here, that so we may serve Thee transfigured from our former selves hereafter. For our long-suffering Saviour's sake. Amen.

"Day and night."—But day unwaning, unending, how then night at all? Perhaps (for one thing) *night* suggests by association that service in Heaven will comport with and not disturb rest. No vigils there, all festivals : equally, no labour there, all rest.

"And He that sitteth on the Throne shall dwell among them,"—or, as in the Revised Version, " . . . shall spread His Tabernacle over them."—The first rendering sets before us Christ All-Gracious walking with His own in the House of God as friends. The second recalls a Divine promise which having had its temporal fulfilment amid drawbacks, awaits its eternal accomplishment in simple unalloyed perfection : " Oh how great is Thy goodness, which Thou hast laid up for them that fear Thee ; which Thou hast wrought for them that trust in Thee before the sons of men ! Thou shalt hide them in the secret of Thy Presence from the pride of man ; Thou shalt keep them secretly in a pavilion from the strife of tongues. Blessed be the Lord : for He hath shewed me His marvellous kindness in a strong city."

I think too that the Revised rendering seems peculiarly suggestive of the unspeakable unity of Christ the Head with His body the Church: as when Ruth, her whole career a prophetic parable, besought Boaz to spread his skirt over her ; or, as when Job protested, "If the men of my tabernacle said not, Oh that we had of his flesh ! we cannot be satisfied."

16. They shall hunger no more, neither thirst any more ; neither shall the sun light on them, nor any heat.

17. For the Lamb which is in the midst of the Throne shall feed them, and shall lead them unto living fountains of waters : and God shall wipe away all tears from their eyes.

"My soul refused to be comforted . . . I complained, and my spirit was overwhelmed," said once the inspired Psalmist.

And now the blessed Elder certifies St. John that the uncomforted faithful shall at last be comforted. They shall be delivered from all they ever endured, relieved from all they ever suffered. Their emptiness shall be fed and filled. " And God shall wipe away all tears [Revised Version: ' every tear '] from their eyes."

Vast is the consolatoriness, satisfaction, of this revelation.

Elsewhere we find rapture, here contentment; elsewhere an overflow, here enough.

Perhaps without presumption we may conjecture that at the moment in question St. John himself was peculiarly open to so comfortable a promise. His work-day had to outlast that of any other of the Twelve; his absence from Christ had to be prolonged beyond theirs. "As cold waters to a thirsty soul, so is good news from a far country."

To the swift and the strong rapture may prove more alluring than relief, triumph than rest. But to the slow and the feeble, to such as trudge on however slowly and toil on however feebly, relief and rest appear a mighty boon; in hope of which the hanging hands and feeble knees are again and again lifted up with piteous indomitable perseverance. Literal hunger and thirst are a keen craving, literal heat intensified and untempered is a sore trial; and the literal are no more than types of the spiritual. If it was not good for man to be alone in Eden, how dreary is loneliness in this outer world. Christ, Himself the Man of sorrows and acquainted with grief, pronounced mourners blessed, but inasmuch as they should be comforted; and when He bade one mourner "Weep not," vouchsafed with the word a foretaste of reunion.

O Lord my God, perfect us in such patience that we may be in no haste to escape from toil or loneliness or suffering; yet ever in haste to serve Thee, to please Thee, and when Thou wilt to go home to Thy Blessed Presence. For our Lord Jesu's sake. Amen.

This beatified multitude in Heaven will be led by "the Lamb." Very meek must they be whom the Lamb shall lead: very pure, not to shame Him Who is without blemish and without spot: very innocent, to be made one flock with Him.

Lest any of us should so stray as to be finally separated from Him Who alone is Love and our own Joy, I pray Him— I pray Thee, O Lord Jesus, to make us also meek, pure, innocent.

O Lamb of God, Who art in the midst of the Throne, show Thy mercy on them that fear Thee; exalt the humble and meek, fill the hungry with good things, help Thy militant Israel; here sanctify us, hereafter glorify us; for Thine own sake, O God our Saviour. Amen.

"Living fountains of waters,"—or as in the Revised Version: "Fountains of waters of life."—These words seem capable of connection with an utterance of our Lord's own lips recorded by St. John in his Gospel: "Jesus stood and cried, saying,

If any man thirst, let him come unto Me, and drink. He that believeth on Me, as the scripture hath said, out of his belly shall flow rivers of living water. (But this spake He of the Spirit, which they that believe on Him should receive : for the Holy Ghost was not yet given; because that Jesus was not yet glorified)."

If it is allowable to assume that the two passages may stand thus connected, we trace here a further harmony with that promise which concerns the "Other Comforter," and discern Him abiding with the elect for ever.

The waters of Baptism, "waters under the firmament," conveyed Him to the called soul ; and "waters that be above the firmament" may haply (at least in a figure) do no less for the chosen and faithful. That would indeed be to drink of the river of Divine pleasures.

It has, I believe, been alleged that a multitude of Christians are but slow of heart and dull of sight and of hearing in what regards an adoring perception of God the Holy Ghost.

It may help myself against so perilous an obtuseness, to search out from what quarter the temptation might advance to encroach on and annul my own faith, thereby vitiating if not totally subverting my practice.

The revelation of the Father implies the Son ; the revelation of the Son implies the Father : but by signification of neither Divine Name is the Holy Spirit implied to our finite apprehension. Even when Christ said : "No man knoweth the Son, but the Father; neither knoweth any man the Father, save the Son, and he to whomsoever the Son will reveal Him," we still see not our tokens.

The very Name "the Holy Spirit" does not necessarily announce Him : inasmuch as we are taught concerning the Godhead that "God is a Spirit" ; Who moreover hath said to man : "Be ye holy; for I am holy."

The actual Graciousness and overflowing Goodness of God the Holy Ghost may be so misused by us as to obscure His Personality. His diffusion throughout the Communion of Saints may be misconstrued as His non-existence independent of that Communion : reducing our conception of Him to a grace, a gift; not a distinct, Divine, Almighty Person.

I think too that the devout formula "Jesus Christ our only Mediator and Advocate," may beguile us into positive though inadvertent misstatement, unless we consciously limit "only" to "Mediator" ; jealously bearing in mind that God the Holy Ghost vouchsafes to be our other Advocate.

O God the Most Holy Trinity, Who seest that Truth itself will not instruct us without Thy preventing, guarding, guiding grace ; grant us to live by every word that proceedeth out of Thy mouth, and to walk and rejoice in the light of Thy Truth ; and give us grace so to bring forth fruits of the Spirit as to attest that Divine Indwelling to all men, and if it please Thee to our own humble consciousness likewise. I plead Jesus. Amen.

CHAPTER VIII.

1. And when He had opened the seventh seal, there was silence in heaven about the space of half an hour.

There seems to be a sense in which heaven waits on earth; in which (if I dare say so) God waits on man. Thus heaven now keeps silence as a prelude to earthly events, portents, vicissitudes.

Yet need not this celestial silence convey to us (I conjecture) any notion of interruption in the day and night harmony of worship before the Throne, any more than time interrupts eternity. For because we dare not think of God Who " inhabiteth eternity " as changing to a habitation of time, we thence perceive that time and eternity co-exist, are simultaneous : if, that is, they be not rather different aspects of one and the same continuity.

If from the songs of heaven we learn to sing and make melody to the Lord with both voice and understanding, equally from the silence of heaven we may learn somewhat.

Whilst heaven kept silence it appears it may have been looking or preparing to look earthwards. And of old David declared : "I will keep my mouth with a bridle, while the wicked is before me. I was dumb with silence, I held my peace, even from good." Thus from Angels above and from a saint below, I may study that meekness of righteous indignation, that discretion of holy zeal, which brings not railing accusations nor risks doing harm even by good words.

. Silence seems unnatural, incongruous, in heaven. On this occasion and remotely we may surmise it to be a result of the Fall, for when earth first saw the light in panoply of beauty the morning stars sang together and all the sons of God shouted for joy : sinless earth, for sinless it then seems to have been whether or not inhabited, called forth instead of silencing an outburst of celestial music.

Q

I think one may view this " silence " as a figure of suspense. Reversing which proposition, I perceive that a Christian's suspense ought to present a figure of that silence.

And if so, suspense should sustain my heart in heavenly peace even whilst fluttering over some spot of earth ; and should become my method of worship, when other modes fail me ; and should be adopted by my free will, whenever by God's Will it befalls me ; and should not hinder heaven from appearing heaven to me, or divorce me from fellowship with angels, or make me speak unadvisedly with my lips. Faithful, hopeful, loving suspense would be rich in evidence of things not seen and not heard ; and would neither lag nor hurry, but would contentedly maintain silence during its imposed " half-hour." A shorter time? no, on pain of rashness : a longer time? no, on pain of sullenness.

This silence followed and waited upon an act of our Lord : " when He had opened the seventh seal."—" Unto Thee lift I up mine eyes, O Thou that dwellest in the heavens. Behold, as the eyes of servants look unto the hand of their masters, and as the eyes of a maiden unto the hand of her mistress ;. so our eyes wait upon the Lord our God, until that He have mercy upon us."

" About the space of half an hour."—Not finally, not for long. " Our God shall come, and shall not keep silence. . . . He shall call to the heavens from above, and to the earth, that He may judge His people. . . . And the heavens shall declare His righteousness."

> The half moon shows a face of plaintive sweetness
> Ready and poised to wax or wane ;
> A fire of pale desire in incompleteness,
> Tending to pleasure or to pain :—
> Lo, while we gaze she rolleth on in fleetness
> To perfect loss or perfect gain.
>
> Half bitterness we know, we know half sweetness ;
> This world is all on wax, on wane :
> When shall completeness round time's incompleteness
> Fulfilling joy, fulfilling pain ?—
> Lo, while we ask, life rolleth on in fleetness
> To finished loss or finished gain.

2. And I saw the seven angels which stood before God ; and to them were given seven trumpets.

Recalling the seven trumpets of rams' horns sounded by the seven priests on seven successive days, whereby was announced and achieved the overthrow of Jericho.

The seven priests blew their trumpets together, the seven

Angels one by one; the seven priests thus appearing as it were equivalent to the single angel; in accordance with St. Peter's declaration: "Angels, which are greater in power and might." And as the agency is greater, so apparently the series of events is greater and the result greater; harmonizing with Isaiah's prophecy, when after foretelling "the day of the great slaughter, when the towers fall,"—he adds: "Moreover the light of the moon shall be as the light of the sun, and the light of the sun shall be sevenfold, as the light of seven days."

Jericho, the outpost of the Promised Land; the earthly Israel shouting and going up straight before them: a figure of the spiritual Israel going out with joy and led forth with peace into the heavenly Canaan.

The destruction of Jericho and entering in of the chosen race, whether considered from the historical or from the emblematical view-point, encourages us to face hopefully the awful unprecedented blast of the seven angelic trumpets. Then the Ark of the Lord encamped before Jericho among the thousands of Israel: and Christ our true and sole Ark of Safety has promised His Church: "Lo, I am with you alway, even unto the end of the world."

His Presence ensures safety and every blessing. Yet it may be—and if such be His Will, Christ grant it may be even so to you, to all, to me—it may be that one day It will ensure these by taking the place to us of any other safety and of every other spiritual blessing. For instance: of old He pronounced, "The Sabbath was made for man, and not man for the Sabbath," upholding its pious though not its superstitious observance; and again He tenderly bade His disciples, "Pray ye that your flight be not . . . on the Sabbath-day." The Sabbath ranks amongst venerable and immutable Divine institutions, dating back to unfallen man in the Garden of Eden; yet may it be reft from us as regards its outward national observance, though never from the faithful as regards its inward hallowing. Already in England (not to glance at other countries) the signs of the times are ominous: Sunday is being diverted by some to business, by others to pleasure; Church congregations are often meagre, and so services are chilled. Our solemn feasts languish, and our fasts where are they? Yet each for himself, and God for us all, we can if we choose "remember the Sabbath-day, to keep it holy"; jealous of its essentials, not wedded to its accidents.

So Joshua and his host when summoned to storm Jericho day after day for seven days, must amongst those days have kept one unexampled Sabbath, if not in the letter yet in the spirit.

> 3. **And another angel came and stood at the altar, having a golden censer; and there was given unto him much incense, that he should offer it with the prayers of all saints upon the golden altar which was before the Throne.**
> 4. **And the smoke of the incense, which came with the prayers of the saints, ascended up before God out of the angel's hand.**

The celestial altar may transcend but can never contradict the terrestrial. One throws light upon the other. To meditate on the altar which we know, seems one safe way of meditating on the altar which we know not.

In heaven "an angel," here a priest ministers; and whether priest or angel, he who stands acceptably before God on behalf of man cannot but represent Christ; "for there is One God, and One Mediator between God and men, the Man Christ Jesus; Who gave Himself a ransom for all, to be testified in due time."

There the altar is of gold; here well might it be of gold. Virtually it becomes of gold when it is of our costliest, choicest, best; but not so, if man's house is of cedar whilst the Lord's is of curtains.

There out of a golden censer prayers ascend by fire. For prayer offered in Christ's Name is such a human work as can stand fire, a worthy superstructure raised on the One Foundation (*see* 1 Cor. iii. 11—15). And since "out of the abundance of the heart the mouth speaketh,". the censer may remind us of that heart which God claims as His own portion (as if He said, "My son, give Me thine heart,") from "the precious sons of Zion, comparable to fine gold." Or rather let it remind us of the Heart of that Only always-acceptable Beloved Son Who, ever living to make intercession for us, presents before the Throne all our needs out of His own heart.

There much incense goes up as smoke with the saints' prayers. Isaiah in vision beheld the Temple of the Lord "filled with smoke"; and perhaps we may compare such smoke to a cloud; figuratively, even to that Cloud which under the elder covenant indicated the Divine Presence. If, so, this sacred smoke may remind us of that Presence of Christ which is plighted to two or three supplicants gathered together in His Name; and of that blessed Advocacy whereby·

Christ and the Holy Spirit deign to effectuate our petitions, rendering them in their degree acceptable like that odour of spikenard wherewith one woman's love filled the house where Jesus supped.

Whereupon the incense and smoke of the incense should kindle us to utmost adoration and love, by thus setting before us Christ Who for our sakes made Himself once for all a whole Burnt Offering, an Offering and a sweet-smelling Savour to the Glory of God the Father ; and Who in the Blessed Sacrament of His Body and Blood having left to His Church a perpetual Memorial of His sole sufficient Sacrifice, receives us and our petitions into the " secret place " of that Presence and sets us in heavenly places with His own Self.

"OUT OF THE ANGEL'S HAND."

No Cherub's heart or hand for us might ache, .
　　No Seraph's heart of fire had half sufficed :
Thine own were pierced and broken for our sake,
　　O Jesus Christ.

Therefore we love Thee with our faint good will,
　　We crave to love Thee not as heretofore,
To love Thee much, to love Thee more, and still
　　More and yet more.

5. And the angel took the censer, and filled it with fire of the altar, and cast it into the earth : and there were voices, and thunderings, and lightnings, and an earthquake.

If I may view this blessed Angel as in any sense representing his and our Lord, then may his casting the fiery censer into the earth recall to my mind a declaration from our Lord's own lips : " I am come to send fire on the earth ; and what will I, if it be already kindled ?　But I have a baptism to be baptized with ; and how am I straitened till it be accomplished !　Suppose ye that I am come to give peace on earth ?　I tell you, Nay ; but rather division."

Then also I may take shelter from terrors of fire, voices, thunderings, lightnings, earthquake, in the sympathy of Jesus : loved He us of old, and doth He not love us now ? loveth He us now, and will He not love us then ?

As the dove which found no rest
　　For sole of her foot, flew back
To the ark her only nest
　　And found safety there ;　.

Because Noah put forth his hand,
· Drew her in fiom ruin and wiack,
And was more to her than the land
    And the air :
So my spirit, like that dove, .
    Fleeth away to an ark
Wheie dwelleth a Heart of love,
    A Hand pierced to save ;
Tho' the sun and the moon should fail,
    Tho' the stars drop into the dark,
And my body lay itself pale
    In a grave.

If I may imagine one petition rather than another to have constituted those prayers of saints which mounted acceptably from the golden censer, it may have been "Thy Kingdom come." For it can never have been in denial of such prayers that the censer, emptied of them, was refilled with fire of the Altar, and cast into the earth.

Because "fire," therefore either purifying as gold or else consuming as dross; because "of the Altar," therefore either sanctifying as Jerusalem or else devoting as Jericho.

Fire of the Altar seems clearly a type of God the Holy Ghost, in conformity with the text : "Christ, Who through the Eternal Spirit offered Himself without spot to God." And if here in St. John's vision we may with reverence so regard it, its descent to earth with the awful phenomena ensuing, sets once more before us how every condescension of God to man must either save or destroy, cannot leave man as he was before the visitation, cannot suffer that the righteous should be finally as the wicked, or the wicked as the righteous. So it befell when "God looked upon the earth, and behold, it was corrupt," in the days of Noah ; so, when " the Lord came down to see the city and the tower, which the children of men builded," and scattered abroad the future nations ; so, when He spake concerning Sodom and Gomorrah, " I will go down now, and see whether they have done altogether according to the cry of it, which is come unto Me "; yet remembered Lot : so, when Christ ministered amongst men ; " Many of His disciples went back, and walked no more with Him. Then said Jesus unto the twelve, Will ye also go away? Then Simon Peter answered Him, Lord, to whom shall we go? Thou hast the words of eternal life " : and even so at Pentecost, when the Holy Spirit descended upon the Church with audible and visible signs, Israel was split asunder into the camp of believers and the hostile camp of unbelievers.

O Lord Almighty, to Whom continually Thy Church reiterates

those awful words "Thy kingdom come"; grant her such
grace that holy love may overcome in her holy fear, and that
like as the hart desireth the water-brooks, so her soul may long
after thee, O God. For Jesus Christ's sake, her Spouse. Amen.

Voices, though uninterpreted, yet exhorting me to prepare
to meet my God. *Thunders*, though inarticulate, yet summon-
ing me to make ready against the Great Day. *Lightnings*,
though evanescent, yet warning me as once the Writing,
Belshazzar. *Earthquake*, though not hitherto beneath my feet,
yet bidding me lay up betimes in heaven treasures indestructible.

6. And the seven angels which had the seven trumpets prepared themselves to sound.

Zephaniah the Prophet foretells a crisis of like sweeping
calamity: "The great day of the Lord is near, it is near, and
hasteth greatly, even the voice of the day of the Lord: the
mighty man shall cry there bitterly. That day is a day of
wrath, a day of trouble and distress, a day of wasteness and
desolation, a day of darkness and gloominess, a day of clouds
and thick darkness, a day of the trumpet and alarm against the
fenced cities, and against the high towers. And I will bring
distress upon men, and they shall walk like blind men, because
they have sinned against the Lord: and their blood shall be
poured out as dust, and their flesh as the dung. Neither their
silver nor their gold shall be able to deliver them in the day of
the Lord's wrath; but the whole land shall be devoured by the
fire of His jealousy: for He shall make even a speedy riddance
of all them that dwell in the land."

The same prophet propounds to us moreover our duty and
privilege on the brink of such destruction: "Gather yourselves
together, yea, gather together, O nation not desired; before the
decree bring forth, before the day pass as the chaff, before the
fierce anger of the Lord come upon you, before the day of the
Lord's anger come upon you. Seek ye the Lord, all ye meek
of the earth, which have wrought His judgment; seek righteousness, seek meekness: it may be ye shall be hid in the day of
the Lord's anger."

Let us not make ourselves like to the horse that hath no understanding, of whom we read, "neither believeth he that it is the
sound of the trumpet. He saith among the trumpets, Ha, ha."

Thy trumpet, Lord Jesus, giveth no uncertain sound: prepare
Thou us to the battle. O Lord God of hosts, blessed is the
man that putteth his trust in Thee.

Angels, whom the result seems to concern only secondarily

sound not without self-preparation : shall man whose all is at
stake not prepare himself ?

O Lord Jesus, Who hast called the Church Thy sister, love,
dove, spouse : Abide close to us, our Brother, our Friend, and
prepare us ;

> Love us unto the end, and prepare us ;
> By indwelling of the Holy Spirit, the Dove, prepare us ;
> For better, for worse, prepare us ;
> That so death itself may not part us.   Amen.

> Thy fainting spouse, yet still Thy spouse ;
>   Thy trembling dove, yet still Thy dove ;
> Thine own by mutual vows,
>   By mutual love.

> Recall Thy vows, if not her vows ;
>   Recall Thy love, if not her love :
> For weak she is, Thy spouse,
>   And tired, Thy dove.

A series of historical events has been compiled as corresponding with the seven trumpet blasts.   But as those blasts
cease not to peal in the Church's ears, I trust we may lawfully
in some degree and on occasion forget concerning them those
things that are behind, and rather reach forward to those
things which are still before : for oftentimes one fulfilment
illustrates, but seems by no means to exhaust prophecy.

7. The first angel sounded, and there followed hail and fire mingled with blood, and they were cast upon the earth : and the third part of trees was burnt up, and all green grass was burnt up.

The Revised Version precedes the other similar clauses of
this verse by the words : " And the third part of the earth was
burnt up."

In the Answer out of the Whirlwind we read : " Hast thou
seen the treasures of the hail, which I have reserved against
the time of trouble, against the day of battle and war ? "—
which weapon was brought forth from the Divine armoury
when the Lord fought for Israel against the Egyptians : " The
Lord sent thunder and hail, and the fire ran along upon the
ground ; and the Lord rained hail upon the land of Egypt.
So there was hail, and fire mingled with the hail, very
grievous. . . .   And the hail smote throughout all the land of
Egypt all that was in the field, both man and beast ; and the
hail smote every herb of the field, and brake every tree of the
field."   And again, when the five infatuated Kings of the

Amorites and their hosts having joined battle with Joshua were discomfited, " it came to pass, as they fled from before Israel . . . that the Lord cast down great stones from heaven upon them, . . . and they died : they were more which died with hailstones than they whom the children of Israel slew with the sword."

But in this Apocalyptic vision of hail, fire, and blood, St. John beheld [earth,] trees, grass, " burnt up " : neither shattered nor crushed that we read, but devoured. Height exempted not the trees, nor lowness the grass.

This hail and fire being " mingled with blood " suggests at once that no mere elemental storm destructive of inanimate nature may here be depicted. " The Voice said, Cry. And he said, What shall I cry? All flesh is grass . . . surely the people is grass." And that trees may stand for men is plain from Jotham's fable: " Then said all the trees unto the bramble, Come thou, and reign over us. And the bramble said unto the trees, If in truth ye anoint me king over you, then come and put your trust in my shadow : and if not, let fire come out of the bramble, and devour the cedars of Lebanon. Now therefore, if ye have done truly and sincerely, in that ye have made Abimelech king . . ."

Between the *trees* and the *grass* a distinction is made : only the *third part* of trees was burnt up, but *all* green grass. Had all trees been burnt, then they all must have perished ; for a charred stump can send up no second sapful trunk : therefore some we see taken, some left. With grass and with green herbs in general the case may, I suppose, be different : the bracken, for instance, renews itself in exquisite verdure after the faded autumn overgrowth has been ignited and consumed.

Which train of thought seems not discordant with a Divine promise : " Fear thou not, O Jacob My servant, saith the Lord : for I am with thee. . . . I will not make a full end of thee, but correct thee in measure ; yet will I not leave thee wholly unpunished."

8. **And the second angel sounded, and as it were a great mountain burning with fire was cast into the sea : and the third part of the sea became blood ;**
9. **And the third part of the creatures which were in the sea, and had life, died ; and the third part of the ships were destroyed.**

Truth confronts us veiled, not in order to baffle us, but rather that our zeal may be redoubled to discern her.

" God is our refuge and strength, a very present help in

trouble.   Therefore will not we fear, though the earth be removed, though the mountains be carried into the midst of the sea ; though the waters thereof roar and be troubled, though the mountains shake with the swelling thereof."   Thus, by aid of God's grace, sang the Psalmist.   And if so he, so at the least ought we : for he looked forward to what would be wrought for his salvation, while we look backward to what has actually been achieved for ours.   Jesus, the Name above every name, is the "desired haven" of our souls : "The Name of the Lord is a strong tower : the righteous runneth into It, and is safe."

O Lord Jesus, the Truth, the Wisdom, the Word of God ; of Thine exceeding Goodness make us, I beseech Thee, so one with Thyself, that cleaving unto Thee we may accept all truth though we cannot express it, and be replenished with wisdom however scant our knowledge, and speak gracious words or keep gracious silence in our daily walk with Thee and with one another.   Amen.

At the first trumpet-blast, fire from heaven did its appointed work of destruction ; now, at the second, this "great mountain burning with fire" seems rather to be of the earth earthy. Both are equally the rod of God's anger ; the latter agent corresponding in some of its effects with that literal Rod of God whereby Aaron, inflicting the first plague upon Egypt, turned the Nile into blood, so that all the fish died and the river stank.

Then *all* the fish perished : now *one-third* part of the living creatures and of the ships.

Those, although mere fish, were set up as false gods ; the Nile itself being for practical purposes also a false god.

We are not informed what offence or what multitude of offences may call for this Apocalyptic destruction of a third part ; but presumably the warning primarily concerns us men and our salvation, rather than any lower creatures involved by Adam's fall in man's punishment.   To quote St. Paul's words in a different context : "Saith he it altogether for our sakes ? For our sakes, no doubt, this is written."

The Prophet Isaiah once for good and once for evil employs the sea as a similitude of mankind.   For good : "The abnndance of the sea shall be converted unto thee,"—but before that for evil : "The wicked are like the troubled sea, when it cannot rest, whose waters cast up mire and dirt."

Considering the parallel with the first Egyptian plague, idolatry suggests itself as a possible provocation here also ; and this the less hazardously, because though we might hesitate to

define idolatry as the only sin, yet has every sin at the least an
idolatrous side; be the sin what it may, its commission
demonstrates that something is preferred before God.

Isaiah exposes the arrant folly of idolatry in its grossly literal
form of image worship: "They have not known nor understood: for He hath shut their eyes, that they cannot see; and
their hearts, that they cannot understand. And none considereth in his heart, neither is there knowledge nor understanding to say,' I have burned part of it in the fire; yea, also
I have baked bread upon the coals thereof; I have roasted
flesh, and eaten it: and shall I make the residue thereof an
abomination? shall I fall down to the stock of a tree? He
feedeth on ashes: a deceived heart hath turned him aside, that
he cannot deliver his soul, nor say, 'Is there not a lie in my
right hand?'"

We are not likely to worship images. Perhaps not. But
our Lord commands all to take heed, and beware of covetousness: and St. Paul warns his Colossian converts that covetousness is idolatry. Stubbornness, too, is as idolatry; as King
Saul found to his cost.

Whatever may be thought about the living sea-creatures, the
mention of ships directs our attention to men. And ships by
association suggest commerce; and commerce, alas! too often
covetousness. Or if we turn to war-ships, stubbornness seems
only too probable in connection with them.

10. And the third angel sounded, and there fell a great star
    from heaven, burning as it were a lamp, and it fell
    upon the third part of the rivers, and upon the
    fountains of waters;

11. And the name of the star is called Wormwood: and the
    third part of the waters became wormwood; and
    many men died of the waters, because they were
    made bitter.

This third fire, for at each trumpet-peal hitherto fire has
appeared, differs from the former two at least as widely as they
from each other.

The first visitation resembles a storm, although in details
and in effect more terrific than storms of this world. To the
first angel summons clouds respond with abundance of water;
lightnings answer and say, Here we are.

The second visitation appears as if a volcano were cast down
headlong. Once Mount Sinai was altogether on a smoke; and
if then Moses, now much more may we exceedingly fear and
quake to witness in a figure the Law avenge itself on transgressors.

The third blast evokes neither an evanescent nor a terrene
fire, but "a great star from heaven, burning as it were a lamp":
thus liable to recall to the mind even involuntarily by verbal
association the sacred verses: "For ever, O Lord, Thy word is
settled in heaven. . .   Thy word is a lamp unto my feet,
and a light unto my path."

This star then is from heaven, and is a luminary, yet is its
name Wormwood, and its effect fatal bitterness. Still, although
it embitters both the third part of rivers and even of springs;
yet we read not that *all* men died of those waters, but *many;*
perhaps intimating that amongst those even who drank, some
survived. "Teach me good judgment and knowledge: for
I have believed Thy commandments. . . .   My soul fainteth
for Thy salvation : but I hope in Thy word."

If such an inference is allowable, then I venture to view as
not incongruous with this passage the dangers which beset
secular knowledge ; a consideration exhibiting an urgently
practical side in this our day of widespread and wider-spreading
culture.

For in the text we behold light introducing men to the darkness of death; an emblem of unsanctified knowledge and its
tendency. The star is a genuine illuminator : so may the
knowledge be genuine knowledge ; yet not being mixed with
faith in them that hold it, it becomes to them perilous or even
deadly.

Whether any given knowledge will prove profitable or unprofitable is a question by itself, independent of any debate as
to its authenticity.   However beguiled, Eve learned the difference between good and evil: so in his turn did Adam, of whom
it is expressly stated that he was not deceived. What they
learned was so far genuine : all the same it proved fatal.
Knowledge and wisdom are quite distinct, though not necessarily sundered.

Again : in the same sense that some see and yet see not,
hear and yet hear not, so some may be said to know without
knowing. As for instance the antediluvians, who were forewarned of the impending catastrophe, and who yet "knew not
until the flood came, and took them all away." Unassimilated
truth avails nothing.

Some there are who, familiarized with both, set the evidence
of their senses above Divine promises: as when Dathan and
Abiram murmured against Moses, "Thou hast not brought us
into a land that floweth with milk and honey . . . wilt thou
put out the eyes of these men?" or as when a certain courtier
weighed probability against an inspired utterance of Elisha.

saying : "Behold, if the Lord would make windows in heaven, might this thing be?" The blind who say they see are brought in guilty.

St. Paul's charge to his "dearly beloved son" seems written afresh for ourselves in this nineteenth century : "O Timothy, keep that which is committed to thy trust, avoiding profane and vain babblings, and oppositions of science falsely so called : which some professing, have erred concerning the faith. Grace be with thee. Amen."

If it be fatal to hold error, what must it be to propagate error?

Amongst all channels of instruction, speech is the readiest and is universal. A noble gift entailing a vast responsibility. St. James sets forth its awful many-sidedness : "If any man offend not in word, the same is a perfect man, and is able also to bridle the whole body. . . . The tongue is a little member, and boasteth great things. Behold, how great a matter a little fire kindleth! And the tongue is a fire, a world of iniquity : so is the tongue among our members, that it defileth the whole body, and setteth on fire the course of nature ; and it is set on fire of hell. . . . The tongue can no man tame; it is an unruly evil, full of deadly poison. Therewith bless we God, even the Father; and therewith curse we men, which are made after the similitude of God. Out of the same mouth proceedeth blessing and cursing. My brethren, these things ought not so to be. Doth a fountain send forth at the same place sweet water and bitter?"

And what is true of the tongue is in ample proportion true of the pen : this likewise may bless, edify, diffuse sweetness ; or may become a fire, a world of iniquity, may propagate defilement, and kindle impious fire, being itself set on fire of hell.

O Longsuffering Lord Jesus, curse not our blessings which we have slighted, but renew them to us. Retrieve for us Thy gifts which we have perverted, and make us blessed and a blessing. Grant us grace by Thy Most Holy Spirit, to devote ourselves and all our powers to Thee, even as Thou by the same Spirit deignest to give Thyself to us. Amen. Is anything too hard for God? Nay.

12. And the fourth angel sounded, and the third part of the sun was smitten, and the third part of the moon, and the third part of the stars ; so as the third part of them was darkened, and the day shone not for a third part of it, and the night likewise.

It seems more marvellous that for earth's sake the stars

should be smitten, than that the sun and moon should be so: for Genesis reveals how sun and moon were created with reference to earth; whilst in the same passage (as I have read in explanation) the stars are mentioned parenthetically, not as simultaneously, but as already created; and are so mentioned not in direct connection with earth's economy, but lest otherwise they might come to be regarded not at all as creatures of the One Universal Creator, their date of existence being assumed as manifestly anterior to the fourth day of creation.

> How great is little man!
>   Sun, moon and stars respond to him,
>   Shine or grow dim
> Harmonious with his span.
>
> How little is great man!
>   More changeable than changeful moon,
>   Nor-half in tune
> With Heaven's harmonious plan.
>
> Ah rich man! ah poor man!
>   Make ready for the testing day,
>   When wastes away
> What bears not fire or fan.
>
> Thou heir of all things man,
>   Pursue the saints by heavenward track:
>   They looked not back;
> Run thou, as erst they ran.
>
> Little and great is man:
>   Great if he will, or if he will
>   A pigmy still;
> For what he will he can.

Again the "third part" smitten, and not the whole: bidding us both "count it all longsuffering," and redeem the time because the days are evil. For surely if this revelation of judgment so bids the men and women of that generation endure and do, whichever generation may be in question; it equally adjures us to-day while it is called to-day: for upon us all alike must finally descend the total night when none can work.

A curtailed day is still a day with daylight opportunities. An ended day is a day done with for good or for evil.

At a first glance it might seem as if no specially appropriate discipline was organized to train us for this diminution of light: by help of grace ordinary bereavement may become that discipline. Bereavement is often a taking away the desire of our eyes with a stroke: if we practise bearing this patiently, thankfully, lovingly, we may entertain a good hope of so bearing the other should our appointed days include that day of darkness and gloominess. "Nevertheless the dimness shall not be such as was in her vexation."

Lord Jesus, how shall I attain to bear patiently the loss of my beloved?—By loving Me more.

How shall I endure when sun, moon, and stars are smitten? —By following Me as thy light Who am alone thy salvation.

One-third taken, *two*-thirds left: I have long dwelt on the threat; I have too long overlooked the promise. Better to lose a third and be thankful, than to retain the whole and be thankless. It is sadly amiss never to perceive how much sunshine gilds our mortal day until that brightness is diminished.

> A moon impoverished amid stars curtailed,
> A sun of its exuberant lustre shorn,
> A transient morning that is scarcely morn,
> A lingering night in double dimness veiled,—
> Our hands are slackened and our strength has failed :
> We born to darkness, wherefore were we born?
> No ripening more for olive, grape, or corn :
> Faith faints, hope faints, even love himself has paled.
> Nay !—love lifts up a face like any rose
> Flushing and sweet above a thorny stem,
> Softly protesting that the way he knows ;
> And as for faith and hope, will carry them
> Safe to the gate of New Jerusalem
> Where light shines full and where the palm tree blows.

13. And I beheld, and heard an angel flying through the midst of heaven, saying with a loud voice, Woe, woe, woe, to the inhabiters of the earth by reason of the other voices of the trumpet of the three angels, which are yet to sound!

"An angel," or in the Revised Version "An eagle."

If every day eagles cannot convey to me any instruction, I dare not flatter myself that actual angels would teach me to much purpose. According to that weighty answer of Father Abraham : "If they hear not Moses and the prophets, neither will they be persuaded, though one rose from the dead" :—the fault in all such cases being chargeable to the listener.

So while waiting for Angels let us utilize eagles. By looking steadfastly toward heaven we are certain to discern something there : whereas by not looking at all in that direction we must inevitably miss both heaven and its population.

The Apostolick Eagle "beheld" and recognized a celestial fellow Eagle : not even he, I suppose, could have beheld without looking.

St. John whilst still a sojourner in this world heard the message, "Woe, woe, woe, to the inhabiters of the earth."

On the point of ascending to heaven Christ had answered His Apostles : "It is not for you to know the times or the seasons, which the Father hath put in His own power."

It is therefore open to conjecture that whilst St. John was satisfied of the advancing Woes he foresaw not the exact moment of their arrival. He may thus have shared the suspense which is our own habitual lot.

Perhaps it may comfort some to think that St. John had a share in the common trial : much more would it comfort us all to undergo it in his spirit. And wherefore not? The disciple whom Jesus loved was not loved to our exclusion.

Our Lord declared : "The things concerning Me have an end." And Christ-like souls can by grace even give thanks because the things concerning themselves likewise have an end, so keenly do they desire to depart and be with Him Whom their soul loveth.

But I woful sinner fear the end which endeth not. In my fear to whom shall I go, save to Him Who hath the words of eternal life? "Hath God forgotten to be gracious? . . . And I said, It is mine own infirmity."

Lord Jesus, Who waitest to be gracious, be gracious to us who tremble, to us who mourn, to us all who many ways offend, to us who are ready to perish. Thou canst not be otherwise than gracious : render us susceptible of Thy grace. Amen.

How weighty must be the three coming woes, since the four preceding seem by comparison not to be called woes. An Angel, himself insusceptible of woe, celebrates those three. Apparently the first four catastrophes are wrought by agencies of inanimate nature. The three woes connect themselves with active wickedness; therefore are they essentially and pre-eminently Woes. "Oh let the wickedness of the wicked come to an end."

Terror of punishment should not swallow up horror of sin. God's act is good; mine evil : shall I recoil from the good rather than from the evil? This were in its degree to choose the evil and refuse the good.

O Lord God Who hast created all things in order and proportion, and requirest us likewise to have a perfect and just weight and measure; grant us grace to judge righteous judgment, and evermore to place our whole trust in Thee. Through Jesus Christ our Lord. Amen.

CHAPTER IX.

1. And the fifth angel sounded, and I saw a star fall from heaven unto the earth : and to him was given the key of the bottomless pit.

THE Revised Version has: "I saw a star from heaven fallen unto the earth,"—not seeming necessarily to imply that St. John witnessed its downfall; but perhaps that he discerned the star, that (so to say) it only then came to light, being *already* fallen.

If such a suggestion may be entertained, then the office assigned to this fallen star may possibly brand it as being one of the rulers of the darkness of this world; once superhuman, but now of its own free choice a subhuman wandering star to whom is reserved the blackness of darkness for ever. "How art thou fallen from heaven, O Lucifer, son of the morning!"

Whatever the star be, one thing is evident: its function is assigned to it; it is not an independent agent, still less an independent potentate. If it be a malevolent power rejoicing in iniquity, yet has it no power at all except under constraint or by sufferance; any more than the sea can overpass its decreed place, or behemoth evade the sword of Him that made him.

A fallen star, not otherwise an outcast star; a self-made outcast. Whoso turns his back on heaven may propose to stop short at earth: but next below yawns the pit. The outcasts of the final day who depart into outer darkness will all be self-made outcasts.

> Oh fallen star ! a darkened light,
> A glory hurtled from its car,
> Self-blasted from the holy height :
> Oh fallen star !
>
> Fallen beyond earth's utmost bar,
> Beyond return, beyond far sight
> Of outmost glimmering nebular:

R

Now blackness, which once walked in white ;
  Now death, whose life once glowed afar ;
Oh son of dawn that loved the night,
    Oh fallen star !

Self-conceit blinds, self-will destroys; self-oblation con-
secrates, self-sacrifice saves : for once our Master taught His
disciples : "If any man will come after Me, let him deny
himself, and take up his cross daily, and follow Me. For
whosoever will save his life shall lose it : but whosoever will
lose his life for My sake, the same shall save it."

The bottomless pit preaches a sermon. It has a lid : which
keep shut, and the pit's bottomlessness remains neutral. But
lift the lid, and none can calculate the volume of deathly outcome from a fathomless abyss, or the depth of a fall into it.

If God permits the lid of evil to be lifted as a test or as a
punishment, the key remains in His hand to secure that lid
again when He will. But if I lift any lid of evil, I have no
power to shut off the dire escape from myself or from others :
death and defilement I may let loose, but I cannot recapture.
Solomon gives us a sample of such deeds and their consequences : "The beginning of strife is as when one letteth out
water" : followed by a precept: "therefore leave off con-
tention, before it be meddled with,"—the precept in spirit
though not in the letter being applicable to all "touching of
pitch."

**2. And he opened the bottomless pit; and there arose a
smoke out of the pit, as the smoke of a great furnace ;
and the sun and the air were darkened by reason of
the smoke of the pit.**

· By the voice of His prophet Isaiah God Almighty declares
concerning one class of offenders : "These are a smoke in
My nose, a fire that burneth all the day" :—thus constituting
smoke a figure of provocation. And touching two formidable
wicked persons He graciously enjoins: "Fear not, neither be
faint-hearted for the two tails of these smoking firebrands."

Whence as regards the Woe summoned by the fifth trumpet-
blast and ushered in by smoke, I yet venture to surmise a
possibility of rescue for sinners of every grade, except, alas,
for the obstinately impenitent.

And this, seeing that the very elect are during their mortal
life sinners : "If we say that we have no sin, we deceive
ourselves, and the truth is not in us. If we confess our sins,
He is faithful and just to forgive us our sins, and to cleanse

us from all unrighteousness. If we say that we have not sinned, we make Him a liar, and His word is not in us."

" My soul fainteth for Thy salvation : but I hope in Thy word. Mine eyes fail for Thy word, saying, When wilt Thou comfort me ? For I am become like a bottle in the smoke ; yet do I not forget Thy statutes. How many are the days of Thy servant ? when wilt Thou execute judgment on them that persecute me ? " Smoke even from the pit will not slay that soul which because it is parched gasps as a thirsty land unto God ; and which in the smoke endures as God's own bottle storing penitential tears. Shrivelled and unsightly it may become to man's eye, " but the Lord looketh on the heart." That smoke offends God Himself, which offends him who is as the apple of the eye.

Yet does the infernal smoke go up as a beacon ominous to the impenitent. Such a smoke of sweeping destruction Abraham descried when " he looked toward Sodom and Gomorrah, and toward all the land of the plain, and beheld, and, lo, the smoke of the country went up as the smoke of a furnace." Such a smoke Isaiah employs figuratively : " For wickedness burneth as the fire : it shall devour the briers and thorns, and shall kindle in the thickets of the forest, and they shall mount up like the lifting up of smoke. Through the wrath of the Lord of hosts is the land darkened, and the people shall be as the fuel of the fire."

Holy Writ saith : " Man is born unto trouble, as the sparks fly upward." And by God's grace he can, while life lasts, in whatever smoke fly upward.

When " the sun and the air were darkened by reason of the smoke of the pit " earth seems once more subjected to a plague of darkness which may be felt. Who shall say but that the faithful once again had light in their dwellings ?

Who knows ? God knows : and what He knows
   Is well and best.
The darkness hideth not from Him, but glows
Clear as the morning or the evening rose
   Of east or west.

Wherefore man's strength is to sit still :
   Not wasting care
To antedate to-morrow's good or ill ;
Yet watching meekly, watching with good will,
   Watching to prayer.

Some rising or some setting ray
   From east or west

> If not to-day, why then another day
> Will light each dove upon the homeward way
>   Safe to her nest.

3. And there came out of the smoke locusts upon the earth : and unto them was given power, as the scorpions of the earth have power.

A defined and limited scourge, a scourge under control and as appears further on for a limited period.   Once more, thanks be to God through Jesus Christ our Saviour.   Amen.

4. And it was commanded them that they should not hurt the grass of the earth, neither any green thing, neither any tree ; but only those men which have not the seal of God in their foreheads.

5. And to them it was given that they should not kill them, but that they should be tormented five months : and their torment was as the torment of a scorpion, when he striketh a man.

Locusts venomous as scorpions, and devastating not vegetation but humankind ; and amongst men discriminating between the holy and the unholy.   Tormenting moreover without slaying, and this no longer than during a prefixed term.   "For the creature that serveth Thee, Who art the Maker, increaseth his strength against the unrighteous for their punishment, and abateth his strength for the benefit of such as put their trust in Thee."

Yet even this extremity of wrathful displeasure seems by possibility to leave open a loophole of hope : it seems haply to fall within the bounds of that Divine Longsuffering which invites and urges to repentance.   For the unsealed are, as it appears, not yet expelled from among the sealed : the wheat and the tares are still growing together until the harvest. While there is life there is hope, according to the time-honoured proverb.

God hath spoken : "Behold, all souls are mine. . . .   The soul that sinneth, it shall die . . .   The wickedness of the wicked shall be upon him.   But if the wicked will turn from all his sins that he hath committed, and keep all My statutes, and do that which is lawful and right, he shall surely live, he shall not die.   All his transgressions that he had committed, they shall not be mentioned unto him ; in his righteousness that he hath done he shall live.   Have I any pleasure at all that the wicked should die? saith the Lord God : and not that he should return from his ways, and live?"   .

6. **And in those days shall men seek death, and shall not find it, and shall desire to die, and death shall flee from them.**

Shall one seek death and not find it, and not rather seek Christ our life Who hath said: "Seek, and ye shall find"? Shall one desire to die, death fleeing from him; and not rather desire life, and obtain a long life even for ever and ever?

"Whoso is wise, and will observe these things, even they shall understand the lovingkindness of the Lord."

To seek death is sinful: yet to desire it may be saintly. St. Paul mentions his "desire to depart, and to be with Christ: which is far better" than even the most spiritual life on earth; thus reminding us of his words on another subject: "For if that which is done away was glorious, much more that which remaineth is glorious."

Mortal life then, even at its utmost perfection, is as the fading face of Moses; and hath comparatively no glory, by reason of the glory that excelleth. Amen. Alleluia.

There is another longing for death, far below St. Paul's, yet on occasion natural to man and not incompatible with eminent holiness. Such longing was Job's when he poured forth the bitterness of his soul: "Wherefore is light given to him that is in misery, and life unto the bitter in soul; which long for death, but it cometh not; and dig for it more than for hid treasures; which rejoice exceedingly, and are glad, when they can find the grave? . . . My soul chooseth strangling, and death rather than my life. I loathe it; I would not live alway. . . . My soul is weary of my life. . . . O that Thou wouldest hide me in the grave!"

St. Paul then desired death not as death but as the passage to Christ. And Job desired death not as death but as release from life well-nigh intolerable. To desire death as death is to love darkness rather than light.

From rebellious death, sudden death, lifeless death, Good Lord, deliver us.

7. **And the shapes of the locusts were like unto horses prepared unto battle; and on their heads were as it were crowns like gold, and their faces were as the faces of men.**
8. **And they had hair as the hair of women, and their teeth were as the teeth of lions.**
9. **And they had breastplates, as it were breastplates of**

iron ; and the sound of their wings was as the sound
of chariots of many horses running to battle.

10. And they had tails like unto scorpions, and there were
stings in their tails : and their power was to hurt
men five months.

11. And they had a king over them, which is the angel of
the bottomless pit, whose name in the Hebrew tongue
is Abaddon, but in the Greek tongue hath his name
Apollyon.

The wording of this passage repeatedly suggests that we are
being instructed not plainly but by figure, similitude, shadow ;
feature after feature being described as " like unto " or "as it
were " or " as." Dark is the glass through which we are
summoned to see, yet is it a glass.

The mysterious horrible smoke whence the locusts issue
teaches us something by analogy. To pass unscathed through
literal suffocating smoke, our way is to crouch low to the
ground : and through that other more deadly smoke surely our
way of safety is not dissimilar; to bow down, to " walk
humbly." Whoso learns humility learns wisdom if not knowledge : and wisdom being better than knowledge, "the word" even
in this occult instance will thus become by no means unfruitful.

That these locusts " had a king over them " illustrates their
allegorical character. For of the natural locusts we read :
" The locusts have no king, yet go they forth all of them by
bands " : which "prophecy" of Agur may be blessed to us as
a helpful Queen Esther prepared " for such a time as this."

Very terrible are these preternatural locusts. Because one
day such a trial may have to be faced by ourselves, and as yet
we know not clearly what thus we may be called upon to face ;
point by point let us endeavour to confront them with that
" Sword of the Spirit, which is the Word of God."

" Like unto horses prepared unto battle."—But if " an horse
is a vain thing for safety," so equally is he in himself a vain
thing for destruction. " The horse is prepared against the day
of battle : but safety is of the Lord." " Thus saith the Lord,
. . . Which bringeth forth the chariot and horse, the army and
the power ; they shall lie down together, they shall not rise :
they are extinct, they are quenched as tow." " I said unto the
Lord, Thou art my God : hear the voice of my supplications,
O Lord. O God the Lord, the strength of my salvation, Thou
hast covered my head in the day of battle."

" Crowns like gold."—Concerning another evil power we

read: "Thy crowned are as the locusts, and thy captains as the great grasshoppers, which camp in the hedges in the cold day, but when the sun ariseth they flee away, and their place is not known where they are." "Weeping may endure for a night, but joy cometh in the morning." "Unto you that fear my name shall the Sun of Righteousness arise with healing in His wings."

"As the faces of men."—But it is written: "He hath said, I will never leave thee, nor forsake thee. So that we may boldly say, The Lord is my helper, and I will not fear what man shall do unto me."

"As the hair of women."—Surely if man is not to be feared, still less aught that can be likened to woman! Concerning a dangerous wicked woman the wise Preacher proclaims: "I applied mine heart to know, and to search, and to seek out wisdom... And I find more bitter than death the woman, whose heart is snares and nets, and her hands as bands: whoso pleaseth God shall escape from her; but the sinner shall be taken by her." "In the way of righteousness is life; and in the pathway thereof there is no death."

"As the teeth of lions."—Yet saith Eliphaz the Temanite: "Remember, I pray thee, who ever perished, being innocent? or where were the righteous cut off? . . . The roaring of the lion, and the voice of the fierce lion, and the teeth of the young lions, are broken. The old lion perisheth for lack of prey, and the stout lion's whelps are scattered abroad."

"As it were breastplates of iron."—The Prophet Daniel interpreting Nebuchadnezzar's first dream, spake of the Stone which was cut out without hands and brake in pieces iron and every such substance; till they became together like the chaff of the summer threshing-floors and the wind carried them away: which figure foreshadowed the destruction of earthly kingdoms by a Heavenly Kingdom. And ages afterwards Christ Himself being questioned declared: "The kingdom of God is within you." Thus the elect have within them what suffices to bring to nought the "iron" of their adversaries. The "breastplate of righteousness" makes each saint in his degree like his Divine Master Who "put on righteousness as a breastplate": behold! an invulnerable breastplate set against a vulnerable: even as Ezekiel's indomitable face was set against the faces of his opponents.

"As the sound of chariots."—"Like the noise of chariots on the tops of mountains shall they leap. . . Before their face the people shall be much pained: all faces shall gather blackness."

Yet still good Christians will be safe. It will be with them as in the days of old when Elisha reassured his terrified servant : "Fear not : for they that be with us are more than they that be with them. . . And behold the mountain was full of horses and chariots of fire round about Elisha." Or according to a yet more excellent confidence : "Some trust in chariots, and some in horses : but we will remember the Name of the Lord our God."

"Be not afraid of their terror, neither be troubled ; but sanctify the Lord God in your hearts." Up to this point their terror only is fallen upon us ; but now we read of their actual ability to hurt : "There were stings in their tails." A base sting, a degrading punishment ; a punishment suited to the offence, for sin is a base thing. What : has sin never a lofty, heroic side? Never the sin, though sometimes the sinner. The sinner may awhile exhibit majestic traces of that lofty heroism which nature richly bestows and grace can transfigure to sanctity : but such birthright nobility when divorced from God can no more endure, than can a severed vine-branch maintain its luxuriance.

I must learn this lesson : must learn to recognize the degradation as well as the sinfulness of Saul's final revolt against humiliation, and of Jezebel's defiant pride.

"And they had a king over them. . . . Whose name . . . is Abaddon, . . . Apollyon."—Whether named King Abaddon or King Apollyon, his English equivalent is King Destroyer. Whatever we call him he remains the same : were we to call him King Preserver it would modify neither his nature nor his office. Being a destroyer, our safety lies in recognizing, acknowledging, fleeing him as such. And further : so far as we are constituted our brother's keeper, our brother's safety similarly lies in our plainly calling him a destroyer ; and never toning him down as a negation of good, or even unloathingly as an archangel ruined ; which last suggestion I cull from my sister's *Shadow of Dante*, where she contrasts Milton's Satan with Dante's Lucifer.

Sins for like reason should be spoken of simply as what they are, never palliatingly or jocosely. Lies and drunkenness should bear their own odious appellations, not any conventional substitute. But some sins "it is a shame to speak of" : true : so let us not speak of them except under necessity ; and under necessity even of them truthfully. "Woe unto them that call evil good, and good evil ; that put darkness for light, and light for darkness ; that put bitter for sweet, and sweet for bitter !"

"The angel of the bottomless pit."—Once an angel of

heaven, now an angel of hell : a self-destroyed destroyer. Such destruction is not annihilation. Happily *angel* still means *messenger*, come from where he may; and a messenger is restrained within the bounds of his commission. Even the Destroyer may thus be overruled to preserve instead of to destroy : as Satan tested Job, sifted Apostles, and by his buffeting messenger promoted St. Paul's well-being. Angels whether fallen or unfallen still envoys, but not plenipotentiaries.

12. One woe is past; and, behold, there come two more woes hereafter.

"One woe is past " shows that none need hesitate to call woe woe, even when short of the final woe : for man is not framed without nerves but with nerves, and many times an horrible dread overwhelmeth him. Creatures of cast-iron or of stone might have different duties from creatures of flesh and blood whereof we are made.

> One woe is past. Come what come will
>   Thus much is ended and made fast :
> Two woes may overhang us still ;
>   One woe is past.
>
> As flowers when winter puffs its last
> Wake in the vale, trail up the hill,
>   Nor wait for skies to overcast :
>
> So meek souls rally from the chill
>   Of pain and fear and poisonous blast,
> To lift their heads : Come good, come ill,
>   One woe is past.

The exceeding mystery of Divine judgments which prophets alone can declare, turns ignorant thought for safety into the channel of supplication. "Who is among you that feareth the Lord, that obeyeth the voice of His servant, that walketh in darkness, and hath no light ? let him trust in the Name of the Lord, and stay upon his God. Behold, all ye that kindle a fire, that compass yourselves about with sparks : walk in the light of your fire, and in the sparks that ye have kindled. This shall ye have of Mine hand : ye shall lie down in sorrow."

> Lord God Whom we fear, protect us.
> Whom we crave grace to obey, accept us.
> Towards Whom we press through darkness, guide and enlighten us.
> Whom we trust, confirm us.
> On Whom we stay our weakness, support us.
> In the Name of Jesus Christ ; in Whom the elect are safe, acceptable,
>   wise, strong, indomitable. Amen.

Study of the Apocalypse should promote holy fear, unflinching obedience, patient progress and patient waiting, unhesitating trust, conformity to the Perfect Will. Time devoted to the cultivation of these cannot be wasted time. Moreover, so long as these are aimed at, to sit down ignorant and even to rise up equally ignorant may along with these virtues help forward humility.

Ignorance with humilty can serve and please God : knowledge without humility cannot. Thus humble ignorance secures the essentials of wisdom, whilst unhumble knowledge is folly.

Would humble knowledge not be better than humble ignorance? Yes, if granted : no, if denied.

St. Peter after mentioning how prophets of old searched for knowledge and angels desired it, winds up with a practical precept to ourselves unto whom the Gospel has been preached : "Wherefore gird up the loins of your mind, be sober, and hope to the end for the grace that is to be brought unto you at the revelation of Jesus Christ; as obedient children, not fashioning yourselves according to the former lusts in your ignorance : but as He which hath called you is holy, so be ye holy in all manner of conversation ; because it is written, Be ye holy ; for I am holy."

Gracious Lord Jesus, grant us so to read, search, desire, pray, that being sober and hoping to the end we may obey Thy Will and be conformed to Thy Sanctity.

The merchantman who found the pearl of great price was one who sought for goodly pearls : not one who never sought at all.

Darkness and thick darkness cover you.—I know it : but if in addition I keep my eyes shut, light itself springing up would fail to enlighten me.—If the blind lead the blind both shall fall into the ditch.—I know it : but if the blind grope in prayer for himself and for all his fellows, who knows but that some of the afflicted company may be advanced to see?

> O Christ our Light Whom even in darkness we
> (So we look up) discern and gaze upon,
> O Christ, Thou loveliest Light that ever shone,
> Thou Light of Light, Fount of all lights that be,
> Grant us clear vision of Thy Light to see ;
> Tho' other lights elude us, or begone
> Into the secret of oblivion,
> Or gleam in places higher than man's degree.
> Who looks on Thee looks full on his desire,
> Who looks on Thee looks full on Very Love :
> Looking, he answers well, ' What lack I yet?'

His heat and cold wait not on earthly fire,
His wealth is not of earth to lose or get ;
Earth reels, but he has stored his store above.

13. And the sixth angel sounded, and I heard a voice from the four horns of the golden altar which is before God,

Here and there a ray seems to be vouchsafed, a broken light. "God is the Lord Who hath shewed us light : bind the sacrifice with cords, yea, even unto the horns of the altar." "Let the words of my mouth, and the meditation of my heart, be alway acceptable in Thy sight, O Lord, my strength, and my Redeemer."

Whatever historical coincidences with St. John's prophetic revelation may be cited as having already in part fulfilled it, these and such as these I leave to the authoritative handling of my teachers. "Whoso boasteth himself of a false gift is like clouds and wind without rain."

Yet meditation is lawful to all of us. Some there must be who shall be blessed according to the promise : "Thine eyes shall see the King in His beauty : they shall behold the land that is very far off. Thine heart shall meditate terror. . . Look upon Zion, the city of our solemnities : thine eyes shall see Jerusalem a quiet habitation, a tabernacle that shall not be taken down."

Whether natural or spiritual, eyes that look are the eyes likely to see. Meditation fixes the spiritual eye on matters worthy of insight : it sees something, it may gradually perceive more and more. At first Pharaoh's daughter discerned only an ark of bulrushes ; next one of the Hebrews' children ; at last Moses. The Brazen Serpent was ordained a channel of healing to those death-stricken Israelites who obediently gazed upon it, although we are not told that even one of them could decipher its Divine symbolism.

In the Jewish tabernacle the Altar of Incense was a golden altar, an altar of acceptance, its horns bearing a distinct part in acts of reconcilement for sins of ignorance. The brazen Altar of Burnt Offering likewise had horns.

The Altar being, so to say, one stronghold of God's Mercy, became so in a minor degree of man's mercy, the lower illustrating the higher : as appeared when Adonijah caught hold on the horns of the Altar, "saying, Let King Solomon swear unto me to-day that he will not slay his servant with the sword. And Solomon said, If he will show himself a worthy man, there shall not an hair of him fall to the earth."

Thus we apprehend this " Voice from the four horns " of the

celestial Golden Altar as a voice of judgment proceeding from a stronghold of mercy. "The yoke of my transgressions is bound by His hand."

14. Saying to the sixth **angel which had the trumpet, Loose the four angels which are bound in the great river Euphrates.**

Amongst the seven Angels of the trumpets the sixth alone is described as executing a double function : he sounds the sixth blast, and he also looses the bonds of four other angels.

That these four angels "were bound in the great river Euphrates" recalls to our mind Jeremiah's prophecy of an anterior judgment : "For this is the day of the Lord God of hosts, a day of vengeance, that He may avenge Him of His adversaries : and the sword shall devour, and it shall be satiate and made drunk with their blood : for the Lord God of hosts hath a sacrifice in the north country by the river Euphrates."

Euphrates had its source in Eden. There it nourished, refreshed, beautified, the fertile Garden ; being constituted a minister of pleasure, an agent of preservation and fecundity. Eden is not more unlike the outer world, than Euphrates at its pure fountain head in Paradise appears unlike the same Euphrates earth-bound, earth-spurning, earth-contaminated, rushing downward to the harvestless sea.

Innocence hedged in Eden : sin breaking through that hedge disparadised Paradise, so far as mortal man was concerned.

Guilt hedges in the world : penitence breaking through that hedge recovers and re-enters Paradise, now made the anteroom of Heaven.

Loss it seems is never simply recouped : the precise forfeit is not restored. Loss may remain irretrievable, or it may be more than compensated.

15. And the four angels were loosed, which were prepared for an hour, and a day, and a month, and a year, for to slay the third part of men.

Once again at the loosing of these four angels it is our comfort that their period of devastation is limited, and that they are not self-ordained but " prepared " for their work. " My times are in Thy hand."

I know not whether so long as we read of the " third part " being destroyed and so by implication the two-thirds remaining, it may systematically be viewed as an indication that the general day of grace is not yet ended, and that probation is prolonged.

If I may so view it, the Judgment in Eden shows forth a sample of such severe compassion : the serpent condemned, Adam and Eve reprieved. "The one shall be taken, and the other left," appears to be a formula of separation beyond appeal.

We read but of one Angel destroying the Egyptian firstborn, Israel numbered under David, Sennacherib's host. What will four do?

O Lord, they will do Thy bidding and no more, Thy will and no more, Thy pleasure and no more. Alleluia. Amen.

16. And the number of the army of the horsemen were two hundred thousand thousand : and I heard the number of them.

Number oftentimes expresses a total by man innumerable.

What St. John heard, that he states: he neither accounts for it, nor requires us to realize it. Simply he knew it by revelation, and through him we in our turn know it.

Which instance exemplifies a general rule as regards revelation. We are not bound to account for, or always even to realize intellectually, its truths : we are bound to accept them, and we are further bound when called upon unhesitatingly and literally to restate them.

"The army of the horsemen" now first mentioned (at least explicitly) comes upon us with startling abruptness. As when Delilah said, "The Philistines be upon thee, Samson,"—or as when "the Lord had made the host of the Syrians to hear a noise of chariots, and a noise of horses, even the noise of a great host."

17. And thus I saw the horses in the vision, and them that sat on them, having breastplates of fire, and of jacinth, and brimstone : and the heads of the horses were as the heads of lions ; and out of their mouths issued fire and smoke and brimstone.

The wise Preacher warns us: "A dream cometh through the multitude of business. . . In the multitude of dreams and many words there are also divers vanities: but fear thou God."

Yet from some dreams otherwise apparently vain may perhaps be derived one illustrative gleam on the passage in hand. Often in such dreams images appear which we identify with certainty as representing cognate objects, which yet they by no means accurately reproduce : so (if the word *horse* is to be understood literally) "the horses in the vision" were recognized by St. John as horses despite their unparalleled features.

"Them that sat on them, having breastplates of fire, and of

jacinth, and brimstone."—As it were an embodiment of fire.
Jacinth displaying tints of fire and smoke might seem petrified
flame.

"The heads of the horses were as the heads of lions":—
behold his neck clothed "with thunder"!—"And out of their
mouths issued fire and smoke and brimstone":—"the glory
of his nostrils is terrible." Yet betide what may all saints are
preserved who fear not, but stand still to see the salvation of
the Lord. Moses and the children of Israel had newly experienced this when they sang: "I will sing unto the Lord, for
He hath triumphed gloriously: the horse and his rider hath
He thrown into the sea . . . And Miriam answered them,
Sing ye to the Lord, for He hath triumphed gloriously; the
horse and his rider hath He thrown into the sea."

18. By these three was the third part of men killed, by the
    fire, and by the smoke, and by the brimstone, which
    issued out of their mouths.

19. For their power is in their mouth, and in their tails:
    for their tails were like unto serpents, and had heads,
    and with them they do hurt.

Thus we are not told definitely that the terrib'e riders, as
distinguished from their horses, slew any.

This visitation reads like a rehearsal, forestalment, foretaste,
of hell itself; fire, smoke, brimstone, and as it were "that old
serpent," working visibly.

I once read of a woman who in her room was converted
from irreligion by hearing a hubbub of drunken folk outside in
the street. She recoiled from an eternity spent with such, and
turned her feet unto the testimonies.

Lord Jesus, grant unto us the like grace and wisdom.

"Above all, taking the shield of faith, wherewith ye shall be
able to quench all the fiery darts of the wicked."

The fire, smoke, brimstone, "killed": the serpent-heads
"do hurt." If we may trace a difference between the two
effects, *killed* may remind us of the second death; *do hurt* may
press home upon us that the second death will not be annihilation but torture.

There is fear, and fear. Wise Abigail's fear sped her, foolish
Nabal's fear paralyzed him.

20. And the rest of the men which were not killed by these
    plagues yet repented not of the works of their hands,
    that they should not worship devils, and idols of gold,
    and silver, and brass, and stone, and of wood: which
    neither can see, nor hear. nor walk:

21. Neither repented they of their murders, nor of their sorceries, nor of their fornication, nor of their thefts.

These two verses by giving a summary of the Ten Commandments remind us that God's Will changes not; that even "if we believe not, yet He abideth faithful: He cannot deny Himself." As St. John points out to the disciples of his day : "Brethren, I write no new commandment unto you, but an old commandment which ye had from the beginning. The old commandment is the word which ye have heard from the beginning."

Whoever worships devils transgresses glaringly the First Commandment, and less obviously that Fourth Commandment which appropriates or hallows the whole of time either to sanctioned labour or to enjoined rest. Certain heathens formally and of set purpose do, as we are assured, worship devils. This literal gross act is not perhaps likely to tempt nineteenth century Christians; or even others who, without being personally Christian, have been born and bred where in a certain sense the world itself is Christian as well as civilized. Wherefore, not so much looking at my remote neighbour, I consider myself; lest I also be tempted, although by means modified to assail my own particular weak points.

PLEASE GOD. I will have nothing to do with spiritualism, whether it be imposture or a black art; or with mesmerism, lest I clog my free will; or with hypnotism, lest wilful self-surrender become my road to evil choice, imagination, conduct, voluntary or involuntary. Neither will I subscribe to any theory which would pursue knowledge by cruel or foul methods; or do evil that good may come. Neither will I either in jest or in earnest tamper with fortune-telling or any other fashion of prying into the future. Moreover, I will aim at avoiding both in speech and in correspondence such expressions as by good luck, or, there seems a spell against us. In performing my daily duties I must strive against the spirit of a frightened slave (which so far as it goes is the spirit of a devil worshipper), and must aim instead at the conformed will of a loving child: I ought to shrink from sin more sensitively than from punishment. In all my dealings temporal and spiritual I must adhere to a just weight, a just measure, even balances, a superhuman standard. I must set conscience above convenience, and Divine law above worldly conventions. I cannot have two masters. I cannot serve God and Mammon. "I have set the Lord always before me," sings David.

The Second Commandment is obviously broken by worshipping idols of any sort, and the mention of their inability to "hear" suggests without stating that kindred breach of the Third Commandment which is involved in misdirected prayer, praise, deprecation, thanksgiving. Studying my own more probable temptations, I pass over idols of brass, stone, wood, to dwell rather upon those of gold and silver. A molten and graven image of gold or of silver is strictly and literally reproduced nowadays and for us moderns, although in altered guise, in the current coin of the realm: it depends on myself whether to make it my minister or my idol. Demas is a warning beacon: set up against him for our encouragement and emulation stands St. Peter, who silver and gold had none. Since I cannot avoid continual contact with that which has the material and make of an idol, I must take good heed that it become not to me an idol. The "almighty dollar" seems to me a phrase simply (however unintentionally) blasphemous: in my mouth it would be blasphemy. May such an estimate of money be far from Christian tongues, and farther from Christian hearts.

Of the other sins enumerated (murders, sorceries, fornication, thefts) three more or less flagrantly transgress the Fifth, Sixth, Seventh, and Eighth Commandments, all belonging to the Second Table (unless so far as the Fifth is concerned, of which I have seen the position discussed). Sorceries alone, at least at first sight, might appear to fall exclusively under the ban of the First Table. But if sorceries, while insulting the Divine Majesty, be regarded as likewise seducing, hoodwinking, misleading, entrapping man; then we recognize in it a distinct breach of the Ninth Commandment: it becomes a fatal false witness borne against our neighbour. One Commandment, the Tenth, remains: and this being spiritual, covetousness may be viewed as underlying and prompting the infractions of the preceding Five. For covetousness, preferring as it does self-interest to alien interest, whether or not co-extensive with selfishness, does at any rate so far as it goes cover the same ground; and is directly contrary to love, which, working no ill to its neighbour, is therefore the fulfilling of the law.

Yet the desperate element as regards these sinners against their own souls was not that they had sinned, but that they did not repent. Repentance would have bleached their scarlet to snow, their crimson to wool. It would have made them like unto ancient Israel when "Samuel said unto the people, Fear not: ye have done all this wickedness: yet turn not aside from following the Lord, but serve the Lord with all your heart; and turn ye not aside: for then should ye go after vain things, which cannot profit nor deliver; for they are vain. For the Lord will not forsake His people for His great Name's sake; because it hath pleased the Lord to make you His people."

All is promised to the penitent, but repentance is not promised to any individual sinner.

Tortures and terrors cannot do the work of love. Nay, more: Love from without cannot accomplish its own work, unless there be some response from love within.

The proportion of men is one taken, two left: and the two repent not. I who write, any who read, are for the present left: God vouchsafe to all, vouchsafe to me, repentance unto amendment of life, for Jesus Christ's sake.

And this thought, that two are as it were "left" even though in such extremity, brings home to all who are not reprobate certain inspired words redolent of hope: "Two are better than one; because they have a good reward for their labour. For if they fall, the one will lift up his fellow: but woe to him that is alone when he falleth; for he hath not another to help him up . . . And if one prevail against him, two shall withstand him."

If then I be one of twain I must comport myself accordingly: be it in labour and in hope of reward; in falls, in arisings, in helps; in contest, in alliance, and in victory; I must as much as in me lies impart to him that hath not, and bear my neighbour's burdens.

Lord Jesus, Thou becamest Man thereby to become One of twain, Thyself and Thy Bride the Church. Thou hast laboured for her; and labourest with her, and sharest with her Thy reward. If she fall Thou liftest her up: happy she who is never alone when she falleth. If the battle go sore against her, yet with Thee she discomfiteth a host: happy she whom Thou hast joined unto Thyself.

Because the Church is moulded after Thy likeness, her least and last member is thus moulded. Lord, give me grace ever thankfully to account myself one of twain; humbly receiving help from my superiors, and myself helping any Thou empowerest me to help. Thou Who createdst all things out of nothing, lay help even on me, making my influence tend to good. Turn, I beseech Thee, my sins to repentance, my repentance to amendment, my amendment to a shining light. Even so of Thy Goodness perfect all and perfect me. Amen.

Life that was born to-day
Must make no stay,
But tend to end
Like bloom of May.

O Lord, confirm my root,
Train up my shoot,
To live and give
A wholesome fruit.

CHAPTER X.

1. And I saw another mighty angel come down from heaven, clothed with a cloud: and a rainbow was upon his head, and his face was as it were the sun, and his feet as pillars of fire:
2. And he had in his hand a little book open: and he set his right foot upon the sea, and his left foot on the earth,
3. And cried with a loud voice, as when a lion roareth: and when he had cried, seven thunders uttered their voices.

We seem to behold "storm fulfilling His word." Arrayed majestically in a cloud, crowned with beauty by a rainbow, his face splendid as the sun, his feet no less splendid than fire : if this mighty Angel appear in some sort as the lightning, his own voice was as a lion's roar, and thunders respond to him.

Not thus at His first advent came the Son of Man down from heaven. His might was not of this world. His first garments were swaddling-bands; and His last, except grave-clothes, were taken away from Him. His crown was of thorns. He hid not His Face from shame and spitting. His Feet after going about to do good were nailed to the Cross. He came to send fire upon the earth; but He strove not, nor cried, neither was His voice heard in the street; and His servants the thunders held their peace.

O Good Lord, Who art above Thy servant, O Good Master, Who art above Thy disciple, grant us grace to ascend to heaven by that way of humility whereby Thou descendedst. Let communion with Thee be our strength. Clothe our children in the Font with the garment of salvation; and guide them and us in robes of righteousness to a holy sepulchre. Grant us patience for a crown, patience for a shield, patience and perseverance in our vocation, patience in suffering. Be

Thy Most Holy Almighty Spirit Fire of Love in our hearts, and His still small Voice more awful to us than thunders. Amen.

One notices a storm : another discerns an Angel. One hears thunder : another divines a message. Well it is, in default of better, to skim the surface and learn a little : though better it is, God willing, to walk in the search of the depth and learn much.

A Christian hero whose ship was about to sink, encouraged his crew by pointing out that heaven is as near the sea as the land. Our assigned level is our nearest point to heaven.

Judge not thy neighbour's walk, except to follow or to lead him.

Those feet "as pillars of fire" stood on earth and sea; the left foot on the earth, the right foot on the sea. As the Left Hand is the hand of rejection, the Right of acceptance, so now this posture of the Angel suggests symbolically that sin is that sole thing which God abominates, and that it is for sin's sake alone that He overturns, overturns, overturns. The barren uninhabited sea sustains the right foot, the populous earth the left.

That Angel was celestial trustee of the "little book open," holding it in trust for St. John; who in his turn received it indeed for his own edification, but also and once more as a trust for others.

If Angels and Apostles, those princes and peers of earth and heaven, are stewards, not owners; we Christian commoners need neither dream nor desire to be constituted more. Our gifts, talents, opportunities, are a trust vested in us for the definite purpose of glorifying God, benefiting man, working out our own salvation. Ours are,—then mine are. In the awful day of account, Good Lord, deliver us.

4. And when the seven thunders had uttered their voices, I was about to write: and I heard a voice from heaven saying unto me, Seal up those things which the seven thunders uttered, and write them not.

Both voices instructed St. John in wisdom and knowledge. I too may learn from both if not knowledge still wisdom.

Privileges entail responsibilities : to be denied the privilege is to be spared the responsibility.

More is entrusted to another than to me. Let not mine eye be evil because God is Good, Who doeth what He will with His own.

Seven voices speak, but not to me. One Voice speaks to me: "Speak, Lord; for Thy servant heareth." Yet do the seven thunders also speak to me without speech; inasmuch as they convince me of ignorance, and further prove that God wills that I should be aware of my own ignorance, and should regulate my conduct with reference to it.

We all might sit down contented and complacent in ignorance, if only ignorant of our ignorance. But our Creator wills otherwise. If the Tree of Knowledge had been planted anywhere except in Eden, Eve might contentedly have obeyed through ignorance; but what was demanded of her was to obey of set purpose. What was demanded of her is what still is demanded of us. Now as to these Seven Thunders we must perforce obey, because we cannot ascertain anything: true: but a thorough obedience excludes even the indulgence of idle curiosity, and as to this we have a choice. Long ago I took into my head that these thunders may have uttered the names of the saved: alas! in so far as with the childish thought I have not yet discarded the childish presumption.

"I was about to write . . . Write them not."—An illustration against depending on "any child of man," on highest, holiest, most Christ-like superiors, beyond their function as channels and mouthpieces of Divine teaching.

O Lord Jesus, Who didst vouchsafe to grow in wisdom, stature, favour; grant us in loving memory of Thee to be in love with our present lowliness. Let grace be our sunshine, grace our dew; that we too may patiently grow in loveliness until we behold Thee face to Face. Amen.

5. And the angel which I saw stand upon the sea, and upon the earth, lifted up his hand to heaven,

"His hand," or as in the Revised Version "his right hand": still a blessing may be hoped for, whatever else may ensue. "God is the Judge: He putteth down one, and setteth up another."

And surely (if from words which concern the servant we may reverently ascend to contemplation of the Master) this present day is still that day wherein Christ comes not to condemn the world, but to save the world. "Blessed be the Glory of the Lord from His place." Both sacred Hands are as yet Hands of blessing, even as when "He lifted up His Hands, and blessed" the Eleven. Or as the Psalm declares: "The Lord is thy shade upon thy right hand"; thus exhibiting the beloved one as at that period of safeguard placed upon the Left. Or as we behold in type when Jacob laid his right hand on Ephraim's head, and his left hand on Manasseh's, blessing both. And indeed (if I may dare say so) there seems a special inherent tenderness in that very Left Hand which condemns at last: it is on the same side as the heart, it belongs to the arm in which mothers enfold and carry their "sucking child." Joy overflowed for the one stray sheep brought back : did Love not overflow for the sheep which refused to return?

<table>
<tr><td>

O mine enemy,
Rejoice not over me !
  Jesus waiteth to be gracious :
    I will yet arise,
Mounting free and far
Past sun and star
  To a house prepared and spacious
    In the skies.

</td><td>

Lord, for Thine own sake
Kindle my heart and break ;
  Make mine anguish efficacious
    Wedded to Thine own :
Be not Thy dear pain,
Thy love in vain,
  Thou Who waitest to be gracious
    On Thy Throne.

</td></tr>
</table>

One hand uplifted to heaven, one foot on sea and one on earth, the Angel thus places himself in contact with the universe; and delivers his message, not as an alien standing aloof, but rather as a fellow-creature so far akin to all whom his words concern. We know that Angels minister to the heirs of salvation: who can doubt that they love them while caring for them?

If contact may be supposed to express sympathy between natures so diverse, much more should it breed sympathy between individuals of one race. In Angels towards men sympathy seems an extra and gratuitous grace : in men towards one another it is an essential grace. Let us not abandon sympathy to the Angels.

An unsympathetic angel would be a devil. An unsympathetic man or woman would be——?

6. **And sware by Him that liveth for ever and ever, Who created heaven, and the things that therein are, and the earth, and the things that therein are, and the sea, and the things which are therein, that there should be time no longer :**

"And sware by Him that liveth for ever and ever . . . that there should be time no longer."—*Delay* has been proposed instead of *time*. As this alternative word would have to do with the interpretation of the sense, not with simple meditation, I leave it to my betters.

Studying the Authorized Version as it actually stands, a contrast is suggested between "for ever and ever" and "time."

He that liveth for ever and ever inhabiteth eternity; His works (enumerated by the angel) are creatures of time. Eternity is duration which neither begins nor ends; time is duration which both begins and ends: the mystery of eternity seems to be its having no beginning; the obscure point of time its having an end.

What is time? It is not subtracted from eternity, which if diminished would fall short of being eternal: neither is it substituted awhile for eternity, which thus would assume both end and beginning: neither is it simultaneous with eternity, because it is in Him Who inhabiteth eternity (not time) that we ourselves day by day live and move and have our being. Perhaps I shall not mislead my own thoughts by defining to myself time as that condition or aspect of eternity which consists with the possibility of probation.

If such indeed be time, then in part I understand how at length there shall be time no longer. The words, "Their time should have endured for ever" (Ps. lxxxi. 15), suggest that no break will occur between time and eternity.

> Time seems not short :
>   If so I call to mind
>   Its vast prerogative to loose or bind,
> And bear and strike amort
>   All humankind.
>
> Time seems not long:
>   If I peer out and see
>   Sphere within sphere, time in eternity,
> And hear the alternate song
>   Cry endlessly.
>
> Time greatly short,
>   O time so briefly long,
>   Yea, time sole battleground of right and wrong;
> Art thou a time for sport
>   And for a song?

The Wise Preacher has bequeathed to us a sermon on time, and I think other texts of Holy Scripture may furnish a running commentary on part of it :—

To everything there is a season, and a time to every purpose under the heaven :

A time to be born,—"That which is born of the flesh is flesh; and that which is born of the Spirit is spirit."

And a time to die;—"Set thine house in order; for thou shalt die, and not live."

A time to plant,—"Neither is he that planteth anything, neither he that watereth; but God that giveth the increase."

And a time to pluck up that which is planted;—"If ye had faith as a grain of mustard seed, ye might say unto this sycamine tree, Be thou plucked up by the root, and be thou planted in the sea; and it should obey you."

A time to kill,—"Whoso sheddeth man's blood, by man shall his blood be shed: for in the image of God made He man."

And a time to heal;—"Is any sick among you? let him call for the elders of the Church; and let them pray over him, anointing him with oil in the Name of the Lord: and the prayer of faith shall save the sick, and the Lord shall raise him up; and if he have committed sins, they shall be forgiven him."

A time to break down,—"Take away her battlements; for they are not the Lord's."

And a time to build up;—"They shall build houses, and inhabit them; and they shall plant vineyards, and eat the fruit of them. They shall not build, and another inhabit; they shall not plant, and another eat: for as the days of a tree are the days of My people, and Mine elect shall long enjoy the work of their hands."

A time to weep,—"Blessed are ye that weep now: for ye shall laugh."

And a time to laugh;—"Behold, God will not cast away a perfect man, ... till He fill thy mouth with laughing, and thy lips with rejoicing."

A time to mourn,—"Blessed are they that mourn: for they shall be comforted."

And a time to dance;—"Praise ye the Lord . . . Praise Him with the timbrel and dance . . . Praise ye the Lord."

A time to cast away stones,—"The priest shall command that they take away the stones in which the plague is, and they shall cast them into an unclean place without the city. . . . And they shall take other stones, and put them in the place of those stones."

And a time to gather stones together;—"They with whom precious stones were found gave them to the treasure of the house of the Lord."

A time to embrace,—"Behold, Jesus met them, saying, All hail. And they came and held Him by the Feet, and worshipped Him."

And a time to refrain from embracing;—"Jesus saith unto her, Touch Me not; for I am not yet ascended to My Father."

A time to get,—"Wisdom is the principal thing; therefore get wisdom: and with all thy getting get understanding."

And a time to lose ;—"There is utterly a fault among you, because ye go to law one with another. Why do ye not rather take wrong? why do ye not rather suffer yourselves to be defrauded?"

A time to keep,—"The foolish said unto the wise, Give us of your oil; for our lamps are gone out. But the wise answered, saying, Not so ; lest there be not enough for us and you."

And a time to cast away ;—"The kingdom of heaven is like unto a net, that was cast into the sea, and gathered of every kind : which, when it was full, they drew to shore ; and sat down, and gathered the good into vessels, but cast the bad away."

A time to rend,—"Rend your heart, and not your garments, and turn unto the Lord your God."

And a time to sew ;—"Coats and garments which Dorcas made, while she was with them."

A time to keep silence,—"I was dumb, I opened not my mouth ; because Thou didst it."

And a time to speak ;—"A word fitly spoken is like apples of gold in pictures of silver."

A time to love,—"A friend loveth at all times."

And a time to hate ;—"If any man come to Me, and hate not his father, and mother, and wife, and children, and brethren, and sisters, yea, and his own life also, he cannot be My disciple."

A time of war,—"Think not that I am come to send peace on earth : I came not to send peace, but a sword."

And a time of peace.—"Peace I leave with you, My peace I give unto you."

> Grant, O Lord,
>   To the natural man regeneration,
>   To regenerate man fulness of Thy Spirit,
>   To man who must die an ordered house,
>   To planters and waterers hundredfo'd increase,
>   To the faithless faith,
>   To the faithful confirmation of faith,
>   To judges righteous judgment,
>   To criminals repentance unto salvation,
>   To sufferers a happy issue out of all their afflictions,
>   To rebels submission,
>   To saints every good and perfect gift,
>   To those who weep consolation,
>   To the elect joy and gladness,
>   To mourners comfort,
>   To the light-hearted Thy fear and love,
>   To spiritual persons discernment,
>   To the rich munificence and devotion,

To friends sanctification of intercourse,
To lonely persons Thy most holy Presence,
To the upright wealth and wisdom,
To the wronged unworldliness and a forgiving spirit,
To the prudent heavenly-mindedness,
To the redeemed mercy in that day,
To sinners contrition and amendment,
To workers good works,
To the rebuked silence,
To the instructed speech,
To lovers Divine love,
To haters Godly hatred,
To Thy soldiers and servants victory,
And after victory peace,
Grant, O Lord.   Amen.

7. But in the days of the voice of the seventh angel, when he shall begin to sound, the mystery of God should be finished, as He hath declared to His servants the prophets.

" Blessed be the Lord God of Israel ; for He hath visited and redeemed His people ; and hath raised up an horn of salvation for us in the house of His servant David ; as He spake by the mouth of His holy prophets, which have been since the world began."

Since a former mystery revealed by prophets is the mystery of man's redemption, let us all the more lovingly lean on God's sustaining grace while He reveals further mysteries.

Faith, hope, love, His gift to us, become in turn our acceptable offering to Him.   Holy fear likewise ; but never such fear as paralyzes those other graces.   Manoah's wife knew far less than Christians know when yet she protested : "If the Lord were pleased to kill us, He would not have received a burnt offering and a meat offering at our hands, neither would He have shewed us all these things, nor would as at this time have told us such things as these."

Faith discerns, embraces.   Hope anticipates, aspires.   Fear curbs, spurs.   Love curbs, spurs, anticipates, aspires, discerns, embraces, cleaves unto, unites.   Love is the panoply of graces.

" Without faith it is impossible to please God."   " Hope maketh not ashamed."   " Let us have grace, whereby we may serve God acceptably with reverence and godly fear."   " God is Love ; and he that dwelleth in love dwelleth in God, and God in him."

An impious species of faith (though unworthy of the name) appertains to devils : so likewise does an impious fear.   In the nature of things devils seem absolutely cut off from hope,

unless from a vile spurious hope of evil doing.   Faith of one
sort or other underlies both hope and fear, obedience and
rebellion.   Hope is a solace, obedience a privilege; both
are proper to the saints.   Despairing faith and rebellious fear
remain for the reprobate.

O Lord God, Who alone knowest my ignorance, have pity
upon me, and mine, and all men.   Weak we are, strengthen
us; afraid, encourage us; rash, sober us; slothful, arouse us;
ignorant, instruct us; destitute, enrich us; dead, quicken us;
lost, find us.   Lost, yet Thy treasure: dead, yet Thine own.
I plead Jesus.

"For what man is he that can know the counsel of God?
or who can think what the Will of the Lord is?   For the
thoughts of mortal men are miserable, and our devices are but
uncertain.   For the corruptible body presseth down the soul,
and the earthy tabernacle weigheth down the mind that museth
upon many things.   And hardly do we guess aright at things
that are upon earth, and with labour do we find the things
that are before us: but the things that are in heaven who hath
searched out?   And Thy counsel who hath known, except
Thou give wisdom, and send Thy Holy Spirit from above?"

I am afraid in foresight of those days when the Mystery of
God shall be finished.   In my fearful and great strait to whom
shall I flee but to Thee, O Unchanging Lord Jesus, Who once
for us men and for our salvation saidst, "It is finished"?

> Thou Who wast straitened till Thy Baptism was accomplished,
>   Pity us, accomplish Thy Will upon us.
> Thou Who finishedst the work Thy Father gave Thee to do,
>   Pity us, finish Thy work by us and in us.
> Thou Who saidst "It is finished" in the ending of Thine Agony,
>   Pity us, bring us to a good end,
>   Yea, Lord most pitiful, pity us.   Amen.

> All that hath begun wasteth,   Plumbs the deep, Fear descending;
> All beneath the sun hasteth;   Scales the steep, Hope ascending;
> Earth-notes change in tune   Faith betwixt the twain
> With the changeful moon,   Plies both goad and rein,
> Which waneth   Half-fearing,
> While earth's chant complaineth.   All hopeful, day is nearing.

Those words, "The Mystery of God should be finished,"
suggest two events: first, its completion so far as it is a dispensation: secondly, its disclosure so far as it is a hidden thing.

Its completion is final, universal, absolute.   Every sanctified
will cannot but concur in it: yet is it independent of all
created wills, equally independent of their concurrence or
demur.   The trumpet-peal of the blessed Angel shall (so to

say) keep time and tune with it ; but the trumpet waits on the mystery, not the mystery on the trumpet. The mystery is " of God " and its " times " are in His hand.

Its disclosure likewise may be final, absolute ; but (assumably) not universal. Almost in Abraham's words the faithful are constrained to protest trembling : " That the wicked should be as the righteous, that be far from Thee." Narrowing my thoughts to humankind, I consider : Whereby do the elect know all things ? By "an Unction from the Holy One." And if it needs This for knowledge now, how shall it not need This for knowledge then ?

It were sad for such as I am to remain in darkness of ignorance for ever and ever. If then for me, how sad and piteous were it for the most aspiring, the most profound, the keenest of insight, the most luminously intellectual ; for a multitude whom I have not known or known of; for some whom I have known and have loved !

My God, Who hast known us all and loved us all ; deliver us, keep us, from outer darkness. For Christ's sake. Amen.

> **8.** And the Voice which I heard from heaven spake unto me again, and said, Go and take the little book which is open in the hand of the angel which standeth upon the sea and upon the earth.
>
> **9.** And I went unto the angel, and said unto him, Give me the little book. And he said unto me, Take it, and eat it up ; and it shall make thy belly bitter, but it shall be in thy mouth sweet as honey.

St. John as a glorious Apostle and as a goodly Prophet may under either aspect appear too exalted for ordinary imitation. Here, however, we behold him instructed step by step what to do, whereupon step by step he obeys. Here then let me not exclaim, Are all Apostles ? are all Prophets ? in order to screen myself while doing nothing : let me rather promptly imitate an imitable obedience by myself waiting on my ministry, whatsoever that ministry may be.

And clearly I must not expect to be spared trouble : St. John had to fetch the Book, it was not brought to him. Neither must I shrink from what is formidable : the Angel was superhuman of aspect. Neither must I choose my instructor : not only was the Voice from heaven obeyed, but likewise the angelic injunction. Neither must I bemoan myself as if duties are sure to be irksome : the little book tasted sweet. Neither

must I cling to comfort, not even to spiritual comfort: the
after flavour thereof was bitter.

Lord, help us.

**10. And I took the little book out of the angel's hand, and
ate it up; and it was in my mouth sweet as honey:
and as soon as I had eaten it, my belly was bitter.**

To sweet souls obedience itself is sweet, and every word of
God acceptable.   The ensuing bitterness may have sprung, at
least in part, from righteous indignation and human sympathy.
Not St. John in his own person, but men of like passions with
him were to encounter the perils, trials, judgments, about to
be revealed.

"How sweet are Thy words unto my taste! yea, sweeter
than honey to my mouth!   Through Thy precepts I get
understanding: therefore I hate every false way."

The Angel knew of that sweetness and bitterness, but tasted
neither: St. John tasted both.

To know without experience is God-like.   To know by
experience is Christ-like.   Christ being our Head, we His
members, it beseems us to have the mind of Christ.

Wherefore, Lord Jesus, grant that sweetness may acquaint
us with such bitterness as Thou approvest, and that bitterness
may be to us safeguard not destroyer of sweetness: until the
bitterness of death pass, and the sweetness of life eternal
ensue, according to Thy Will.   Amen.

**11. And he said unto me, Thou must prophesy again before
many peoples, and nations, and tongues, and kings.**

"And he said unto me,"—or as in the Revised Version:
"And they say unto me."—Herein lies a difference, not a
contradiction: let me not ignorantly and obstinately insist on
confounding differences with contradictions.

The earthly Communion of Saints tolerates differences but
cannot subscribe to contradictions.

The heavenly Communion of Saints knows neither differences
nor contradictions.

"I believe in the Communion of Saints."

"Thou must prophesy again."—A sorrowful saying, it may
be, even to St. John; who already having entered heaven and
rejoined Christ, found that he had still to turn back from that
beloved Visible Presence and revert to earth.

Yet thus doing he became the more Christ-like, and if so
surely the more blessed.   Christ had Himself left heaven, or
ever He bade His disciple leave heaven.   He put him forth

indeed, but not until He had Himself gone before him. And now the disciple of Love knowing the voice of Love made ready to follow it whithersoever it might send him. "Hast thou not known? hast thou not heard, that the everlasting God, the Lord, the Creator of the ends of the earth, fainteth not, neither is weary? there is no searching of His understanding. He giveth power to the faint."

St. John's example of patient obedience speaks to us as with the precept and promise of St. Paul: "Let us not be weary in well-doing: for in due season we shall reap, if we faint not."

"Brethren, be not weary in well-doing."

Patience wears no crown, but acts as a crown to her fellow-virtues. Will Patience herself never be crowned? Not until she be transfigured; and transfigured, Patience will no longer appear as Patience.

I suppose this charge to prophesy again "before many peoples, and nations, and tongues, and kings," though partially fulfilled by word of mouth during St. John's after life, was further and in ampler measure fulfilled by promulgation of those writings which throughout the remainder of time prophesy to the Church and to the world, to high and low, to rich and poor, to one with another. Thus he being dead yet speaketh: thus he tarrieth till our Lord shall come.

And thus in every precept of duty a sequent glory is bound up.

The *great* things we are forbidden to ask for ourselves bear no proportion to the *good* things which God layeth up for them that love Him. So lips say: but does conduct say so?

Lord, if not hitherto, henceforward. Amen.

> Lord, grant us eyes to see
> Within the seed a tree,
>   Within the glowing egg a bird,
>   Within the shroud a butterfly:
> Till taught by such, we see
> Beyond all creatures Thee,
>   And hearken for Thy tender word
>   And hear it, "Fear not: it is I."

CHAPTER XI.

1. And there was given me a reed like unto a rod: and the angel stood, saying, Rise, and measure the temple of God, and the altar, and them that worship therein.

When Philip the Deacon inquired, "Understandest thou what thou readest?" the Ethiopian replied: "How can I, except some man should guide me?" Yet were that Bible student's meditations acceptable and profitable even before light sprang up. Since I cannot sit at the feet of an inspired interpreter, I may at least essay to mount the chariot of devout meditative ignorance, which went forward in the direction of undiscovered truth. And in virtue of that promise, "Man shall not live by bread alone, but by every word that proceedeth out of the mouth of God," I will doubt not, but earnestly believe that the mere words of Holy Writ can by God's grace avail to teach the teachable.

"A reed,"—the emblem of weakness, becomes consecrated as the measure of what is holy.

Christ accepts our weakness, not accounting it as weakness, but associating it with His own Holiness and Strength. Once He held a reed in His right Hand, making it the sceptre and visible sign of His invincible patience: if we following Him make of our own weakness the measure of our patience, it will become transmuted into strength. Once in the Almighty Strength of His dying weakness He accepted vinegar on a reed: if in our weakness we give but a cup of cold water for love of Him, He will accept this also, and strengthen and sanctify us.

When we shrink appalled from the holiness of our calling, privileges, vocation, there is comfort for us in the reed. For not the strength of iron, or the indestructibility of gold, was employed for measurement of the holy place and people, but the frailty of a reed. Am I frailer than other reeds, verily a bruised reed? Yet a bruised reed will He not break.

"We will not boast of things without our measure; but according to the measure of the rule which God hath distributed to us."

A reed shaken with the wind dwells trembling in the wilderness. Lord, I am such. But King Solomon has written: "Who is this that cometh up from the wilderness, leaning upon her Beloved?" Lord, is it I? Lord, is it not I? *Amen.*

"A reed like unto a rod."—"Hear ye the rod, and Who hath appointed it." Centuries before St. John's day the Prophet Ezekiel records how "in the visions of God . . . behold, there was a man, whose appearance was like the appearance of brass, with a line of flax in his hand, and a measuring reed"—who measured the holy house and holy precincts; until we read: "He measured it by the four sides: it had a wall round about, five hundred reeds long, and five hundred broad, to make a separation between the sanctuary and the profane place."

The Temple, not the Lord of the Temple, is measurable; the Altar, not the One Sacrifice upon the Altar. The measured worshippers are themselves temples, and in their degree sacrifices; worshipping in spirit and in truth, for the Father seeketh such to worship Him. "In His Temple doth every one speak of His glory."

The practice of the celestial Temple is the theory of each terrestrial temple, whether of hewn stone and carved work, or of flesh and blood. There is one temple whereof I am custodian and votaress; of its services, devotions, worship, I alone shall have to render an account: "Know ye not that ye are the temple of God, and that the Spirit of God dwelleth in you? If any man defile the temple of God, him shall God destroy; for the temple of God is holy, which temple ye are."

All creatures being God's servants, any at His behest become His messengers. Yet perhaps we may think that God as God hath eminently angels for His messengers, whilst as Man men; although under the Old Dispensation prophets were sent as well as angels, and at the outset of the New Dispensation angels as well as apostles.

Perhaps the Apostle rather than the Angel was commissioned to measure the worshippers of St. John's present vision, in order to encourage all worshippers, even weepers barely within the sacred precincts, and tremblers in dread of final expulsion, by a feeling of kinship.

Assumably St. John was greater than those worshippers whom he was commanded to measure; and yet to do so he was called upon to "rise." Each act of dutiful service, though for its performance the elect soul abases itself, yet raises that soul to a loftier level and augments its glory. So long as Christ be all in all, to descend "upon the Son of Man" is as elevating as to ascend. Indeed, neither ascent nor descent comes any longer into question, when Christ is felt to be that true and only and living Centre to which all *living* life gravitates.

> Alone Lord God, in Whom our trust and peace,
>   Our love and our desire, glow bright with hope ;
>   Lift us above this transitory scope
> Of earth, these pleasures that begin and cease,
> This moon which wanes, these seasons which decrease :
>   We turn to Thee ; as on an eastern slope
>   Wheat feels the dawn beneath night's lingering cope,
> Bending and stretching sunward ere it sees.
> Alone Lord God, we see not yet we know ;
> By love we dwell with patience and desire,
>   And loving so and so desiring pray :
>   Thy Will be done in earth as heaven to-day ;
> As yesterday it was, to-morrow so ;
> Love offering love on love's self-feeding fire.

2. But the court which is without the temple leave out, and measure it not; for it is given unto the Gentiles: and the holy city shall they tread under foot forty and two months.

A spur to missionary zeal. For of these excluded Gentiles may not some by dint of brotherly love be compelled to come in, pending the "forty and two months" allowed them?

The Gentiles here in question are apparently virulent rebels within reach and sound of the truth. What they tread underfoot is the holy city; what they inhabit is an outskirt of the temple. Their case appears more appalling than the case of any who being without a preacher sit still afar off in the region and shadow of death, and may in some sort plead: No man hath hired us. The more appalling, the more urgent.

"Forty and two months"—three years and a half. Whether or not this is to be understood literally, it doubtless forms a goodly period for such persons as by patient continuance in well-doing have habituated themselves to redeem the time. But it may prove a fearfully brief period into which to crowd neglected duties, work behindhand, a worthy course and a good end.

Besides : although the extent of the period be indicated, I

know not when it commences. It may be passing away whilst I sit waiting for it to begin.

It is the period of a Woe, or perhaps a pause between two Woes: not any leisure time for worldly gaiety or worldly care. It is the period preceding a Woe. In prospect of which Woe, as I am ignorant when it begins, I shall do wisely *at once* to rend my heart if not my garments, and turn unto the Lord my God; for He is gracious and merciful, slow to anger, and of great kindness, and repenteth Him of the evil.

From our Lord's Ascension to the end of time is holy Church's season of Advent. Each Christian's whole life then is one continuous Advent season.

O Lord Almighty, Who by Thy Psalmist hast said that one day in Thy courts is better than a thousand, grant that forty and two months be not spent there altogether in vain; but of Thine inexhaustible Goodness save souls, though it be as brands snatched from the burning. For our Mercy's sake, our Lord Jesus Christ's sake. Amen.

3. And I will give power unto My two witnesses, and they shall prophesy a thousand, two hundred and threescore days, clothed in sackcloth.

It has been conjectured that these twain are Enoch and Ebas; who not having hitherto died the common death of all men, will then being sent back to earth taste of death. If so, in accordance with those words of St. Paul: "By one man sin entered into the world, and death by sin; and so death passed upon all men, for that all have sinned."

If Christ had not died, it might have appeared almost the chief of human exemptions not to die; but since Christ elected to die, which of us would dare choose not to die?—as though to be less Christ-like could be more excellent.

"And I will give power."—The Speaker, as occurs more than once in this Divine Apocalypse, seems without announcement to have changed. Mighty as are the two Witnesses, yet could even they have no power at all except it were given them from above. So Joseph answered Pharaoh: "It is not in me: God shall give . . ."

O God Almighty, Who to them that have no might increasest strength, strengthen us to do and suffer Thy good Will and pleasure. For the honour of Jesus Christ, Thy Blessed Son, in Whom Thou art well pleased. Amen.

"One thousand two hundred and threescore days" amount

to very nearly those "forty and two months" mentioned above (ver. 2).

"Clothed in sackcloth."—They are sent to bear witness for God in a world which lieth in wickedness. Such, however, is the daily vocation of each Christian in his or her degree. If then we put not on actual sackcloth of hair outside and visibly to all men, yet let us beware of falling short of that very faulty King of Israel, who wore sackcloth within upon his flesh; he literally, we at the least in spirit.

"Therefore said I, Look away from me; I will weep bitterly, labour not to comfort me, because of the spoiling of the daughter of my people. For it is a day of trouble, and of treading down, and of perplexity by the Lord God of hosts in the valley of vision. . . . And in that day did the Lord God of hosts call to weeping, and to mourning, and to baldness, and to girding with sackcloth: and behold joy and gladness, slaying oxen, and killing sheep, eating flesh and drinking wine: let us eat and drink, for to-morrow we shall die."

From a seared conscience, good Lord, deliver us.

4. These are the two olive trees, and the two candlesticks standing before the God of the earth.

A marginal reference directs me to the fourth chapter of Zechariah: "What are these two olive trees upon the right side of the candlestick, and upon the left side thereof? . . . What be these two olive branches which through the two golden pipes empty the golden oil out of themselves? . . . These are the two anointed ones, that stand by the Lord of the whole earth."

This fourth chapter of Zechariah refers to the building of the Second Temple. If its mysterious revelation of "the two anointed ones" does in truth (although haply in a subordinate sense) correspond with the Apocalyptic "two witnesses," then I fortify hope that besides those worshippers already harboured within the sanctuary (ver. 1), some living stones from without may even during the forty-two months be built in with them. For if the final Temple be still in building, "yet there is room."

"The God of the earth,"—or, as in Zechariah, "The Lord of the whole earth." The two phrases correspond, claiming all men by right for God. "Is He the God of the Jews only? is He not also of the Gentiles? Yes, of the Gentiles also: seeing it is one God."

My God, Who hast revealed to us hope as a most opportune grace, endow us with it as our own anchor of the soul sure and steadfast. Keep us by holy hope from presumption, as it were a waterspout, and from despair as it were a quicksand, that we shipwreck not ourselves by the one or in the other. For Jesus Christ's sake. Amen.

5. **And if any man will hurt them fire proceedeth out of their mouth, and devoureth their enemies: and if any man will hurt them, he must in this manner be killed.**
6. **These have power to shut heaven, that it rain not in the days of their prophecy: and have power over waters to turn them to blood, and to smite the earth with all plagues, as often as they will.**

Very similarly it is recorded concerning Elijah in his contest with evil: "Then the king sent unto him a captain of fifty with his fifty. And he went up to him: and, behold, he sat on the top of an hill. And he spake unto him, Thou man of God, the king hath said, Come down. And Elijah answered and said to the captain of fifty, If I be a man of God, then let fire come down from heaven, and consume thee and thy fifty. And there came down fire from heaven, and consumed him and his fifty. Again also he sent unto him another captain of fifty with his fifty. And he answered and said unto him, O man of God, thus hath the king said, Come down quickly. And Elijah answered and said unto them, If I be a man of God, let fire come down from heaven, and consume thee and thy fifty. And the fire of God came down from heaven, and consumed him and his fifty." But as now in prophecy, so then in history, that devouring fire touched only aggressors. "And he sent again a captain of the third fifty with his fifty. And the third captain of fifty went up, and came and fell on his knees before Elijah, and besought him, and said unto him, O man of God, I pray thee, let my life, and the life of these fifty thy servants, be precious in thy sight. Behold, there came fire down from heaven, and burnt up the two captains of the former fifties with their fifties: therefore let my life now be precious in thy sight. And the angel of the Lord said unto Elijah, Go down with him: be not afraid of him. And he arose, and went down with him unto the king." And before his invocation of fire, Elijah had by his word shut and reopened the floodgates of heaven.

The turning waters to blood, and smiting with all plagues, recall the joint mission of Moses and Aaron to Pharaoh.

Elijah stood alone: his, at least under one prominent aspect, were deeds of vengeance in a day of vengeance. Moses and

Aaron wrought together: theirs was primarily a work of redemption, though accomplished at all costs; " I gave Egypt for thy ransom."

A few are charged to do judgment: every one without exception is charged to show mercy. I may doubt whether I am one of *a few*: I cannot doubt whether I am one of *every one*. A clue in obscure cases.

" Behold, the Lord will come with fire, . . . to render . . . His rebuke with flames of fire." Already by the word of His Scriptures, of His priests, of my own conscience, of my fellowmen, and especially of any good Christians, the Divine word of rebuke comes to me.

O Merciful Lord Jesus, grant that now Thy rebuke may enlighten and enkindle us, lest then it should consume us.

Thou Who once madest Thyself as a man in Whose mouth are no reproofs, rebuke us, but with judgment, not in Thine anger, lest Thou bring us to nothing.

Thou Who becamest a reproof among Thine enemies and Thy neighbours, save us from the reproof of him that would eat us up.

Thou Who knowest our reproof, our shame and our dishonour, deliver us from our adversaries, who are all in Thy sight. Blessed be Thou. Amen.

"The exhortation which speaketh unto you as unto children, My son, despise not thou the chastening of the Lord, nor faint when thou art rebuked of Him: for whom the Lord loveth He chasteneth, and scourgeth every son whom He receiveth." The temper I should cultivate is love, which endureth all things. " Rebuke a wise man, and he will love thee." St. Peter loved St. Paul, writing: " Our beloved brother Paul." The influence entrusted to me I cannot choose but exert, by it promoting and countenancing, directly or indirectly, good or else evil. " He that saith unto the wicked, Thou art righteous; him shall the people curse, nations shall abhor him; but to them that rebuke him shall be delight, and a good blessing shall come upon them." No extremity stays the flow of influence.

"As often as they will."—Storm, pestilence, earthquake, the sea, lightning, wild beasts, these all have oftentimes destroyed men. It is yet to be seen, more terrific will it be to see, saints wielding all weapons of destruction. Saints who resemble Christ.

O Christ, the Saint of saints, Who callest us to be saints; in the dire day of destruction save us. Christ our Refuge, exclude us not; our Redeemer, despise us not; our Surety, deny us not; our Saviour, destroy us not; our Brother, abhor us not; our Friend, forsake us not; our All in all, fail us not. Amen.

7. And when they shall have finished their testimony, the beast that ascendeth out of the bottomless pit shall make war against them, and shall overcome them, and kill them.

"But we have this treasure in earthen vessels, that the excellency of the power may be of God, and not of us. We are troubled on every side, yet not distressed; we are perplexed, but not in despair; persecuted, but not forsaken; cast down, but not destroyed; always bearing about in the body the dying of the Lord Jesus, that the life also of Jesus might be made manifest in our body. For we which live are alway delivered unto death for Jesus' sake, that the life also of Jesus might be made manifest in our mortal flesh. So then death worketh in us."

An overthrow which redounds to the glory of God is not defeat, but victory. Nor indeed is such an overthrow any genuine overthrow; any more than prostration is a fall, or self-sacrifice destruction. Bear witness, Gethsemane and Calvary!

I being weak and timid would fain serve God without great terrors or tortures; but I comprehend that amongst His most noble and ardent lovers some are so rapt out of themselves in Jesus Christ that terrors appal them not, nor tortures abate their spirit. God is good in their height, and in my lowness, accepting the one and not having rejected the other.

As flames that consume the mountains, as winds that coerce the sea,
Thy men of renown show forth Thy might in the clutch of death :
Down they go into silence, yet the Trump of the Jubilee
Swells not Thy praise as swells it the breathless pause of their breath.

What is the flame of their fire, if so I may catch the flame ;
What the strength of their strength, if also I may wax strong?
The flaming fire of their strength is the love of Jesu's Name,
In Whom their death is life, their silence utters a song.

"When they shall have finished their testimony :"—and not till then. "Lord, now lettest Thou Thy servant depart in peace."

"The beast that ascendeth out of the bottomless pit."—As said the Angel to Zechariah: "This is wickedness"—knowing which I know enough: "Wickedness shall be broken as a tree."

Curiosity may remain as to aspect, features, mode of warfare;

but happy I am inasmuch as I cannot, like my mother Eve, gratify my curiosity. For what once I know, I cannot at a wish unknow; and to hanker after knowledge of wickedness seems too often akin to hankering after wickedness.

This my ignorance being Providential, and therefore beyond cavil safe and right, teaches me that to gaze at sin for any purpose except learning to avoid it, has a dangerous side. It was the serpent fascinated Eve when they met face to face, not Eve the serpent. If Elijah complained: "I am not better than my fathers," well may I acknowledge as much, and fear to disport myself in any place where they stumbled.

Lord, I beseech Thee, deliver and preserve us from sinful and sympathetic study of evil. Evil communications corrupt good manners; awaken us to righteousness that we sin no more, but be made of Thee blameless and acceptable in Jesus Christ our Redeemer. Amen.

8. And their dead bodies shall lie in the street of the great city, which spiritually is called Sodom and Egypt, where also our Lord was crucified.

Our Master had aforetime declared: "It cannot be that a prophet perish out of Jerusalem."

Sodom, Egypt, Jerusalem: who but for the Inspired Word had dared class them as, under any aspect, spiritual equivalents?

The Jerusalem of our day is holy Church, the outward and visible Church Catholic. A net she is full of good and bad, a field green with tares and wheat, a floor laden with grain and chaff. In her the not-good are bad, the not-wheat are tares, the not-grain is chaff: *in* her they all are, but some not *of* her; all in her now, but some not always; all borne with to-day, but some not to be borne with to-morrow. Each one of us inevitably is good or else bad; is wheat or else a tare; is grain or else chaff.

According to another similitude we all are either sheep or goats. Now mixed together; but at last to be sorted and severed, and to depart one from another. Yet those millions of souls destitute of help, who have never so much as known their right hand from their left: what of them? God knoweth. We read that even the hallowed Passover Lamb might be taken out either from the sheep or from the goats; the kid, the infant goat, being thus classed with the lamb, the infant sheep, and proved capable of Divine acceptance.

O Lord the Good Shepherd, Whose is the holy flock; the

cattle upon a thousand hills are also Thine. Thou art good and gracious, and my trust is in Thy word.

" Love righteousness, ye that be judges of the earth : think of the Lord with a good (heart), and in simplicity of heart seek Him. For He will be found of them that tempt Him not ; and sheweth Himself unto such as do not distrust Him."

" Their dead bodies shall lie."—" But though the righteous be prevented with death, yet shall he be in rest. For honourable age is not that which standeth in length of time, nor that is measured by number of years. But wisdom is the gray hair unto men, and an unspotted life is old age."

Where never tempest heaveth,	Where never shame bewaileth,
Nor sorrow grieveth,	Nor serpent traileth,
Nor death bereaveth,	Nor death prevaileth,
Nor hope deceiveth,	Nor harvest faileth,
Sleep.	Reap.

" Where also our Lord was crucified."—Following Whom afar off, " Blessed are they which are persecuted for righteousness' sake : for theirs is the kingdom of heaven."

It is " our Lord " Who was crucified : theirs, and equally ours ; theirs, no more than ours, no more than mine.

O our Lord, because of Thy gracious word touching the corn of wheat, make us all, make me, of its living abundant fruit. O our Lord, because Thou hast been lifted up from the earth, fulfil Thy gracious word and draw all men, draw me, unto Thee.

9. And they of the people and kindreds and tongues and nations shall see their dead bodies three days and an half, and shall not suffer their dead bodies to be put in graves.

" Why do . . . the people imagine a vain thing? . . . The Lord shall have them in derision."

The chief priests and Pharisees, Christ's murderers, remembered that He had said : " After three days I will rise again. . . . So they went, and made the sepulchre sure, sealing the stone, and setting a watch." Now on the contrary these miscreants suffer not the holy bodies to be hidden out of sight, but keep an eye upon them.

If this be the lesson they learned from that former experience, what a lesson from the ways and works of God !

Under either precaution the result is the same. Thus of old it was equally possible for Samson mured up in Gaza to arise at midnight and break forth ; or for the same Samson

openly and under all men's eyes in Dagon's temple to overthrow both idol and idolaters.

**10. And they that dwell upon the earth shall rejoice over
them, and make merry, and shall send gifts one to
another; because these two prophets tormented them
that dwelt on the earth.**

"The heart of fools is in the house of mirth. It is better to
hear the rebuke of the wise, than for a man to hear the song
of fools. For as the crackling of thorns under a pot, so is the
laughter of the fool : this also is vanity."

All such impious sending of gifts is in its degree as when
Pilate "sent" our Lord to Herod, and Herod again "sent"
Him back to Pilate, whereupon the two were made friends.
"Though hand join in hand, the wicked shall not be un-
punished."

They that dwelt upon the earth rejoiced over twain who
doubtless were well content no longer to dwell upon such an
earth. Short-sighted, those sinners rejoiced because of a
cessation of torment, a lull before a storm.

To slay the two prophets produced at the utmost a pause of
torment. Yet might those tormented sinners have clean
escaped if they would, as out of the snare of the fowler.
Whereby? By ceasing to "dwell upon the earth," and trans-
ferring conversation, treasure, heart, to heaven.

As then, so now, so always while the day of grace endures.
Would any not be afraid of the power? Whoso doeth that
which is good shall have praise of the same; for he is the
minister of God to such for good.

> Toll, bell, toll. For hope is flying
> Sighing from the earthbound soul :
> Life is sighing, life is dying :
> Toll, bell, toll.
>
> Gropes in its own grave the mole
> Wedding darkness, undescrying,
> Tending to no different goal.
>
> Self-slain soul, in vain thy sighing :
> Self-slain, who should make thee whole?
> Vain the clamour of thy crying :
> Toll, bell, toll,

Living branches are borne by the root, and through the root
only have commerce with the earth. What cannot be compassed or indulged in as by Christ's member, is unfit to be
compassed or indulged in at all.

The saints are strangers and pilgrims, dwellers in tents, sojourners as all our fathers were. They resemble air plants rather than earth plants, yet are by no means tossed about with every wind. They may be likened to birds of paradise, having feet as well as pinions, yet pinions more conspicuous and more characteristic than feet.

> Yet earth was very good in days of old,
>   And earth is lovely still :
> Still for the sacred flock she spreads the fold,
>   For Sion rears the hill.
>
> Mother she is and cradle of our race,
>   A depth where treasures lie,
> The broad foundation of a holy place,
>   Man's step to scale the sky.
>
> She spreads the harvest-field which Angels reap,
>   And lo ! the crop is white ;
> She spreads God's Acre where the happy sleep
>   All night that is not night.
>
> Earth may not pass till heaven shall pass away,
>   Nor heaven may be renewed
> Except with earth : and once more in that day
>   Earth shall be very good.

11. And after three days and an half the Spirit of life from God entered into them, and they stood upon their feet; and great fear fell upon them which saw them.

"Three days and an half" apparently of total failure. "Thou hast made us as the offscouring and refuse in the midst of the people." "We are made as the filth of the world, and are the offscouring of all things unto this day." *Unto*, but not beyond. "If a man die, shall he live again ? all the days of my appointed time will I wait, till my change come. Thou shalt call, and I will answer Thee."

I may or may not be numbered amongst those who with eyes of flesh and blood shall behold when the Spirit of God entering into the two Witnesses they shall stand upon their feet. But the general resurrection all must see.

The rejoicers in iniquity must gaze horror-struck. The rejoicers in the truth may indeed gaze with "great fear"; yet, please God, with greater hope ; with at least some trembling joy amid the general lamentation and mourning and woe.

That so (God grant it !), that so it may assuredly be with us in that day, it must in this day be so with us in spirit, will, strenuous endeavour : by our siding with God against Satan, with righteousness against sin, with truth against falsehood, with law against revolt; by our siding with those against these in our secret aim, heart ; in our open conduct ; in our circle by example, influence ; in the Church by loyalty, consistency ; in the world by courage, zeal, endurance.

A saint or a sinner : one or other each must come to light in the resurrection. No neutrals then : therefore no neutrals now.

It is an alarming symptom when sympathy leans to the wrong side, or when taste and curiosity lie beyond the pale. " Remember Lot's wife."

O Lord Jesus Christ, Who being Infinite didst for our sake deign to encompass Thyself with limitations ; curb our eyes, hearts, wills, imaginations, desires : that law and instruction may be our ornament of grace and chains of dignity, and that Thy service may be our perfect freedom.

12. And they heard a great voice from heaven saying unto them, Come up hither. And they ascended up to heaven in a cloud ; and their enemies beheld them.

If these two witnesses be Enoch and Elias, then is their career pre-eminently Christ-like. In a subordinate sense, they like their Master first came down from heaven to earth in order to die ; and having died and risen again, they afterwards re-ascended to heaven in a cloud, as we read that our Lord Himself ascended.

"Come up hither."—And they went up.

To us day by day the word is "Come." "Come unto Me, all ye that labour and are heavy laden, and I will give you rest." "Come ; for all things are now ready." "Come unto the marriage." Alas ! for any with whom the Truth is pleading : "Ye will not come to Me, that ye might have life";—to whom He will never say : " Come up hither."

"See that ye refuse not Him that speaketh. For if they escaped not who refused Him that spake on earth, much more shall not we escape, if we turn away from Him that speaketh from heaven."

Lord, this blessed day while Thou commandest, invitest, beseechest us to come, grant us grace obediently to come : lest another day Thou say to us, Go, depart ; and disobedient even in our obedience we must then depart. From which utter destruction preserve us, Good Lord Jesus. Amen.

> Lord, grant us grace to mount by steps of grace
> From grace to grace nearer, my God, to Thee :
>   Not tarrying for to-morrow
>   Lest we lie down in sorrow,
>   And never see
> Unveiled Thy Face.

Life is a vapour vanishing in haste ;
  Life is a day whose sun grows pale to set ;
    Life is a stint and sorrow,
    One day and not the morrow ;
  Precious, while yet
It runs to waste.

Lord, strengthen us ; lest fainting by the way
  We come not to Thee, we who come from far :
    Lord, bring us to that morrow
    Which makes an end of sorrow,
  Where all saints are
On holyday.

Where all the saints rest who have heard Thy call,
  Have risen and striven and now rejoice in rest :
    Call us too home from sorrow
    To rest in Thee to-morrow ;
  In Thee our Best,
In Thee our All.

"And their enemies beheld them."—Not (please God) that there were not also friends left on earth to see them ; for besides those dead in Christ who will rise first, St. Paul particularizes some who being alive at His coming will be caught up to meet Him in the air.

Hidden saints : Mephibosheths of the Better David. Yet as "Open rebuke is better than secret love," we must by a sort of parallel be on our guard lest any "hidden" aspect of our own depend on our not being saints at all, and therefore and for that reason only not shining to the glory of our Heavenly Father. Lest in lieu of dark lanterns lighted, we be simply lightless lanterns.

"A people scattered and peeled . . . a people terrible from their beginning hitherto ; a nation meted out and trodden under foot" :—to less than this, even at her very least, the Church Militant can never dwindle.

13. And the same hour was there a great earthquake, and the tenth part of the city fell, and in the earthquake were slain of men seven thousand : and the remnant were affrighted, and gave glory to the God of heaven.

"Ye are the salt of the earth," said our Blessed Master to His disciples : by which statement we recognize Christians as the preservative element of this world. So Noah barricaded the old world against the Deluge, until he was shut into the Ark. So Lot screened the cities of the plain from fire, until he entered into Zoar. So now the earthquake forbore, until the two Witnesses had ascended. So to the very end earth cannot perish, until the last saint has been caught up.

Salt pleases not every palate, nor preaching every ear, nor warning every temper. If it be possible, as much as lieth in him, each Christian is charged to live peaceably with all men. Beyond what lieth in him he is not answerable: up to what lieth in him he is.

One who aspires to teach must first become teachable. And if no time should remain afterwards for teaching? Then like a Deacon such an one will have purchased to himself a good degree; good, although another may be better and higher.

If we may connect the overthrown tenth of the city as bearing a traceable arithmetical proportion to the seven thousand slain; then the full number of inhabitants was seventy thousand, of whom sixty-three thousand being affrighted glorified God. So far this dire destruction resembles the amputation of one limb to relieve a whole body; as one says, to afford one last chance for life.

The sixty-three thousand presumably included, if they did not altogether consist of, a remnant of those outrageous rebels of whom we have just been reading as revelling and rejoicing over the slain Witnesses. They were impressed, aroused, at the least momentarily as it would seem brought to a better mind, by the death of seven thousand in a great earthquake.

I myself have lived in a period though not in a region of earthquakes. Inhabited places have fallen, an unknown number of my fellow-creatures have perished. I have been affrighted and I have been spared.

Now, Lord God of Heaven, grant me grace to give Thee glory; lest it had been better for me to be cut off short, not living out half my days. Multiply upon us Thy mercy; pleading Jesus Christ I multiply my prayer for every soul within the possibility of Thine infinite mercy. Amen.

14. The second woe is past; and, behold, the third woe cometh quickly.

That third woe, that most awful woe inasmuch as we read not that it passes!

It is in great measure with the contrary source of grief that we are for the present familiar. Half earth's sadness takes its rise from her transitory habit. Spring or summer might satisfy a light heart, if only they could abide. Autumn is a very parable of passing away and sorrowfulness. Only winter is cheered by our foresight of its coming to an end; winter the death of each year.

That winter which will be the death of Time has no promise of termination. Winter that returns not to spring, night that returns not to day, death that returns not to life, woe that returns not to bliss,—who can bear it?

Thou Who didst endure for us the cold night of Thy Passion; deliver us from the winter, the night, the woe, of eternal death. Thou Who didst die and revive for us; deliver us from the fruitless woeful eternity of death.

15. And the seventh angel sounded; and there were great voices in heaven, saying, The kingdoms of this world are become the kingdoms of our Lord, and of His Christ; and He shall reign for ever and ever.

At the opening of the seventh seal there was silence in heaven: now at the sounding of the seventh trumpet there are "great voices in heaven." In divers manners God speaketh to us.

A Woe was predicted: and behold! joy as the joy of harvest, and as when men rejoice who divide the spoil. But the Woe is bound up in the joy; overthrow introduces the triumph.

The Woe is mentioned first, reminding us to bear each other's burdens while we may. As yet, God prospering our poor endeavour, we may by influence, example, sympathy, a helping hand, intercession, lighten our brethren's load: even as the saints by holy influence, pious example, warm hands stretched out to help, Christ-like sympathy and intercession, spend themselves to lighten ours.

"The kingdoms of this world" are those which are to become "the kingdoms of our Lord, and of His Christ." But the Revised Version in each clause gives the singular instead of the plural, *kingdom* instead of *kingdoms*.

Since I know not which translation to prefer, it seems lawful to learn from both.

Strength attaches to union, resource to multiplicity. The kingdom of death (notwithstanding that death is dissolution) retains strength while it coheres; for our Lord Himself declared that were Satan divided against himself his kingdom could not stand. How much more would the kingdom of life, which is the Church Catholic, wax invincibly strong if all Christendom were to become as at the first of one heart and one mind! Alas! for the offences of former days and of this day, for our fathers' offences and our own, which have torn to shreds Christ's seamless vesture.

Nevertheless inasmuch as multiplicity is allied to resource, let us, until better may be, make capital even of our guilty disadvantage. Let us be provoked to good works by those with whom we cannot altogether agree, yet who many ways set us a pattern. Why exclusively peer after defects while virtues stare us in the face? Cannot we—I at least can learn much from the devotion of Catholic Rome, the immutability of Catholic Greece, the philanthropic piety of Quakerism, the zeal of many a "protestant." And when the Anglican Church has acquired and reduced to practice each virtue from every such source, holding fast meanwhile her own goodly heritage of gifts and graces, then may those others likewise learn much from her : until to every Church, congregation, soul, God be All in all.

This present dying life has to end in final death or final life. Time must be superseded by eternity.

Then the kingdom will pass away utterly from whatsoever is not "of our Lord, and of His Christ."

Death will abide in evil unity, the lost in evil multiplicity : unity of impotence not of strength, multiplicity of antagonism not of alliance.

Life, created but immortal, will be bound up as one in that "bundle of life," the love of God ; and at the same time will be what "no man could number" in its offering of love to God. One in joy, innumerable in pleasures ; one in sanctification, innumerable in graces.

"And He shall reign for ever and ever." Amen.

> Marvel of marvels, if I myself shall behold
> With mine own eyes my King in His city of gold ;
> Where the least of lambs is spotless white in the fold,
> Where the least and last of saints in spotless white is stoled,
> Where the dimmest head beyond a moon is aureoled.
> O saints my beloved, now mouldering to mould in the mould,
> Shall I see you lift your heads, see your cerements unrolled,
> See with these very eyes? who now in darkness and cold
> Tremble for the midnight cry, the rapture, the tale untold,
> "The Bridegroom cometh, cometh, His Bride to enfold."
>
> Cold it is, my beloved, since your funeral bell was tolled,
> Cold it is, O my King, how cold alone on the wold.

16. And the four and twenty elders, which sat before God on their seats, fell upon their faces, and worshipped God,

17. Saying, We give Thee thanks, O Lord God Almighty, which art, and wast, and art to come ; because Thou hast taken to Thee Thy great power, and hast reigned.

Judgment, mercy, salvation, destruction, all elicit worship
from the citizens of heaven ; amongst whom we here behold
the four and twenty elders prostrate themselves in adoration,
thereby enhancing not abating their proper dignity. Throughout this Apocalypse the chorus of rapturous praise occurs and
recurs ; like the burden of that 136th Psalm of which each
verse, whatever it recounts, culminates in the words : " For His
mercy endureth for ever." God's Goodness, His supremacy,
His marvellous acts, His Wisdom in creation, His Providence,
His destruction of the Egyptian firstborn, His rescue of
enslaved Israel, His wonders at the Red Sea, His longsuffering
in the wilderness, His overthrow of hostile kings, His bestowal
of the promised land, His faithful remembrance, His ever-
ready help, His bounty,—all called forth the Psalmist's
impartial praise. Which chant of praise from his day to our
own has echoed in the Church generation after generation,
and echoes still and still will echo while faith remains in the
earth.

"Justice and judgment are the habitation of Thy Throne ;
mercy and truth shall go before Thy face. Blessed is the
people that know the joyful sound : they shall walk, O Lord,
in the light of Thy countenance."

Lord, make us, I beseech Thee, like-minded with all saints
whether on earth or in heaven ; that we may worship Thee as
they worship, trust Thee as they trust, rejoice in Thee as they
rejoice, love Thee as they love. Even for the sake of our
Saviour Jesus Christ the Saint of saints. Amen.

" O Lord God Almighty, Which Art, and Wast, and Art to
come."—The Revised Version omits " and Art to come " : thus
setting before us (by suggestion) that perpetual *now* of eternity
which ensues from the unchanging Perfection of the Divine
Being. For since He Whose Name is Holy " inhabiteth
eternity," therefore eternity is so to say moulded upon Him ;
and to Him in his own Nature there exists neither past nor
future, nothing ended, nothing beginning. "Which Wast"
expresses the creature's experience throughout time, and the
creature's mode of apprehending that eternity which (in a
sense) preceded time ; while, as the passage under consideration commemorates the transference of the creature out of
time into eternity, the text stopping short (if in truth it does
so stop short) at the words " and Wast," indicates how time
has at length passed away even for the creatures of time, who
thenceforward for good or for evil are conformed to the law of
eternity.

"Thou hast taken to Thee Thy great power, and hast reigned"—as it were responding to the prayer and prophecy: "Awake, awake, put on strength, O arm of the Lord; awake, as in the ancient days, in the generations of old. Art thou not it that hath cut Rahab, and wounded the dragon? Art thou not it which hath dried the sea, the waters of the great deep; that hath made the depths of the sea a way for the ransomed to pass over? Therefore the redeemed of the Lord shall return, and come with singing unto Zion; and everlasting joy shall be upon their head: they shall obtain gladness and joy; and sorrow and mourning shall flee away."

"Thy Throne, O God, is for ever and ever: the sceptre of Thy kingdom is a right sceptre."

18. And the nations were angry, and Thy wrath is come, and the time of the dead, that they should be judged, and that Thou shouldest give reward unto Thy servants the prophets, and to the saints, and them that fear Thy Name, small and great; and shouldest destroy them which destroy the earth.

St. Paul writes: "Be ye angry, and sin not: let not the sun go down upon your wrath: neither give place to the devil."

Here at the sunset of time the nations are angry; and God suffering His whole displeasure at length to arise destroys them which destroy the earth. "Thou sattest in the Throne judging right. Thou hast rebuked the heathen, Thou hast destroyed the wicked, Thou hast put out their name for ever and ever. O thou enemy, destructions are come to a perpetual end."

"It is appointed unto men once to die, but after this the judgment." After life, death: after death, judgment: after judgment, life everlasting or death everlasting. "My comeliness was turned in me into corruption, and I retained no strength."

> So brief a life, and then an endless life
> 　Or endless death:
> So brief a life, then endless peace or strife.
> 　Whoso considereth
> How man but like a flower
> 　Or shoot of grass
> Blooms an hour,
> 　Well may sigh "Alas!"
>
> So brief a life, and then an endless grief
> 　Or endless joy:
> So brief a life, then ruin or relief.
> 　What solace, what annoy

Of Time needs dwelling on ?
   It is, it was,
It is done,
   While we sigh " Alas ! "
Yet saints are singing in a happy hope
   Forecasting pleasure,
Bright eyes of faith enlarging all their scope.
   Saints love beyond Time's measure :
Where love is, there is bliss
   That will not pass ;
Where love is,
   Dies away " Alas ! "

O Lord Jesus, Who knowest them that are Thine; when Thou rewardest Thy servants the prophets, remember, I beseech Thee, for good those who have taught me, rebuked me, counselled me, guided me; and in that day show them mercy.

When Thou rewardest the saints, remember, I beseech Thee, for good those who have surrounded me with holy influences, borne with me, forgiven me, sacrificed themselves for me, loved me; and in that day show them mercy.

When Thou rewardest the great that fear Thy Name, remember, I beseech Thee, for good those who have been my patterns of any virtue or grace, of repentance, acknowledgment of offences, begging of pardon, obedience, patience, perseverance; and in that day show them mercy.

When Thou rewardest the small that fear Thy Name, remember, I beseech Thee, for good, ignorant disciples, halting followers, weak cross-bearers, the kneelers on feeble knees, the faint believers who faint not utterly; and in that day show them mercy.

Nor forget any, nor forget me; but in that day show us mercy. Amen.

I think of the saints I have known, and lift up mine eyes
To the far-away home of beautiful Paradise,
Where the song of saints gives voice to an undividing sea
On whose plain their feet stand firm while they keep their jubilee.
As the sound of waters their voice, as the sound of thunderings,
While they all at once rejoice, while all sing and while each one sings ;
Where more saints flock in, and more, and yet more, and again yet more,
And not one turns back to depart thro' the open entrance door.
O sights of our lovely earth, O sound of our earthly sea,
Speak to me of Paradise, of all blessed saints to me ;
Or keep silence touching them, and speak to my heart alone
Of the Saint of saints, the King of kings, the Lamb on the Throne.

" And that Thou . . . shouldest destroy them which destroy

the earth "— or according to a marginal reading :—" which corrupt the earth " :—corrupting, that worst method of destroying ; and which sooner or later draws down a righteous retributive destruction penal and purgative, as was foreshown in the days of Noah : " The earth also was corrupt before God, and the earth was filled with violence. And God looked upon the earth, and, behold, it was corrupt ; for all flesh had corrupted his way upon the earth. And God said unto Noah, The end of all flesh is come before Me ; for the earth is filled with violence through them ; and, behold, I will destroy them with the earth."

And even as Noah kept himself unsullied by the antediluvian corruption ; so by Divine assistance must and can each living soul now in these dangerous days by sanctity of innocence or sanctity of penitence escape the corruption that is in the world through lust, though it dwell all alone without son or daughter, and as holy Job speaking of himself complained : " My friends scorn me : but mine eye poureth out tears unto God."

" Whosoever will be saved " must so do : I who would be saved must so do. To which end certain Bible texts admonish me.

The Incarnate Truth Himself has given this Counsel of Prudence : " Sell that ye have, and give alms ; provide yourselves bags which wax not old, a treasure in the heavens that faileth not, where no thief approacheth, neither moth corrupteth. For where your treasure is, there will your heart be also "—and this Instruction of Righteousness : " Either make the tree good, and his fruit good ; or else make the tree corrupt, and his fruit corrupt : for the tree is known by his fruit."

And holy men of old moved by the Holy Ghost have taught us :—

Eye servants are men pleasers : " It came to pass, when the judge was dead, that they returned, and corrupted themselves more than their fathers."

Misbelief breeds misdoing : " The fool hath said in his heart, There is no God. They are corrupt, they have done abominable works, there is none that doeth good."

Inward defilement exudes : " They are corrupt, and speak wickedly concerning oppression : they speak loftily."

Hold fast integrity : " A righteous man falling down before the wicked is as a troubled fountain, and a corrupt spring."

Mercy rejoices against judgment : " Ye shall know that I

am the Lord, when I have wrought with you for My Name's sake, not according to your wicked ways, nor according to your corrupt doings."

Make a covenant with the eyes: "Corrupt in her inordinate love."

Boast not thyself as if thou hadst not received it: "Thine heart was lifted up because of thy beauty, thou hast corrupted thy wisdom by reason of thy brightness."

There is an evil diligence: "They rose early, and corrupted all their doings."

Take heed what ye hear: "Evil communications corrupt good manners."

Beware of false teachers: "Many, which corrupt the word of God."

Believe not every spirit: "Lest by any means, as the serpent beguiled Eve through his subtilty, so your minds should be corrupted from the simplicity that is in Christ."

What we sow we reap: "He that soweth to his flesh shall of the flesh reap corruption."

The time past may suffice us: "Put off concerning the former conversation the old man, which is corrupt according to the deceitful lusts."

Curb the tongue: "Let no corrupt communication proceed out of your mouth."

Be not wise above that which is written: "Perverse disputings of men of corrupt minds, and destitute of the truth."

Walk not in the counsel of the ungodly: "These also resist the truth: men of corrupt minds, reprobate concerning the faith."

Woe to him that coveteth an evil covetousness: "Your riches are corrupted."

The folly of presumption: "These . . . speak evil of the things that they understand not; and shall utterly perish in their own corruption."

The besottedness of folly: "What they know naturally, as brute beasts, in those things they corrupt themselves."

"They are all grievous revolters, walking with slanders: they are brass and iron; they are all corrupters." "O my soul, come not thou into their secret; unto their assembly, mine honour, be not thou united."

19. And the temple of God was opened in heaven, and there was seen in His temple the ark of His testament: and there were lightnings, and voices, and thunderings, and an earthquake, and great hail.

" I will lift up mine eyes unto the hills, from whence cometh my help. My help cometh from the Lord, which made heaven and earth."

From this opening of the celestial Temple (whatever of higher and deeper it may signify) I venture to infer a promise of future insight : so that what I know not now I may, by following on, attain to know hereafter. And because the Ark of the Testament symbolizes the Divine Son's sacred Humanity, I trust that even as now Christ is the central Mystery revealed to man on probation, so the crowning Mystery revealed to man made perfect will still be Christ : Christ in Whom dwelleth all the Fulness of the Godhead bodily ; the Son Who reveals to whomsoever He will the Father ; the Son Whom to have seen is to have seen the Father ; the Incarnate Son in Whom the Spirit dwelleth not by measure.

O Lord God Almighty, Who out of Thy treasure bringest things new and old for man's instruction, let nature become to us a parable of grace. By Thy lightnings enlighten us and consume us not, by Thy thunders awe us without terror, sit we loose to that earth which may quake and must depart, shelter Thou us in a peaceable habitation when it shall hail coming down on the forest, and this world shall be low in a low place. Let voices of the past persuade us to repentance and faith, of the present to amendment and hope, of the revealed future to holiness and charity ; yea, let all voices persuade us to charity. Speak, Lord, for Thy servant heareth. Grant us grace to hear though both our ears tingle ; and to obey, though taking our life in our hand. For His sake, Whose merit exceeds our demerit, Jesus Christ our Lord. Amen.

Tempest and terror below : but Christ the Almighty above.
Tho' the depth of the deep overflow, tho' fire run along on the ground,
Tho' all billows and flames make a noise,—and where is an Ark for the
    dove ?—
Tho' sorrows rejoice against joys, and death and destruction abound .
Yet Jesus abolisheth death, and Jesus Who loves us we love ;
    His dead are renewed with a breath, His lost are the sought and the
    found.

Thy wanderers call and recall, Thy dead men lift out of the ground :
O Jesus, Who lovest us all, stoop low from Thy Glory above :
Where sin hath abounded make grace to abound and to superabound,
    Till we gaze on Thee face unto Face, and respond to Thee love unto
    Love.

CHAPTER XII

1. And there appeared a great wonder in heaven; a woman clothed with the sun, and the moon under her feet, and upon her head a crown of twelve stars:

The Preacher, the son of David, King in Jerusalem, has left on record : " I know that, whatsoever God doeth, it shall be for ever : nothing can be put to it, nor anything taken from it ; and God doeth it, that men should fear before Him. That which hath been is now ; and that which is to be hath already been ; and God requireth that which is past." Thus the past which we know, presages the future which we know not.

And Greater than that King and Wiser than that Preacher, our Lord Himself said to His disciples : " Have ye understood all these things? They say unto Him, Yea, Lord. Then said He unto them, Therefore every scribe which is instructed unto the kingdom of heaven is like unto a man that is an householder, which bringeth forth out of his treasure things new and old." Now as every Christian " is instructed unto the kingdom of heaven," he cannot be destitute of a treasure whence to bring forth somewhat ; new it may be, old it cannot but be.

Of this Apocalypse the occult unfulfilled signification will be new ; the letter is old. Old, not merely because these eighteen hundred years it has warned us to flee from the wrath to come ; but also because each figure appeals to our experience, even when it stands for some object unprecedented or surpassing.

A rose might preach beauty and a lily purity to a receptive mind, although the ear had not yet heard tell of the Rose of Sharon and Lily of the Valleys.

" A woman clothed with the sun, and the moon under her feet, and upon her head a crown of twelve stars."—Whatever else may here be hidden, there stands revealed that " great wonder," weakness made strong and shame swallowed up in celestial glory. For thus the figure is set before our eyes.

Through Eve's lapse, weakness and shame devolved on woman as her characteristics, in a manner special to herself and unlike the corresponding heritage of man.

And as instinctively we personify the sun and moon as *he* and *she*, I trust there is no harm in my considering that her sun-clothing indicates how in that heaven where St. John in vision beheld her, she will be made equal with men and angels; arrayed in all human virtues, and decked with all communicable Divine graces: whilst the moon under her feet portends that her sometime infirmity of purpose and changeableness of mood have, by preventing, assisting, final grace, become immutable; she has done all and stands; from the lowest place she has gone up higher. As love of his Lord enabled St. Peter to tread the sea, so love of the same Lord sets weak woman immovable on the waves of this troublesome world, triumphantly erect, despite her own frailty, made not "like unto a wheel," amid all the changes and chances of this mortal life.

Eve's temptation and fall suggest the suitableness and safety of much (though by no means of all) ignorance, and the wholesomeness of studying what is open without prying into what is secret. We have no reason to doubt that the forbidden fruit was genuinely "pleasant to the eyes": as such she might innocently have gazed upon it with delight, and for that delight might profitably have returned thanks to the Author and Giver of all good. Not till she became wise in her own conceit, disregarding the plain obvious meaning of words, and theorizing on her own responsibility as to physical and intellectual results, did she bring sin and death into the world. The Tree of the Knowledge of Good and Evil was as it were a standing prophet ever reiterating the contingent sentence, Thou shalt surely die. This sentence, plain and unmistakable, she connived at explaining away, and being deceived, was undone.

Eve exhibits one extreme of feminine character, the Blessed Virgin the opposite extreme. Eve parleyed with a devil: holy Mary "was troubled" at the salutation of an Angel. Eve sought knowledge: Mary instruction. Eve aimed at self-indulgence: Mary at self-oblation. Eve, by disbelief and disobedience, brought sin to the birth: Mary, by faith and submission, Righteousness.

And yet, even as at the foot of the Cross, St. Mary Magdalene, out of whom went seven devils, stood beside the "lily among thorns," the Mother of sorrows: so (I humbly hope and trust) amongst all saints of all time will stand before the Throne, Eve the beloved first Mother of us all. Who that has loved and revered her own immediate dear mother, will not echo the hope?

Again and eminently, the heavenly figure under consideration presents an image of the Church: "the King hath brought me into His chambers."

"Who is she that looketh forth as the morning, fair as the moon, clear as the sun, and terrible as an army with banners?" All glorious she is within by the Indwelling of the Holy Spirit, and effluent glory envelopes her as with the sun for a garment. The moon, set below, may never again eclipse the sun; yet inasmuch as the perfect life had to be developed out of the imperfect, the unchangeable out of the changeable, therefore the moon abides underlying that consummated glory. Twelve stars compose her crown, a twelvefold splendour. I have seen the Twelve Apostles suggested as the interpretation of this symbol; and well may it direct our thoughts to their glorious company, the illumination of their doctrine, the shining light of their example. Perhaps there will be no harm in an additional gloss. The eternal state of the Church Triumphant is expressed by her sun-vesture; the moon beneath her feet memorializes her temporal probation while militant in this world; the twelve stars may—may they not? for earth's day is as night when compared with heaven's day—may remind us of those twelve hours in the day during which she was bound to walk and work in accordance with our Lord's own words and practice. Thus her probation issues in glory, a glory all the more glorious because of that probation. "Give her of the fruit of her hands; and let her own works praise her in the gates." Or if *stars* seem too incongruous an emblem of any *daylight* hours; I call to mind both that there shall be no night there, and that certain benefactors have for their allotted dignity to shine as the stars for ever and ever: whereby stars take rank in the everlasting day.

Or rather, what real connection is there between stars and night more than between stars and day? Earth's shadows approach them not in their high places; nor so far as we can trace, affect them in any way, or do aught in their regard beyond revealing them to mortal ken. Our perception varies, not their lustre.

2. And she being with child cried, travailing in birth, and pained to be delivered.

Wending my way amid inscrutable mysteries, the *words* of each verse suggest at least detached matter for thought.

The 87th Psalm (1—6: Prayer-book version) narrates how

"he" was born in divers places and apparently of different parentages. Which comes to pass concerning Christ: Who being formed in each elect soul of whatever kindred, nation, people, tongue, locality, is thus "born" wheresoever such happy souls are born; holy Church being their mother. "Her foundations are upon the holy hills: the Lord loveth the gates of Sion more than all the dwellings of Jacob. Very excellent things are spoken of thee: thou city of God. I will think upon Rahab and Babylon: with them that know me. Behold ye the Philistines also: and they of Tyre, with the Morians; lo, there was he born. And of Sion it shall be reported that he was born in her: and the Most High shall stablish her." Thus out of Egypt again and again God vouchsafes to call His Son. Thus may Philistia a thousand times be glad of Him. Is any spot excluded? Nay: "The Lord shall rehearse it when He writeth up the people: that He was born there."

Cries and travail pangs:—no marvel then that not without effort, suffering, fear, sometimes agony, missionaries do and must do their work of travailing for souls. But they shall remember no more the anguish for joy of the birth: "In that day shall there be a highway out of Egypt to Assyria, and the Assyrian shall come into Egypt, and the Egyptian into Assyria, and the Egyptians shall serve with the Assyrians. In that day shall Israel be the third with Egypt and with Assyria, even a blessing in the midst of the land: whom the Lord of hosts shall bless, saying, Blessed be Egypt My people, and Assyria the work of My hands, and Israel Mine inheritance."

Eve, the representative woman, received as part of her sentence "desire": the assigned object of her desire being such that satisfaction must depend not on herself but on one stronger than she, who might grant or might deny. Many women attain their heart's desire: many attain it not. Yet are these latter no losers if they exchange desire for aspiration, the corruptible for the incorruptible: "Thou shalt no more be termed Forsaken; neither shall thy land any more be termed Desolate: but thou shalt be called Hephzibah, and thy land Beulah: for the Lord delighteth in thee, and thy land shall be married." "The desolate hath many more children than she which hath an husband." "Give me children, or else I die," was a foolish speech: the childless who make themselves nursing mothers of Christ's little ones are true mothers in Israel.

> O Lord, when Thou didst call me, didst Thou know
>   My heart disheartened thro' and thro',
>   Still hankering after Egypt full in view,

Where cucumbers and melons grow ?
—"Yea, I knew."—

But, Lord, when Thou didst choose me, didst Thou know
How marred I was and withered too,
Nor rose for sweetness nor for virtue rue,
Timid and rash, hasty and slow?
—"Yea, I knew."—

My Lord, when Thou didst love me, didst Thou know
How weak my efforts were, how few,
Tepid to love and impotent to do,
Envious to reap while slack to sow ?
•   —"Yea, I knew."—

Good Lord Who knowest what I cannot know
And dare not know, my false, my true,
My new, my old ; Good Lord, arise and do
If loving Thou hast known me so.
—"Yea, I knew."—

3. And there appeared another wonder in heaven: and behold a great red dragon, having seven heads and ten horns, and seven crowns upon his heads.

A wonder: and not least a wonder because beheld "in heaven." The monster has seven heads, which perhaps may be viewed as indicating pseudo self-completeness and assumption of independence ; ten horns, pseudo-strength ; seven crowns, pseudo-supremacy. For these seven crowns appear (*see* Revised Version) to be correctly translated "seven diadems"; and to be consequently not wreaths of victory but insignia of dominion. *Power* therefore the dragon wields, yet only under sufferance and until it be reclaimed from him : *victory* is not his, nor shall be. He is that "swift" to whom the race is not, that "strong" to whom is not the battle.

Even his "red" colour may possibly express a pseudo-sanctity: for of the Stronger than he we read : "Wherefore art Thou red in Thine apparel?" Thus would Satan himself be transformed into much more than an angel of light.

And at the present day when so open-mouthed an antagonism has set in against Christ and Revelation ; and when so many "devout and honourable" persons (if following the Inspired text I dare call them so) are arrayed against the truth as it is in Jesus ; and when signal virtues of philanthropy, with self-spending and alacrity in being spent, take the field like Goliath the Giant in defiance of the armies of the Living God ; I think the pseudo-Christ-like aspect of error becomes prominently urged upon our gravest consideration : especially as of necessity we know not how close upon us may already be the actual personal Antichrist in whom human wickedness appears to culminate; that Antichrist who will, it seems, be a foul human agent and copy of the old original Evil one. Let us pause a moment to face this last great adversary, who not as our open enemy but as one of ourselves, will do us this dishonour.

Some then presage in the Antichrist a pseudo- or mock-Christ. And that his adherents will be not rebels merely, but eminently dupes, St. Paul by Inspiration intimates; when touching the Second Advent and the awful period preceding it, he writes: "Let no man beguile you in any wise: for it will not be, except the falling away come first, and the man of sin be revealed, the son of perdition, he that opposeth and exalteth himself against all that is called God or that is worshipped; so that he sitteth in the temple of God, setting himself forth as God. . . . And then shall be revealed the lawless one, whom the Lord Jesus shall slay with the breath of His mouth, and bring to nought by the manifestation of His coming; even he, whose coming is according to the working of Satan with all power and signs and lying wonders, and with all deceit of unrighteousness for them that are perishing; because they received not the love of the truth, that they might be saved. And for this cause God sendeth them a working error, that they should believe a lie: that they all might be judged who believed not the truth, but had pleasure in unrighteousness."

I have here quoted the Revised Version in preference to the Authorized because, whilst in my ignorance of Greek I can only take either text upon trust, I note some difference between the two renderings. The words "bring to nought by the manifestation of His coming," seem pointedly to express how the simple revelation of truth must supersede and abolish error: whereas "destroy with the brightness of His coming" (Authorized Version), may suggest a physical destruction as by fire from heaven. Again: "all deceit of unrighteousness for them that are perishing," is perhaps more easy to be understood, than "all deceivableness of unrighteousness in them that perish" (Authorized Version); and by suggesting that the perishing persons in question entertain no idea of their death-struck condition, the phrase recalls those piteous words of Hosea concerning Ephraim: "Strangers have devoured his strength, and he knoweth it not: yea, gray hairs are here and there upon him, yet he knoweth not."

4. And his tail drew the third part of the stars of heaven, and did cast them to the earth: and the dragon stood

before the woman which was ready to be delivered, for to devour her child as soon as it was born.

" Yea, the stars are not pure in His sight." " How is the gold become dim! how is the most fine gold changed! the stones of the sanctuary are poured out in the top of every street. . . . They that were brought up in scarlet embrace dunghills."

Temptation, whatever guise it assumes, remains essentially and unalterably base : not even the head, but the tail of the dragon drew and cast down those stars. Temptation, however urgent, remains powerless to compel : the stars were "drawn," not swept along, their free will being seduced, not overborne. At least, they preach to ourselves by such a parable ; to ourselves who are free to stand or to fall.

"He that dwelleth in the secret place of the Most High shall abide under the shadow of the Almighty. I will say of the Lord, He is my refuge and my fortress : my God ; in Him will I trust. . . . Because thou hast made the Lord, which is my refuge, even the Most High, thy habitation ; there shall no evil befall thee. . . . The dragon shalt thou trample under feet. Because he hath set his love upon Me, therefore will I deliver him."

As to this dragon, he appears to be that "murderer from the beginning," whom our Lord thus characterized plainly to His hearers. As he was, so he is ; and his lusts he will do so far as in him lies.

Yet is God Almighty able to break the heads of the dragons in the waters. Meanwhile, what is the mind of the saints? "Our heart is not turned back, neither have our steps declined from Thy way ; though Thou hast sore broken us in the place of dragons, and covered us with the shadow of death."

A travailing woman and a new-born babe : truly these might have seemed souls destitute of help. But even concerning doomed Edom, the word of prophecy saith : "Leave thy fatherless children, I will preserve them alive ; and let thy widows trust in Me." Not fathoming the profound signification, let me be thankful for the encouragement of a homely mercy. If my song cannot be of "mercy and judgment," it can at least be "of mercy . . . unto Thee, O Lord, will I sing. O let me have understanding : in the way of godliness."

Behold in heaven a floating, dazzling cloud,
So dazzling that I could but cry Alas !
Alas, because I felt how low I was ;
Alas, within my spirit if not aloud,

Foreviewing my last breathless bed and shroud :
  Thus pondering, I glanced downward on the grass ;
  And the grass bowed when airs of heaven would pass,
Lifting itself again when it had bowed.
That grass spake comfort ; weak it was and low.
  Yet strong enough and high enough to bend
    In homage at a message fiom the sky :
    As the grass did and prospeied, so will I :
Tho' knowing little, doing what I know ;
  And strong in patient weakness till the end.

Gracious Lord Jesus, regard Thy creation for good : men, to befriend them ; women, to protect them ; babes, to nurture them ; sufferers, to ease them ; tremblers, to reassure them ; wanderers, to reclaim them ; the sick, to heal them ; sinners, to convert them ; saints, to perfect them ; the dying, to receive them ; the dead, to keep them. Yea, our compassionate Saviour : Who of Thine own free Will and for our sakes didst become an Infant of days, wast born of a woman, didst grow up to perfect Manhood, wert pleased to share human sufferings, to face fear, to seek the lost, to heal the sick, to forgive sinners, to lead saints, to open Paradise to the dying, and there Thyself to receive the dead. Amen.

Elijah said : "Thou hast asked a hard thing."

But the Lord hath said : "Is anything too hard for the Lord ? "

5. And she brought forth a man child, who was to rule all nations with a rod of iron: and her child was caught up unto God, and to His Throne.

Recalling these words of the second Psalm : "I will declare the decree : the Lord hath said unto Me, Thou art My Son ; this day have I begotten Thee. Ask of Me, and I shall give Thee the heathen for Thine inheritance, and the uttermost parts of the earth for Thy possession. Thou shalt break them with a rod of iron ; Thou shalt dash them in pieces like a potter's vessel " :— an appalling prediction ; but behold as it were a city of refuge !—" Be wise now therefore, O ye kings : be instructed, ye judges of the earth. Serve the Lord with fear, and rejoice with trembling. Kiss the Son, lest He be angry, and ye perish from the way, when His wrath is kindled but a little. Blessed are all they that put their trust in Him."

Behold, Lord Jesus : to love and trust Thee is our place of shelter. Give us thankful hearts while we seek Thee by such ways of pleasantness and paths of peace. Yea, Lord, that we may please Thee and abide with Thee for ever. Amen.

6. And the woman fled into the wilderness, where she hath

a place prepared of God, that they should feed her there a thousand two hundred and threescore days.

This period of "a thousand two hundred and threescore days," being coextensive with that already assigned for the prophesying of the two Witnesses, suggests (by no means proves) that the two periods are in fact identical, and the two groups of events not successive but simultaneous.

If so, and regarding the Woman as a figure of the Church, she and her champions compose an awful harmony. She flees out of heaven to her refuge in a wilderness : they (comparing as before Zechariah iv., especially ver. 14, with the relevant text) appear to emerge from the Lord's immediate Presence to put on sackcloth and bear witness. She is divinely provided for during the days of seclusion ; they abide impregnable until their testimony is completed. Meanwhile her Child, her Representative, the Man she has gotten from the Lord, hath heaven for throne and earth for footstool.

So great a King and Child appears to be a figure of Christ, if he be not Christ Himself.

Lord Jesus, Accessible, Gracious, Winning, Merciful ; purge our eyes to discern Thee wheresoever as the morning spread upon the mountains Thou showest Thyself unto us. And if sometimes we think to recognize Thee where not so much as Thy shadow passeth by, pardon our error, instruct our ignorance. Nevertheless, because whoso goeth up into heaven, or down into hell, or on wings of the morning betaketh himself to the uttermost parts of the sea, leaveth Thee not but still encountereth Thee ; grant us ever to be as Jacob when he became aware that God was close at hand, ever as St. Mary Magdalene in the garden when lo ! the Unknown was Thyself. Amen.

I do not know whether it is allowable to connect texts as follows :

We are expressly certified that during the thousand two hundred and threescore days the Woman was to be fed. But the "forty and two months" of Gentile supremacy slightly exceed that period. So also does the time allotted to the two Witnesses, if the "three days and an half" of their exposure be added to the term of their mission. Thus supposing all three periods to be simultaneous (and whether computed literally or by some figurative scale, their relative proportion amongst themselves continues apparently unaffected), a brief space remains unaccounted for as concerns the Woman ; which brief space is not apparently furnished with food ; reminding us of the words of Gabriel the Archangel to Daniel the Prophet:

"And in the midst of the week "—a half week being equivalent to three days and a half—" He shall cause the sacrifice and the oblation to cease, and for the overspreading of abominations He shall make it desolate, even until the consummation, and that determined shall be poured upon the desolate."

In this cessation of the sacrifice and oblation devout insight has, I believe, apprehended a cessation of the Blessed Sacrament of Christ's Body and Blood : if so, a withdrawal of that very Bread of Life and Cup of Blessing which are the Church's daily Food and Drink.

Whilst It abides in our midst God grant us grace to partake of It to life eternal. For Jesus Christ's sake. Amen.

"That they should feed her there."—We are not informed who "they" are. Angels ministered to Our Lord in the wilderness of His temptation, an Angel in the Garden of His Agony. Wilderness and Garden appear as one lot in the same fair ground in Isaiah's lovely words of promise : "The wilderness and the solitary place shall be glad for them ; and the desert shall rejoice, and blossom as the rose. It shall blossom abundantly."

Or if this fallen world's wilderness never rejoice, nor its desert ever blossom, yet wherever holy Church abides she herself is "a garden inclosed"; where even one holy soul sojourns there blooms a "lily among thorns."

Any wilderness whither God sends His be'oved is sure to turn out a place of safety and of food convenient, if not of flowers. And were it possible for the whole Church or for one single soul to take up its abode in Heaven against the Divine Will, Heaven itself would be found thenceforward a stronghold not of peace, but of unrest. There is no peace outside "the peace of God."

7. And there was war in heaven: Michael and his angels fought against the dragon ; and the dragon fought and his angels,

8. And prevailed not; neither was their place found any more in heaven.

9. And the great dragon was cast out, that old serpent called the Devil, and Satan, which deceiveth the whole world : he was cast out into the earth, and his angels were cast out with him.

Whatever other and subsequent meaning may attach to this revelation, thought reverts instinctively to that occult primitive sin before which sin was not ; that primæval rebellion which, though long ago trodden down, has not yet been stamped out.

What of disorder cannot sin achieve, if it can turn heaven itself into a battlefield?

" Michael "—which signifies, Who is like God? a name of self-oblation, of self-obliteration. Wherefore all holy intelligences on earth, and haply all holy intelligences in heaven, may discern latent in that old name the new name of one " Who is like God," inasmuch as he glorified not himself.

O Lord All Holy Almighty, let our definition be that we are members of Christ, and our praise be not of men but of Thee, and our memorial be names written in heaven. For His sake Whose Name is as ointment poured forth, Jesus. Amen.

I speak only so far as *my own* present powers of apprehension are concerned :—the mystery inherent in evil is its existence ; not, assuming that existence, its punishment.

Absolute darkness engulfs me when I attempt to realize the origin of evil. Yet even in that darkness which may be felt and which I feel, one point I dare not hesitate to hold fast and assert : evil had its origin in the free choice of a free will. Without free will there can be neither virtue nor vice ; without free choice neither offence nor merit.

The authoritative voice of Holy Church expounding Holy Scripture certifies evil to be positive, not merely negative. If ever I tend to question this, let me look within and consider envy, perhaps at first sight the most irretrievably dead of the seven deadly sins : its sepulchre is incapable of being whited ; it pretends not to be so much as the travestie of any virtue. Envy, surely, is positive evil.

From gratuitous envy, as of the serpent who without gain to himself robbed mankind of innocence : deliver us, O Lord.

From reckless envy, as when to ruin man he aggravated his own doom : deliver us, O Lord.

From far-reaching envy, as when he defaced a perfection distinct from that he had forfeited : deliver us, O Lord.

Yet as the root is answerable for the shoot, not the shoot for the root ; not envy but pride, the deadly root of the other six must I suppose stand first in the hideous array. Pride is that one of the seven which might subsist in a being absolutely solitary, a being constituting (so to say) its own universe. The other six with however evil an eye yet do look out of self, and have regard or disregard to something that is not self : pride, self-centred, fears not God neither regards man.

Pride worships self as self : envy hates good as not-self.

One can conceive some sort of affinity between anger and zeal, lust and love, gluttony and appreciation of blessings, avarice and prudence, sloth and contentment; even between pride and self-respect; but for envy there seems no possible next of kin except a devil.

"Pride goeth before destruction, and an haughty spirit before a fall." If this text may be construed as conveying a double lesson : the obvious admonition which deters from particular sin on pain of consequent disaster; and the distinct statement that pride it is which entails destruction, and an haughty spirit it is which precedes a fall ; then is light thrown on the sin and downfall of angels.

"Michael and his angels," who excel in strength, overcame not the dragon and his angels but by dint of battle.

The strong against the strong, spirit against spirit, *then :* the weak against the strong, flesh and blood against spirit, *now.* Nevertheless weakness indomitable, flesh and blood invulnerable, when they come "to the help of the Lord, to the help of the Lord against the mighty." Alleluiah ! Amen !

If not with hope of life,
  Begin with fear of death :
Strive the tremendous lifelong strife
  Breath after breath.

Bleed on beneath the rod ;
  Weep on until thou see ;
Turn fear and hope to love of God
  Who loveth thee.

Turn all to love, poor soul ;
  Be love thy watch and ward ;
Be love thy starting-point, thy goal,
  And thy reward.

As to the fall of the rebel angels, our very paucity of knowledge certifies us that there is no need for our knowing much. Unless this passage of the Apocalypse throws light upon it, its direct history is, I suppose, not on record. Yet one or two passages of the elder prophecies fulminated against human rebels, seem further to wake a mysterious chord out of incalculable remoteness. "How art thou fallen from heaven, O Lucifer, son of the morning ! how art thou cut down to the ground, which didst weaken the nations ! For thou hast said in thine heart, I will ascend into heaven, I will exalt my throne above the stars of God : I will sit also upon the mount of the congregation, in the sides of the north : I will ascend above the heights of the clouds ; I will be like the Most High. Yet thou shalt be brought down to hell, to the sides of the pit."—"Thou sealest up the sum, full of wisdom, and perfect in beauty. Thou hast been in Eden the garden of God ; every precious stone was thy covering, the sardius, topaz, and the diamond, the beryl, the onyx, and the jasper, the sapphire. the emerald, and the carbuncle, and gold : the workmanship of thy tabrets and of thy pipes was prepared in thee in the day that thou wast created. Thou art the anointed cherub that covereth; and I have set thee so : thou wast upon the holy mountain of God ; thou hast walked up and down in the midst of the stones of fire. Thou wast perfect in thy ways from the day that thou wast created, till iniquity was found in thee. . . . I will cast thee as profane out of the mountain of God : and I will destroy thee, O covering cherub, from the midst of the stones of fire. Thine heart was lifted up because of thy beauty, thou hast corrupted thy wisdom by reason of thy bright-ness : I will cast thee to the ground, I will lay thee before kings, that they may behold thee. Thou hast defiled thy sanctuaries by the multitude of thine iniquities . . . therefore will I bring forth a fire from the midst of thee, and I will bring thee to ashes upon the earth in the sight of all them that behold thee. All they that know thee among the people shall be astonished at thee : thou shalt be a terror, and never shalt thou be any more."

Whilst studying the devil I must take heed that my study become not devilish by reason of sympathy. As to gaze down a precipice seems to fascinate the gazer towards a shattering fall ; so is it spiritually perilous to gaze on excessive wickedness, lest its immeasurable scale should fascinate us as if it were colossal without being monstrous. A quotation from my sister's *Shadow of Dante* speaks to the point :—

"Some there are who, gazing upon Dante's Hell mainly with their own eyes, are startled by the grotesque element traceable throughout the Cantica as a whole, and shocked at the even ludicrous tone of not a few of its parts. Others seek rather to gaze on Dante's Hell with Dante's eyes; these discern in that grotesqueness a realized horror, in that ludicrousness a sovereign contempt of evil. . . . They remember that the Divine Eternal Wisdom Himself, the Very and Infallible Truth, has, not once nor twice, characterized impiety and sin as Folly ; and they feel in the depths of the nature wherewith He has created them that whatever else Folly may be and is, it is none the less essentially monstrous and ridiculous. . . . A sense of the utter degradation, loathsomeness, despicableness of the soul which by deadly sin besots Reason and enslaves Free Will passes from the Poet's mind into theirs ; while the ghastly definiteness and adaptation of the punishments enables them to touch with their finger the awful possibility and actuality of the Second Death, and thus for themselves as for others to dread it more really, to deprecate it more intensely. Dante's Lucifer does appear 'less than Archangel ruined,' immeasurably less; for he appears Seraph wilfully fallen. No illusive splendour is here to dazzle eye and mind into sympathy with rebellious pride; no vagueness to shroud in mist things fearful or things abominable. Dante's Devils are hateful and hated, Dante's reprobates loathsome and loathed, despicable and despised, or at best miserable and commiserated. . . . Dante is guiltless of seducing any soul of man towards making or calling Evil his Good."

"Which deceiveth the whole world "—not, thank God, the whole Church. And already it behoves us to walk warily if we would not be of the deceived : " It is the last time : and as ye have heard that antichrist shall come, even now are there many antichrists; whereby we know that it is the last time—"; and to lay to heart our dear Lord's own words of prophetic warning : "Except those days should be shortened, there should no flesh be saved : but for the elect's sake those days shall be shortened. Then if any man shall say unto you, Lo, here is Christ, or there; believe it not. For there shall arise false Christs, and false prophets, and shall shew great signs and wonders; insomuch that, if it were possible, they shall deceive the very elect."

WORDS AS GOADS AND AS NAILS.

"When anyone heareth the word of the kingdom, and understandeth it not, then cometh the wicked one, and catcheth away that which was sown in his heart."

"My daughter is grievously vexed with a devil."

"A man, which had a spirit of an unclean devil."

"Legion : because many devils were entered into him."

"Satan hath desired to have you, that he may sift you as wheat."

"The devil having now put into the heart of Judas Iscariot, Simon's son, to betray Him . . . . After the sop Satan entered into him."

"Ananias, why hath Satan filled thine heart to lie to the Holy Ghost, and to keep back part of the price of the land?"

"O full of all subtilty and all mischief, thou child of the devil, thou enemy of all righteousness, wilt thou not cease to pervert the right ways of the Lord?"

"Lest Satan should get an advantage of us : for we are not ignorant of his devices."

"Satan himself is transformed into an angel of light. Therefore it is no great thing if his ministers also be transformed as the ministers of righteousness."

" Neither give place to the devil."

" Put on the whole armour of God, that ye may be able to stand against the wiles of the devil."

" Now the Spirit speaketh expressly, that in the latter times some shall depart from the faith, giving heed to seducing spirits, and doctrines of devils ; speaking lies in hypocrisy ; having their conscience seared with a hot iron."

. " Some are already turned aside after Satan."

" Him that hath the power of death, that is, the devil."

" Resist the devil, and he will flee from you."

" Be sober, be vigilant ; because your adversary the devil, as a roaring lion, walketh about, seeking whom he may devour : whom resist stedfast in the faith."

" He that committeth sin is of the devil; for the devil sinneth from the beginning. . . . In this . . . are manifest . . . the children of the devil : whosoever doeth not righteousness is not of God, neither he that loveth not his brother."

" He was cast out into the earth, and his angels were cast out with him."—Yet is not humankind given over for a prey unto their teeth. For He Who is not ashamed to call us brethren, saith : " Behold I and the children which God hath given Me." And " hath He said, and shall He not do it ? or hath He spoken, and shall He not make it good ? "

> O Lamb of God, slain from the foundation of the world, save us.
> O Lamb of God, slain for us men and for our salvation, save us.
> Thou without blemish and without spot, save us.
> Thou the only and all-sufficient Sacrifice, save us.
> O Lamb of God, the Avenger of our blood, save us.

10. **And I heard a loud voice saying in heaven, Now is come salvation, and strength, and the kingdom of our God, and the power of His Christ: for the accuser of our brethren is cast down which accused them before our God day and night.**

11. **And they overcame him by the blood of the Lamb, and by the word of their testimony; and they loved not their lives unto the death.**

12. **Therefore rejoice, ye heavens, and ye that dwell in them. Woe to the inhabiters of the earth and of the sea ! for the devil is come down unto you, having great wrath, because he knoweth that he hath but a short time.**

If I may still ponder the text as bearing any reference to that fall of certain angels whereby they remade themselves as devils ; by preference exchanging glory for shame, righteousness for guilt, life for spiritual death ; their experience as here set forth teaches me (as heretofore I was taught) how absolute is the repulsion between good as good and evil as evil. Exclude all possibility of repentance, and sympathy between the twain is annihilated. So long as in any depth of degradation repentance can rear its ladder, that ladder. reaching heaven may become a very pleasure-ground of celestial spirits jubilant over each penitent, ministering to each imperfect perfectible soul. But if once "that which is crooked cannot be made straight ; and that which is wanting cannot be numbered," the recoil becomes mutual and final. No sweet apparent analogies of this present temporal world must mislead me : in the eternal world to come, the world of the Right Hand and the Left, we read nothing of intermediate neutral ground, but only of a great gulf; nothing of twilight, but only of outer darkness or else of a city where is no night ; nothing of mixed characters. Perhaps the pit is revealed to us as bottomless, that we may flee from it as from a place of boundless, endless, unarrestable downfall.

More awful than the triumph burst of Heaven over the expulsion of evil, is that word of Incarnate Love when Judas went out "and it was night. . . . Now is the Son of Man glorified, and God is glorified in Him."

Whoso loveth God will also trust Him.

Whoso loveth God will not so dwell on the impending retribution as to remain cold towards the accomplishment of salvation, indifferent to the perfecting of strength, reluctant that God's Kingdom should come, unwilling to behold the day of Christ's power. "Thy people shall be willing in the day of Thy power, in the beauties of holiness."

Nevertheless "O Lord, I am oppressed ; undertake for me. What shall I say ? He hath both spoken unto me, and Himself hath done it."

"The accuser of our brethren . . . which accused them before our God day and night."—As when Satan accused Job : perhaps also as when in the vision concerning Joshua the High Priest, Satan "resisted" before the Angel of the Lord. On a third occasion the Presence Chamber is as it were opened to us; but then we hear no accusing voice ; the life at stake is the life of Ahab whose sins are his crying accusation.

A reprobate spirit accuses the brethren. Sometimes also a saint accuses sinners ; for as to certain misbelievers our Blessed Lord declared : " There is one that accuseth you, even Moses, in whom ye trust."

Thus while Satan maliciously accuses the saints, those very saints cannot but righteously arraign sinners. If not by word or by writing, yet by their lives and deaths they testify against the ungodly. The mere proverb, What man has done man may do, condemns defaulters : let us not use it lightly lest it condemn ourselves. And no more than an outer accuser can we avoid that inner tribunal before which even the Gentiles are set by St. Paul when he writes : " Their conscience also bearing witness, and their thoughts the meanwhile accusing or else excusing one another."

Not the Last Day alone : every day is a Judgment Day.

" Therefore if thou bring thy gift to the altar, and there rememberest that thy brother hath ought against thee ; leave there thy gift before the altar, and go thy way ; first be reconciled to thy brother, and then come and offer thy gift. Agree with thine adversary quickly, whiles thou art in the way with him ; lest at any time the adversary deliver thee to the judge, and the judge deliver thee to the officer, and thou be cast into prison. Verily I say unto thee, Thou shalt by no means come out thence, till thou hast paid the uttermost farthing."

> Day and night the Accuser makes no pause,
> Day and night protest the Righteous Laws,
> Good and Evil witness to man's flaws :
> Man the culprit, man's the ruined cause,
> Man midway to death's devouring jaws
> And the worm that gnaws.

> Day and night our Jesu makes no pause,
> Pleads His own fulfilment of all laws,
> Veils with His Perfections mortal flaws,
> Clears the culprit, pleads the desperate cause,
> Plucks the dead from death's devouring jaws
> And the worm that gnaws.

If from this passage we may think of elect Angels as in any sense overcoming " by the blood of the Lamb," it reminds us that the Lamb is slain from the foundation of the world. Not that we should entertain carnal thoughts on so sacred a mystery ; our thoughts should ever be moulded and spiritualized by the Inspired Word : " Nor yet that He should offer Himself often . . . for then must He often have suffered since the foundation of the world : but now once in the end of the world hath He appeared to put away sin by the sacrifice of Himself."

Of " their testimony " we know one word : " Michael," Who is like God?

Their not having loved " their lives unto the death " must convey a far different meaning from what the same phrase

wou!d import if used of mortal men ; but the true death being
that spiritual death which to man is the second death, this
latter in the case of angels may be glanced at. Thus "Michael
and his angels" may, like Queen Esther, though after a loftier
fashion, have taken their life in their hand ; even whilst by any
apparent peril they braved, they entrenched themselves im-
pregnably within the Divine safeguard. For hazard of life or
of aught else in God's quarrel, can at the very utmost and for
any creature amount to no more than a surface risk : "He
that hateth his life in this world shall keep it unto life eternal."

Meanwhile, however skill may fail me to work out such a
problem in matters celestial, in matters terrestrial the lesson is
obvious. All must, I must, overcome Satan and his crew "by
the Blood of the Lamb"; by faith in His Atonement, and by
fast hold of His Strength ever accessible to us in the Blessed
Sacrament of His Body and Blood : also, according to our
several vocations, by the word of our testimony ; by never
denying but constantly upholding His eternal Verity ; and
finally by not loving life beyond His blessed Will for us either
to live or to die.

When speculation fails resort to practice.

Whatever period may be in question, "Woe" is denounced
to earth and sea. Yet the declared reason of this woe includes
an element of encouragement. For the devil's wrath is great
"because he knoweth that he hath but a *short* time."

Courage! For aught we know courage may shorten the
short time : as when David "hasted, and ran" to meet the
Philistine.

> "Launch out into the deep," Christ spake of old
>   To Peter : and he launched into the deep ;
>   Strengthened should tempest wake which lay asleep,
> Strengthened to suffer heat or suffer cold.
> Thus, in Christ's Prescience : patient to behold
>   A fall, a rise, a scaling Heaven's high steep ;
>   Prescience of Love which deigned to overleap
> The mire of human errors manifold.
> Lord, Lover of Thy Peter, and of him
>   Beloved with craving of a humbled heart
>   Which eighteen hundred years have satisfied ;
> Hath he his throne among Thy Seraphim
>   Who love ? or sits he on a throne apart,
>   Unique, near Thee, to love Thee human-eyed ?

**13. And when the dragon saw that he was cast unto the
earth, he persecuted the woman which brought forth
the man child.**

Did I not fear to offend by bringing a railing accusation, I would say that Satan is a fool: he adds sin to sin, heaps up wrath against the day of wrath,—a cowardly fool: he uses his strength to persecute the weak,—an incorrigible fool: punishment exasperates him.' "Though thou shouldest bray a fool in a mortar among wheat with a pestle, yet will not his foolishness depart from him."

14. **And to the woman were given two wings of a great eagle, that she might fly into the wilderness, into her place, where she is nourished for a time, and times, and half a time, from the face of the serpent.**

Or as in the Revised Version " . . . the two wings of the great eagle." Whatever further sense may attach to the words, they pointedly convey to us a figure of the succour and safeguard of God; inasmuch as they recall a passage of the Song of Moses: "As an eagle stirreth up her nest, fluttereth over her young, spreadeth abroad her wings, taketh them, beareth them on her wings: so the Lord alone did lead him." Thus in her wilderness "the daughter of Jerusalem" may shake her head at her persecutor and sing her song: "Bless the Lord, O my soul, and forget not all His benefits. . . . Who redeemeth thy life from destruction; Who crowneth thee with lovingkindness and tender mercies; Who satisfieth thy mouth with good things; so that thy youth is renewed like the eagle's":— for "They that wait upon the Lord shall renew their strength; they shall mount up with wings as eagles; they shall run, and not be weary; and they shall walk, and not faint."

Salvation is of grace: wings are given to the Woman. The soul must co-operate with grace: the Woman herself has to fly with the wings.

"From the face of the serpent":—he keeping his malicious abominable eye still upon her. As when of old "the enemy said, I will pursue, I will overtake, I will divide the spoil; my lust shall be satisfied upon them," and perished by reason of his boast. Or as when ages earlier the serpent himself eyed Eve, and she, alas! fled not.

15. **And the serpent cast out of his mouth water as a flood after the woman, that he might cause her to be carried away of the flood.**

16. **And the earth helped the woman, and the earth opened her mouth, and swallowed up the flood which the dragon cast out of his mouth.**

For unless "the faithful city become an harlot" her end

shall not be with a flood. "Thou stretchest out Thy right hand, the earth swallowed them."

The serpent cast that flood "out of his mouth." From such a source can scarcely issue less than rank poison : for consider our Lord's words as to what may proceed out of even a man's mouth : "Those things which proceed out of the mouth come forth from the heart ; and they defile the man. For out of the heart proceed evil thoughts, murders, adulteries, fornications, thefts, false witness, blasphemies."

So that, at least, for an immediate practical purpose, this pursuing "flood" may, I trust, be viewed as a flood of temptations ; and in particular of such temptations as are best coped with by flight. Joseph found safety in flight, before the searching and strengthening iron had entered into his soul.

Now because "righteousness is immortal" and the memorial of virtue immortal, this august Woman, if we may regard her as a figure of Mother Church, is immortal and blessed. Yet even thus there remains a mortal side to the members who make up her immortal personality; and since "the earth opened her mouth, and swallowed up the flood," we are re- . minded that the flood of besetting temptation can be finally arrested and annulled only in the grave. "There the wicked cease from troubling ; and there the weary be at rest." "For he that is dead is freed from sin."

A holy grave is the true bed of heartsease. And already the flowers appear on the earth although the winter is not yet past.

> Lord, grant us grace to rest upon Thy word,
>   To rest in hope until we see Thy Face ;
> To rest thro' toil unruffled and unstirred,
>   Lord, grant us grace.
>
> This burden and this heat wear on apace :
> Night comes, when sweeter than night's singing bird
>   Will swell the silence of our ended race.
>
> Ah, songs which flesh and blood have never heard
>   And cannot hear, songs of the silent place
> Where rest remains ! Lord, slake our hope deferred,
>   Lord, grant us grace.

17. And the dragon was wroth with the woman, and went to make war with the remnant of her seed, which keep the commandments of God, and have the testimony of Jesus Christ.

This word has a distinct bearing upon all future time until the end. Whoever keeps the commandments and accepts and champions the faith, must expect and will one way or other experience not peace alone, but peace and a sword.

At this point, ignorance of prophecy need not deprive the simplest student of a life and death lesson.

"The testimony of Jesus Christ."—By this I hope I may understand two things :—

That testimony which each Christian bears to Christ by conformity of life and death to his dear Master's Life and Death,—

That testimony which Jesus Christ bears to each Christian by endowing him with gifts superhuman and Divine graces, so that no Christian can be accounted for on a merely natural theory.

Great saints by spiritual lustre outshine the visible lustre of Moses. But every Christian is in his or her degree Veronica (true Image) of Christ. A flower we name veronica springs up here and there without will or culture of man, lowly and lovely ; its small blossom is celestial blue, its leaf and seed-vessel show something of a heart shape.

Christ-likeness in high or low is eloquent witness to Christ.

"The remnant of her seed."—Is there not a forlorn sound of weakness in the words ? yet with an undertone of triumph. If these beleaguered persons are only a remnant, a great concourse of the same family may be looked for elsewhere : in Paradise.

O my God, to Whom have gone home so many souls beloved on earth and in heaven, and of my own beloved, I humbly trust not a few : grant grace to us who are the present remnant to live as they lived and die as they died. And so grant grace to remnant after remnant through all generations for ever, until it please Thee to make an end in righteousness. So may we awake and sing out of our dust, or exult when in a moment our change comes, and give Thee thanks world without end, through Jesus Christ our Lord. Amen, Amen.

CHAPTER XIII.

1. And I stood upon the sand of the sea, and saw a beast rise up out of the sea, having seven heads and ten horns, and upon his horns ten crowns, and upon his heads the name of blasphemy.

In the Revised Version the opening clause of this chapter forms on the contrary the final clause of Chapter xii., and reads thus: "And he stood upon the sand of the sea"; thus apparently referring not to St. John but to the dragon. Whence it ensues that at this point I remain dubious between a saint and a reprobate; and by a sort of illustration the warning of the Parable of the Tares is brought home to me: "Lest while ye gather up the tares, ye root up also the wheat with them."

My God Who art Love, so purge our hearts by love that we may hate implicitly any who hate Thee, and love explicitly all to whom Thou givest or wilt give grace to love Thee; yea, all whom Thou lovest. Through Jesus Christ our Lord. Amen.

This "beast" seems in some sense a development of evil beyond the original dragon. Both have seven heads and ten horns; but the diadems of the dragon were seven, encircling his heads; those of the beast ten, surmounting his doubly salient horns. Moreover of this beast only do we read that he had "upon his heads the name of blasphemy"; or as in the Revised Version: "and upon his heads names of blasphemy." And as we shall find him (ver. 2) under the patronage of the dragon, we are thus reminded of our Lord's denunciation of the hypocritical Scribes and Pharisees: "Ye compass sea and land to make one proselyte, and when he is made, ye make him twofold more the child of hell than yourselves."

The beast is base: he rises out of that sea whose troubled waters cast up mire and dirt. "He maketh the deep to boil like a pot: he maketh the sea like a pot of ointment." Whilst we fear, it befits us also to loathe and despise him. Never let us forget that the sea hath said concerning Wisdom : "It is not with me."

2. And the beast which I saw was like unto a leopard, and his feet were as the feet of a bear, and his mouth as the mouth of a lion : and the dragon gave him his power, and his seat, and great authority.

This Apocalyptic beast combines in its one aspect features of three distinct and successive beasts of Daniel's vision : "Behold, the four winds of the heaven strove upon the great sea. And four great beasts came up fiom the sea, diverse ore from another. The first was like a lion, and had eagle's wings : I beheld till the wings thereof were plucked, and it was lifted up from the earth, and made stand upon the feet as a man, and a man's heart was given to it. And behold another beast, a second, like to a bear, and it raised up itself on one side, and it had three ribs in the mouth of it between the teeth of it : and they said thus unto it, Arise, devour much flesh. After this I beheld, and lo another, like a leopard, which had upon the back of it four wings of a fowl ; the beast had a'so four heads ; and dominion was given to it. After this I saw in the night visions, and behold a fourth beast, dreadful and terrible, and strong exceedingly ; and it had great iron teeth : it devoured and brake in pieces, and stamped the residue with the feet of it : and it was diverse from all the beasts that were before it ; and it had ten horns. I considered the horns, and, behold, there came up among them another little horn, before whom there were three of the first horns plucked up by the roots : and, behold, in this horn were eyes like the eyes of man, and a mouth speaking great things."

Daniel's vision has been expounded as concerning the successive empires of Babylon, Persia, Greece ; personified respectively as lion, bear, leopard. The fourth yet more mysteriously appalling beast stands over to what was then and may still be the future. St. John's vision may haply already concern ourselves, or at any rate will concern others like us. Its lesson is for all and is for me.

Whatever this Apocalyptic beast may prove in fulness of time, it exhibits some likeness to that world, flesh, devil, which are my daily antagonists ; of which I must daily, hourly, momentarily beware.

The world is like a leopard. Beautiful but spotted ; soft, graceful, sportive, yet a devourer, a destroyer. "A leopard shall watch over their cities." Nor can the leopard change his spots. " Love not the world, neither the things that are in the world. If any man love the world, the love of the Father is not in him. For all that is in the world, the lust of the flesh, and the lust of the eyes, and the pride of life, is not of the Father, but is of the world. And the world passeth away, and the lust thereof: but he that doeth the Will of God abideth for ever."

The flesh is like a bear. Its hug is deadly. " How long wilt thou sleep, O sluggard? when wilt thou arise out of thy sleep? Yet a little sleep, a little slumber, a little folding of the hands to sleep: so shall thy poverty come as one that travelleth, and thy want as an armed man." The bear treads with his whole foot upon the earth, and his gross aspect is prominently of the earth earthy.

The devil is like a lion: as a roaring lion he walketh about seeking whom he may devour. He is as a lion's whelp lurking in secret places. " Rescue my soul from their destructions, my darling from the lions."

World, flesh, devil, comprise all sources and varieties of my temptations. Repelling these three wherever found, I shall not fail to repel them even if in my own mortal day they appear concentrated into one ghastly head, one obscene monster.

On the other hand: if I succumb to them separately, how shall I cope with them should they rise up against me as one?

But that word *the world* is frequently used to denote a great portion of the human race. How little must I love the world? How much may I love it?—Love it to the fulness of thy heart's desire, so thou love it with self-sacrifice; for thus to love it is after the Mind of God, the Pattern of Christ: "God so loved the world, that He gave His Only Begotten Son, that whosoever believeth in Him should not perish, but have everlasting life. For God sent not His Son into the world to condemn the world; but that the world through Him might be saved."

> Love is alone the worthy law of love :
>   All other laws have pre-supposed a taint :
>   Love is the law from kindled saint to saint,
> From lamb to lamb, from tender dove to dove.
> Love is the motive of all things that move
>   Harmonious by free will without constraint :
>   Love learns and teaches : love shall man acquaint
> With all he lacks, which all his lack is love.
> Because Love is the fountain, I discern
>   The stream as love : for what but love should flow
>   From fountain Love ? not bitter from the sweet !
>   I ignorant, have I laid claim to know ?
>   Oh teach me, Love, such knowledge as is meet
> For one to know who is fain to love and learn.

This world is not my orchard for fruit or my garden for flowers. It is however my only field whence to raise a harvest.

What is the world? Wherein resides its harmfulness, snare, pollution? Left to itself it is neither harmful, ensnaring, nor polluting. It becomes all this as the passive agent, passive vehicle if I may so call it, of the devil, man's outside tempter, and of the flesh, man's inside tempter. There is no inherent evil in cedar and vermilion, horses and chariots, purple and fine linen; nay, nor in sumptuous fare, in down, silk, apes, ivory, or peacocks. St. Peter himself objects not to hair, gold, apparel, but to women's misuse of them. An alabaster box of precious ointment becomes good or bad simply according to the use it is put to. Through envy of the devil death came into the world, and man hath sought out many inventions; but the heavens and the earth, and all the host of them when made and finished were beheld to be "very good."

Lord Jesus, everywhere and always inspire us to refuse the evil and to choose the good; and I beseech Thee, give us grace never to judge our neighbour rashly, whilst one by one we ourselves endeavour to learn and perform Thy Will.

Christ exchanged heaven for earth to enable man to exchange earth for heaven. Hast Thou done that for me, and will I not do this for Thee?

"The dragon gave him his power, and his seat, and great authority"—constituting him, so to say, diabolical viceroy. The flesh is even now such a viceroy, having the world for a throne, while the devil keeps out of sight ruling by deputy.—Or the world is a stage, the flesh an actor, the devil prompter and scene-shifter.

3. And I saw one of his heads as it were wounded to death; and his deadly wound was healed : and all the world wondered after the beast.

Again we are reminded that *any* and not only *the final* Antichrist may appear as a pseudo-Christ. This death-wound so healed that a sort of life survives, seems a hideous mockery of the All-Holy Death and Resurrection. "Surely in vain the net is spread in the sight of any bird."

"All the world wondered after the beast."—What go they out for to see? If a reed, a broken reed, "the staff of this bruised reed . . . on which if a man lean, it will go into his hand, and pierce it." If a man clothed in soft raiment, a courtier of the prince of this world; like prince, like courtier. If a prophet, less than a prophet, a lying prophet.

"'A wonderful and horrible thing is committed in the land ; the prophets prophesy falsely, and the priests bear rule by their means; and My people love to have it so : and what will ye do in the end thereof?"

It is a time-long and world-wide curiosity, time-long at least so far as we know the tendencies of fallen human nature, this which wonders after the monstrous and the inexplicable.

I must beware lest my own curiosity be morbid, perverse, unbridled. To-day the monstrous may be simply abnormal, to-morrow it may be "the mystery of iniquity." To-day the inexplicable may be a secret of nature, to-morrow a secret of hell. O my soul, come not thou into such a secret! "All darkness shall be hid in his secret places : a fire not blown shall consume him; it shall go ill with him that is left in his tabernacle. The heaven shall reveal his iniquity ; and the earth shall rise up against him.".

Likewise I must beware lest my study of holy subjects degenerate into curious investigation instead of pious exercise. Lest I *wonder* after my risen Saviour instead of adoring Him. Which God for His gracious sake forbid !

4. And they worshipped the dragon which gave power unto the beast : and they worshipped the beast, saying, Who is like unto the beast ? who is able to make war with him ?

Once more a point of distorted, degraded resemblance. "Who is like unto the beast?" as it were the "Michael" of besotted blasphemy.

"And they worshipped. . . ."—This impious worship seems to be worship without any reference to goodness. World and devil worship paid by flesh: curiosity and comparative weak-ness worshipping unexplained power. "Who is able to make war with him?" In a like spirit spoke Goliath when "he stood and cried unto the armies of Israel, and said unto them, Why are ye come out to set your battle in array? am not I a Philistine, and ye servants to Saul? choose you a man for you, and let him come down to me. If he be able to fight with me, and to kill me, then will we be your servants : but if I prevail against him, and kill him, then shall ye be our servants, and serve us. And the Philistine said, I defy the armies of Israel this day ; give me a man, that we may fight together."

"Who is able . . . ?" "Yea, if God will, things which are not are able to bring to nought things which are. Loving fear befits the creature toward the Creator : craven fear befits

not the creature toward the creature. Ponder Isaiah's Divine
message: "I, even I, am He that comforteth you: who art
thou, that thou shouldest be afraid of a man that shall die, and
of the son of man which shall be made as grass; and forgettest
the Lord thy Maker, that hath stretched forth the heavens,
and laid the foundations of the earth; and hast feared continually every day because of the fury of the oppressor, as if
he were ready to destroy? and where is the fury of the
oppressor?" Ponder Daniel's prophecy interpreted touching
Antiochus Epiphanes, that Antichrist of the elder dispensation:
"And in the latter time of their kingdom, when the transgressors are come to the full, a king of fierce countenance, and
understanding dark sentences, shall stand up. And his power
shall be mighty, but not by his own power: and he shall
destroy wonderfully, and shall prosper, and practise, and shall
destroy the mighty and the holy people. And through his
policy also he shall cause craft to prosper in his hand; and
he shall magnify himself in his heart, and by peace shall destroy
many: he shall also stand up against the Prince of princes;
but he shall be broken without hand."

**5. And there was given unto him a mouth speaking great
things and blasphemies; and power was given unto
him to continue forty and two months.**

Turning for a moment from the ultra-human element in
these appalling revelations, I consider the parallel case of a
human "excessive sinner": his primary gifts, like all gifts, are
from God. His mouth might speak truly great things, even
the Divine praises. With his power he might like Jacob
prevail to work wonders by prayer. His prefixed period he
might so use as to extend it into the long life for ever and
ever. To deny this would be to deny his free will, and so his
accountability. To admit it shows me that every degree of
sin is a step in that direction where this one of whom we now
are reading occupies an advanced station.

"Hazael said, But what, is thy servant a dog, that he should
do this great thing?" Nevertheless "on the morrow" he
took the first step.

O Lord Jesus, Who knowest the number of our sins that
they are more in number than the hairs of our head, give us
grace henceforward to walk circumspectly, not as fools, but as
wise, redeeming the time because the days are evil.

"Forty and two months."—The former period, the same
suggestion. If the periods be successive, how long-drawn is

the agony : if simultaneous, how do the "fat bulls of Basan" close in on every side !

6. And he opened his mouth in blasphemy against God, to blaspheme His Name, and His tabernacle, and them that dwell in heaven.

St. Paul writes : "That man of sin . . . the son of perdition ; who opposeth and exalteth himself above all that is called God, or that is worshipped ; so that he as God sitteth in the temple of God, shewing himself that he is God."

If a deep-seated difference may be traced between these closely-parallel passages, St. John perhaps speaks of an intellectual, spiritual antagonism, St. Paul of a self-worshipping atheism.

He who blasphemes God does to his own destruction recognize Him. He who assumes the position of God supersedes Him,—were that possible.

God Almighty has deigned to reveal Himself to man's adoration as Three in One. So the blasphemy may be regarded as both one and threefold ; against God in His own Person and Nature ; against Him in that sacred Name which Christ the Head shares with His members ; against Him in that tabernacle which is the Church indwelt by the Holy Spirit ; against Him in that Communion of Saints whereby already elect souls, whether in the body or out of the body, sit with Christ in heavenly places, and have their conversation in heaven.

Devils are not atheists : we are emphatically certified that they believe and tremble. During our Lord's earthly ministry, devils even proclaimed Him in the audience of men.

Atheism appears to be a possibility confined to a lower nature. A body seems to be that which is capable of blocking up spirit into unmitigated materialism. "No man hath seen God at any time" : that flesh and blood which cannot inherit the kingdom of God may, if it will, deny His existence.

Satan, a master of his weapons, brings out of his counterfeit treasure things new and old : his own blasphemy, along with worldly deceits and carnal obstructions.

Alas ! for many wise after the flesh, many mighty, many noble ; for many an one who is confident of being a guide of the blind, an instructor of the foolish, a teacher of babes ! "He feedeth on ashes : a deceived heart hath turned him aside, that he cannot deliver his soul, nor say, Is there not a lie in my right hand?"

From knowledge that is foolishness, Good Lord deliver us.
From ignorance that is blindness, Good Lord deliver us.

Words are chaff: obedience is grain. I must beware of "polished corners" which form no part of the sole Temple ; of fair-seeming superstructures which are not founded upon the one only Rock ; of spiritualism which is not spirituality ; of philanthropy divorced from dogma ; of socialism in lieu of Christian brotherhood ; of indifferentism to truth simulating charity ; of charity degraded into an investment. I will mistrust any newfangled name for an old-established Biblical virtue : if such modern designations mean old familiar virtues, I love these best under their old familiar hallowed names ; if the new word means less or more, well may I say, " The old is better."

7. And it was given unto him to make war with the saints, and to overcome them : and power was given him over all kindreds, and tongues, and nations.

War is no one-sided matter. Because the beast makes war, therefore the saints on their side are waging corresponding war. The whole world is at war, the whole Church at war ; the battle is set in array army against army.

The foregone foretold conclusion—" It was given unto him . . . to overcome them,"—makes no difference as to the duty involved ; indeed, it enforces the duty. If the saints strove not they could not be overcome ; and the Divine decree, inscrutable and ever venerable, purports that they shall be overcome. And inasmuch as they suffer for righteousness' sake, happy are they : whilst they die, yet by that very sentence of death, as by every other word proceeding out of the mouth of God, they live. They have resisted unto blood striving against sin, and dear shall their blood be in His sight.

Slain in their high places :—fallen on rest
Where the eternal peace lights up their faces,
In God's sacred acre breast to breast —:
Slain in their high places.

From all tribes, all families, all races,
Gathered home together ; east or west
Sending home its tale of gifts and graces.

Twine, oh twine, heaven's amaranth for their crest,
Raise their praise while home their triumph paces ;
Kings by their own King of kings confessed,
Slain in their high places.

By a heavenly paradox those whom the beast overcomes are those over whom he has no power. They over whom he has power are such as make an agreement with him by a present, and come out to him; and truly it shall be until one come and take them away, but not to any desirable land, "even to the land of darkness and the shadow of death; a land of darkness, as darkness itself; and of the shadow of death, without any order, and where the light is as darkness." For: "Though hand join in hand, the wicked shall not be unpunished."

> In tempest and storm blackness of darkness for ever,
> A fire unextinguished, a worm's indestructible swarm ;
> Where no hope shall ever be more, and love shall be never,
> In tempest and storm ;
> Where the form of all things is fashionless, void of all form ;
> Where from death that severeth all, the soul cannot sever
> In tempest and storm.

8. And all that dwell upon the earth shall worship him, whose names are not written in the Book of Life of the Lamb, slain from the foundation of the world.

In the Book of Life: or not in the Book of Life. Once more, no neutral book, no neutral ground: no names "written in water," as one death-stricken man predicted of himself, presumably with reference to earthly fame.

"Verily I say unto you, This generation shall not pass away, till all be fulfilled. Heaven and earth shall pass away: but My words shall not pass away." Such are our Lord's own words when He prophesied concerning His Second Advent, and the end of the world.

Centuries earlier King David uses the word generation in a broadly comprehensive sense where he says: "God is in the generation of the righteous"—"This is the generation of them that seek Him."

If we may reverently understand our Lord also as speaking not exclusively of any one generation, but of the entire human race under its temporal conditions,—even as the wise Preacher in man's very transitoriness seems to feel a sort of continuity: "One generation passeth away, and another generation cometh: but the earth abideth for ever"—then perhaps we may equally read verses of another Psalm, with an additional and widened signification: "Let Satan stand at his right hand. . . . Let his posterity be cut off; and in the generation following let their name be blotted out."

Thus understood, "this generation" would indicate man throughout time; "the generation following" man throughout eternity. (Let us note that the prayer or decree imports the *extinction,* not the condemnation, of the posterity.) The names recorded in the Lamb's Book of Life are those of the Famous Men who shall have praise of God; the names not there recorded are blotted out into blackness of darkness.

"That which hath been is named already, and it is known that it is man: neither may he contend with Him that is mightier than he."

It is the Book of Life of the Lamb, slain from the foundation of the world, of the Lamb slain for us, in which our names, yours, mine, will or will not be found written. If we love ourselves so little as to be ready to slight our chance, do we love Him Who loved us unto death so little as to be ready to slight Him?

> Slain for man, slain for me, O Lamb of God, look down;
>   Loving to the end, look down, behold and see:
> Turn Thine Eyes of pity, turn not on us Thy frown,
>   O Lamb of God, slain for man, slain for me.
>
> Mark the wrestling, mark the race for indeed a crown;
>   Mark our chariots how we drive them heavily;
> Mark the foe upon our track blasting, thundering down,
>   O Lamb of God, slain for man, slain for me.
>
> Set as a Cloudy Pillar against them Thy frown,
>   Thy Face of Light toward us gracious utterly;
> Help granting, hope granting, until Thou grant a crown,
>   O Lamb of God, slain for man, slain for me.

9. If any man have an ear, let him hear.

Have interest, attention, flagged? "Awake, thou that sleepest." If we be not less than men, let us hear.

O Lord God, Who knowest that every warning, opportunity, gift, grace, magnifieth Thy Goodness and augmenteth our responsibility; suffer us not to impoverish ourselves by the overflow of Thy bounty. Nothing have we except of Thy bestowal. Along with Thy call supply our response, with Thy talent our increase, with Thy Love our love. So shall it be well with us all the days of our life in the Presence of Jesus Christ our Intercessor. Amen.

10. He that leadeth into captivity shall go into captivity: he that killeth with the sword must be killed with the sword. Here is the patience and the faith of the saints.

The Revised Version in its margin defines the Greek text of this verse as "somewhat uncertain." The first clause in that Version runs: "If any man is for captivity, into captivity he goeth"—but as an alternative marginal rendering restores it to (apparently) nearly the same sense as that adopted by the Authorized Version, I betake myself simply to the latter, leaving all complications to competent students.

Behold the Triumph of Evil sweeping by! Wickedness laurelled and in purple, righteousness despoiled and in fetters.

Nevertheless, "The Lord hath made all things for Himself: yea, even the wicked for the day of evil."

That triumph is itself the omen of ruin. For who is he that shall go into captivity? he that leadeth into captivity. Who is he that must be killed with the sword? he that killeth with the sword.

Not, alas! that all Satan's captives have promise of freedom: the captive whose will consents to bondage is so far a lawful captive, and incapable of enfranchisement. St. Paul reads an awful lesson to both men and women whose lot is cast in the perilous times of the last days: "For men shall be lovers of their own selves, covetous, boasters, proud, blasphemous, disobedient to parents, unthankful, unholy, without natural affection, truce-breakers, false accusers, incontinent, fierce, despisers of those that are good, traitors, heady, high-minded, lovers of pleasure more than lovers of God; having a form of godliness, but denying the power thereof. . . . For of this sort are they which creep into houses, and lead captive silly women laden with sins, led away with divers lusts, ever learning, and never able to come to the knowledge of the truth. . . . These also resist the truth: men of corrupt minds, reprobate concerning the faith. But they shall proceed no further: for their folly shall be manifest unto all men."

"He that killeth with the sword must be killed with the sword." Whether we restrict our thoughts to the proposition that sword-takers shall perish by stroke of sword, or reflect further that they who have recourse to the sword shall perish along with the weapon of their vain reliance, our Lord's own precious words to St. Peter emphasize, if they do not forestall, this revelation: "Put up again thy sword into his place: for all they that take the sword shall perish with the sword."

Christ at His Ascension led captivity captive. Thenceforward voluntary captivity was constituted rebellion, so that not even towards God is the Christian spirit to be a spirit of bondage.

Man must indeed be enamoured of rebellion! Proclaim the law of liberty, and he hugs his chains: proclaim the blessedness of freewill obedience, and he breaks this band asunder.

Chains for freemen:—"My son, hear the instruction of thy

father, and forsake not the law of thy mother : for they shall be an ornament of grace unto thy head, and chains about thy neck— ;" St. Paul said, "For the hope of Israel I am bound with this chain— ;" "The love of Christ constraineth us."

O Lord Jesus Christ, Who in our stead wast bound on the night of Thy most holy Passion ; be love of Thee our yoke, wisdom from Thee our rule, hope in Thee the limit of our desire.

"Here is the patience and the faith of the saints."—O Gracious God, Whose longsuffering beareth with the unthankful and the evil, make us like-minded with Thee : so shall we wax intolerant of no sins except our own. Far be it from us suddenly to curse our brother's habitation : in our prayers and blessings let all our brethren have a share. So may we intercede one for another, and do good one to another ; and edifying one another upbuild ourselves in faith and patience. For the sake of Jesus Christ our Intercessor with Thee. Amen.

"Thorns also and thistles shall it bring forth to thee." Let the "it" in question be my allotment, my field, my garden : "I said, I will water my best garden, and will water abundantly my garden bed." Thorns should stir up my faith to look on Him Whom all men pierced, Whom I pierced, wearing the Crown of Thorns and the Purple Robe. Thistles should exercise me in patience ; it will tax patience to weed out what can be extirpated, it will strain patience to put up with the remainder. And lo ! the lot is fallen unto me in a fair ground : faith is cheaply bought by many a thorn-wound, and patience by many a thistle-prick.

> Grant us, O Lord, that patience and that faith :
>   Faith's patience imperturbable in Thee,
>   Hope's patience till the long-drawn shadows flee,
> Love's patience unresentful of all scathe.
> Verily we need patience breath by breath ;
>   Patience while faith holds up her glass to see,
>   While hope toils yoked in fear's copartnery,
> And love goes softly on the way to death.
> How gracious and how perfecting a grace
>   Must patience be on which those others wait :
> Faith with suspended rapture in her face,
>   Hope pale and careful hand in hand with fear,
> Love—ah, good love, who would not antedate
>   God's Will, but saith, Good is it to be here.

11. And I beheld another beast coming up out of the earth ; and he had two horns like a lamb, and he spake as a dragon.

Once more a suggestion that Antichrist may wear the mask of a pseudo-Christ: "he had two horns like a lamb."

Our Lord Himself, in His Sermon on the Mount, forewarned His hearers of such a Satanic device: "Beware of false prophets, which come to you in sheep's clothing, but inwardly they are ravening wolves. Ye shall know them by their fruits. Do men gather grapes of thorns, or figs of thistles? Even so every good tree bringeth forth good fruit, but a corrupt tree bringeth forth evil fruit. A good tree cannot bring forth evil fruit, neither can a corrupt tree bring forth good fruit. Every tree that bringeth not forth good fruit is hewn down, and cast into the fire. Wherefore by their fruits ye shall know them."

Having this clue we are inexcusable if we use it not. Even at once we need it; for this is already a day of "false prophets," of evil veneered with good, of hollow heights. If by help of grace we make due use of our clue to-day, to-morrow it will not fail us, though the danger be intensified, the crisis final.

Alleged ignorance is not admitted as a justifying plea if thou save not another's life; how should it justify thee if thou save not thine own soul? "If thou forbear to deliver them that are drawn unto death, and those that are ready to be slain; if thou sayest, Behold, we knew it not; doth not He that pondereth the heart consider it? and He that keepeth thy soul, doth not He know it? and shall not He render to every man according to his works?"

But my reader (if I have one) may object: By treating figure after figure as Antichrist, you practically deny the one revealed final individual personal Antichrist.

I earnestly trust I have not done so; if any sentence of mine implies such error, I retract and repudiate that sentence. The whole subject is beyond me; the prophecies leave me in anxious ignorance. But St. John himself has declared that already in his own day many Antichrists were in the world; if it was so then, presumably it has gone on so ever since, and will so continue to the end. All serpents are serpents, however there may be one great sea-serpent most of all to be feared and fled. (This is merely for illustration; not alleged as a fact of natural history.)

The dragon fell from heaven, the first beast emerged from the sea. This second beast, as "coming up out of the earth," seems more akin to humankind; perhaps we are thus certified that here at last comes the literal "*man* of sin." Something he exhibits of lamb, something of dragon: but the *lamb* is on his outside, the *dragon* is deep-seated within.

If these two beasts are to emerge from sea and earth—and
to come out thence in any sense, they must needs first be
there : perhaps already they lurk there potentially and in embryo—let me not cling too fondly to the earth and sea I love.
"Arise ye, and depart; for this is not your rest : because it is
polluted. . . ."

Earth is a race-course, not a goal.   Instead of mansions she
pitches tents.   Her nearest approach to a permanent abode is
the grave.   "And My people shall dwell in a peaceable habitation, and in sure dwellings, and in quiet resting places; when
it shall hail, coming down on the forest; and the city shall be
low in a low place."

> Hail, garden of confident hope !
> Where sweet seeds are quickening in darkness and cold :
> For how sweet and how young will they be
> When they pierce thro' the mould.
> Balm, woodbine, and heliotrope,
> There watch and there wait out of sight for their Sun :
> While the Sun which they see not, doth see
> Each and all one by one.

**12. And he exerciseth all the power of the first beast before
him, and causeth the earth and them which dwell
therein to worship the first beast, whose deadly wound
was healed.**

"Before him" is varied in the Revised Version to "in his
sight"; so that the two monsters appear thus to be acting and
reacting in presence of each other, and for a while if not to the
very end to be thenceforward simultaneous.

One appears to act as vicegerent of the other, being apparently the same as "the false prophet" mentioned afterwards
(ch. xvi. 13).   Thus he claims not worship for himself, but
for that other.

"Because sentence against an evil work is not executed
speedily, therefore the heart of the sons of men is fully set in
them to do evil.   Though a sinner do evil an hundred times,
and his days be prolonged, yet surely I know that it shall be
well with them that fear God, which fear before Him : but it
shall not be well with the wicked, neither shall he prolong his
days, which are as a shadow; because he feareth not before
God."

**13. And he doeth great wonders, so that he maketh fire
come down from heaven on the earth in the sight
of men,**

The false prophet, as it were the Elias of falsehood.

If reverently I may think so, the witness of fire from heaven, true and venerable under the Jewish dispensation, seems to be withdrawn or actually to be reversed as regards the Christian Church.

Of old Elias invoked and was answered by fire from heaven. This the convened prophets of Baal having clamoured for in vain, they were cut off in their impotence. But when St. James and St. John, sons of Zebedee, quoted and would have copied the example of Elias, our Lord "turned, and rebuked them, and said, Ye know not what manner of spirit ye are of."

And now the same St. John beholds fire brought from heaven by a liar to endorse a lie.

Venomous and deadly beyond all others as may be this last false prophet, yet has he from time to time been foreshadowed by evil predecessors more or less like him. Former generations of the elect have had to contend with such, and by Divine grace have won the victory. In proportion to man's peril is God's succour. The law and the history of the elder Church constitute a treasury of wisdom amassed for the Church of the latter days:—

"If there arise among you a prophet, or a dreamer of dreams, and giveth thee a sign or a wonder, and the sign or the wonder come to pass, whereof he spake unto thee, saying, Let us go after other gods, which thou hast not known, and let us serve them; thou shalt not hearken unto the words of that prophet, or that dreamer of dreams: for the Lord your God proveth you, to know whether ye love the Lord your God with all your heart and with all your soul. Ye shall walk after the Lord your God, and fear Him, and keep His commandments, and obey His voice, and ye shall serve Him, and cleave unto Him."

"Mine heart within me is broken because of the prophets. . . . For both prophet and priest are profane; yea, in My house have I found their wickedness, saith the Lord. Wherefore their way shall be unto them as slippery ways in the darkness: they shall be driven on, and fall therein: for I will bring evil upon them, even the year of their visitation, saith the Lord."

"Hearken not ye to your prophets, nor to your diviners, nor to your dreamers, nor to your enchanters, nor to your sorcerers, which speak unto you . . . for they prophesy a lie unto you."

"There is a conspiracy of her prophets in the midst thereof, like a roaring lion ravening the prey; they have devoured souls "

"The days of visitation are come, the days of recompense are come; Israel shall know it: the prophet is a fool, the spiritual man is mad, for the multitude of thine iniquity, and the great hatred. . . . The prophet is a snare of a fowler in all his ways, and hatred in the house of his God."

"If a man walking in the spirit and falsehood do lie, saying, I will prophesy unto thee of wine and of strong drink; he shall even be the prophet of this people."

"Thus saith the Lord concerning the prophets that make my people err, that bite with their teeth, and cry, Peace; and he that putteth not into their mouths, they even prepare war against him. Therefore night shall be unto you, that ye shall not have a vision; and it shall be dark unto you, that ye shall not divine; and the sun shall go down over the prophets, and the day shall be dark over them. Then shall the seers be ashamed, and the diviners confounded: yea, they shall all cover their lips; for there is no answer of God."

"It shall come to pass in that day, saith the Lord of hosts, that I will cut off the names of the idols out of the land, and they shall no more be remembered: and also I will cause the prophets and the unclean spirit to pass out of the land."

Our neighbours' gifts invite us to hope: our own to fear. Graces are the safest gifts to rejoice in: yet even as to graces joy has a dangerous side. It might seem safe for the humble to rejoice over his humility; but then the humble soul, discerning defect where others observe excellence, is of all men slow to exult over his own gifts.

It is safer to rejoice in the Giver than in the gift.

To value our neighbours' gifts in such a manner as to sympathize with their misuse, is so far to share in the misuse though not at all in the gifts. It is to go halves not even in a bubble investment, but simply in an impending bankruptcy.

14. And deceiveth them that dwell on the earth by the means of those miracles which he had power to do in the sight of the beast; saying to them that dwell on the earth, that they should make an image to the beast, which had the wound by a sword, and did live.

The beast evinces no relish for shame; his wound by a sword and in the head appears in the sight of men honourable.

The Crucifix is the Image made to our dearest Lord. There heaven and earth behold His Likeness Almighty in weakness, All-glorious in shame; red in His apparel but not because of woven garments; Very Life while tasting death for every man.

As said a Saint of old : Shall I wear a crown of roses, while Thou didst wear a Crown of Thorns?

> " 'Tis like frail man to love to walk on high,
> But to be lowly is to be like God."

"And deceiveth them. . . ."—Wherein consists the deceit? Not, apparently, in the actuality of the miracles, but in the inference drawn from them.

A warning to sift both witness borne and witness bearer. Truth may be wrested to endorse a lie.

I must mistrust the impulse which answers, "Charity begins at home," to an appeal; "Prudence is the better part of valour," to an alarum of conscience; "Least said, soonest mended," when duty urges to speech; "A penny saved is a penny got," when brotherly kindness demands my "two pence" and marks me fumbling for a mite, when I might cast in much. At the very least I must *mistrust* such impulses.

History repeats itself, is a familiar adage, and true doubtless in a measure : yet it repeats itself with a difference. So in one sense the leaves of an oak are similar; in another, no two may be alike : its twigs tally, yet the midsummer-shoot stands out distinct.

Isaiah centuries ago exposed to his fellow-countrymen the stupidity no less than the guilt of their idolatries : "They that make a graven image are all of them vanity; and their delectable things shall not profit; and they are their own witnesses; they see not, nor know; that they may be ashamed. Who hath formed a god, or molten a graven image that is profitable for nothing? Behold, all his fellows shall be ashamed. . . . The smith with the tongs both worketh in the coals, and fashioneth it with hammers, and worketh it with the strength of his arms. . . . The carpenter stretcheth out his rule; he marketh it out with a line; he fitteth it with planes, and he marketh it out with the compass, and maketh it after the figure of a man, according to the beauty of a man; that it may remain in the house. . . . He planteth an ash, and the rain doth nourish it. Then shall it be for a man to burn : for he will take thereof, and warm himself; yea, he kindleth it, and baketh bread; yea, he maketh a god, and worshippeth it; he maketh it a graven image. . . . He falleth down unto it, and worshippeth it, and prayeth unto it, and saith, Deliver me; for thou art my god. . . . And none considereth in his heart, neither is there knowledge nor understanding to say, I have burned part of it in the fire; yea, also I have baked bread upon the coals thereof; I have roasted flesh, and eaten it; and shall I make the residue thereof an abomination? shall I fall down to the stock of a tree? He feedeth on ashes: a deceived heart hath turned him aside, that he cannot deliver his soul, nor say, Is there not a lie in my right hand?"

The image thus described seems by its unhelpfulness, inertia, senselessness, lifelessness, an embodiment of St. Paul's phrase: "We know that an idol is nothing in the world."

15. And he had power to give life unto the image of the beast, that the image of the beast should both speak, and cause that as many as would not worship the image of the beast should be killed.

This outcome of idolatry seems to go beyond all that preceded it. This image speaks, originates, to all appearance wills. It invades that prerogative of Almighty God which even an unsanctified King of Israel ascribed to Him alone when "he rent his clothes, and said, Am I God, to kill and to make alive?"

The Prophet Habakkuk having proclaimed the futility of ordinary idolatry, goes on to fulminate "Woe" against a virulent form of it: "What profiteth the graven image that the maker thereof hath graven it; the molten image, and a teacher of lies, that the maker of his work trusteth therein, to make dumb idols? Woe unto him that saith to the wood, Awake; to the dumb stone, Arise, it shall teach! Behold, it is laid over with gold and silver, and there is no breath at all in the midst of it."

Setting this prophecy over against St. John's vision, the thought arises that in neither case may there be genuine life of any sort; so that not even dead-life can become inherent in the image of the beast: such life perhaps there will be as a devil-possessed oracle might have exhibited, a life as execrable as that ascribed by superstition to the doubly dead vampire.

Is this then, is this hideous spectacle of obscene death the legitimate end of will worship, beauty worship, intellect worship, humanity worship, creature worship whatsoever? The slow sifting process carried on age after age, revelation after revelation, experience after experience, seems gradually to bring more and more to light by separation two and only two possibilities: God, and that which is united to God; not-God, even all which is divorced from God.

Hitherto our Fatherly Creator has not made a full end or suffered His whole displeasure to arise. If so He please, ever such an "ass" may still wax mighty to forbid the madness of the most acute towering headlong prophet. Therefore the least or last to whom He has given a tongue must not dare answer, I cannot, or, I will not, should He deign to put a word in such a mouth.

16. **And he causeth all, both small and great, rich and poor, free and bond, to receive a mark in their right hand, or in their foreheads:**
17. **And that no man might buy or sell, save he that had the mark, or the name of the beast, or the number of his name.**

The Revised Version restricts the mark as twofold: ". . . the mark, even the name of the beast or the number of his name."

"He causeth all . . ."—all who by saving their lives have lost them. Meanwhile the genuinely alive are those slain whose silence utters a song emphasizing the words of holy Job: "Whence then cometh wisdom? and where is the place of understanding? Seeing it is hid from the eyes of all living, and kept close from the fowls of the air. Destruction and death say, We have heard the fame thereof with our ears." "Weep ye not for the dead, neither bemoan him."

As to the others, all distinctions are levelled to the dead level of present evil and approaching ruin. The evil is present, because to choose being present with them they choose evil: the ruin approaches, because bound up in that evil they have chosen death.

"Because to every purpose there is time and judgment, therefore the misery of man is great upon him. For he knoweth not that which shall be: for who can tell him when it shall be? There is no man that hath power over the spirit to retain the spirit; neither hath he power in the day of death: and there is no discharge in that war; neither shall wickedness deliver those that are given to it. . . . Because sentence against an evil work is not executed speedily, therefore the heart of the sons of men is fully set in them to do evil."

Since at the day of final reckoning insignificance will not screen the small, or importance exempt the great, or gold ransom the rich, or penury excuse the poor, or liberty furnish an escape to the free, or chains exonerate the bond, all these will clearly count as nothing then; not as chaff on the wind, not as dust in the balance.

From appraising molehills as mountains, Good Lord, deliver us.

"To receive a mark"—To receive is voluntary: "They are all gone aside, they are altogether become filthy."

". . . In their right hand, or in their foreheads."—The *right hand* suggests active, practical life ; the *forehead* studious, intellectual. Every career may be consecrated or desecrated, every gift used or abused.

This *mark* seems to be in effect a diabolical trading licence, the temptation and snare into which persons who at that critical moment *will* be rich, fall. Indeed, not mere poverty, but actual destitution appears to be the alternative for faithful souls, who in the sight of the unwise become for a little moment no better than children of fools, of base men, viler than the earth : " For want and famine they were solitary ; fleeing into the wilderness in former time desolate and waste. Who cut up mallows by the bushes, and juniper roots for their meat. They were driven forth from among men, (they cried after them as after a thief;) to dwell in the cliffs of the valleys, in caves of the earth, and in the rocks." Yet blessed are they if cliffs of valleys be made to them humility, and caves self-denial, and rocks a sure foundation.

But are not coming events already casting their shadows before ? Glance at recent troubles in Ireland : mark boycotting and its results. Look at home ; at strikes and unions, so far as any terrorism resorted to is concerned. God in His mercy restrain men from misusing tremendous edge-tools, launching out on unfathomed waters, rehearsing and forestalling on a minor scale the last awful days. Man is a microcosm : a microcosm may be either a miniature heaven or a miniature hell.

18. Here is wisdom. Let him that hath understanding count the number of the beast: for it is the number of a man; and his number is six hundred threescore and six.

For the special purpose in question, he "that hath understanding" excludes, I should surmise, most men, and very likely all women. For the masses Wisdom resides elsewhere, is an immediately practical grace, and is far more readily accessible. " Happy is the man that findeth wisdom, and the man that getteth understanding. For the merchandise of it is better than the merchandise of silver, and the gain thereof than fine gold."

"Behold, the fear of the Lord, that is wisdom; and to depart from evil is understanding."

" Multitude of years should teach wisdom."

"The mouth of the righteous speaketh wisdom, and his tongue talketh of judgment. The law of his God is in his heart; none of his steps shall slide."

"The Lord giveth wisdom : out of His mouth cometh knowledge and understanding. He layeth up sound wisdom for the righteous."

"Wisdom is better than rubies; and all things that may be desired are not to be compared to it. I, Wisdom, dwell with prudence."

"The fear of the Lord is the beginning of wisdom : and the knowledge of the Holy is understanding."

"With the lowly is wisdom."

"The rod and reproof give wisdom."

"God giveth to a man that is good in His sight wisdom, and knowledge, and joy."

"Christ Jesus, Who of God is made unto us wisdom, and righteousness, and sanctification, and redemption : that, according as it is written, He that glorieth, let him glory in the Lord."

"If any of you lack wisdom, let him ask of God, that giveth to all men liberally, and upbraideth not; and it shall be given him."

I must beware of scrutinizing any text of Holy Scripture as if it were a puzzle or a riddle. I must beware of making guesses at what is withheld from me. "Blessed are the poor in spirit : for theirs is the kingdom of heaven."

St. John himself, and touching his own future, was once contented to repeat his Lord's precise words without attempt at elucidation.

Whoever by loving submission turns intellectual poverty into voluntary spiritual poverty, has discovered a super-excellent philosopher's stone, apt to transmute ignorance into wisdom.

"Six hundred, threescore and six" is not universally set down as the indicative number : some read "six hundred and sixteen."

Lord, give me grace
To take the lowest place;
Nor even desire,
Unless it be Thy Will, to go up higher.

Except by grace,
I fail of lowest place;
Except desire
Sit low, it aims awry to go up higher.

CHAPTER XIV

1. And I looked, and, lo, a Lamb stood on the mount Sion, and with Him an hundred, forty and four thousand, having His Father's Name written in their foreheads.

" Yet have I set My King : upon My holy hill of Sion."

" For the gifts and calling of God are without repentance." This certainly blessed text, rich in comfort and promise (however to me obscure) seems here to receive an illustrative fulfilment. The holy hill and holy city of Palestine were rejected, after the Jews' rejection of Messiah : yet now we behold the Lamb standing on a spot which His own Blood alone could purge from the crying blood-guilt of His crucifixion. How beautiful upon that mountain are those Feet which bring good tidings of good ! For although this be a celestial and not any earthly Sion, surely after some super-sensual manner it still may be that Sion, whose gates the Lord loved more than all the dwellings of Jacob.

Whatever angels or men bent on self-destruction may do or leave undone, yet God Almighty suffereth not, nor can suffer loss. The lightnings ever answer Him " Here we are," though Satan as lightning be fallen from heaven.

" An hundred, forty and four thousand " is the sum of those twelve twelve-thousands sealed (chap. vii.) out of the tribes of Israel. If in both chapters these be the same blessed persons, a double light is thus thrown on their beatitude : if they be different, then with Solomon we see the Church " the Shulamite, as it were the company of two armies."

With Solomon, sounds a bold proposition ; yet *above* Solomon, need not be over-bold ; for he at his highest and holiest could but belong to that company of prophets and kings who desired to see the things which Christians see.

" Having His Father's Name written in their foreheads "— or according to the Revised Version, " Having His Name, and the Name of His Father, written . . . ." This inscription, perhaps, discloses in what the sealing (chap. vii.) consisted ; and so far may suggest that the two elect companies are in fact the same. It corresponds also in great measure with that promise to him that overcometh, in which the charge to the Church of Philadelphia culminates (chap. iii. 12).

2. **And I heard a voice from heaven, as the voice of many waters, and as the voice of a great thunder: and I heard the voice of harpers harping with their harps:**
3. **And they sung as it were a new song before the Throne, and before the four beasts, and the elders: and no man could learn that song but the hundred and forty and four thousand, which were redeemed from the earth.**

The voice is (so to say) the saint's self, the harp is his possession ; the voice is what he had to train, the harping what he had to acquire : all that he has, and all that he is, make up his perpetual offering " before the Throne." To present this offering is his inexhaustible contentment, his rapture. Even on earth, who that sings or plays well on an instrument knows not the joy of waking music? Merely to listen oftentimes moves to tears, to light-heartedness, to longings, to feelings one would not or could not utter. What will it be in heaven to be singer, musician, listener ; to be one voice in a harmony, yet as individually listened to, approved, commended, as if summoned to sing all alone in heaven's half-hour of silence ?

Under one aspect hearing, although stirring and thrilling the heart depths, seems the least sensual of the five senses. Touch, taste, even smell, demand contact grosser or more subtle, as the case may be : sight, though eschewing contact, yet takes cognizance of what might be touched. Hearing is addressed by the intangible and invisible.

Heaven is revealed to earth as the home-land of music : of music, thus remote from what is gross or carnal ; exhibiting likewise an incalculable range of variety, which rebukes and silences perverse suggestions of monotonous tedium in the final beatitude. If we desired a reassuring figure of variety, could we devise one more apt and more refined than music?

"Sing, O heavens ; and be joyful, O earth."

> As the Voice of many waters all saints sing as one,
> As the Voice of an unclouded thundering ;
> Unswayed by the changing moon and unswayed by the sun,
> As the Voice of many waters all saints sing.
>
> Circling round the rainbow of their perfect ring
> Twelve thousand times twelve thousand voices in unison
> Swell the triumph, swell the praise of Christ the King.

Where raiment is white of blood-steeped linen slowly spun,
  Where crowns are golden of Love's own largessing,
Where eternally the ecstasy is but begun,
  As the voice of many waters all saints sing.

Before, when the Living Creatures and the Elders sung a
new song, the words of their anthem were set down (chap. v.
8—10: unless it be possible to understand that the Elders
alone sang): while of this second, "as it were a new song,"
the words are not revealed ; at least, if at all, not in this place.
And as we are certified that no man but the singers themselves
"which were redeemed from the earth" could learn this song,
if we aspire to know somewhat of its meaning it seems our
hopeful course to study reverently and copy affectionately the
characteristics of the choice ones of her that bare them.

> **4. These are they which were not defiled with women ; for
> they are virgins. These are they which follow the
> Lamb whithersoever He goeth. These were redeemed
> from among men, being the firstfruits unto God and
> to the Lamb.**
>
> **5. And in their mouth was found no guile : for they are
> without fault before the Throne of God.**

Mother Church has appropriated this beatitude to her
beloved Holy Innocents. On their Feast Day we behold the
unspotted little souls, guiltless of actual sin, drooping for a
moment with the drooping grace of a snowdrop, subdued for
a moment with the subdued lustre of pearls. "Their Lord
and Lover," Who gave His life in ransom of all lives, is exalt-
ing these babes to give their lives in ransom of His life.
Speech was scarcely in their mouths, much less guile. On
earth their feet could barely have trotted or tottered after a
literal lamb. Thus Rachel beheld them, and weeping for her
children refused to be comforted. " Refrain thy voice from
weeping, and thine eyes from tears." Who now beholds them
sees them "follow the Lamb whithersoever He goeth." Hath He
gone up to glory ? so have they : to dominion and power ? so
have they. Their grace is eternized, their lustre eternized ; their
feet rank with wings, their speech has become song. Alleluia !

Unspotted lambs to follow the one Lamb,
  Unspotted doves to wait on the one Dove ;
To whom Love saith, "Be with Me where I am,"
  And lo ! their answer unto Love is love.
For tho' I know not any note they know,
  Nor know one word of all their song above,
I know Love speaks to them, and even so
  I know the answer unto Love is love.

I think not to infringe obedience by considering how much of this blessedness, secured as it were by birthright (though none the less by grace) to innocence, may also permanently abide within the reach of penitence. To me, to most of us, the heritage of penitence is of more practical importance than the heritage of innocence.

Innocence we cannot recover, but purity and guilelessness we, by God's help, may; and if these graces have led the innocent to glory, us also they may yet lead to glory. Innocence walks with God on earth, and follows Him in heaven: purity and guilelessness tread on earth in the steps of Jesus Christ; and they who follow Him to the gate of heaven will assuredly not be forbidden to follow Him through and within that gate.

Let us encourage ourselves. We may say either that we follow Him, or that He leads us; for the two propositions are practically the same. And if it is unimaginable that one who has followed Him below will not care to follow Him above, much more is it unimaginable—it were blasphemous to imagine that our Leader out of great tribulation will fail to lead us hereafter beside the waters of comfort.

Whatever else is conjecturable, this is certain: these hundred and forty and four thousand sanctified persons whom St. John beheld, were "firstfruits" of the human family unto God and to the Lamb. And since, as St. Paul avers, "If the firstfruit be holy, the lump is also holy," it becomes clear that nothing unholy can find place in the final harvest-home.

I dare not then say simply, Penitence may:—I am driven to say with self-mistrust and trembling, Penitence *must*, on pain of ultimate rejection, recover purity and guilelessness.

> Can peach renew lost bloom,
> Or violet lost perfume;
> Or sullied snow turn white as overnight?
> Man cannot compass it, yet never fear:
> The leper Naaman
> Shows what God will and can;
> God Who worked there is working here;
> Wherefore let shame, not gloom, betinge thy brow,
> God Who worked then is working now.

6. And I saw another angel fly in the midst of heaven, having the everlasting gospel to preach unto them that dwell on the earth, and to every nation, and kindred, and tongue, and people,

7. Saying with a loud voice, Fear God, and give glory to Him; for the hour of His judgment is come: and

worship Him that made heaven, and earth, and the sea, and the fountains of waters.

An angel, as his title imports, is a messenger. If this be a literal winged Angel visibly traversing the local heaven, the prophecy appears hitherto unfulfilled. Meanwhile the Church has her own consecrated Gospel messengers, the Bishops, Priests, Deacons of the Apostolical Succession : and their mission in great measure assimilates them to this Angel.

Though their person is human, their vocation is superhuman : their home is heaven rather than earth. But no sluggish heaven of dreams and premature repose ; heaven where they "fly" on a definite urgent errand, as the Archangel Gabriel flew swiftly (literally, "with weariness") on his embassy to Daniel. "In the midst of heaven" must their path be, inclining neither to the right hand nor to the left ; without partiality, without respect of persons, preaching the self-same Divine Will and Word to all alike. As in matters of this world we say, "Bird's-eye view," because a bird poised aloft looks down upon, and so can estimate the point it aims at ; so with an enhanced elevated meaning, let us say "Angel's-eye view" of those who watch for our souls, as they who must give account, and from a habitual heaven appraise earth. In heart and hand they carry the Everlasting Gospel, that word which passeth not away, though heaven and earth pass away ; which word they proclaim, commanding all men everywhere to repent, and in Christ's stead beseeching them : "How long, ye simple ones, will ye love simplicity? and the scorners delight in their scorning, and fools hate knowledge? Turn you at My reproof: behold, I will pour out My Spirit unto you, I will make known My words unto you." For they know that it is the last time, and that the Judge standeth before the door, even while they know not the day or the hour of His coming. They cry aloud to all people of all languages : He Who made all demands and will accept from all fear, glory, worship. He Who made heaven and earth, the sea, and the fountains of waters, He it is Who gives all blessings, Who gives, and Who can take away : "In Whose hand is the soul of every living thing, and the breath of all mankind." They cry aloud, they spare not, they lift up the voice like a trumpet, and show the people their transgression and their sins. Yet must they not glory in themselves, but cultivate the temper of St. Paul when he wrote : "For though I preach the gospel, I have nothing to glory of: for necessity is laid upon me ; yea, woe is unto me, if I preach not the gospel! For if I do this thing willingly, I have a reward : but if against my will, a dispensation of the gospel is committed unto me."

In functions spiritual the clergy occupy the heights, the laity the levels. Yet as the Church at large is "a royal priesthood," even the least and last of us may win something practical by contemplating an angelic preacher traversing heaven.

"Now there are diversities of gifts, but the same Spirit. And there are differences of administrations, but the same Lord. And there are diversities of operations, but it is the same God which worketh all in all."

"The everlasting Gospel"—unaltered, unalterable. To its immutability St. Paul bears witness : "Though we, or an angel from heaven, preach any other gospel unto you than that which we have preached unto you, let him be accursed. As we said before, so say I now again, If any man preach any other gospel unto you than that ye have received, let him be accursed."—A text for my times and for myself.

"For the hour of His judgment is come."—Yet notwithstanding, and indeed therefore ("for"), men being summoned to fear God are further called upon to give Him glory; worshipping Him as the Creator. The Lord's hand is not shortened that it cannot save : it is man's eleventh hour; Achan may yet appease Him in death Whom in life he provoked; the Thief extirpated from earth may yet sit down in Paradise.

O my God, regard man at his last chance; regard man setting himself to make his final choice ; regard man in the poised balance which must dip. By Thy dear Son's last agony, by His giving up the Ghost, regard, regard man for whom He died, and suffer him not for ever to say Thee nay.

When the end of all things is at hand, it is a comfort to be reminded that heaven, earth, sea, fountains of waters, overwhelmed as they are about to be by awful judgments, are yet all of them God's work, and therefore good. Let me not be more perverse than the clay, which saith not to the potter, Why hast thou made me thus?

8. And there followed another angel, saying, Babylon is fallen, is fallen, that great city, because she made all nations drink of the wine of the wrath of her fornication.

Some have thought to identify the site and structure of a local "Babylon." As to me, who can by no means identify them, I think not I need therefore miss my practical lesson from her greatness and her fall.

Wherefore fell she? The Angel declares, because of what she did; not otherwise because of what she was. Let me (if I may) consider her as that World, which in some sort seems to form common ground, a point of contact, a link, a conductor, between flesh and devil.

Long ago Satan boasted to Christ's very Face that "all the kingdoms of the world, and the glory of them" were delivered unto him; nor did the Truth then and there give the lie to the father of lies. If, then, we may assume an ingredient of truth in the assertion, that element of truth supplies a clue to the fascination and domination of the world; a fascination which is deadly, a domination which is tyrannous. For Satan is the showman of her goodly show: he who can himself appear as an angel of light understands how to inflate her scale, tint her mists and bubbles with prismatic colours, hide her thorns under roses and her worms under silk. He can paint her face, and tire her head, and set her on a wall and at a window, as the goal of a vain race, and the prize of a vain victory. David, superb in his kingliness, made to himself instruments of music; and so has she her men singers and women singers, her brazen wind instruments and her hollow drums. She spreads a feast: first her best, afterwards that which is worse; apples of Sodom to follow forbidden fruit. And as to her cup, "all nations" have not unwarned drunk of it: "Look not thou upon the wine when it is red, when it giveth his colour in the cup, when it moveth itself aright. At the last it biteth like a serpent, and stingeth like an adder. Thine eyes shall behold strange women, and thine heart shall utter perverse things." If this be true of earth's vintage, how tenfold true of the world's!

The City and Woman appear so indistinguishable in the Apocalyptic vision as to justify (I trust) my confusion of personification. Temptation, by a common instinct, seems to be personified as feminine: let us thence derive courage; the symbol itself insinuating that as woman is weaker than man, so temptation is never so strong as the individual assailed. "There hath no temptation taken you but such as is common to man: but God is faithful, Who will not suffer you to be tempted above that ye are able; but will with the temptation also make a way to escape, that ye may be able to bear it."

We daughters of Eve may beyond her sons be kept humble by that common voice which makes temptation feminine.

Woman is a mighty power for good or for evil. She constrains though she cannot compel. Potential for evil, it becomes her to beware and forbear ; potential for good, to spend herself and be spent for her brethren. In the Bible the word *tempt* (or its derivatives) is used in a good or in an evil sense, according to the agent or to the object aimed at.

The wisest of three wrote : " Women are strongest " ; and said : " Many also have perished, have erred, and sinned, for women."

" Babylon is fallen," saith the Angel : he saith not, Is cast down. Though she be cast down, yet is the impulse of her casting down in herself ; she hath undermined herself. Sin is the essential destroyer : the sinner is self-destroyed. Drunkenness especially sets this truth as in a picture before our eyes ; drunkenness being the example of a general rule, not its exception.

Taking physical corruption as the foul image of sin, we see how it consists not with stability, permanence ; but dissolves, disintegrates its prey. It turns bone to dust, muscle as it were to pulp : we loathe to look upon it in a body ; who shall bear to look upon it in a soul ?

9. **And the third angel followed them, saying with a loud voice, If any man worship the beast and his image, and receive his mark in his forehead, or in his hand,**
10. **The same shall drink of the wine of the wrath of God, which is poured out without mixture into the cup of His indignation ; and he shall be tormented with fire and brimstone in the presence of the holy angels, and in the presence of the Lamb :**
11. **And the smoke of their torment ascendeth up for ever and ever : and they have no rest day nor night, who worship the beast and his image, and whosoever receiveth the mark of his name.**

" I have seen the wicked in great power, and spreading himself like a green bay tree. Yet he passed away, and, lo, he was not : yea, I sought him, but he could not be found."

Before when we read of these beast and image worshippers they appeared, as David beheld their predecessors, flourishing and exalted. But alas ! it is only as regards earth that such pass away and cannot be found : " in the presence of the holy angels, and in the Presence of the Lamb " they reappear ; but tormented, smoking, without rest, without apparent help or hope.

Nor perhaps does it clearly transpire *when* it is that their interminable unrest begins : whether before, or consequent upon the decree of judgment. As later on we shall read of darkness pervading the kingdom of the beast, while apparently it continues as yet to be a kingdom ; so now haply the restlessness begins even before it writhes impotently amid the fire, brimstone, smoke.

This retribution is "in the Presence of the Lamb" ; by which awful word I discern not whether there be implied the finishing sting of all agony, or some lessening of horror. Yet is not "Depart from Me" a more overwhelming sentence than even this? To be "clean forgotten" seems a desperateness of forlornness.

"The wine of the wrath of God, which is poured out without mixture into the cup of His indignation."—Indignation is ominous of justice : is His mercy clean gone for ever? We see not our tokens.

"They have no rest day nor night, who worship the beast and his image."—Another worship there is carried on elsewhere, there is another company of worshippers of whom we read (chap. iv. 8), that "they rest not day and night." But (if having no power to study the original text, I may dwell on the wording of the translation) an absolute contrast is suggested by the two statements. Not to rest, is voluntary : to have no rest, is involuntary. The Beatified rest not from adoration, because adoration is the joy of their hearts, the breath of their nostrils : rest (could such a dispensation be conceived) would inflict on them the restlessness as it were of a pent-up conflagration ; to keep silence from their good words would be not rest, but pain and grief to them. The accursed have and can have no rest, because they abide at enmity with Him by Whose grace there remaineth rest for His people.

12. Here is the patience of the saints : here are they that keep the commandments of God, and the faith of Jesus.

"Here"—where? Wherever else, "in the Presence of the Lamb."

That Presence indeed is everywhere ; and all saints clad in patience, keeping the commandments, and cleaving to the faith, inhabit the all-embracing Presence. A shadowed life is no hardship to loving souls consciously abiding under the shadow of the Almighty ; weary indeed would this world's land be without the shadow of that Great Rock !

Patience is an advanced grace. In children we try to fore-stall reason by faith, and by early habit to constitute obedience their second nature; but patience we wish not to characterize them at the outset. Of course nothing contrary to patience can we desire for them at any period; but we remember that "tribulation worketh patience," and if we can we shelter our harmless little ones awhile from tribulation.

At this point of the Revelation, after so many Fatherly Lovingkindnesses and terrors of the Lord have been laid bare —for amid unfathomable mystery the great Love wherewith God loves us, and the tremendous woe from which He would fence us, stand out as clear as day—at this point, patience once more meets the pilgrim soul. All I have read, then, is to lead me up to patience: patience under ignorance, patience under fear, patience under hope deferred, patience so long as free will entails the terrific possibility of self-destruction; patience until (please God) my will freely, finally, indefectibly, becomes one with the Divine Will. Pending which beatific moment, it ought to be with each of us according to St. Paul's description: "Being justified by faith, we have peace with God through our Lord Jesus Christ: by Whom also we have access by faith into this grace wherein we stand, and rejoice in hope of the glory of God. And not only so, but we glory in tribulations also: knowing that tribulation worketh patience; and patience, experience; and experience, hope: and hope maketh not ashamed, because the love of God is shed abroad in our hearts by the Holy Ghost which is given unto us."

"Who is there among you of all His people? The Lord his God be with him, and let him go up."

Obedience is the fruit of faith; patience, the bloom upon the fruit.

> Sweetness of rest when Thou sheddest rest,
> Sweetness of patience till then;
> Only the Will of our God is best
> For all the millions of men:
>
> For all the millions on earth to-day,
> On earth and under the earth;
> Waiting for earth to vanish away,
> Waiting to come to the birth.

13. **And I heard a voice from heaven saying unto me, Write, Blessed are the dead which die in the Lord from henceforth · Yea, saith the Spirit, that they may rest from their labours; and their works do follow them.**

In an earlier age the prophet Isaiah, speaking as in the Person of Christ, proclaimed comfort to the living faithful: "The Spirit of the Lord God is upon Me; because the Lord hath anointed Me to preach good tidings unto the meek; He hath sent Me to bind up the broken-hearted, to proclaim liberty to the captives, and the opening of the prison to them that are bound; to proclaim the acceptable year of the Lord, and the day of vengeance of our God; . . . to appoint unto them that mourn in Zion, to give unto them beauty for ashes, the oil of joy for mourning, the garment of praise for the spirit of heaviness; that they might be called trees of righteousness, the planting of the Lord, that He might be glorified." And now God Almighty Himself comforts the faithful dead. Indeed I think both the former and the latter message may reverently and affectionately be delighted in as conveying hope and solace to living and dead together.

"The acceptable year of the Lord, and the day of vengeance of our God," may (may they not?) be viewed as the period of the final supreme restitution of all things, as well as of the Gospel dispensation; the one sense not excluding but preceding the other. Good will be those tidings to the meek, which summon them to inherit and occupy the everlasting earth wherein dwelleth righteousness. The broken-hearted will be bound up, when mourners are comforted never to mourn again. Liberty will come to light, the iron prison-door will stand ready to open of his own accord, while holy souls rejoicing in their beds, reach forward to regain their resurrection bodies. Then will ashes resume beauty, and the face of mourning shine, and praise obliterate reproach; even self-reproach. Already God's Acre abounds in trees of righteousness planted by Him, and waiting to spring up skywards to His glory. "Is it not yet a very little while, and Lebanon shall be turned into a fruitful field, and the fruitful field shall be esteemed as a forest?"

And now once more St. John hears, and we hear without any ambiguity, a Voice from heaven: "Blessed are the dead which die in the Lord from henceforth." Blessed year after year, blessed century after century, blessed be the death what it may, whereby one by one the long not half-recorded series of the elect die in the Lord: martyrs on death-beds of torture, or in winding-sheets of flame; confessors upraised in loneliness against the world; virgins unflinching in self-oblation; workers wearing out inch by inch; the sick wrung by agony or burdened with long-drawn weariness; men suffering the more because strength holds out; women the more because weakness shrinks; children in their degree but spared foresight.

We understand at a glance that blessed it is for these, and such as these, to die "in the Lord."

Yea, and blessed also is it for these, and such as these, to live: life is their work-day, and their works will follow them. The slothful servant desires to rest without labour; the good and faithful servant after labour.

"Labours . . . works."—There is such a thing as nnproductive labour, strenuously to be eschewed on pain of having no "works" at the critical moment. "Wherefore do ye spend . . . your labour for that which satisfieth not?" Thus did the slothful servant in the Parable of the Talents: he hid his talent in the earth, although nought else would he do with it.

Labour not for the world: "I made me great works; I builded me houses; I planted me vineyards: I made me gardens and orchards, and I planted trees in them of all kind of fruits: I made me pools of water, to water therewith the wood that bringeth forth trees: I got me servants and maidens, and had servants born in my house; also I had great possessions of great and small cattle above all that were in Jerusalem before me: I gathered me also silver and gold, and the peculiar treasure of kings and of the provinces: I gat me men singers and women singers, and the delights of the sons of men, as musical instruments, and that of all sorts. So I was great, and increased more than all that were before me in Jerusalem: also my wisdom remained with me. And whatsoever mine eyes desired I kept not from them, I withheld not my heart from any joy; for my heart rejoiced in all my labour: and this was my portion of all my labour. Then I looked on all the works that my hands had wrought, and on the labour that I had laboured to do: and, behold, all was vanity and vexation of spirit, and there was no profit under the sun."

Labour not for the flesh: "All the labour of man is for his mouth, and yet the appetite is not filled."

"But, beloved, we are persuaded better things of you, and things that accompany salvation. . . . For God is not unrighteous to forget your work and labour of love, which ye have showed toward His Name, in that ye have ministered to the saints, and do minister. And we desire that every one of you do show the same diligence to the full assurance of hope unto the end: that ye be not slothful, but followers of them who through faith and patience inherit the promises."

Labour with and in God: "Every man shall receive his

own reward according to his own labour.   For we are labourers together with God."   "Be ye steadfast, unmovable, always abounding in the work of the Lord, forasmuch as ye know that your labour is not in vain in the Lord."

So shall Christians render thanks for one another : " We give thanks to God always for you all, ... remembering without ceasing your work of faith, and labour of love, and patience of hope in our Lord Jesus Christ."

Lord, that afterwards we may rest, give us grace at once to labour; that at last works may follow us, enable us now to work Thy works Who sendest us, in the Strength of Jesus Christ, Whose Name we plead.   Amen.

Without hazarding conjecture beyond my depth, the verse under consideration reminds me of the Manifestation of the Divine Trinity at our Lord's Baptism, and again (?) at His Transfiguration.   Now " a Voice " speaks, as it were the Paternal Fountain-head of Blessing; and refers that Blessing to union with the Son, the Spouse of souls; finally, " the Spirit " ratifies and seals all.

" The Spirit Itself beareth witness with our spirit, that we are the children of God : and if children, then heirs ; heirs of God, the joint-heirs with Christ ; if so be that we suffer with Him, that we may be also glorified together."

14. And I looked, and behold a white cloud, and upon the cloud one sat like unto the Son of Man, having on His head a golden crown, and in His hand a sharp sickle.

Both in chap. i. 13, *ante*, where the same words occur, and here, R.V. has *a*, not *the* " Son of Man " : in each instance, however, supplying *the* as an alternative marginal reading. As " *the* Son of Man " I adore my Lord as Head indeed of the race, but as so separate from sinners that Him alone it befits to be constituted Judge of human-kind.   As " *a* Son of Man " I worship Him as the Representative Man in Whose perfect Will all sanctified human wills concur, Whose righteous Acts all holy souls approve.

If reverently I may assume this " White Cloud " to be that awful Cloud which intimates the Presence of God the Holy Spirit, the Cloud apparently of the Transfiguration, the Cloud haply of the Ascension ; then I behold the Two Comforters, the Two Advocates of mankind, now concurring in that supreme judgment to which mercy and justice have led up. Pauseless Intercession, groanings unutterable, dew of grace, inspirations of sanctity, have fulfilled their day, done their work, accomplished their mission. And this, whether souls have or have not responded to the saving call.

The done is done once and for ever. The undone remains undone and past doing. The eleventh hour of man's long working-day closes: that day was the preparation, and the Sabbath draws on. Let us not lose heart even while contemplating the end of all things as at hand: "If thou . . . call the Sabbath a delight, the holy of the Lord, honourable; and shalt honour Him, not doing thine own ways, nor finding thine own pleasure, nor speaking thine own words: then shalt thou delight thyself in the Lord."

"For My thoughts are not your thoughts, neither are your ways My ways, saith the Lord. For as the heavens are higher than the earth, so are My ways higher than your ways, and My thoughts than your thoughts. For as the rain cometh down, and the snow from heaven, and returneth not thither, but watereth the earth, and maketh it bring forth and bud, that it may give seed to the sower, and bread to the eater: so shall My word be that goeth forth out of My mouth: it shall not return unto Me void, but it shall accomplish that which I please, and it shall prosper in the thing whereto I sent it."

"On His Head a golden crown."—"We see Jesus, Who was made a little lower than the angels for the suffering of death, crowned with glory and honour." For love of us Christ once abased Himself to wear "a corruptible crown," the Crown of Thorns, that with Him we might eternally wear incorruptible crowns of glory. It seems a very simple, natural thing, yet does it foreshadow a mystery when we read of Ahasuerus: "The king loved Esther . . . and she obtained grace and favour in his sight . . . so that he set the royal crown upon her head."

Sharp though it be, our dear Lord holds a sickle, not a scythe: He mows not, but reaps. With a mower it is far otherwise; but the reaper embraces and draws to his bosom that good grain which he cuts down.

15. **And another angel came out of the temple, crying with a loud voice to Him that sat on the cloud, Thrust in Thy sickle, and reap: for the time is come for Thee to reap; for the harvest of the earth is ripe.**
16. **And He that sat on the cloud thrust in His sickle on the earth; and the earth was reaped.**

"Another angel" does not perhaps carry us back to the preceding verse, but to one more remote: the last individual angel clearly mentioned was at ver. 9. But I take this opportunity of calling attention to my ignorance of, sometimes, a very critical point in the text on which I venture to meditate; and if in consequence I misrepresent the person of the speaker or the word spoken, I ask pardon for my involuntary error. Only should I have readers, let me remind them that what I write professes to be a *surface* study of an unfathomable depth: if it incites any to dive deeper than I attain to, it will so far have accomplished a worthy work. My suggestions do not necessarily amount to beliefs; they may be no more than tentative thoughts compatible with acknowledged ignorance.

Our Lord said: "Whoso shall swear by the temple, sweareth by it, and by Him that dwelleth therein." Whence it appears that this Angel came forth from the immediate Presence of God Almighty to utter his exhortation. Straight from that Presence he doubtless spake the Divine words and Will. And because concerning such a day and hour as this of the supreme harvest our Lord had once declared that not the Angels in heaven at that moment knew the prefixed period; this Angel by now announcing the time as come, suggests that accessions of knowledge are possible in the case of Angels; and thereby further suggests that man in consummated perfection made equal to the Angels, may like them remain open to the delight of increasing knowledge. I think a study of the final beatitude resembles so far a study of precious stones: the more we ponder on the heavenly beatitude, the wider seems to expand the field of ever-multiplying possibilities of bliss; similarly, to read even a little about jewels discloses how many different colours and shades of colour may vary and adorn gems which we commonly assume to be of one fixed colour; for the ruby need not be red, nor the sapphire blue, nor need the diamond be colourless. "O Lord, how manifold are Thy works! in wisdom hast Thou made them all."

"Thrust in Thy sickle"—"He . . . thrust in His sickle."—The Revised Version gives (and similarly at vers. 18, 19): "Send forth Thy sickle"—"He . . . cast His sickle." If this be the more accurate rendering, may it not convey a modified meaning? According to the Authorized Version we seem to behold the Divine Lord of the harvest reap with His own Hand; whilst the Revised Version by treating the sickle rather as an agent than as a mere implement brings the passage into more obvious harmony both with one point in our Master's Parable of the Wheat and the Tares, and with the

corresponding portion of His subsequent key to its meaning :
"In the time of harvest I will say to the reapers, Gather ye
together first the tares, and bind them in bundles to burn them :
but gather the wheat into My barn. . . . The harvest is the
end of the world ; and the reapers are the angels. As therefore the tares are gathered and burned in the fire ; so shall it
be in the end of this world. The Son of Man shall send forth
His angels, and they shall gather. . . ."

"For the harvest of the earth is ripe"—or "over-ripe"
according to the Revised Version, or "dried up" given there
marginally as the literal Greek. Thus long hath God waited !
So of old He spake unto Abram : "In the fourth generation
they shall come hither again : for the iniquity of the Amorites
is not yet full." Meanwhile pious souls on both sides of the
veil (it may be) call out of the deep : "As the hart panteth
after the water brooks, so panteth my soul after Thee, O God.
My soul thirsteth for God, for the Living God : when shall I
come and appear before God ? "

That is a very wonderful rule (if it may be deemed a rule)
which sweetly ordering both nature and grace, oftentimes for
the moment appears to postpone the righteous to the wicked :
so that the ninety-nine are left in the wilderness for the sake of
one, and that one no more after all than contingently recover-
able. "If so be that he find it. . . ."

Imperfectly good people may feel such postponement a
keen trial ; whether it befall them immediately by direct
Providences, or mediately by (for instance) ruinous lifelong
family sacrifices to save a vicious child. St. James has left an
encouraging exhortation and a warning suited to such un-
finished Christians : "Be patient therefore, brethren, unto the
coming of the Lord. Behold, the husbandman waiteth for
the precious fruit of the earth, and hath long patience for it,
until he receive the early and latter rain.· Be ye also patient ;
stablish your hearts : for the coming of the Lord draweth nigh.
Grudge not one against another, brethren, lest ye be condemned : behold, the Judge standeth before the door." And
the spirit if not the letter of the Parable of the Prodigal
Son invites them with the elder son to triumph over self :
"And he was angry, and would not go in : therefore came his
father out, and intreated him. And he answering said to his
father, Lo, these many years do I serve thee, neither transgressed
I at any time thy commandment : and yet thou never gavest me
a kid, that I might make merry with my friends : but as soon
as this thy son was come, which hath devoured thy living

with harlots, thou hast killed for him the fatted calf. And he said unto him, Son, thou art ever with me, and all that I have is thine. It was meet that we should make merry, and be glad : for this thy brother was dead, and is alive again ; and was lost, and is found."

"And the earth was reaped"—at last. Not as yet do we discern the unearthly reapers, the flying sickle ; but we are forewarned of their imminence. If then by watching as well as by prayer we desire to make ready against the moment of their actual inevitable arrival, let us strive to rise above our natural and high above our present level; for the farthest view is from the loftiest standpoint. Doves at windows command a much wider horizon than moles on hillocks : whilst a mole who takes his ease or grubs inside a hillock, what chance has he of seeing ?

> 17. And another angel came out of the temple which is in heaven, he also having a sharp sickle.
> 18. And another angel came out from the altar, which had power over fire ; and cried with a loud cry to him that had the sharp sickle, saying, Thrust in thy sharp sickle, and gather the clusters of the vine of the earth ; for her grapes are fully ripe.

At first sight there seems a striking likeness, on further observation a marked distinction, between that reaping of the earth and this vintage of the clusters of her vine. In both cases the authoritative judicial sentence is pronounced as from the Temple; but the angel of the harvest invokes One Who "sitteth upon the circle of the earth, and the inhabitants thereof are as grasshoppers; that stretcheth out the heavens as a curtain, and spreadeth them out as a tent to dwell in " : while the Angel of the vintage, apparently a minister of the Altar, calls upon a fellow Angel (for so the sequence of verses at least suggests), who sickle in hand has issued from the Temple, to execute his office.

Such a resemblance harmonizing with such a difference suggests that though harvest and vintage are congruous figures, they yet are not here employed simply and absolutely as equivalents; whence arises a further suggestion : that the corn corresponds with the general human race, the vine with the Church. A like distinction, but in reverse order, seems at least conjecturable between the Servants in the Parable of the Talents and the Sheep and Goats in the Prophecy of the Doom (*see* St. Matt. xxv. 14—46).

Our Lord expressly claimed the Vine as a figure of the Church made one with and in Himself: "I am the Vine, ye are the branches." So in the Old Testament the Jewish Church, so far as comported with that dispensation, appears under the same symbol: "Thou hast brought a vine out of Egypt. . . . Look down from heaven, and behold, and visit this vine":—"Yet I had planted thee a noble vine, wholly a right seed: how then art thou turned into the degenerate plant of a strange vine unto Me?"

When our Lord employs the figure of corn it is (at least sometimes) without any restrictive stamp of unity: "The harvest truly is plenteous—"; "Lift up your eyes, and look on the fields; for they are white already to harvest." Even when He deigns to symbolize Himself by "a corn of wheat," the characteristic stated is not simple expansion, but multiplication: "If it die, it bringeth forth much fruit." And though (blessed be His Holy Name) this much fruit is self-evidently His death-bought Church, it yet remains true that one obvious lesson from the corn is neither exclusion nor unity, but likeness. The function of each branch is to abide in the vine: the function of each grain in the ear is to do like the parent seed.

To return to our text, if I may thus consider it. He Who reaps the corn reaps it not from the Temple, but seated at large in the open firmament of heaven; that heaven which canopies the whole earth, the evil and the good, the just and the unjust. "The heavens declare the glory of God; and the firmament sheweth His handywork. Day unto day uttereth speech, and night unto night sheweth knowledge. There is no speech nor language, where their voice is not heard. Their line is gone out through all the earth, and their words to the end of the world." Every man, woman, child, must undergo the judgment: whence it ensues that every one, whatever the issue, was created susceptible of salvation; less than this St. Paul in the universal brotherhood of his zealous heart does surely not imply: "The righteous judgment of God; Who will render to every man according to his deeds: to them who by patient continuance in welldoing seek for glory and honour and immortality, eternal life: but unto them that are contentious, and do not obey the truth, but obey unrighteousness, indignation and wrath, tribulation and anguish, upon every soul of man that doeth evil, of the Jew first, and also of the Gentile; but glory, honour, and peace, to every man that worketh good, to the Jew first, and also to the Gentile: for there is no respect of persons with God. For as many as have sinned without law shall also perish without law: and as many as have sinned in the law shall be judged by the law; . . . in the day when God shall judge the secrets of men by Jesus Christ." And perhaps I may without rashness notice how in this Apocalyptic vision the last word concerning earth's harvest is that it " was reaped "; nothing further do we here read of wheat or tares, barn or fire; reminding us of St. Paul's words to his Corinthian converts : " What have I to do to judge them also that are without? . . . Them that are without God judgeth."

As to the vine, wide is the difference. The armed messenger of judgment comes forth from the Temple; and the exhorting Angel from as it were the very heart of the temple, the Altar. if not the Fire of the Altar. From the days of Isaiah the elect vine was forewarned of the inevitable future reckoning, each intermediate judgment prefiguring that final judgment which is to be without appeal : " My Well-Beloved hath a vineyard in a very fruitful hill : and He fenced it, and gathered out the stones thereof, and planted it with the choicest vine, and built a tower in the midst of it, and also made a winepress therein : and He looked that it should bring forth grapes, and it brought forth wild grapes. . . . What could have been done more to My vineyard, that I have not done in it? wherefore, when I looked that it should bring forth grapes, brought it forth wild grapes? And now go to; I will tell you what I will do to My vineyard : I will take away the hedge thereof, and it shall be eaten up; and break down the wall thereof, and it shall be trodden down : and I will lay it waste." And in the passage of the Apocalypse under consideration, now that the final judgment is come (for so it seems to be), I suppose we may parallel the clusters of fully ripe grapes with the " wild grapes " of the former provocation; observing that at the utmost they apparently rank no higher than barren branches, both alike being doomed to severance from the root of their only life. Degenerate clusters, they have left their wine which cheereth God and man, and have made themselves like the vine of God's enemies whose "vine is of the vine of Sodom, and of the fields of Gomorrah : their grapes are grapes of gall, their clusters are bitter : their wine is the poison of dragons, and the cruel venom of asps."

" Fully ripe."—Not (so far as either the translated text or the margin informs me) either *dried up* or *over ripe:* such excess befell the corn, as if this had been made to wait on the vine. Even so the world is tolerated until the number of the elect be fulfilled.

A A

19. And the angel thrust in his sickle into the earth, and gathered the vine of the earth, and cast it into the great winepress of the wrath of God.

20. And the winepress was trodden without the city, and blood came out of the winepress, even unto the horse bridles, by the space of a thousand and six hundred furlongs.

As to the harvest we are told nothing further than that it was reaped; but plainly are we told what befalls the condemned clusters of this awful vine. So are all Christians warned of what awaits unworthy Christians: "If we sin wilfully after that we have received the knowledge of the truth, there remaineth no more sacrifice for sins, but a certain fearful looking for of judgment and fiery indignation, which shall devour the adversaries. He that despised Moses' law died without mercy under two or three witnesses: of how much sorer punishment, suppose ye, shall he be thought worthy, who hath trodden under foot the Son of God, and hath counted the Blood of the covenant, wherewith he was sanctified, an unholy thing, and hath done despite to the Spirit of grace? For we know Him that hath said, Vengeance belongeth unto Me, I will recompense, saith the Lord. And again, The Lord shall judge His people. It is a fearful thing to fall into the hands of the Living God."

These "clusters" are men, for they yield blood, and their winepress is the wrath of God. Such are they who once trod under foot the Son of God, that very Saviour Who for their sakes trod the winepress alone: now are they ground as it were to powder under His wrath Whom they outraged. They despised and rejected His saving Blood: now must their own be as dung on the face of the field. They went not forth unto Him without the camp bearing His reproach: now are they themselves crushed without the city. They did despite to the Spirit of grace; and now there remaineth no more sacrifice for sins. "Put ye in the sickle, for the harvest is ripe: come get you down; for the press is full, the fats overflow; for their wickedness is great."

God's righteous vengeance, even when He maketh a way to His indignation and spareth not souls from death, is proportioned, due, not in excess: the horses are bridled, the area is circumscribed.

CHAPTER XV

1. And I saw another sign in heaven, great and marvellous, seven angels having the seven last plagues; for in them is filled up the wrath of God.

Twice before (ch. xii.) St. John saw a "wonder"; or as the Revised Version in each instance translates the word, a "sign"; in heaven. First, when he beheld there "the King's Daughter" all glorious without as well as within, made indomitable in weakness. Secondly, when he beheld there a great red dragon, God's adversary and hers, at work yet baffled in his evil purpose. Now thirdly (if I may assume the Greek word still to be the same), when Seven Angels appear having the Seven last Plagues wherein is filled up the wrath of God.

Many points as I may miss, I perceive the marvel of "a woman" (for such is the figure, whatever may be the signification) appearing as the centre of such concurrent glories: I readily perceive the marvel of a rebel working wickedness and waging war in heaven itself. But angels being (so to say) natives of heaven, and St. John having already mentioned as present there ten thousand times ten thousand and thousands of thousands, the third marvel seems not to consist in Seven Angels thence confronting us, but rather in their being the bearers of Seven Plagues. This is the third and last *Seven* of the Apocalypse, "for in them is filled up the wrath of God." The previous Sevens were the Seals and the Trumpets; and however the three series may have to be viewed in historical sequence, yet to any uninstructed reader they convey with one voice one reiterated warning to love righteousness and hate iniquity and flee from the wrath to come.

"The wrath of God" admits of being filled up: nowhere do we read of His mercy being filled up. Equally, "seven last plagues" are here defined; but nowhere seven last blessings.

2. And I saw as it were a sea of glass mingled with fire: and them that had gotten the victory over the beast, and

over his image, and over his mark, and over the number of his name, stand on the sea of glass, having the harps of God.

If I may venture to assume this sea to be the same as that which St. John originally beheld "before the Throne . . . of glass like unto crystal" (ch. iv. 6), a fresh point of glory has now been added to its former glory; or if not truly added, has yet been added so far as our knowledge is concerned.

The former vision magnified God as Creator. Of that vision the sea appeared pure, perfect, unbroken, unperturbed; it spread double against that overarching sky which is strong and as a molten looking-glass. Itself flawless, there could occur no flaw in its reflection of the firmament.

Now fire is added not to consume, but "mingled" with that sea to illuminate, flash, augment beauty; even as the fiery milky opal would not be half itself without its spark. For Redemption now excels Creation; and the fiery trial through which the elect have pressed after Christ, being past as a trial endures as a perpetual splendour. None but victors stand upon that sea "having the harps of God," for "he that is feeble among them at that day shall be as David." "Awake, awake, utter a song: arise . . . and lead thy captivity captive."

> Jerusalem of fire
>   And gold and pearl and gem,
> Saints flock to fill thy choir,
>   Jerusalem.
>
> Lo, thrones thou hast for them;
> Desirous they desire
>   Thy harp, thy diadem,
>
> Thy bridal white attire,
>   A palm branch from thy stem:
> Thy holiness their hire,
>   Jerusalem.

Though the sea be "of glass mingled with fire," yet if we may regard it as in any sense equivalent to a sea of *water* thus mingled, we immediately recognize and revere two conspicuous types of God the Holy Spirit; and we discern as in a glass darkly how it is His Presence, Gift, Grace, which sustains the Church universal. The Altar has clearly reappeared in the celestial Temple: now (if I may) I behold the Font also, that "womb of the morning," whence as Christ's members we derive the dew of immortal birth.

"O Lord, how manifold are Thy works! in wisdom hast

Thou made them all : the earth is full of Thy riches. So is
the great and wide sea."

An alternative reading (Revised Version) makes these more
than conquerors stand not *on* but *by* the glassy sea ; thus supplying us with an additional thought by contrasting the Church
Triumphant for evermore with sometime the Church Militant :
" By the rivers of Babylon, there we sat down, yea, we wept,
when we remembered Zion. We hanged our harps upon the
willows in the midst thereof. . . . How shall we sing the
Lord's song in a strange land ? "

**3. And they sing the song of Moses the servant of God, and
the song of the Lamb, saying, Great and marvellous
are Thy works, Lord God Almighty, just and true are
Thy ways, Thou King of saints.**

" Consider the Apostle and High Priest of our profession,
Christ Jesus ; Who was faithful to Him that appointed Him, as
also Moses was faithful in all His house. . . And Moses
verily was faithful in all His house, as a servant. . . . But
Christ as a Son over His own house." Hence it appears how
wide and not to be bridged over is the gulf between Son and
servant ; yet Christ setting aside that inequality is pleased to
combine with Himself Moses His friend in a song of triumph,
ennobling with transcendent significance Solomon's proverb :
" A wise servant . . . shall have part of the inheritance among
the brethren."

Surely this also is a sign and a great wonder brought to light
in heaven.

> The Passion Flower hath sprung up tall,
>   Hath east and west its arms outspread ;
>   The heliotrope shoots up its head
> To clear the shadow of the wall :
> Down looks the Passion Flower,
>   The heliotrope looks upward still,
> Hour by hour
>   On the heavenward hill.
>
> The Passion Flower blooms red or white,
>   A shadowed white, a cloudless red ;
>   Caressingly it droops its head,
> Its leaves, its tendrils, from the light :
> Because that lowlier flower
>   Looks up, but mounts not half so high,
> Hour by hour
>   Tending toward the sky.

On earth long ages before Moses had had his triumph and
his song of triumph when Israel stood safe on the further shore of

the Red Sea : so that in heaven it is no new thing for him to sing unto the Lord because He hath triumphed gloriously. Throughout the Gospel, on the contrary, no trace appears of any triumph song "of the Lamb," unless it be that Hymn which He sang with His disciples while He stood on the brink of deep waters whose floods were presently to run over Him. Moses had said, " Fear ye not, stand still and see the salvation of the Lord," when a type of supreme salvation was about to be enacted; and Christ said, " Be of good cheer; I have over- come the world," when He was about with His own right hand and with His holy arm to get Himself the victory.

Lord Jesus, there is none like unto Thee, none beside Thee.

This " Song " is rendered somewhat differently in the Revised Version—

"Great and marvellous are Thy works, O Lord God, the Almighty ; righteous and true are Thy ways, Thou King of the ages [*margin*, "nations "]. Who shall not fear, O Lord, and glorify Thy Name ? for Thou only art Holy ; for all the nations shall come and worship before Thee; for Thy righteous acts have been made manifest."

4. Who shalt not fear Thee, O Lord, and glorify Thy Name ? for Thou only art Holy: for all nations shall come and worship before Thee; for Thy judgments are made manifest.

O Lord God Almighty, All Holy, Whom we fear, Whom we trust, Whose Name we desire to glorify ; Thou Who hast vouchsafed to constitute man not least amongst Thy marvellous works ; on wings of grace enable us like Thine Angel of old to do wondrously, ascending spiritually from the rock of faith and altar of obedience in the flame of love. O King of saints, of nations, of the ages, Thou Whose ways are just and true ; Thou Unapproachable Who callest us unto Thee, Thou Inimitable Who requirest us to become like unto Thee ; grant us grace ever worshipping to follow Thee by justice and truth. In this age of probation prepare Thou generation after generation for the eternal ages of perfected sanctity; until the knowledge of Thy glory shall fill the earth as the waters cover the sea, and all saints shall be co-extensive with all nations. Father, Son, Holy Spirit, Co-Eternal Trinity in Unity, we plead the Merits of Jesus Christ. Amen.

5. And after that I looked, and behold, the temple of the tabernacle of the testimony in heaven was opened :

6. And the seven angels came out of the temple, having

the seven plagues, clothed in pure and white linen, and having their breasts girded with golden girdles.

Surely this also is a time appointed, a solemn feast day. Because to the saints it is meat and drink to do the Will of God and to finish His work : if to do it, likewise to suffer it ; if to finish it, likewise to behold it finished. " He that is our God is the God of salvation ; and unto God the Lord belong the issues from death."

Yet of old far different was that procession which the sweet Psalmist of Israel contemplated when he uplifted heart and voice in the Divine praises : " They have seen Thy goings, O God ; even the goings of my God, my King, in the sanctuary. The singers went before, the players on instruments followed after ; among them were the damsels playing with timbrels." Then the thousands of the chosen nation flocked up to the earthly Tabernacle of the Mercy Seat ; now from the heavenly Temple of the Tabernacle of the Testimony emerge the ministers of Judgment. Song, music, mirth, befitted that interlude of time : awe, silence, this prelude of eternity.

> Time lengthening, in the lengthening seemeth long :
>   But ended Time will seem a little space,
> A little while from morn to evensong,
>   A little while that ran a rapid race ;
> A little while, when once Eternity
>   Denies proportion to the other's pace.
> Eternity to be and be and be,
>   Ever beginning, never ending still,
> Still undiminished far as thought can see ;
>   Farther than thought can see, by dint of will
> Strung up and strained and shooting like a star
>   Past utmost bound of everlasting hill :
> Eternity unswaddled, without bar,
>   Finishing sequence in its awful sum ;
> Eternity still rolling forth its car,
>   Eternity still here and still to come.

At the sounding of the Seventh Trumpet (ch. xi. 15, 19), " the Temple of God was opened in heaven, and there was seen in His Temple the Ark of His Testament." Now once more " the Temple of the Tabernacle of the Testimony in heaven was opened," but no word indicates that the Stronghold of Mercy and Comfort was again revealed to sight. There, doubtless, It abode ; but hidden, it may be, as when the Cloudy Pillar of Fire turned unbroken darkness against Pharaoh and his host.

So likewise Moses, that luminous type of Christ, answered

Pharaoh who in his hardheartedness made himself a type of all obstinate rebels :—"Pharaoh said unto him, Get thee from me, take heed to thyself, see my face no more. . . . And Moses said, Thou hast spoken well, I will see thy face again no more."

"Clothed in pure and white linen"—in the Revised Version : "Arrayed with precious stone, pure and bright."— This latter translation, strange to my unlearned ears, set me to search whether I could find in the Authorized Version any other instance of an angel being described in so many words, and beyond question as clad *in linen :* I have failed to find one, and though this may merely prove my ignorance it suggests a thought.

In the Prophecy of Ezekiel (xxviii. 13, &c.) the King of Tyrus is twice designated by the word *cherub,* and in the same passage we read concerning him : "Every precious stone was thy covering, the sardius, topaz, and the diamond, the beryl, the onyx, and the jasper, the sapphire, the emerald, and the carbuncle, and gold." Robed in these or in such as these, including gold ("girded with golden girdles"), it may haply be that these seven angels came forth ; themselves and their vestments alike in the flawless perfection of direct Divine workmanship, upright, unimpaired, as at the beginning. Even so was it with the first Tables of the Law : "The tables were the work of God, and the writing was the writing of God, graven upon the tables."

If thus we may deem of elect Angels, it leaves linen for the appropriate vestment of redeemed men. Christ wears it, for He is not ashamed to call us brethren ; and after Him and with Him all saints wear it. Linen differs essentially from jewels inasmuch as it is a manufacture, needing human agency whereby to be steeped and bleached and wrought finely, and to have harshnesses and coarsenesses discarded from the web as this grows into beauty. God indeed provides the flax, the skill, the patience, and all else that comes into requisition ; but still man it is who must sow and reap, steep and bleach, weave and finish that fine linen which is the righteousness of saints.

If Angels who inherit no weak points need girding for their work ; how much more man who is made up of weak points, and who has for incitement to gird himself and run Christ's All-Holy Example : "Righteousness shall be the girdle of His loins, and faithfulness the girdle of His reins." Truth is man's girdle, "Stand therefore, having your loins girt about with truth"; gold the Angels' : by faith man apprehends and cleaves to truth, and comparing faith with gold, St. Peter awards the preference to faith : "The trial of your faith, being much more precious than of gold that perisheth, though it be tried with fire."

Now the gold of *that* land we know is good, while what it may signify we know not ; and well we know that man in his mortality ranks lower than angels. Yet weighing the preciousness of his allotted girdle here below, he may well lift up his heart unto the Lord, and thanking God take courage : "For thou hast girded me with strength unto the battle."

7. And one of the four beasts gave unto the seven angels seven golden vials full of the wrath of God, Who liveth for ever and ever.

" Wisdom is justified of all her children."

Every celestial creature subserves the Will of its Creator, approves His decree, executes His behest, forwards His work. So faithfully do the elect reproduce His Image, that to fall into their hands becomes a fearful thing to any to whom it is fearful to fall into His hands. Point after point in this awful Revelation presses home the conviction that, cost what it may, and to whom it may, God and His elect will in heaven be of one heart, and one mind, and one will. Implicitly it has been so in time, explicitly it will be so in eternity.

Man's perversity has made gold the occasion and instrument of so much sin, that no wonder it one day reappears as vials full of Divine wrath. Happy will he be at the last who with St. Peter has had neither silver nor gold, with St. Paul has coveted no man's gold ; he miserable who made gold his hope, or against whom hire fraudulently kept back crieth.

From sordid self-ruin, Good Lord, deliver us.

> Seven vials hold Thy wrath : but what can hold
>   Thy mercy save Thine own Infinitude
>   Boundlessly overflowing with all good,
> All lovingkindness, all delights untold ?
> Thy Love, of each created love the mould ;
>   Thyself, of all the empty plenitude ;
>   Heard of at Ephrata, found in the Wood,
> For ever One, the Same, and Manifold.
> Lord, give us grace to tremble with that dove
>   Which Ark-bound winged its solitary way
>   And overpast the Deluge in a day,
>   Whom Noah's hand pulled in and comforted :
> For we who much more hang upon Thy Love
>   Behold its shadow in the deed he did.

8. And the temple was filled with smoke from the glory of

God, and from His power; and no man was able to enter into the temple, till the seven plagues of the seven angels were fulfilled.

When the Mosaic Tabernacle was finished and set up, "Then a Cloud covered the tent of the congregation, and the Glory of the Lord filled the Tabernacle. And Moses was not able to enter into the tent of the congregation, because the Cloud abode thereon, and the Glory of the Lord filled the Tabernacle." So likewise at the Dedication of Solomon's Temple: "It came to pass, when the priests were come out of the Holy Place, that the Cloud filled the house of the Lord, so that the priests could not stand to minister because of the Cloud: for the Glory of the Lord had filled the house of the Lord."

If these two historical incidents may be viewed as prefiguring this of which we read in St. John's vision: "The Temple was filled with smoke from the Glory of God, and from His power; and no man was able to enter into the Temple. . . .": then perhaps without rashness I may here think to discern a token of Christ being pleased in His own good time to fulfil and end His Mediatorial Kingdom, His perpetual Intercession. For not only (ver. 5) has "the Temple of the Tabernacle of the Testimony" been opened, without the Ark of the Testament (so far as is stated) becoming visible; but that "no man" should be able to enter into the Temple suggests that Christ Himself has ceased or is nigh ceasing to appear in the Presence of God for incorrigible offenders; so that thenceforward, to quote St. Paul's phrase, God (as God) wills to be All in All.

That such a termination impends seems certain. That the point has been reached in St. John's Revelation appears conjecturable when, as now by looking forward, we mark one unbroken course of punitive judgments untempered by any answering sign of repentance. Of this we have an appalling type in the history of Joshua's war against the accursed nations: "It was of the Lord to harden their hearts, that they should come against Israel in battle, that he might destroy them utterly, and that they might have no favour, but that he might destroy them." Yet first doubtless they had hardened themselves, according to the inspired Proverb: "He, that being often reproved hardeneth his neck, shall suddenly be destroyed, and that without remedy."

"A certain man had a fig-tree planted in his vineyard; and he came and sought fruit thereon, and found none. Then said he unto the dresser of his vineyard, Behold, these three years I come seeking fruit on this fig tree, and find none : cut it down ; why cumbereth it the ground ? And he answering said unto him, Lord, let it alone this year also, till I shall dig about it, and dung it : and if it bear fruit, well : and if not, then after that thou shalt cut it down."

"Every man in his own order: Christ the firstfruits ; afterward they that are Christ's at His coming. Then cometh the end, when He shall have delivered up the kingdom to God, even the Father ; when He shall have put down all rule and all authority and power. For He must reign, till He hath put all enemies under His feet. The last enemy that shall be destroyed is death. For He hath put all things under His feet. But when He saith, all things are put under Him, it is manifest that He is excepted, which did put all things under Him. And when all things shall be subdued unto Him, then shall the Son also Himself be subject unto Him that put all things under Him, that God may be all in all."

"And the Temple was filled with smoke. . . ." If this "Smoke" corresponds with the Ineffable Cloud of the Divine Presence, then we surmise here an intimation of the Double Procession of God the Holy Spirit, "Who proceedeth from the Father and the Son" : inasmuch as the Smoke proceeded from "the Glory of God" and from "His Power."

And one step further. If simultaneously with a plenary Effusion of the Holy Spirit the day of grace will terminate, we are thus reminded of that most awful declaration : "Verily I say unto you, All sins shall be forgiven unto the sons of men, and blasphemies wherewith soever they shall blaspheme : but he that shall blaspheme against the Holy Ghost hath never forgiveness, but is in danger of eternal damnation."

Thank God, that when the Seven Plagues are over, the Temple shall be reopened to man : where Christ is, there shall also His servant be. "When Thou hadst overcome the sharpness of death : Thou didst open the Kingdom of Heaven to all believers."

CHAPTER XVI.

1. And I heard a great voice out of the temple saying to the seven angels, Go your ways, and pour out the vials of the wrath of God upon the earth.

"Now is the end come upon thee, and I will send Mine anger upon thee, and will judge thee according to thy ways, and will recompense upon thee all thine abominations. And Mine eye shall not spare thee, neither will I have pity: but I will recompense thy ways upon thee, and thine abominations shall be in the midst of thee: and ye shall know that I am the Lord. Thus saith the Lord God; An evil, an only evil, behold, is come. An end is come, the end is come: it watcheth for thee; behold, it is come."

Seven offences had not sufficed to draw down this sevenfold judgment, nay, nor seventy times seven, had man but turned and said, I repent. For certainly God All-Holy proposeth not to any a higher standard than His own (*see* St. Matt. xviii. 21, 22).

Nor may I so frame my thoughts as to represent God as like the forgiving man: it is the forgiving man who faintly, feebly, inadequately, amid flaws and shortcomings is in his degree like God. The antitype determines the type, not this that. If such a distinction might seem purposeless, I come to perceive its purpose when (for instance) Divine Truths having first been confounded with heathen myths are interpreted as on a par with them; as if all alike symbolized various processes, phases, of nature. It is pious to contemplate autumn, winter, spring, summer, as emblematical of our dear Lord's death, burial, resurrection, ascended glory; but to treat these as if they were a parable of those, is to deny the faith.

2. And the first went, and poured out his vial upon the earth; and there fell a noisome and grievous sore upon the men which had the mark of the beast, and upon them which worshipped his image.

O Lord, correct us, but with judgment; not in Thine anger, lest Thou bring us to nothing.

If Thou smite us, let it be with the sores of holy Job unto amendment and perfection: not with the sores of obstinate Egypt, or of reprobation. By pain bring back our pleasure.

3. And the second angel poured out his vial upon the sea; and it became as the blood of a dead man: and every living soul died in the sea.

If thou curse our blessings, let it be that losing less we may gain more; that in exchange for bitterness we may inherit sweetness, and for sterility fruit. By death instruct us unto life.

4. And the third angel poured out his vial upon the rivers and fountains of waters; and they became blood.

If Thou assure us not water nor give us bread, grant us grace by hungering and thirsting after righteousness to feast in famine, in destitution to have enough. By want enrich us.

5. And I heard the angel of the waters say, Thou art righteous, O Lord, which art, and wast, and shalt be, because Thou hast judged thus.

6. For they have shed the blood of saints and prophets, and Thou hast given them blood to drink; for they are worthy.

Deliver us from blood-guiltiness, O God, Thou that art the God of our health: that with Angels and Archangels and all the company of heaven our tongue may laud and magnify Thy Glorious Name, evermore praising Thee and Thy Righteousness. Be reproofs of instruction to us the way of life.

7. And I heard another out of the altar say, Even so, Lord God Almighty, true and righteous are Thy judgments.

Grant us to be of one mind with Thine Angel of the Altar, and with Abraham Thy friend, who bear witness that the Judge of all the earth doeth right. So may we trust Thee though Thou slay us. By Thy loving correction make us great.

8. And the fourth angel poured out his vial upon the sun; and power was given unto him to scorch men with fire.

9. And men were scorched with great heat, and blasphemed the Name of God, which hath power over these plagues: and they repented not to give Him glory.

Though the sun smite us by day and the moon by night, yet

to us let the Sun of Righteousness arise with healing in His wings. Though Thou destroy our flesh, save our spirit. Be the seven times heated furnace of affliction our upper chamber wherein to adore the Son of God, and by repentance to glorify His Name. Walk with us in the fire, Good Lord.

10. And the fifth angel poured out his vial upon the seat of the beast; and his kingdom was full of darkness; and they gnawed their tongues for pain,

11. And blasphemed the God of heaven because of their pains and their sores, and repented not of their deeds.

Not unto us the outer darkness, not unto us the gnashing of teeth. Deliver us from penal darkness, from darkness which may be felt, from paralyzing darkness forbidding us to arise and go to our Father. Be our pangs schoolmasters to bring us to Christ.

12. And the sixth angel poured out his vial upon the great river Euphrates; and the water thereof was dried up, that the way of the kings of the east might be prepared.

If Thou change the elements by a kind of harmony making dry land where was water; bringing upon us evil, and not good as once by the Red Sea or the beloved Jordan, but gloom from the sun-rising and terror from afar, yet support us though Thou rescue us not. As to Thee, so to us, be darkness and light both alike.

13. And I saw three unclean spirits like frogs come out of the mouth of the dragon, and out of the mouth of the beast, and out of the mouth of the false prophet.

14. For they are the spirits of devils, working miracles, which go forth unto the kings of the earth and of the whole world, to gather them to the battle of that great day of God Almighty.

If all wickedness spread nets for our feet or set the battle in array against us, strengthen us to shake our head at the adversary and laugh him to scorn, although he work miracles and stir up the earth and the whole world, O Lord God, against Thee and Thine. Bring forth the spear, and stop the way against them that persecute us: say unto our soul, I am thy salvation. Out of weakness make us strong.

15. Behold, I come as a thief. Blessed is he that watcheth, and keepeth his garments, lest he walk naked, and they see his shame.

Until Thou comest, kindle our desires to go forth to meet Thee, our watchfulness to rehearse Thy welcome. Be purity our veil, obedience our walk, Thyself our righteousness. Yea, be Thyself our all in all.

16. And he gathered them together into a place called in the Hebrew tongue Armageddon.

Lord, to Whom the gathering of the people shall be, Lord Most Mighty, Most Holy, Most Merciful ; when summoned without appeal multitudes stand before Thee in the Valley of Decision, set us not on Thy Left Hand of rejection but on Thy Right Hand of acceptance. Turn not Thy Face from us poor men.

17. And the seventh angel poured out his vial into the air; and there came a great voice out of the temple of heaven, from the Throne, saying, It is done.

When an end is come, the end is come, the endless end, the end which is the final beginning ; when every eye sees, and all kindreds of the earth wail, and the undone cannot be done, neither the done undone ; be Thy word to each of us, Come. In us see of the travail of Thy Soul, and be satisfied.

18. And there were voices, and thunders, and lightnings; and there was a great earthquake, such as was not since men were upon the earth, so mighty an earthquake, and so great.

When earth is passing away with a great noise, and there is trembling in the field, in the host, and among all the people, and the earth quakes, so that it is a very great trembling ; put us in the clift of Thy Rock, in the place by Thee, O Lord Thou Rock of Ages. Defer not for Thine own sake, O our God : for behold, Thou hast it by Thee.

19. And the great city was divided into three parts, and the cities of the nations fell: and great Babylon came in remembrance before God, to give unto her the cup of the wine of the fierceness of His wrath.

When woe is to them who have coveted an evil covetousness to their house, and the stone is crying out of the wall, and the beam out of the timber is answering it ; and the mourners go about the streets because mankind is going to its long home, for good or for evil to its long home, for life or for death to its long home ; then be our remembrance a sweet savour unto Thee, O God. Find Thou a ransom.

20. And every island fled away, and the mountains were not found.

When all faileth save Thou, fail us not Thou; Thou Who never failest them that seek Thee. Lord, Lord, give us grace to seek and find Thee.

21. And there fell upon men a great hail out of heaven, every stone about the weight of a talent: and men blasphemed God because of the plague of the hail; for the plague thereof was exceeding great.

Suffer us not to fall into desperateness, suffer us not to curse Thee and die. Suffer us not by despairing of mercy to forfeit mercy. Are we stronger than Thou? Nay, Good Lord. O be Thou our help in trouble, for vain is the help of man.

We plead Jesus Christ, having a good hope because of Thy word. Amen.

"A noisome and grievous sore."—Recalling the "boil breaking forth with blains upon man . . . throughout all the land of Egypt," which plague came in answer to ashes of the furnace sprinkled toward heaven by Moses, as though at that moment the provocation of earth went up visibly toward heaven. "A people that provoketh Me to anger continually to My Face. . . . These are a smoke in My nose, a fire that burneth all the day." But to St. John's vision no stated challenge from earth then and there calls down heaven's vengeance, which rather seems a pouring out of that wrath which human wickedness has treasured up unto itself against the day of wrath; which overflows and cannot but overflow at length; which can no longer be shut up with doors, or obscured in cloudy garment, or swaddled in thick darkness. "The morning is come unto thee, O thou that dwellest in the land: the time is come,.the day of trouble is near, and not the sounding again of the mountains. Now will I shortly pour out my fury upon thee, and accomplish Mine anger upon thee: and I will judge thee according to thy ways, and will recompense thee for all thine abominations. And Mine eye shall not spare, neither will I have pity: I will recompense thee according to thy ways and thine abominations that are in the midst of thee; and ye shall know that I am the Lord that smiteth."

> Tremble, thou earth, at the Presence of the Lord
> Whose Will conceived thee and brought thee to the birth,
> Always everywhere thy Lord to be adored:
> Tremble, thou earth.

Wilt thou laugh time away in music and mirth?
Time hath days of pestilence, hath days of a sword,
    Hath days of hunger and thirst in desolate dearth.

Till eternity wake up the multicord
    Thrilled harp of heaven and breathe full its organ's girth
For joy of harvest and infinite reward,
    Tremble, thou earth.

"The sea; and it became as the blood of a dead man."—
Fresh water too will be turned into blood; but of the sea
alone is it said that it became "as the blood of a dead man,"
or that in it "every living soul died." Perhaps this prominent
connection of the sea with death prepares us for its mysterious
exclusion from the new heaven and new earth (ch. xxi. 1).

"The rivers and fountains of waters; and they became
blood."—This seems at first sight almost identical with the
corresponding Egyptian plague: "Take thy rod, and stretch
out thine hand upon the waters of Egypt, upon their streams,
upon their rivers, and upon their ponds, and upon all their
pools of water, that they may become blood; and that there
may be blood throughout all the land of Egypt, both in vessels
of wood, and in vessels of stone. . . . And he lifted up the
rod, and smote the waters that were in the river . . . and all
the waters that were in the river were turned to blood. And
the fish that was in the river died; and the river stank, and
the Egyptians could not drink of the water of the river; and
there was blood throughout all the land of Egypt. . . . And
all the Egyptians digged round about the river for water to
drink; for they could not drink of the water of the river."

Yet a difference may be observed. In the case of Egypt
the "fountains of waters" are not particularized; so that if
the digging Egyptians succeeded in finding springs independent
of the Nile, such springs may (so far as is stated) have gushed
forth in intact purity, and have served instead of the transmuted
waters.

St. John, on the contrary, beheld the springs and all the
waters contaminated; so that the Angel of the waters extolling
the Divine Equity names "blood" as the drink of those
murderers. Whereupon another out of the Altar responds
with like lands. The Revised Version however translates as
if not an Angel from the Altar but the Altar itself uttered
praises: reminding us of our Lord's emphatic saying, "The
stones would immediately cry out,"—thus the very Altar, the
stronghold of reconciliation, would at length condemn the
ungodly.

B B

"I will also water with thy blood the land wherein thou swimmest, even to the mountains; and the rivers shall be full of thee."

"Because thou hast had a perpetual hatred, and hast shed the blood of the children of Israel by the force of the sword in the time of their calamity, in the time that their iniquity had an end: therefore, as I live, saith the Lord God, I will prepare thee unto blood, and blood shall pursue thee: sith thou hast not hated blood, even blood shall pursue thee."

"Upon the sun."—At the Fourth Trumpet the light of the sun was abridged (ch. viii. 12). At the Fourth Vial its heat is intensified so as to scorch yet not to consume. Combining in thought the two phases, we see in emblem the outer darkness of hell no way lit up by the unquenchable fire, and that fire ever feeding upon without devouring its prey.

But the sun is earth's vivifier, benefactor, guardian, friend. Even so. It will not be otherwise, alas! with any lost soul which at length makes of Mercy an enemy.

Without pressing every word, I think these two prophecies may be harmonized as at least a dim allegory touching the mystery of Redemption.

The Sun oftentimes symbolizes Christ. Here in a figure we behold Christ by voluntary Self-abasement and Self-sacrifice first taking upon Himself the plagues due to us, before He suffers us to be touched by them. At the Fourth Trumpet the Sun itself is smitten. On the Sun itself the Fourth Vial of Wrath is poured out, or ever the wrath descends to mankind at large: yet is it the Sun and none other which at length smites. Of the elect we read elsewhere, but not here. Of the incorrigible we are reading, and their personal rankling raging hatred of God in Christ persists in venting blasphemy and abhorring repentance. Could they, would they, repent, they might . . . yea, so surely as God Almighty is Faithful and True, they *must* up to and beyond the eleventh hour go home out of the horrible pit to Paradise. Thus did one Malefactor, but not (so far as is recorded) the other.

"And blasphemed . . . and they repented not to give Him glory."—Far below Achan, who through the grave and gate of temporal death was (please God!) delivered from death eternal: "Joshua said unto Achan, My son, give, I pray thee, glory to the Lord God of Israel, and make confession unto Him; and tell me now what thou hast done; hide it not from me. And Achan answered Joshua, and said, Indeed I have sinned against the Lord God of Israel, and thus and thus have I done."

[But darest thou when reading of impenitence, once and again urge penitence?

Yea; because impenitence is set before us to that very end that we should repent.]

O Loving Lord Jesus, Who revealest hell that we may flee to heaven, and lest we should loose hold on Thee warnest us that souls may fall away; Thou Who on the Cross didst love saint and sinner, and on Thy Throne of Intercession lovest saints and sinners still; there is nothing but Thy Love or some fruit of Thy Love which we can plead with Thee. Such I plead. Amen.

Well spake that soldier who being asked what he would do if he became too weak to cling to Christ, answered, "Then I will pray Him to cling to me."

"The seat of the beast; and his kingdom was full of darkness."—Prefigured but only faintly by the three days' darkness in Egypt: for at that time Moses was within reach, within hearing; Moses, type of Christ, still accessible to Pharaoh. Three days, and then presumably renewal of light. And as we expressly read: "Neither rose any from his place for three days" (in strong contrast with those blinded men of doomed Sodom who wearied themselves to find the door), it suggests that the door of repentance continued open: for considering that three days' darkness by way of a spiritual parable, and connecting it with our Lord's figurative declaration: "If the blind lead the blind, both shall fall into the ditch," we are invited humbly to hope that the Egyptian darkness was by no means necessarily outer darkness; but rather in the case of impressionable souls that it shut such up awhile in a corner of safety, affording them leisure to consider their ways and become wise; to purge themselves from such blindness as by misleading or misfollowing falls into the ditch; and to watch for the morning with eyes apt and anxious to see, should God of His bounty rekindle light and sight.

"They gnawed their tongues for pain, and blasphemed . . . because of their pains and their sores."—To harden heart and stiffen neck under any chastisement predisposes towards final virulence of misery and impotence of hatred. The consummated horrible end appears as if a scorpion hedged in by fire stung itself and could not die. "Death and life are in the power of the tongue: and they that love it shall eat the fruit thereof." The power of choice is limited to time: the consequences who shall limit?

Bitter it is to long for life and die; more bitter to long for death and it cometh not. Christ in His boundless mercy preserve us through bitterness of life and from bitterness of death.

Bitterness that may turn to sweetness is better than sweetness that must turn to bitterness.

Nothing which can end is unbearable.

The lost must not shift their perdition off their own shoulders on to Satan's: their own load they must bear. Though the wretched persons of our text were subjects and confederates of the beast, yet they themselves gnawed their own tongues and plied their own tongues in blasphemy: themselves, not he.

Satan is guilty, and none the less each soul is guilty, of that same soul's death; guilt being like flame, capable of communication not of transference.

"And repented not of their deeds."—At the Fourth Vial, and now again at the Fifth, but not previously, impenitence is clearly alleged as one sin of those sinners. At the Fourth it seems characteristically a revolt of will against faith : "Men . . . blasphemed the Name of God, which hath power over these plagues: and they repented not to give Him glory." At the Fifth it seems characteristically a rebellion of flesh (the lower nature) against spirit : "They . . . blasphemed the God of heaven because of their pains and their sores, and repented not of their deeds." The result of such obduracy is differently stated in each case : first it refuses glory to God, thereby shutting the door of heaven against man; afterwards it bereaves man of his last vestige of hope, even of the bare wish to amend.

"And even as they did not like to retain God in their knowledge, God gave them over to a reprobate mind, to do those things which are not convenient. . . . Who knowing the judgment of God, that they which commit such things are worthy of death, not only do the same, but have pleasure in them that do them."

> Lord, I believe, help Thou mine unbelief :
>   Lord, I repent, help mine impenitence :
>   Hide not Thy Face from me, nor spurn me hence,
> Nor utterly despise me in my grief ;
> Nor say me nay, who worship with the thief
>   Bemoaning my so long lost innocence :—
>   Ah me ! my penitence a fresh offence,
> Too tardy and too tepid and too brief.
> Lord, must I perish, I who look to Thee ?
>   Look Thou upon me, bid me live, not die ;
>   Say "Come," say not "Depart," tho' Thou art just :
>   Yea, Lord, be mindful how out of the dust

I look to Thee while Thou dost look on me,
Thou Face to face with me and Eye to eye.

Euphrates flowed out of Eden, and (at least in its fountain head, if not after being parted into one of four) its first recorded use was to water Paradise. Its last recorded use is negative: to be dried up and afford a free passage.

Euphrates in Eden was congruous with sinless Adam: one watered, the other tilled, both obeyed.

Euphrates in the end of the world is congruous with many sons of Adam: both parched, both done away with.

Dost thou deplore the fate of high-born Euphrates? Deplore rather the fate of multitudes of higher born men. Deplore what thou hast made thyself: deprecate what thou mayest yet make thyself.

I can alone destroy myself: from myself, Good Lord, deliver me.

If the way to destruction lie open before me; from that way, Good Lord, deliver me.

Though they that be better than I destroy themselves; from self-destruction, Good Lord, deliver me.

From following a multitude to do evil, from apostasy, from depravity; Good Lord, deliver me.

From angels executing wrath; Good Lord, deliver me.

From Thyself my Judge, to Thyself my Saviour, I appeal. Good Lord, deliver me. Amen.

"The kings of the east"—Revised Version: "The kings that come from the sun rising."—With whom, whatever their purpose, the Wise Men from the east will rise up in the Judgment together.

"I saw under the sun the place of judgment, that wickedness was there; and the place of righteousness, that iniquity was there. I said in mine heart, God shall judge the righteous and the wicked: for there is a time there for every purpose and for every work."

"We must prevent the sun to give Thee thanks, and at the dayspring pray unto Thee."

"Three unclean spirits like frogs . . . are the spirits of devils, working miracles, which go forth unto the kings of the earth." — Contemptible as well as formidable: "frogs; yea even in their kings' chambers." Long before, "the magicians . . . with their enchantments . . . brought up frogs upon the land of Egypt"—brought them up, but presumably lacked power to suppress them, for Moses it was who by intercession delivered Pharaoh from that plague.

The likeness of these unclean spirits to frogs recalls our Lord's mysterious declaration : " The unclean spirit . . . walketh through dry places, seeking rest, and findeth none." Now however, they seek not rest in a dry place, but go forth to stir up war.

Vile emissaries befit vile potentates. Are all the kingdoms of the world and the glory of them to be mustered against God Almighty at the summons of three frogs ? " The harvest of the river is her revenue ; and she is a mart of nations. Be thou ashamed, O Zidon."

" Hold thy peace at the presence of the Lord God : for the day of the Lord is at hand : for the Lord hath prepared a sacrifice, He hath bid His guests. And it shall come to pass in the day of the Lord's sacrifice, that I will punish the princes, and the king's children, and all such as are clothed with strange apparel. In the same day also will I punish all those that leap on the threshold, which fill their masters' houses with violence and deceit."

Because these unclean spirits come " out of the mouth " of dragon, beast, false prophet, it should set me on my guard against all words whereby a pernicious tongue may offend. " Why boastest thou thyself, thou tyrant, that thou canst do mischief ; whereas the goodness of God endureth yet daily ? Thy tongue imagineth wickedness, and with lies thou cuttest like a sharp razor. Thou hast loved unrighteousness more than goodness, and to talk of lies more than righteousness. Thou hast loved to speak all words that may do hurt, O thou false tongue. Therefore shall God destroy thee for ever : He shall take thee, and pluck thee out of thy dwelling, and root thee out of the land of the living."

Lord, grant us grace to make Thy Goodness our trust : shutting our hearts against pride, our mouths against evil words, our ears against foul knowledge ; and using Thy gifts to the promotion of Thy Glory and of man's salvation. For His Blessed sake in Whom we have all and are full and abound, Jesus Christ. Amen.

" Behold, I come as a thief."—This or a kindred expression our Blessed Master and after Him His Apostles and Evangelists have employed repeatedly in reference to the Second Advent and ensuing Judgment Day. SS. Matthew and Luke record in great measure the same Divine words, although spoken (it seems) on two separate occasions : " Watch therefore : for ye know not what hour your Lord doth come. But know this ; that if the goodman of the house had known in what watch the thief would come, he would have watched, and would not have suffered his house to be broken up. Therefore be ye also ready: for in such an hour as ye think not the Son of Man cometh." St. Paul reminds the Thessalonians: "Yourselves know perfectly that the day of the Lord so cometh as a thief in the night. . . . But ye, brethren, are not in darkness, that that day should overtake you as a thief." St. Peter forewarns the Church Catholic: "But the day of the Lord will come as a thief in the night."

Still more striking is the likeness of our present text to part of our Lord's message to the Church in Sardis (ch. iii. 3, 4): "If therefore thou shalt not watch, I will come on thee as a thief, and thou shalt not know what hour I will come upon thee. Thou hast a few names even in Sardis which have not defiled their garments; and they shall walk with Me in white."

Blessed indeed then is he that watcheth! he shall escape overwhelming shame: yea, much more, he shall abide in eternal fellowship with Christ.

> Solomon most glorious in array
>   Put not on his glories without care :—
> Clothe us as Thy lilies of a day,
>   As the lilies thou accountest fair,
>   Lilies of Thy making,
>   Of Thy love partaking,
>   Filling with free fragrance earth and air :
> Thou Who gatherest lilies, gather us and wear.

"Armageddon"—is, I see, interpreted "The destruction of the troops," and (on the same authority) is supposed to allude to the overthrow of Sisera and his hosts before Barak and his ten thousand (*see* Judges iv. 14, 15 ; v. 19—21).

"And the seventh angel poured out his vial into the air."— I trust that since modern accuracy has not yet forbidden our speaking of sunrise and sunset, we may also venture on occasion to revive the Four Elements of my youth.

Three elements have in turn been smitten ; earth by the first vial, water by the second and third, fire (the sun) by the fourth. Then recommencing the series ; earth (perhaps, the world) by the fifth ; water (Euphrates) by the sixth : but fire (if the dragon and the spirits of devils may be assumed to represent it) musters on the contrary its rebellious force apparently for a final effort ; not recking that the kingdom and the battle and the great day are all alike "of God Almighty."

The seventh vial is poured out "into the air," that element which may be termed the vital breath both of man and of fire : and we are reminded of St. Paul's phrase : "The prince of the power of the air, the spirit that now worketh in the children of disobedience."

" And there came a great Voice out of the Temple of heaven."
—I do not know whether I perceive or merely fancy a distinction.
In previous passages (ch. xi. 19; xiv. 17; xv. 5) the Temple is spoken of as *in* heaven, the context having reference to God the Son, man's Redeemer and Judge. In this passage, "the Temple of heaven" (harmonizing with the words, " The heaven is My Throne ") might seem to speak of heaven at large as being itself that Temple ; and to do so at this point of the Revelation because the imminent Judgment and consummation will affect much more than humankind only. The Revised Version, however, by omitting the words " of heaven " precludes any such notion.

" It is done."—"God requireth that which is past."

Holy fear incites faith to humility, hope to prudence, love to obedience. Faith without humility presumes, hope without prudence misleads, love without obedience—there is no genuine love without obedience. " He that hath My commandments, and keepeth them, he it is that loveth Me," saith the Sole Fountain of Truth and Love.

> Fear, Faith, and Hope have sent their hearts above :
> Prudence, Obedience, and Humility
> Climb at their call, all scaling heaven toward Love.
> Fear hath least grace but great expediency ;
> Faith and Humility show grave and strong ;
> Prudence and Hope mount balanced equally.
> Obedience marches marshalling their throng,
> Goes first, goes last, to left hand or to right ;
> And all the six uplift a pilgrim's song.
> By day they rest not, nor they rest by night :
> While Love within them, with them, over them,
> Weans them and woos them from the dark to light.
> Each plies for staff not reed with broken stem,
> But olive branch in pledge of patient peace ;
> Till Love being theirs in New Jerusalem,
> Transfigure them to Love, and so they cease.
> Love is the sole beatitude above :
> All other graces, to their vast increase
> Of glory, look on Love and mirror Love.

" A great earthquake, such as was not since men were upon the earth."—The latter clause is perhaps a saving clause, reserving pre-Adamite convulsions of which geology (if I am not mistaken) appears to detect tremendous indications.

O Lord God Only Wise, keep us or deliver us, I beseech Thee, from ignorant assertions and ignorant denials, from confusing probabilities with certainties and opinions with beliefs.

So be it to Thy Glory and our salvation, for the honour of Jesus Christ. Amen.

"And the great city was divided into three parts."—If we may understand by this division not simply one material result of the earthquake, but also internal dissension and a splitting asunder into parties, then the "three parts" may perhaps correspond with the dragon (devil), beast (world?), false prophet (man): and we behold as in a picture that mutual hatred, inextinguishable ire, reviling, loathing, in which must end the cajoleries, befoolments, besottedness, of any congregation and assembly whose bond of union is evil deliberately chosen and finally adhered to.

"Because ye have said, We have made a covenant with death, and with hell are we at agreement. . . . Your covenant with death shall be disannulled, and your agreement with hell shall not stand."

Whatever the secondary cause, a bitter foretaste of such mutual damage befell the Philistines when of old the Lord saved Israel by the hand of Jonathan and his armour-bearer: "And there was trembling in the host, in the field, and among all the people: the garrison, and the spoilers, they also trembled, and the earth quaked: so it was a very great trembling. . . . And, behold, the multitude melted away, and they went on beating down one another. . . . And, behold, every man's sword was against his fellow, and there was a very great discomfiture."

If our Lord's "parable" spoken to certain impious Scribes and Pharisees conveyed a prophecy as well as a lesson, may not this passage of the Apocalypse be reverently studied in connection with it?—"If a kingdom be divided against itself, that kingdom cannot stand. And if a house be divided against itself, that house cannot stand. And if Satan rise up against himself, and be divided, he cannot stand, but hath an end."

"And great Babylon came in remembrance before God, to give unto her the cup of the wine of the fierceness of His wrath."—Great Babylon incurs but the greater destruction: better was it for "little" Zoar than for its neighbour cities in the day of retribution. Ill fares it with him that layeth up treasure for himself and is not rich toward God.

"And every island fled away, and the mountains were not found."—"I beheld the earth, and, lo, it was without form, and void; and the heavens, and they had no light. I beheld the mountains, and, lo, they trembled, and all the hills moved lightly. I beheld, and, lo, there was no man, and all the birds of the heavens were fled. I beheld, and, lo, the fruitful place was a wilderness, and all the cities thereof were broken down at the presence of the Lord, and by His fierce anger."

"And there fell upon men a great hail out of heaven . . . and men blasphemed God."—Jeremiah dwelling on the prolonged agony which in his day wrung Jerusalem, declared: "The punishment of the iniquity of the daughter of my people is greater than the punishment of the sin of Sodom, that was overthrown as in a moment, and no hands stayed on her." Incomparably great is the woe beheld by St. John, when extension of time is abused to enhance provocation: for in Jeremiah's experience some men even in extremity may so have numbered their days as to apply their hearts unto saving wisdom.

This crushing hail recalls the corresponding Egyptian plague: but then a shelter was provided; not so now.

Man's extremity is God's opportunity: so long as this proverb holds good true extremity has not been reached. But Wisdom has forewarned man of such extremity: "Because I have called, and ye refused; I have stretched out My hand, and no man regarded; but ye have set at nought all My counsel, and would none of My reproof: I also will laugh at your calamity; I will mock when your fear cometh; when your fear cometh as desolation, and your destruction cometh as a whirlwind; when distress and anguish cometh upon you. Then shall they call upon Me, but I will not answer; they shall seek Me early, but they shall not find Me: for that they hated knowledge, and did not choose the fear of the Lord: they would none of My counsel: they despised all My reproof. Therefore shall they eat of the fruit of their own way, and be filled with their own devices."

Divine gifts are called by our Master "talents." Every gift must turn to the recipient's impoverishment, unless it be so used as to secure the true riches: of goodly talents misused nothing will at last remain but as it were the avenging weight. First, gift; afterwards, reward or penalty: they all equally come "out of heaven."

"Every stone about the weight of a talent":—of a talent I have done amiss with, or done nothing with. God forbid.

"Thus saith the Lord of hosts: Consider your ways. Ye have sown much, and bring in little; ye eat, but ye have not enough; ye drink, but ye are not filled with drink; ye clothe you, but there is none warm; and he that earneth wages, earneth wages to put it into a bag with holes. Thus saith the Lord of hosts; Consider your ways."

CHAPTER XVII

1. **And there came one of the seven angels which had the seven vials, and talked with me, saying unto me, Come hither; I will shew unto thee the judgment of the great whore that sitteth upon many waters:**
2. **With whom the kings of the earth have committed fornication, and the inhabitants of the earth have been made drunk with the wine of her fornication.**

As to its subject, the vision of this chapter does not in order of time appear to follow passages which more or less remotely precede it; but rather to be at least partially simultaneous, elucidatory, and so to say parenthetical. The very words "Babylon is fallen" (ch. xiv. 8), "Great Babylon came in remembrance" (ch. xvi. 19), show that her existence antedates either mention of her. So far then it becomes conjecturable that this present chapter will exhibit a traceable connection with previous portions of the Apocalypse; will, as it were, fit into what we have already studied.

Lord, Who by Thy Most Holy Spirit hast inspired Thy Prophets to speak and to write Thy word, grant us by help of the Same Spirit to study that blessed word which for each of us contains an individual lesson. Give us one by one grace to learn our own lesson, neither vexing nor envying one another; but so imbued with wisdom that we may become pure, peaceable, gentle, easy to be intreated, full of mercy and good fruits, void of partiality and hypocrisy, sowing righteousness in peace while we make peace. For our Peacemaker's sake, Jesus Christ. Amen.

Isaiah instructs us how profitably to contemplate God's judgments, while putting our whole trust in Him and honouring His Holy Name and His word: "Thou wilt keep him in perfect peace, whose mind is stayed on Thee: because he trusteth in Thee. Trust ye in the Lord for ever: for in the Lord Jehovah is everlasting strength. For He bringeth down them that dwell on high; the lofty city, He layeth it low; He layeth it low, even to the ground; He bringeth it even to the dust. . . . Yea, in the way of Thy judgments, O Lord, have we waited for Thee; the desire of our soul is to Thy Name, and to the remembrance of Thee. With my soul have I desired Thee in the night; yea, with my spirit within me will I seek Thee early: for when Thy judgments are in the earth, the inhabitants of the world will learn righteousness."

Far from being necessarily an insurmountable disadvantage, I think that ignorance of the historical drift of prophecy may on occasion turn to a humble but genuine profit. Such ignorance entails (or wisely utilized might entail) that a general lesson, a fundamental principle, essence not accident, will be elicited from the abstruse text. Further:—instead of attention being directed to the ends of the earth, our eye must be turned within; elsewhere at a future moment additional light will doubtless be vouchsafed, but for the present the message is delivered pointedly to ourselves; as when "there fell a voice from heaven, saying, O king Nebuchadnezzar, to thee it is spoken";—and could no more be evaded than could that other message; "I have an errand to thee, O captain. . . . Unto which of all us? . . . To thee."

Wherefore "one of the Seven Angels" talks with *me*, saying: "Come hither; I will shew unto thee. . . ." And what he shows me (at any rate) amounts to the vileness and ruinousness of idolatrous defection in every form subtle or gross. Assume what shape it may, its nature remains the same: kings may idolize all the kingdoms of the world and the glory of them; whilst subjects bow down to wealth, influence, fame, genius, beauty, or even to success. But under one aspect or other the sin infects "kings of the earth" and "inhabitants of the earth"; and whilst mighty men shall be mightily tormented, the meaner sort cannot go unpunished.

The First and Second Commandments concur to forbid idolatry: misplaced preference breaks the First, misdirected worship the Second. The first holds out neither threat nor promise, neither reward nor punishment: it is one, simple, featureless, absolute; and being equally incumbent upon all rational beings, addresses man on his spiritual side, not taking account of the earthy. The Second commands, but it also reasons: it sets before man his own interest, adjures him for his children's sake, deters him by a threat, allures him by a promise; remembers whereof he is made, and appeals to him both as flesh and as spirit. Perhaps even the Fifth Commandment is less persuasively formulated than the Second : the Fifth guarantees a contingent blessing to ourself, the Second to our cherished "thousands." And even in the appalling entail of contingent judgment "upon the children, unto the third and fourth generation," a door of hope, howbeit of a trembling hope, remains open, when we turn to a Divine exposition of mercy and judgment; for by the mouth of Ezekiel the Lord God deigned to refute the Jewish proverb, "The fathers have eaten sour grapes, and the children's teeth are set on edge," and to declare concerning a hypothetical heinous offender : "Now, lo, if he beget a son, that seeth all his father's sins which he hath done, and considereth, and doeth not such like, that . . . hath executed My judgments, hath walked in My statutes ; he shall not die for the iniquity of his father, he shall surely live." Thus the second generation can by righteous obedience in some measure retrieve the error of the first, thereby recovering mercy as an inheritance to his posterity ; so that (may we not hope ?) even the visiting upon them of their more remote forefathers' sins will be so far reversed as to help them, if they choose, to walk humbly. To the next of kin appertained a twofold office : as avenger of blood he executed judgment, as nearest in blood he filled the vacant place. Moreover though the fathers may not, yet may the children take courage and rejoice in their grievous liability because of Christ-likeness : for Christ was born for this very end, that on Him might be visited the iniquity of father Adam and of all mankind.

I suppose it is no exaggeration to say that every sin, fleshly or spiritual, is a sin of idolatry, inasmuch as it is the preference of some object tangible or intangible to God All Good : indeed further reflection recognizes sin as simply the preference of *self* to God ; self-pleasing, self-will, self-indulgence, self in a word, being the universal lure. St. Paul brands covetousness as idolatry : thus the First, Second and Tenth Commandments concur in forbidding idolatry ; whilst to break any of the remaining seven involves a breach of the spirit common to all.

If three Commandments out of Ten be explicit, and if the other seven implicit against one and the same wickedness, let us pray to be delivered and evermore kept safe from the wide-spread snare without and from the foolhardy traitor within :—

From love that cleaveth not to Thee,
From worship that waiteth not on Thee,
From a tongue that extolleth not Thee,
From labour and rest that serve not Thee,

From defrauding Thy representatives of honour,
From defacing Thine image,
From defiling Thy temple,
From misappropriating Thy gifts,
From perverting Thy truth,
From lust of that which shall pass away,
   Good Lord, deliver us.
 Wanderings of heart,
Crookedness of intention,
Unsanctified speech,
Vain labour, slothful rest,
Disrespect and stubbornness,
Hasty spirit and hasty hand,
Corrupt eye,
Grasping fingers,
False tongue,
Evil covetousness,
   Forgive to us, O Lord.   Good Lord, amend us.   Amen.

What would move me to love one who loved me?—If he sacrificed himself for me, changed places with me that I might be safe, impoverished himself to discharge my ruinous debts, preferred me at every turn to himself, bore and shared my griefs, planned and wrought for my happiness, earned and laid up treasure for me, remembered me when I forgot him and myself, put me on the best robe when I had shamed him, and a ring after I had deserted him, won back for me alienated friends, released me from bonds on his own suretyship, sought me where I was straying among quicksands, found me, carried me, rejoiced over me.

What can withhold me from loving such an One Who loveth me?

Lord, give me love that I may love Thee much,
  Yea, give me love that I may love Thee more,
  And all for love may worship and adore
And touch Thee with love's consecrated touch.
I halt to-day ; be love my cheerful crutch,
  My feet to plod, some day my wings to soar :
  Some day ; but, Lord, not any day before
Thou call me perfect having made me such.
This is a day of love, a day of sorrow,
  Love tempering sorrow to a sort of bliss ;
    A day that shortens while we call it long :
A longer day of love will dawn to-morrow,
  A longer, brighter, lovelier day than this,
    Endless, all love, no sorrow, but a song.

3. So he carried me away in the spirit into the wilderness: and I saw a woman sit upon a scarlet-coloured beast, full of names of blasphemy, having seven heads and ten horns.

He who exhibits is an angel, and he who inspects is a saint :
yet does this exalted pair betake themselves into "the wilderness," there and not elsewhere to set themselves face to face
with an impersonation of abominable wickedness. So likewise
did their and our Divine Master do when He deigned to confront Satan. And if the Standard Bearer among ten thousand,
and if the flower of His armies did thus, it leaves us an example
that we should tread in their steps.

Some innocent souls there are who from cradle to grave
remain as it were veiled and cloistered from knowledge of evil.
As pearls in their native deep, as flower-buds under Alpine snow,
they abide unsullied : the lot has fallen unto them in a fair
ground. But for most persons contact with evil and consequent knowledge of evil being unavoidable, is clearly so far
ordained : they must achieve a more difficult sanctity, touching
pitch yet continuing clean, enduring evil communications yet
without corruption of good manners.

To each such imperilled soul, Angel and Apostle here set a
pattern. If we too would gaze unscathed and undefiled on
wickedness, let us not seek for enchantments, but set our face
toward the wilderness. Strip sin bare from voluptuousness
of music, fascination of gesture, entrancement of the stage,
rapture of poetry, glamour of eloquence, seduction of imagina-
tive emotion ; strip it of every adornment, let it stand out bald
as in the Ten stern Commandments. Study sin, when study it
we must, not as a relishing pastime, but as an embittering
deterrent. Lavish sympathy on the sinner, never on the sin.
Say, if we will and if we mean it, Would God I had died for
thee : nevertheless let us flee at the cry of such, lest the earth
swallow us up also.

Wherever the serpent is tolerated there is sure to be dust for
his pasture : he finds or he makes a desolate wilderness of
what was as the Garden of Eden. Only an illusion, a mirage,
can cause a barren desert to appear in our eyes as a city of
palaces, an orchard of fruits.

This woman Babylon sits upon a scarlet beast, it appears
not whether as upon a throne or as upon a chariot : if a throne,
steadfast in evil ; if a chariot, swift unto perdition. Moreover,
in a former verse we read of her as sitting "upon many
waters " : a point to be noted further on.

The woman and the beast by a foul congruity seem to make
up a sort of oneness, after the fashion of a snail and its shell.
If she removes he is the motor ; she is lifted aloft to the
extent of his height ; her stability depends on his. In semblance
he is her slave, in reality her master.

4. And the woman was arrayed in purple and scarlet
   colour, and decked with gold and precious stones and
   pearls, having a golden cup in her hand full of abominations and filthiness of her fornication :
5. And upon her forehead was a name written, Mystery,
   Babylon the Great, The Mother of Harlots and Abominations of the Earth.

The beast is scarlet, and the woman wears scarlet. He is
full of names of blasphemy, and her names are of the same
sort.

He is scarlet as sin. She is both scarlet and particoloured,
decked with such gauds as St. Paul warns us women against.
As it seemed possible to study the sun-clothed exalted Woman
(ch. xii.) as a figure of the all-glorious destiny awaiting the
Virtuous Woman, so now I think this obscene woman may (on
the surface) be studied as illustrating the particular foulness,
degradation, loathsomeness, to which a perverse rebellious
woman because feminine not masculine is liable.

Execrable, for aught we know, as any devil, beast, man, of
them all, the resources and so to say the tactics of Babylon
differ from theirs : she and they proceed to a common goal by
distinct paths. They have (such as it is) counsel and strength
for war : she less astute in counsel, less hardy in war, makes of
her own self a trap, a bait, a ruinous prize. She seduces, not
coerces. She tyrannizes by influence, not by might. Filthy
she is, but she proffers filthiness in a golden cup. No heart
of husband safely trusts in her, no children arise up and call
her blessed : vile mother is she of vile daughters, all alike be-
dizened, perfumed, debased to hell; all alike blood-suckers,
as we read : " The horseleach hath two daughters, crying,
Give, give."

Some have opined that a woman's wickedness even exceeds
that of a man ; as Jezebel stirred up Ahab, and Herodias out-
stripped Herod on feet swift to shed blood. But this point
must stand over for decision to the Judgment of that Only
Judge to whom each and all of us will one day stand or fall.
Solomon meanwhile by warning man against woman has virtually warned woman against herself : " When wisdom entereth
into thine heart, and knowledge is pleasant unto thy soul; discretion shall preserve thee, understanding shall keep thee. . . .
To deliver thee from the strange woman, even from the
stranger which flattereth with her words ; which forsaketh the
guide of her youth, and forgetteth the covenant of her God.
For her house inclineth unto death, and her paths unto the

dead. None that go unto her return again, neither take they hold of the paths of life ":—"The lips of a strange woman drop as an honeycomb, and her mouth is smoother than oil: but her end is bitter as wormwood, sharp as a two-edged sword. Her feet go down to death; her steps take hold on hell. Lest thou shouldest ponder the path of life, her ways are moveable, that thou canst not know them ":—"A foolish woman is clamourous: she is simple, and knoweth nothing. For she sitteth at the door of her house, on a seat in the high places of the city, to call passengers who go right on their ways: Whoso is simple, let him turn in hither. . . . But he knoweth not that the dead are there; and that her guests are in the depths of hell."

Our Mothers, lovely women pitiful ;
  Our Sisters, gracious in their life and death ;
  To us each unforgotten memory saith
"Learn as we learned in life's sufficient school,
Work as we worked in patience of our rule,
  Walk as we walked much less by sight than faith,
  Hope as we hoped despite our slips and scathe,
Fearful in joy and confident in dule."
I know not if they see us or can see :
  But if they see us in our painful day,
    How looking back to earth from Paradise
    Do tears not gather in those loving eyes ?—
  Ah, happy eyes ! whose tears are wiped away
Whether or not you bear to look on me.

" Upon her forehead was a name written, Mystery . . . "— The mystery is announced to all; but is ·not explained to all, if to any.

Intelligence may be required of some : faith is required of all.

Is it disappointing to be restricted to faith? Faith, the grace, is a higher endowment than intelligence, the gift.

A revealed unexplained mystery is (as it were) my Tree of Knowledge accessible whilst forbidden ; a theme for prayer, not a bait for curiosity. Ignorance by virtue of good will takes rank as a part of obedience.

To be of one mind with God is universal knowledge in embryo.

6. And I saw the woman drunken with the blood of the saints, and with the blood of the martyrs of Jesus : and when I saw her, I wondered with great admiration.

Whatever evil power confronts us under this figure of Babylon, she, in some degree, corresponds in temper with such rich men as St. James addresses; which correspondence as with a redoubled alarum urges whosoever will be saved to choose if not actual poverty at least not riches: "Go to now, ye rich men, weep and howl for your miseries that shall come upon you. Your riches are corrupted, and your garments are motheaten. Your gold and silver is cankered; and the rust of them shall be a witness against you, and shall eat your flesh as it were fire. Ye have heaped treasure together for the last days. . . . Ye have lived in pleasure on earth, and been wanton; ye have nourished your hearts, as in a day of slaughter. Ye have condemned and killed the just; and he doth not resist you. Be patient therefore, brethren, unto the coming of the Lord."

> Crimson as the rubies, crimson as the roses,
>   Crimson as the sinking sun,
> Singing on his crimsoned bed each saint reposes,
>   Fought his fight, his battle won;
> Till the rosy east the day of days discloses
>   All his work save waiting done.
>
> Far above the stars while underneath the daisies,
>   Resting for his race is run,
> Unto Thee his heart each quiet saint upraises,
>   God the Father, Spirit, Son;
> Unto Thee his heart, unto Thee his praises,
>   O Lord God the Three in One.

St. John "wondered with great admiration" at what he beheld.

Deliver us, I beseech Thee, Good Lord Jesus, from indifferentism, superciliousness, shallow judgments, crooked judgments; from curiosity without faith, superstition instead of faith, opinions subversive of faith. For whatsoever is not of faith is sin, and without faith it is impossible to please God. To Whom, O Lord, in Thine all-gracious, well-beloved Self, bring us near and make us well pleasing. Amen.

7. And the Angel said unto me, Wherefore didst thou marvel? I will tell thee the mystery of the woman, and of the beast that carrieth her, which hath the seven heads and ten horns.

The voice of conscience echoing the angelic question, asks reader after reader, Wherefore didst thou marvel? Athenian curiosity of old was eager to hear some new thing, and readily inquired concerning "certain strange things," promulgated by inspired lips; but in the end some mocked, some postponed investigation, few it seems were converted and clave to the truth. Of these timely wise few we know one man by name, Dionysius, the Areopagite, and one woman, Damaris: and to this very day the Word of God, quick, and powerful, and sharper than any two-edged sword, divides the new man from the old man, Dionysius and Damaris from their fellows.

Thou art or art not as Dionysius: I am or am not as Damaris. God Most Merciful, imbue us with such love of the truth, that being likeminded we may have the same love, and desiring the sincere milk of the word may grow thereby. For Christ's sake. Amen.

God reveals what He pleases, as much as He pleases, no more than He pleases. The faithful soul is as Issachar: he secs that the land is pleasant, and bowing down rests between his burdens.

> 8. **The beast that thou sawest was, and is not; and shall ascend out of the bottomless pit, and go into perdition: and they that dwell on the earth shall wonder, whose names were not written in the book of life from the foundation of the world, when they behold the beast that was, and is not, and yet is.**

(If I may venture so far out of my depth—) This seems by various indications to be the very beast which St. John saw rise up out of the sea (ch. xiii.). If it be the same, in the present chapter (ver. 3) for the first time is its colour defined as scarlet : yet since at its former appearing the red dragon gave it "his power, and his seat, and great authority," it seems not incongruous to surmise that such foul dominion may have been expressed by the imperial scarlet colour.

If it be the same beast, then we discern how the woman can sit at once on the sea beast and on "many waters" (ver. 1). Though all be symbolic, the symbols may presumably harmonize. (It follows not, however, that I can harmonize them.)

Moreover the "woman" whom now of a sudden we encounter: have we under a different aspect already met her? Chapter xiii. exhibits various points of apparent correspondence with the present chapter. Besides the sea beast, it clearly mentions the dragon, and an earth beast : which three monsters (assuming the earth beast to be identical with the false prophet of ch. xix. 20) are destroyed further on (ch. xix. 20; xx. 10), and thus are accounted for and done with. With them, like them, yet not the same as any of them, appears "an image" (ch. xiii. 14, 15) of the sea beast, itself instinct with at least a semblance of hideous life, endowed with the faculty of speech, moved apparently by an impious and perhaps an independent volition. Can this *image* be a diverse presentment of the *woman*? So much in the kingdom of darkness seems an awful mockery of the Divine Kingdom, that I think the image and woman assume a possible interchangeableness when we recall St. Paul's sentence: "A man . . . is the image and glory of God : but the woman is the glory of the man."

That this woman does in an appreciable degree resemble the beast which carries her has, I think, transpired. And whilst the end of the image, as such, is not revealed, that of the woman is made abundantly clear.

Each symbol suggests thought, however the veiled reality may elude discovery. Interpretation is the gift of some, thought of all. Lack of interpretation dispenses not from the duty of thought.

"And shall ascend out of the bottomless pit, and go into perdition."—The Revised Version expresses with vividness imminence and movement : "And is about to come up out of the abyss, and to go into perdition." St. John witnessed such a rising out of the sea as before narrated, whether or not both passages refer to the same incident. If the same, the substance of this present vision seems authoritatively displaced from its apparent order of time.

"And they that dwell on the earth shall wonder."—Recalling the words of Habakkuk as quoted by St. Paul: " Behold, ye despisers, and wonder, and perish."

"Whose names were not written in the Book of Life from the foundation of the world " :— or as in the Revised Version : " They whose name hath not been written in the Book of Life from the foundation of the world." — Although the two translations can (I think) be understood in precisely the same sense, I yet feel or fancy a possible difference betwixt them : the Authorized Version conveying the idea of election and predestination once for all and irreversible ; the Revised, of a period of probation and contingent election from the foundation of the world onwards.

"The beast that was, and is not, and yet is."—

O Lord Jesus Christ, Who changest not, but art the Same yesterday and to-day and for ever, support us in all dangers and carry us through all temptations. From open and secret foes, from snares and pitfalls, Good Lord, deliver us.

9. And here is the mind which hath wisdom. The seven heads are seven mountains, on which the woman sitteth.

So teach us to number our days that we may apply our hearts unto wisdom; that we may receive the instruction of wisdom, justice and judgment and equity. O Lord, Who givest wisdom, Who layest up sound wisdom for the righteous; teach us in the way of wisdom, lead us in right paths. Furnish our lips with wisdom: let us not die for want of wisdom. Grant us wisdom with the just, the lowly, the well advised; that with the prudent we may understand our way, and ceasing from our own wisdom may learn of Thee, Lord Jesus Christ our Wisdom. Amen.

The Virtuous Woman whose price is far above rubies "openeth her mouth with wisdom; and in her tongue is the law of kindness." Wisdom, then, associates with kindness: to cultivate kindness is to frequent the society of wisdom. A clue especially vouchsafed to us women.

I observe that while to Moses celestial patterns were displayed and on him was poured the radiance of direct revelation; and that whereas "Bezaleel and Aholiab, and every wise-hearted man, in whom the Lord put wisdom and understanding to know how to work all manner of work for the service of the sanctuary," so wrought: "all the women that were wise-hearted did spin with their hands, and brought that which they had spun, both of blue, and of purple, and of scarlet, and of fine linen. And all the women whose heart stirred them up in wisdom spun goats' hair." Thus coverings, curtains, veils, were assigned to the women: to the men those sacred things enshrined beneath and within.

So long as he or she who "standeth without" can hear the Bridegroom's Voice, surely it is joy fulfilled.

"The seven heads are seven mountains, on which the woman sitteth."—The interpretation lies above and beyond my range: the symbol conveys a lesson.

Mortal life is, so to say, a tissue of sevens; and each seven must be guarded against the fascination of that World whereof "the woman" (be she ultimately what she may) exhibits characteristics.

Guard, so far as in thee lieth, innocence in infancy, reverence in childhood, holiness in youth, aspiration in maturity, patience on the decline, perseverance in age, hope in death. Is it too late for thyself? Then guard them in others: and as to thyself, at least redeem the remaining time from waste and snatch thy grave from desecration. Guard others and thyself against that world which defiles innocence by contact, substitutes foolhardiness and false shame for reverence, violates

holiness, paralyzes aspiration ; which breeds selfishness instead
of patience, frivolity instead of perseverance; which is too
corrupt, too dead, too twice dead for hope in death. And
whilst the seven stages of life compose thus a sort of week,
each stage is itself composed of weeks of days, seven within
seven, seven after seven, each and all needing the Gift of
Sevenfold Grace to consecrate labours and hallow rest.

Yet as St. Paul exhorts not his converts to go out of the
world, but to act rightly in it ; and much more as our Divine
Master offering up His High Priestly Prayer spake, saying :
" I pray not that Thou shouldest take them out of the world,
but that Thou shouldest keep them from the evil,"— let us
not be afraid of her terror, but sanctify the Lord God in our
hearts. We cannot prevent the World's besetting, haunting,
overshadowing us : only let us not suffer her to *sit down*.

Dante in the Divina Commedia (*see* my sister's *A Shadow
of Dante*) tells us how he " dreamed of a woman stammering,
squinting, lame of foot, maimed of hands, and ashy pale. He
gazed on her, and lo ! under his gaze her form straightened,
her face flushed, her tongue loosed to the Siren's song."

> Foul is she and ill-favoured, set askew :
>   Gaze not upon her till thou dream her fair,
>   Lest she should mesh thee in her wanton hair,
> Adept in arts grown old yet ever new.
> Her heart lusts not for love, but thro' and thro'
>   For blood, as spotted panther lusts in lair ;
>   No wine is in her cup, but filth is there
> Unutterable, with plagues hid out of view.
> Gaze not upon her ; for her dancing whirl
>   Turns giddy the fixed gazer presently :
> Gaze not upon her, lest thou be as she
>   When at the far end of her long desire
> Her scarlet vest and gold and gem and pearl
>   And she amid her pomp are set on fire.

" Seven heads . . . seven mountains "—seven deadly sins :
these sustain the World, and the World fosters these. High
crested Pride, volcanic Anger, smooth sloped Lust, overhanging
Envy, undermined Avarice, swine pasturing Gluttony, landslip
Sloth. A dark continent of spiritual geography.

**10. And there are seven kings : five are fallen, and one is
and the other is not yet come ; and when he cometh,
he must continue a short space.**

From evil rulers and pernicious laws, from obeying man by
disobeying God, from misusing our short space, for short is our
space, .   Good Lord, save us :

Lest we become as a plant that buds not, as a bud that blows not, as a flower that fruits not, in our short space until the harvest, our only space.

11. And the beast that was, and is not, even he is the eighth, and is of the seven, and goeth into perdition.

From comradeship with devils and disciples of devils, from persisting in sin and passing away into perdition,

Good Lord, save us :

Lest it had been better for us never to have been born, never to have known the way of life, never to have heard of Thee by the hearing of the ear, never to have beheld the Kingdom of Heaven set open to all believers.

12. And the ten horns which thou sawest are ten kings, which have received no kingdom as yet; but receive power as kings one hour with the beast.

From selling our birthright for a mess of pottage, from bartering eternity for one hour,

Good Lord, save us :

Lest we receive our good things in this life, and after that be tormented.

13. These have one mind, and shall give their power and strength unto the beast.

From the counsel and deed of them,

Good Lord, save us :

Lest we spend money for that which is not bread, and our labour for that which satisfieth not.

14. These shall make war with the Lamb, and the Lamb shall overcome them: for He is Lord of lords, and King of kings: and they that are with Him are called, and chosen, and faithful.

From choosing the evil and refusing the good, from setting ourselves in no good way, from the tactics of Balak and the end of Balaam, Good Lord, save us :

Lest we who are dust set ourselves in the balance against Thee : and lo ! we are dust in the balance.

15. And he saith unto me, The waters which thou sawest, where the whore sitteth, are peoples, and multitudes, and nations, and tongues.

From following a multitude to do evil, from sinful compliances, from saving our life but not with Thy salvation,

Good Lord, save us :

Lest amid multitudinous glory and pomp and rejoicing we be put to open shame and perish together.

16. And the ten horns which thou sawest upon the beast, these shall hate the whore, and shall make her desolate and naked, and shall eat her flesh, and burn her with fire.

From such hatred of sin as is not love of righteousness, from hating not sin but sinners, from casting the stone of condemnation whereby we condemn ourselves,
Good Lord, save us:
Lest out of our own mouth we be condemned where there is no respect of persons.

17. For God hath put in their hearts to fulfil His will, and to agree, and give their kingdom unto the beast, until the words of God shall be fulfilled.

From fulfilling a Divine behest in the spirit of rebellious Absalom, apostate Jeroboam, bloodthirsty Edom, Caiaphas harder than flint,
Good Lord, save us:
Lest in us be fulfilled that other word also: "Depart from Me, ye cursed, into everlasting fire, prepared for the devil and his angels."

18. And the woman which thou sawest is that great city, which reigneth over the kings of the earth.

From the lust of the flesh and the lust of the eyes and the pride of life, from foreheads of brass and hearts of stone,
Good Lord, save us:
Lest in the end we be past renewing unto salvation, and there be none to save us.
Yea, Good Lord, save us. Amen.
"And there are seven kings."—The Revised Version preserves this reading marginally, whilst the text gives: "And they [*i. e.* the 'mountains' mentioned in the previous verse] are seven kings." Suggesting a many-sided significance in at least one of the images employed: if in one, perhaps in others. For here the original figure is "seven heads" *mountains* and *kings* alike belong to the angelic interpretation.
"And the beast . . . even he is the eighth, and is of the seven":—in the Revised Version "... is himself also an eighth, . . ."—As moral goodness or depravity finds expression in the face, whilst the seat of life is the heart; so a seven-

headed monster may infuse into every head his own hideous vitality, whilst each head acts independently of its fellows as mouthpiece and intelligent agent to the abominable animating principle. Perhaps the beast's being "also an eighth" may inspire a dread that in the final death-struggle of Satan against Christ, wickedness superhuman or subhuman (whichever it should be termed) will take the field openly and visibly ; and will act in person, as well as through the instrumentality of its miserable mortal allies.

The seven heads have not only the beast for a basis, but have moreover the seated woman for a superincumbent load : the one detaches them from earth, the goodness of nature ; the other blocks them out from the sky, the goodness of grace.

I think not as interpretation but as meditation such thoughts may spring from the text.

Have we sought great things for ourselves ? Seek them not. Ten kings receive authority, but it is with the beast, and for one hour. "Yea, even like as a dream when one awaketh."

"The Lamb shall overcome them : for He is Lord of lords, and King of kings."—Although both the Lion and the Lamb are titles belonging to our Lord, here in the day of battle we read of Him as the Lamb, not as the Lion. Whatever inscrutable reasons there may be for this choice of a designation, one or two obvious ones suggest themselves. Thus is accomplished one of the Beatitudes : "Blessed are the meek : for they shall inherit the earth." Thus Christ in His own adorable Person heads the army of those who "out of weakness were made strong, waxed valiant in fight, turned to flight the armies of the aliens." Thus "the weakness of God" stands forth as "stronger than men." "Not by might, nor by power, but by My Spirit, saith the Lord of hosts." And thus also by a condescension of grace, Jael, a certain woman (*see* Judges ix. 53), Esther, Judith, become figures illustrative of like truth.

Weakness, however, is not *as* weakness this more than conqueror. Our Redeemer's weakness was rather the triumph of His strength, because to become weak and work mightily through weakness He laid aside His strength and kept it in abeyance. Our weakness, if it is to win a victory, must include a voluntary element ; at the least so far as to will in concert with the Divine Will, and never to have recourse to illicit weapons.

And I think that in these days of women's self-assertion and avowed rivalry with men, I do well to bear in mind that in a contest no stronger proof of superiority can be given on either side than the *not* bringing into action all available force. As yet, I suppose, we women claim no more than equality with our brethren in head and heart: whilst as to physical force, we scout it as unworthy to arbitrate between the opposed camps. Men on their side do not scout physical force, but let it be.

Does either man or woman doubt where superiority resides, when at chess one player discards a pawn in favour of the other?

Society may be personified as a human figure whose right hand is man, whose left woman; in one sense equal, in another sense unequal. The right hand is labourer, acquirer, achiever: the left hand helps, but has little independence, and is more apt at carrying than at executing. The right hand runs the risks, fights the battles: the left hand abides in comparative quiet and safety; except (a material exception) that in the *mutual* relations of the twain it is in some ways far more liable to undergo than to inflict hurt, to be cut (for instance) than to cut.

Rules admit of and are proved by exceptions. There are left-handed people, and there may arise a left-handed society!

> Content to come, content to go,
> Content to wrestle or to race,
> Content to know or not to know,
> Each in his place;
>
> Lord, grant us grace to love Thee so
> That glad of heart and glad of face
> At last we may sit high or low
> Each in his place:
>
> Where pleasures flow as rivers flow,
> And loss has left no barren trace,
> And all that are, are perfect so
> Each in his place.

"And they that are with Him are called, and chosen, and faithful":—or according to the Revised Version: "And they also shall overcome that are with Him, called and chosen and faithful":—thus, towards the end, sending thought back to the beginning, to the ever-recurring "overcometh" of the Messages to the Seven Churches, that "overcometh" on which depends each consummating benediction.

God of His free Love calls and chooses: man's faithfulness certifies the call, until by overcoming he crowns all by final perseverance.

Lord Jesus, give us hearing ears, responsive wills, some fear, much faith, much hope, most love.

"'The waters . . . where the whore sitteth, are peoples, and multitudes, and nations, and tongues."—"Raging waves of the sea, foaming out their own shame."

"The ten horns which thou sawest upon the beast, these shall hate the whore."—The Revised Version supplies a noticeable variation: "The ten horns . . . and the beast, these shall hate . . . ," thus uniting all in one close confederacy, as in ver. 13 *ante:* "These have one mind, and shall give their power and strength unto the beast."

Whatever further the wise may elicit from this passage and its sequel, even the foolish may deduce somewhat. The kingdom of the beast is essentially unalterably a kingdom of hatred, hatred underlying any and every appearance of its spurious love: sift such love, and the residuum will be hatred. In the day of her foul attractiveness the lost woman was idol, mistress, plaything: in the day of her decay she becomes a prey, and there is none to help her. The drunken with blood must herself be devoured.

Evil may subserve evil, yet be overruled for good. Thus the horns spring from the beast, and in their turn give their kingdom unto the beast: wherefore? because "God hath put in their hearts to fulfil His Will."

"The woman . . . is that great city, which reigneth over the kings of the earth."—"Without controversy" who then, what then, is she?

She seems to include or invite all which tempts man at his earthly proudest and mightiest: ambition shedding blood as water, with garments rolled in blood scarlet as her array; enervating luxury, as she herself sits inert on her scarlet beast; sensual excess foul as her cup; licence that is not liberty, but is chains and fetters like her bravery of gold and pearls and precious stones. Woe to her dupes! "Lo, this is the man that made not God his strength; but trusted in the abundance of his riches, and strengthened himself in his wickedness."

Such as this, then, is she. From all this and from whatsoever besides she may be, may we every one of us great or small be delivered. Amen.

CHAPTER XVIII

1. And after these things I saw another angel come down from heaven, having great power; and the earth was lightened with his glory.

If chapter xvii. may be treated as parenthetical, the present chapter appears to supply a sequel to chapter xvi., and particularly to ver. 19 of that chapter.

St. John beheld and recognized a frequent recurrence of Angels : here one, there seven, there again ten thousand times ten thousand, and thousands of thousands. What he records affords a presumption of what may encompass or cross my own path any day, any hour. I ought not to imagine omens or supernatural indications with rashness; yet neither ought I to feel positive that the rainbow I discern has no connection with an Angel. I discern not, or that the blaze which appears to be lightning may not dart from a descending Angel.

Great St. John knew; and unfolds his knowledge in order that others should reverently surmise things they know not. "That which had not been told them shall they see; and that which they had not heard shall they consider."

2. And he cried mightily with a strong voice, saying, Babylon the great is fallen, is fallen, and is become the habitation of devils, and the hold of every foul spirit, and a cage of every unclean and hateful bird.

Compare "The burden of Babylon, which Isaiah the son of Amoz did see. . . . Babylon, the glory of kingdoms, the beauty of the Chaldees' excellency, shall be as when God overthrew Sodom and Gomorrah. It shall never be inhabited, neither shall it be dwelt in from generation to generation : neither shall the Arabian pitch tent there; neither shall the shepherds make their fold there. But wild beasts of the desert shall lie there; and their houses shall be full of doleful creatures; and owls shall dwell there, and satyrs shall dance there. And the wild beasts of the islands shall cry in their desolate houses, and dragons in their pleasant palaces : and her time is near to come, and her days shall not be prolonged."

Is not this great Babylon? is it not also a hell? For what but a hell can be "the habitation of devils?" If they find not a hell they make one.

The Revised Version writes "hold" (a second time) instead of "cage"; and as a marginal alternative proposes in each instance "prison" : according to which it might appear that even foul spirits and unclean and hateful birds consort with the fallen mother of luxury not of free will but by constraint. Devils (Revised Version : "demons") her inhabitants are perhaps at home in her.

Shall I choose my good things here? or hereafter?

Shall I choose sweet that turns to bitterness? or bitter that turns to sweetness?

Shall I choose life that leads to death? or death that leads to life?

Shall I choose . . . nay : what am I choosing?

> I peered within, and saw a world of sin :
> Upward, and saw a world of righteousness :
> Downward, and saw darkness and flame begin
> Which no man can express.
>
> I girt me up, I gat me up to flee
> From face of darkness and devouring flame :
> And fled I had, but guilt is loading me
> With dust of death and shame.
>
> Yet still the light of righteousness l eams pure,
> Beams to me from the world of far-off day :—
> Lord, Who hast called them happy that endure,
> Lord, make me such as they.

3. For all nations have drunk of the wine of the wrath of her fornication, and the kings of the earth have committed fornication with her, and the merchants of the earth are waxed rich through the abundance of her delicacies.

"All nations . . . kings . . . merchants."—Her spell has been cast upon them all.

So far, then, all are alike : yet it may be that in guilt they are not altogether alike. The first class, *nations* (which indeed includes both kings and merchants), have more or less "as natural brute beasts" succumbed to her seductions. *Kings*, in the position to exercise a royally untrammelled choice, have of free will and voluntary preference wallowed in her company.

Merchants substituting gain for godliness have trafficked in her gauds, dealt in her poisons, filled their purses by help of her abominations; and thus ruining others, have ruined themselves both at first and at second hand.

The *national* sin illustrates what nature may lapse to divorced from grace. The *regal* sin, how far more perilous it is to sit high than to sit low. The *sordid* sin, how easily those who will be rich fall into temptation and a snare. "Corrupt are they, and have done abominable iniquity : there is none that doeth good. God looked down from heaven upon the children of men, to see if there were any that did understand, that did seek God. Every one of them is gone back : they are altogether become filthy; there is none that doeth good, no, not one."

4. **And I heard another voice from heaven, saying, Come out of her, My people, that ye be not partakers of her sins, and that ye receive not of her plagues.**
5. **For her sins have reached unto heaven, and God hath remembered her iniquities.**

"Woe to her that is filthy and polluted, to the oppressing city ! She obeyed not the voice; she received not correction."

A "Voice from heaven."—Alas ! that oftentimes I have not heard, have not heeded, have not obeyed, have not returned thanks. Lord, forgive me.

"Come out of her."—Alas ! that oftentimes I have sat still, have looked back, have not escaped for my life, have not fled to the mountain, have not praised the Lord for His Goodness. Lord, forgive me.

"My people."—Alas ! that when Thou hast chosen me, many times I have not chosen Thee. Lord, forgive me.

"That ye be not partakers of her sins."—Alas ! that I have ere now if not now walked in the counsel of the ungodly, have stood in the way of sinners, have sat in the seat of the scornful. Lord, forgive me.

"That ye receive not of her plagues."—Alas ! that I have been afraid where no fear was, that I have fled when no man pursued, but have not put my whole trust in God, nor honoured Thee my Father, nor feared Thee my Master. Lord, forgive me.

"Her sins have reached unto heaven."—Alas ! that when Thou hast looked for judgment, behold oppression ; for righteousness, behold a cry. Lord, forgive us.

"God hath remembered her iniquities."—Alas, Lord ! According to Thy lovingkindnesses, according unto the multitude of Thy tender mercies, blot out our transgressions, blot out all our iniquities. Lord, forgive us.

God the Father, God the Son, God the Holy Spirit, forgive us. I plead the Blood of Jesus Christ Who took away the handwriting that was against us, nailing it to His Cross. Amen.

6. Reward her even as she rewarded you, and double unto her double according to her works: in the cup which she hath filled fill to her double.

The Revised Version furnishes a variation of the first clause: "Render unto her even as she rendered." By thus omitting the pronoun *you*, the precept seems no longer so pointedly addressed to the once persecuted faithful, but simply to form part of a sentence of condemnation which the Strong Lord God Alone pronounces upon her directly from Himself without specification of secondary agency.

I write under correction,—but whilst I recollect that Angels are mentioned as executing final Divine Judgment on human kind, I recollect not that men are thus unequivocally mentioned in regard to their fellow-men; although the saints are to *judge* the world and to judge angels, as St. Paul intimates to the Corinthian Church. All saints are to sympathize indeed with the triumph of good over evil, but not with their own hands (?) to set fire to the great pile. "He shall take them away as with a whirlwind, both living, and in His wrath. The righteous shall rejoice when he seeth the vengeance: he shall wash his feet in the blood of the wicked. So that a man shall say, Verily there is a reward for the righteous: verily He is a God that judgeth in the earth."

A secondary human agent indeed there is, a human second cause in every man's penalty: the selfsame man himself.

For similarly: what reward is the foul woman to receive? such as she gave. Her own works are to be doubled unto her, her own cup is to be filled double to her.

Obstinate disobedience sifted, meted, weighed, is the unerring measure of that vengeance which God measures to it.

Utmost obedience is no measure of that blessing wherewith God overfills and overflows any measure.

"Wherefore doth a living man complain, a man for the punishment of his sins? Let us search and try our ways, and turn again to the Lord. Let us lift up our heart with our hands unto God in the heavens."

7. **How much she hath glorified** herself, and lived deliciously, **so** much torment and sorrow give her : for she
· saith in her heart, I sit a queen, and am no widow, and
shall see no sorrow.

8. **Therefore** shall her plagues come in one day, death, and
mourning, and famine ; and she shall be utterly burned
with fire : for strong is the Lord God Who judgeth
her.

Because this type of transcendent wickedness is presented
under the feminine aspect, doubtless we women may elicit
thence our own appropriate lesson.   When we behold gauds
and frivolities go up toward heaven in smoke of hell, they
become a beacon fire to warn us from making shipwreck be it
on a mudbank of vileness or on a curious reef of luxury.
Scant comfort would it be to perish, though on a very miracle
of beauty.

"Moreover the Lord saith, Because the daughters of Zion
are haughty, and walk with stretched forth necks and wanton
eyes, walking and mincing as they go, and making a tinkling
with their feet. . . .   The Lord will take away the bravery of
their tinkling ornaments about their feet, and their cauls, and
their round tires like the moon, the chains, and the bracelets,
and the mufflers, the bonnets, and the ornaments of the legs,
and the headbands, and the tablets, and the earrings, the rings,
and nose jewels, the changeable suits of apparel, and the
mantles, and the wimples, and the crisping pins, the glasses,
and the fine linen, and the hoods, and the vails.   And it shall
come to pass, that instead of sweet smell there shall be stink ;
and instead of a girdle a rent ; and instead of well set hair
baldness ; and instead of a stomacher a girding of sackcloth ;
and burning instead of beauty."

"How much she hath glorified herself. . . ."—On the other
hand, who would choose to live and die inglorious ? and who
shall glorify us, if we ourselves achieve not glory.   No mere
surface glory though it stream down from heaven can abide :
were Coniah the signet upon God's right hand, yet would
wickedness pluck him thence.   Moses in his sanctity illustrates
the difference between outward albeit genuine glory, and glory
everlasting, assimilated, inalienable : he comes forth from the
earthly Tabernacle of the Divine Presence, and the glory of his
countenance fades away ; he reappears from the unseen world
" in glory " on the Mount of the Transfiguration, changed from
glory to glory, clothed upon with glory.   The all glorious

within can afford to wait patiently for clothing of wrought gold.

O Soul insatiable of glory, covet earnestly the best gifts, pursue them along the more excellent way. Barter not for Cleopatra's dissolving pearl the pearls which are entrance-gates to New Jerusalem; for Dives's sumptuous daily fare the marriage-supper of eternity; for black tents of Kedar the curtains of Solomon; for Nabal to-day, David to-morrow; for what hath been told us, that whereof the half hath not been told us; for sight of eye, and hearing of ear, and heart's present desire, that which eye hath not seen nor ear heard, neither hath entered into the heart of man.

Crouch lowest to spring highest. Disperse abroad and give to the poor, so shall thy riches make themselves wings and fly away as eagles toward heaven. Strip off thine ornaments now, that they may become chains about thy neck hereafter. To-night turn from the west in its fading purple, and set thy face steadfastly toward the east, where out of darkness golden glory and roses of a dawn that sets not will be revealed.

Dear Brother, dear Sister, God grant thee such grace, and deny it not to me. For Jesus' sake. Amen.

"In one day, death, and mourning, and famine."—At once corpse and mourner: a famishing corpse. It recalls Zechariah's awful prediction: "And this shall be the plague wherewith the Lord will smite all the people that have fought against Jerusalem; Their flesh shall consume away while they stand upon their feet, and their eyes shall consume away in their holes, and their tongue shall consume away in their mouth."

> "I sit a queen, and am no widow, and shall see no sorrow"—
> Yea, scarlet woman, to-day : but not yea at all to-morrow.
> Scarlet queen on a scarlet throne all to-day without sorrow,
> Bethink thee : to-day must end ; there is no end of to-morrow.

O Strong Lord God, Who judgest her and wilt judge all mankind, grant to the exalted humility, to the desolate thankfulness, to the happy sympathy with sorrow; that so earthly eminence may become a stepping-stone to heavenly heights, and loneliness may introduce to the full communion of saints, and joy blossoming in time may bear eternal fruit. Be we high or low, prosperous or depressed, wheresoever, whatsoever we be, make us and evermore keep us well pleasing in Thy sight. Through Jesus Christ our Lord. Amen.

9. And the kings of the earth, who have committed fornication and lived deliciously with her, shall bewail her,

D D

and lament for her, when they shall see the smoke of
her burning,

10. Standing afar off for the fear of her torment, saying,
Alas, alas, that great city Babylon, that mighty city!
for in one hour is thy judgment come.

"It is better to trust in the Lord than to put confidence in
man. It is better to trust in the Lord than to put confidence
in princes."

"Put not your trust in princes, nor in the son of man, in
whom there is no help." Least of all in wicked men can there
be any help.

Adam seems not to have found one word to plead for Eve in
the terrible hour of judgment.

To-day is the day of helpfulness : the Day of Doom will be
a day of helplessness. Moreover, the relative attitude of the
righteous and the wicked as now it exists will then be
reversed.

Now they are the wicked who stand callous amidst the fears,
torments, miseries of others; not investigating human claims,
not mourning with them that mourn, not moving burdens with
one of their fingers, not heeding the burning questions of their
day, neighbourhood, nay sometimes of their own hearths.
Now they are the righteous who quake in horrible fear for the
ungodly, and all but enter within the vortex of evil in rescue
work, and cry out, Alas the pity of it! over perishing souls,
and with Christ-like tears bewail the impenitent; saying, How
often would I, and ye would not.

Then it will be the obdurate wicked who weep and lament,
having reached the end of softness and sweetness, beholding
the lap of their luxury set on fire, foretasting in that perdition
their own perdition. *Then* it will be the righteous who of one
mind, will, desire, with God All-Holy, at the execution of His
sentence become as it were "Yea and Amen" to His Glory:
of old all His promises have been unto His glory and unto
them "Yea and Amen" in Christ; and now they themselves
shine forth and glow as reflections of the Just Judge, renewed
in His image, perfected in His likeness.

STANDING AFAR OFF FOR THE FEAR OF HER TORMENT.

Is this the end? is there no end but this?
  Yea, none beside :
  No other end for pride
And foulness and besottedness.

Hath she no friend? hath she no clinging friend?
Nay, none at all :
Who stare upon her fall,
Quake for themselves with hair on end.
Will she be done away? vanish away?
Yea, like a dream ;
Yea, like the shades that seem
Somewhat, and lo ! are nought by day.
Alas for her amid man's helpless moan,
Alas for her !
She hath no comforter :
In solitude of fire she sits alone.

"In one hour is thy judgment come."—"Sit thou silent, and get thee into darkness, O daughter of the Chaldeans : for thou shalt no more be called, The lady of kingdoms. . . . And thou saidst, I shall be a lady for ever : so that thou didst not lay these things to thy heart, neither didst remember the latter end of it. Therefore hear now this, thou that art given to pleasures, that dwellest carelessly, that sayest in thine heart, I am, and none else beside me ; I shall not sit as a widow, neither shall I know the loss of children : but these two things shall come to thee in a moment in one day, the loss of children, and widowhood : they shall come upon thee in their perfection for the multitude of thy sorceries, and for the great abundance of thine enchantments."—"Flee out of the midst of Babylon, and deliver every man his soul : be not cut off in her iniquity ; for this is the time of the Lord's vengeance ; He will render unto her a recompence. Babylon hath been a golden cup in the Lord's hand, that made all the earth drunken : the nations have drunken of her wine ; therefore the nations are mad. Babylon is suddenly fallen and destroyed : howl for her ; take balm for her pain, if so be she may be healed. We would have healed Babylon, but she is not healed : forsake her, and let us go every one into his own country : for her judgment reacheth unto heaven, and is lifted up even to the skies."

11. And the merchants of the earth shall weep and mourn over her ; for no man buyeth their merchandise any more.

Those *kings* did at least bewail Babylon for herself : these *merchants* bewail her because of their own impoverishment. They all alike are "of the earth," yet is there a finer and a coarser clay.

Only I must beware of reckoning that sympathy with evil *in itself* is nobler than sympathy with evil *in its effects*. Neither is nobler : one may be baser. From both, O Lord, deliver us.

12. The merchandise of gold, and silver, and precious stones, and of pearls, and fine linen, and purple, and silk, and scarlet, and all thyine wood, and all manner vessels of ivory, and all manner vessels of most precious wood, and of brass, and iron, and marble,

13. And cinnamon, and odours, and ointments, and frankincense, and wine, and oil, and fine flour, and wheat, and beasts, and sheep, and horses, and chariots, and slaves, and souls of men.

"A man's life consisteth not in the abundance of the things which he possesseth." We know that it is so now : we shall see that it is so then. If either, his death rather than his life consisteth in such.

"Brethren, the time is short: it remaineth," that they that buy be "as though they possessed not ; and they that use this world, as not abusing it : for the fashion of this world passeth away."

Yet on the same principle that we are bidden redeem the time because the days are evil, Christians find ways to redeem these other creatures despite their evil tendency. Gold and silver they lend unto the Lord : He will pay them again. Precious stones and pearls they dedicate to the service of His Altar. With fine linen, purple, silk, scarlet, they invest His Sanctuary ; and fragrant "thyine" wood they carve delicately for its further adornment. Vessels of ivory, of most precious wood, of brass, iron, marble, are refined to serve as lavers, ennobled to become alms coffers or alms dishes. They burn cinnamon, odours (the Revised Version for "odours" gives "spice and incense"), frankincense, for a sweet savour in the Divine Presence. Wine, fine flour, wheat, constitute their most pure Oblation. With ointments and oil they comfort Christ in His beloved sick members. With beasts and sheep they spread a feast for His poor. On horses and in chariots they carry His Gospel afar. And ministering rather than being ministered unto, they tend bodies and travail for souls. (For "slaves" the margin gives as literal "bodies.")

"The glory of the Lord shall endure for ever: the Lord shall rejoice in His works."

Whoso has the spirit of Elijah, though his horse and chariot have come up out of Egypt, yet shall they receive virtue as "of fire" to forward him on his heavenward course. And this despite a horse being but a vain thing to save a man.

14. And the fruits that thy soul lusted after are departed

> from thee, and all things which were dainty and goodly are departed from thee, and thou shalt find them no more at all.

Or according to the Revised Version: "And the fruits which thy soul lusted after are gone from thee, and all things that were dainty and sumptuous are perished from thee, and men shall find them no more at all":— reminding us of St. Paul's words to the Colossians: ". . . The rudiments of the world . . . (Touch not; taste not; handle not; which all are to perish with the using)."

As regards the second clause of the doom (*in this verse*), the two Versions suggest each its own sense. The Authorized, as if those objects of desire may have been not destroyed but withdrawn whilst the craving remains insatiable. According to both texts the loss appears absolute, final, irreparable; but (collating the two) that which *departs* instead of *perishing* leaves behind it in addition to the agony of loss the hankering, corroding misery of absence.

> 15. The merchants of these things, which were made rich by her, shall stand afar off for the fear of her torment, weeping and wailing,
> 16. And saying, Alas, alas, that great city, that was clothed in fine linen, and purple, and scarlet, and decked with gold, and precious stones, and pearls!
> 17. For in one hour so great riches is come to nought. And every shipmaster, and all the company in ships, and sailors, and as many as trade by sea, stood afar off,

This desolation which we have not yet seen must one day be seen. Meanwhile we have known preludes, rehearsals, foretastes of such as this: so that looking back through the centuries we may take up our lamentation and say :—

Alas Sodom once full of bread! From empty fulness, Good Lord, deliver us.

Alas Tyre whose merchants were princes! From riches but not toward God, Good Lord, deliver us.

Alas the man whose barns sufficed not! From heart and hands shut close, Good Lord, deliver us.

Alas Dives clothed in purple and fine linen! From remediless destitution, Good Lord, deliver us.

And looking forward we may say :—

Alas any whom the unknown day and hour find unprepared! From the folly of the foolish virgins, Good Lord, deliver us.

And looking around us trembling we needs must say :—

Alas England full of luxuries and thronged by stinted poor, whose merchants are princes and whose dealings crooked, whose packed storehouses stand amid bare homes, whose gorgeous array has rags for neighbours! From a canker in our gold and silver, from a moth in our garments, from blasted crops, from dwindling substance, from righteous retribution abasing us among the nations, Good Lord, deliver us. Amen.

18. And cried when they saw the smoke of her burning, saying, What city is like unto this great city!

If any shipmasters and crews, sailors and sea-traders, have yet to lament and quake, well may arrogant England amid her seas quake and lament betimes.

"What city is like unto this great city!"—Like what she was, like what she is: her present tallying with her past.

For purposes of probation height and depth are at once distinguishable and continuous: man, the probationer set midway between their extremities, has it within his option to reclaim either from the other. Probation over, height and depth, whilst still of two aspects, will yet form one evidently undivided sequence; to the summit or to the base of which consummated man has worked his way. And why not all the baptized to the summit? "Ye did run well; who did hinder you that ye should not obey the truth?"

19. And they cast dust on their heads, and cried, weeping and wailing, saying, Alas, alas, that great city, wherein were made rich all that had ships in the sea by reason of her costliness! for in one hour is she made desolate.

To cast dust on the head with penitence attests death unto sin. To cast dust on the head with impenitence prefigures the second death.

Sin conducts all to one goal. The land sinner finds dust in plenty; the seafaring sinner shall inherit dust enough.

Thank God, ample provision is stored for every penitent wheresoever and whatsoever: dust, ashes, are ready to hand for all.

Lord, array us in spiritual sackcloth, that by penitence we may bear witness to Thy Goodness.

20. Rejoice over her, thou heaven, and ye holy apostles and prophets; for God hath avenged you on her.

In the Revised Version: "Rejoice over her, thou heaven,

and ye saints, and ye apostles, and ye prophets; for God hath judged your judgment on her."

This second rendering endears itself to us all the more because in it we meet with simple "saints," saints of any shade or degree. All are not "apostles" or "prophets," neither can be: "heaven" suggests (for the time being) the exceeding nobility of the ninefold angelic host, too exalted for the Church's fellowship during her prolonged exile. But high and low, rich and poor, young and old, great and small meet together as "saints" in a general beatitude; not one is absent, overlooked, forgotten.

Behold them at last! All His saints are in His hand, He has kept their feet, they are rejoicing in goodness, singing unto the Lord, loving the Lord, fearing the Lord but without torment, gathered together unto Him, a congregation, an assembly, their souls preserved, their death precious in His sight, shouting aloud for joy, blessing God Who is their praise, joyful in glory, every one honourable, having attained unto the kingdom. Behold saints from Lydda, beloved ones of God called to be saints from Rome, poor saints from Jerusalem, saints known to us by name and other saints with them, saints from Achaia, from Ephesus, all in Christ Jesus from Philippi; now fellow-citizens of no mean city, partakers of the inheritance in light. "My love be with you all in Christ Jesus. Amen."

The hills are tipped with sunshine, while I walk
In shadows dim and cold:
The unawakened rose sleeps on her stalk
In a bud's fold,
Until the sun flood all the world with gold.

The hills are crowned with glory, and the glow
Flows widening down apace:
Unto the sunny hill-tops I, set low,
Lift a tired face,—
Ah, happy rose, content to wait for grace!

How tired a face, how tired a brain, how tired
A heart I lift, who long
For something never felt but still desired;
Sunshine and song—
Song where the choirs of sunny heaven stand choired.

21. And a mighty angel took up a stone like a great millstone, and cast it into the sea, saying, Thus with violence shall that great city Babylon be thrown down, and shall be found no more at all.

So of old Noah beheld the whole wicked world "like a

great millstone" vanish beneath the flood. So after Lot fled, the cities of the plain "salted with fire" were superseded by the Dead Sea. So the Red Sea swallowed up the strength of Egypt. [I am aware that a different site has been proposed for the cities of the plain, and that I only follow one opinion.]

"We have heard with our ears, O God, our fathers have told us, what work Thou didst in their days, in the times of old."

The deed of this "mighty Angel" seems at first sight inimitable by man. Yet ponder our Lord's injunction to the Twelve: "Have faith in God. For verily I say unto you, That whosoever shall say unto this mountain, Be thou removed, and be thou cast into the sea; and shall not doubt in his heart, but shall believe that those things which he saith shall come to pass; he shall have whatsoever he saith ":—sacred words which besides any literal promise doubtless convey a profound spiritual lesson.

Feeling our way amongst these Apocalyptic symbols, these mysteries of life and death, we observe the mother of abominations and mistress of kings and peoples seated upon seven mountains; dark mountains whereon our feet stumble. The darkness conceals much, but not all. For so long as there are seven stumbling-blocks (well known, alas! to most of us) upholding and upheld by the world,—overtopping Pride, Anger flaming and fuming in the face of heaven, Gluttony bloated as a toad in a stone, Lust a slippery precipice, Avarice hard as a flint, Envy barren as peaks above the snow-line, Sloth deadly as sleep amid that snow,—by labouring to remove these stumbling-blocks from our own heavenward path, and so far as in us lies from our neighbour's, we can and shall do somewhat towards undermining the throne of the world. "Who art thou, O great mountain?" Before faith working by prayer thou shalt be swept away. "He that is slow to anger is better than the mighty; and he that ruleth his spirit than he that taketh a city ":—thus may any earnest person help to take, and taking to overthrow, Babylon. Moreover, by aspiring to become that which "is better," we shall also one by one take another city, a city which hath foundations, and wherein we may abide for ever.

O Lord God, Whose Strength is sufficient for all who lay hold on it, grant us in Thee to comfort our hearts and be strong. Humility, meekness, temperance, purity, large-heartedness, sympathy, zeal, grant us these evidences of faith, handmaids of hope, fruits of love. For the sake of Jesus

Christ our Strength, our Righteousness, our Hope of gloiy. Amen.

This great lewd Babylon which "shall be found no more at all," becomes (whatever else she may be) a figure to us of strong temptation : harassing, persistent, insistent, all but irresistible to-day ; to-morrow nothing.

It is not merely that the world will be abolished ; my own temptation from the world must end in one of two ways : either I shall have sunk below any pleasures, or I shall have risen above polluting pleasures. If only I could realize to practical purpose that even long-drawn incessant temptation is yet not interminable.

What is this above thy head,
  O Man ?—
The World, all overspread
With pearls and golden rays
And gems ablaze ;
A sight which day and night
  Fills an eye's span.

What is she while time is time,
  O Man ?—
In a perpetual prime
Beauty and youth she hath ;
And her footpath
Breeds flowers thro' dancing hours
  Since time began.

What is this beneath thy feet,
  O Saint ?—
The World, a nauseous sweet
Puffed up and perishing ;
A hollow thing,
A lie, a vanity,
  Tinsel and paint.

While time lengthens what is she,
  O Saint ?—
Nought : yea, all men shall see
How she is nought at all,
When her death pall
Of fire ends their desire
  And brands her taint.

Ah, poor Man, befooled and slow
  And faint !
Ah, poorest Man, if so
Thou turn thy back on bliss
And choose amiss !
For thou art choosing now :
  Sinner,—or Saint.

22. And the voice of harpers, and musicians, and of pipers, and trumpeters, shall be heard no more at all in thee ; and no craftsman, of whatsoever craft he be, shall be found any more in thee ; and the sound of a millstone shall be heard no more at all in thee ;

23. And the light of a candle shall shine no more at all in thee ; and the voice of the bridegroom and of the bride shall be heard no more at all in thee : for thy merchants were the great men of the earth ; for by thy sorceries were all nations deceived.

No more in Babylon. But in New Jerusalem we shall hear once more (God grant it !) the voice of harpers harping with their harps.

.No more in Babylon. But in New Jerusalem we shall behold once more (God grant it!) every craftsman of whatsoever craft who hath wrought a good work toward Christ or toward His disciples.

No more in Babylon. But in New Jerusalem we shall rejoice (God grant it!) with some taken from grinding at the mill while others were left.

No more in Babylon. But in New Jerusalem (God grant it!) we shall walk in the light that has no need of a candle.

No more in Babylon. But in New Jerusalem we shall keep high festival (God grant it!) with bridegrooms and brides reunited in the communion of saints and fellowship of angels.

No more in Babylon. But in New Jerusalem (God grant it!) we shall exult amongst the company of merchantmen who once sold all for the treasure field or for the pearl of great price.

God grant it to every one of us, for Jesus Christ's sake. Amen.

" . . . No more at all in thee."—Whether the enumerated multitude has been involved and for ever silenced in the ruin of Babylon, or whether it has clean escaped among those legions of whom the world was not worthy, in either contingency one faculty common to all has saved or lost each : free will.

Not Nemesis, Destiny, Predestination, hast cast the lot : man's own free will has been the factor of good or of evil.

Lord God Almighty, Who hast promised to Thy servants deliverance from their enemies, much more deliver us, I implore Thee, from ourselves. We, only we, can destroy ourselves : Thou, Thou alone canst rescue and save us. I plead our Saviour Jesus. Amen.

From all kinds of music which worship an idol in Thy stead,
From craft which fashioning a golden image dishonoureth Thee,
From labour for the meat which perisheth and not for that which endureth
  unto life eternal,
From lamps going out, gone out ; from any light that shineth not to the
  glory of our Heavenly Father,
From such temporal love and joy as forfeit eternal love and joy,
From earthly gain which is heavenly loss,
From the whole world in exchange for our souls,
             Deliver us, deliver all men, O Lord.   Amen.

24. And in her was found the blood of prophets, and of saints, and of all that were slain upon the earth.

" O earth, cover not thou my blood, and let my cry have no

place. Also now, behold, my witness is in heaven, and my record is on high."—" O daughter of Babylon, who art to be destroyed."

Well may the virgin, the daughter of Zion, despise and laugh to scorn her adversary; well may the daughter of Jerusalem shake her head at her.

Yet so long as time lasts, probation lasts; and so long as probation lasts, the end of individuals is not assured. It were folly to boast in girding on the harness, or at any moment short of putting it off. ·

Because he is not a Jew which is one outwardly, but he only which is one inwardly, the Church militant here in earth must still give diligence to make her calling and election sure. All her members must : each must.

It is awe-striking to observe the similarity between our Lord's accusation against the Jerusalem of His mortal day, and this final allegation against lost Babylon. In both cases a surface life overlaid a deep-seated death.

"Then spake Jesus. . . . Wherefore, behold, I send unto you prophets, and wise men, and scribes : and some of them ye shall kill and crucify; and some of them shall ye scourge in your synagogues, and persecute them from city to city : that upon you may come all the righteous blood shed upon the earth, from the blood of righteous Abel unto the blood of Zacharias son of Barachias, whom ye slew between the temple and the altar. Verily I say unto you, All these things shall come upon this generation. O Jerusalem, Jerusalem, thou that killest the prophets, and stonest them which are sent unto thee. . . . "

" Of all that were slain upon the earth."—Since no exception is made, may we understand not the immortal righteous. only, but the twice dead unrighteous also, *all* ? Her smooth words have been very swords, and her tender mercies cruel. Her hatred slays bodies, her love souls : better her hatred than her love.

From both, Good Lord, deliver us.

CHAPTER XIX.

1. And after these things I heard a great voice of much people in heaven, saying, Alleluia; Salvation, and glory, and honour, and power, unto the Lord our God:
2. For true and righteous are His judgments: for He hath judged the great whore, which did corrupt the earth with her fornication, and hath avenged the blood of His servants at her hand.

While a great voice of earth uplifts Alas! (ch. xviii. 10, &c.) the "great voice" of heaven will uplift Alleluia. Even now already it is so, whether or not we have ears to hear. One laments, the other exults, over the selfsame doom.

The prefixed day will come upon all the earth. With one or other company, I in the flesh or in the spirit shall then be saying Alas! or Alleluia!

What shall I say then? Presumably the same substantially as I am saying now.

At present, if I utter not Alas! I as it were am feeling Alas for disappointment, pain, trouble, anxiety, weariness, failure. For these and for such as these I may feel it perchance unblamed: yet only perchance: each grievance and each pang must be tested and brought to the light ere safely I can acquit myself. Disappointment should not dishearten, nor pain exasperate, nor trouble overwhelm, nor anxiety sour, nor weariness exhaust, nor failure hinder me. Verily I dare not acquit myself.

Moreover my Alleluias, when and wherefore come they? Few, cold, tearful, far between; more like the high octave of Alas than is seemly; too unlike the peaceful song of saints.

> Alleluia! or Alas! my heart is crying :—
> So yours is sighing :
> Or replying with content undying,
>   Alleluia!

> Alas ! grieves overmuch for pain that is ending,
> Hurt that is mending,
> Life descending soon to be ascending,
> Alleluia !

"I will consider Thy testimonies. I see that all things come to an end : but Thy commandment is exceeding broad."

When amid the luminous obscurity of prophecy insight fails, obedience remains. "I see that all things come to an end": yet see it not in such wise as to forecast times and seasons, modes and details. None the less things better than these lie within my scope : already I can ascribe to my God all "glory and honour" of every dispensation or event; I can long after His salvation, rely upon His power and goodness, justify His judgments, divorce my heart from perverse sympathies, cast in my lot come what may with His servants.

I can, or I cannot, already do all this. If I can, the term of my mortal life will not exhaust such gracious employments : if I cannot, the same term will be wholesomely spent in acquiring so blessed a temper.

In hope and fear, glory and abasement, honour and dishonour, power and weakness; by purifying and ruling our sympathies, recognizing and magnifying Thy judgments, loving and emulating Thy faithful servants; while evermore we wait patiently for Thee, O Lord, and for Thy salvation; give us grace to cry Alleluia, through Jesus Christ to the Glory of God the Father. Amen.

> I lift mine eyes to see : earth vanisheth.
> I lift up wistful eyes and bow my knee :
> Trembling, bowed down, and face to face with Death,
> I lift mine eyes to see.
>
> Lo, what I see is Death that shadows me :
> Yet whilst I, seeing, draw a shuddering breath,
> Death like a mist grows rare perceptibly.
>
> Beyond the darkness light, beyond the scathe
> Healing, beyond the Cross a palm-branch tree,
> Beyond Death Life, on evidence of faith :
> I lift mine eyes to see.

3. And again they said, Alleluia. And her smoke rose up for ever and ever.

If Amen did not appear and reappear in the celestial vocabulary, one might have supposed that Alleluia had taken its place. As it is, both words being at once terrestrial and celestial, link earth to heaven: here Amen prevails, there Alleluia.

It emphasizes to our apprehension the momentous difference between eternity and time, to read that "her smoke rose up for ever and ever." Throughout time smoke is an emblem of transitoriness, evanescence, as both the Canonical Scriptures and the Apocryphal Books teach us :—"As smoke is driven away, so drive them away"—"My days are consumed like smoke"—"They shall be . . . as the smoke out of the chimney "—"The breath in our nostrils is as smoke "—"The hope of the ungodly is like . . . as the smoke which is dispersed here and there with a tempest."

Time with all its possibilities is yet a day when that which is wanting cannot be numbered. Eternity with all its impossibilities is yet the day when God will require that which is past.

4. And the four and twenty elders and the four beasts fell down and worshipped God that sat on the throne, saying, Amen; Alleluia.

Whatever else varies, one condition abides invariable : the heavenly host is absolutely at one with God Omnipotent in will, choice, approval, pleasure. The Free Will of the Creator and the free will of the creature, in heaven coalesce in one eternal concord, one indissoluble harmony. Nevertheless from first to last (so far as *last* can be predicated of aught which ends not) both wills were and are and will be free.

Free will is the foundation of heaven. Free will at the opposite pole is the basis of hell. Free will may not elect hell *per se*, but by rejecting God it leaves itself no other alternative. Perhaps hell may even be the least degree of ruin compatible with man's dogged, unwavering freedom of choice. Not of course that he chooses it purposely ; only virtually, by repudiating whatever is not hell or hellish.

If man has a right to his free will, so also has God to His. "He hath shewed thee, O man, what is good."

5. And a voice came out of the throne, saying, Praise our God, all ye His servants, and ye that fear Him, both small and great.

The little one has become a thousand, and the small one a strong nation : the zeal of the Lord of hosts hath done this.

A very dear and saintly person years ago called home, once in my hearing exulted at this appearance of the small that fear God : viewing it as a vast encouragement. Even they will be there, not on sufferance, but taken account of, brought forward, called upon to enhance the acceptable rapture.

O Loving Lamb of God, Who for love of us didst sacrifice

all which Thou couldest sacrifice, cast out envy from our hearts and fill them with love like Thine.

That in the day of rejoicing we one and all may rejoice with Thee in the Communion of Saints, by virtue of love like Thine.

That Apostles, Prophets, Patriarchs, Martyrs, all Saints, even ourselves also, may love one another for pure love of Thee : yea, with love like Thine.

That the great rich in tenderness, and the small rich in veneration, may praise Thee each for other, overflowing with love like Thine.

That as heaven is heaven to Thee because of love, so it may be heaven to every one of us because of love, of love like Thine.

That we who can carry away nothing when we die, may yet carry love from earth to heaven, love in its measure like Thine.

That thither works may follow us, works of love, even of love like Thine.

And to the end that there we may superabound in love, grant us here to abound in love, in love like Thine. Amen. Alleluia.

> The least, if so I am ;
> If so, less than the least,
> May I reach heaven to glorify the Lamb,
> And sit down at the Feast.
> I fear and I am small, .
> Whence am I of good cheer :
> For I who hear Thy call, have heard Thee call
> To Thee the small who fear.

6. And I heard as it were the voice of a great multitude, and as the voice of many waters, and as the voice of mighty thunderings, saying, Alleluia: for the Lord God Omnipotent reigneth.

Hearken to music of the deaf whose spirit was not deaf, and a song of the dumb whose heart was not dumb; for in this chorus all the redeemed, whatever their sometime gift or blemish, sing together. Deafness, dumbness, every imperfection has been left behind with the dust of death ; and God hath put a new song into all mouths, even a thanksgiving unto our God. "Many shall see it, and fear ; and shall put their trust in the Lord." (Lord, so be it for Jesu's sake.)

May I be one of those wise master singers ! If *then* I would be so, *now* I must become so. The talents vouchsafed me I must use and improve thankfully ; the gifts withheld I must forego ungrudgingly and thankfully.

O Lord my God the Omnipotent, Who searchest all hearts ; Who knowest my heart through and through ; Who in many

hearts discernest lifelong disappointment, mortification, aching
rankling soreness; O Lord our God, grant us such grace that
Thy Will may be to us glory and Thine award satisfaction;
so in our solitary place shall we be glad, awaiting that day of
days when patient mourners shall come forth in the dances of
them that make merry. Amen, for the honour of Jesus Christ,
Who for our sake exhausted human bitterness.

If reverently I may say so :—In the Bible God condescends
to employ multiform overtures of endearing graciousness,
wooing, beseeching, alluring, encouraging. We love beauty;
He lavishes beauty on the sacred text. We desire knowledge;
He tells us much, and promises that one day He will tell us
all. We are conscious of feelings inexpressible and as yet
insatiable; He stirs up such feelings, at once directing them
and guaranteeing their ultimate satisfaction. He works upon
us by what we can and by what we cannot utter; He appeals
in us to what we can and to what we cannot define.

Whence it seems to ensue that not only words and thoughts
compose such a commentary on Revelation as may lawfully
be brought by man for his offering of firstfruits; but that
painting, sculpture, music, all are sources capable of swelling
that store.

Without cavilling or doubt then let us worship God in
wordless aspiration aroused by any form of beauty, let us
praise Him in musical yearnings and ecstasies. Or if not thou,
at least I; who remember how one highly endowed by nature
and by grace and by me èver to be venerated, was affected by
one movement in the overwhelming harmony of the Hallelujah
Chorus.

> When wickedness is broken as a tree
>   Paradise comes to light, ah holy land !
>   Whence death has vanished like a shifting sand
> And barrenness is banished with the sea.
> Its bulwarks are salvation fully manned,
>   All gems it hath for glad variety,
>   And pearls for pureness radiant glimmeringly,
> And gold for grandeur where all good is grand.
> An inner ring of saints meets linked above,
>   And linked of angels is an outer ring :
>   For voice of waters or for thunders' voice
>   Lo ! harps and songs wherewith all saints rejoice,
>   And all the trembling there of any string
> Is but a trembling of enraptured love.

**7. Let us be glad and rejoice, and give honour to Him; for
the marriage of the Lamb is come, and His wife hath
made herself ready.**

Let us meanwhile "be glad and rejoice, and give honour to Him," because this which shall come will come, and will not tarry.

As God brought Eve to Adam, so now is He bringing each pure and lovely soul to Christ. As He conducted fair Rebekah to Isaac unseen yet the chosen of her heart, so is He now calling and guiding the elect to Christ. As Jacob loved and served for Rachel, so and much more Christ loves His own, and will accept no different guerdon. As Joseph amid home joys forgot his toil, so Christ makes no account of His toil in comparison with the love of His beloved. As Moses was first champion, then husband; even such Christ is and will be to every sanctified soul. As Moses sang and Miriam answered, so will there be "the song of the Lamb," and the responsive adoring song of the Church. As Moses prayed for leprous Miriam, so is Christ now interceding for the heirs of salvation. As the daughters of Zelophehad were espoused by their near kinsmen, so to blessed souls Christ deigns to say, "My sister, My spouse." As at Achsah's request Caleb bestowed on her water-springs, so does our Heavenly Father reserve "a pure River of Water of Life" for them who ask in His Son's Name. As Jephthah's daughter became the glory of her father's house, so will the King's daughter arise, shine, to His glory, never more lamenting on her mountain-tops, but exulting on the height of heavenly Zion. As Ruth by untried paths journeyed home to Boaz, so are sweet souls by untried paths journeying home to Christ. As Elkanah was better to downcast Hannah than ten sons, so is Christ now to His faithful mourners; what will He be *then?* As Rizpah's self-devotion to the slain for sin won for her everlasting renown, so even now all who devote themselves to Christ, the Sole Sacrifice for sin, are winning a far more exceeding and eternal weight of glory; winning, not earning. As the Queen of Sheba exchanged gifts with King Solomon, so gracious souls to-day exchange love with Christ, and will carry on the exchange for ever; unlike that Queen who returned to her own country, they, born in the region and shadow of death, will return no more, nor see their native country, but will stand continually before Christ and hear His Wisdom: "Because the Lord loved Israel for ever, therefore made He thee king." As the Widow of Zarephath entertaining Elijah received a prophet's reward, so all ministries to Christ in His poor and afflicted shall one day by no means lose their reward. As Elisha at the Widow's word turned her penury into wealth, so God is giving good gifts to them that

E E

ask Him, and withholds no good thing from them that live a godly life. As the great Shunammite according to Elisha's promise embraced a son, so Christ bestows a name better than of sons or of daughters on such as choose the things that please Him. As the daughters of Shallum helped their father to rebuild the wall of Jerusalem, so now feeble souls are strengthened to edify others, while they themselves are being built as lively stones into Christ's living temple. As Esther excelled Vashti and assumed her forfeited crown, so the Christian vocation at once human and superhuman hath the promise of that which now is, and of that which is to come ; and as after a brief fast, mourning, trembling terror, Queen Esther attained to the half of her husband's kingdom, so the Church looks onward, upward, to the moment of sitting down with her Divine King and Spouse in His Throne.

All· this and much more I profess when I say: I believe in the Communion of Saints, and the life everlasting. Amen.

As everything human that is masculine is or should be typical of Christ, so all that is feminine of the Church. Why then break off our parallel with the galaxy of holy maids and matrons memorialized in the Old Testament, and not carry it further by help of their sister saints in the Gospel?

Because it is so lovely a privilege to have stood really and truly in some direct relation to Christ that it may well take precedence of aught figurative. There is no title by which to indicate the Blessed Virgin Mary half so august as that of His Mother. The glory of righteous Elizabeth was her worship of His unseen Presence. It was enough for ascetic Anna to behold Him and to speak of Him. And so each named or unnamed personage appears invested with her proper halo. To the Woman of Samaria He announced Himself as the Messiah. The Widow of Nain He consoled. He accepted love and tears from a woman a sinner, and faith from her who had suffered many things from many ˋphysicians. Jairus's Daughter He took by the hand. On the Canaanitish Mother He bestowed an unique commendation. Martha and her sister Mary He loved. The woman bowed with infirmity He acknowledged as a daughter of Abraham. He set store by the Widow's two mites. And His last recorded words before the Seven Sentences from the Cross were addressed to the wailing and lamenting Daughters of Jerusalem.

O Christ our God, remember Thy strong and weak ones, great and small, men and women, for good. Remember the

nursing Fathers and nursing Mothers of Holy Church for good.
Remember the righteous who worship Thee by faith, and
bestow on them the blessing of those who not having seen
have believed. Remember and advance all who worship Thee
with fasting and prayer, and reveal Thy gracious Presence unto
them. Remember any overthrown through frailty, raise them
up and perfect Thy strength in their weakness. Remember
the bereaved in their anguish, and make their latter end better
than their beginning. Furnish the fallen with love, and accept
their love. Grant to sufferers faith, and reward their faith.
Raise sinners now from sin to righteousness, that Thou mayest
hereafter raise them as saints to perfection. Remember the
love of Parents; remember not except to forgive them the
offences of children. Love us all, that we all may love Thee.
Remember the despised, the overlooked, the misunderstood,
reserving mercy for them in the day of Thy justice. Remember
munificent hands to refill them, and generous hearts to
spiritualize them. Remember all who mourn in Zion. My
God, forget not any mourner. Remember us all, O Lord our
God, for good. Amen.

Who shall decide whether to be constituted in the first
instance strong or weak holds out the greater promise of
ultimate strength? And it is the end crowns the beginning,
never the beginning the end.

St. James erects a standard as it were of equality in inequality: "Let the brother of low degree rejoice in that he
is exalted; but the rich, in that he is made low."

"The marriage of the Lamb is come."

O Gracious Master, Who of old forgavest Thy disciples
when they believed not for joy and wondered, so now, so
always forgive us. We believe; help Thou our unbelief. If
we believe not, let it be for joy and not for unwillingness;
through mistrust of self, not of Thy word; for a moment, not
for ever. Open Thou our understanding that we may
understand the Scriptures; understand somewhat, believe all.
So, Good Lord, make us ready. Amen.

"And His wife hath made herself ready." To Jacob by
reason of his great love seven years seemed but a few days;
we read not that they seemed so to Rachel. He by desire shortened delay; she by responsive desire may have
lengthened it.

Christ saith: "Surely I come quickly"— while the Church
ceases not to cry: "How long, O Lord, Holy and
True?"

At length in St. John's vision her mystical week is fulfilled. The Bridegroom cometh forth out of His chamber; let the Bride come forth out of her closet.

Many times heretofore has she come forth fasting, praying, weeping between the porch and the altar, imploring mercy. Now is she called forth to rejoice in the dances of them that make merry. "Then were we like unto them that dream."

She hath made herself ready; but in what royal closet, what dainty bower? She who comes out of great tribulation hath made herself ready in great tribulation, which yet was to her the secret of His Tabernacle.

As swelled by a thousand confluents from a thousand sources some unmeasured river at last attains the measureless ocean, so she comes forth from the thousand battle-fields of the fierce fight of her afflictions. Beds of weariness, haunts of starvation, hospital wards, rescue homes, orphanages, leper colonies, fires of martyrdom, in these and such as these did she set up mirrors whereby to fashion herself after Christ's likeness; workhouses, prisons (thank God !), the sea, the land, the rocks for a shelter, each and all send up their contingent of saints; palaces, hovels, houselessness, homelessness, again saints; east, west, north, south, still saints. Every gift, every grace, arrays and adorns her; innocence, penitence, purity, purification, largeness of heart as the sand of the sea; weighty judgment, mercy, faith; carefulness in well doing, as mint and anise and cummin; no longer patience, yet fruits of patience; no longer chastening, yet its peaceable fruit of righteousness; hope that maketh not ashamed, love superseding all that is not love or love's. She has forgotten her own people and her father's house, has forgotten all who are not of her or with her, in the supreme moment of going home to Him Whom her soul loveth. She has come up from the wilderness leaning upon her Beloved, and leaning upon Him she will sit down in the Promised Land flowing with milk and honey.

"The Voice of my Beloved! . . . Arise, My love, My fair one, and come away."

8. And to her was granted that she should be arrayed in fine linen, clean and white; for the fine linen is the righteousness of saints.

Or in the Revised Version: "And it was given unto her that she should array herself in fine linen, bright and pure; for the fine linen is the righteous acts of the saints."

Collated, the two texts suggest that revealed paradox which

teaches both that we cannot, and that we must, array ourselves in righteousness: Whence one conclusion appears both safe and reasonable : what we can, do ; what we cannot, trust God to do.

Till one tries, it is easy to fancy oneself doing everything : when one tries, it is not difficult to despair of doing anything. Neither delusion will work us ultimate harm if we so let these extremes meet as to curb, balance, counteract each other. Presumption should at least fight lustily; despondency should at least pray urgently. Genuine prayer in conjunction with genuine fighting must sooner or later overthrow presumption and dissipate despondency.

If I may venture to say so, I think the Revised Version of this passage appears eminently consonant with those Providential circumstances which day by day dictate our duties. It exhibits the Bride as arraying herself " in fine linen, bright and pure " ; but not for her is such vesture provided, as were the cloud garment and swaddling-band of thick darkness for the primeval sea : hers is a nobler law, " Give her of the fruit of her hands." " Righteous acts " have woven that lustrous linen, acts of all saints from the beginning to the end. Spotless and radiant now, it has been steeped in tears and bleached in the heat of the day : woven and at length without flaw from the top throughout it forms one fair unbroken web ; but held up to that light which manifests all works, behold ! its warp and woof have not been wrought into a perfect whole except by an interweaving of cross threads, of *crosses.* The acts and crosses of each day and of every day, your acts and crosses and my own, are capable of reappearing in that achieved glory.

If the Revised Version incites us to abound in labour to-day while it is called to-day, the Authorized promotes no different result by enamouring us of that final perfection when all having been done both for and by the Church (for the things concerning her also have an end), she shall be presented as a chaste virgin to Christ : and so shall the king have pleasure in her beauty.

> **9. And he saith unto me, Write, Blessed are they which are called unto the marriage supper of the Lamb. And he saith unto me, These are the true sayings of God.**

Speech ends, writing endures. Wherefore this " Write " has respect even to children that are yet unborn : for the promise

is unto us and to our children and to all that are afar off, even
as many as the Lord our God shall call.

My neighbour's call I may not apprehend : my own I recognize.   All things, all events, knowledge, even ignorance, speak
to me.   Thou knowest? " thou oughtest therefore ": thou
knowest not? none the less "how dreadful is this place."
"There are, it may be, so many kinds of voices in the world,
and none of them is without signification " :—or according to
a marginal rendering of the concluding phrase, "and nothing
is without voice."

This Revelation of St. John the Divine excepts from its
summons none who have ears to hear.   By trumpets and harps,
by thunders and voices, it calls on all men everywhere to
repent.   What or how we may learn hereafter stands over until
that hereafter.   What we cannot yet know will not yet be
demanded of us.

At present and at once all earthly things teach some lesson
to the teachable.   " For the invisible things of Him from the
creation of the world are clearly seen, being understood by
the things that are made, even His eternal power and Godhead."   And whereas (if I may reverently use the word)
accessories in this Inspired Book seem in great measure
emblematical rather than actual ; I can at least infer thence
that every such figure must have an original, every type an
antitype.   Only a substance can cast a shadow.

To-day while daylight lasts let us study the shadows vouchsafed us : when our night falls they for us will vanish.   Hezekiah had his faith confirmed by a shadow.   "The shadow of
Peter passing by " was not lightly to be regarded.

Let us sit down amid Divinely cast shadows with great
delight : it is good for us to be here.

Fulness of beauty and reality of perfection belong to substance, not to shadow.   Meanwhile shadows, although they
reproduce neither details nor colours, familiarize us with broad
outlines.

However weary the land of our sojourn, the "great rock "
extends for us a refreshing shadow; itself, and not its shadow,
being our ultimate benefactor.

Shadows befit probation, but befit not the promised beatitude.
Whilst set in their midst I must thankfully utilize them, yet
must not make myself so comfortable in their region as to
settle down or to drop asleep.   Symbolism affords a fascinating
study : wholesome so long as it amounts to aspiration and
research ; unwholesome when it degenerates into a pastime.

As literal shadows tend to soothe, lull, abate keenness of vision ; so perhaps symbols may have a tendency to engross, satisfy, arrest incautious souls unwatchful and unprayerful lest they enter into temptation.

> Lord, to Thine own grant watchful hearts and eyes ;
>> Hearts strung to prayer, awake while eyelids sleep ;
>> Eyes patient till the end to watch and weep.
> So will sleep nourish power to wake and rise
> With Virgins who keep vigil and are wise,
>> To sow among all sowers who shall reap,
>> From out man's deep to call Thy vaster deep,
> And tread the uphill track to Paradise.
> Sweet souls ! so patient that they make no moan,
>> So calm on journey that they seem at rest,
>>> So rapt in prayer that half they dwell in heaven
>>> Thankful for all withheld and all things given ;
>> So lit by love that Christ shines manifest
> Transfiguring their aspects to His own.

"Blessed are they which are called unto the Marriage Supper of the Lamb."—This beatitude is specially vouched for as a true saying of God, and baptized Christians have received the call ; yet so long as mortal life endures each soul must use all diligence to secure the blessing, probation rendering every promise contingent.

Two Divine Parables warn us that the call of grace condemns whom it does not save :—

"One . . . said unto Him, Blessed is he that shall eat bread in the kingdom of God. Then said He unto him, A certain man made a great supper, and bade many : and sent his servant at supper time to say to them that were bidden, Come ; for all things are now ready. And they all with one consent began to make excuse. . . . So that servant came, and shewed his lord these things. Then the master of the house being angry said to his servant . . . Go out into the highways and hedges, and compel them to come in, that my house may be filled. For I say unto you, That none of those men which were bidden shall taste of my supper."

"The kingdom of heaven is like unto a certain king, which made a marriage for his son, and sent forth his servants to call them that were bidden to the wedding : and they would not come. . . . Then saith he to his servants, The wedding is ready, but they which were bidden were not worthy. Go ye therefore into the highways, and as many as ye shall find, bid to the marriage. So those servants went out into the highways, and gathered together all as many as they found, both bad and good : and the wedding was furnished with guests. And when the king came in to see the guests, he saw there a man which had not on a wedding garment : and he saith unto him, Friend, how camest thou in hither not having a wedding garment? And he was speechless. Then said the king to the servants, Bind him hand and foot, and take him away, and cast him into outer darkness; there shall be weeping and gnashing of teeth. For many are called, but few are chosen."

Lord, with a call give responsive grace, with grace diligence, with diligence perseverance, with final perseverance an entrance into Thy glory, with glory a seat at Thy Feast full of pleasure. For the sake and worthiness of Jesus Christ. Amen.

10. And I fell at his feet to worship him. And he said unto me, See thou do it not : I am thy fellow-servant, and of thy brethren that have the testimony of Jesus : worship God : for the testimony of Jesus is the spirit of prophecy.

Looking back (ch. xvii. 1) it seems as if this personage who converses with St. John may still be one of the seven Angels of the vials. Marvellous indeed is it to behold that beloved disciple who had lain on the Master's Bosom fall down at the servant's feet to worship him. What motive led St. John to such exuberance of humility concerns me not. But for myself I learn from the celestial disallowance of his act how safe it is for me to be set low on a lowly level and one bounded by a misty horizon, so that thence I can neither explore height nor depth nor distance to any great extent : for to say the least of it, " I am not better than my fathers." Even St. Paul felt how it would have been possible for himself to be exalted above measure.

"Let no man beguile you of your reward in a voluntary humility and worshipping of angels, intruding into those things which he hath not seen, vainly puffed up by his fleshly mind, and not holding the Head."

Self-willed humility is pride in masquerade.

> As violets so be I recluse and sweet,
>   Cheerful as daisies unaccounted rare,
> Still sunward-gazing from a lowly seat,
>   Still sweetening wintry air.
>
> While half-awakened Spring lags incomplete,
>   While lofty forest-trees tower bleak and bare,
> Daisies and violets own remotest heat
>   And bloom and make them fair.

"See thou do it not."—" He that rebuketh a man afterwards shall find more favour than he that flattereth with the tongue."

Lord Jesus, give us grace in charity to rebuke and in humility to bear rebuke; until that day when Thou shalt swallow up death in victory, and wipe away tears from off all faces, and take away from off all the earth the rebuke of Thy people.

"I am thy fellow-servant, and of thy brethren that have the testimony of Jesus."—This definition exalted the Creator and abased the creature, it edified and did not puff up, it satisfied loyal hearts, not itching ears.

Such a specimen of "conversation in heaven" (if I may treat the word when thus used as including *conversation* in its colloquial sense: and this notwithstanding that the Revised Version substitutes *citizenship*, or marginally *commonwealth*)— such a specimen suggests various practical points for everyday guidance.

"Fellow-servants" are more or less on a par: "brethren" are equals: if Jesus Christ is the Object of my own faith, hope, love; then all to whom He is the same are my fellow-servants to be courteously entreated, my brethren to be beloved. A system which spiritually exalts valleys and makes low mountains and hills takes no more account of inequalities of birth, breeding, education, than of those roughnesses on an orange to which in proportion to her magnitude the excrescences of our globe have been likened. "If there be therefore any consolation in Christ, if any comfort of love, if any fellowship of the Spirit, if any bowels and mercies, fulfil ye my joy, that ye be likeminded, having the same love, being of one accord, of one mind. Let nothing be done through strife or vainglory; but in lowliness of mind let each esteem other better than themselves. Look not every man on his own things, but every man also on the things of others."

Curiosity is starved; piety fed and feasted. Gossip is indirectly discouraged by a contrary model.

"The testimony of Jesus" is an essential characteristic of true servants and brethren. Whatever more it may import, it cannot consist with less than neither through fear nor favour our being ashamed of Christ and of His words.

From a fleshly mind vainly puffed up, from lack of natural affection, from respect of persons; Thou, Lord, Who lovest us all, deliver us.

From fastidiousness, exclusiveness, pride, conceit; Thou, Lord, Who condescendest to us all, deliver us.

From undue curiosity, vain hankerings, idle words, wasted irrecoverable time; Thou, Lord, Who understandest our thoughts long before, deliver us.

From false fear and false shame ; Thou, Lord, Who art not ashamed to call us brethren, deliver us.

. Into Thy hands I commend us, for Thou hast redeemed us. Thou, Lord, Who hast redeemed us all, for Thine own sake sanctify and save us.   Amen.

"WORSHIP GOD."

Lord, if Thy word had been " Worship Me not,
  For I than thou am holier : draw not near "—
  We had besieged Thy Face with prayer and tear
And manifold abasement in our lot,
Our crooked ground, our thorned and thistled plot ;
  Envious of flawless Angels in their sphere,
  Envious of brutes, and envious of the mere
Unliving and undying unbegot.
But now Thou hast said ; " Worship Me : and give
  Thy heart to Me, My child " ;—now therefore we
Think twice before we stoop to worship Thee ;
  We proffer half a heart while life is strong
And strung with hope ; so sweet it is to live !
  Wilt Thou not wait?   Yea, Thou hast waited long.

"The testimony of Jesus is the spirit of prophecy."—By this "testimony of Jesus" I will (if I may) understand, as included in the angelic definition, such witness as all Christians are bound to bear, and all good Christians do bear to their Master.

And this, although St. Paul emphatically intimates that disciples are not all prophets.   For whilst a spirit of prediction is obviously confined to a few, a virtue of revelation (if I may term it so) is diffused throughout the area of Christendom. As certain believers were St. Paul's epistle known and read of all men, but beyond this were manifestly "the epistle of Christ " ; so all believers should be and may be epistles of Christ, instinct with His Spirit, stamped with His image, exemplifying His Will.   As St. Peter and St. John could only be accounted for as having "been with Jesus," so should it come to pass with any and every Christian in the face of the world. One who cannot be so much as a teacher of babes, may yet by Divine Grace become a lesson, a revelation, bearing on eternity as well as on time: such were even the least gifted of our elect fathers and mothers before us, who being in multitude as the stars of the sky and as the sand by the sea shore innumerable, "all died in faith, not having received the promises, but having seen them afar off, and were persuaded of them, and embraced them, and confessed that they were strangers and pilgrims on the earth.   For they that say such things declare plainly that they seek a country." The grace of our probation is itself a present glory; and this faithfully lived and died in announces, prefigures, guarantees the glory of future final acceptance and perfection: even as the face of St. Stephen, while the Council beheld it as it had been the face of an angel, may have set forth before them the latent aspect of those who shall be made equal to the angels.

"Prophesy, son of man."—And Ezekiel prophesied by promulgating Divine decrees; and thereupon the answering dry bones prophesied by foreshowing the far-off resurrection. Two sorts of prophecy independent of any miraculous concomitant are open to us all: to declare the Will of God, and to do it.

Is it a mistake to think that prophecy (in the sense of prediction) may often address us when we fail to recognize its voice? Surely the "Thou shalt not" of the Decalogue, being an expression of the Almighty Will, may be not merely an injunction but also a prophecy: man can set it at nought in this life, but not in the next. For as the first death which kills the body cuts short all physical possibility of image worship, verbal profanity, Sabbath breaking, murder, sensuality, theft, lying speech; so the second death, which destroys both body and soul, will (as a probable inference) annul any power to transgress any commandment as a pleasurable self-indulgence, whilst not—alas! alas!—abating one jot or one tittle of rebellious will; so that lost souls hating goodness with impotent undying hatred appear like tortured bodies under the influence of curari, all the more excruciated whilst outwardly paralyzed. Thus sinners sell their souls for that which as a gratification cannot last, but turns to loathing and rancour. Truly a vanity and a vexation of spirit.

In the Egyptian darkness men saw not one another, neither did any arise from his place. So in the outer darkness thereby typified, how should there not be an end of the lust of the eyes and the pride of life!

Lord, pardon and amend us whenever we doubt, misunderstand, misstate. Suffer us not to go astray. Suffer us not to mislead each other. Whatsoever we be enlighten our minds and enkindle our affections, for the honour of Jesus Christ our Redeemer. Amen.

> Grant us such grace that we may work Thy Will, ·
> And speak Thy words and walk before Thy Face,
> Profound and calm like waters deep and still:
> Grant us such grace.

> Not hastening and not loitering in our pace
> For gloomiest valley or for sultriest hill,
>   Content and fearless on our downward race.
>
> As rivers seek a sea they cannot fill
>   But are themselves filled full in its embrace,
> Absorbed, at rest, each river and each rill :
>   Grant us such grace.

11. And I saw heaven opened, and behold, a white horse; and He that sat upon him was called Faithful and True, and in righteousness He doth judge and make war.

This vision by recalling the former vision of the white horse and his rider (ch. vi. 2), reminds us that we are contemplating Him Who is the Same yesterday and to-day and for ever, " greatly to be feared in the assembly of the saints, and to be had in reverence of all them that are about Him. O Lord God of hosts, who is a strong Lord like unto Thee? or to Thy faithfulness round about Thee? "

[What then am I that I should dare speak? or how shall I dare be silent? O Lord Jesus, forgive me my speech, my silence. " Death and life are in the power of the tongue."]

It is wise to obey in fear, foolish to fear to obey: wise to worship trembling, foolish to tremble instead of worshipping. A talent must neither be misused nor laid away unused.

" He . . . was called Faithful and True."—" O Lord, Thou art my God; I will exalt Thee, I will praise Thy Name; for Thou hast done wonderful things; Thy counsels of old are faithfulness and truth."—" I will say of the Lord, He is my refuge and my fortress: my God; in Him will I trust. . . . His truth shall be thy shield and buckler."—" It is a good thing to give thanks unto the Lord, and to sing praises unto Thy Name, O Most High: to show forth Thy lovingkindness in the morning, and Thy faithfulness every night."

In the former vision the Rider on the white horse " went forth conquering, and to conquer," His reward with Him, His work before Him. Now because He " doth judge " as well as " make war," this latter war seems to be rather of extirpation than of conquest; the carrying out of a righteous sentence rather than a subdual and receiving to amity of sometime enemies. The beginning has been seen, and the end must be seen.

O Lord God, Holy and True, grant that in the Mount of the Lord it may be seen by us Thy servants and trembling children. And to the end that thither at last we may attain, now give us grace to use this embittered world as our mountain of myrrh by self-denial, our hill of frankincense by self-oblation. For His only sake, the Rock of Ages, Jesus Christ. Amen.

12. His eyes were as a flame of fire, and on His head were many crowns; and He had a Name written, that no man knew, but He Himself.

" His eyes were as a flame of fire."—Word for word as our Lord revealed Himself in the first vision (ch. i. 14): then standing (it might seem) on earth, heaven not being opened till afterwards (ch. iv. 1). Awful in His Unchangeableness.

His eyes did see our substance yet being imperfect. Now they see it worse than imperfect, marred, contorted. At the last day they will see it such as then it will be. Yea, before the beginning they have foreseen the end. Awful in His Unchangeableness.

Lord, suffer not awe to turn in us to slavish fear, nor godly fear to degenerate into mistrust: but give us grace fearing Thee to put our whole trust in Thee; fearing Thee much, to love Thee much more. For Thine own sake, Lord Jesus, Who lovest us. Amen.

"And on His head were many crowns."—"And a crown was given unto Him" (ch. vi. 2). The Authorized Version in both passages gives *crown* or *crowns :* the Revised *crown* in the earlier chapter, *diadems* in the present text. This distinction (which my ignorance of Greek leads me to adopt on trust) suggests the Victor's Wreath as that first crown : when Christ having already with His own right hand and with His holy arm gotten Himself the victory, sets forth anew conquering and to conquer as Captain of man's salvation; that at last where He is there all His faithful ones may be also.

This second time He wears many "diadems" indicative of dominion. He is no longer enrolling recruits, raising an army : His veteran invincible troops are mounted ready to follow Him (*see* ver. 14).

But wherefore "many" diadems? Lord, when I cannot adore Thee in knowledge, in ignorance I will adore Thee.

Lord Jesus, Thou art God, Alone Supreme in absolute Supremacy. As God I worship Thee.

Thou art Man, Whose is the Human Name supreme above every name, that at the Name of Jesus every knee should bow. As Man I worship Thee.

Thou hast created all things, and without Thee was not anything made that was made. As Creator I worship Thee.

Thou hast become Man, and hast taken the Manhood into God indissolubly for ever and ever. As the Firstborn of every creature I worship Thee.

Thou art the Wisdom of ·God Whom He possessed in the beginning of His way. As the Divine Wisdom I worship Thee.

Thou hast made Thyself man's wisdom. As my only Hope of wisdom I worship Thee.

Thou art the Word, God and with God. As the Divine Word I worship Thee.

Thou art the Word speaking to us as never man spake. As my Teacher of absolute authority I worship Thee.

Thou art the Lord Who hath declared: My ways are not your ways. Having a good hope because of Thy word I worship Thee.

Thou art the Way whereby alone man cometh unto the Father. A wayfarer liable to error, beseeching safeguard, I worship Thee.

Thou art the King of Heaven, all Whose works are truth. I, a little one among Thy works, worship Thee.

Thou art the Truth: in Thee mercy and truth are met together, kindness and truth are shown forth. In the paths of Thy mercy and of Thy truth I worship Thee.

Thou art the Living God into Whose hands it is a fearful thing to fall. Yet calling to remembrance the former days, to-day while it is called to-day I worship Thee.

Thou art the Life. Thou Who hadst power to lay Thy Life down and power to take it again, Who art Life manifested, and Who givest Thy flesh for the life of the world, I worship Thee.

O Thou Who hearest prayer, and unto Whom all flesh shall come, draw all my brethren and all my sisters and myself not outcast from their gracious company, to worship Thee. Amen.

"And He had a Name written, that no man knew, but He Himself."—This gracious revelation corresponds apparently not with any previous Apocalyptic description of Christ in Person, but rather with His promise to "him that overcometh. . . . I . . . will give him . . . a new name written, which no man knoweth saving he that receiveth it" (ch. ii. 17).

By many Names, by many Titles, we recognize Him now. Jesus, Saviour: Christ, Anointed: Emmanuel, God with us: the Good Shepherd seeking, fetching back, dying for His sheep: the Good Samaritan healing, nourishing: the Master·

teaching: the Lord ruling, providing, instituting: the Captain, but of salvation: the Chiefest, but girt by His ten thousand: the First-born among many brethren: the Bridegroom. Who tarrieth, Who cometh: the Lamb of Atonement: the Bread of Life: the Salvation of the Cup: the Vine sap-diffusing: the Corn of Wheat multiplied after its own likeness: the Way from earth to heaven: the Door of access to the Father: the Life to all who living and believing shall never die: the Resurrection and the Life. "Lord, now lettest Thou Thy servant depart in peace . . . for mine eyes have seen Thy Salvation."

Moreover, we recognize all saints as the complement, so to say, of these Names as ointment "poured forth." In divers lovely degrees of grace and glory they are saved, have the Unction from the Holy One, walk with God, are sheep who know their Shepherd's Voice, are wounded wayfarers whom the Good Physician heals and tends, are disciples of the One Master, servants and ministers of the One Lord, crusading soldiers, like-minded courtiers, brethren beloved, Virgins who wait, Brides who watch; they are accepted through the Only Atonement, are made partakers of the Body and Blood of Christ, flourish as fruitful branches of the only Vine, ripen as wheat for the eternal garner, follow Jesus from earth to heaven, enter through His merits, and being indissolubly His members, have part in the first blessed resurrection and live for evermore. " By the Name of Jesus Christ . . . for there is none other name under heaven given among men, whereby we must be saved."

"That no man knew, but He Himself."—St. John writes not, That no man shall know: but "that no man knew.". God alone knoweth the limit of man's future knowledge.

Meanwhile it is a Divine and comfortable promise that when He shall appear we shall be like Him, for we shall see Him as He is. Recognition, then, is one revealed point of Christ-likeness: He recognizing us, we all must recognize Him. And because "every one that is perfect shall be as his Master," surely that supreme beatific recognition involves all congruous blessed recognitions : Christ recognizing us all, we should so far be un-Christlike if we recognized not each other.

As Israel of old spake unto Joseph, " I had not thought to see thy face: and, lo, God hath shewed me also thy seed "; so shall all saints, monuments and miracles of Divine Mercy, attest no less in the supreme day of union and of reunion.

Moreover in the surpassing rapture of that day recognition will not be all: discovery likewise (please God !) awaits us.

As one has strikingly suggested : some that glanced at afar off appear stones, when viewed close at hand may turn out to be sheep. God all along has beheld them as sheep, and sheep they were : the misapprehension (thank God) was ours.

To-day I read "Samaria"; to-morrow I may redecipher the selfsame letters as "S^a. Maria."

Passing away the bliss,
　The anguish passing away :
Thus it is
　　To-day.

Clean past away the sorrow,
　The pleasure brought back to stay :
Thus and this
　　To-morrow.

13. And He was clothed with a vesture dipped in blood: and His Name is called The Word of God.

"Wherefore art Thou red in Thine apparel, and Thy garments like him that treadeth in the winefat? I have trodden the winepress alone ; and of the people there was none with Me : for I will tread them in Mine anger, and trample them in My fury ; and their blood shall be sprinkled upon My garments, and I will stain all My raiment. For the day of vengeance is in Mine heart, and the year of My redeemed is come." Thus does Isaiah's prophecy provide as it were an answer to St. John's revelation : between the twain the Cross of Calvary standing forth as an intermediate fulfilment of the elder prophecy and a rehearsal of the later revelation.

Prophecy couples the day of vengeance with the year of the redeemed. Visions link together salvation and destruction. The blessed Cross, with on either hand the cross of a malefactor hardened or penitent, shows forth the same verity in a figure. For Divine Mercy is not contrary to Divine Justice, neither is that Justice at feud with that Mercy.

"I was dumb with silence, I held my peace, even from good ; and my sorrow was stirred."

"Without shedding of blood is no remission." None the less, "The voice of thy brother's blood crieth,"—and man's blood shall be required "at the hand of man." The Red Sea saved whom it did not destroy, and destroyed whom it did not save.

His "vesture dipped in blood" seems to challenge heaven and earth : "What could have been done more to My vineyard, that I have not done in it ?"

"His Name is called The Word of God."—Whatever that Other Name may be which abides hidden, this Name reveals to us our nearness and dearness to our Heavenly Father. It is His good Will, His gracious pleasure to speak to us, converse with us, maintain intercourse with us. Jesus Christ is the Divine Word to us : and if out of the abundance of man's heart his mouth speaketh, much more fully and infallibly God Omniscient. Jesus is Truth, Wisdom, the Word : " O God . . . the Lord . . . I am not worthy of the least of all the mercies, and of all the truth, which Thou hast shewed unto Thy servant." " Lord, if it be Thou, bid me come unto Thee."

We need everything in Christ, nothing out of Christ : that is, we simply need Christ. To need is a blessed thing, to lack is quite a different thing. " O fear the Lord, ye that are His saints : for they that fear Him lack nothing." But I will not be content to fear Christ : I will love Him. Amen.

Because Christ being Wisdom is the Word, and being the Truth is the Word, therefore Christians must speak words of wisdom and truth, or else must keep silence. Yet remember truth-telling Balaam and his end, oracular Ahithophel and his end : accuracy without charity, or astuteness without charity, profits nothing.

Gifts become a curse and no blessing when divorced from graces. Imagine a gift of tongues without either wisdom or truth !

O God the Son, Who being the Brightness of the Father's Glory and the Express Image of His Person, art to mankind His gracious Word, His revealed Truth, His imparted Wisdom ; grant us grace to speak the truth in love, to show forth meekness of wisdom ; not to speak except truthfully, not to be wise except unto salvation. From idle words deliver us, O Lord, from wisdom of the children of this world : from words that may do hurt deliver us, O Lord, from wisdom that is foolishness. From all which Thou acceptest not, to which Thou bearest not witness, which beareth not witness unto Thee, which hath not praise of God, deliver us. Amen.

14. And the armies which were in heaven followed Him upon white horses, clothed in fine linen, white and clean.

In the former vision (ch. vi. 2) the Rider on the White Horse went forth (so far as we read) alone : now the armies of heaven follow Him. Thus we behold and adore Christ *alone* in His work : *in fellowship* in His triumph. He reappears clad in the unique glory of man's redemption, the " vesture dipped in blood " : whilst His elect follow Him all alike

F F

decked in the joyful glory of the redeemed, " clothed in fine linen, white and clean."

> As one red rose in a garden where all other roses are white
> Blossoms alone in its glory, crowned all alone
> In a solitude of own sweetness and fragrance of own delight,
> With loveliness not another's and thorns its own ;
> As one ruddy sun amid million orbs comely and colourless,
> Among all others, above all others is known ;
> As it were alone in the garden, alone in the heavenly place,
> Chief and centre of all, in fellowship yet alone.

" Followed Him."—Cross-bearers, crown-wearers. " If any man serve Me, let him follow Me ; and where I am, there shall also My servant be : if any man serve Me, him will My Father honour."

15. And out of His mouth goeth a sharp sword, that with it He should smite the nations : and He shall rule them with a rod of iron : and He treadeth the wine-press of the fierceness and wrath of Almighty God.

So at the first St. John beheld Him (ch. i. 16) with a sword. In that vision we are certified that it was two-edged as well as sharp : now we read of it only as sharp. During man's probation, the Divine Sword has (so to say) two edges, whereof one wounds, but not incurably ; yea, wounds with the very intent to heal : as St. Paul teaches : " When we are judged, we are chastened of the Lord, that we should not be condemned with the world." The other edge, the edge of extirpation, hangs all along suspended over our heads ; yet need never fall upon us, God helping our own earnest endeavour.

The final sentence upon incorrigible sinners is as the fall of that fatal edge. Christ All-Merciful has forewarned us what sort of life leads down to such a death :—

" God sent not His Son into the world to condemn the world ; but that the world through Him might be saved. He that believeth on Him is not condemned : but he that believeth not is condemned already, because he hath not believed in the Name of the only begotten Son of God. And this is the condemnation, that light is come into the world, and men loved darkness rather than light, because their deeds were evil. For every one that doeth evil hateth the light, neither cometh to the light, lest his deeds should be reproved."

" Wide is the gate, and broad is the way, that leadeth to destruction, and many there be which go in thereat."

" Every tree that bringeth not forth good fruit is hewn down, and cast into the fire."

" Many will say to Me in that day, Lord, Lord, have we not prophesied in Thy Name? and in Thy Name have cast out devils? and in Thy Name done many wonderful works? And then will I profess unto them, I never knew you : depart from Me, ye that work iniquity."

" The hour is coming, in the which all that are in the graves shall hear His Voice, and shall come forth . . . they that have done evil, unto the resurrection of damnation."

"Every idle word that men shall speak, they shall give account thereof in the day of judgment. For by thy words thou shalt be justified, and by thy words thou shalt be condemned."

" . . . Except ye repent, ye shall all likewise perish."

" Whosoever shall deny Me before men, him will I also deny before My Father which is in heaven."

"Whosoever shall be ashamed of Me and of My words, of him shall the Son of Man be ashamed, when He shall come in His own Glory, and in His Father's, and of the holy angels."

" Except ye be converted, and become as little children, ye shall not enter into the kingdom of heaven."

" He that rejecteth Me, and receiveth not My words, hath one that judgeth him : the word that I have spoken, the same shall judge him in the last day."

" . . . Which devour widows' houses, and for a pretence make long prayers : these shall receive greater damnation."

"Take heed to yourselves, lest at any time your hearts be overcharged with surfeiting, and drunkenness, and cares of this life, and so that day come upon you unawares."

" . . . With the hypocrites : there shall be weeping and gnashing of teeth."

"Then shall He say also unto them on the left hand, Depart from Me, ye cursed, into everlasting fire, prepared for the devil and his angels : for I was an hungred, and ye gave Me no meat : I was thirsty, and ye gave Me no drink : I was a stranger, and ye took Me not in : naked, and ye clothed Me not : sick, and in prison, and ye visited Me not. Then shall they also answer Him, saying, Lord, when saw we Thee an hungred, or athirst, or a stranger, or naked, or sick, or in prison, and did not minister unto Thee ? Then shall He answer them, saying, Verily I say unto you, Inasmuch as ye did it not to one of the least of these, ye did it not to Me. And these shall go away into everlasting punishment."

"He shall rule them with a rod of iron."—" It is the Lord : let Him do what seemeth Him good."

"HE TREADETH THE WINEPRESS OF THE FIERCENESS AND WRATH OF ALMIGHTY GOD."

I lift mine eyes, and see
Thee, tender Lord, in pain upon the Tree,
Athirst for my sake and athirst for me.

"Yea, look upon Me there
Compassed with thorns and bleeding everywhere,
For thy sake bearing all and glad to bear."

I lift my heart to pray :
Thou Who didst love me all that darkened day,
Wilt Thou not love me to the end alway?

"Yea, thee My wandering sheep,
Yea, thee My scarlet sinner slow to weep,
Come to Me, I will love thee and will keep."

Yet am I racked with fear :
Behold the unending outer darkness drear,
Behold the gulf unbridgeable and near !

"Nay, fix thy heart, thine eyes,
Thy hope upon My boundless Sacrifice :
Will I lose lightly one so dear-bought prize ? "

Ah, Lord ; it is not Thou,
Thou that wilt fail ; yet woe is me, for how
Shall I endure who half am failing now?

" Nay, weld thy resolute will
To Mine : glance not aside for good or ill :
I love thee ; trust Me still and love Me still."

Yet Thou Thyself hast said,
When Thou shalt sift the living from the dead
Some must depart shamed and uncomforted.

"Judge not before that day,
Trust me with all thy heart even tho' I slay :
Trust Me in love, trust on, love on, and pray."

16. And He hath on His vesture and on His thigh a Name written, King of kings, and Lord of lords.

"On His vesture and on His thigh."—Herein (if I may) I discern an intimation of Christ's Twofold Nature. As He is from eternity to eternity in Himself "Equal to the Father, as touching His Godhead," so is He throughout that same eternity inalienably and supremely, potentially if not actually " King of kings, and Lord of lords." Before any kings or any lords were, beyond human faculty of expression or grasp of understanding, the All-Holy Trinity Was. " I opened my mouth, and panted." Kings bowing down as bulrushes before Him, lords at the beck of His sceptre, though they be kings in heavenly places and lords beyond the bounds of the everlasting hills, of these we can form a conception, we can attest the

seemliness of their adoration, prostrate with them we can
adore; but the antecedent of these, of such as these, of all
creatures, of any creature, silences us.   God the Son is King
of kings and Lord of lords, and on His thigh the Name is
written.

Equally "on His vesture" is that Same Name written; on
the Nature He has assumed, on the Manhood He has taken
into God.   For although He was made a little lower than the
angels for the suffering of death, yet hath He "by inheritance
obtained a more excellent Name than they."

In Eve, the mother of all living, man desired in vain.to make
himself like God.   But when God deigned to desire with
desire to make Himself like Man, He spake and it was done:
and all desire human and Divine was appeased.

"We have walked to and fro through the earth, and, behold,
all the earth sitteth still, and is at rest."

O God, the God of our Lord Jesus Christ, the Father of
Lights, grant unto us all the Spirit of Wisdom and revelation
in the knowledge of Him.   Enlighten the eyes of our understanding that we may know the hope of His calling, and the
riches of the glory of His inheritance in the saints, and the
greatness of His power to usward.   Reveal to us ever more
and more Christ risen from the dead, and set at Thine own
Right Hand in the heavenly places: Whose dominion is
above all dominion, and Whose Name above every name.   In
which supreme Name, the Name of Jesus, we shelter ourselves and plead with Thee.   Amen.

O everliving God, let this mind be in us which was also in
Christ Jesus: that as He from His loftiness stooped to the
death of the Cross; so we in our lowliness may humble
ourselves and become obedient unto death, though of constraint yet likewise willingly, believing and obeying, living and
dying, to the glory of God the Father.   For the Same Jesus
Christ's sake.   Amen.

KING OF KINGS, AND LORD OF LORDS.

Is this that Name as ointment poured forth
  For which the virgins love Thee: King of kings
  And Lord of lords?   All Seraphs clad in wings;
All Cherubs and all wheels which south and north,
Which east and west turn not in going forth;
  All many-semblanced ordered Spirits, as rings
  Of rainbow in unwonted fashionings;
Might answer, Yes.   But we from south and north,
From east and west, a feeble folk who came
  By desert ways in quest of land unseen,

A promised land of pasture ever green
And ever-springing ever-singing wave,
Know best Thy Name of Jesus : Blessed Name,
Man's life and resurrection from the grave.

17. And I saw an angel standing in the sun; and he cried with a loud voice, saying to all the fowls that fly in the midst of heaven, Come and gather yourselves together unto the supper of the great God;

18. That ye may eat the flesh of kings, and the flesh of captains, and the flesh of mighty men, and the flesh of horses, and of them that sit on them, and the flesh of all men, both free and bond, both small and great.

This elect Angel "standing in the sun" seems, as it were, elder brother to such elect souls as shall prevail to "dwell with the devouring fire . . . with everlasting burnings." And so the description of such souls throws lovely light (may it not?) on the character of this and of all angels.

An angel, then, walks righteously in his own order of perfection: he is holy because God is Holy, and merciful in homage to the Divine Mercy. Loving the truth, hating a lie, he speaks uprightly whatever word is put in his mouth, neither calling bitter sweet nor sweet bitter. Self weighs nought with him, the equity of God's perfect Will absorbing his will and fulfilling his pleasure. He delights not in destruction for destruction's sake, yet as a step in the equal ways of God he delights in it : nor does he investigate evil for evil's sake, but rather as an agent towards the bringing in of Everlasting Righteousness. Thus he dwelleth on high.

And thus by grace we may dwell below while we await the call to go up higher.

Nerve us with patience, Lord, to toil or rest,
Toiling at rest on our allotted level ;
Unsnared, unscared by world or flesh or devil,
Fulfilling the good Will of Thy behest :
Not careful heie to hoard, not here to revel ;
But waiting for our treasure and our zest
Beyond the fading splendour of the west,
Beyond this deathstruck life and deathlier evil.
Not with the sparrow building here a house :
But with the swallow tabernacling so
As still to poise alert to rise and go
On eager wings with wing-outspeeding wills
Beyond earth's gourds and past her almond boughs,
Past utmost bound of the everlasting hills.

"To all the fowls."—All, apparently the clean and doubtless the unclean, must obey that summons, concur in that act.

No man can count on an eagle as his devourer : it may be a vulture. Is it a degradation to be torn piecemeal by a carrion bird ? Worse degradation it is to have made oneself the carrion it gorges upon.

Alas for kings, captains, champions, cavaliers, freemen, great men, who are no longer those excellences at all, but carrion ! Alas for slaves and mean men, carrion no less and no more ! All carrion, like that "flesh of horses" which in this catalogue appears mixed up undistinguishedly with the human refuse.

> Before the beginning Thou hast foreknown the end,
>   Before the birthday the deathbed was seen of Thee :
> Cleanse what I cannot cleanse, mend what I cannot mend,
>   O Lord All-Merciful, be merciful to me.
>
> While the end is drawing near I know not mine end ;
>   Birth I recall not, my death I cannot foresee :
> O God, arise to defend, arise to befriend,
>   O Lord All-Merciful, be merciful to me.

19. And I saw the beast, and the kings of the earth, and their armies, gathered together to make war against Him that sat on the horse, and against His army.

If this which St. John now sees be consequent upon that which he saw in a former vision (ch. xvi. 13—16) where we read : ". . . . The spirits of devils, working miracles, which go forth unto the kings of the earth and of the whole world, to gather them to the battle of that great day of God Almighty "—the overthrow of so huge a power there only to be anticipated is here accounted for : God the Almighty Son heads and leads His army to destroy the destroyer. Every day and all day the Church Militant discerns such a muster of evil ; not as yet does she discern the advance of that heavenly host : yet because the things which are seen are temporal, whilst the things which are not seen are eternal, she thanks God and takes courage.

She always did, always does, always will thank God and take courage. Shall I be the one traitor in her councils, the one craven in her camp ? God forbid !

And what after all can Satan and his legions effect against the elect ? They can give an immortalizing stroke to that flesh and blood which cannot as they stand inherit the kingdom of God. They can minister incorruption to corruption. They can kindle a fire which will turn to a glory. They can kill the body, but cannot cause one hair to perish. They can dig a grave, but cannot bar resurrection. "Shall not all these take up a parable against him, and a taunting proverb against him ? ”

20. **And the beast was taken, and with him the false prophet that wrought miracles before him, with which he deceived them that had received the mark of the beast, and them that worshipped his image. These both were cast alive into a lake of fire burning with brimstone.**

Brimstone is solid sulphur, sulphur which has neither been fused nor sublimated, which has not undergone elevation by fire, which abides as originally it was of the earth earthy. Of sulphur (*see* Latham's Dictionary) I read that it is an “elementary substance so called ; the name, unlike the majority of similar ones, being destitute of any technical termination indicative of its character. . . . This suggests the likelihood of the characters of sulphur being negative rather than positive.” *Sulphur* thus becomes a parable of mankind in general : *brimstone* of any in particular who may be condemned to the lake of fire. Sulphur is not evil by original constitution, but to become actually good it needs the elevating action of fire : not consigned to the purifying crucible it remains gross though capable of refinement : capable of refinement yet unrefined it is at last condemned as fuel to the flame. [I mean not my little parable for scientific experts, but for verbal dabblers like myself.]

“The beast was taken, and with him the false prophet ” —: bound up as it were in a bundle to be burnt. “Fear not, neither be faint-hearted for the two tails of these smoking firebrands.”

O Christ Who once wast condemned that we might never be condemned, pity us.
Who once enduredst shame that we might never fall into everlasting contempt, pity us.
Who once wast forsaken of all that we might never be forsaken of God, pity us.
Who once wast slain that we might never die, pity us.
Who once madest Thy bed in a grave that we might not come short of a blessed resurrection, pity us.
O Christ Who showest us hell that we may flee from it, pity us.
Who showest us heaven that we may thither ascend, pity us.
Because, O Christ, we deserve condemnation, pity us.
Because shame hath covered our face, pity us.
Because many times we have forsaken God, pity us.
Because we have destroyed ourselves, pity us.
Because we have said to corruption father, to the worm mother and sister, pity us.
O Christ Who knowest and we know not the depth of hell, pity us.

Who knowest and we know not the height of heaven, pity us.
Joseph yearned over Benjamin. O Christ, Lord God Almighty, Who
hast deigned to become our Brother, pity us. Amen.

**21. And the remnant were slain with the sword of Him
that sat upon the horse, which sword proceeded out
of His mouth: and all the fowls were filled with
their flesh.**

" With the breath of His lips shall He slay the wicked."

The deceivers are cast alive into a lake of fire, the deceived
are slain with the sword : " With Him is strength and Wisdom :
the deceived and the deceiver are His." Thus the seducer
being incomparably more guilty than the seduced, incurs a
proportionate doom ; the scale of condemnation being poised
as accurately, equitably, subtly, as even the scale of salvation.

According to which Divine model of Justice and Mercy,
Holy Mother Church now disciplines or would fain discipline
her children : "Of some have compassion, making a difference : and others save with fear, pulling them out of the fire ;
hating even the garment spotted by the flesh."

"And all the fowls were filled with their flesh."—"The eye
that mocketh at his father, and despiseth to obey his mother,
the ravens of the valley shall pick it out, and the young eagles
shall eat it " :—a proverb with a natural meaning and a supernatural suggestion.

> The end of all things is at hand.   We all
>   Stand in the balance trembling as we stand ;
> Or if not trembling, tottering to a fall.
>   The end of all things is at hand.
>
> O hearts of men, covet the unending land !
> O hearts of men, covet the musical,
>   Sweet, never-ending waters of that strand !
>
> While Earth shows poor, a slippery rolling ball,
>   And Hell looms vast, a gulf unplumbed, unspanned,
> And Heaven flings wide its gates to great and small,
>   The end of all things is at hand.

Earth is pre-eminently that rolling stone which gathers no
moss. She has treasure, but it can be laid up in heaven only :
she has a harvest, but her harvest-home is in heaven.

CHAPTER XX.

1. And I saw an angel come down from heaven, having the key of the bottomless pit and a great chain in his hand.

"An evil man seeketh only rebellion: therefore a cruel messenger shall be sent against him." Not that I dare misdeem of this avenging Angel as tinged with any taint of cruelty, but only as merciless when God All-Merciful shuts up His loving-kindness in displeasure. If "the tender mercies of the wicked are cruel," no less are the "cruelties" of the righteous merciful; for the casting away of all evil is the restitution of all things.

Who forged that chain? Surely the dragon himself. So Goliath furnished the sword which smote off his own head, and Haman reared the gallows on which he himself came to be hanged. Thus we are self-bound in the chain of sin before God tightens it upon us as a chain of penalty.

"O God, Whose nature and property is ever to have mercy and to forgive, receive our humble petitions; and though we be tied and bound with the chain of our sins, yet let the pitifulness of Thy great mercy loose us; for the honour of Jesus Christ, our Mediator and Advocate. Amen."

In the same sense that "God made not death," made He not punishment.

O God our God, Who hast no pleasure in the death of him that dieth, from death deliver fleshly sinners, spotted, stained, leprous, hideous, one and all and me a sinner.

From destruction deliver worldly sinners, clogged, weighed down, glued fast to perishing earth, one and all and me a sinner.

From the bottomless pit, from the lake of fire, deliver spiritual sinners, wilful, rebellious, defiant, braving vengeance, one and all and me a sinner.

For the love of Jesus, Who laid aside His Glory, Who learned obedience, Who was crucified, Who made His grave with the wicked and with the rich in His death, for love of one and all and of me a sinner. Amen.

2. And he laid hold on the dragon, that old serpent, which is the Devil, and Satan, and bound him a thousand years,

3. And cast him into the bottomless pit, and shut him up, and set a seal upon him, that he should deceive the nations no more, till the thousand years should be fulfilled: and after that he must be loosed a little season.

Truly a joyful day when these "former things" shall come to pass. Meanwhile if it was not for Apostles to know the times and the seasons which the Father hath put in His own power, how much less for me !

The date is hidden, the event revealed : the date therefore concerns me not at present, the event concerns me at once.

But what? must we fall a helpless prey to the strong raging dragon, the insinuating serpent, until an angel secure him with chain and seal and the lid of hell? Not so. Even now already thou hast thy chain at hand, my brother, my sister : I, if I will, have mine.

> "Satan trembles when he sees
> The weakest saint upon his knees."

Prayer is a chain apt presently to bind him, and which he cannot snap; prayer which links earth to heaven, human weakness to Divine Strength, me (if I will), even me to my Redeemer. Though the great and wide sea be Leviathan's playground, yet to him and to his habitation alike God hath assigned a bound by a perpetual decree so that neither can pass over it.

Lord Jesus, Who Alone makest our prayers acceptable to the Father, shelter us under prayer, hide us in prayer, give us breathings of prayer wherewith to quench the fiery breath of the dragon, wisdom of prayer whereby to silence the lying subtilty of the serpent. Amen.

Not dragon simply, or serpent simply; but serpent-dragon to be fled from when met raging, and still more to be feared when gliding unobtrusively. Not a novice, but an "old serpent," surpassingly subtil when Eve encountered him, and having now the accumulated experience of thousands of years and millions of victories.—Good Lord, deliver us.

"A seal upon him, that he should deceive the nations no more, till. . . ."—If upon *himself*, Cain's mark as it were. If upon his *prison*, then we are reminded of the irreversible act of Darius : " A stone was brought, and laid upon the mouth of the den; and the king sealed it with his own signet, and with the signet of his lords; that the purpose might not be changed."

Hell has no bottom, but has a lid : I need not fall in. Hell has indeed no bottom, yet has it one only exit and that upwards. A figure to me of the folly of piling sin on sin in hopes of self-extrication. To cover one lie by a second lie thickens the lid over me.

> Lord, grant us wills to trust Thee with such aim
>   Of hope and passionate craving of desire,
>   That we may mount aspiring, and aspire
> Still while we mount ; rejoicing in Thy Name
> Yesterday, this day, day by day the Same :
>   So sparks fly upward scaling heaven by fire,
>   Still mount and still attain not, yet draw nigher
> While they have being to their fountain flame.
> To saints who mount, the bottomless abyss
>   Is as mere nothing : they have set their face
>   Onward and upward toward that blessed place
>   Where man rejoices with his God, and soul
> With soul, in the unutterable kiss
>   Of peace for every victor at the goal.

"The thousand years . . . a little season."—I can compute a *thousand*, but not *a little*. The thousand years I might call long : the little season I incline to figure to myself as much shorter. Either would appear brief if compared with the whole of time ; and time from beginning to end would itself dwindle to mere brevity if set against eternity. Nevertheless eternity hangs on time. " Behold, how great a matter a little fire kindleth !"

The thousand years of exemption are to be " fulfilled." We read not that the little season of final horror is to be *fulfilled*. Perhaps Divine Compassion may cut it short ; if so, it appears in harmony with Christ's promise : " For the elect's sake those days shall be shortened."

"He must . . . "—What is to be understood by this *must ?* an irresponsible, inflexible fate overbearing the Will of the Almighty?—Not so : it expresses to us the fiat of that Almighty Will.—*Shall* would have conveyed the same without ambiguity.—Possibly so : and if so, a surface ambiguity is here superadded for my profit.—How should it profit one ?—By pressing home upon me to acquiesce in any case and to trust in every case. By practising me in discerning truth and eschewing error.—But suppose the other should be the true sense?—I cannot suppose what contradicts everything I know. —But suppose it for argument's sake.—I will not even for argument's sake suppose that to be true which I know to be a lie.

4. And I saw thrones, and they sat upon them, and judgment was given unto them: and I saw the souls of them that were beheaded for the witness of Jesus, and for the word of God, and which had not worshipped the beast, neither his image, neither had received his mark upon their foreheads, or in their hands; and they lived and reigned with Christ a thousand years.

Lord Jesus, grant us grace to live not by bread alone, but by every word which proceedeth out of Thy mouth.

Grant us in Thy Revelation to see as it were thrones whereon sitteth that word which Thou hast spoken, and which is to judge us at the last day.

Grant us to understand somewhat and to obey all. Here am I, send me.

Grant us to understand somewhat and to believe all. Speak, Lord, for Thy servant heareth.

Remember Thy sigh, Gracious Saviour, remember Thy word Ephphatha, and evermore open deaf ears. Amen.

Glorious as is the lot of these princes and peers of the Millennium, I yet perceive one thing: the causes—secondary causes, of course; the primary cause being Divine gratuitous Love—the secondary causes of their lofty beatitude are, with a single exception, within the reach of every Christian; of whom not one need pollute himself by devil worship or idolatry, or need befoul his mind by evil thoughts, or his will by evil choice, or his hands by evil deeds. The qualification not open to all is the being " beheaded " for witnessing their good confession; and this qualification was not bestowed even on St. John himself, bosom friend, beloved disciple, true witness (*see* St. John xxi. 24) though he was.

To be excluded with St. John surely excludes not from the innermost blessedness, from the deepest heart of Divine Love. And who shall realize St. John's joy, his peace, his overflowing gratitude and unspoken " It is enough," when he realized St. James his brother as fulfilling every condition of this great exaltation?

They who love as brethren, they who love neighbours as self, can best surmise such a rapture.

Souls who aspire to the millennial glory, yet who involuntarily fall more or less short of the revealed qualification, may all together be likened to the spiral tendril of a passion-flower climbing skyward, each curve advanced one grade in approximation, none touching the goal. Thus some confessors have borne prolonged witness in instant hazard of life, and some have endured bitterness of persecution bitter as bitterness of death, and some have taken their life in their hands to reap the mission field, and some have sacrificed earthly prospects to spiritual fidelity, and some have offered up earthly love on the altar of heavenly love. And beside or below this galaxy coruscate resplendent souls who laden with a daily Cross have followed Christ in weariness and painfulness, in watchings and fastings often, in poverty submitted to with Christ or assumed for Christ, in that contented lack of all things which is their true possession, in perfecting work of patience, in self-abasement, self-forsaking, self-oblation; and amongst them behold unobtrusive saints who rejoice in beds of loathsomeness or of agony.

What reward shall these and such as these inherit? What reward shall they not inherit? O Jesus Christ, King of Joy and of Glory, bring us also to see the felicity of Thy chosen, and rejoice in the gladness of Thy people, and give thanks with Thine inheritance. Amen.

Unless, which let me not for a moment suppose, the desecration of the Jewish Seventh Day preceded the consecration of the Christian First Day, it follows that two "Sabbaths" must once at least in the course of time have occurred in undivided succession. Thus (if lawfully I may) I endeavour to realize to myself one aspect of the Millennium: it is the closing Sabbath of time, scarcely disjoined from the permanent Sabbath of eternity; it is one marked fulfilment of that promise to the Meek, "they shall inherit the earth." Time receives a blessing as it gives place to more blessed eternity: for " Godliness is profitable unto all things, having promise of the life that now is, and of that which is to come."

"But, beloved, be not ignorant of this one thing, that one day is with the Lord as a thousand years, and a thousand years as one day."

"Fulfil her week." Leah and Rachel, recognized figures of the Active and Contemplative Lives, seem consequently to become figures of Time and Eternity. Each claims her rights,

the week of each must be fulfilled : Leah takes precedence of
Rachel, Rachel supersedes Leah.

Whether we speak of Leah or of Time, either is characterized
by craving, aspiring, unsatisfied love : whether of Rachel or of
Eternity, either is characterized by satisfaction of love.

Leah herself declares her fruitfulness to be that which gives
her a hold upon her husband : similarly, works wrought in time
secure to the creatures of time their hold upon the Divine
Spouse. Leah said : "Now this time will my husband be
joined unto me, because I have born him three sons. . . .
God hath endued me with a good dowry; now will my husband
dwell with me, because I have born him six sons." How indissoluble was the tie thus woven between them Jacob himself
suggests when he makes his last bed where he "buried
Leah." Time passes away, but the result of Time passes not
away.

"Her children arise up, and call her blessed; her husband
also, and he praiseth her. . . . Give her of the fruit of her
hands; and let her own works praise her in the gates "—please
God, the gates of pearl.

> Time passeth away with its pleasure and pain,
>   Its garlands of cypress and bay,
> With wealth and with want, with a balm and a bane,
>   Time passeth away.
>
> Eternity cometh to stay,
> Eternity stayeth to go not again :
> Eternity barring the way,
>
> Arresting all courses of planet or main,
>   Arresting who plan or who pray,
> Arresting creation,—while grand in its wane
>   Time passeth away.

"With Christ a thousand years."—Whilst in Thy sight a
thousand years are but as yesterday, seeing that it is past ; in our
sight they would be less than yesterday, than a moment, than
the twinkling of an eye, if a millennium could end in parting.
If after knowledge of Thee our Lord and Saviour Jesus Christ,
if after having known Thee our Way of Righteousness, saints
could at last be severed from Thee, they would indeed be of
all men most miserable. As now foresight of death straitens
and disenchants life, so then would foresight of divorce balk
and embitter union. If in order to hasten and have done with
the last pang even downcast Elijah requested for himself that
he might die, how much more might those !

Lord, Good Lord, suffer not one who hath had knowledge

that Thou art Jesus, ever for any pains of life or death to fall from Thee.

To know and love God in this mortal life argues immortality.

> O Lord, fulfil Thy Will
> Be the days few or many, good or ill :
> Prolong them, to suffice
> For offering up ourselves Thy sacrifice ;
> Shorten them if Thou wilt,
> To make in righteousness an end of guilt.
> Yea, they will not be long
> To souls who learn to sing a patient song :
> Yea, short they will not be
> To souls on tiptoe to flee home to Thee.
> O Lord, fulfil Thy Will :
> Make Thy Will ours, and keep us patient still
> Be the days few or many, good or ill.

5. But the rest of the dead lived not again until the thousand years were finished. This is the first resurrection.

"The rest of the dead"—prisoners of hope, prisoners of fear, waiting a thousand years, waiting thirteen thousand moons : years which will terminate, yet which in some sort are already the beginning of the endless end ; moons (if I may call them moons) without phases, unchangeable, irrevocably fixed ; without terror for the prisoners of hope, without hope for the prisoners of fear.

The popular saying "While there is life there is hope" implies also that while there is life there is fear. Hope and fear in this life are interdependent. Indeed hope without fear might perhaps be viewed no longer as hope but rather as longing expectation, fear without hope as desperate anticipation. But during probation such distinctions are beside the question. Fear is the ballast of Hope, Hope the buoy of Fear.

O my God, Who demandest of us patient hope and trustful fear, give us, I beseech Thee, that which pleaseth Thee : contented fear, resigned hope, unexhausted patience, all based on faith, and faith itself based on love. For Jesus Christ's sake. Amen.

6. Blessed and holy is he that hath part in the first resurrection : on such the second death hath no power, but they shall be priests of God and of Christ, and shall reign with Him a thousand years.

"Whosoever will save his life shall lose it ; but whosoever

shall lose his life for My sake and the gospel's, the same shall save it,"—said once our Lord.

These "blessed and holy" of the First Resurrection experience this privilege in its plenitude. Literally they fulfilled the annexed condition, literally does God fulfil to them His promise. "On such the second death hath no power," it has no hold upon them, it does not apply to them : thus indeed are the children free !

Behold the host of men, the host of women, yea, even the host of young children also, who on such wise lost life and saved it. Once over them devout persons made great lamentation, a grief they were to their fathers, a pang to the mothers that bare them, for love of them brethren and sisters sat alone and kept silence, for love of them kindred faces gathered blackness. Now and for evermore these are they whom their brethren praise, whom virgins love, with whom all saints claim kinship, whom fathers bless, and because of whom mothers forget sorrow for joy that such are born into the world, the deathless world.

A priest must of necessity have somewhat to offer. Wherefore well may they be priests of God and of Christ, who have offered themselves and have kept back nothing. Now they who kept nothing lack nothing, they who gave all receive all. They counted the cost, and having counted gave their all : this better all which they receive they count not and cannot count.

These are champions of hosts, alphas of constellations. Their consummate glory lies not within reach of every man.

Nevertheless it is their gift which is exclusive, not their grace. One who cannot be martyr in deed may yet be martyr in will. Man recognizes the first dazzling company : our God recognizes (thank God) both the first and the last. "Praise ye the Lord. Praise the Lord, O my soul." "Let every thing that hath breath praise the Lord."

"They shall be priests . . . and shall reign."--"Melchizedek king of Salem . . . was the priest of the Most High God." On earth kings exercise a Royal Priesthood when they intercede for and bless their people : Priests a Spiritual Royalty when they rule their flocks with wisdom and self-postponement. Such functions, virtues, dignities, appertain in various degrees to all superiors ; and every intercessor (and what Christian is there debarred from intercession ?) becomes so far a superior. "Covet earnestly the best gifts," and secure them by the "more excellent way."

O Jesus Christ, the Great High Priest, Who knowest all and

lovest all, give unto each one of us grace to shine as Thy spark, Thy flame, Thy conflagration, as best may please Thee, and best may glorify Thee. We are called by Thy Name and lack nothing, we are dear unto Thee and it is enough.

Yea, blessed and holy is he that hath part in the First Resurrection !
  We mark well his bulwarks, we set up his tokens, we gaze even we
On this lustre of God and of Christ, this creature of flawless perfection :
    Yea, blessed and holy is he.

  But what? an offscouring of earth, a wreck from the turbulent sea,
A bloodstone unflinchingly hewn for the Temple's eternal erection,
  One scattered and peeled, one sifted and chastened and scourged and set
    free ?
Yea, this is that worshipful stone of the Wise Master Builder's election,
  Yea, this is that King and that Priest where all Hallows bow down the
    knee,
Yea, this man set nigh to the Throne is Jonathan of David's delection,
  Yea, blessed and holy is he.

7. And when the thousand years are expired, Satan shall be loosed out of his prison,

8. And shall go out to deceive the nations which are in the four quarters of the earth, Gog and Magog, to gather them together to battle: the number of whom is as the sand of the sea.

As Satan went in, so comes he out : a liar and the father of lies ; a murderer from the beginning and to the end.

He is loosed but not freed. He appears lord of sin: but like the whole wretched rabble of his fellow-sinners he too is merely servant of that sin to which he obeys.

The wages of sin is death : to penitence the first death, to impenitence the second death. " The sting of death is sin ; and the strength of sin is the law. But thanks be to God, which giveth us the victory through our Lord Jesus Christ."

God's chastisement is always good : my response may be either good or evil. On what does my response depend? on my own will.

Lord Jesus, Who didst so bind Thyself with cords of love, that having saved others Thyself Thou couldst not save : constraining us by love save us.

Thou Who wast bound and led captive by wicked men, agents of the devil: by Thy captivity free us.

Bind us if Thou wilt ; but tenderly as in Thine own swaddling bands, guards of weakness, screens from peril. Amen.

That thousand years' imprisonment wrought no reformation : therefore hell ensued.

The thousand years of paralyzed wickedness seem on com-

parison better rather than worse than the little season of
rampant wickedness ;—I mean, even as regards the wicked
one. By inference : hell itself in all its horror may so far be
better than ante-hell.

[Nevertheless:—From fancied wisdom, presumptuous guesses,
vain speculations, unauthorized conclusions, Good Lord, deliver
all, deliver me.]

A spiritual-minded and very dear person once suggested to
me (and to me the suggestion was new and unheard of) that
this final insurrection of Gog and Magog seduced and stirred
up by diabolical deceit, may not be as heretofore a rebellion
of the living ; but rather a closing death-struggle of the already
dead, occurring in the interval between the first and the second
death. My friend dropped no more than a very few words, but
thus I attempt to state her idea. Years ago she went home
from shadows to substances, and happy should I be were I a
mirror to others of some of her wisdom. Only let not errors
of mine be imputed to her.

Contemplating the text under such a borrowed light, the
deceit may apparently consist not in sophistries such as erst
entrapped the living fool to say in his heart, There is no God ;
but in equally futile sophistries now encouraging the creature
to a trial of strength with its Creator : a much more desperate
undertaking than if earth should so challenge the sun.

As such a scheme, however, trenches upon interpretation, I
pursue it no further, except to note how vividly it sets before
me that he who dies a rebel rises a rebel ; and that lost souls
are punished not for sins left behind, but for sin clung to,
persisted in, chosen with unrelaxed, inflexible choice.

Ezekiel in three successive chapters (xxxvii., xxxviii., xxxix.)
sets before us in vision or in prophecy a resurrection to life of
perished Israel, and an upsurging and destruction of Gog with
his hosts of Magog. However these three chapters may admit
of a previous temporal interpretation, they exhibit no less a
vivid symbol of events which will close time and open eternity.

That there is difference as well as likeness between these two
revelations touching Gog and Magog, is suggested by Ezekiel's
Gog and Magog being derived expressly "out of the north
parts," whilst St. John's muster from "the four quarters of the
earth." The first host is a multitude, the second a multitude
of multitudes : and even of the former it is predicted : "Thou
shalt ascend and come like a storm, thou shalt be like a cloud
to cover the land, thou, and all thy bands, and many people
with thee."

" The number of whom is as the sand of the sea."—Nearly the same simile is used of faithful Abraham's descendants : " As the sand which is by the sea shore innumerable." So that sand which is neither good nor evil, by being compared to something good and to something evil indifferently, reminds us once more how a simile is not a proof, neither is an illustration evidence.

I in my degree must bear this in mind. Sand may curb excursiveness, but cannot serve for a foundation.

" Fear ye not Me ? saith the Lord : will ye not tremble at My presence, which have placed the sand for the bound of the sea by a perpetual decree, that it cannot pass it ? "—" Every one that heareth these sayings of Mine, and doeth them not, shall be likened unto a foolish man, which built his house upon the sand : and the rain descended, and the floods came, and the winds blew, and beat upon that house ; and it fell : and great was the fall of it."—" The sand [is] weighty," says the Proverb.

9. And they went up on the breadth of the earth, and compassed the camp of the saints about, and the beloved city: and fire came down from God out of heaven, and devoured them.

" If it had not been the Lord Who was on our side, now may Israel say ; if it had not been the Lord Who was on our side, when men rose up against us : then they had swallowed us up quick, when their wrath was kindled against us : then the waters had overwhelmed us, the stream had gone over our soul : then the proud waters had gone over our soul. Blessed be the Lord, Who hath not given us as a prey to their teeth."

" On the breadth of the earth."—Hast thou perceived the breadth of the earth ? declare if thou knowest it all." Broad yet finite : narrower than a hairbreadth by comparison with infinity. " I see that all things come to an end : but Thy commandment is exceeding broad."

" The camp of the saints."—For the last time we thus behold the Church Militant ; shortly she will reappear as the Church Triumphant : for the last time terrible as an army with banners ; then and for evermore fair as the moon, clear as the sun.

The saints form a camp, but we perceive not that at this juncture they fight. It may be that like their Divine Captain they neither strive nor cry ; but now are called to stand still and see the salvation of God, as Israel once on the

Red Sea coast awaited deliverance. "Vengeance is Mine; I will repay, saith the Lord." Having done all, they stand.

All along their weapons had been superhuman, their warfare spiritual, not carnal. They fought the battles of the Lord not only to save their own souls alive, but likewise so far as in them lay to subdue the adversaries to His obedience; in themselves and in all mankind aiming to promote the Divine glory and supremacy. Theirs was a long-drawn fight in hope and charity, in faith, zeal, and obedience. It may be that as to any active agency they are mercifully exempted from the war of extermination.

"The beloved city."—"The Lord loveth the gates of Zion more than all the dwellings of Jacob. Glorious things are spoken of thee, O city of God." "The Lord hath chosen Zion; He hath desired it for His habitation. This is My rest for ever: here will I dwell; for I have desired it."

"Fire came down from God out of heaven, and devoured them."—Nevertheless, why will we die? Fire from heaven once reclaimed an apostate nation; once carried up a saint by a whirlwind into heaven. This day is still the day of salvation; there is yet time, there is yet room. Why will we die? If we die it is by our own obstinacy.

O Merciful Lord God, O Lord most Merciful, so replenish us with grace that whatever else may be hidden from us we may always everywhere and in all things discern Thy mercy. For if being Truth Thou canst not deny Thyself, neither being Love canst Thou be other than Thyself. In which Thine Unchangeableness grant us quiet hearts, assurance of holy hope, peace, patient confidence of love. For Jesus Christ's sake, Who is our All in all. Amen.

For folly give us wisdom, Good Lord, for heart of stone heart of flesh, for rebellion loyalty, for sin righteousness, for death resurrection, for mortal life, life immortal. Good Lord, for Thine own sake. Amen.

Sodom perished by fire for pride, fulness, idleness, neglect of the poor, haughtiness, depravity: from crying sin and signal punishment, Good Lord, deliver us, as Thou didst deliver righteous Lot vexed of soul.

Nadab and Abihu perished by fire for offering strange fire: from presumption and sacrilege, from fellowship in evil and not in good, Good Lord, deliver us.

Certain Israelites perished by fire for murmuring in the wilderness: from thankless discontent, Good Lord, deliver us.

Two hundred and fifty Levites perished by fire for invading

the Priest's Office : from exceeding our rights and outstepping our order, Good Lord, deliver us.

Two Captains of Fifty for slighting a Prophet perished by fire with their Fifties : from like sin and like destruction, Good Lord, deliver us, as Thou didst deliver with his Fifty the third Captain humbling himself and deprecating wrath.

10. And the devil that deceived them was cast into the lake of fire and brimstone, where the beast and the false prophet are, and shall be tormented day and night for ever and ever.

"The getting of treasures by a lying tongue is a vanity tossed to and fro of them that seek death."

Did Satan then seek death? Yes, even if he named not death that which he sought. He sought not life : and thereupon seeking somewhat he sought death. A fearful parallel holds good : as he, so we, if we seek not life seek death.

O Christ our only Life, our Life immortal, Who of old hast declared, "I am found of them that sought Me not"; say to us also "Behold Me, behold Me," and with the word give the grace. So shall we not die but live and declare Thy works, O Lord : so with all living shall we praise Thee as I do this day. Amen.

Satan is "that old serpent"; and in the serpent tribe we observe ghastly, loathly, emblematic likenesses of Satan. Constrictors some of them, some vessels of venom ; flat heads, unemotional eyes, forked darting tongues are amongst them : silent, insinuating, gliding, they are upon us before we know that they are near. Yet of all living creatures which my memory records no one in Satanic suggestion approaches, to my own thinking, the octopus.

One single small octopus in an aquarium is all I have seen. It had a fascination for me. Inert as it often appeared, it bred and tickled a perpetual suspense : will it do something? will it emerge from the background of its water den? I have seen it swallow its live prey in an eyewink, change from a stony colour to an appalling lividness, elongate unequal feelers and set them flickering like a flame, sit still with an air of immemorial old age amongst the lifeless refuse of its once living meals. I had to remind myself that this vivid figure of wickedness was not in truth itself wickedness.

"Where the beast and the false prophet are."—"Art thou also become weak as we : art thou become like unto us?"

Recognition appears no less essential to the rancorous horror of hell than to the felicity of heaven. Recognition points and clenches hatred as well as love. If so be they are immured eternally together, what other soul could be to Caiaphas as Judas, or to Judas as Caiaphas? or to the Pharisee as his own twofold more child of hell, or to that child as that Pharisee?

Alas for seducer and seduced who once called their bond love, and behold it is loathing! "Day and night for ever and ever."

11. And I saw a great white Throne, and Him that sat on it, from Whose Face the earth and the heaven fled away; and there was found no place for them.

"Great," and all other thrones are as footstools before it: "white," for it is the tribunal of absolute equity. "Fear before Him, all the earth." "And I will wait on Thy Name; for it is good before Thy saints."

This fleeing away of earth and heaven, of irresponsible nature, may serve as a symbol how neutrality (if in truth neutrality can be said ever to have existed) will be abolished at the last day. Either the Right Hand or the Left, no middle region : either saint or reprobate, no mixed character.

Where two bodies touch the dividing line is imaginary.

Earth, heaven, neutrals: "there was found no place for them."

O Christ our God, inasmuch as Thy sacred footsteps conferred not perpetuity on this present earth, let us not harbour a grudge because endeared familiar places must one day know us no more.

O Christ our God, inasmuch as Thy triumphant Ascension conferred not perpetuity on the heaven that now is, let us not lose patience while we await the unseen heaven Thou preparest for them that love Thee.

> Lift up thine eyes to seek the invisible :
> Stir up thy heart to choose the still unseen :
> Strain up thy hope in glad perpetual green
> To scale the exceeding height where all saints dwell.
> —Saints, is it well with you?—Yea, it is well.—
> Where they have reaped, by faith kneel thou to glean :
> Because they stooped so low to reap, they lean
> Now over golden harps unspeakable.
> —But thou purblind and deafened, knowest thou
> Those glorious beauties unexperienced
> By ear or eye or by heart hitherto?—
> I know Whom I have trusted : wherefore now
> All amiable, accessible tho' fenced,
> Golden Jerusalem floats full in view.

That which one faces, modifies, and is reflected from the face.

Alas! what fire is it which flushes the world's face to an "angry and brave" rose?

The Church Militant exhibits a pale, ascetic face, because the pale forecast of the "Great White Throne" abides upon it. A light heart is not for her, but rather the weight of an ever-conscious responsibility. Idle words are not for her, for of such an account must be given in the Day of Judgment. Revellings and such like are not for her, for though one eat and drink to-morrow he must die. Her courage is curbed by fear, her fear spurred by courage. She lifts not up her face to a window, neither cries she to an arm of flesh, Who is on my side? who? But she lifts up her eyes to the unearthly hills from whence cometh her help, even from the Lord Who hath made heaven and earth.

"It is better to go to the house of mourning, than to go to the house of feasting : for that is the end of all men ; and the living will lay it to his heart. Sorrow is better than laughter : for by the sadness of the countenance the heart is made better. The heart of the wise is in the house of mourning : but the heart of fools is in the house of mirth. It is better to hear the rebuke of the wise, than for a man to hear the song of fools. For as the crackling of thorns under a pot, so is the laughter of the fool : this also is vanity."

12. And I saw the dead, small and great, stand before God; and the books were opened : and another book was opened, which is the book of life : and the dead were judged out of those things which were written in the books, according to their works.

On the dead for whom once Thou diedst, Lord Jesus, have mercy.
On the living for whom Thou ever livest, have mercy.
Thou Who wast arraigned before a corrupt judge, O Incorruptible Judge, have mercy.
Thou Who knowest what is in man, O Son of Man, have mercy.
Thou Whose works were all good, have mercy.
Thou Whose life, in the sight of the unwise, once hung in suspense before Pilate, have mercy.
Thou Who Thyself ever knowest what Thou wilt do, have mercy.
On the small, mercy.
On the great, mercy.
Thou Who art unlike us in Thy sinlessness, on us sinners have mercy.
Thou Who art like us in Thy Humanity, on us Thy brethren and Thy sisters, have mercy.
Blot out our evil works from Thy Book of Works, and have mercy.
Write our names in Thy Book of Life, and have mercy.

Blot not out our names, but have mercy.
Give us tears from the Fountain of Thy Mercy.
Store our tears in Thy bottle, with Thine own tears shed for us in pure
    mercy.
And whatever we lack let us not lack Thy mercy. Amen.

"Stand before God"—past kneeling, past praying ; not to
be converted, but sentenced. *Now*, not *then*, is the day of
salvation : not *then* except for the already saved.

My page in the Book of Works is to me awful : the contents
are my own, the record is not my own. It is my life's record
without oversights, without false entries or suppressions : any
good set down accurately as good ; all evil, unless erased by
Divine Compassion, set down accurately as evil. Nothing
whatever is there except what I have genuinely endeavoured,
compassed, done, been : I meant it all, though I meant not to
meet it again face to face. It is as if all along one had walked
in a world of invisible photographic cameras charged with
instantaneous plates.

The Book of Life may seem yet more awful, kept secret as
it has been from the foundation of the world in the knowledge
of God Omniscient.

Yet is it really so? It is in fact no independent statement,
but appears to be essentially an index or summary of the other.
I who composed although I compiled not my Book of Works,
I myself virtually entered or entered not my name in the
corresponding Book of Life : to dread this beyond the other,
is to dread a sum total rather than those very items which
produce the total.

For whilst we read that "the dead were judged out of those
things which were written in the Books," it was none the less
"according to their works."

**13. And the sea gave up the dead which were in it ; and
death and hell delivered up the dead which were in
them : and they were judged every man according to
their works.**

If I make my bed in hell, if I dwell in the uttermost parts of
the sea, the darkness will not cover me, but Thy right hand will
find me and fetch me back. To saints a promise, to sinners a
threat : a blessing, an anathema, "according to their works,"
and not otherwise.

"The sea gave up the dead which were in it."—The dead,
but nought else was as it would seem reclaimed : the diver, but
not the pearl which cost him his life ; the crews, but not the

bullion of foundered ships of Tarshish. Thus complicated civilization produces or amasses riches : and the riches come to nothing except as accusers, and the lives cannot be silenced in the day of account. In that day many luxuries may turn out to have been unlawful, and the price of blood. Ahab was requited in Naboth's vineyard. "So teach us to number our days, that we may apply our hearts unto wisdom."

Death (if I may so express myself) has an enormous swallow, but no digestion : Hades may be viewed as rather a pound than a prison. Like the feaster with him who hath an evil eye, they twain shall " vomit up " the eaten morsel : they have feasted with Satan, and like that evil-eyed host they must be excluded from the land of blessed life everlasting.

Yet Death presents two aspects, Hades two regions: a kindly aspect for Christ-lovers, a twilight bright with afterglow for any who have worked the work of Christ. So that we may pray :—

Lord Jesus Who livest, from the sting of death deliver us.

Lord Jesus Who hast died, to the peace of death bring us.

Lord Jesus Who art risen, let not our grave have the victory.

Lord Jesus Who wast buried, prepare for us a quiet resting-place.

> Clother of the lily, Feeder of the sparrow,
>   Father of the fatherless, dear Lord,
> Tho' Thou set me as a mark against Thine arrow,
>   As a prey unto Thy sword,
> As a ploughed-up field beneath Thy harrow,
>   As a captive in Thy cord,
> Let that cord be love ; and some day make my narrow
> Hallowed bed according to Thy word. Amen.

14. And death and hell were cast into the lake of fire. This is the second death.

"God hath not given us the spirit of fear; but of power, and of love, and of a sound mind. Be not thou therefore ashamed of the testimony of our Lord . . . but be thou partaker of the afflictions of the gospel according to the power of God; Who hath saved us, and called us with an holy calling, not according to our works, but according to His own purpose and grace, which was given us in Christ Jesus before the world began, but is now made manifest by the appearing of our Saviour Jesus Christ, Who hath abolished death, and hath brought life and immortality to light through the gospel."

Thus St. Paul points out that our being called " with an holy calling," *precedes* our duty of working and guarantees our ability to achieve those works according to which we shall be judged. This premised, I think we may infer that each man's lot must inevitably be either to partake of the sanctifying afflictions of the gospel along with its life and immortality ; or else so to cling to death (for this mortal life is a slow death, and sin a superadded death) that at last death and he must be abolished together.

I suppose that amongst so many things which I understand not, thus much I may understand. Because death and Hades are "cast into the lake of fire," impenitent man may expect to find every plague which he has ever known, rankled against, kicked against, there amongst unknown plagues ready to receive him, and to become unto him as the cloak that he hath upon him, and as the girdle that he is alway girded withal. Superb strength must writhe bound hand and foot with grave-clothes, dainty beauty corroded by obscene corruption. Hades the intermediate prison reappears intensified as Hell the final prison, the first death as the second death.

"By Thine Agony, by Thy precious Death and Burial, Good Lord, deliver us."

15. And whosoever was not found written in the book of life was cast into the lake of fire.

Or according to the Revised Version : "And if any was not found written in the Book of Life, he was cast into the lake of fire."

This latter translation may suggest (if I dare so think) a Divine tenderness, yearning, regret. No summary sentence was pronounced, but the Book was searched : " who knoweth if—? "—"and if so be that he find it—." Not that God Omniscient before the beginning foresaw not the end, or that in the ultimate issue of all courses any (except to their own cost) will have resisted His Will; but Holy Scripture being written for our learning, that we through patience and comfort of the Scriptures might have hope, condescends to the limitation of our intelligence and the faintings of our heart, and deals tenderly with us, showing us at a first glance the Fatherly Divine Love ; then at a second anxious look, more vivid and deeper becomes the revelation of that same Love ; so that the more we look the more Love we perceive ; until other aspects fall into the background, and sometime afraid though we are and cannot but be, yet (by God's grace) we put our trust in Him.

"God is Love." Yet I must not so pervert that most comfoitable word as to make it mean that He will exercise a mercy contrary to justice. Beyond a doubt "God is Love": it is my own conception of love which may not in truth be love.

What in the height and depth of my soul, transcending far my level of attainment, "as high as heaven . . . deeper than hell"; what is in truth my own ideal of love?

Such love, at once an affection and a mystery, would sacrifice not myself alone but the beloved object also to his (or her) highest good. Which faithful "for better for worse" chooses the utmost good attainable; or if perfection or even genuine good has become unattainable, then chooses the least evil within possibility.

I fall back on "God is Love."

"Into the lake of fire."—". . . Into hell, into the fire that never shall be quenched: where their worm dieth not, and the fire is not quenched. . . . For every one shall be salted with fire." Not consumed, but conserved; not devoured by fire, but salted with fire.

Whether for good or for evil, to be consumed appertains to time, to be unconsumed appertains to eternity.

CHAPTER XXI.

1. And I saw a new heaven and a new earth: for the first heaven and the first earth were passed away; and there was no more sea.

Behold, one heaven and one earth have passed away, but Christ's word has not passed away. Blessed are now the poor in spirit and the persecuted for righteousness' sake, for theirs is the kingdom of heaven. Blessed are now the meek, for they inherit the earth. Well might St. John who " saw," look up and lift up his head; for however remote, his redemption, the general redemption, was drawing nigh.

Meanwhile the first heaven and the first earth make up our own present lot. Of those others God giveth us not as yet so much as to set our foot on, although He promises them to us for a possession.

The temporary heaven and earth above, around, beneath us, import us now, supply now things convenient for us. These we are bound to use, and by no means to misuse or neglect. "He that is faithful in that which is least is faithful also in much: and he that is unjust in the least is unjust also in much. If therefore ye have not been faithful in the unrighteous mammon, who will commit to your trust the true riches? And if ye have not been faithful in that which is another man's, who shall give you that which is your own?" And though the things which are seen be but temporal, yet a work of the Great Creator is and cannot but be so great, that I suppose neither the profoundest and most illuminated saint, nor all saints summed up together will have exhausted the teaching of things visible, even when the hour comes for them to give place to things invisible. "Ye shall not have gone over the cities of Israel, till the Son of Man be come."

Heaven and earth are to be renewed. Not so the sea: "There was no more sea." And wherefore not the sea?

Regarding the first creation as symbolical, one answer (however inadequate: please God, not contradictory of truth) suggests itself. The harvest of earth ripened, was reaped, was garnered: the sea nourished and brought up no harvest. It bore no fruits which remain, it wrought no works which follow it. It was moreover originally constituted as a passage, not as an abode: across it man toiled in rowing to the haven where he would be, but itself never was and never could become that haven. Thus it presents to us a picture of all which must be left behind. In Ezekiel's vision of the healing river, we yet read concerning a portion of the sea-space: "But the miry places thereof and the marishes thereof shall not be healed; they shall be given to salt,"—given over, it would seem, to reprobation.

"Ye are the salt of the earth," said our Divine Teacher: *salt* in reference to earth and its prevalent corruption, not apparently in any immediate reference to the kingdom of immortality and perfection. "Have salt in yourselves," He said again; but still apparently in reference to man's conduct during probation.

That is an accursed region whereof we read: "That the whole land thereof is brimstone, and salt, and burning, that it is not sown, nor beareth, nor any grass groweth therein." Again, the accursed man "that trusteth in man, and maketh flesh his arm, and whose heart departeth from the Lord , . . shall inhabit the parched places in the wilderness, in a salt land and not inhabited." And the Prophet Zephaniah associates "the breeding of nettles, and saltpits, and a perpetual desolation." Also we "Remember Lot's wife."

Yet how shall we be consoled for our lost sea with its familiar fascination, its delights, its lifelong endearedness? Lo! heaven enshrines its own proper sea of glass as it were mingled with fire, and the uplifted voice of the redeemed is as the sound of many waters. There at last is fulness of that joy, whereas the sea never yet was full; there plenteousness of pleasures as a river. There music unheard hitherto, unimaginable, in lieu of the long-drawn wail of our bitter sea.

Or if after all we cannot during our actual weakness be thoroughly and consciously consoled on this point, let it at least bring home to us that better it is to enter into life, halt, or maimed, or one-eyed, than having two feet, hands, eyes, to be shut out. To suffer loss and be saved is better than to forego nothing and be lost.

"There was no more sea."—As in a far different matter, "For our sakes, no doubt, this is written."

O my God, bestow upon us such confidence, such peace, such happiness in Thee, that Thy Will may always be dearer to us than our own will, and Thy Pleasure than our own pleasure. All that Thou givest is Thy free gift to us, all that Thou takest away Thy grace to us. Be Thou thanked for all, praised for all, loved for all. Through Jesus Christ our Lord. Amen.

> The sea laments with unappeasable
>   Hankering wail of loss,
>   Lifting its hands on high and passing by
>   Out of the lovely light :
> No foambow any more may crest that swell
>   Of clamorous waves which toss ;
>   Lifting its hands on high it passes by
>   From light into the night.
> Peace, peace, thou sea ! God's Wisdom worketh well,
>   Assigns It crown or cross :
>   Lift we all hands on high, and passing by
>   Attest : God doeth right.

2. And I John saw the holy city, new Jerusalem, coming down from God out of heaven, prepared as a bride adorned for her husband.

" For, behold, I create new heavens and a new earth : and the former shall not be remembered, nor come into mind. But be ye glad and rejoice for ever in that which I create : for, behold, I create Jerusalem a rejoicing, and her people a joy. And I will rejoice in Jerusalem, and joy in My people : and the voice of weeping shall be no more heard in her, nor the voice of crying."

(If I am not mistaken) a double point of likeness here connects St. John with his Adorable Master. Throughout the Gospel record of Christ's sayings whilst on earth He never once calls Himself by His Blessed Name of Jesus ; but speaking from heaven first to Saul of Tarsus, afterwards in this Apocalypse (ch. xxii. 16) in reference to the Churches, He nameth Himself by that Name which is above every name, whereat every knee shall bow and which every tongue shall confess. Even so the beloved disciple who in his Gospel enters not his own name so much as once, now speaking as from within the door opened into heaven names himself thrice, and of these times twice in the emphatic form " I John."

To ourselves an alluring lesson of present abasement, future exaltation. Thus pearls submerged awhile in deep waters come to light hereafter in the City of God.

I think too that our eager hope of recognition, the craved

for " I am I and you are you " of eternal reunion, is hereby solaced and strengthened ; whilst we perceive one such identity as might even have eluded observation on earth proclaimed triumphantly in heaven.

My Lord, my Lord Jesus, Thou art enough, Thou by Thyself art enough. Yet withholdest Thou no good thing from them that live a godly life. And Thou discernest the heart's desire of every man, and Thou hearest the request of all lips. Every heart's desire and request I commend to Thee, most loving Lord. Amen.

What will it be at last to see a " holy " city ! for Londoners, for Parisians, for citizens of all cities upon earth to see a holy city. Truly as yet this also " eye hath not seen." Not such is or ever was Jerusalem that now is, or Rome though styled eternal or sacred, or Moscow albeit called holy : neither does any continent or island rear such, nor is any ruin extant of such, nor is so much as one material foundation-stone laid of such.

Nevertheless whoever seeks citizenship at last in that all holy City must now day by day watch, pray, labour, agonize it may be, to sanctify his allotted dwelling in his present mean city ; though this be as Babylon awaiting destruction, as an actual city of the plain clamouring for the vengeance of eternal fire.

Art thou as Lazarus? Hold fast godliness and contentment, earnests and precursors of great gain. Art thou as Dives? Heed betimes the voice of Lazarus :—

> I, laid beside thy gate, am Lazarus ;
>   See me or see me not I still am there,
>   Hungry and thirsty, sore and sick and bare,
> Dog-comforted and crumbs-solicitous :
> While thou in all thy ways art sumptuous,
>   Daintily clothed, with dainties for thy fare :
>   Thus a world's wonder thou art quit of care,
> And be I seen or not seen I am thus.
> One day a worm for thee, a worm for me :
>   With my worm angel songs and trumpet burst
>   And plenitude an end of all desire :
> But what for thee, alas ! but what for thee?
>   Fire and an unextinguishable thirst,
>   Thirst in an unextinguishable fire.

New Jerusalem has been gathered from the uttermost part of the earth to the uttermost part of heaven : stone by stone, soul by soul, here a little and there a little. Laps of luxury, fire of temptation, ease of riches, squalor of destitution, pinnacles of giddy exaltation, mountains of difficulty, valleys of humiliation, each has sent up its prefixed weight, number, measure, nothing lacking, nothing over. Redeemed, called by name, claimed, precious, honourable, beloved, brought from the east and gathered from the west, given up by the north and by the south kept not back, God's sons have been brought from far and His daughters from the ends of the earth ; even every one that is called by the Divine Name, formed of God, created for His glory. Alleluia !

New Jerusalem comes down "from God out of heaven," not as leaving God, but inasmuch as His Presence goeth with her. As when of old that Adorable Presence led the elder Israel in the stages of their Exodus, so now that Same Adorable Inalienable Presence leads her out and brings her in, is beneath her for stability, over her for benediction, around her for acceptance. As a chaste virgin espoused she comes down, longed for, toiled for, Self-sacrificed for, bought with a great price by Him Who gave His whole Substance for love.

She has received all and now she gives back all. She is " adorned for her Husband," for her Beloved Who is indeed more than another beloved. He loved her first, and now she returns His love. He is the Sun, and now as His moon-mirror she appears clear as the sun. He is the Life, and now she has received life from Him and lives to Him. She is His lily, no longer among thorns because He once wore those thorns that so He might take them out of her way. He is All-Holy : and now, her heart purified by His Blood and sanctified by His Spirit, she sees Him Whom to see beatifies. His graces shed on her form the ornament to her head and the chains about her neck. Beautiful are her feet shod with the preparation of the Gospel · of His peace. Behold her in tenderness His dove, in likeness His sister, in union His spouse.

Behold her ! yea, also, and behold thyself, O thou called to be a saint. Her perfections are thy birthright ; thou art what she was, what she is thou mayest become. That Goodness which is her fountain of good overflows to thee likewise. Covet earnestly gifts such as hers, practise self-adornment for love of Him who loveth thee. Reserve gems and pearls for immortality when thou shalt be flawless as they. Adorn thyself meanwhile with flower-like graces : humility the violet, innocence the snowdrop, purity the· lily ; with sweetness for a honeysuckle, with penitence for a fruitful thorn. To-day put on the garments of salvation prepared for thee, that to-morrow'

H H

thou mayest be promoted to wear the garments of praise. "Then shall every man have praise of God."

> A lovely city in a lovely land,
>> Whose citizens are lovely, and whose King
>> Is Very Love; to Whom all angels sing;
> To Whom all saints sing crowned, their sacred hand
> Saluting Love with palm-branch in their hand:
>> Thither all doves on gold or silver wing
>> Flock home thro' agate windows glistering
> Set wide, and where pearl gates wide open stand.
> A bower of roses is not half so sweet,
>> A cave of diamonds doth not glitter so,
>> Nor Lebanon is fruitful set thereby:
>> And thither thou, beloved, and thither I
> May set our heart and set our face, and go
> Faint yet pursuing home on tireless feet.

3. And I heard a great voice out of heaven saying, Behold, the tabernacle of God is with men, and He will dwell with them, and they shall be His people, and God Himself shall be with them, and be their God.

I know not whether the following train of thought is allowable: if not, I repudiate it.

"Out of heaven"—or according to the Revised Version: "Out of the Throne." By this double reading two immutable things, the consensus of heaven and the Supreme Decree from the Throne, may be suggested. Not that in either case it is other than a Divine behest; but thus I seem to see once again and vividly the final absolute unity of all sanctified wills with the Supreme Will. Will, pleasure, approval, choice, in these, in all, the perfected elect are at one with their Father, Redeemer, Sanctifier. "God . . . with men" pervades, so to say, the verse: three times it is expressed; three times, the number of completeness.

"The Tabernacle" itself appears as threefold. It is Christ in Whom dwelleth all the Fulness of the Godhead Bodily. It is the one Church built up in Him and constituted a dwelling of the Holy Spirit. It is each individual saved soul instinct with the Divine Life and Presence. For ever and ever, one by one, each soul a separate, self-conscious, loving, adoring, rejoicing entity: not a drop swallowed up in an ocean, a flame merged in a conflagration, but what it was that it is and that it will be for ever and ever.

Glory be to the Father, and to the Son, and to the Holy Ghost;

As it was in the beginning, is now, and ever shall be world without end. Amen.

"The Tabernacle."—Here where all is perfected, final, irreversible, one might perhaps have expected the word to be Temple rather than Tabernacle. Yet Tabernacle it is, and so has special associations proper to itself.

It carries thought back to that outset (if I may call it so) of Divine Love to the chosen nation when the Angel of His Presence saved them, and He led them and carried them. And to the tenderness of that wonderful word to David: "Shalt thou build Me an house for Me to dwell in? Whereas . I have not dwelt in any house since the time that I brought up the children of Israel out of Egypt, even to this day, but have walked in a tent and in a tabernacle. In all the places wherein I have walked with all the children of Israel spake I a word with any of the tribes of Israel, whom I commanded to feed My people Israel, saying, Why build ye not Me an house of cedar?" And indirectly to that mystery of grace: "The gifts and calling of God are without repentance." "Go and cry in the ears of Jerusalem, saying, Thus saith the Lord; I remember thee, the kindness of thy youth, the love of thine espousals, when thou wentest after Me in the wilderness, in a land that was not sown. Israel was holiness unto the Lord, and the firstfruits of His increase." "God is faithful."

Moreover the word Tabernacle, by recalling to our mind the older progressive journey day after day, may perhaps encourage us to look for progress throughout the days of the years of eternity. Further on indeed we shall encounter the word Temple with all its associations of accomplishment, perpetuity, · rest. But here the word written for our learning is Tabernacle, which thus becomes our "word of exhortation."

"God Himself shall be with them, and be their God."— Yet in some measure it has been so all along as to the righteous. The Goodness of God awaits not a new earth, then and not till then to begin being with His beloved and being their God. Of old He declared, "I change not": it is men that shall be changed. Sin forgiven, guilt abolished, infirmity healed, the possibility of lapse ended, we ourselves (please God) shall be renewed when all things are made new.

In the house not made with hands, eternal in the heavens, shall be brought forth out of. its treasure things new and old.

"With them" and "their" is a promise made unto us and to our children, and to as many as the Lord our God shall call. Yet is it not a promise, or of the nature of a promise, except to such as are willingly His people : to obstinate sinners it would be no promise at all, "but a certain fearful looking for of judgment and fiery indignation."

God made man, Satan unmade man, Christ remaketh man. Yet is it also true that man makes or unmakes himself by virtue of his free will.

From our foes protect us, from ourselves rescue us, let not freewill turn to selfwill and curse our blessings. Good Lord, Kind Lord, Longsuffering Almighty Lord Jesus. Amen.

> Whiteness most white. Ah, to be clean again
>   In mine own sight and God's most holy sight !
> To reach thro' any flood or fire of pain
>   Whiteness most white :
>
> To learn to hate the wrong and love the right,
> Even while I walk thro' shadows that are vain,
>   Descending thro' vain shadows into night.
>
> Lord, not to-day : yet some day bliss for bane
>   Give me, for mortal frailty give me might,
> Give innocence for guilt, and for my stain
>   Whiteness most white.

4. And God shall wipe away all tears from their eyes; and there shall be no more death, neither sorrow, nor crying, neither shall there be any more pain: for the former things are passed away.

It needeth God and it will be God to "wipe away all tears." " As one whom his mother comforteth, so will I comfort you ; and ye shall be comforted in Jerusalem. And when ye see this, your heart shall rejoice, and your bones shall flourish like an herb."

> Together with my dead body shall they arise.
>   Shall my dead body arise ? then amen and yea
> In quest of a home beyond the uttermost skies
>   Together with my dead body shall they.
>
> We know the way : thank God Who hath showed us the way !
> Jesus Christ our Way to beautiful Paradise,
>   Jesus Christ the Same for ever, the Same to-day.
>
> Five Virgins replenish with oil their lamps being wise,
>   Five Virgins awaiting the Bridegroom watch and pray :
> And if I one day spring from my grave to the prize,
>   Together with my dead body shall they.

My brother, my sister, thus shall it be with thee, and thus can I well believe that it will be with thee. Blessed are they that weep now, then to laugh ; that mourn now, then to be comforted. And right dear in the sight of the Lord is the death of His saints. And on the birthday of life immortal anguish of pain shall be forgotten for joy of being born into the eternal world. Therefore are they wise who as yet scarce smile a little, and frequent the house of mourning rather than the house of feasting, and die daily, and groan and travail in patient pain waiting for the redemption of the body. My brother, my sister, happy in knowing these things, and happier still in doing them.

I recollect in a fine sermon meeting with a thought which substantially remains with me. Devout souls, steeped as it were in the anguish of Holy Week, may by stress of that very love and sorrow be unable at a moment's notice to unfurl bright Easter wings and soar triumphant heavenward : so that Easter may overtake them less like giants rejoicing at the goal than like strengthless convalescents still with no more than one step between them and death, carried in kind arms out into the reviving sunshine, laid down in a pleasant spot to inhale the sweet free air, learning gradually to assimilate a renewed hope, joy, peace.

To some such phases a student of the Apocalypse appears liable : "I am afflicted, and ready to die from my youth up : while I suffer Thy terrors I am distracted." Pardonable, laudable up to a certain point ; but beyond that point not to be indulged. Let us not persist in remaining as Zion, who said, "The Lord hath forsaken me, and my Lord hath forgotten me," even when the message came : "Sing, O heavens ; and be joyful, O earth ; and break forth into singing, O mountains : for the Lord hath comforted His people, and will have mercy upon His afflicted."

It is possible to substitute an actual meditation on tears, death, sorrow, crying, pain, for a professed meditation on their abolition. (Whereof I should beware. The homely old proverb bears witness : It is a poor heart that never rejoices.)

If I can scarcely forecast a wiping away of my own tears, I can trustfully contemplate that blessed consummation for all tears of some whom I have loved and revered, who in earlier days set before me examples of things lovely and of good report.

With one such holy cherished memory I connect the text : " O how plentiful is Thy goodness, which Thou hast laid up for them that fear Thee : and that Thou hast prepared for them that put their trust in Thee, even before the sons of men ! Thou shalt hide them privily by Thine own presence from the provoking of all men : Thou shalt keep them secretly in Thy tabernacle from the strife of tongues."

With a second : " Hearken, O daughter, and consider, incline
thine ear : forget also thine own people, and thy father's house.
So shall the King have pleasure in thy beauty : for He is thy
Lord God, and worship thou Him."

With a third : " For to their power, I bear record, yea, and
beyond their power they were willing. . . ."

Two of these I watched to the last breath, and the third
nearly to the end. I have witnessed tears, death, sorrow,
crying, pain. God grant that I may witness the general and
particular abolition of all these when death shall at length be
swallowed up in victory : that I, that we all, may witness and
share in that rapture.

A CHURCHYARD SONG OF PATIENT HOPE.

All tears done away with the bitter unquiet sea,
    Death done away from among the living at last,
Man shall say of sorrow—Love grant it to thee and me !—
        At last, " It is past."

Shall I say of pain, "It is past," nor say it with thee,
    Thou heart of my heart, thou soul of my soul, my Friend?
Shalt thou say of pain, "It is past," nor say it with me
        Beloved to the end ?

" For the former things are passed away."—The word is *for*,
not by any means *although*. The flesh and blood endeared to
us by a lifetime, the marrying and giving in marriage which
formed the vocation and felicity of our fathers and mothers
from Adam and Eve downwards, have passed away. Had
they not, neither would death and its associates have passed
away.

What is good must often be given up in favour of something
better. Who would perpetuate blossom and forego fruit?

To over-cultivate, develop, double a flower, destroys its
fruitfulness. Such double flowers have no future.

**5. And He that sat upon the Throne said, Behold, I make
all things new. And He said unto me, Write : for
these words are true and faithful.**

O Blessed Jesus, Bridegroom of souls, remember how once
Thou saidst : " Can the children of the bridechamber mourn,
as long as the Bridegroom is with them? but the day will
come, when the Bridegroom shall be taken from them, and
then shall they fast." Now, Lord, we fast and mourn : till
Thou return, to mourn is better. But when Thou returnest,
how will it be with Thine own faithful ones? No more sorrow,
because no more sin; no more death, because nothing more

worthy of death.   Again Thou sayest: "Behold, I make all things new": Good Lord, renew us to fresh powers of loving Thee in the joy of Thine unveiled Presence.   Yet to each of us be Thou the Same, and be each soul to Thee the same: say Thou, "It is I," and give each of us grace to answer, It is I.   Amen.

> New creatures; the Creator still the Same
>   For ever and for ever: therefore we
>   Win hope from God's unsearchable decree
> And glorify His still unchanging Name.
> We too are still the same: and still our claim,
>   Our trust, our stay, is Jesus, none but He:
>   He still the Same regards us, and still we
> Mount toward Him in old love's accustomed flame.
> We know Thy wounded Hands: and Thou dost know
>   Our praying hands, our hands that clasp and cling
> To hold Thee fast and not to let Thee go.
>   All else be new then, Lord, as Thou hast said:
>   Since it is Thou, we dare not be afraid,
> Our King of old and still our Self-same King.

"He said unto me, Write: for these words are true and faithful."—*True* is isolated, absolute, self-sufficient: *faithful* is relative, tenderly considerate.   True is an announcement: faithful a promise.   Were every man a liar, God and His Word would abide unalterably true; but (blessed be God!) as the case stands, to all who loving and doing the truth are joyful in Him, God and His Word abide no less unalterably faithful.

O Lord, Whose mercy reacheth unto the heavens and Whose faithfulness unto the clouds, seal to us Thy mercy.

Thou Who of very faithfulness causest us to be troubled, bring Thou our soul out of trouble that we may praise Thee among much people.

Thou Whose loving mercy and faithfulness preserved our Lord Christ, while by life and death He fulfilled Thy pleasure, in Him behold us; that having pleased Thee on earth we may glorify Thee out of our graves, trusting Thy faithfulness even in destruction.

Thou Whose faithfulness and truth are man's shield and buckler, by Thy light and Thy truth lead us evermore; that so all saints together may praise Thee and Thy faithfulness, O God, playing upon instruments of music celestial, and may sing to Thee upon golden harps, O Thou Holy One of Israel.

Through Him in Whom all Thy promises are Yea and Amen, Jesus Christ our only hope.

O Lord Jesus, Whose words are true and faithful, I am full of frailties, faults, falls. Set a watch before my mouth : keep the door of my lips. Except Thy grace curb me I shall offend : yea, except Thy grace inspire me I cannot so much as utterly purpose that my mouth shall not offend. Lord, Who knowest my foolishness, give me wisdom and truth in my heart, that out of the abundance of my heart my mouth may speak worthily. And I pray for all others with me, give us honest and good hearts and acceptable words. Amen.

A fall is a signal not to lie wallowing but to rise.

It is not the signal I should choose, yet it is the signal I have chosen.

Having chosen it wrongly, let me at least obey it rightly.

6. And He said unto me, It is done. I am Alpha and Omega, the Beginning and the End. I will give unto him that is athirst of the fountain of the water of life freely.

If one of our difficulties in striving to rejoice with celestial joy arises from our having hitherto no experience of any un-alloyed delight—for what we know, that we can contemplate, meditate upon, and by kindling of grace anticipate; but what we know not, how are we to lay hold upon?—an efficacious aid towards joy is, I think, vouchsafed us by the wording of this blessed Apocalypse whereby we are sent back again and again to earlier utterances of the same Revelation. Our Lord Jesus Christ, Who many times has called us to worship Him in fear, serve Him by sustained and ever-renewed effort, flee from His wrath, take refuge in His mercy, die daily while we live to Him, and when we die by dying to Him live eternally, now by proclaiming Himself under His former title certifies us that He abideth faithful and cannot deny Himself. "There is therefore now no condemnation to them which are in Christ Jesus, who walk not after the flesh, but after the Spirit."

This, then, Who changes not is He Who now says, "It is done." When hanging on the Cross He said, "It is finished," the work of man's Redemption was finished. Now that He says, "It is done," Salvation, "the fountain of the water of life," is freely proffered to all who thirst. Alas! for any who thirsting refuse to drink : their blood is on their own heads.

Lord, Thy saints know their beginning, for Thou art their Beginning of life; and their end, for Thou art their endless End; and the number of their days, for Thou givest them a long life even for ever and ever, the length of the years of Thine own immortality. Thy saints know this and know all things : Thou Who lovest all, grant unto us all, I pray Thee, to know all things ; and in all, by all, beyond all to know Thee, love Thee, cleave unto Thee, trust Thee, attain unto Thee. Amen, Amen.

It is our own heart that needs to be tuned aright as His Heart is with our heart.

> Tune me, O Lord, into one harmony
>> With Thee, one full responsive vibrant chord ;
> Unto Thy praise all love and melody,
>> Tune me, O Lord.
>
> Thus need I flee nor death, nor fire, nor sword :
> A little while these be, then cease to be,
>> And sent by Thee not these should be abhorred.
>
> Devil and world, gird me with strength to flee ;
>> To flee the flesh, and arm me with Thy word :
> As Thy Heart is to my heart, unto Thee
>> Tune me, O Lord.

" Unto him that is athirst."—The thirsty soul stands between a Divine promise and its fulfilment. " I will give," saith our Gracious Lord : as when to one suppliant leper He spake, " I will," and it was done,—" I will give . . . of the Fountain of the Water of Life freely." Christ's word is pledged ; the Well of Water is springing up into everlasting life : what doth hinder ? Nothing doth hinder, unless it be that I thirst not, neither go thither to draw. Free is the gift, but I also am free to accept or to decline it.

There is a mystery of evil which I suppose no man during his tenure of mortal life will ever fathom. But there is a second mystery of evil (unless I ought rather to call it a branch of the original mystery under a special aspect) which every infected soul must track, must run to earth if I may use the phrase, each for itself; following upon and overtaking it, neither turning again till it be destroyed. I pursuing my own evil from point to point find that it leads me not outward amid a host of foes laid against me, but inward within myself: it is not mine enemy that doeth me this dishonour, neither is it mine adversary that magnifieth himself against me : it is I, it is not another, not primarily any other; it is I who undo, defile, deface myself. True, I am summoned to wrestle on my own scale against principalities, powers, rulers of the darkness of this world, spiritual wickedness in high places ; but none of these can crush me unless I simultaneously undermine my own citadel. That tremendous endowment of Free Will which can even say nay to God Almighty, is able tenfold to say nay to the strong man armed. Nothing outside myself can destroy me by main force and in my own despite : so that as regards my salvation the abstract mystery of evil concerns me not practically; my own inherent evil is what I have to cope with. Thus the universe seems to stand aside, leaving me already all alone face to face with my Judge; at once and for ever as utterly alone with Him as I can be at the last day when set before His tribunal.

So long as I live I must, I cannot but, resist, wrestle with somewhat. . . . Evil or good, Satan or Christ, I am resisting, I am setting myself against. To fight against Satan is to engage on my side the Stronger than he. To fight against Christ . . . .

Dear Lord, by Thy mercies, Thy compassions, boundless compassions, mercies innumerable, keep me, keep all from ever knowing what it is to fight against Thee.

He "that is athirst" is alone he .to whom this free gift is promised.

The · gift, being free, cannot be claimed : yet being by promise, the promise can be claimed.

To desire the gift is to desire the terms of the gift. If I thirst not, at least let me thirst to thirst. " Open thy mouth wide."

Although I cannot at a wish command thirst, at least let me at once practise free giving: for as this is the duty of those who have freely received, though I be not as yet conscious of having received the free gift, perhaps by behaving myself as having it in possession, it may the more copiously be vouchsafed me.

For there is no limit to the Fatherly Bounty of my God.

Refreshing texts for people "hungry, and weary, and thirsty, in the wilderness":—

"And they came to Elim, where were twelve wells of water, and threescore and ten palm trees : and they encamped there by the waters."—"And from thence they went to Beer; that is the well whereof the Lord spake unto Moses, Gather the people together, and I will give them water. Then Israel sang this song, Spring up, O well; sing ye unto it. . . . "— "Ye shall not see wind, neither shall ye see rain; yet that valley shall be filled with water, that ye may drink."—"Thou gavest also Thy Good Spirit to instruct them, and withheldest not Thy manna from their mouth, and gavest them water for their thirst."—"Blessed is the man whose strength is in Thee. . . . Who passing through the valley of Baca make it a well;

the rain also filleth the pools."—"He turneth the wilderness into a standing water, and dry ground into watersprings. And there He maketh the hungry to dwell."—"When the poor and needy seek water, and there is none, and their tongue faileth for thirst, I the Lord will hear them, I the God of Israel will not forsake them. I will open rivers in high places, and fountains in the midst of the valleys : I will make the wilderness a pool of water, and the dry land springs of water." —"I will pour water upon him that is thirsty, and floods upon the dry ground : I will·pour My Spirit upon thy seed, and My blessing upon thine offspring : and they shall spring up as among the grass, as willows by the watercourses."

"Understanding is a wellspring of life unto him that hath it : but the instruction of fools is folly."—"The words of a man's mouth are as deep waters, and the wellspring of wisdom as a flowing brook."

7. He that overcometh shall inherit all things ; and I will be his God, and he shall be My son.

In the Revised Version : " . . . shall inherit these things " : —by which perhaps we may understand either the whole uninterrupted train of glories and blessings enumerated thus far from the opening of this chapter ; or more particularly the " all things new " of ver. 5. Not, it may be, that there is any real difference between the two ideas ; but even the smallest verbal distinction in a document so all-important invites notice ; as when with accurate humility St. John recorded : " Jesus said not unto him . . . but . . . . " If it became St. John, how much more does it become us not to be wise above that which is revealed. " For vain man would be wise, though man be born like a wild ass's colt."

Returning to the Authorized Version, we once more observe how the end reproduces the beginning : as at the starting-point "he that overcometh" was the only hero, so he alone reappears at the goal. At the outset, however, temptation after temptation, snare after snare, each having special features, was enumerated : and one soldier and servant was· summoned to face, despise, triumph over one form of evil ; whilst another was summoned to oppose and conquer a diverse foe. The temptation being special to each man, man by man ; so each victory would have its special point of vantage, ray of glory, guerdon. Now on the contrary at the beatific consummation when the King deigns to be glorified in His saints and admired in all them that believe, "he that overcometh" is rewarded without measure: he inherits not one thing, not many things, but even "all things." As indeed was long ago sung by the Psalmist: "The Lord God is a sun and shield: the Lord will give grace and glory: no good thing will He withhold from them that walk uprightly."

Surely then these who finally inherit all things guaranteed to any soul, must while probation endured have had within themselves at least the germ of every grace anywhere developed. A surmise full of joy when the thralls of lifelong involuntary disadvantages are in question: ". . . A poor and a wise child. . . . Out of prison he cometh to reign." Tending also, I think, to allay party feeling and party cries; St. Paul and Faith! St. James and Works!—if so be we arrive at last within sight of those blessed Saints we shall behold both of them invested with glory because of faith, and with glory because of works; alike in unlikeness, as one star differeth from another star yet both in glory.

"And I will be his God, and he shall be My son."— "Behold, what manner of love the Father hath bestowed upon us, that we should be called the sons of God. . . . Beloved, now are we the sons of God, and it doth not yet appear what we shall be: but we know that, when He shall appear, we shall be like Him; for we shall see Him as He is. And every man that hath this hope in him purifieth himself, even as He is pure. . . . Little children, let no man deceive you. . . . In this the children of God are manifest, and the children of the devil: whosoever doeth not righteousness is not of God, neither he that loveth not his brother."

Thus must he do, such must he become, thus must he persevere unto the end, whosoever desires at the end to have God for his God and to be to Him a son. It will take a life-long overcoming if we, if such as I, are to purify ourselves thoroughly, do righteousness consistently, love all our brethren without exception.

A lifelong overcoming,—but worth the long anxious agonizing strain to be like Him and see Him as He is at last.

"I will . . . and he shall . . . "—"Blessed be the God and Father of our Lord Jesus Christ, Who hath blessed us with all spiritual blessings in heavenly places in Christ: according as He hath chosen us in Him before the foundation of the world, that we should be holy and without blame before Him in love: having predestinated us unto the adoption of children by Jesus Christ to Himself, according to the good pleasure of His Will, to the praise of the glory of His grace, wherein He hath made us accepted in the Beloved."—"For it is God which worketh in you both to will and to do of His good pleasure."

8. But the fearful, and unbelieving, and the abominable, and murderers, and whoremongers, and sorcerers, and idolaters, and all liars, shall have their part in the lake which burneth with fire and brimstone: which is the second death.

O Lord, by might of Whose grace trembling Esther took her life in her hand to the saving of her people and of her own soul; grant us such salutary fear of Thee as may tread underfoot all other fear: even so from the second death defend us.

O Lord, Whose word by Elisha convicted a certain lord of unbelief, wherefore he partook not of the abundance which his eyes beheld; grant us so implicitly to believe Thy promises and threatenings that we may evermore refuse the evil and choose the good: even so from the second death defend us.

O Lord, Who by Thine Angel smotest Herod highly-esteemed among men but making himself an abomination in Thy sight; grant us wisdom to choose the praise of God rather than the praise of men, that our praise may indeed be not of men but of Thee, until that day when every man shall have his praise of God: even so from the second death defend us.

O Lord, the Avenger of Blood, Who for the devil, that murderer from the beginning, hast prepared everlasting fire; deliver us from blood-guiltiness that we fall not into the same condemnation; that slain bodies or slain souls should rise up against us at Thy Judgment Seat, avert, O Lord: even so from the second death defend us.

O Lord, Who by Thine Apostle St. Paul hast instructed us that to the defiled and unbelieving is nothing pure, even their mind and conscience being defiled; purify us that unto us all things may become pure, yea, purify our hearts that we may see Thee, our God: even so from the second death defend us.

O Lord, Who by the same blessed Paul didst smite Elymas the sorcerer with blindness, that so others seeing and fearing might be converted and live and flee from the wrath to come; deliver us from unhallowed curiosity, from superstition, from tampering with unlawful arts: even so from the second death defend us.

O Lord, Who by the arm of Samson destroyedst the worshippers of Dagon, and afterwards without might of man abasedst that impotent idol; take away all idols out of our hearts and any stumbling-block of iniquity from before our face : even so from the second death defend us.

O Lord the Word, Wisdom, Truth, Who having warned us that he that telleth lies shall not tarry in Thy sight, afterwards by Elisha the Prophet didst condemn Gehazi, and by St. Peter the Apostle Ananias and Sapphira ; from the heinous besetting sin of falsehood purge every soul of man, woman, child : even so, Good Lord, from the second death defend us.　Amen.

Texts by way of antidote :—

" The fear of man bringeth a snare : but whoso putteth his trust in the Lord shall be safe."—" Lord, I believe ; help Thou mine unbelief."—" Every one that is proud in heart is an abomination to the Lord : though hand join in hand, he shall not be unpunished."—" Whosoever hateth his brother is a murderer : and ye know that no murderer hath eternal life abiding in him."—" God shall bring every work into judgment, with every secret thing, whether it be good, or whether it be evil."—" There shall not be found among you any one . . . that useth divination, or an observer of times, or an enchanter, or a witch, or a charmer, or a consulter with familiar spirits, or a wizard, or a necromancer.　For all that do these things are an abomination unto the Lord."—" What say I then? that the idol is anything, or that which is offered in sacrifice to idols is anything?　But I say, that the things which the Gentiles sacrifice, they sacrifice to devils, and not to God : and I would not that ye should have fellowship with devils.　Ye cannot drink the Cup of the Lord, and the cup of devils : ye cannot be partakers of the Lord's Table, and of the table of devils."— "Deliver my soul, O Lord, from lying lips, and from a deceitful tongue.　What shall be given unto thee ? or what shall be done unto thee, thou false tongue?　Sharp arrows of the mighty, with coals of juniper."

9. And there came unto me one of the seven angels which had the seven vials full of the seven last plagues, and talked with me, saying, Come hither, I will shew thee the bride, the Lamb's wife.

Flesh and blood shrink from "the seven angels which had the seven vials full of the seven last plagues"; but behold! the vials are emptied, the plagues accomplished, the righteous abide unscathed, one of the angels draws nigh with a joyful message.

All souls have been searched, sifted, tested ; have been weighed, and have been found wanting or not wanting.　Those who have endured to the end, the same are saved. And to them the messenger of vengeance turns out to be their own commissioned messenger of peace.

What Christ-like condescension may we not look for from St. John the beloved! Surely here he stands as representative of all his brethren, yea, of one the least of those his brethren. His gifts, graces, illumination, privileges, vouch for ours, if so be we watch and pray to believe as he believed, hope as he hoped, love as he loved.

If I desire the consummation, it is in my power to practise its antecedents and to rehearse it day by day. Hourly, momentarily, there come to me mercies or chastisements. The chastisements themselves are veiled mercies, as it were veiled angels. The mercies I name chastisements are no less merciful than those which at once I recognize as mercies: no less so, if filially I bow my will to the Divine Will. Open-faced angels are no more celestial than are angels unawares.

> Lord, whomsoever Thou shalt send to me,
> Let that same be
>   Mine Angel predilect:
> Veiled or unveiled, benignant or austere,
> Aloof or near;
>   Thine, therefore mine, elect.
> So may my soul nurse patience day by day,
> Watch on and pray
>   Obedient and at peace;
> Living a lonely life in hope, in faith;
> Loving till death;
>   When life, not love, shall cease.
> . . . . Lo, thou mine Angel with transfigured face
> Brimful of grace,
>   Brimful of love for me!
> Did I misdoubt thee all that weary while,
> Thee with a smile
>   For me as I for thee?

St. John, who has already beheld "the Lamb," is now permitted and invited to see "the Bride, the Lamb's Wife." Christ First, Nearest, Dearest: the Communion of Saints second, near, dear. Christ our All in all: and with Him not nothing, but all things.

Lord, bring with Thee my beloved, according to Thy Will: and to them and much more to Thee bring me at last unworthy. Amen for us all. Amen.

> Lord, by what inconceivable dim road
>   Thou leadest man on footsore pilgrimage!
>   Weariness is his rest from stage to stage,
> Brief halting-places are his sole abode.

Onward he faies thro' rivers overflowed,
  Thro' deserts where all doleful creatures rage ;
  Onward from year to year, from age to age,
He groans and totters onward with his load.
Behold how inconceivable his way ;
  How tenfold inconceivable the goal,
    His goal of hope deferred, his promised peace :—
  Yea but behold him sitting down at ease,
Refreshed in body and refreshed in soul,
At rest from labour on the Sabbath-day.

10. And he carried me away in the spirit to a great and high mountain, and shewed me that great city, the holy Jerusalem, descending out of heaven from God,

11. Having the glory of God : and her light was like unto a stone most precious, even like a jasper stone, clear as crystal;

"A great and high mountain."—A mystical Pisgah. As from Pisgah Moses beheld the Holy Land, so now from this mountain St. John the Holy City. Thus far similarity : afterwards contrast. That earthly mountain becomes as a beacon-height of disappointment and death, the holy land having no power to ascend and meet the longing saint. The unearthly mountain of vision becomes as a watch-tower of hope, a threshold of possession, because the holy city descends to appease desire.

Not that aught created, however "great," can of itself appease desire. But He Who made her and Who sends her forth invests her with His own Glory, so that her resplendence is an image and outcome of His own according to a former revelation : "He that sat was to look upon like a jasper and a sardine stone." She comes down from Him, nevertheless He comes down with her ; she goes not forth except He goes with her ; she is no void shrine, but a tabernacle of God ; a sacred vessel, not empty but full of the Divine Presence. God within her is her Holiness, without her, her Glory : He is above her for her Crown and exceeding great Reward, beneath her for a sure Foundation, around her for Satisfaction without satiety in the indissoluble union of mutual Love inexhaustible. St. John who gazes upon her is of her. She is the Body of Christ, and he a Member in particular. Now beholdeth he what he shall be when seeing Christ as He is he shall be like Him.

The King's Daughter is all glorious within,
  Her clothing of wrought gold sets forth her bliss ;
Where the endless choruses of heaven begin
    The King's Daughter is :

Perfect her notes in the perfect harmonies ;
With tears wiped away, no conscience of sin,
Loss forgotten and sorrowful memories ;

Alight with Cherubin, afire with Seraphin,
Lily for pureness, rose for charities,
With joy won and with joy evermore to win,
The King's Daughter is.

Souls full of grace, highly favoured, may deduce a higher
and more inward lesson : even very weak poor souls may learn
their own lowly lesson. "The Bride" appears not under the
semblance of a woman, but as a "great city" beautiful for
situation, the joy of the whole earth, the city of the Great
King : thus repelling mortal frailty from any sensual, equivocal,
unworthy image of transcendent spiritual truths which demand
purged hearts for their contemplation, purged lips for their
utterance.

Not Holy Jerusalem but obscene Babylon flaunts forth
under the figure of a woman.

Lord Jesus, show us what Thou wilt, that above all else we
may prefer Thee. Hide from us what Thou wilt, that we may
fall back on Thee. Show us not what would hide Thee :
hide not what would reveal Thee. Say unto us, "It is I";
and if it please Thee say unto us, "Be not afraid."

**12. And had a wall great and high, and had twelve gates,
and at the gates twelve angels, and names written
thereon, which are the names of the twelve tribes of
the children of Israel:**

Wherefore "a wall," and wherefore "gates"? "Thou shalt
call thy walls Salvation, and thy gates Praise." Isaiah writes
walls, St. John *a wall*. New Jerusalem standing foursquare
possesses under one aspect four walls; yet these being continuous and all four corner-stoned into unity seem to be one
at least as indisputably as to be four. And (if so I may take
the sense) Isaiah's *walls* reappearing as St. John's *wall*, sets
forth the universal salvation as being one free gift from the
alone Will, Might, Love, of God : whilst the *gates* are twelve,
because multitudinous mankind offering praise for so great a
gift uplifts an innumerable voice.

Or I may connect the wall with the One all-pervading, all-
containing Indwelling Presence : the gates with the inflow of
every confluent stream of humankind. That wall is inclusive,
not exclusive, for its gates stand open (*see* ver. 25) : those
gates are of ingress not of egress, for none who enter thereby
shall go out any more (*see* ch. iii. 12).

I I

That New Jerusalem has a wall expresses to me a local, distinct, defined heaven (at least, as by a condescension to our present faculties); not indiscriminate as were the waters before the formation of a firmament, nor without form like void chaos; but a genuine home, with recognizable features and amiabilities of a home meet for those who have weaned themselves from earth on the promise and faith of heaven. For now we too "desire a better country, that is, an heavenly," which is far different from not desiring any country at all; the home feeling being congruous with that other human craving not to be unclothed but clothed upon.

Truly that Great Householder Whose house is the universe will be no man's debtor, but will bring forth from His treasure things new and old. All holy desires shall be fulfilled,—nor shall even mere blameless desires be nothing accounted of, please God.

Noah's Ark, that primitive type of the Church, was built with a window as is expressly stated. As a type it prefigured the Church not perfected but on probation, corresponding with that Gospel net which enclosed both bad and good: thus its raven went in and out at the window, and its dove needing shelter and comfort found both there. Again: Isaiah foresaw the Church as built of fair colours and sapphires, of carbuncles and pleasant stones, and as having windows of agates; but this is still the Church Militant, whose children must yet be taught, and against whom there would yet be a gathering together foredoomed to overthrow.

What is the one most obvious purpose of a window? To admit light. The Holy of Holies fashioned after an unearthly pattern had no windows, neither can it apparently have had any light save what (man knoweth not) may have been vouchsafed by the Presence within. No light of day was worthy to enter into that Presence compared with which it became as outer darkness. So likewise we read not of windows as appertaining to the Holy Jerusalem, the Church perfected and triumphant: she herself is consecrated as a veritable Holy of Holies, a shrine of the Uncreated Light, illuminated from within; arising for ever, shining for ever, because the Glory of the Lord is risen upon her.

Almighty God, I beseech Thee, deliver and keep us from over care, vain trouble, profitless anxiety. Give us wisdom to learn somewhat by all Thy wonderful works and ways; and to feel sure that heaven will be better than earth; and that if any earthly good reappear not there, it will be superseded not lost.

For the sake of Jesus Christ in Whom we have all and abound. Amen.

"'Twelve gates, and at the gates twelve angels, and . . . written thereon . . . the names of the twelve tribes of the children of Israel."—O Lord, Who hast said, " Friend, I do thee no wrong," enlarge, I pray Thee, our wills and hearts to embrace the whole Communion of Saints with welcoming jubilee. Give us such wealth of charity that we may rejoice with all who rejoice, even with the thousand times ten thousand and thousands of thousands of Thine elect: until their crowns and joys become to us as our own crowns and joys, and their exaltation be as it were our own. So may we mirror One Love and all love, the Saint of saints and all saints; so may every loveliness which pleaseth Thee become reflected in each lovely soul, and as it were multiplied to Thy Glory, O Lord God our Father: Whom we approach through Jesus Christ Thy Well Beloved Son, in Whom Thou art always well pleased. Amen.

By every human instinct, taste, desire, God is ready to help man onward and upward: this the Twelve Gates, opening to us what we know not with what partially we know, serve to illustrate. They who pant for knowledge shall at last understand what as yet they cannot fathom: they shall see whether the Twelve Angels be angels (as we commonly interpret the word) by nature, or only by office; whether they belong to the flying nation of heaven, or whether from citizenship on earth they have mounted to equality with those elder angels. For *angel*, that is *messenger*, may of course indicate either a celestial or a human delegate: in an earlier portion of this Book of Revelation the Angels of the Seven Churches are acknowledged to be Bishops, not superhuman guardians. What manner of faces shall be then revealed to all who enter those gates with thanksgiving and those courts with praise? countenances like lightning, or aspects of just men made perfect? If we long to know let us follow on to know.

Or if we cling to early lessons and experiences, behold set before us the patriarchal names familiar to us from childhood, taught us by dear maternal lips, each name having its proper context of hope or fear, praise or blame. Thus on earth; but in heaven all by God's grace purged from fear and blame inherit His benediction. And so too a great door and effectual is opened to our aspiration.

All melodious choirs whose vocal melody sprang from a melody-making heart unto the Lord, may enter heaven by the

Gate of Praise, the Gate of Juda.   Such as out of weakness
have waxed strong, an innumerable multitude, through the
Gate of Reuben.   The fallen but risen again, the sanctified of
the eleventh hour whose wickedness shall be mentioned no
more, through the Gate of Gad.   They who lived not by
bread alone but by every word of God, through the Gate of
Aser.   The great company of preachers whose portion and
inheritance was the Lord, through the Gate of Nepthalim.
The stewards of five talents who have made other five, through
the Gate of Manasses.   The wrathful become meek for love of
our Meek Lord, through the Gate of Simeon.   The heroic
Priesthood, the pure Diaconate, and joined to them by self-
oblation the poor and lowly for Christ's sake, through the
Gate of Levi.   They who sat down in the lowest place
esteeming earth no mansion but a tent, through the Gate of
Issachar.   They who made not shipwreck of faith as they
voyaged across the waves of this troublesome world, through
the Gate of Zabulon.   The stewards of ten talents who have
made other ten, through the Gate of Joseph.   The called and
chosen who repented and went, through the Gate of Benjamin.

> What are these lovely ones, yea, what are these?
>   Lo, these are they who for pure love of Christ
> Cast off the trammels of soft silken ease
>   Beggaring themselves bytimes, to be sufficed
> Throughout heaven's one eternal day of peace :
>   By golden streets, thro' gates of pearl unpriced,
> They entered on the joys that will not cease,
>   And found again all firstfruits sacrificed.
> And wherefore have you harps, and wherefore palms,
>   And wherefore crowns, O ye who walk in white?
> Because our happy hearts are chanting psalms,
>   Endless Te Deum for the ended fight ;
> While thro' the everlasting lapse of calms
>   We cast our crowns before the Lamb our Might.

13. On the east three gates; on the north three gates; on the south three gates; and on the west three gates.

East, north, south, west, the four points of the compass at
present so divided not to say opposed that the Psalmist
employs east and west as a standard of remoteness, finally
exhibit absolute equality ; each having its three gates and its
triple influx of confluent saints.   The Holy City erects no
walls of partition : all its citizens as Children of God, Members
of Christ, Inheritors put into actual possession of the Kingdom
of Heaven, are so far equal.   "Sirs, ye are brethren."
Equality, which noble hearts have vainly craved after on

earth, meets and greets mankind in heaven. Not a level:—
gradation, precedence, a Right Hand and a Left, we look for:
but underlying all is essential equality, inasmuch as all are
Christ's.

There the sunny south will have nothing over, the auroral
north no lack: there the region of sunrise will not prevent the
region of sunset. Then supremely shall come to pass that
which Isaiah foretold: " I will bring thy seed from the east,
and gather thee from the west; I will say to the north, Give
up; and to the south, Keep not back: bring My sons from
far, and My daughters from the ends of the earth; even every
one that is called by My Name: for I have created him for
My glory, I have formed him; yea, I have made him."

. We dwell on the reversal in heaven of earth's relative
positions: "Many that are first shall be last; and the last
shall be first." We anticipate that there many monarchs will
range below subjects, many teachers below learners, many
masters and mistresses below servants. Perhaps in our own
person we look forward to taking without shame the lowest
place, if by God's grace we find entrance:—without shame,
for shame is sharp pain, and pain may not invade the final
beatitude; and indeed with satisfaction and good will, for
the justified cannot but love judgment and justice. Such
reversals seem natural and easy to be conceived. Not so,
at least not necessarily so, the celestial equality: this, it may
be, taxes our faith and acquiescence, in a sense even our
imagination more severely. Perhaps one source of such difficulty is that while lifelong experience displays before all eyes
reverses and inequalities, never has this world beheld universal
or even prevalent equality. We exercise by nature the instinct
of inequality: by grace only can we acquire the intuition of
equality.

Which then will it be wise to practise, to rehearse, at once:
equality or inequality? Equality, surely; as the more abstruse,
the far more difficult to assimilate. Equality tends to annihilate pride: *proud* humility may plant itself in the lowest
place; only *humble* humility can revel and rejoice in sitting
altogether undistinguished amid peers. Besides, as most of
us do not suppose ourselves on a par with the "very chiefest,"
we are prepared to see St. Peter placed higher, St. John nigher:
comparison is simply impossible, and we repeat contentedly
" First, Apostles," not needing argument to prove such inequality.

For the present, meanwhile, every one occupies his own

level, and on that particular level occurs his personal temptation. It is easier, often, to stoop low than to stoop slightly:
in the former case all see and acknowledge the condescension;
in the latter many may not admit that there is any condescension
at all.

O Gracious Lord Jesus, by Thine inconceivable Self-abasement in Thy most holy Incarnation: by Thy daily Self-abasement in Thy Life as a Man amongst fellow-men: by Thine
utter Self-abasement through Thy Cross and Passion: by Thy
crowning Self abasement in Crucifixion between two male-
factors: grant us humility.

Lest we put Thee to an open shame: lest we fall from Thee:
lest we never see Thee as Thou art, Thou Who art the Same
yesterday, and to-day, and for ever: grant us humility.
Amen.

14. And the wall of the city had twelve foundations, and in them the names of the twelve apostles of the Lamb.

"Known unto God are all His works from the beginning of
the world." And now in and beyond the end of the world the
strong foundations of New Jerusalem bear witness to His
Faithfulness by Whose grace the Twelve Apostles became
"called, and chosen, and faithful": they fell not, being themselves founded upon a rock, and that Rock was Christ. Truly
are the "twelve foundations" of costly stones; according to
the prophetic word: "I will make a man more precious than
fine gold; even a man than the golden wedge of Ophir";—for
any handwriting of old that was contrary to man, Christ took it
clean away; so that it shall no more be said in reproach of him:
"Behold He put no trust in His servants; and His angels He
charged with folly: how much less in them that dwell in
houses of clay, whose foundation is in the dust, which are
crushed before the moth!" "Her foundations are upon the
holy hills," the Twelve being as those gracious mountains
which bring peace to the people. By faith they stood fast
like the immovable Mount Zion: for "the righteous is an
everlasting foundation." That Lord Almighty Who spake by
Cyrus to the second Temple, saying, "Thy foundation shall
be laid," hath built up His House not made with hands on the
glorious foundation of the Apostles.

O Lord, by grace sustain us, so that in will and affection we
may now by faith dwell in tabernacles with Abraham, Isaac,
and Jacob; and being heirs with them of the same promise
may look for that city which hath foundations, whose Builder

and Maker Thou art. Through Jesus Christ our Redeemer. Amen, so be it.

Wherefore are those twelve names inscribed on those twelve foundation-stones? Mighty princes amongst us were the Saints that bore them. St. Peter loved much, St. John was greatly beloved, St. James the Great drank of Christ's cup, St. Andrew was a succourer of many, St. Philip led his friend in the way of salvation, St. Thomas confessed the Faith, St. Matthew left all, St. James the Less instructed the Church, St. Jude sought out heavenly knowledge, the glory of St. Bartholomew is certified. though not set forth, the mighty deeds of St. Simon are vouched for though not chronicled, St. Matthias repaired the breach and restored paths to dwell in. Yet not unto them, O Lord, not unto them but unto Thy Name give the praise, for Thy loving mercy and for Thy truth's sake.

Not because they were what otherwise they were, but because they were "Apostles of the Lamb" are their names graven in the everlasting rock. For that which is not of the Lamb passes away; that which is of the Lamb abides for ever.

O Lamb of God, Very God, Who hast shown us the love of St. Peter, make us like-hearted: the nearness of St. John, draw us unto Thee: the loftiness of St. James the Great, grant us spiritual growth: the brotherly kindness of St. Andrew, replenish us with charity: the friendship of St. Philip, let us never forget our friend or our father's friend: the adoration of St. Thomas, strengthen our faith: the self-oblation of St. Matthew, wean us from the world: the wisdom of St. James the Less, instruct our teachers: the wisdom of St. Jude, instruct us learners. Thou Who certifiest to us the hidden glory of St. Bartholomew, give us our best things last: the acceptableness of St. Simon, accept us unworthy. Thou Who calledst St. Matthias at the eleventh hour of the apostolic call, call us to any office at any hour, giving us ears to hear and wills to obey.

O Lamb of God, that takest away the sins of the world, take away my sins and all sins. Amen.

15. And he that talked with me had a golden reed to measure the city, and the gates thereof, and the wall thereof.

A reed the image of frailty and fragility: "A reed shaken with the wind," "A bruised reed." Thanks be to the Lord of all, Who broke not the bruised reed of earth.

Behold earth's reed transplanted to heaven: its feeble **poverty** has been transmuted into golden indestructible strength, its crookedness is restored to rectitude. It has become the standard measure whereby the perfect City of God is measured: that city where unto the God of gods appeareth every one of the elect, through whose gates the redeemed pour, within whose walls they abide all glorious.

As the Sabbath is made for man, and not man for the Sabbath, in such a sense is New Jerusalem made for man, and not man for New Jerusalem: he is accepted according to that he hath, and not according to that he hath not. Whatsoever God condescends to reap He has first sown, whatsoever He condescends to gather He has first strawed.

. But the golden reed recalls another and infinitely transcendent glory. Christ in His saving Passion held a reed in His Right Hand, and endured to be smitten therewith upon the Sacred Divine Head. Thus deigned He for man's sake Himself to be measured as it were with a reed; the height of His Love, the extent of His Patience, His long-suffering, to be meted with a span. All for love of us; that so at last the perfect man might attain to "the measure of the stature of the fulness of Christ."

> Lord, hast Thou so loved us : and will not we
>   Love Thee with heart and mind and strength and soul,
>   Desiring Thee beyond our glorious goal,
> Beyond the heaven of heavens desiring Thee ?
> Each saint, all saints, cry out : Yea me, yea me,
>   Thou hast desired beyond an aureole,
>   Beyond Thy many crowns, beyond the whole
> Ninety and nine unwandering family.
> Souls in green pastures of the watered land,
> Faint pilgrim souls wayfaring thro' the sand,
>   Abide with Thee and in Thee are at rest :
>   Yet evermore, kind Lord, renew Thy quest
> After new wanderers ; such as once Thy Hand
>   Gathered, Thy Shoulders bore, Thy Heart caressed.

16. And the city lieth foursquare, and the length is as large as the breadth: and he measured the city with the reed, twelve thousand furlongs. The length and the breadth and the height of it are equal.

" Foursquare " :—that city's angles therefore are right angles. Turn such angles inward from circumference to centre, and they form a perfect cross.

The Cross is the nucleus of heaven. Already faith beholds it thus, and loves it for that which it is, and for that which shall unfold from it.

Angles inward, the cross of probation : angles outward, the square of perfection.

Lord, enable us to love the cross because it was Thy Cross, and to love New Jerusalem because it is Thy Shrine.

> A chill blank world. Yet over the utmost sea
> The light of a coming dawn is rising to me,
>   No more than a paler shade of darkness as yet ;
> While I lift my heart, O Lord, my heart unto Thee
>   Who hast not forgotten me, yea, Who wilt not forget.

> Forget not Thy sorrowful servant, O Lord my God,
> Weak as I cry, faint as I cry underneath Thy rod,
>   Soon to lie dumb before Thee a body devoid of breath,
> Dust to dust, ashes to ashes, a sod to the sod :
>   Forget not my life, O my Lord, forget not my death.

"Length . . . breadth . . . height . . . are equal,"—*there.* *Here* human ways and works are deplorably out of scale, out of relative proportion. Pride towers, Envy is straitened in its own bowels, Anger spurns barriers, Avarice burrows, Lust saps limits, Gluttony overheaps the measure, Sloth drones out of time.

Yet length, breadth, height, are settled quantities not amenable to mortal whims and ways. O Man, O Woman, whether thou be acute-angled or obtuse-angled, accommodate thyself betimes to the rigid squareness of thine optional habitat : for if thou fit not thyself to it by rectification of every line and angle, never will it fit itself to thee by so much as a hairbreadth.

Meanwhile be of good cheer. "Twelve thousand furlongs" may suffice thee for space, and an Angel as surveyor enhances thy dignity. If here thou must be squeezed or stretched to bring thee into shape, look outward and upward to the ensuing amplitude.

Time is short : long is eternity.

> Short is time, and only time is bleak ;
>   Gauge the exceeding height thou hast to climb :
> Long eternity is nigh to seek :
>   Short is time.

> Time is shortening with the wintry rime :
> Pray and watch and pray, girt up and meek ;
>   Praying, watching, praying, chime by chime.

> Pray by silence if thou canst not speak :
>   Time is shortening ; pray on till the prime :
> Time is shortening ; soul, fulfil thy week :
>   Short is time.

17. And he measured the wall thereof, an hundred and forty and four cubits, according to the measure of a man, that is, of the angel.

This is that wall whose battlements shall never be taken away, for they are the Lord's. This is that just measure which applies to unfallen angels, and equally to fallen man when at length he is raised to equality with angels.

Both the city furlongs and the wall cubits being multiples of twelve appear traceable back to twelve as to their secondary origin. So in Isaiah's Prophecy are the thousand to the little one, and the strong nation to the small one.

The Jewish Church had its Twelve Patriarchs, the Christian Church its Twelve Apostles; those Patriarchs natural fathers of their nation, those Apostles spiritual fathers of their community. Nevertheless when the hundred and forty and four thousand (ch. vii. 4—8) are numbered for salvation, Dan is not numbered amongst them; and the name of Judas Iscariot, erased from the Apostolick College on earth and replaced by the name of St. Matthias, cannot be looked for on any foundation-stone of New Jerusalem.

Yet in neither case doth God Almighty suffer loss: twelve He hath summoned, and twelve make answer, "Here we are." Abraham shall not lack children, nor praise keep silence, so long as there be "stones" (*see* St. Matt. iii. 9: St. Luke xix. 40).

Gracious Lord Jesus, let not Thine own brethren and sisters be stonier than stones, having hearts of stone incapable of loving Thee, and more dumb and graceless than stones of the highway.

O Loving Lord Jesus, in Whose Heart there yet is room, I thank Thee that the good of any is the good of all. Dan and Manasses might have entered into rest together : Judas and St. Matthias might have been fellow Saints if not fellow Apostles. Grant us grace to rejoice with Thee and with Thy holy angels over every sinner that repenteth; and to be ourselves, to be myself, numbered with those over whom Thou rejoicest.

18. And the building of the wall of it was of jasper: and the city was pure gold, like unto clear glass.

Well may the wall be built of jasper, be great and high. For whatever be here beyond my scrutiny, let me seek to connect what I perceive with the Love of God in Christ.

He Who sat upon the Throne (ch. iv. 3) "was to look upon like a jasper. . . ." Holy Jerusalem is the Shrine of Him

Whom no words can express : and whatever else its jasper wall may indicate, surely it may lawfully represent to some who fear His Name the effusion, embrace, all-inclusion of His Love. He Who within is the life of His own, without is their habitation. The Centre in which all meet, unifies : the Circumference which contains all, unites. The gracious City is pervaded through and through by grace : the Builder radiates throughout the building : the beauty of the Bride is the 'Beauty of the everywhere-present Bridegroom : He Who rejoiceth over her is her joy : He Who is glorified in her is her glory.

The "pure gold" of the city, inasmuch as it is "like unto clear glass," lets not nor hinders the universal permeation of light. Earthly gold is opaque, heavenly gold translucent : yet a blessed alchemy resorted to betimes transmutes 'the baser into the more precious : "Sell that ye have, and give alms ; provide yourselves bags which wax not old, a treasure in the heavens that faileth not, where no thief approacheth, neither moth corrupteth. For where your treasure is, there will your heart be also." Thus far the Greater than Solomon. King Solomon in his wisdom instructs us as to the transitoriness of terrestrial riches, at the same time suggesting that they may find their way to heaven, although he explains not on what terms : "Wilt thou set thine eyes upon that which is not? for riches certainly make themselves wings ; they fly away as an eagle toward heaven."

I think that from this glass-like gold of the flawless heavenly city we may devise a test for our own earthly possessions, whether they be lawful, safe, expedient, or otherwise. Such as in our contemplation eclipse not God belong to the former class, such as eclipse Him to the latter. Which test secures the further advantage of setting us to judge ourselves without at all judging our neighbour, whose view-point we stand not at and whose powers of vision we cannot estimate.

Moreover, that the ultimate imperishable gold should reappear "like glass," suggests how little genuine inequality there need be between the many and various earthly lots. The rich must refine their gold as glass, or woe is them. The poor can make their paltry perishable belongings like gold, durable, precious, and laid up in the eternal storehouse.

"Pure gold" and "clear glass" alike have stood the fire. Any residuum which man neither brings nor takes away with him is but a minor matter.

19. And the foundations of the walls of the city were

garnished with all manner of precious stones. The
first foundation was jasper; the second, sapphire; the
third, chalcedony; the fourth, an emerald;
20. The fifth, sardonyx; the sixth, sardius; the seventh,
chrysolyte; the eighth, beryl; the ninth, a topaz;
the tenth, a chrysoprasus; the eleventh, a jacinth; the
twelfth, an amethyst.

Twelve foundation-stones, and in them the names of the
Twelve Apostles. Our not being informed which stone bears
which name, seems to leave us fiee to meditate at large on the
subject; tracing out if we can a variety of analogies or of
symbols, widening our perception of graces bestowed and
rewards vouchsafed.

Jasper (*see ante* on ver. 18) reminded us of the Love of God
in Christ. Our Lord Christ being by right the Rock, jasper
seems by grace congruous with the Apostolic rock St. Peter;
once Simon, but at his call renamed by the Master as "Cephas,
which is by interpretation, a stone," and afterwards confirmed
in that name by the same Divine lips: "I say also unto thee,
That thou art Peter, and upon this rock I will build My
Church." St. Peter, Primate of the Apostles.

Sapphire exhibits a heavenly blue. Sky-colour suits St.
John the Divine, that Sun-gazing, heaven-exploring, Apostolic
eagle, whose Evangelical Symbol is the Eagle. Such an eagle
becomes to us our bird of Paradise.

Chalcedony is characterized by a variety of subdued tints;
gems of a bright striking colour would throw it into the background. Its shape is likewise so to say subdued: for it is
formed within rock cavities, and in subordination to their
contour and capacity moulds itself. St. Andrew brought to
Christ a brother who at least in human estimation eclipsed
him; yet none the less did he himself live, move, and have his
being in the God Whom he glorified and loved; exhibiting
very tender and endearing gifts such as may be shadowed forth
by chalcedony.

Emerald, by its intense fadeless green constituted an emblem
of hope, at once recalls St. James the Great; that fiist among
the Twelve to attain the goal of hope and the crown incorruptible.

Sardonyx being compounded of two substances, sard and
onyx, may (so far and fancifully) suggest St. Thomas "called
Didymus," or *Twin*. Moreover, as that tender-spirited saint
needed the most tender handling of his Divine Lord and

Friend to bring out, invigorate, establish his graces, so the many-layered sardonyx discloses not half its beauties until a master-hand by probing, as it were, its substance brings to light its full scale of harmonious loveliness.

Sardius, a choice sort of carnelian, is found in rocks. Red it is, the more vividly red the more costly: thus may it symbolize the awful ensanguined glory wherewith tradition invests the memory of St. Bartholomew.

Chrysolyte (whether or not this Apocalyptic Chrysolyte be that self-same yellowish-green stone which now bears the name) clearly from its name should be some stone of more or less golden hue. Which *gold* reminds us of *treasure hid ;* and thus by association of St. Philip's announcement, " We have found " the Messiah. Discovery indeed, the craving to see and know, becomes inseparably linked with our idea of St. Philip, for he it is who said : " Lord, show us the Father, and it sufficeth us."

Beryl, amongst various Biblical allusions, has for ourselves one that is pre-eminent, inasmuch as Solomon in his mystical Song of Songs says of the Beloved : " His hands are as gold rings set with the beryl." Whence I venture to associate this gem with that Apostle whom tradition dignifies by physical as well as spiritual likeness to our Adorable Lord, St. James the Less, " the Lord's brother."

Topaz because yellow and brilliant so far resembles gold ; and the two are brought together in the saying : " But where shall wisdom be found? . . . The topaz of Ethiopia shall not equal it, neither shall it be valued with pure gold." Thus of old are topaz and gold weighed in the balance and found wanting by Job, a man " perfect and upright, and one that feared God, and eschewed evil " : and thus centuries later did St. Matthew estimate all such wealth when the Uncreated Wisdom vouchsafed to summon him : " Follow Me. And he left all, rose up, and followed Him."

Chrysoprase derives its name from gold and a leek. Gold passes unharmed through fire : the leek can stand no such test. This combination of dissimilars seems not incongruous with the memory of St. Jude, whose one recorded speech contrasts the Church and the world : " Lord, how is it that Thou wilt manifest Thyself unto us, and not unto the world?" and whose Epistle dwells on the general mixture of good and evil, which having been many times already partially divided, yet ever remingle until the final supreme sifting of the Judgment Day.

Jacinth is often flame- or fire-coloured : some specimens of
this mimic fire exhibit also a mimic smokiness of tint. The
virtue of heavenly zeal is as it were pure flame ; but human
zeal even in a righteous cause too often kindles not without
contamination of smoke. We are not told whether St. Simon
received his title of Zelotes from our Lord's own lips : in any
case, presumably it fitted him. By conjecture and before his
call he has been assigned to the Jewish sect of Zealots : if
correctly so, the smoky jacinth may remind us of his beginning,
the smokeless jacinth of his end.

Amethyst is of two qualities : in the west, the region of
sunset where light dies away into darkness, it is a soft stone of
little worth ; in the east, the region of sunrise where darkness
turns to light, it is a gem hard and precious. Impressions
made on a comparatively soft substance can be worn away,
obliterated, lost : on a hard substance they endure. Both
qualities of amethyst display violet tints, the tints of Church
mourning. The noble amethyst in its beauty seems naturally,
as forming the Twelfth and last Foundation, to fall to St.
Matthias : and since the action of fire purging this jewel of
colour can impart to it the appearance of a lustrous diamond,
we may if we please even think of it in its final glory as divested
of any tinge of sometime mourning. None the less while the
earth remaineth thoughts of St. Matthias involve thoughts of
Judas Iscariot the expunged Apostle, and as it were the un-
retentive base amethyst : whose fall may well make us not
fearful only but also sorrowful, remembering how in the
moment of victory David mourned for lost Absalom and
triumphant Judah mourned with him. "The King was much
moved, and went up to the chamber over the gate, and wept :
and as he went, thus he said, O my son Absalom, my son, my
son Absalom! would God I had died for thee, O Absalom,
my son, my son! . . . And the victory that day was turned
into mourning unto all the people : for the people heard say
that day how the King was grieved for his son. And the
people gat them by stealth that day into the city, as people
being ashamed steal away when they flee in battle. But
the King covered his face, and the King cried with a loud
voice, O my son Absalom, O Absalom, my son, my son!"

Lord Jesus, Who lovest great and small, first and last, build
us up, I beseech Thee, on the foundation of the Apostles.
Grant us impregnable faith with St. Peter, unearthly wisdom
with St. John; brotherly love with St. Andrew, heavenly hope
with St. James the Great, confirmation with St. Thomas, self-

oblation with St. Bartholomew, thirst for Divine knowledge with St. Philip, spiritual Christ-likeness with St. James the Less, unworldliness with St. Matthew, just judgment with St. Jude, righteous zeal with St. Simon, final perseverance with St. Matthias. Provoke us to good works by all holy examples, O Lord our only Perfect Example, Who hast deigned to say to each one of us, Follow Me. Amen.

21. And the twelve gates were twelve pearls; every several gate was of one pearl: and the street of the city was pure gold, as it were transparent glass.

After all, the vanished sea has a representative in the eternal holy city: "the twelve gates were twelve pearls." Though no mention shall be made of coral or of pearls in comparison with Wisdom whose price is above rubies, yet are pearls also admitted there white and lustrous: "every several gate was of one pearl."

Still, since in this world (according to St. Paul's rule for women) pearls are not to be clung to and delighted in, so by a figure even those celestial pearls set forth how God prepares better things for His dutiful children: a gate is to be passed through, not resided in. They who on earth contending for truth and righteousness spake unashamed with their enemies in the gate, may now through the everlasting doors pass onward and inward. "Open ye the gates, that the righteous nation which keepeth the truth may enter in."

Before (ver. 18) we read of the city in general that it "was pure gold, like unto clear glass." Now we read of the street in particular that it was "pure gold, as it were transparent glass." Here on earth a saint walking with God needeth "to wash his feet," because being flesh and not altogether spirit he is beset by infirmity, and is liable to contract defilement even in the path of duty: he must wash over and over again in penitential tears, he must wash and never cease to wash in the Only and all-cleansing Blood of Christ. Not so there: for there is neither anything that causeth sweat, nor mire of the streets, nor dust of death.

We who go softly, can we if we will press forward towards the perfection of that better country? Yea, by God's grace! Whoso barters earthly gold for meat for the hungry, drink for the thirsty, clothing for the destitute, any good gift for any forlorn soul or body, shall find it after many days refined into the glass-like gold of the eternal city. A profitable exchange and a goodly: for this supersensual gold is as precious metal with the virtue of glass superadded ; not like poverty-stricken glass gilded over to simulate gold. Mere surface gilding belongs to earth not to heaven, and with earth it vanishes. "Make to yourselves friends of the mammon of unrighteousness; that, when ye fail, they may receive you into everlasting habitations."

22. And I saw no temple therein: for the Lord God Almighty and the Lamb are the temple of it.

Truly in that Temple will every man speak of God's honour. They who shall be accounted worthy to obtain that world and the resurrection from the dead shall understand and experience in its fulness the ineffable mutual indwelling whereof Christ spake : "That they all may be one : as Thou, Father, art in Me, and I in Thee, that they also may be one in Us. . . . And the glory which Thou gavest Me I have given them ; that they may be one, even as We are One : I in them, and Thou in Me, that they may be made perfect in one." In that Divine Temple the worshippers themselves are temples of God the Holy Spirit.

Childlike souls know much which they understand not; and what is required of them is not to understand but to know.

"I will both lay me down in peace, and sleep: for Thou, Lord, only makest me dwell in safety."

O Lord, before Whom I say, "I will lay me down in peace" : Thou beholdest me harassed by cares, fears, perils without, evil within. What I should choose I know not, if the choice lay with me : I thank Thee that the choice lieth with Thee, not with me. Yet this I choose, even whilst I cannot choose : I choose Thy choice, my Lord, I will Thy Will, I by help of Thy grace will be pleased with Thy good pleasure. Even so, Lord Jesus, for me and for all. Amen.

23. And the city had no need of the sun, neither of the moon, to shine in it : for the glory of God did lighten it, and the Lamb is the light thereof.

Be its plenary fulfilment far off or imminent, already man can bask in some furthest ray of this promised glory. Wean thyself from sensible objects, and thou shalt relish the unseen, untouched, unhandled. Look beyond sun and moon, and thou shalt see greater things than they. Stint bodily indulgence, and thou shalt enlarge spiritual capacity. Make a covenant with thine eyes, and thou shalt be full of light. Lean not to thine own understanding, and the Lord shall even now be thy Light, and the Lamb thy Light and thy salvation.

Not in the future only, but now are the elect constituted

living stones of the deathless city. And already they are themselves deathless, though in the teeth of death and corruption : for he that liveth and believeth in Christ shall never die.

The longest and keenest trials of time become comparatively petty, trivial, inconsiderable when strong faith weighs and measures them. Though his eyes be sealed against sun and moon, he is not blind who sees Christ. The hungry man will not starve outright whose spiritual mouth is opened wide and being filled. The veiled and downcast eye discerns fairer objects than it foregoes. The simplest illiterate keeper of commandments is wise and hath understanding beyond many aged and many teachers. Rule thyself : and already thou art king, freeman, citizen of no mean city.

> Love builds a nest on earth and waits for rest,
> Love sends to heaven the warm heart from its breast,
> Looks to be blest and is already blest,
> And testifies : " God's Will is alway best."

Whilst man needs sun and moon he has them : so long as he needs them he will have them. This is a sample of the Providential Bounty lavished upon him without stint or failure ; an antidote for his cares and fears, a reassurance of his hope. Which reassurance (so to say) acts both backwards and forwards : for by guaranteeing to him all necessaries it likewise proves that aught he lacks cannot be a genuine necessary.

" What lack I yet ? " asked the beloved Young Ruler eager for salvation in the lap of prosperity. The answer returned by the Very Truth broke up his earthly comfort and convenience : " One thing thou lackest : go thy way, sell whatsoever thou hast, and give to the poor, and thou shalt have treasure in heaven : and come, take up the cross, and follow Me." Whereat the rich young man turned away sorrowful. Yet if he had stayed to sift those unexpected words of grace he might rather have thanked God and taken courage. " Sell . . . and give " : it is not " give " merely, but " sell " also : the spiritual price would have remained to the obedient seller, and have been invested in the secure treasury. The material gift he might retain at the longest for a lifetime : its intangible, substantial price for ever and ever.

I see the pity of it, that the Young Ruler appreciated not, so far as is recorded, his unique chance. I see it as regards him : what see I as regards myself? If I see it as regards myself, what then do I ? If I do nought in accordance with

K K

what I see, who shall deliver me not from snares or foes but from myself?

24. And the nations of them which are saved shall walk in the light of it: and the kings of the earth do bring their glory and honour into it.

Experience worketh hope. As yet my own experience attests nothing whatever as to " nations " of the saved. To have known here one and there another individual self-evidently rich in grace and goodness has, however, been my happy lot: so that experience has actually already familiarized me with samples of elect communities, units of the sum-total which no man can number.

Patience it is which works experience: no wonder that a vast amount of human experience is limited. To stint patience stints hope at one remove.

Patience is irksome, experience tedious; but then without hope which is their result life were a living death. Every course of life at any level affords scope for patience. Let us not despond as if destined to stick fast in patience and there come to an end; the fault is mine if my patience shoot not up into experience, or if my experience bud and blossom not into hope.

When past history strikes us as a tissue of crimes, and present history as a tangle of unrighteousness; when a backward glance scares, and a forward glance scares yet more ; then the word of this sure prophecy revives a comfortable hope : "The kings of the earth do bring their glory and honour into it." Not kings of a new creation, of a superior dynasty, but literal kings of this literal earth. From their palaces of pomp, from their giddy pinnacles of dominion, they too have gone up on high and have led their captivity captive ; as Barak son of Abinoam from his high places, or as Deborah wife of Lapidoth from palm tree of earth to palm trees of heaven.

If hard it is for any rich man to enter into the kingdom of heaven, how hard must it be for those royal rich men to whom tribute, custom, fear, honour, are due it may be from subject millions. Wise indeed was Agur when he prayed, "Remove far from me vanity and lies : give me neither poverty nor riches "—wiser, so far, than wisest Solomon who lost himself in luxuries and pleasures for a while, if not (as God forbid!) for ever.

Every man's vocation exhibits a twofold aspect. Primarily, it is allotted to him for himself, that therein he may glorify

God and save his own soul ; secondarily, it is allotted to him
for his brethren, that therein he may serve them and promote
their salvation.

Children, servants, subjects, exist in right of parents,
masters, monarchs; and *vice versâ ;* each equally in right of
the other, each complementarily to the other. I see this at
once as to parents and children : I accept it readily as to
monarchs and subjects : I must take heed to admit it practically
as to superiors and inferiors, employers and employed.

O Perfect Lord Jesus, Who being the Creator wert pleased
to abase Thyself to become a Creature, and amongst creatures
a dutiful Son, a submissive Subject, and though not a servant
of men yet toward Thine own as he that serveth ; grant us a
faint shadow of Thy humility whereby we too may become
dutiful, submissive, serviceable. Make us in our several
stations affectionate, loyal, helpful, to one another ; and in
and above all earthly ties, absorb us in self-devotion to Thyself,
the Source of our life, the King of our race, the Master to
Whom we must stand or fall. For none of which things are
we sufficient, but our sufficiency is of Thee. Make us as Mary
when she turned and said Rabboni.

> Bring me to see, Lord, bring me yet to see
> Those nations of Thy glory and Thy grace
> Who splendid in Thy splendour worship Thee.
> Light in all eyes, content in every face,
> Raptures and voices one while manifold,
> Love and are well-beloved the ransomed race :—
> Great mitred priests, great kings in crowns of gold,
> Patriarchs who head the army of their sons,
> Matrons and mothers by their own extolled,
> Wise and most harmless holy little ones,
> Virgins who making merry lead the dance,
> Full-breathed victorious racers from all runs,
> Home-comers out of every change and chance,
> Hermits restored to social neighbourhood,
> Aspects which reproduce One countenance,
> Life-losers with their losses all made good,
> All blessed hungry and athirst sufficed,
> All who bore crosses round the Holy Rood,
> Friends, brethren, sisters, of Lord Jesus Christ.

25. And the gates of it shall not be shut at all by day : for there shall be no night there.

" The evening and the morning " made up the former day :
the latter day shall consist of morning without evening. The
sun of that former day went down even while it was yet day,
because rebellious Adam set his face toward death and

darkness. Then was the gate shut, Eden gate; and no man remained within, neither could any return thither whence once for all man had gone out. Inside stood the Tree of Life inaccessible; outside stood the live man death-stricken. A gate that is shut fulfils an obvious purpose.

But wherefore gates at all if never to be shut? The full *wherefore* may abide hidden, yet in this as in many another instance one may elicit a lesson without fathoming any mystery.

The gates bear perpetual witness that man inhabits heaven not of right but of grace. The morning stars which sang together, the sons of God who shout for joy, are (so to say) aborigines of the celestial country: not so man, whose life is a resurrection from death, whose sonship is by adoption, whose freedom commenced in enfranchisement, whose citizenship is conferred, not natal. "We are strangers before Thee, and sojourners, as were all our fathers: our days on the earth are as a shadow, and there is none abiding."

The open gates bear permanent witness to human free will, still free even when made indefectible. "A brother or a sister is not under bondage": Love alone constrains such. But whilst God's eternal Love endures, and their own everlasting love endures, and the immortal mutual love of the whole Communion of Saints endures, so long will a threefold cord not quickly broken, "cords of a man . . . bands of love," hold them fast.

The gate of Eden honours Law: the gates of New Jerusalem honour Love. Art thou weary of Law and enamoured of love? St. Paul teaches us a short cut out of law into love: "The fruit of the Spirit is love, joy, peace, longsuffering, gentleness, goodness, faith, meekness, temperance: against such there is no law."

Lord, by Thy Most Holy Life-giving Spirit plant, I beseech Thee, love in every heart. Living, growing, flourishing love: with joy as a fair flower, peace as a refreshing fruit, longsuffering for a steadfast prop; by gentleness kept ever pliant to the Husbandman, by goodness meet to stand every test, by virtue of faith fadeless, by meekness bending not breaking, by temperance concentrated as under the pruning-knife. Grant us these graces which please Thee, and deign to be pleased with us sheltered in the grace of Jesus Christ. All for His sake. Amen.

I suppose some ears are liable to be involuntarily caught as by an illogical sequence on hearing: "And the gates of it shall not be shut at all by day: *for* there shall be no night there,"—which latter clause the Revised Version segregates in a parenthesis. Yet as it stands in the Authorized Version much may be made of that very *for :* it will teach the teachable.

Days which alternate with nights make up Time, Time fraught with danger at its best. This temporal mortal life needs restrictions as it were both by day and night : its virtues may run into excess, while its vices call for bit and bridle at every turn if we are not to be destroyed by them. "Keep the door of my lips," is the Psalmist's prayer; although within the lips dwells the praise-giving member, that "best member" . that man has. The door of Noah's Ark continued shut both day and night, after "the Lord shut him in," and until he received the command to go forth : at least, so we may infer the more readily because the raven was sent out at the opened window. The closet of prayer has a shut door (*see* St. Matt. vi. 6). The sheepfold of salvation has a door, evidently sometimes shut, inasmuch as on occasion it is opened (*see* St. John x. 1—4).

Seclusion, exclusion, befit Time.

But Eternity! The Eternity of the beatified knows nought of seclusion when all are brethren beloved, or of exclusion when all are saints. Time shut its gates even by day, because of night being there : Eternity opens them and leaves them wide open "by day : for there shall be no night there."

O Gracious Lord God, enlarge our hearts, wills, intellects, that more and more we may love, choose, worship Thee. Through Jesus Christ our Redeemer. Amen.

> Day that hath no tinge of night,
>   Night that hath no tinge of day,
> These at last will come to sight
>   Not to fade away.
>
> This is twilight that we know,
>   Scarcely night and scarcely day;
> This hath been from long ago
>   Shed around man's way :
>
> Step by step to utter night,
>   Step by step to perfect day,
> To the Left Hand or the Right
>   Leading all away.
>
> This is twilight : be it so ;
>   Suited to our strength our day :
> Let us follow on to know,
>   Patient by the way.

26. And they shall bring the glory and honour of the nations into it.

Nearly the same as we read of the kings of the earth (ver. 24 *ante*), yet not quite the same. For those kings appear themselves to "bring their glory and honour into it." Glorious and honourable was their vocation : they reigned in righteousness and ruled in judgment; until invested with the untarnished glory and honour of their proper calling they at length ascend the Hill of the Lord and rise up in His Holy Place.

Not so the nations at large. They have not like King Solomon worn glory as a robe, or amid popular acclamations received honour of men. Their majesty has been inward, their dignity without insignia. Like the Holy Innocents they have put on unsuspected splendours, not seeking praise of men. Neither have they honoured themselves, nor borne witness to themselves; but copying their Blessed Master they have committed themselves to Him that judgeth righteously, saying with St. Paul, " Yea, I judge not mine own self." And since we read not that they shall with their own hands present their offering, we cannot tell whether themselves or others on their behalf shall do so : "they shall bring it," whoever *they* may be on whom so felicitous a charge devolves. Perhaps those elect kings commending to God their people's offerings, as did David : or those elect angels who have ministered to these heirs of salvation : or it may be these same heirs of salvation one for another, in honour preferring one another in perfection, as heretofore in imperfection ; still looking every man not on his own things, but also on the things of others.

It were to be a stone, a clod, dust in our native dust, not to kindle and glow, flame and mount heavenward amid the great cloud of witnesses our brethren and sisters in Christ. Shall others go up from the extreme outposts of peril, the heights or depths of difficulty ; they the forlorn hope of the Christian army, they the violent whose violence the kingdom of heaven suffers : and will not we go up from our peaceable habitation, sure dwellings, quiet resting-places ? Forbid it, honour—forbid it, shame !

"Now set your heart and your soul to seek the Lord your God ; arise therefore, and build ye the sanctuary of the Lord God."

O Lord my God, by honour or dishonour, through evil report or good report, give us grace to seek Thee, greater grace to find Thee, greatest grace to abide with Thee, for ever and ever, world without end. By the Indwelling of Thy Most Holy Spirit, and for the only Merits and sake of Thy Son Jesus Christ. Amen.

Lord Jesu, Thou art sweetness to my soul :
    I to myself am bitterness :
Regard my fainting struggle toward the goal,
    Regard my manifold distress,
        O Sweet Jesu.

Thou art Thyself my goal, O Lord my King :
    Stretch forth Thy hand to save my soul :
What matters more or less of journeying ?
    While I touch Thee I touch my goal,
        O Sweet Jesu.

27. And there shall in no wise enter into it anything that defileth, neither whatsoever worketh abomination, or maketh a lie : but they which are written in the Lamb's book of life.

St. Paul writes : "We must all appear before the judgment seat of Christ ; that every one may receive the things done in his body, according to that he hath done, whether it be good or bad. Knowing therefore the terror of the Lord, we persuade men." And St. John in the verse we have now to study shows whom that Judgment will exclude from final blessedness, and whom it will admit.

Everything foul and everything false will be excluded. Perhaps we can still trace the inveterate hostility of free will in the persons excluded : not merely are they in their own persons tainted and hollow ; but afford them scope, and they still are such as defile, as work abomination, as make a lie. Never must I picture to myself lost souls as ready to repent were penitence attainable, ready to be reconciled were a door opened to reconciliation ; as more ready to pray than God to hear. While there was life there was hope ; and once Christ's tender Hand touched and healed the leper : "But put forth Thine Hand now, and touch his bone and his flesh, and he will curse Thee to Thy face."

We are taught here what manner of folk will be shut out, not what manner will find entrance. But almost at the outset of this Revelation (ch. iii. 5) we learned the "he that over-cometh" is he whose name will not be blotted out of the Book of Life.

Temptations are what I have to overcome, and at the root of every possible temptation I have to overcome myself. The rest God will do for me, unless I frustrate His gracious purpose. So that works and faith here combine : self-conquest and trust in God.

The Bible is open to all, not so the Book of Life. The

Bible then is what man needs at present, however curiosity may hanker after the other.

Profit now by the open Bible, and hereafter the Book of Life will not be closed to thee.

It is characteristic of Divine Revelation to kindle and sustain instead of satisfying curiosity. Is thy curiosity evil? Desire not its gratification. Is it good? Wait patiently and it will be gratified.

The Bible is well worth prolonged study, and the Book of Life prolonged expectation. And already in the Bible man holds the key to the Book of Life.

Curiosity though it be not a sin forms a highway for sin. The curiosity of Eve brought sin into the world and death by sin. Curiosity may have seduced Lot's wife into looking back, whereupon she became a pillar of salt.

These two instances suggest Curiosity as a feminine weak point inviting temptation, and doubly likely to facilitate a fall when to indulge it woman affects independence. Thus we see Eve assume the initiative with Adam, and Lot's wife take her own way behind her husband's back.

CHAPTER XXII

1. And he showed me a pure river of water of life, clear as crystal, proceeding out of the Throne of God and of the Lamb.

Or as the Revised Version arranges the text: "... the Throne of God and of the Lamb, in the midst of the street thereof"—thus adding to the end of ver. 1 a clause which the Authorized Version places at the beginning of ver. 2. This latter reading favours a collation of the verse we have now to consider with a Divine utterance recorded by St. John:

"Jesus stood and cried, saying, If any man thirst, let him come unto Me, and drink. He that believeth on Me, as the Scripture hath said, out of his belly shall flow rivers of living water. (But this He spake of the Spirit, which they that believe on Him should receive ...)" The two passages taken together suggest how ineffably real and close is regenerate man's union with his dearest Lord and Head: so that every thing communicable which is Christ's He shares verily and indeed with His brethren; yea, even with each of the least of those His brethren.

That the "Pure River of Water of Life" proceeded "out of the Throne of God and of the Lamb" confirms that clause of the Nicene Creed: "The Holy Ghost, The Lord and Giver of Life, Who proceedeth from the Father and the Son, Who with the Father and the Son together is worshipped and glorified."

That It flows forth through the golden street of New Jerusalem (*see* Revised Version as quoted above) certifies us that the Divine All Gracious Spirit will abide for ever in the human temple He has deigned to edify and hallow. No more than will our Lord Himself, will God the Holy Spirit, the "Other Comforter," ever leave His own comfortless.

Pure It is and purifying, Living and quickening. The

Waters of Baptism in a mystery have already conveyed it to us by grace of the Most Holy Trinity. "He that believeth and is baptized shall be saved."

"Clear as crystal"—not concealing, but revealing. According to Christ's promise to St. Peter : "What I do thou knowest not now; but thou shalt know hereafter." For in the day of eternity all faithful children shall be as that Father of the Faithful of whom the Lord once said : "Shall I hide from Abraham that thing which I do?"

If I may without presumption, I connect symbolically the reflecting power of "a pure river" with another saying of Christ's when on the eve of His most sacred Passion· He poured Himself forth in love to His disciples : "Howbeit when He, the Spirit of Truth, is come, He will guide you into all truth: for He shall not speak of Himself; but whatsoever He shall hear, that shall He speak : and He will show you things to come. He shall glorify Me : for He shall receive of Mine, and shall show it unto you. All things that the Father hath are Mine : therefore said I, that He shall take of Mine, and shall show it unto you." This promise, relating to time, seems not necessarily limited to time.

I suppose that the river of Eden, which from being one became parted into four heads, may correspond figuratively with the Apocalyptic "Pure River of Water of Life." From the Paradise which could be lost and which it watered, the single fountain-head poured forth in fourfold stream Pison and Gihon, Hiddekel and Euphrates, to fertilize the world and sprinkle many nations : in the regained Paradise That which it typified appears as One, having accomplished the Divine Pleasure.

O Most Holy, Almighty, Eternal, Divine Spirit, Who art of one Authority and Dominion with the Father and the Son ; set up Thy throne in our hearts, indwell us, gather us into Thine obedience, reign over us.

Thou Who art Lord and Giver of Life, grant us life, a long life, even for ever and ever.

Thou Who art a Loving Spirit, ever willing to give Thyself to whoso will receive Thee, give Thyself to us, give Thyself to us more and more, and never withdraw Thyself from us.

Thou Who art Purity, purify us : Who art Light, enlighten us : Who art Fulness and Refreshment, make us Thine, keep us Thine, fill us, refresh us.

Thou Who lovest us, grant us grace to love Thee.

O Lord God Almighty, Most Holy Trinity, Jesus Christ is our sole plea for any gift, for any grace. Amen.

We know not a voice of that River,
If vocal or silent it be,
Where for ever and ever and ever
It flows to no sea.

More deep than the seas is that River,
More full than their manifold tides,
Where for ever and ever and ever
It flows and abides.

Pure gold is the bed of that River
(The gold of that land is the best),
Where for ever and ever and ever
It flows on at rest.

Oh goodly the banks of that River.
Oh goodly the fruits that they bear,
Where for ever and ever and ever
It flows and is fair.

For lo ! on each bank of that River
The Tree of Life, life-giving grows,
Where for ever and ever and ever
The Pure River flows.

2. In the midst of the street of it, and on either side of the river, was there the tree of life, which bare twelve manner of fruits, and yielded her fruit every month: and the leaves of the tree were for the healing of the nations.

According to one or other Version " In the midst of the street of it " either closes the first verse or opens the second.

If now I may treat it as opening ver. 2, it appears to belong to the revelation of where and how stood the Tree of Life ; that figure of Christ Crucified for our salvation, and constituting Himself our Meat indeed and Drink indeed in the Sacrament of His most Blessed Body and Blood : which how should we name without words of love, yet how shall words of our love worthily name it ?

It is the greatness of Thy Love, dear Lord, that we would celebrate
With sevenfold powers.
Our love at best is cold and poor, at best unseemly for Thy state,
This best of ours.
Creatures that die, we yet are such as Thine own hands deigned to create :
We frail as flowers,
We bitter bondslaves ransomed at a price incomparably great
To deck heaven's bowers.
Thou callest : " Come at once "—and still Thou callest us : " Come late,
tho' late "—
(The moments fly)—
" Come, every one that thirsteth, come "—" Come prove Me, knocking at
My gate "—
(Some souls draw nigh !)—

" Come thou who waiting seekest Me "—" Come thou for whom I seek
    and wait "—
    (Why will we die ?)—
" Come and repent : come and amend : come joy the joys unsatiate "—
    —Christ passeth by . . .
Lord, pass not by—I come—and I—and I.   Amen.

Perhaps the banyan tree (of which I have read) was created
with its exceptional habit of self-multiplication in unbroken
unity, to show us one natural tree capable of standing " in the
midst . . . and on either side," for the more confirmation of
our faith.

If, on the other hand, ver. 2 should be considered as not
commencing until the words, "And on either side of the river,"
then the double (and no more than double) presence of the
Tree of Life recalls to adoring love those Two Natures of our
Redeemer, distinct whilst inseparable, which the Two Candlesticks upon Christian Altars are designed to express.

In the Revised Version a marginal reading substitutes
" twelve crops " for " twelve manner of fruits." This alternative
word bears witness to the inadequacy of eternity itself to empty
into the creature's apprehension a full knowledge of the Creator :
because the crops are yielded and the nations fed (*see* ch. ii. 7 :
and ver. 14 of the present ch.), satisfied, fed again, for ever and
ever. For the twelve crops corresponding with the twelve months
appear to provide for them, that is, for the entire year ; but
twelve months when heaven is in question seem perforce a
figure not of the years of time but of some aspect of eternity.
In accordance with which surmise I remark, that these mystical
months being twelve are not paralleled by the thirteen moons
of a temporal year, moons which wax and wane in an ever
renewed incompleteness. That moon which was ordained to
rule over the night, rules not the perpetual day.

The other reading, " twelve manner of fruits," reminds us
that the flavour of the wilderness Manna is said to have been
mysteriously adapted to the palate of each eater. And if the
type, much more will the True Bread from Heaven satisfy and
still excite and still appease every taste and craving of the
many thousands of the perfected Israel ; those tribes and
families whose thousands of thousands dwell at last in the
Lord's Tabernacle and rest upon His holy hill.

" And the leaves of the Tree were for the healing of the
nations."—To this revelation, so mysterious by reason of its
context, I attempt not to assign conjectural time or place. I
rest in Christ's declaration even to His assembled Apostles :

"It is not for you to know the times or the seasons. . . ."
Still, something it does teach me if I learn from it that what-
ever the multitudes of the redeemed need, that our tender
Saviour Himself becomes to them.

Lord Jesus, so long as seemeth Thee good, give us faith
rather than knowledge, and hope than assurance. Feed us
when we need feeding, heal us when we need healing. Grant
us to find peace by conforming ourselves lovingly to Thy good
Will and pleasure, peace here and peace hereafter. Amen.

**3. And there shall be no more curse: but the Throne of God
and of the Lamb shall be in it; and His servants shall
serve Him:**

**4. And they shall see His face; and His Name shall be in
their foreheads.**

Where the Throne of God and of the Lamb is established
in uncontested dominion; where His servants serve Him with
no more fightings without or fears within; where in Beatific
Vision they see His Face; where His Name is in their foreheads: there is and can be "no more curse."

What may I understand by "His Name shall be in their
foreheads?" (If I may) I will not think of it as a Name then
newly impressed there; but rather as the consummated, in-
effaceable, fully-developed glory of that Name into which the
elect were once baptized in weakness who finally must bear it
in power. To participate in the Name is (by adoption) to
participate in the Nature (*consider* 1 St. Peter i. 2—4): to
bear the Name in full view, "in their foreheads," is to show
forth the restored Divine Image and Likeness before the face
of all people. The forehead expresses thought, reason,
intellect; and these supernaturalized by grace become wisdom
in union with the Uncreated Wisdom. One Name, one
Wisdom, one Love, with God: this is what we hope for—we
dare not hope for less than this—when unto the God of gods
we appear every one of us.

If the Name in the forehead do indeed (amongst whatever
else) express the consummation of a gift conferred in Baptism,
then surely day by day, hour by hour, moment by moment, the
Divine Likeness should be developing, augmenting, deepening
in each of us. The progressive work may be hidden,—

"Who ever saw the earliest rose first open her sweet breast?"—

and well is it that from our too self-conscious eyes it is
hidden! but none the less line upon line, here a little and

there a little, the transfiguring process must be going on: or else, woe is us! the latent likeness is inevitably weakening, diminishing, even if not yet ready to vanish away.

God, for Christ's sake, nerve us to stake all on the inconceivable hope set before us.

> Alas, alas! for the self-destroyed
> Vanish as images from a glass,
> Sink down and die down by hope unbuoyed :—
> Alas, alas!
>
> Who shall stay their ruinous mass?
> Besotted, reckless, possessed, decoyed,
> They hurry to the dolorous pass.
>
> Saints fall a-weeping who would have joyed,
> Sore they weep for a glory that was,
> For a fulness emptied into the void,
> Alas, alas!

O Lord Jesus, Who biddest us here serve Thee, and promisest that hereafter Thy servants shall serve Thee; make Thy command dear to us as Thy promise. Now give us grace to fulfil Thy command, and afterwards of exceeding grace fulfil to us Thy promise; that we may serve Thee now in love and then in love, and may see Thy Face of Love for ever and ever. Amen.

5. And there shall be no night there; and they need no candle, neither light of the sun; for the Lord God giveth them light: and they shall reign for ever and ever.

"By night on my bed I sought Him Whom my soul loveth: I sought Him, but I found Him not." Night represents to us separation, privation, baffled endeavour, unsuccessful search: none of which will baulk heavenly bliss. "There shall be no night there."

Candle or light of sun is not for them whose whole body shall be full of light: such illumination from without applies not to children of light conformed to their Original. That which is outward is lent, and may be withdrawn: God's crowning gifts to His elect become so to say their attributes, inseparable from their persons to all eternity, "for the Lord God giveth them light."

"And they shall reign for ever and ever."—Joseph's dungeon was antechamber to the second throne-room of a kingdom: our own case, unless by our own fault. Bonds and bars seem a strange preparation for a throne, yet such they become when

God wills it. May it please Him by the weakness, endurance, inferiority, obedience, patience, of our present lot, to train us for future grandeur! A little here : all there. "Sing unto the Lord, O ye saints of His, and give thanks at the remembrance of His Holiness. For His anger endureth but a moment; in His favour is life : weeping may endure for a night, but joy cometh in the morning."

It is possible to be so disheartened by earth as to be deadened towards heaven. Israel groaning under the Egyptian bondage fell into such a temper : "Say unto the children of Israel, I am the Lord, and I will bring you out from under the burdens of the Egyptians, and I will rid you out of their bondage, and I will redeem you with a stretched out arm, and with great judgments : and I will take you to Me for a people, and I will be to you a God : and ye shall know that I am the Lord your God, which bringeth you out from under the burdens of the Egyptians. And I will bring you in unto the land, concerning the which I did swear to give it to Abraham, to Isaac, and to Jacob ; and I will give it you for an heritage : I am the Lord. And Moses spake so unto the children of Israel : but they hearkened not unto Moses for anguish of spirit, and for cruel bondage."

O my God, by Whose loving Providence sorrows, difficulties, trials, dangers, become means of grace, lessons of patience, channels of hope, grant us good will to use and not abuse those our privileges ; and of Thy great goodness keep us alive through this dying life, that out of death Thou mayest raise us up to immortality. For His sake Who is the Life, Jesus Christ our Lord. Amen.

6. And he said unto me, These sayings are faithful and true : and the Lord God of the holy prophets sent His angel to shew unto His servants the things which must shortly be done.

"These sayings are faithful and true" :—"Write : for these words are true and faithful" (ch. xxi. 5). The two texts are nearly similar, but whilst that from the earlier chapter calls upon St. John to execute his prophetic office, the other goes on to mention God's "servants" in general. St. John's gift and glory are personal and unique ; yet are the gift and glory of all saints like unto them. Apostles and Prophets take precedence among the brethren ; yet are constituted such not for their own exclusive weal, but pointedly for the edifying of the body of Christ.

" Freely ye have received, freely give." " Go, and do thou likewise."

" The things which must shortly be done."—*Shortly :* nevertheless our Master Himself in condescension to His hearers once said : " After a *long* time the lord of those servants cometh, and reckoneth with them." On earth the word appears to be spoken from the viewpoint of time, in heaven from the viewpoint of eternity.

Creatures of time, such as were those whom Christ instructed, are as children, speaking as children, understanding as children, thinking as children. The full grown man of eternity puts away childish things.

O Lord our Wisdom, so teach us to number our days that we may apply our hearts unto wisdom. Amen.

In so far as time is long, I comprehend that it suffices for the work of salvation. In so far as it is short, I comprehend that it contains not one superfluous moment.

7. Behold, I come quickly : blessed is he that keepeth the sayings of the prophecy of this book.

Here at first sight and according to what precedes and follows, the *angel* (ch. xxi. 9) might seem still to be the speaker. But rather with the Bride let us recognize the Voice of the Beloved, saying, " Open to Me." For what were it to us that another should come quickly? Or who but He Whom our soul loveth should pronounce upon us a benediction?

Even if in this and in much beside I be mistaken, I hope to be held at least in some degree excused. For not (please God) as courting error do I err, but rather as seeing very darkly through my glass.

O Gracious Master, Thou seekest us and we seek Thee : find us and be found of us. If not the illumination of Jacob, yet give us his good will and holy fear when he awaked out of sleep and said : " Surely the Lord is in this place ; and I knew it not. How dreadful is this place !" Everywhere Thou art present : teach us everywhere to discern Thee, rejoicing unto Thee with reverence. Amen.

Once before (ch. iii. 11), our Lord being then undoubtedly the Speaker, He used the same words to the Church of Philadelphia, but followed by an injunction : " Behold, I come quickly : hold that fast which thou hast, that no man take thy crown." And twice hereafter shall we meet with the same promise of His coming vouchsafed by His own lips.

On this occasion we receive it coupled with a blessing on the very act which now by His grace we are endeavouring to perform, and which at the outset of this Book of Revelation (ch. i. 3) was commended to us under sanction of a similar blessing. For with the Father of Lights is no variableness, neither shadow of turning: He is the Same yesterday and to-day and for ever. Thus Christ referred the lawyer simply to the old established Law for the terms of salvation : " A certain lawyer stood up, and tempted Him, saying, Master, what shall I do to inherit eternal life? He said unto him, What is written in the law? how readest thou? And he answering said, Thou shalt love the Lord thy God with all thy heart, and with all thy soul, and with all thy strength, and with all thy mind; and thy neighbour as thyself. And He said unto him, Thou hast answered right : this do, and thou shalt live." And in St. John's First Epistle we read : " Brethren, I write no new commandment unto you, but an old commandment which ye had from the beginning. The old commandment is the word which ye have heard from the beginning."

So also in the Parable of the Two Sons, the injunction remained in force however long obedience was delayed : " Son, go work to-day in my vineyard. He answered and said, I will not : but afterwards he repented, and went."

Once by night the Apostles supposed that they saw a spirit; and Jesus said unto them, " It is I, be not afraid." Once in the morning St. Mary Magdalene supposed that she talked with the gardener; and Jesus said unto her, " Mary."

If we had love like theirs the more we looked for Him the more we should behold Him. [Yet as I read not anywhere that any pious soul ever mistook for Jesus one who was not Jesus, so I beseech Him to forgive me the thought of my heart whereinsoever I err.]

" In all thy ways acknowledge Him, and He shall direct thy paths."

A SONG FOR THE LEAST OF ALL SAINTS.

Love is the key of life and death,
　Of hidden heavenly mystery :
Of all Christ is, of all He saith,
　Love is the key.

As three times to His Saint He saith,
　He saith to me, He saith to thee,
Breathing His Grace-conferring Breath :
　" Lovest thou Me ? "

L L

> Ah, Lord, I have such feeble faith,
> Such feeble hope to comfort me :
> But love it is, is strong as death,
> And I love Thee.

8. And I John saw these things, and heard them. And when I had heard and seen, I fell down to worship before the feet of the angel which shewed me these things.

I think this passage (on which I cannot attempt any sort of full comment) may safely suggest that no height of holiness attainable on this side of the grave can afford positive proof that the saint is already fully ripe for beatitude ; with not one weak point still to be fortified, not one defect to be made good.

For behold St. John the beloved, at the very moment when he calls our attention to his having seen and heard things such as might well make man go softly all his years, if not in the bitterness at least in the solemn aspiration of his soul,—behold St. John for the second time offering to do that which was not lawful.

Sometimes the harvest is white and garnered before the harvest months are fulfilled. Sometimes it stands unreaped long after we would fain have chanted harvest home. Thank God that "the reapers are the angels" and not our short-sighted selves : and that not even angels may reap unsent.

But St. John is habitually our example. Here he sets us a pattern of affectionate gratitude and veneration towards one who ministers in things spiritual ; which we in just measure may thankfully imitate towards our own spiritual pastors, accounting them worthy of double honour and esteeming them very highly in love.

9. Then saith he unto me, See thou do it not: for I am thy fellowservant, and of thy brethren the prophets, and of them which keep the sayings of this book: worship God.

"For I am . . ."—All is in the present: by no means ended and consigned to the past. The speaker (apparently a deathless Angel) not merely *was* but *is* St. John's fellow-servant, of his brethren the prophets, of them who keep the sayings of this Book. Thus are the lives of any such twain lovely and pleasant, being such as neither immortality nor mortality shall divide.

We too, I too, the first of us and the last, may aspire to

the same blessed fellowship. By *service*,—spending and self-spending for God: by *prophecy*,—illustrating in our daily life the pleasantness of His ways and peace of His paths: by *keeping the sayings*,—watching, praying, obeying, in preparation for the day of the consummation of all things. This we can do : this will we not do?

For our all is at stake : and that which momentarily draws nearer and nearer to us is inevitable, be it gain or loss, salvation or ruin. Let us worship God by consecrated life and offered substance; by will, desire, affection; not grudgingly or of necessity, for He loveth a cheerful giver. Martyrs have worshipped Him exultant in torture, Confessors unashamed in shame, lofty Saints in self-sacrifice, lowly Saints in self-discipline. All Saints have worshipped, are worshipping, will worship Him for ever and ever. This we also can do : and this will we not do?

"The Grace of our Lord Jesus Christ, and the Love of God, and the Fellowship of the Holy Ghost, be with us all evermore. Amen."

I suppose that no insight or profundity of mortal man ever has been adequate to the full exploration of this Apocalypse. I feel certain that no natural shallowness need render it a dead letter to man, woman, or child. We may wonder in vain over the personality of the Angel and over his vocation, but his practical precept is as clear as day : "Worship God."

Indeed all through the Book of Revelation lessons enforcing what we must or must not do or be, are as clear and as definite as in the rest of Holy Writ. What can be easily understood furnishes occupation for a lifetime : "The wayfaring men, though fools, shall not err therein." But this promise can be claimed only by wayfarers along "the Way of Holiness" neither by standers-still in that way, nor by vagrants along any other way, can it be claimed.

To study the Apocalypse out of idle curiosity would turn it, so far as the student's self were concerned, into a branch of the Tree of the Knowledge of Good and Evil. And what came of Eve's curious investigation of the original Tree we all know.

Obey to the limit of knowledge, and in all probability obedience may extend knowledge.

10. And he saith unto me, Seal not the sayings of the prophecy of this book: for the time is at hand.

Once more it appears as if the Personality of the Speaker

may have changed, inasmuch as this verse seems to form one unbroken sequence with those which immediately follow.

If eighteen hundred years ago the time was "at hand," how urgently at hand must it now be! If then it behoved disciples to read, mark, learn, and inwardly digest the prophecy, how urgently now! If then it was of the Divine Grace and Mercy that the Book was left unsealed, still is it of the Divine Grace and Mercy that it continues unsealed to our own day. If then it was high time to awake out of sleep, truly is it so now.

> The night is far spent, the day is at hand :
>   Let us therefore cast off the works of darkness,
>   And let us put on the armour of light.
>   Night for the dead in their stiffness and starkness !
>   Day for the living who mount in their might
> Out of their graves to the beautiful land.
>
> Far far away lies the beautiful land :
>   Mount on wide wings of exceeding desire,
>   Mount, look not back, mount to life and to light,
>   Mount by the glow of your lamps all on fire,
>   Up from the dead men and up from the night.
> The night is far spent, the day is at hand.

A disobedient and gainsaying people withstood the stretched forth Divine hands. A blinded people rejected the sheltering wing of Divine Love.

Alas for the disobedient, gainsaying, blinded multitude before whom the Book now stands open! Alas for them : and what for ourselves?

Our eyes we can open or shut ; but the opened Book never can we shut. Whom it cannot instruct it must judge.

O Lord our only Saviour, we cannot bear alone our load of responsibility : upbear us under it. We look without seeing unless Thou purge our sight : grant us sight. We read without comprehending unless Thou open our understanding : give us intelligence. Nothing can we do unless Thou prosper the work of our hands upon us : oh prosper Thou our handiwork. We are weak : out of weakness make us strong. We are in peril of death : come and heal us. We believe : help Thou our unbelief. We hope : let us not be disappointed of our hope. We love : grant us to love much, to love ever more and more, to love all, and most of all to love Thee.

11. He that is unjust, let him be unjust still: and he which is filthy, let him be filthy still: and he that is righteous, let him be righteous still: and he that is holy, let him be holy still.

Or as in the Revised Version: "He that is unrighteous, let him do unrighteousness still: and he that is filthy, let him be made filthy still: and he that is righteous, let him do righteousness still: and he that is holy, let him be made holy still." Despite the correspondence of the two translations, the Authorized may perhaps be understood to convey a doom of fixedness whether in good or evil; the Revised, a sentence of freedom to persist in the same good or evil: such determined persistence amounting to actual progress in either quality, if we are to adopt a marginal alternative reading which at each clause of the verse substitutes "yet more" for "still."

Thus once more pressing home on us that man is his own destroyer: especially if stress may be laid upon the word *let* as permissive rather than imperative. More horrible than what he incurs is what he makes himself: it has become his habit to be wicked, foul; and not only his habit, it has become his taste. "Let him."

On the other hand, how safe and glorious thus transpires the lot of the righteous man and the holy. On him too a doom passes, on him a sentence of freedom, on him a permissive fiat. He too by God's grace has made himself what he is: it has become his habit to be just and pure; and not merely his habit, it has become his taste. "Let him."

God saves the saved: the destroyed destroy themselves.

Then let us not merely flee from the wrath to come. Let us court righteousness, make love to holiness.

Yet how court righteousness? "For the Righteous God trieth the hearts and reins." How dare make love to holiness when "Great and terrible" is God's most Holy Name?

O God, Whose Presence fills space, take away our ungodliness and Thou shalt find none.

Thou Whose Presence we cannot flee, do away our offences and cleanse us from all defilements of flesh and spirit.

Thou Whose Righteousness is from everlasting, impute to us righteousness.

Thou with Whom is mercy, grant us fear, grant us hope.

Thou with Whom is mercy, show mercy upon us.

In the Name of Jesus Christ. Amen.

12. And, behold, I come quickly; and My reward is with Me, to give every man according as his work shall be.

A dear and saintly person, one of my own nearest and dearest, who had been aforetime a great reader and lover of pious literature, when near her end expressed as at that period her almost exclusive love of Holy Scripture : the Inspired Text itself, no longer the comment; although still she prized such human work as elucidated the blessed Text. She fed on the Word of Life, being evidently fed with food convenient for her. Thus she prepared for death : thus went out to meet the Bridegroom, having oil in her lamp.

If this closing chapter of the Apocalypse finds some with few words of their own, God's grace may yet be teaching them by it, and by all that went before, a solemn preparation for death or for the Second Advent. Either may be very near : one at least cannot be very far distant : "Behold, I come quickly."

Every ending includes a solemn element : the ending of God's Revelation to humankind is solemn indeed. Every ending, winding up, cutting short, foreshadows the ending, winding up, cutting short of life and of probation.

The reiterations of the Apocalypse emphasize this finality, this note of preparation. There is nothing new under the sun. "That which hath been is named already, and it is known that it is man : neither may he contend with Him that is mightier than he." "Let that therefore abide in you, which ye have heard from the beginning. If that which ye have heard from the beginning shall remain in you, ye also shall continue in the Son, and in the Father. And this is the promise that He hath promised us, even eternal life."

He Who once had His reward with Him and His work before Him, has fed His flock like a shepherd, gathering and carrying and gently leading the tender ones. Now has He His reward in readiness to give to every man according as his work shall be. Christ worked for man the work of Redemption : the Holy Spirit worked in man the work of sanctification : all men one by one have or have not worked out their own individual salvation with fear and trembling.

The reward is for all work in general, but is assigned to each work in proportion. "He which soweth sparingly shall reap also sparingly; and he which soweth bountifully shall reap also bountifully." The far more exceeding and eternal weight of glory though incommensurate with any desert will yet be harmonized with each desert. Sun, moon, stars, differ in glory : star from star in glory.

"Behold, I come quickly."—Quickly He cometh, whether we behold or whether we forbear. "Behold, He cometh with clouds" :—blessed are they to whom the brightness of His Presence dissipates every cloud.

And His reward is with Him. What know we of that reward? It is Himself, as He declared to Abram: "I am thy shield, and thy exceeding great reward." It is Himself above all and beyond all: this, and beside this "such and such things," as of yore He spake concerning David His beloved.

Faith spurning the world claims kindred with Moses: "By faith Moses, when he was come to years, refused to be called the son of Pharaoh's daughter; choosing rather to suffer affliction with the people of God, than to enjoy the pleasures of sin for a season; esteeming the reproach of Christ greater riches than the treasures in Egypt: for he had respect unto the recompence of the reward."

Whoso trusts in Him shall be as Ruth: "The Lord recompense thy work, and a full reward be given thee of the Lord God of Israel, under Whose wings thou art come to trust."

Whoso waxes strong in the Lord's quarrel, his "work shall be rewarded."

Whoso desires and is warned by His judgments, "In keeping of them there is great reward."

"Verily there is a reward for the righteous."

"He that feareth the commandment shall be rewarded."

The knowledge of wisdom is sweet and good: "When thou hast found it, then there shall be a reward, and thy expectation shall not be cut off."

"If thine enemy be hungry, give him bread to eat; and if he be thirsty, give him water to drink: for thou shalt heap coals of fire upon his head, and the Lord shall reward thee."

"When thou doest alms, let not thy left hand know what thy right hand doeth: that thine alms may be in secret: and thy Father which seeth in secret Himself shall reward thee openly."

"When thou prayest, enter into thy closet, and when thou hast shut thy door, pray to thy Father which is in secret; and thy Father which seeth in secret shall reward thee openly."

"When thou fastest, anoint thine head, and wash thy face; that thou appear not unto men to fast, but unto thy Father which is in secret; and thy Father, which seeth in secret, shall reward thee openly."

"Whosoever shall give you a cup of water to drink in My Name, because ye belong to Christ, verily I say unto you, he shall not lose his reward."

"Blessed are ye, when men shall hate you, and when they shall separate you from their company, and shall reproach you, and cast out your name as evil, for the Son of Man's sake.

Rejoice ye in that day, and leap for joy: for, behold, your reward is great in heaven."

"Whatsoever ye do, do it heartily, as to the Lord, and not unto men ; knowing that of the Lord ye shall receive the reward of the inheritance : for ye serve the Lord Christ."

Confidence under trials "hath great recompence of reward."

For God "is a Rewarder of them that diligently seek Him."

" For the Son of Man shall come in the Glory of His Father with His angels ; and then He shall reward every man according to his works." Amen.

13. I am Alpha and Omega, the Beginning and the End, the First and the Last.

" I am Alpha and Omega " is here declared for the fourth time.   Thus is it at the beginning (ch. i. 8), and still thus at the end ; thus at the first, and still thus at the last.   We change, He changes not.   Yet even in ourselves constitutional changeableness cannot annul a certain inherent unchangeableness, which so far corresponds with His in Whom we live and move and have our being: for we are His offspring.   His Immutability is reflected in our identity : as He cannot deny Himself, so neither can we deny ourselves.   Rocks may fall on us, mountains cover us ; but under mountain and rock remains the inextinguishable I.

Not but the Omnipotent Creator could if He willed annihilate His creature : " With God all things are possible."   But no such decree is revealed.

14. Blessed are they that do His commandments, that they may have right to the Tree of Life, and may enter in through the gates into the city.

Or as in the Revised Version : " Blessed are they that wash their robes. . . ."

The two readings taken together suggest the sanctity of obedience, the sanctity of repentance, and the exceeding great reward of both.   Nor indeed were either excluded could the other possibly find admission ; for human obedience being at best imperfect so far needs repentance ; and repentance is the particular form of obedience practicable by even the most imperfect.

Our last opportunity is not lost so long as repentance remains accessible.   This snatches the brand from the burning, this wrenches the prey from between the teeth of the mighty.

Lord, I repent : help Thou mine impenitence.

Almost beyond belief it seems blessed in the eternal kingdom to " have right to the Tree of Life."

All is of God's grace, nothing of man's desert. Of His grace it pleases Him to constitute such a privilege our " right "; and our right thenceforward it becomes, whilst first and last all is of grace. " For He spake, and it was done; He commanded, and it stood fast."

As the hart desireth the water-brooks, doth our soul so long after that Tree of Life ? Surely yes, if we be not lower than the beasts that perish.

. . . Alas! not "surely" at all, unless our present longings can stand one test which too often shames them. For already we have a right to our own precious Tree of Life, Christ in the Sacrament of His most Blessed Body and Blood.

Whoso longs not for Christ here, wherefore should he long for Him there?

Because our Saviour longed for us on earth we are convinced that He longs for us in heaven.

If we long not for Him on earth, who shall kindle our longing for Him in heaven?

To "do His commandments" is the condition on which depends our " right to the Tree of Life." One of His commandments is : " Do this in remembrance of Me." St. James warns us : " Whosoever shall keep the whole law, and yet offend in one point, he is guilty of all."

Good Lord Jesus, our only Hope ; because we cannot help ourselves, help Thou us. Because we cannot quicken ourselves, quicken Thou us. Because we cannot kindle ourselves, kindle Thou us. Because we cannot cleanse ourselves, cleanse Thou us. Because we cannot heal ourselves, heal Thou us. For Thou hast no pleasure in our impotence, lifelessness, coldness, pollutions, infirmity. If Thou desire our love, who shall give us love wherewith to love Thee except Thou Who art Love give it us? Helpless we are, and our helplessness appeals to Thee.

" 'Through the gates into the city."—Such gates as Isaiah celebrates, and whereunto he indicates the approach : " Open ye the gates, that the righteous nation which keepeth the truth may enter in. . . . The way of the just is uprightness : Thou, most upright, dost weigh the path of the just. Yea, in the way of Thy judgments, O Lord, have we waited for Thee ; the desire of our soul is to Thy Name, and to the remembrance of Thee. With my soul have I desired Thee in the night ; yea, with my spirit within me will I seek Thee early :

for when Thy judgments are in the earth, the inhabitants of the world will learn righteousness."

> Hark ! the Alleluias of the great salvation
>   Still beginning, never ending, still begin,
> The thunder of an endless adoration :
> Open ye the gates, that the righteous nation
>   Which have kept the truth may enter in.
>
> Roll ye back, ye pearls, on your twelvefold station :
>   No more deaths to die, no more fights to win !
> Lift your heads, ye gates, that the righteous nation
> Led by the Great Captain of their sole salvation
>   Having kept the truth may enter in.

15. For without are dogs, and sorcerers, and whoremongers, and murderers, and idolaters, and whosoever loveth and maketh a lie.

Here the entire evil company must be understood literally, with the exception of "dogs," which seems figurative. Various texts of Holy Writ under this same figure exhibit wickedness, or alienation from goodness, or brand certain tempers or habits as abominable ; whilst an enactment of the Mosaic Law suggests typically this final exclusion of dogs : "Thou shalt not bring the hire of a whore, or the price of a dog, into the house of the Lord thy God for any vow : for even both these are abomination unto the Lord thy God."—"Against any of the children of Israel shall not a dog move his tongue." "Dogs have compassed Me : the assembly of the wicked have enclosed Me. . . . Deliver My soul from the sword ; My darling from the power of the dog." "Deliver me from' the workers of iniquity, and save me from bloody men. . . . And at evening let them return ; and let them make a noise like a dog, and go round about the city. Let them wander up and down for meat, and grudge if they be not satisfied." "His watchmen . . . are all dumb dogs, they cannot bark ; sleeping, lying down, loving to slumber. Yea, they are greedy dogs which can never have enough." "Give not that which is holy unto the dogs." "Beware of dogs, beware of evil workers." "It had been better for them not to have known the way of righteousness, than, after they have known it, to turn from the holy commandment delivered unto them. But it is happened unto them according to the true proverb, The dog is turned to his own vomit again ; and the sow that was washed to her wallowing in the mire."

"Dogs" may perhaps be viewed as representing brutal, bestial, gross, rampant, low-type opposition. "Whoremongers and murderers" degrade man's lower nature, "sorcerers . . . and idolaters" his higher nature. "Whosoever loveth and maketh a lie," whilst it seems to start with heart idolatry and go on to material idolatry, may also surely include liars in general, who, misusing the best member that they have, and loving darkness rather than light, put darkness for light and light for darkness.

If all lying great or small is here branded with infamy, we may fairly assume that any and every taint of the other sins indicated is likewise here condemned by that Gracious God and Saviour, Who threatens that He may not smite, and often smites that He may not cast off for ever; and Who condescends to entertain a plea for the very dogs, even for some whom large-hearted Job himself had haply disdained to set with the dogs of his flock : " Jesus said unto her, Let the children first be filled : for it is not meet to take the children's bread, and to cast it unto the dogs. And she answered and said unto Him, Yes, Lord : yet the dogs under the table eat of the children's crumbs. And He said unto her, For this saying go thy way ; the devil is gone out of thy daughter." It behoves us to barricade the approaches of our souls against the creeping tide of evil : though the tide may scarce have turned, the danger has begun.

" Whosoever looketh on a woman to lust after her hath committed adultery with her already in his heart."—" Whosoever is angry with his brother without a cause shall be in danger of the judgment."—" Rebellion is as the sin of witchcraft."—" If I have made gold my hope, or have said to the fine gold, Thou art my confidence ; if I rejoiced because my wealth was great, and because mine hand had gotten much ; if I beheld the sun when it shined, or the moon walking in brightness ; and my heart hath been secretly enticed, or my mouth hath kissed my hand : this also were an iniquity to be punished by the judge : for I should have denied the God that is above."

16. I Jesus have sent Mine Angel to testify unto you these things in the churches. I am the root and the offspring of David, and the bright and morning star.

" It is I, be not afraid." Yea, Lord, so bring us unto the haven where we would be.

The countenance of Thy messenger may be like the countenance of an Angel of God very terrible : we ask him not whence he is, neither telleth he us his name.

Thee, Lord, we know : Thee we trust. Thy Name we know : in Thy Name we take refuge. Grant us grace to do so of a truth : grant steadfastness, patience, faith, hope, love, to Thy Church expectant.

O Root of David, mould us after Thine own Heart. O Offspring of David, be formed in us by the operation of Thy Most Holy Spirit.

O Bright and Morning Star, kindle us to shine as stars for ever and ever ; all differing in glory, yet one and all resplendent to Thy glory. Amen and Amen.

It is " in the Churches " that these things are testified. To myself it is in the beloved Anglican Church of my Baptism : a living branch of that one Holy Catholic Apostolic Church which is authoritatively commended and endeared to every Christian by the Word of God. "The Lord added to the Church daily such as should be saved." "And so were the Churches established in the faith, and increased in number daily." "The Church of God, which He hath purchased with His own Blood." "God is not the author of confusion, but of peace, as in all Churches of the saints." "Christ . . . the Head over all things to the Church, which is His Body, the fulness of Him that filleth all in all." "Now unto Him that is able to do exceeding abundantly above all that we ask or think, according to the power that worketh in us, unto Him be glory in the Church by Christ Jesus throughout all ages, world without end. Amen." "Christ is the Head of the Church. . . . The Church is subject unto Christ. . . . Christ also loved the Church, and gave Himself for it ; that He might sanctify and cleanse it with the washing of water by the word, that He might present it to Himself a glorious Church, not having spot, or wrinkle, or any such thing ; but that it should be holy and without blemish." "The house of God, which is the Church of the Living God, the pillar and ground of the truth." "Let us hold fast the profession of our faith without wavering ; (for He is faithful that promised;) and let us consider one another to provoke unto love and to good works : not forsaking the assembling of ourselves together, as the manner of some is ; but exhorting one another : and so much the more, as ye see the day approaching."

Our Lord is designated as the "Sun of Righteousness" by a Prophet : the sun without peer rules over the planetary system. But Christ with lips full of grace deigns to call Himself "the Bright and Morning Star ": which star solitary in office and in dignity lights up hope for the darkened world and promises and ushers in day after night. Yet is it a veritable star amid fellow stars; incomparably the Chiefest, but among ten thousand.

> The shout of a King is among them. One day may I be
> Of that perfect communion of lovers contented and free
> In the land that is very far off, and far off from the sea.
> The shout of the King is among them. One King and one song,
> One thunder of manifold voices harmonious and strong,
> One King and one love and one shout of one worshipping throng.

If in itself we care not for our own glorification, still let us care, long, pray for it, that so our glory may by a condescension of grace enhance Christ's excelling glory, and that even in the great day of final award He may not be ashamed to call us brethren.

Turning to a parable of nature, we perceive the bright and morning star which renews our gladness, to be none other than the sweet calm evening star of our twilight solace. So and much more art Thou, Good Lord Jesus, the consolatory Star of this vigil of our mortality; and so dost Thou reveal Thyself as the all-surpassing Star of the festival of our immortality.

17. And the Spirit and the bride say, Come. And let him that heareth say, Come. And let him that is athirst come. And whosoever will, let him take the water of life freely.

The Church has no independent existence. Christ, Whose mystical body she is, is her Head: the Holy Ghost, Whose temple she is, is her overruling Will and Power. Severed from the Head she would die: emptied of the Indwelling Presence she would return to corruption.

Yet is not all this even on her side by constraint, but willingly. The Bridegroom chooses the Bride by free will of Divine Love: the Bride by free will of love human and super-human chooses the Bridegroom. The Most Holy Spirit freely chooses His Temple: the living and breathing Temple in the fortress of her will and the secret place of her affections freely enshrines her God.

In the peaceful verse under contemplation, " the Spirit and the Bride " speaking with one voice say " Come " with one will. The Indweller is Love: and therefore the Temple is full of love. God the Holy Spirit is that Person of the All Holy Trinity Who " Proceedeth ": He has imparted Himself to Christ's mystical Bride, and by His Divine impulse she pants to share every good and every perfect gift which is. hers with the worldwide family of man. Because a Flowing River is His emblem, therefore a stagnant pool never can be hers.

Fire also is His symbol. His Flame has kindled hers: and therefore from her spreading flame the hearer who hath ears to hear likewise catches fire, and echoes and cries and cannot but cry " Come."

" And let him that is athirst come."—We thirst: with the call to come give us the will to come, most Bountiful Lord Jesus. Thou Who turnedst water into wine ; Who saidst, " Give Me to drink"; Who criest, " If any man thirst let him come unto Me and drink"; Who saidst, " With desire I have desired "; Who declarest, " My Blood is drink indeed"; Who saidst in extremity, " I thirst"; suffer us not to make ourselves as Dives, but join us to Thyself and quench our thirst.

When the Spirit saith, " Come," He fulfils in our ears that all-gracious promised ministry whereby He brings to our remembrance the blessed sayings of Christ; Who in the course of His earthly ministry said likewise, "Come," sometimes to one, sometimes to another, sometimes to a multitude ; and Who while addressing each however individually conveyed also a message, charge, lesson, to many others, and even by analogy or inference to all. Let us arise and go to Him Who came to us before He bade us come to Him.

" The Voice of my Beloved! behold, He cometh . . ."

" Come ye after Me."—Lord Jesus, Whose call the blessed brothers Peter and Andrew obeyed with warm hearts, grant to each of us like warmth and like obedience ; a good start, a good course, a good goal. Call us all, I beseech Thee, grant saving grace to us all.

" First be reconciled to thy brother, and then come and offer thy gift."—Lord Jesus, since I can never deliver my brother, grant me at least never to wrong him. Enable us by love to serve one another and to offer ourselves unto Thee.

> Me and my gift ; kind Lord, behold,
> Be not extreme to test or sift :
> Thy Love can turn to fire and gold
> Me and my gift.
>
> Myself and mine to Thee I lift :
> Gather us to Thee from the cold
> Dead outer world where dead things drift.
>
> If much were mine, then manifold
> Should be the offering of my thrift :
> I am but poor, yet love makes bold
> Me and my gift.

"All that are in the graves shall hear His Voice, and shall come forth."—Lord Jesus, Who in pure Love madest Thy grave with the wicked and with the rich in Thy death, for that same Love's sake turn the wicked from their evil ways, and enrich all souls with heavenly treasure : that so when a great company hearing Thy Voice shall come forth from their graves, they may have their portion in the resurrection of life.

"Whosoever cometh to Me, and heareth My sayings, and doeth them, I will shew you to whom he is like : he is like a man which built an house, and digged deep, and laid the foundation on a rock."—Lord Jesus, grant us grace to come to Thee in obedience, and by constant obedience to abide with Thee ; that our foundation may be upon the Rock of Ages, and that underneath us may be the Everlasting Arms. Hold us fast that we may cleave unto Thee ; embrace us that we may cling unto Thee.

"I will come and heal him."—Lord Jesus, Who knowing whereof we are made, and remembering that we are but dust, beholdest all our palsies and grievous torments of body and soul, have compassion on us and heal us. We are not worthy : yet speak the word.

"Come unto Me, all ye that labour and are heavy laden, and I will give you rest."—Lord Jesus, help us to take Thy yoke upon us, and learn of Thee : that being meek and lowly our souls may rest in Thee all the while we labour and bear our due appointed burden patiently.

"I am not come to call the righteous, but sinners to repentance."—Lord Jesus, Who camest from heaven to earth to call us, wean us from earth that we may ascend to Thee in heaven. Thou leftest heaven for love of us : forbid it, that we should not leave anything or everything for love of Thee ! Thou sinless camest in contact with sin for love of us : enable us for love of Thee to repent and sin no more.

"Ye shall not have gone over the cities of Israel, till the Son of Man be come."—Lord Jesus, Who art Thyself our Way and our End, suffer not persecution or pleasure or any circumstance to hinder our pressing forward to meet Thee at Thy coming. Be Thou here our city of refuge, and hereafter our home.

"Come."—Lord Jesus, Whom holy Peter loved and Who didst much more love Peter, grant us faith all-venturesome for Thy sake, hope for an anchor sure and steadfast, love responsive to Thy loving call.

"I am the Bread of Life : he that cometh to Me shall never

hunger."—Lord Jesus, evermore give us this Bread, give us Thyself. Thou Who in love givest Thyself to us in the Blessed Sacrament of Thy Body and Blood, grant us grace in love to receive Thee, in love to retain Thee, in love to be joined to Thee eternally.

"All that the Father giveth Me shall come to Me ; and him that cometh to Me I will in no wise cast out."—Lord Jesus, draw us, we will run after Thee. Bring us into the many mansions of Thy Father's house that we may be glad, and rejoice in Thee remembering Thy Love. Make us upright that we may love Thee.

"I came down from heaven, not to do mine own Will, but the Will of Him that sent Me."—Lord Jesus, Who for us men and for our salvation camest down from heaven, I beseech Thee assist us by Thy grace so to do Thy Will and the Will of Him that sent Thee, that in heart and soul we may mount up and abide with Thee in heaven.

"No man can come to Me, except the Father which hath sent Me draw him : and I will raise him up at the last day."— Lord Jesus, our Great High Priest, vouchsafe to intercede for us with the Father that He may draw us. Receive Thou us, and raise us up at the last day. Whom have we in heaven but Thee? and sinners as we are, whom hast Thou on earth but us?

"No man can come unto Me, except it were given unto him of My Father."—Lord Jesus, we plead Thy Strength, we plead with Thee our own weakness. Can a woman forget her sucking child? Yea, Lord : yet wilt not Thou forget us.

"If any man will come after Me, let him deny himself, and take up his cross daily, and follow Me."—Lord Jesus, grant us daily grace for daily need. Daily patience for a daily cross. Daily, hourly, incessant love of Thee, to take up our cross daily and bear it after Thee.

-"If any man thirst, let him come unto Me, and drink."— Lord Jesus, if we thirst not, give us thirst ; if we thirst, give us to drink. Withhold not from us Thyself and Thy Most Holy Spirit, that we thirst no more, neither go elsewhere to draw.

"I am come that they might have life, and that they might have it more abundantly."—Lord Jesus, in Whose hand is the soul of every living thing and the breath of all mankind, to the lifeless impart life, to the living increase life : for Thou Thyself art the Life, and apart from Thee we have no life.

"Lazarus, come forth."—Lord Jesus, Who in love to Martha and her sister and Lazarus gavest them back to one another

for yet a brief space of mortal life; give back to us, I beseech
Thee, our beloved whom Thou hast taken to Thyself: reunite
us not in mortal life but immortal, not for a little while but for
ever.   This I pray for generation after generation of mankind
until all be fulfilled ; and the last acceptable souls going home
to Thee, find with Thee those also who shall not return to them.

"They shall come from the east, and from the west, and
from the north, and from the south, and shall sit down in the
kingdom of God."—Lord Jesus, grant us wisdom with the
Wise Men and with all who tread in their steps, not to grudge
any long journey that leadeth to Thee, but in patience to
possess our souls.

"If any man come to Me, and hate not his father, and
mother, and wife, and children, and brethren, and sisters, yea,
and his own life also, he cannot be My disciple."—Lord Jesus,
what Thou requirest enable us to do and be, for verily flesh
and blood enter not into the kingdom of God.   Grant us self-
restraint, self-denial, self-oblation, the lesser love enhancing
the greater; the pure sacrifice which is acceptable to Thee.

"Suffer the little children to come unto Me, and forbid them
not : for of such is the kingdom of God."—Lord Jesus, give
us Thine own grace of love and care for little children, that we
may bring them to Thee in Holy Baptism, and watch over them
body and soul.   And I beseech Thee make us like them, that
so Thou mayest love and care for us with them.

"If thou wilt be perfect, go and sell that thou hast, and
give to the poor, and thou shalt have treasure in heaven : and
come and follow Me."—Lord Jesus, with Thy call pour forth
grace responsive to that call ; that so high saints may walk on
high with Thee, perfect as Thou art perfect.   Yet call to mind,
I beseech Thee, that compassion whereby Thou saidst, "He
that is able to receive it, let him receive it,"—call to mind Thy
condescension when by the mouth of St. Peter Thou pro-
testedst, "Whiles it remained, was it not thine own? and
after it was sold, was it not in thine own power?"—and
pardon even every one that prepareth his heart to seek God,
the Lord God of his fathers, though he be not cleansed
according to the purification of the sanctuary.   Be merciful to
first and last.

"Zacchæus, make haste, and come down; for to-day I
must abide at thy house."—Lord Jesus, when Thou biddest
us come down, give us grace to humble ourselves.   Thou art
our salvation : come Thou to our hearts and abide there this
day, every day, for ever.

"The Son of Man is come to seek and to save that which was lost."—Lord Jesus, Only Sacrifice, Only Saviour, Thou Who seekest us to save us, give us gracious yearnings that seeking Thee we may be saved. We are lost if Thou seek us not : self-lost if we seek not Thee. From utter irretrievable loss, O Saviour of the lost, deliver us.

"I am come a light into the world, that whosoever believeth on Me should not abide in darkness."—Lord Jesus, suffer us not to love darkness rather than light ; but help us so to do good works and come into the light, that our deeds may be made manifest that they are wrought in God.

"Watch therefore : for ye know not what hour your Lord doth come."—Lord Jesus, we know not, but Thou knowest. Thou Who in loving pity watchest over us, grant us in longing love to watch for Thee. Alas for me ! grant me, even me, such great love.

"When the Son of Man shall come in His glory . . . then shall He sit upon the Throne of His glory : and before Him shall be gathered all nations."—Lord Jesus, when rocks cannot hide us or mountains cover us, be Thou our shield and hiding-place from the wrath to come.

"Come, ye blessed of My Father, inherit the kingdom prepared for you from the foundation of the world."—Lord Jesus, Thou waitest to be gracious. We wait for Thy loving-kindness in the midst of Thy temple. The eyes of all wait upon Thee : give us, I pray Thee, our meat in due season, now that meat which endureth unto everlasting life, hereafter the marriage supper of Thy kingdom.

"If I go and prepare a place for you, I will come again, and receive you unto Myself."—Lord Jesus, let us not faint, but have patience, awaiting the fulfilment of this Thine all-consolatory promise. For Thou the Truth art True, though every man were a liar.

"I will not leave you comfortless : I will come to you."—Lord Jesus, never suffer us to despond, saying, the Lord hath forsaken me, and my Lord hath forgotten me. Heaven and earth shall pass away, but Thy word shall not pass away.

"If a man love Me, he will keep My words : and My Father will love him, and We will come unto him, and make Our abode with him."—Lord Jesus, Blessed be Thou Who for love of us becamest lonely in life, while men hid as it were their faces from Thee, and unutterably lonely in Thy last Agony, when the Father Himself hid His Face from Thee.

It was our loneliness Thou enduredst in our stead : Blessed be Thou.

" Come and dine."—Lord Jesus, mortal life is our night of abstinence : grant us eternal life for our day of feasting. Blessed is he that eateth Bread in the kingdom of God : in the Church Militant here, in the Church Triumphant hereafter. With Thee here in a Mystery : with Thee hereafter face to Face.

" If I will that he tarry till I come, what is that to thee ? follow thou Me."—Lord Jesus, Who sweetly orderest all things, give to each one of us, I beseech Thee, the special grace proper to his vocation : that the contemplative may sit ever at Thy Feet in spirit, and the active may follow in Thy blessed footsteps which went about doing good. Amen and Amen.

" Come. . . . And whosoever will, let him take the water of life freely."—Once more our will is made the turning-point. God's Will is revealed in that word of mercy " Come " : man's will is still in question.

Do I then ignore or deny the doctrines of Prevenient Grace and Predestination ? God forbid ; but neither when He saith Come, can I deny or ignore that so He saith. He Who is the Truth cannot but mean Come when He saith Come.

Yet Christ declares plainly : " No man can come unto Me, except it were given unto him of My Father "—establishing the necessity of Prevenient Grace.

I know it : yet saith He to me, Come.

And St. Paul writing under Inspiration states : " Whom He did predestinate, them He also called."

This also I know : yet surely He Who saith to me Come, calleth me.

What then do I think ? God helping me, I will think this. The Divine Call has been addressed to me, has reached me, has urged my will, convinced my understanding, moved my heart. At the Judgment Bar never can I plead, No man hath hired me ; never can I claim the few stripes of one who knew nothing of his Lord's Will. I observe moreover that my call being a practical one, demanding not intellect on my side but obedience, enjoins practice rather than subtil theory, and is responded to by simplest obedience. My understanding breaks down : so be it. Please God, my will shall not break down, nor my faith make shipwreck.

O Love of Christ, constrain me, constrain all.

" Rejoice greatly, O daughter of Zion ; shout, O daughter of Jerusalem : behold, thy King cometh unto thee : He is just, and having salvation."

This Call which cries "Come," and addresses "whosoever will," is a call to refreshment, solace, overflowing plenty, boundless endless supply, sustenance of immortality. A call without stint, without bar: "Whosoever will, let him take the water of life freely."

Yet some Christians traverse the world like walking funerals rather than like wedding-guests! (Know thyself.) "But be ye doers of the word, and not hearers only, deceiving your own selves. For if any be a hearer of the word, and not a doer, he is like unto a man beholding his natural face in a glass: for he beholdeth himself, and goeth his way, and straightway forgetteth what manner of man he was."

18. For I testify unto every man that heareth the words of the prophecy of this book, If any man shall add unto these things, God shall add unto him the plagues that are written in this book.

19. And if any man shall take away from the words of the book of this prophecy, God shall take away his part out of the book of life, and out of the holy city, and from the things which are written in this book.

Our Lord deigns to testify "unto every man that heareth . . .": thus acting in accordance with a revelation vouchsafed of His own Nature: "That was the true Light, which lighteth every man . . .," and in harmony with His declaration before Pontius Pilate: "To this end was I born, and for this cause came I into the world, that I should bear witness unto the truth."

O Lord, if I myself have fallen into either deadly error against which Thou here testifiest: "I acknowledge my transgressions. . . . Against Thee, Thee only, have I sinned, and done this evil in Thy sight: that Thou mightest be justified when Thou speakest, and be clear when Thou judgest. . . . Hide Thy Face from my sins, and blot out all mine iniquities."

Were it not for the blessing (ch. i. 3) pronounced on him that readeth and on them that hear the words of this Prophecy, and keep those things which are written therein, well might we weep much, confessing our utter unworthiness to open and to read the Book, or so much as to look thereon.

It is well to fear and obey. It is ill to fear instead of obeying.

Some can meditate and interpret. All can meditate and pray.

To interpret should do good. To pray will do good.

Interpretation may err and darken knowledge. Prayer fetches down wisdom from the Father of lights.

Prayer is the safeguard of interpretation, and without interpretation is still profitable.

We seem to bring something of our own to interpretation, and if puffed up may destroy ourselves. Prayer avows destitution, and lays hold on the riches of Him Who made us.

Interpretation is safe and seemly for some. Prayer is safe and seemly for all.

"If any man shall add. . . . And if any man shall take away. . . ."—The ruinous sin here denounced of adding to this Revelation to be punished by added plagues, or of taking away from it to be punished by expulsion from blessings, is foreshadowed in two Prophecies of Jeremiah: "Thus saith the Lord concerning Shemaiah the Nehelamite; Because that Shemaiah hath prophesied unto you, and I sent him not, and he caused you to trust in a lie; therefore thus saith the Lord; Behold, I will punish Shemaiah the Nehelamite, and his seed: he shall not have a man to dwell among this people; neither shall he behold the good that I will do for My people, saith the Lord; because he hath taught rebellion against the Lord"— "Thou shalt say to Jehoiakim king of Judah, Thus saith the Lord; Thou hast burned this roll, saying, Why hast thou written therein, saying, The king of Babylon shall certainly come and destroy this land, and shall cause to cease from thence man and beast? Therefore thus saith the Lord of Jehoiakim king of Judah; He shall have none to sit upon the throne of David: and his dead body shall be cast out in the day to the heat, and in the night to the frost."

"God shall take away his part out of the Book of Life, and out of the holy city, and from the things which are written in this book."—The Revised Version gives a noteworthy variation: "God shall take away his part from the Tree of Life, and out of the holy city, which are written in this book." Sad it were to forfeit the Book of Life and the holy city: sadder still to forfeit the Tree of Life, which represents to us Jesus.

Jesus alone :—if thus it were to me ;
Yet thus it cannot be ;
Lord, I have all things if I have but Thee.

Jesus and all :—precious His bounties are,
Yet He more precious far ;
Day's-eyes are many, one the Morning Star.

Jesus my all :—so let me rest in love,
Thy peaceable poor dove,
Some time below till timeless time above.

The wilfully dead sever themselves from the Tree of Life, the wilfully foul from the holy city. Dreadful were it simply to be shut up with self in the darkness of a grave-like solitude. What will it be to be shut up as in a grave where the worm dieth not, and where the whole congregation of the defiled dead being dead yet cannot die? Yet if I can face the being divorced from that Tree of Life which is Christ, well may I face any and every other loss. Yea, let Ziba take all! nor will I cry unto the King of any lesser matter.

20. He which testifieth these things saith, Surely I come quickly. Amen. Even so, come, Lord Jesus.

If up to this point we have, however feebly, feared, hoped, believed, loved with St. John, now on once again hearing the Voice, "Surely I come quickly," we should be prompt with him to answer: "Even so, come, Lord Jesus."

No hope or fear, faith or love of ours, is worthy to welcome Christ: yet woe is us if they welcome Him not. Woe is us if amid and above terror and clouds of His approach we hail not His Presence as the very bow in the cloud. And as sometimes a second bow fainter, less perfect, further off, appears in the train of the chief rainbow, so in His train will reappear our lost beloved ones who loved us much and Him much more; a hem as it were to His garment, an outer edge to His glory, an over-flow to our full cup of bliss. "And now men see not the bright light which is in the clouds." "He shall pray unto God, and He will be favourable unto him: and he shall see His Face with joy."

O Thou Who art as the light of the morning when the sun riseth, even a morning without clouds, revive our drooping souls as the tender grass springing out of the earth by clear shining after rain, springing out of the earth toward Thee. Although Thy Church be not so with God, in Whose sight no man living shall be justified, yet have respect unto Thine everlasting covenant ordered in all things and sure; and bring to pass her full salvation, and fulfil all her desire, and make us all to grow. Amen.

> Can man rejoice who lives in hourly fear?
>   Can man make haste who toils beneath a load?
>   Can man feel rest who has no fixed abode?
> All he lays hold of or can see or hear
> Is passing by, is prompt to disappear,
>   .Is doomed, foredoomed, continueth in no stay:
>   This day he breathes in is his latter day,
> This year of time is this world's latter year.

Thus in himself is he most miserable :—
Out of himself, Lord, lift him up to Thee,
Out of himself and all these worlds that flee;
Hold him in patience underneath the rod,
Anchor his hope beyond life's ebb and swell,
Perfect his patience in the love of God.

21. The grace of our Lord Jesus Christ be with you all. Amen.

Or according to the Revised Version : ". . . be with the saints."

If a doubt exists as to which is the more accurate translation, by becoming saints we shall in any case secure St. John's benediction.

At the very commencement (ch. i. 1) "The Revelation of Jesus Christ" addressed us : here at the very end "The grace of our Lord Jesus Christ" waits for us. All that lies between has not effected towards ourselves its purpose unless we conclude the whole matter in a culminating grace by fearing God and keeping His commandments.

We have heard enough when God ceases to speak, and have learned enough when we have learned His Will.

Jesus Christ, our Starting Point, our Way, our Goal, look upon us with Thy most gracious eyes, with the eyes of Thy most overcoming pity, with the eyes that recalled St. Peter to himself, to the Communion of Saints, to Thee. Amen.

———————

If I have been overbold in attempting such a work as this, I beg pardon.

FOR EACH.

My harvest is done, its promise is ended,
Weak and watery sets the sun,
Day and night in one mist are blended,
My harvest is done.

Long while running, how short when run,
Time to eternity has descended,
Timeless eternity has begun.

Was it the narrow way that I wended?
Snares and pits was it mine to shun?
The scythe has fallen so long suspended,
My harvest is done.

FOR ALL.

Man's harvest is past, his summer is ended,
  Hope and fear are finished at last,
Day hath descended, night hath ascended,
  Man's harvest is past.

  Time is fled that fleeted so fast :
All the unmended remains unmended,
  The perfect, perfect : all lots are cast.

Waiting till earth and ocean be rended,
  Waiting for call of the trumpet-blast,
Each soul at goal of each way it wended,—
  Man's harvest is past.

THE END.

Richard Clay & Sons, Limited, London & Bungay.

PUBLICATIONS

OF THE

Society for Promoting Christian Knowledge.

THE FATHERS FOR ENGLISH READERS.

A Series of Monograms on the Chief Fathers of the Church, the Fathers selected being centres of influence at important periods of Church History, and in important spheres of action.

Fcap. 8vo, cloth boards, 2s. each.

Leo the Great.
By the Rev. CHARLES GORE, M.A.

Gregory the Great.
By the Rev. J. BARMBY, B.D.

Saint Ambrose: his Life, Times, and Teaching.
By the Ven. Archdeacon THORNTON, D.D.

Saint Athanasius: his Life and Times.
By the Rev. R. WHELER BUSH. (2s. 6d.)

Saint Augustine.
By the Rev. E. L. CUTTS, D.D.

Saint Basil the Great.
By the Rev. RICHARD T. SMITH, B.D.

Saint Bernard, Abbot of Clairvaux, A.D. 1091—1153.
By the Rev. S. J. EALES, M.A., D.C.L. (2s. 6d.)

Saint Hilary of Poitiers, and Saint Martin of Tours.
By the Rev. J. GIBSON CAZENOVE, D.D.

Saint Jerome.
By the Rev. EDWARD L. CUTTS, D.D.

Saint John of Damascus.
By the Rev. J. H. LUPTON, M.A.

Saint Patrick: his Life and Teaching.
By the Rev. E. J. NEWELL, M.A. (2s. 6d.)

Synesius of Cyrene, Philosopher and Bishop.
By ALICE GARDNER.

The Apostolic Fathers.
By the Rev. Canon SCOTT-HOLLAND.

The Defenders of the Faith; or, The Christian Apologists of the Second and Third Centuries.
By the Rev. F. WATSON, D.D.

The Venerable Bede.
By the Rev. Canon BROWNE.

THE ROMANCE OF SCIENCE.

A Series of Books which shows that Science has for the masses as great interest as, and more edification than, the romances of the day.

Small Post 8vo, cloth boards.

COAL: and what we get from it. .
By Professor RAPHAEL MELDOLA, F.R.S., F.I.C. With numerous illustrations. 2s. 6d.

COLOUR, MEASUREMENT, AND MIXTURE.
By Captain W. DE W. ABNEY, C.B., R.E., F.R.S. With several illustrations. 2s. 6d.

THE MAKING OF FLOWERS.
By the Rev. Professor GEORGE HENSLOW, M.A., F.L.S., F.G.S. With several illustrations. 2s. 6d.

DISEASES OF PLANTS.
By H. MARSHALL WARD, M.A., F.R.S., F.L.S. With numerous illustrations. 2s. 6d.

OUR SECRET FRIENDS AND FOES.
By Professor P. FARADAY FRANKLAND, PH.D., B.Sc. (Lond.), F.R.S. Second Edition, revised and enlarged. 3s.

TIME AND TIDE: a Romance of the Moon.
By Sir ROBERT S. BALL, F.R.S. Second Edition, revised. Illustrated. 2s. 6d.

THE STORY OF A TINDER-BOX.
By the late C. M. TIDY, M.B.M.S., F.C.S. With illustrations. 2s.

THE BIRTH AND GROWTH OF WORLDS.
A Lecture by Professor GREEN, M.A., F.R.S. 1s.

SOAP-BUBBLES, and the Forces which mould them.
By C.V. BOYS, A.R.S.M., F.R.S. With numerous diagrams. 2s. 6d.

SPINNING-TOPS.
By Prof. J. PERRY, M.E., F.R.S. With numerous diagrams. 2s. 6d.

NON-CHRISTIAN RELIGIOUS SYSTEMS.

A Series of Manuals which furnish in a brief and popular form an accurate account of the great Non-Christian Religious Systems of the World.

Fcap. 8vo, cloth boards, 2s. 6d. each.

BUDDHISM: Being a Sketch of the Life and Teachings of Gautama, the Buddha.
By T. W. RHYS DAVIDS, M.A., PH.D. With Map.

BUDDHISM IN CHINA.
By the Rev. S. BEAL. With Map.

CHRISTIANITY AND BUDDHISM.
By the Rev. T. STERLING BERRY, D.D.

CONFUCIANISM AND TAOUISM.
By Professor R. K. DOUGLAS, of the British Museum. With Map.

HINDUISM.
By Sir M. MONIER WILLIAMS, M.A., D.C.L. With Map.

ISLAM AND ITS FOUNDER.
By J. W. H. STOBART. With Map.

ISLAM, as a Missionary Religion.

DIOCESAN HISTORIES.

*This Series furnishes a perfect Library of English Ecclesiastical History.
Each volume is complete in itself, and the possibility of repetition has
been carefully guarded against.*

Fcap. 8vo, cloth boards.

Bath and Wells.
By the Rev. W. HUNT. With Map, 2s. 6d.

Canterbury.
By the Rev. R. C. JENKINS, Hon. Canon of Canterbury. With Map, 3s. 6d.

Carlisle.
By RICHARD S. FERGUSON, Esq. With Map, 2s. 6d.

Chichester.
By the Rev. W. R. W. STEPHENS. With Map and Plan, 2s. 6d.

Durham.
By the Rev. J. L. LOW. With Map and Plan, 2s. 6d.

Hereford.
By the Rev. Canon PHILLOTT. With Map, 3s.

Lichfield.
By the Rev. W. BERESFORD. With Map, 2s. 6d.

Norwich.
By the Rev. A. JESSOPP, D.D. With Map, 2s. 6d.

Oxford.
By the Rev. E. MARSHALL. With Map, 2s. 6d.

Peterborough.
By the Rev. G. A. POOLE, M.A. With Map, 2s. 6d.

Salisbury.
By the Rev. W. H. JONES. With Map and Plan, 2s. 6d.

Sodor and Man.
By A. W. MOORE, M.A. With Map, 3s.

St. Asaph.
By the Ven. Archdeacon THOMAS. With Map, 2s.

St. David's.
By the Rev. Canon BEVAN. With Map, 2s. 6d.

Winchester.
By the Rev. W. BENHAM, B.D. With Map, 3s.

Worcester.
By the Rev. I. GREGORY SMITH, M.A., and the Rev. PHIPPS ONSLOW,
M.A. With Map, 3s. 6d.

York.
By the Rev. Canon ORNSBY, M.A., F.S.A. With Map, 3s. 6d.

CHIEF ANCIENT PHILOSOPHIES.

Fcap. 8vo, cloth boards, 2s. 6d. each.

Aristotelianism.
The Ethics of Aristotle, by the Rev. I. GREGORY SMITH, M.A., Hon.
LL.D. The Logical Treatises, the Metaphysics, the Psychology, the
Politics, by the Rev. W. GRUNDY, M.A.

Epicureanism.
B. W. WALLACE, Es. Fellow and Tutor of Merton College, Oxford.

CHURCH HYMNS, with Tunes.
Edited by Sir ARTHUR SULLIVAN. Crown 8vo, Fcap. 4to, and Folio (Organ copy), in various Bindings, from 2s. to £1 1s.

COMMON PRAYER-BOOK AND CHURCH HYMNS.
Bound in one Volume, and in Two Volumes in Cases. Can be had in various Sizes and Bindings, from 5d. to 4s.

COMMON PRAYER-BOOK AND CHURCH HYMNS, with Tunes.
Brevier, 8vo, limp paste grain roan, red edges, 6s.

COMMENTARY ON THE BIBLE.

By various Authors. With Maps and Plans.

Crown 8vo, cloth boards, red edges, 4s.; *half calf,* 10s.; *whole calf,* 12s.; *half morocco,* 12s. *each volume.*

OLD TESTAMENT.
Vol. I., containing the Pentateuch.

OLD TESTAMENT.
Vol. II., containing the Historical Books, Joshua to Esther.

OLD TESTAMENT.
Vol. III., containing the Poetical Books, Job to Song of Solomon.

OLD TESTAMENT.
Vol. IV., containing the Prophetical Books, Isaiah to Malachi.

OLD TESTAMENT.
Vol. V., containing the Apocryphal Books.

NEW TESTAMENT.
Vol. I., containing the Four Gospels.

NEW TESTAMENT.
Vol. II., containing the Acts, Epistles, and Revelation.

ANCIENT HISTORY FROM THE MONUMENTS.

This Series is chiefly intended to illustrate the Sacred Scriptures by the results of recent Monumental Researches in the East. The Volumes have, however, an independent value, as furnishing, as far as they go, trustworthy histories of the ancient Monarchies of the Eastern World.

Fcap. 8vo, cloth boards, 2s. each.

ASSYRIA, from the Earliest Times to the Fall of Nineveh.
By the late GEORGE SMITH, of the British Museum.

BABYLONIA, the History of.
By the late GEORGE SMITH. Edited by the Rev. A. H. SAYCE, Professor of Comparative Philology, Oxford.

EGYPT, from the Earliest Times to B.C. 300.
By the late S. BIRCH, LL.D.

PERSIA, from the Earliest Period to the Arab Conquest.
By the late W. S. W. VAUX, M.A., F.R.S. A New and Revised Edition by the Rev. Professor SAYCE.

SINAI, from the Fourth Egyptian Dynasty to the Present Time.
By the late H. SPENCER PALMER, Major R.E., F.R.A.S. A New Edition, revised throughout by the Rev. Professor SAYCE.

MISCELLANEOUS PUBLICATIONS.

DEVOTIONAL (A) LIFE OF OUR LORD.   *s. d.*
By the Rev. EDWARD L. CUTTS, D.D., author of "Pastoral
Counsels," &c. Post 8vo..................................*Cloth boards* 5 0

DISPENSATION OF THE SPIRIT (THE).
Being Readings on the Person and Work of the Holy Ghost
in Relation to the World, the Church, and the Individual.
By the Rev. C. R. BALL, M.A. Small Post 8vo. *Cloth boards* 2 6

**DIVINE SOCIETY (THE); or, The Church's Care of Large
Populations.**
Cambridge Lectures on Pastoral Theology, 1890. By the Rev.
Canon JACOB. Small Post 8vo.......................*Cloth boards* 2 6

GOSPELS, THE FOUR.
Arranged in the Form of an English Harmony, from the Text
of the Authorised Version. By the late Rev. J. M. FULLER.
With Analytical Table of Contents and Four Maps. *Cloth boards* 1 0

LAND OF ISRAEL (THE).
A Journal of Travel in Palestine, undertaken with special
reference to its Physical Character. By the Rev. Canon TRIS-
TRAM. With two Maps and Illustrations. Large Post 8vo.
Cloth boards 10 6

**LECTURES ON THE HISTORICAL AND DOGMATICAL
POSITION OF THE CHURCH OF ENGLAND.**
By the Rev. W. BAKER, D.D. Post 8vo.............*Cloth boards* 1 6

LESSER LIGHTS.
By the Rev. F. BOURBILLON, M.A. SERIES I and II. Post 8vo.
Cloth boards, each 2 6

LETTER AND SPIRIT.
Notes on the Commandments. By the late CHRISTINA G.
ROSSETTI. Post 8vo.....................................*Cloth boards* 2 0

MANUAL OF PAROCHIAL WORK (A).
For the Use of the Younger Clergy. By various Writers.
Edited by the late Rev. Canon ELLERTON. Large Post 8vo.
Cloth boards 6 0

**MARTYRS AND SAINTS OF THE FIRST TWELVE
CENTURIES. Studies from the Lives of the Black-
Letter Saints of the English Calendar.**
By Mrs. RUNDLE CHARLES. Crown 8vo............*Cloth boards* 5 0

OURSELVES, OUR PEOPLE, OUR WORK.
Six Addresses given in the Divinity Schools, Cambridge, by
the Rev. E. T. LEEKE, M.A. Small Post 8vo.......*Cloth boards* 2 0

PALEY'S HORÆ PAULINÆ.
A New Edition, with Notes, Appendix, and Preface. By
the Rev. J. S. HOWSON, D D., Dean of Chester. Post 8vo.
Cloth boards 3 0

PARISH PRIEST OF THE TOWN.
Lectures delivered in the Divinity School, Cambridge, by the
Right Rev. J. GOTT, D.D. Post 8vo.............*Cloth boards* 3 0

PASTORAL COUNSELS; or, Words of Encouragement and Guidance to Holy Living.
By the Rev. E. L. CUTTS. Crown 8vo.............*Cloth boards* 1 6

PASTORAL THEOLOGY (LECTURES ON), with Special Reference to the Promises required of Candidates for Ordination.
By the late Venerable J. R. NORRIS, B.D., Archdeacon of
Bristol. Post 8vo...................................*Cloth boards* 2 0

PEACE WITH GOD.
A Manual for the Sick. By the Rev. E. BURBIDGE, M.A.
Post 8vo...*Cloth boards* 1 6

PLAIN WORDS FOR CHRIST.
Being a Series of Readings for Working Men. By the late
Rev. R. G. DUTTON. Post 8vo.....................*Cloth boards* 1 0

PRAYER OF CHRISTENDOM, THE GREAT.
By Mrs. RUNDLE CHARLES, author of "The Schönberg-Cotta
Family." Post 8vo................................*Cloth boards* 1 6

PROMISED SEED (THE).
Being a Course of Lessons on the Old Testament, for Schools
and Families, arranged for every Sunday in the Year. By the
Rev. C. R. BALL, M.A. Post 8vo.................*Cloth boards* 1 6

RELIGION FOR EVERY DAY.
Lectures for Men. By the Right Rev. A. BARRY, D.D.
Fcap. 8vo.......................................*Cloth boards* 1 0

SCENES IN THE EAST.
Consisting of Twelve Coloured Photographic Views of Places
mentioned in the Bible, beautifully executed, with Descriptive
Letterpress. By the Rev. Canon TRISTRAM.
Cloth, bevelled boards, red edges 6 0

SEEK AND FIND.
A Double Series of Short Studies of the Benedicite. By
the late CHRISTINA G. ROSSETTI. Post 8vo........*Cloth boards* 2 6

SERVANTS OF SCRIPTURE (THE).
By the late Rev. J. W. BURGON, B.D. Post 8vo. *Cloth boards* 1 6

SINAI AND JERUSALEM; or, Scenes from Bible Lands.   *s. d.*
Consisting of Coloured Photographic Views of Places mentioned
in the Bible, including a Panoramic View of Jerusalem, with
Descriptive Letterpress.   By the Rev. F. W. HOLLAND, M.A.,
Demy 4to.............................*Cloth, bevelled boards, gilt edges*   6   0

SOME CHIEF TRUTHS OF RELIGION.
By the Rev. E. L. CUTTS, D.D., author of "St. Cedd's Cross."
Crown 8vo...*Cloth boards*   2   6

THOUGHTS FOR MEN AND WOMEN.
THE LORD'S PRAYER.   By EMILY C. ORR.   Post 8vo.
                                                    Limp cloth   1   0

THOUGHTS FOR WORKING DAYS.
Original and Selected.   By EMILY C. ORR.   Post 8vo.
                                                    Limp cloth   1   0

THREE MARTYRS OF THE NINETEENTH CENTURY:
Studies from the Lives of Livingstone, Gordon, and
Patteson.
By Mrs. RUNDLE CHARLES.   Crown 8vo............*Cloth boards*   3   6

TIME FLIES; a Reading Diary.
By the late CHRISTINA G. ROSSETTI.   Post 8vo.   *Cloth boards*   2   6

TRUE VINE (THE).
By Mrs. RUNDLE CHARLES, author of "The Schönberg-Cotta
Family," &c.   Printed in red and black.   Post 8vo.   *Cloth boards*   1   6

TURNING-POINTS OF ENGLISH CHURCH HISTORY.
By the Rev. E. L. CUTTS, D.D., Vicar of Holy Trinity, Haver-
stock Hill.   Crown 8vo......................................*Cloth boards*   3   6

TURNING-POINTS OF GENERAL CHURCH HISTORY.
By the Rev. E. L. CUTTS, D.D., author of "Pastoral Counsels."
Crown 8vo...*Cloth boards*   5   0

VERSES.
By the late CHRISTINA G. ROSSETTI.   Sm. Post 8vo.   Printed
in Red and Black on hand-made paper ....*Cloth boards*   3   6

WITHIN THE VEIL.
Studies in the Epistle to the Hebrews.   By Mrs. RUNDLE
CHARLES, author of "Chronicles of the Schonberg-Cotta
Family."   Small Post 8vo.............................*Cloth boards*   1   6

LONDON:

NORTHUMBERLAND AVENUE, CHARING CROSS, W.C. ;
43   QUEEN VICTORIA STREET, E.